MW01092198

SOUTHERN EUROPE IN THE AGE OF REVOLUTIONS

Southern Europe in the Age of Revolutions

Maurizio Isabella

PRINCETON UNIVERSITY PRESS

PRINCETON & OXFORD

Copyright © 2023 by Princeton University Press

Princeton University Press is committed to the protection of copyright and the intellectual property our authors entrust to us. Copyright promotes the progress and integrity of knowledge. Thank you for supporting free speech and the global exchange of ideas by purchasing an authorized edition of this book. If you wish to reproduce or distribute any part of it in any form, please obtain permission.

Requests for permission to reproduce material from this work should be sent to permissions@press.princeton.edu

Published by Princeton University Press
41 William Street, Princeton, New Jersey 08540
99 Banbury Road, Oxford OX2 6JX

press.princeton.edu

All Rights Reserved

Library of Congress Cataloging-in-Publication Data

Names: Isabella, Maurizio, author.
Title: Southern Europe in the age of revolutions / Maurizio Isabella.
Description: Princeton ; Oxford : Princeton University Press, 2023. |
    Includes bibliographical references and index.
Identifiers: LCCN 2022019166 (print) | LCCN 2022019167 (ebook) |
    ISBN 9780691181707 (hardback) | ISBN 9780691246192 (ebook)
Subjects: LCSH: Europe, Southern—Politics and government—19th century. |
    Europe, Southern—History—19th century. | Political culture—Europe,
    Southern—History—19th century. | Revolutions—History—19th century.
Classification: LCC D974 .I83 2023 (print) | LCC D974 (ebook) |
    DDC 940.2/7—dc23/eng/20220513
LC record available at https://lccn.loc.gov/2022019166
LC ebook record available at https://lccn.loc.gov/2022019167

British Library Cataloging-in-Publication Data is available

Editorial: Ben Tate & Josh Drake
Production Editorial: Ali Parrington
Jacket Design: Heather Hansen
Production: Danielle Amatucci
Publicity: Alyssa Sanford & Charlotte Coyne

Jacket Image Credit: Partida de la fragata Constitución by Louis Martinet, 19th century. Courtesy of the Zumalakarregi Museum / San Telmo Museoa

This book has been composed in Miller

Printed on acid-free paper. ∞

Printed and bound by CPI Group (UK) Ltd, Croydon, CR0 4YY

10 9 8 7 6 5 4 3 2 1

To my parents Duilio and Graziella Isabella

CONTENTS

ACKNOWLEDGEMENTS

I STARTED WORKING on this book in 2013, and since then a number of institutions have supported its completion. I am grateful to the Center for European Studies at Harvard where I held a fellowship in 2013; the Leverhulme Foundation which awarded me a one-year fellowship to carry out research in Greece, Naples and Sicily; the Instituto de Ciências Sociais in Lisbon (and in particular its then director José Luís Cardoso); the Casa de Velázquez in Madrid (and especially Michel Bertrand, its then director, and Nicolas Morales, then head of its École des hautes études hispaniques et ibériques); the Madrid Institute of Advanced Studies (and its president Antonio Álvarez-Ossorio), where I held a year-long EURIAS mobility fellowship; the École normale supérieure, rue d'Ulm in Paris (Hélène Blais and Antonin Durand in particular); the European University Institute in Florence where I was privileged to be a Fernand Braudel fellow; the Max Weber Institute in Erfurt, where I spent one term as Senior Fellow in the Urbanity and Religion programme (and especially Susanne Rau and Jörg Rüpke). Successive heads of school at Queen Mary College, Miri Rubin, Julian Jackson, Colin Jones and Dan Todman, have done all they could to help me complete this project.

All history books are based on the research and ideas produced by other scholars, but some books are especially reliant on the practical expertise and intellectual engagement of colleagues from many countries. This is certainly the case with this work, which attempts to synthesise, combine and reinterpret a variety of national historiographical traditions. I could not have written this book without participating in the dozens of seminar activities and discussions of the Leverhulme-funded project 'Re-imagining Democracy in the Mediterranean', held in many different cities across Europe between 2012 and 2015. I am indebted to Joanna Innes, Mark Philp and Eduardo Posada-Carbó for inviting me to take part in it and for their friendship and advice since then.

The book could never have taken shape without the generosity too of fellow historians who shared their knowledge concerning Portuguese, Spanish, Italian and Greek history. Doing research in so many different countries and interacting with so many scholarly communities has been an immensely rewarding and pleasurable aspect of working on southern European history. In Lisbon I received much support from Grégoire Bron,

Carmine Cassino, Hugo Gonçalves Dores, Maria de Fátima Sá e Melo Ferreira, Maria Alexandre Lousada, Sérgio Campos Matos, Nuno Gonçalo Monteiro, Miriam Halpern Pereira and Rui Ramos; and in Spain from Ramon Arnabat Mata, Sophie Bustos, Emilio La Parra López, Javier Martínez Dos Santos, Darina Martykánová, Juan Pan-Montojo, Álvaro París Martín, Florencia Peyrou, the late Jean-Philippe Luis, Pedro Rújula, Juan Luis Simal and Víctor Sánchez Martín. In Naples, Renata De Lorenzo, Pierre-Marie Delpu, Laura Di Fiore, Viviana Mellone, Marco Meriggi, Giovanni Muto, Carmine Pinto, Anna Maria Rao, Jens Späth did much to facilitate my research. In this same city I enjoyed the warm hospitality of Daniela Luigia Caglioti over many years. In Athens, I benefited from the guidance of Marios Hatzopoulos, Antonis Liakos, Christos Loukos, Nassia Yakovaki and Dimitris Stamatopoulos; in Palermo from that of Nino Blando, Salvatore Lupo and Carlo Verri; and in Catania I had memorable conversations with the late Giuseppe Giarrizzo, and was supported by Giuseppe Barone, Alessia Facineroso, Paolo Militello, Chiara Maria Pulvirenti, Lina Scalisi and the late Mons. Gaetano Zito. In all of these countries the staff of the local archives were exceptionally generous and went out of their way to offer assistance.

David Armitage's encouragement in 2013 was decisive in overcoming my initial hesitation to embark on such a long-term project. He has been wonderfully supportive of it throughout the years. I had the privilege of discussing this project in its early stages with the late Christopher Bayly, whose work has been a great source of inspiration. John Davis has always been solicitous in promoting my project in very many different ways. In recent years, conversations with Lucy Riall, Sujit Sivasundaram, Marcela Ternavasio and Clément Thibaud have helped me to rethink the relationship between southern European events and their global revolutionary context. The scholarship of Carlo Capra has remained a constant point of reference, and his belief in my ability to finish this book essential for its completion.

Many colleagues have read my work in progress. Mark Philp commented on most of the manuscript, offering penetrating and detailed feedback. Gianluca Albergoni, David Bell, Carlo Capra, Ada Dialla, Joanna Innes, Antonis Liakos, Julian Jackson, Marco Meriggi, Álvaro París Martín, Nuno Monteiro, Alessio Petrizzo, Michalis Sotiropoulos and Konstantina Zanou shared their critical insights on individual chapters.

Konstantina Zanou, Michalis Sotiropoulos and Haris Malamidis translated and summarised for me documents and publications from Greek, a language I started to study too late and I know insufficiently well.

Konstantina and Michalis in particular shared with me their knowledge of the period, and their perceptive and wholly original views on the Greek revolution and the existing literature on this topic. I have learned a great deal about Neapolitan and British exchanges from my former PhD student Giuseppe Grieco, who also drafted the chronology for this book.

I have had the privilege of being able to discuss my ideas in a number of workshops: at the school of history at Queen Mary, where Colin Jones, James Ellison and Georgios Varouxakis in particular commented on my draft introduction, along with many other generous colleagues; with Mark Mazower at the Italian Colloquium of Columbia University run by Konstantina Zanou; with Gabriel Paquette and Konstantina at the Noether Dialogues in Italian and Modern History organised by Sergio Luzzatto at the University of Connecticut; with Holly Case in one of the 'Conversations about Greece' convened by Elsa Amanatidou at Brown University; in a lecture series run by Luca Fruci at the University of Pisa; at the graduate seminar of the Scuola normale superiore di Pisa convened by Ilaria Pavan; with Ada Dialla and Yanni Kotsonis in Athens and London. The European University Institute has been an exceptionally stimulating place to test my arguments, and I am thankful in particular for the numerous invitations from Lucy Riall and Ann Thomson. Appreciation is also due to the manuscript's evaluators, who read it carefully and offered timely reports with constructive criticism. All of these readers and audiences improved the book immensely. The remaining errors are of course mine alone. As usual, Martin Thom did much to clarify my style and my arguments. At Princeton University Press my editor Ben Tate, who took on my book proposal with great enthusiasm, has given me invaluable advice across the years. Francis Eaves was an exceptionally meticulous copyeditor of my book manuscript, and I feel very lucky to have enjoyed his support in the final stages of its production.

My greatest debt during these long years is however to my parents, who always made their loving presence felt during my hours of solitary work, and have proved to be the most loyal champions. This book is dedicated to them.

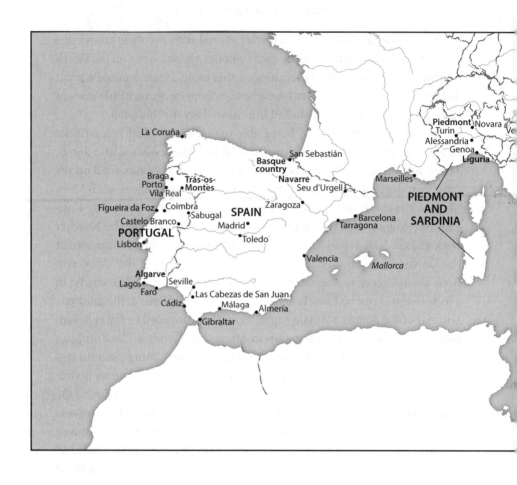

Jassy
Moldavia
Odessa
Izmail
Trieste
Târgoviște
Drăgășani
Bucharest
Wallachia

Constantinople

O T T O M A N   E M P I R E

Foggia
Bari
ola
Avellino
Moschopolis
es
Salerno
NGDOM
Corfu
Yannina
THE TWO
Cosenza
Souli
Roumeli
CILIES
(Sterea Ellada)
Smyrna
Pizzo
Messolonghi
Patras
alermo
Ionian Islands
Athens
Messina
Argos
Epidavros
icily
Tripolitsa
Nafplion
Catania
Morea
(Peloponnese)
Cyprus

Malta
Crete

Alexandria

Map of southern Europe and
detail showing the area around the
Aegean Sea

Macedonia
Mount Athos

Thessaly
Psara
Salona
(Amfissa)
Chios
Samos
Corinth
Aegina
Tripolitsa
Ermioni
Mykonos
Arcadia
Syros
Naxos
Hydra
Navarino
Spetses
Mani
Karpathos
Rethymno
Crete

Southern Europe and the Making of a Global Revolutionary South

WAS THERE EVER a revolutionary South, and if so when did it manifest itself, what did it look like, and what was peculiar about it? This book attempts to answer these questions by exploring a wave of simultaneous and interconnected revolutions that broke out in Spain, Portugal, Piedmont, Naples, Sicily and Greece between 1820 and 1821. In this moment it was the southern peripheries of Europe that took the revolutionary initiative. In January 1820, Rafael Riego's military uprising launched outside the city of Cádiz triggered a set of similar events led by army officers in Naples, Portugal, Piedmont and the Ottoman world. Taking inspiration from Riego's initiative in Spain, officers such as Guglielmo Pepe outside Naples, Bernardo Correia de Castro e Sepúlveda and Sebastião Cabreira in the Portuguese city of Porto, Giacomo Garelli and Isidoro Palma in Piedmont and Alexandros Ypsilantis in the Danubian Principalities led army rebellions in favour of representative government. This set of events was marked not only by chronological convergence, but also by a convergence in aims and consequences. The political initiatives taken by these officers and their troops in fact enjoyed substantial popular support, and led to the introduction of constitutions. Their interventions further encouraged a popular participation in revolutionary politics that had no precedents in their countries.

In the historiography of the age of revolutions, southern Europe is largely absent or plays, to say the least, a very marginal role.[1] The conventional

---

1. A noticeable recent exception is Richard Stites, *The Four Horsemen: Riding to Liberty in Post-Napoleonic Europe* (Oxford: Oxford University Press, 2014). For earlier

narrative of this age is therefore a francocentric one that, starting with 1789, moves on to 1815 as a turning point that is required to explain the revolutions of 1830 and 1848.[2] Traditional narratives of European history tend to grant the continent's southern peripheries just a few pages, or even a few lines, which generally focus on the Spanish reaction to Napoleonic rule, the Greek war of independence and the participation of the Italian states in the 1848 European revolution. If mentioned at all, the 1820s uprisings are treated as half-hearted attempts to subvert the new geopolitical order created by the Congress of Vienna. They have been dismissed as elitist events noteworthy for the lack of any substantial social basis. Their weakness is deemed to be borne out by the easy success of the military expeditions by the Austrian army in Piedmont and Naples in 1821, and by the French army in Spain in 1823. Historians have seen these interventions, along with the belated European agreement to underwrite the autonomy of Greece, as evidence of the efficacy of the newly created principle of intervention serving to guarantee the peace and stability of Europe.[3]

The global turn of historiography has had a major impact on our understanding of the age of revolutions. First of all, it has resulted in a revision of its map and extent. Second, it has at the same time firmly rejected the derivative model that dominated the work of Robert Palmer and Eric Hobsbawm, which, based as it was on the assumption that modernity was the product of the ideas of the American and French revolutions, lay at the origins of this chronology. It has had the merit of shifting the focus from western Europe, and from the North Atlantic space in particular, to other parts of the world, incorporating into the narrative of the period between the second half of the eighteenth century and the first half of the nineteenth century spaces such as the Indian Ocean, Africa and the South Atlantic. It has also entailed a rejection of the derivative approach to revolutionary ideologies as by-products of the French revolution. Finally, this historiography has treated the age of revolutions as a by-product of a broader world crisis. Some, among them David Armitage and Sanjay Subrahmanyam, have suggested that such a crisis was initiated in

---

appreciations of the role played by the European southern peripheries in the age of revolutions, see Franco Venturi, 'Le rivoluzioni liberali', in *Le rivoluzioni borghesi*, ed. Ruggiero Romano, 5 vols (Milan: Fratelli Fabbri, 1973), 4, pp. 193–208.

2. Eric Hobsbawm, *The Age of Revolution: 1789–1848* (London: Weidenfeld & Nicolson, 1962); Jonathan Sperber, *Revolutionary Europe, 1780–1850* (Harlow: Longman, 2000).

3. Paul W. Schroeder, *The Transformation of European Politics 1763–1848* (Oxford: Oxford University Press, 1994).

the early eighteenth century.[4] For Christopher Bayly, this crisis was inaugurated by the Seven Years' War (1756–63), a conflict between Europeans in America and Asia that precipitated the end of the ancien régime, and was directly associated with its financial bankruptcy. The increasing costs of war determined by imperial competition became unsustainable and caused the existing monarchies to lose their legitimacy.[5] The expansion of, and conflicts between, empires led to a generalised crisis of sovereignty, in which state power and state independence were combined in novel ways, and projected within state borders and beyond.[6] In this context, the relationship between the boundaries of political communities and the rights and obligations of citizens, between peoples and monarchs, between territories within the same polity or between different ones, was questioned, rethought and reconstituted.[7] Southern Europe and the Mediterranean are still largely absent, however, from this recent scholarship on the global age of revolution. The idea of Europe behind this otherwise revisionist scholarship remains virtually unchanged, although it does integrate Spain and Portugal with France and Britain as the centres of empires.[8]

The 1820s revolutions in southern Europe belonged to this long-term global crisis of sovereignty. However, if we give due importance to the revolutionary space stretching from Portugal to Greece, then not only the chronology offered by the histories of Europe, but also that suggested by global approaches to the age of revolutions requires some revision. In fact, neither 1763, nor 1776, 1789 or 1815 can be considered as the key moments unleashing the crisis that led to the revolutionary wave of the 1820s in southern Europe. Rather, the onset of this crisis should be associated with a set of dates related to the direct or indirect impact that the Napoleonic wars had on the countries and empires of this continental periphery, and with their repercussions on the Ottoman world. This moment following on from the American (1776–83), and the French (1789–99) revolutions,

4. David Armitage and Sanjay Subrahmanyam, eds, *The Age of Revolutions in Global Context, c. 1760–1840* (Basingstoke: Palgrave Macmillan, 2010).

5. Christopher Bayly, *The Birth of the Modern World 1780–1914: Global Connections and Comparisons* (Oxford: Blackwell, 2004), pp. 93–96.

6. On this notion, see Jeremy Adelman, 'An Age of Imperial Revolutions', *The American Historical Review* 113, no. 2 (2008): 319–40.

7. Jeremy Adelman, *Sovereignty and Revolution in the Iberian Atlantic* (Princeton, NJ: Princeton University Press, 2006), p. 391.

8. Armitage and Subrahmanyam, *Age of Revolutions*; Susan Desan, Lynn Hunt and William Max Nelson, eds, *The French Revolution in Global Perspective* (Ithaca, NY: Cornell University Press, 2013); Sujit Sivasundaram, *Waves across the South: A New History of Revolution and Empire* (London: William Collins, 2020).

led to the dissolution of the Ibero-American empires, and had political, ideological, financial and economic consequences for empires and states worldwide.[9]

The first and most tangible side-effect of the Napoleonic expansion towards the southern peripheries of the continent was the physical displacement and replacement of existing monarchs. The foundations of authority and the sources of its legitimacy in southern Europe and the Ibero-Atlantic world were thereby shaken. In Spain this crisis was triggered by the forced abdication of Fernando VII in 1808. Both Spain and its American empire were left without a legitimate king, with individuals on both sides of the hemisphere having to establish new institutions acting on behalf of the absent monarch. The absence of the monarch provided the preconditions for the drafting of the Cádiz Constitution of 1812. In the Ibero-American colonies it led, at least in a first phase, to the recognition of provinces and *juntas* (committees, councils) as the legitimate holders of monarchical sovereignty in the ruler's absence, and to demands for the equal treatment of the American provinces within the Iberian empires. But once the principles of autonomy and equality underpinning the claims of the colonial elites had been challenged or rejected, this crisis led to a more radical hostility against the metropolis and to independence, an outcome that coincided with the revolutionary explosion of southern Europe described in this book. The military occupation of the Iberian peninsula by the French resulted also in the departure of Dom João, the prince regent of Portugal, from Lisbon for Brazil in 1807, an event that transformed dramatically the mutual relations between centre and periphery in the Portuguese Empire, turning Brazil into the new metropolis, and leaving Portugal in the hands of the British army. The prolonged civil war that broke out during the 1820s as a result of the crisis of the dynasties in Portugal and Spain was another dramatic consequence of the physical displacement and revision of authority that had taken place after 1808.[10]

The French invasion of the Italian peninsula in 1796 produced equally dramatic effects: existing monarchies were deprived of their authority there too. Ferdinando IV of Naples and Sicily was first displaced, albeit temporarily, in 1799 when, under the protection of the French revolutionary army, a republic was declared in Naples by a group of Enlightenment intellectuals. The republic was immediately crushed, and Ferdinando

9. Bayly, *Birth of the Modern World*, pp. 106–7, 125–27.

10. Gabriel Paquette, *Imperial Portugal in the Age of Atlantic Revolutions: The Luso-Brazilian World, c. 1770–1850* (Cambridge: Cambridge University Press, 2013).

restored to power, although it was not until the end of 1801 that he went back from Sicily to Naples. Ferdinando lost the continental part of his kingdom again in January 1806. In that year, Naples was turned into a Napoleonic satellite state, and the king once again found shelter in Sicily, by then a British imperial protectorate, until the end of the Napoleonic wars in 1815. Likewise, in December 1798 King Carlo Emanuele was forced to leave Turin in the hands of the French and to retire to his only remaining possession, the island of Sardinia (in fact he owed the title of king to this territory, not Piedmont). In 1802 a separate republican administration in Piedmont came to an end, and its territories were directly annexed by France. Carlo Emanuele abdicated the throne in favour of his brother Vittorio Emanuele, who was only able to return to Turin in 1814. Popular opposition to French rule in the territories annexed to Napoleon's empire or in the satellite states taught Italian patriots that republicanism was not a viable political option. Notions of popular sovereignty, however, had an enduring impact. As revolutions in Piedmont and Naples show, although loyalties to the old dynasties were not replaced by new ones, their foundations had nonetheless been shaken and were therefore open to revision.[11]

This attack on monarchical authority in southern Europe coincided with a dramatic dynastic crisis in the Ottoman Empire. Between 1807 and 1808 two sultans, Selim III and Mustafa IV, were deposed and murdered in quick succession. These dramatic events were not the direct result of the Napoleonic occupation, as after Napoleon's invasion of Egypt in 1798 the Ottoman Empire had been only tangentially affected by French military expansion. However, the crisis of sovereignty affecting southern Europe and the Ottoman world were interconnected. The latter's internal crisis was in fact due to its almost permanent state of war between 1787 and 1812, mainly against Russia. The Napoleonic conflicts indirectly increased the pressure on Constantinople. From 1806 onwards the Danubian Principalities of Wallachia and Moldavia were occupied by Russian forces. Attempts at reform driven by this external military pressure, and the domestic resistance to them, explain the dramatic events between 1807 and 1808. The glaring inadequacies of the traditional military forces of the Ottoman Empire, the Janissaries, revealed in their encounters with European armies, led to the decision by Selim III to establish the 'New Order' (*nizam-ı cedid*), an alternative standing army trained and

---

11. Stuart Woolf, *Napoleon's Integration of Europe* (London: Routledge, 1993); John A. Davis, *Naples and Napoleon: Southern Italy and the European Revolutions (1780–1860)* (Oxford: Oxford University Press, 2006).

organised according to the Western system. Unsurprisingly, the Janissaries themselves, along with popular groups, clerical elites and notables, who deemed the innovation incompatible with Islam, resented Selim III's creation. It was a rebellion on the part of the Janissaries that led in 1804 to a revolution of the Christian population of Serbia and to the recognition of its autonomy as a vassal state of the empire in 1817. Furthermore, it was a coalition between the Janissaries, their affiliates and the crowds of Constantinople (Istanbul) that brought about the deposition and murder of Selim III in 1807. The following year, a coalition of provincial notables led by Alemdar Mustafa Pasha marched on Constantinople, deposed Mustafa IV and reintroduced the New Order under the new Sultan Mahmud II. As in Spain or in Sicily, this crisis of authority occasioned some experimentation with a new 'constitutional' arrangement: the short-lived Deed of Agreement. This document, signed in 1808 by the new sultan and by the notables of the empire, provided a mutual guarantee of the rights and duties of all the central and provincial authorities to ensure its stability and peace, repress any rebellion and support the financial and military needs of the empire.[12]

Napoleonic military expansion more directly threatened Ottoman sovereignty in its Mediterranean peripheries. The French occupation of the Ionian islands in particular offered further opportunities for provincial groups within the Ottoman Empire to undermine its sovereignty and challenge its integrity. In 1808 Mavromichalis, a leading notable from the peninsula of Mani in the Peloponnese, entered into communication with the French in the hope that they would replace the Ottomans as a superior authority and provide a protectorate over an autonomous Beylik. In the same year a coalition between Christian and Muslim leaders from the Peloponnese, all equally hostile to a newly appointed Ottoman governor and his local allies, entertained similar plans to reject Ottoman authority and submit themselves to French protection.[13]

What further contributed to the rethinking of the monarchical authority in southern Europe and the Mediterranean was the British military presence. British imperial agents and officers did not simply provide a concrete defence of the pre-existing political order, and ideological weapons against Napoleonic rule. They showed the existence of alternative political models to both pre-revolutionary absolutism and Napoleonic

---

12. Ali Yaycioglu, *Partners of the Empire: The Crisis of the Ottoman Order in the Age of Revolutions* (Stanford, CA: Stanford University Press, 2016).

13. Dean J. Kostantaras, 'Christian Elites of the Peloponnese and the Ottoman State, 1715–1821', *European History Quarterly* 43, no. 4 (2013): 628–56 at pp. 637–38.

despotism. In response to the Napoleonic expansion in southern Europe, the British Empire had in fact extended its presence at the expense of the French and Dutch empires, not only in the Caribbean, South Africa and South-East Asia, but also in the Mediterranean. While the occupation of Sicily would prove to be temporary (1806–15), Britain acquired Malta in 1800, and Corfu and the rest of Ionian islands in 1815. Portugal was not directly annexed, but the presence of the British army there, poised to fight the French on the Iberian peninsula, continued for some years after 1815. British military occupation and colonial rule were bitterly resented for their despotic character in particular in Portugal, where under Marshal William Carr Beresford the British prevented any form of constitutional government until the outbreak of the 1820 revolution. However, besides military occupation, the British brought with them constitutions. It was in the Mediterranean during the Napoleonic wars that the British first toyed with the idea of transferring constitutions as a tool to consolidate their hegemonic power. They did this in Sicily under William Bentinck, who in 1812 had introduced a constitution inspired by the Britain's own. There, at least temporarily, they demonstrated that imperial expansion and protectorates could be compatible with liberal institutions. This is why, in the following decade, revolutionaries in the region (in Greece, Sicily and Genoa in particular) came to see the British Empire as a potential guarantor for their new political aspirations.[14]

The impact of these events was so dramatic that the efforts made at the Congress of Vienna in 1815 to find a lasting peace and to reconstitute the monarchical authority shattered during the previous decade were never likely to succeed.[15] Between 1808 and 1815 the populations of southern European states and empires had all been directly affected by military occupation, had fought for and against their legitimate sovereigns both in national and foreign armies travelling far and wide, had experienced new forms of government and had acquired novel political ideas. By 1815 army officers, members of the clergy and civil servants, as well as ordinary citizens, had new expectations for political participation—expectations that were disappointed by the authorities restored after the Congress of Vienna. The impact of wars on society, and the new social and political role played

---

14. On the constitutional experiment in Sicily, see John Rosselli, *Lord William Bentinck and the British Occupation of Sicily, 1811–1814* (Cambridge: Cambridge University Press, 1956).

15. Brian Vick, *The Congress of Vienna: Power and Politics after Napoleon* (Cambridge, MA: Harvard University Press, 2016); Glenda Sluga, *The Invention of International Order: Remaking Europe after Napoleon* (Princeton, NJ: Princeton University Press, 2021).

by armies during the Napoleonic era, account for the military revolutionary activism of the following years. In 1820 and 1821, in Spain, Portugal,
Piedmont and Naples, revolutionary military leaders such as Riego, Pepe
and Ypsilantis all argued that after the Napoleonic struggles a return to
absolute rule was inconceivable. The people had fought to defend their
monarchs and therefore their sacrifices (or so the insurgents maintained)
deserved to be rewarded with new constitutional pacts. The scant resistance that the insurrections encountered when they broke out between
1820 and 1821, and the fact that only diplomatic and military intervention
by stronger countries was able to determine their fate, points to the weak
legitimacy of the restored regimes in these countries, and the existence of
substantial political and social support for change. My claim here is that
it is therefore insufficient to treat these revolutions as minor events in the
context of the newly found stability of the European continent after 1815.
Rather, the 1820s uprisings in southern Europe demonstrate the fragility,
not the solidity, of the political order re-established in 1815.

Admittedly, in this decade France, Britain, Austria and Russia, by interfering with, and limiting, the sovereignty of the states on the southern and
eastern peripheries of the continent, constrained the possible outcomes
of revolutionaries' attempts in this area in both direct and indirect ways.
Indeed, southern Europe experienced every possible type of diplomatic,
political or military intervention on the part of the European hegemonic
powers—both those that they adopted elsewhere within the continent
itself and those that they were testing in other parts of the world. It is
in southern Europe that, as a result of the Vienna settlement, new types
of military and political intervention were tried out (as in the invasion of
Naples and Spain) with a view to guaranteeing the stability of the continent. To these forms of intervention we must add heightened European
interference in Ottoman affairs in the aftermath of the Greek revolution
(which led to the recognition of Greece as a state whose sovereignty was
guaranteed by the European powers) as well as the consolidation of an
existing colonial presence (with the strengthening of British colonial rule
in Malta and the Ionian Islands), limited military intervention as a form of
police action (such as the 1816 bombardment of Algiers, or the naval battle
of Navarino against the Ottomans in 1827) and colonial expansion (for
the decade closes with the conquest of Algiers in 1830): all new forms of
gunboat diplomacy.[16] These forms of interference forced southern patriots to imagine possible solutions to the question of freedom that would

---

16. Joanna Innes, 'Popular Consent and the European Order', in Innes and Philp, *Re-
imagining Democracy*, pp. 271–99 at 284–85.

be compatible with the European geopolitical preponderance in their territories. Such interventions did not succeed, however, in repressing the revolutionary potential of southern populations.

At the same time, southern Europe is the geographical space that best demonstrates the interconnection and convergence between European, Ibero-American and Asian uprisings. The 1820s revolutions coincided with a much broader revolutionary wave that affected the entire global South, from the Ibero-American world to the Indian Ocean. This were not just a matter of random simultaneous events; a number of shared causes and a set of global transformations account for the emergence of this global revolutionary South. These revolutions thus invite us to consider southern Europe as part of the Ibero-American world, and vice versa, and to think about both the Mediterranean Sea and the Indian Ocean as interconnected imperial and revolutionary maritime spaces.

A first crucial global consequence of the Napoleonic wars was a considerable strengthening of the military and fiscal apparatuses of states and empires alike, which resulted in more assertive central government through the expansion of administrative controls, fiscal impositions and military reforms. Linda Colley has forcefully argued and demonstrated that, in the age of revolutions, it was the intensification of warfare that led to an unprecedented circulation and adoption of constitutions across the globe. Constitutions served the purpose of legitimising the expansion of empires, but also represented tools of resistance to them among local populations and armies alike.[17] The uprisings of the 1820s across the global South confirm the validity of these claims. However, as I argue in this book, constitutions were also a response to the reorganisations of territory that took place in this period as a result of such imperial expansion, and served the purpose of reconfiguring these to meet the expectations of a variety of local provincial and imperial groups. Such administrative and fiscal transformations in fact carried with them demands that autonomy be safeguarded, as well as resistance to the increasingly intrusive financial and administrative structure of the states that emerged from this era of global warfare. The debates about constitutional government that characterised these revolutions, especially from Latin America to southern Europe, can only be understood in relation to the conflicts triggered by these processes.[18]

17. Linda Colley, *The Gun, the Ship, and the Pen: Warfare, Constitutions, and the Making of the Modern World* (New York: W. W. Norton & Co., 2021).

18. Defence of self-government against centralisation emerged also in France at the same time. See Annelien de Dijn, *French Political Thought from Montesquieu to Tocqueville: Liberty in a Levelled Society?* (Cambridge: Cambridge University Press, 2009).

Demands for autonomy from increasing central controls were, without exception, by-products of the Napoleonic period, and represent a shared cause for revolution in the global South up to the 1820s. In the Spanish Empire after 1808, the determination of local and regional authorities to participate in new constituent powers stemmed from a vacuum of authority occasioned by the decapitation of the monarchy in Spain. Between then and the 1820s in the revolutionary contexts of the Spanish Empire, the relationship between state structures, provinces and local authorities was contested and rethought, while regions, provinces and communes sought to reaffirm their autonomy.[19] However, attempts by the metropolis to reassert state authority and to crush self-government in an unprecedented fashion very soon followed, exacerbating resistance. Between 1812 and 1814 first, and in 1820 yet again, Spanish governments attempted to extend to the colonies those parts of the Cádiz Constitution which envisaged a single imperial nation with a centrally controlled administration. Failure by Spanish liberals to take into account aspirations for self-government that had emerged after 1808 resulted in revolution and the full independence of the Spanish colonies. Metropolitan Spain itself was not untouched by such reaffirmations of autonomy: the declaration of the Cádiz Constitution in 1820 triggered counterrevolutionary movements that defended the traditional territorial privileges or *fueros* of the Basque country and Navarre that had been abolished by the constitution.[20]

By contrast with the territories of the Spanish Empire after 1808, the revolution in Naples and Sicily in 1820 did not originate from a temporary power vacuum. Rather, it represented a reaction to, and an act of resistance against, the new centralised state structures that the Neapolitan Bourbon dynasty inherited from the Napoleonic occupation after 1815. In Naples the local and provincial authorities that hoped to participate in exercising the new constituent powers of 1820 did so because they resented the abolition of traditional self-government. They aspired to re-found the monarchy by combining constitutional rights with local self-rule. Thus in this monarchy too, as in the Spanish Empire, revolution was marked by a quest for local autonomy. As a consequence, in spite of the different circumstances leading to revolution, the Cádiz Constitution was understood in strikingly similar ways both in the Mediterranean and in Spanish

19. José M. Portillo Valdés, *Crisis atlántica: Autonomía e independencia en la crisis de la monarquía hispana* (Madrid: Marcial Pons, 2006), p. 158.

20. Portillo Valdés, *Crisis atlántica*, p. 48; Pedro Rújula and Manuel Chust, *El Trienio Liberal en la monarquía hispánica: Revolución e independencia (1820–1823)* (Madrid: Catarata, 2020).

America. In Central America and New Spain, support for Cádiz was conflated with the defence of the *pueblos* (Spanish colonial towns), according to the colonial administrative tradition. Here the *pueblo* in the sense of nation was conceived first and foremost, as in Sicily and the Neapolitan provinces, as being made up of communes.[21] The elites of both the Spanish colonies and Sicily, a separate state within an ancient composite monarchy, could only accept constitutional government if it guaranteed the reorganisation of their monarchies on a federative basis. Those Spanish American patriots who wished to remain loyal to the Spanish monarchy demanded that their territories be put on an equal footing with those of Spain. They requested either equal representation in the Cortes in Madrid or the creation of Cortes on both sides of the Atlantic. Sicilian patriots likewise demanded the establishment of two separate parliaments, one in Naples and one in Palermo. Similar requests were put forward in 1822 by the representatives of Brazil in the Portuguese Cortes, with the object of federalising the empire with assemblies on both sides of the Atlantic.

Like the Neapolitan and Sicilian revolutions, the Greek revolt represented an affirmation of autonomy against an increasingly intrusive central power. Although the nature of 'centralisation' was different, outcomes were similar. In the Ottoman context, central power was exerted not though new administrative structures, but rather in a violent and unprecedented way by sultanic determination to crush any form of independent power. Following the end of the war against Russia in 1812, Mahmud II embarked on new policies aimed at strengthening his authority, and set about repressing any form of insubordination from the notables who controlled the provinces of the empire and constituted its main military forces. Mahmud intervened against all of those who were acting no longer as representatives of the empire but merely as independent rulers, reaffirming his authority by killing them and replacing them with loyalists. Among those disposed of was Ali Pasha of Yannina, who had carved out a semi-independent state around Epirus and controlled parts of the Morea and mainland Greece. His presence provided a modicum of stability and protection to these territories previously subject to constant

21. Jordana Dym, *From Sovereign Villages to National States: Cities, State, and Federation in Central America, 1759–1839* (Albuquerque, NM: University of New Mexico Press, 2006); Antonio Annino, 'Cádiz y la revolución territorial de los pueblos mexicanos 1812–1821', in *Historia de las elecciones en Iberoamérica, siglo XIX*, ed. Antonio Annino (Buenos Aires: Fondo de Cultura Económica, 1995), pp. 177–226. On reactions to Cádiz, see also Brian R. Hamnett, *The End of Iberian Rule on the American Continent, 1770–1830* (Cambridge: Cambridge University Press, 2017).

incursions by Albanian bandits. In 1820 the sultan decided to launch a military campaign against him headed by the new governor of the Morea, Hursid Pasha. Thereupon the Greek notables, fearful that they might be the next target of Ottoman repression, rebelled and triggered the Greek revolution.[22]

The Greek revolution was not the only uprising to shake the Ottoman Empire in this turbulent decade in response to increasing pressures from the centre. Another revolt broke out in Lebanon in 1821, where the Christian communities reacted to unprecedented fiscal demands from local notables that had disrupted traditional community bonds; and a major rebellion broke out in Bosnia in 1829, in reaction to the abolition of the Janissaries carried out in 1826 in Constantinople, but resisted across the empire. Among all of these Ottoman events the Greek revolution was the only one to take on a clear-cut confessional dimension—the Mount Lebanon insurrection remained multiconfessional in nature—and the only one to converge with other southern European insurrections in terms of its political and constitutional culture.[23]

Administrative and fiscal reforms and enhanced state interference account for the explosion of anticolonial rebellions in the British and Dutch empires in the same years. Although it was only later that the language of constitutionalism would be adopted in the Asian and Mediterranean territories of these empires, the resulting grievances had origins similar to those arising in the lands already mentioned that were subject to other imperial regimes.[24] This phase of extension and consolidation of British imperial rule across the world represented a specific moment of its history marked by colonial or 'proconsular' despotism, aristocratic and military government, neo-mercantilist economic policies and attacks on feudal privileges and local oligarchies, accompanied by the establishment

22. Frederick F. Anscombe, *State, Faith, and Nation in Ottoman and Post-Ottoman Lands* (Cambridge: Cambridge University Press, 2014). On these policies, see also Sukru Huseyin Ilikak, 'A Radical Rethinking of Empire: Ottoman State and Society during the Greek War of Independence (1821–1826)', unpublished PhD dissertation, Harvard University, 2011, pp. 27–93.

23. Frederick F. Anscombe, 'The Balkan Revolutionary Age', *The Journal of Modern History* 84, no. 3 (2012): 572–606; Peter Hill, 'How Global Was the Age of Revolutions? The Case of Mount Lebanon, 1821', *Journal of Global History* 16, no. 1 (2021): 65–84; Hill, 'Mount Lebanon and Greece: Mediterranean Crosscurrents, 1821–1841', *Historein* 20, no. 1 (2021), DOI: https://doi.org/10.12681/historein.24937.

24. But for early engagement with southern European constitutionalism by an Indian liberal such as Rammohan Roy, see Christopher Bayly, *Recovering Liberties: Indian Thought in the Age of Liberalism and Empire* (Cambridge: Cambridge University Press, 2011), pp. 42–50.

of racial hierarchies and a commitment to 'civilise' local populations. In spite of the obvious ideological differences, its style of governance had similarities to that introduced by Napoleon and, after 1815, was politically consistent with the absolutism dominant in continental Europe, aiming as it did at strengthening state power. After 1815 the experiment of exporting constitutions to the Mediterranean was abandoned, as imperial agents came to be convinced that the local aristocracies were not capable of self-government. The circulation of imperial administrators among colonies across the world guaranteed a degree of consistency in outlook and objectives. Sir Thomas Maitland, who had ruled over Saint-Domingue in 1797 and acted as governor of Ceylon between 1805 and 1811, was appointed governor of Malta in 1813, and from the following year to 1823 also lord high commissioner of the Ionian Islands.[25] In subsequent years the administrative reforms introduced in the colonies of Malta and the Ionian Islands were also inspired by the example of what the French had done after conquering Naples. Unsurprisingly, the grievances of the local elites in these insular dominions were similar to those of their counterparts in the Neapolitan provinces and in Sicily, where the Bourbons had retained the French centralised system. As a consequence, in Britain's recently established colonial dependencies within and beyond the Mediterranean, attempts at curbing local autonomy and aristocratic self-rule produced either resentment or outright rebellion. In the Ionian Islands, the distaste for administrative despotism that triggered revolution in the Kingdom of the Two Sicilies did not lead to a fully-fledged revolution. Only very localised disturbances associated with the outbreak of the Greek revolution occurred in 1821 on these islands. Most members of its elites remained loyal to Britain, but some of them considered service with imperial Russia, and were drawn to the new ideas of Greek and Italian nationality.[26] More substantial resistance to colonial rule than in the Mediterranean came, however, from the aristocracies in Ceylon and in Java, under the British

25. Christopher Bayly, *Imperial Meridian: The British Empire and the World 1780–1830* (London: Routledge, 1989); Lauren Benton and Lisa Ford, *Rage for Order: The British Empire and the Origins of International Law (1800–1850)* (Cambridge, MA: Harvard University Press, 2016).

26. On the Ionian islands in the 1820s, see Konstantina Zanou, *Transnational Patriotism in the Mediterranean, 1800–1850: Stammering the Nation* (Oxford: Oxford University Press, 2018); Sakis Gekas, *Xenocracy: States, Class and Colonialism in the Ionian Islands, 1815–1864* (New York: Berghahn, 2016). On Napoleonic influence over the Ionian administrative reorganisation, see Giuseppe Grieco, 'The British Empire and the Two Sicilies: Constitutions and International Law in the Revolutionary Mediterranean, ca. 1800–60', unpublished PhD dissertation, Queen Mary University of London, 2022.

and the Dutch respectively. The colonial rebellions in Ceylon between 1817 and 1818, and subsequently in 1821 and 1823, and the long and bloody anti-Dutch revolution led by Prince Diponegoro in Java between 1825 and 1830 are cases in point.[27] In the Pacific Ocean and Asia anticolonial rebellions and wars resulted in the strengthening and centralisation of kingdoms and empires and not, as in the Ibero-American world and the Mediterranean, in their temporary fragmentation. Faced with British military pressures, monarchies superseded local and tribal identities in Burma, New Zealand and Tonga alike.[28]

A second global interrelated consequence of the Napoleonic wars was that by permanently transforming the relationship between centres and peripheries in states and empires alike, they unleashed a multiplicity of territorial crises. The wars between 1808 and 1815 and the administrative reforms that followed them resulted in radical revisions of territorial relationships. These revisions in turn triggered new rivalries between urban centres and provinces, and renewed long-standing conflicts. In other words, the 1820s revolutions in both southern Europe and Latin America were either rebellions against metropolitan centres, or reactions to the transformation of former centres into new peripheries; they might be civil wars opposing different provinces within the same polities, as well as conflicts between secondary cities and their capitals within colonial and European territories. It was through constitutions that attempts were made to settle these conflicts, but their implementation in turn produced new disagreements and alternative constitutional projects.

The revolutions that affected the Portuguese Empire on both sides of the Atlantic between 1817 and 1824 are a case in point. The transfer of the seat of power of the Bragança dynasty from Lisbon to Rio de Janeiro in 1808 changed the internal balance of the empire, and produced long-lasting shocks on both sides of the Atlantic. It left Portugal at the mercy of Great Britain, and with a very distant monarch. The 1820 revolution in Porto was caused by the transformation of Portugal, formerly the centre of the empire, into a provincial appendage ruled from Brazil.[29] But this transfer triggered territorial conflicts also within Brazil, where some provinces resented the excessive power of the new imperial centre, which they

---

27. Kingsley M. De Silva, *A History of Sri Lanka* (London: C. Hurst & Co., 1981); James Wilson, 'Reappropriation, Resistance, and British Autocracy in Sri Lanka, 1820–1850', *The Historical Journal* 60, no. 1 (2017): 47–69; Peter Carey, *The Power of Prophecy: Prince Diponegoro and the End of the Old Order in Java, 1785–1855* (Leiden: Brill, 2008).

28. Sivasundaram, *Waves*, pp. 53–55, 59–61, 62–64, 77, 207.

29. Paquette, *Imperial Portugal*.

would have preferred to remain in Portugal. The republican revolutions of Pernambuco in 1817 and 1821–25 were not only antimonarchical in nature, but also a defence of provincial autonomy against Rio de Janeiro.[30]

Yet the explosion of these multiple conflicts was not unique to the Portuguese Empire. In 1820 in Sicily, the city of Catania engaged in a civil war with the capital of the island, Palermo. Like Pernambuco, Catania preferred the rule of the distant centre, Naples, to the renewed oppression of its ancient insular capital that was now leading an independentist revolt. In the same years other striking parallels can be found: between the territorial crisis and revolutionary events of Spanish America and the Ottoman world, for example. In both empires, independence first resulted in the affirmation of provincial sovereignty, not national emancipation. The transition to independence of the viceroyalty of the Río de la Plata, which was declared in 1816, resulted first and foremost in the self-rule of its constituent provinces. When the former capital of the viceroyalty, Buenos Aires, tried to assert its primacy over the provinces, exert control over them and advance a unitary notion of the nation, civil war ensued. The province of Córdoba attempted to create an alternative and federal governmental structure, against the claims of Buenos Aires. It was only the urgent need to create a common front to defeat the royalist army in Peru that forced the provinces to arrive at a compromise and establish some form of administrative cooperation.[31] The Greek revolution, meanwhile, was strikingly similar in nature to that of the Río de la Plata. It was a revolt of discrete and sovereign territories that first joined the revolution as separate entities in 1821. Attempts to coordinate and centralise government led to clashes between these territories and civil war between the Peloponnese, the islands and continental Greece. As in Río de la Plata, so too in Greece the emergency of the war forced the insurgents to find a compromise. In Greece as in South America, nation building was therefore the result of war pressures.[32] Likewise, the revolution that broke out

30. On Pernambuco in particular, see also Evaldo Cabral de Mello, *A outra Independência: O federalismo pernambucano de 1817 a 1824* (São Paulo: Editora 34, 2004); Denis Antônio de Mendonça Bernardes, *O patriotismo constitucional: Pernambuco 1820–1822* (São Paulo: Editora Universitária UFPE, 2001).

31. Geneviève Verdo, 'L'Organisation des souverainetés provinciales dans l'Amérique indépendante: Le cas de la république de Córdoba, 1776–1827', *Annales* 69, no. 2 (2014): 349–81; Marcela Ternavasio, *Gobernar la revolución: Poderes en disputa en el Río de la Plata, 1810–1816* (Buenos Aires: Siglo XXI, 2007).

32. Clément Thibaud, *Républiques en armes: Les armées de Bolívar dans les guerres d'indépendance du Venezuela et de la Colombie* (Rennes: Presses Universitaires de Rennes, 2006).

in the coastal city of Genoa in the Kingdom of Piedmont-Sardinia represented the rebellion of a former capital (the centre of the ancient republic
absorbed by Piedmont in 1814) turned into a provincial city against its new
capital, Turin.

   The complex nature of the territorial crises associated with the southern European revolutions is reflected in the declarations of national independence they produced. Besides the famous declaration of independence
of Greece in 1821, a number of lesser known such documents were issued
in southern Europe. Independence was thus declared in Sicily in 1820, in
Portugal in 1821 and in Piedmont (Alessandria) and Naples in 1821. These
declarations bear witness to the 'global contagion of sovereignty' that
followed the American declaration of 1776, to cite David Armitage's
felicitous description. They belong to a 'first Eurasian rights moment'
of dissemination of these documents across the world that lasted until
1848.[33] Yet these declarations each meant something entirely different, as
did the idea of nation that each embodied. The affirmations of sovereignty
contained in them can only be understood in relation to the variety of
their domestic, imperial, international, trans-imperial and transnational
contexts. The Greek declaration of independence was an anti-despotic
document that challenged the sovereignty of the Ottoman Empire, but
did not exclude an accommodation with it. The Portuguese declaration
of 1821 was a declaration of independence from Brazil, but by no means a
request that the empire be dissolved; rather it sought the return of its centre to its European component. In the citadel of Alessandria in Piedmont, a
reference to the future independence of Italy conveyed hopes for a federation of autonomous Italian states after the expulsion of the Austrians
from the peninsula. The declaration of Italian independence endorsed by
the Neapolitan parliament was for its part compatible with the existence
of the Neapolitan nation, and similarly the Piedmontese declaration was
an act in defiance of Austrian imperial hegemony over the peninsula.
For the Neapolitan revolutionaries, therefore, pushing the claims of Italy
was a means of revising the international order, not an attempt to abolish or undermine the separate existence of their kingdom. The Sicilian
declaration served the purpose primarily of protecting the autonomy of
the island: this could be achieved either within a federalised kingdom—
one which contained many elements of continuity with the old composite

33. David Armitage, *The Declaration of Independence: A Global History* (Cambridge,
MA: Harvard University Press, 2007), pp. 103, 107.

Sicilian monarchy—or, alternatively, by the establishment of a separate state under the protection of the British Empire.

The revolutionaries in southern Europe were aware of the global space within which their own demands were articulated. The trans-Atlantic space in particular caught the attention not only of supporters of the constitution in Portugal and Spain, who aimed at reforming their empires, but also of observers in Naples, Sicily and Greece. In these countries, revolutionaries related their own aspirations to those of the Latin American movements for independence. While colonial rebellions in Asia were only scantily known of, southern European revolutionaries were aware of the global outreach of the British Empire and its increasing direct or indirect geopolitical influence. Nonetheless, they often saw its presence in the Mediterranean and its role in European politics as compatible with their own agenda, and went so far as to call for British imperial protection as a guarantee for their constitutions.

At the same time, contemporaries in these countries understood this revolutionary wave as a peculiarly southern European phenomenon. It is even more remarkable that it was mainly the Portuguese, whose revolution was quintessentially Atlantic (rebelling as they did also to call their monarch back from Brazil), who came to perceive their revolt as part of a wave that stretched all the way to the Aegean. The existence of a specific revolutionary space between Portugal and Greece is not an ahistorical projection of our own understanding of these events. The idea that they represented a set of relatively peaceful military uprisings in the name of the constitution, when set against the memory of the French revolutionary conquest and destruction of preceding years, echoed among constitutionalists in Portugal, Spain and Naples. It was only the Greek revolutionaries, concerned as they were to disassociate themselves from the other uprisings, who rejected the notion of a 'southern regeneration'. The Greeks preferred to define their insurrection as an assertion of Europe's Christian civilisation against Ottoman despotism.

Another reason to treat these southern European events together is that they shared many converging, or at least comparable, features. Revolutionaries from Portugal to Greece came up with a similar set of answers in response to a number of similar problems related to the question of sovereignty. What encapsulates the peculiarity of all of these revolutions, if compared to the French revolution, is the existence of a widespread hostility to excessive centralisation among large social sectors supporting them. In addition, right across southern Europe, revolutionaries remained resolutely in favour of monarchies, if constitutional ones, and considered the republican option embraced in Latin America or in France in the past as inconceivable. Finally, what justifies further a focus specifically upon the southern European/Mediterranean region within the context of the global 1820s is the existence of multiple forms of exchange, not only within the various imperial and colonial spaces to which each of the countries involved belonged, or with which they interacted, but also within southern Europe itself. These were the result of the circulation of individuals, information and ideas. The revolutions enhanced existing bonds between these countries and created new ones. One of these was their constitutional culture.

What constitution did revolutionaries fight for? A few introductory remarks

What constitutions did revolutionaries fight for, defend and implement in the 1820s? This book does not focus on theoretical debates in which constitutional thinkers were engaged. Its main object is to explore the ways in which constitutions were experienced by the population at large, and understood by revolutionary agents in particular. Nonetheless, a few introductory words are needed here about the texts that were introduced during this revolutionary wave in southern Europe, and how they related to each other. This brief sketch suggests that the constitutional cultures of this period were not only interconnected, but also constantly evolving, even within the narrow chronology of this specific revolutionary period. Local contexts and shifting national and international circumstances, as well as the different agendas and expectations of a variety of revolutionary leaders, account for these cultures' complexity.

As has been observed, by 1820, 'more than 60 different constitutions had been attempted within continental Europe'.[34] Among them, there is no doubt that by 1820 the Cádiz Constitution was the most widely known and favoured in southern Europe. It was this charter that revolutionaries saw fit to introduce not only in Spain in 1820, but also in Naples and Palermo in the same year, and in Piedmont in 1821.[35] Its association with the anti-Napoleonic struggle and its religious definition of the nation—evocative

34. Linda Colley, 'Empires of Writing: Britain. American and Constitutions, 1776–1848', *Law and History Review* 32, no. 2 (2014): 237–66 at p. 237.
35. On its southern European fame, see Jens Späth, 'Turning Constitutional History Upside Down: The 1820s Revolutions in the Mediterranean', in *Re-mapping Centre and Periphery: Asymmetrical Encounters in European and Global Contexts*, ed. Tessa Hauswedell, Axel Körner and Ulrich Tiedau (London: UCL Press, 2019), pp. 111–34.

connotations combining with an indirect electoral system—accounted for its widespread popularity. The peculiarities of this text owed much to the context in which it had been conceived. Its drafting and implementation had in fact been the consequence of the dynastic and political crisis precipitated by the French invasion of the Spanish monarchy and Napoleon's replacement of the Bourbons with a member of his own family, his brother Joseph, in 1808. In order to defend its independence from Napoleon's despotism, first local juntas were set up, then a central junta, and finally a Cortes Constituentes was elected to draft the constitution. The Spanish insurgents against Napoleon claimed that the legitimacy of these new bodies stemmed from the fact that, in the absence of the monarch, sovereignty had reverted to the nation.[36] The idea of the nation as sovereign lay at the centre of the constitution approved in Cádiz in 1812. The constituents conceived it in communitarian terms, as a sovereign entity that subsumed the rights of its citizens and was defined by Catholicism. It was a religious text that protected the Catholic unity of the monarchy and did not tolerate any other cult. This communitarian understanding of the Spanish nation accounted for the fact that the constitution lacked a separate catalogue of rights: these were in fact scattered through the document. To reflect the unity of the nation, the constitution introduced one single representative assembly, the Cortes, elected by quasi-universal male suffrage, albeit indirect. The Cortes had a central function in the architecture of the state and enjoyed very broad competences, not only legislative, but also in the sphere of international relations and military affairs. The monarch shared legislative powers with the Cortes, and was the sole executive authority. However, the Cádiz Constitution substantially reduced his prerogatives. Besides the Cortes, what limited his powers was the Council of State. This institution, whose members were appointed from a list chosen by the Cortes, was created to support him in his executive authority, but also to limit and contain his sphere of action.

While the Spanish liberals had dramatically transformed their political system, they did not seek to define their act as a revolutionary one. On the contrary, they strove to highlight the historical continuities of the text with the ancient institutions of a monarchy gradually eroded by absolutism. They did so firstly to demonstrate its national origin and deny the influence of any foreign documents (and in particular French revolutionary

---

36. José M. Portillo Valdés, *Revolución de nación: Orígenes de la cultura constitucional en España, 1780–1812* (Madrid: Centro de Estudios Políticos y Constitucionales, 2000); Ignacio Fernández Sarasola, *La Constitución de Cádiz: Orígen, contenido y proyección internacional* (Madrid: Centro de Estudios Políticos y Constitucionales, 2001).

doctrines), and secondly to appease those loyal monarchists who were fearful of any radical innovation. According to this national historicism, apparent in the 'Discurso preliminar' of the constitution, the origins of the sovereignty of the Spanish nation could be found in its ancient laws and institutions. By these means, the constitution was presented as a reformist text. This historicist attitude to constitution-making was not, however, simply a useful fiction: it also underpinned the way in which the constitution was implemented as a reformist document. It did not in fact abolish pre-existing legislation and institutions, but left it to the Cortes to repeal selectively those elements that were deemed to be despotic, without questioning in their entirety the *leyes fundamentales* of the monarchy.[37]

The 1820s represented a new context for the reception of the 1812 Spanish constitution, both nationally and internationally. The political realignments that emerged during the revolution in Spain, the so-called *Trienio Liberal* (or *Trienio Constitucional*; hereafter 'the Trienio'; for Portugal, 'the Triénio') of 1820–23, gave rise to alternative interpretations of the Cádiz Constitution. The most radical wing of the revolutionary front, the so-called *exaltados*, set themselves up as defenders of popular sovereignty. As a consequence, they not only supported any and every form of direct and indirect popular participation in the decision-making process, but defended in particular the prerogatives of the Cortes as the central institution of the constitutional regime. The more conservative supporters of the revolution, the so-called *moderados*, on the contrary wished drastically to limit the suffrage guaranteed by the constitution, to introduce a second chamber, or turn the Council of State into a fully-fledged senate, and to reinforce the powers of the monarch at the expense of those enjoyed by the Cortes.[38] Another key factor that affected the workings of the constitution was the monarch's resistance to any limitations upon his absolute power. The possibility of replacing the 1812 constitution with a more conservative document temporarily gathered momentum at the end of the constitutional period. In 1823, at the time of the French invasion of Spain that put an end to the revolution, the French government, along with some of these Spanish moderate liberals, pushed for the adoption of

37. Carlos Garriga and Marta Lorente, *Cádiz 1812: La constitución jurisdiccional* (Madrid: Centro de Estudios Políticos y Constitucionales, 2007), pp. 36–38.

38. Joaquín Varela Suanzes-Carpegna, *La monarquía doceañista (1810–1837)* (Madrid: Marcial Pons, 2013), pp. 243–317; Antonio Elorza, 'La ideología moderada en el Trienio Liberal', *Quadernos Hispanoamericanos* 288 (1974): 584–652.

the bicameral French 'Charte' of 1814 as a means of preventing the return to absolutism, but this project failed due to the hostility of the monarch.[39]

Outside Spain, the Spanish constitution provided a way of getting the constituent process off the ground with a minimum of complication and a measure of consensus. Yet even in those foreign countries where the Spanish constitution was declared and implemented, substantial groups of its supporters were keen to make some revisions to its text. This was due to a variety of reasons. First of all, revolutionaries drew upon a variety of other sources of inspiration when reflecting upon their own local political problems. In particular, although not exclusively, they were inspired by the French revolutionary constitutions and by the United States of America. Moreover, although the constitutional culture of the 1820s was defiantly international, there was a widespread consensus that constitutional texts and institutions could not simply be transferred from one country to another without taking into account national traditions and historical peculiarities. While revolutionaries resolutely rejected climatic theories employed to argue or insinuate that only some peoples were suited to constitutional government, they tended to agree that local circumstances should be taken into account when adopting a constitution.[40] As a Neapolitan admirer of the Spanish constitution claimed, this 'very wise constitution had to be accommodated to our own needs'; otherwise 'a religious esteem is easily turned into superstitious adoration'.[41] Finally, as had happened in Spain in 1823, the perceived radicalism of the Spanish monocameral constitution, and the hostility of the kings to it, along with an unfavourable diplomatic context, led the most moderate fringe of the revolutionary elite to consider the possibility of an alternative constitution. These moderate groups hoped that an entirely different document, often inspired by British institutions or the French bicameral Charte, would be more agreeable to the monarchs while still guaranteeing limited government.

For all of the above reasons, outside Spain, the Cádiz Constitution was often interpreted in diverging ways in 1820, and adapted to local circumstances. In the Italian states, the immediate adoption of the Spanish

39. Emilio La Parra López, *Fernando VII: Un rey deseado y detestado* (Barcelona: Tusquets Editores, 2018), p. 476; Gonzalo Butrón Prida, 'From Hope to Defensiveness: The Foreign Policy of a Beleaguered Liberal Spain, 1820–1823', *The English Historical Review* 133, no. 562 (2018): 567–96.

40. See the article in a Portuguese periodical, 'On How to Translate a Constitution from One Country to Another' (my translation), *O Liberal*, no. 24, 14 March 1821, p. 4.

41. *L'Amico della Costituzione*, 4 August 1820, p. 1.

constitution was due to the fact that, as a symbol of anti-despotic resistance, it had already acquired considerable popularity among conspirators. As such, it was the document most likely to obtain the broadest consensus, and for this reason all revolutionaries initially rallied behind it. This, however, meant neither that it was universally supported nor that it was interpreted univocally. In Naples the provisional government decided that a constituent assembly was not needed in adopting this constitution, but the Neapolitan parliament elected according to the system of the Spanish charter then proceeded to discuss in detail the adaptation of each of its provisions, although it rarely modified them dramatically. As mentioned above, it was nonetheless interpreted by the majority of Neapolitan revolutionaries as an anti-Napoleonic, anti-centralising and quasi-federal document that sought to recast the state as an assemblage of communes and provinces. In addition, more than anywhere else in the region, in Naples the revolution was marked by the publication of an array of old and more recent constitutions and by the translation of the writings of constitutional thinkers such as Benjamin Constant and Jeremy Bentham.[42] In Palermo, the two key social groups behind the revolt, the aristocracy and the artisans' corporations, had both agreed that a national assembly elected by the communes of western Sicily and the capital would use the Spanish text as a basis of discussion for the future constitution of the island. However, artisans and aristocrats assuredly entertained different expectations and objectives. Many aristocrats wished for their part to reintroduce the 1812 Sicilian constitution approved during the British occupation. This was a document that, being inspired by the institutional architecture of the unwritten constitution of Great Britain, granted separate representation to the island's aristocracy. This constitution had introduced a bicameral system with an elective Camera dei comuni (Chamber of commons) appointed by restricted suffrage. The aristocracy of Palermo saw it as a peculiarly national constitution, as its new Camera de' pari (Chamber of peers, modelled on the British House of Lords), of 1812, granted membership to the members of the two *bracci* of the ancient medieval Sicilian parliament, aristocrats and churchmen.[43] For their part, artisans defended

42. Werner Daum, *Oscillazioni dello spirito pubblico: Sfera pubblica, mercato librario e comunicazione nella rivoluzione del 1820–21 nel Regno delle Due Sicilie* (Naples: Società napoletana di storia patria, 2015); Carlos María Rodríguez López-Brea, 'La Constitución de Cádiz y el proceso revolucionario en las Dos Sicilias (1820–1821)', *Historia Contemporánea* 47 (2013): 561–94.

43. Rosselli, *Lord William Bentinck*; Andrea Romano, 'Introduzione', in Andrea Romano, ed., *Costituzione di Sicilia stabilita nel Generale Parlamento del 1812* (Soveria Mannelli: Rubbettino editore, 2000 [Palermo, 1813]), pp. xix–lvii.

the Spanish constitution but wanted to blend its principles and universal suffrage with the recognition of their corporations' authority.

In Piedmont, too, the introduction of the Spanish charter in 1821 concealed the fact that supporters of constitutionalism were split on the institutional future of the kingdom. Support for the Spanish charter had been a strategic decision taken to maximise consensus across the conspiratorial networks that had organised the revolution.[44] A number of prominent aristocratic liberals were critical of it, however. This group included both those who had taken a leading role in the conspiracy, such as Count Santorre di Santarosa, and those who would have preferred a transition towards representative government without violent means (a group that included intellectuals and officers such as Cesare Balbo, Emanuele Pes di Villamarina and Cesare D'Azeglio). This second group favoured instead either the Sicilian constitution, or the French Charte. What rendered these alternative models appealing was the role that they granted to the nobility and the greater powers they assigned to the monarch. For Santarosa, the Sicilian constitution turned the British constitution into a written document, but without its original flaws, as it abolished feudalism, and corrected the glaring deficiencies of Britain's electoral system. These aristocrats deemed the Spanish constitution too radical and revolutionary. For Villamarina it amounted in fact to nothing less than 'true democracy', a term that pointed to its popular nature, disregard for any aristocratic institutional role and de facto destruction of monarchical power. For him, democracy and monarchy were incompatible.[45]

In Portugal, the Spanish constitution represented an unavoidable point of reference for the constituents assembled between 1820 and 1822, but the constitution approved in the latter year in Lisbon did not simply replicate its Spanish equivalent.[46] The constituent assembly elected on December 1820 on the basis of the indirect system borrowed from the

44. On Piedmontese constitutional debates, see Jens Späth, *Revolution in Europa 1820–23: Verfassung und Verfassungskultur in den Königreichen Spanien, beider Sizilien und Sardinien-Piemont* (Cologne: SH Verlag, 2012); Gonzalo Butrón Prida, *Nuestra sagrada causa: El modelo gaditano en la revolución piamontesa de 1821* (Cádiz: Fundación Municipal de Cultura del Ayuntamiento de Cádiz, 2006), esp. pp. 51–70.

45. Quoted in Butrón Prida, *Nuestra sagrada causa*, p. 57.

46. A comparison between the two constitutions is in Joaquín Varela Suanzes-Carpegna, 'El constitucionalismo español y portugués durante la primera mitad del siglo XIX (un estudio comparado)', *Estudos Íbero-Americanos* 33, no. 1 (2007): 38–85. See also Paquette, *Imperial Portugal*, pp. 130–34; António Manuel Hespanha, *Guiando a mão invisível: Direitos, Estado e lei no liberalismo monárquico português* (Coimbra: Almedina, 2004); Hespanha, 'O constitucionalismo monárquico português: Breve síntese', *Historia Constitucional* 13 (2012): 477–526.

Cádiz Constitution approved, one year later, a working document, the *Bases da constituição*, heavily dependent on the Spanish charter, to draft the new constitution. Similar to the Cádiz Constitution, the *Bases*—as also the Portuguese constitution approved the following year—retained a historicist approach. Both proclaimed that they did not represent revolutionary acts or a breach with the past, but were rather reforming documents aiming at the re-establishing of traditional rights and forgotten fundamental laws. This cautious reformist rhetoric was designed to reassure its audiences that it had nothing to do with French Jacobinism.

At the same time, the 1822 Portuguese constitution differed in a number of important ways from the Spanish one. It was a much more concise text. While it reaffirmed the sovereignty of the nation, unlike the Spanish constitution it included a separate list of the rights and duties of the citizen that owed much to the French declarations of 1789. It retained a single representative chamber, but it replaced the Spanish indirect electoral system, used in 1820 to appoint the Portuguese constituent assembly, with a direct one. Finally, although like the Spanish constitution it proclaimed that the religion of the nation was the Catholic faith, it diverged from it in affording toleration to other denominations.

In addition, it should be noted that Portugal was the only southern European state among those undergoing revolution in the 1820s in which the demise of monocameral constitutions led to a new compromise between liberals and the monarchy. Such a compromise proved impossible in Spain, Piedmont and Naples because of the resolute opposition of their kings. In Portugal, the consecutive repression of the revolutions in Naples, Piedmont and Spain, and increasing hostility towards the 1822 constitution, paved the way to its repeal in 1823. Yet when Dom João VI died, his heir Dom Pedro of Brazil approved in 1826 a new and more moderate constitution, the so-called 'Carta'. This new text, in force for a biennium, retained a role for representative government but gave the monarch greater powers than those stipulated by the previous constitution. It ceased to operate only because of the re-establishment of absolutism by Dom Miguel in 1828. This moderate constitution, heavily influenced by the Brazilian constitution of 1824, introduced a second aristocratic chamber (Câmara dos Pares) which included a hereditary nobility, and a chamber of deputies (Câmara dos Deputados) appointed through an indirect electoral system limited by census. The monarch was given a central role in the new institutional architecture of the state. The constitution endowed him with executive authority, and legislative powers shared with the Cortes, and declared him to represent the nation along with the Cortes. But additional attributes were granted to him as holder of the so-called 'moderating power', a fourth power beyond the judicial, legislative and executive ones listed by the constitution. By virtue of this fourth power (a notion borrowed from the writings of Benjamin Constant), the monarch was entitled to appoint an unlimited number of peers to the upper chamber, to summon and dissolve the Cortes and to appoint and dismiss ministers. It crucially also gave the sovereign an absolute veto over legislative measures.[47]

A further factor limiting the impact of the Spanish constitution upon southern Europe was its absence from the constitutional debates of the Greek revolution. While Greek constitutional culture reveals an array of foreign influences, the Spanish text was not among them. During the Greek revolution the process of constitution-making was led primarily by members of the Greek Phanariot families, an elite with a tradition of service to the Ottoman Empire as interpreters and as governors of the Danubian Principalities, and by Greek scholars who had studied at German, Italian and French universities. Frequent travel to France and Britain by members of these groups had exposed them to a variety of legal and constitutional texts. One of the authors of the first constitution, Prince Mavrokordatos, was widely known to be a fervent admirer of the institutions of Great Britain. One of the authors of the declaration of independence of 1821, Anastasios Polyzoidis, a jurist who had studied in Vienna and Göttingen, had taken inspiration from the American Declaration of Independence. His publications reveal a breadth of interest in a variety of international texts. They included translations of Jeremy Bentham's essays and the American constitution, as well as of Magna Charta. At the same time, like most contemporary Portuguese and Neapolitan revolutionaries too, Polyzoidis argued against an unthinking and unqualified transfer of foreign political models, as Greeks had to 'imitate and transfer within our own polity what is transferable, imitable and implementable'.[48]

47. Paquette, 'The Brazilian Origins of the 1826 Portuguese Constitution', *European History Quarterly* 41, no. 3 (2011): 444–71; Hespanha, 'O constitucionalismo monárquico'.

48. On Polyzoidis, see Anastasios Polyzoidis, *Κείμενα για τη δημοκρατία, 1824–1825* (Texts on democracy, 1824–1825), ed. Filimon Paionidis and Elpida Vogli (Athens: Ekdoseis Okto, 2011). Quotation from Anastasios Polyzoidis, *Προσωρινό Πολίτευμα της Ελλάδος και σχέδιον οργανισμού των επαρχιών αυτής. Αμφότερα επιδιορθωμένα και επικυρωμένα υπό της Δευτέρας Εθνικής Νομοθετικής των Ελλήνων Συνελεύσεως εν Άστρει, οις έπονται το πολιτικόν σύνταγμα της Βρεταννίας και το των Ηνωμένων Επικρατειών της Αμερικής, μετά της διατυπώσεως του συνεδρίου αυτών, εξ Αγγλικών και Γαλλικών συγγραμμάτων μεταφρασθέντα υπό Α. Πολυζωίδου* (Provisional polity of Greece and a plan of the organisation of its provinces. Both revised and ratified by the second national assembly of the Greeks in Astros, accompanied by the Political Constitution of Britain and that of the United States of

Like the Cádiz Constitution, the three main revolutionary constitutions of 1821, 1823 and 1827 were deeply religious documents. The first national charter, the Provisional Constitution of Epidavros, approved in January 1822, included in its preamble a declaration of the independence of the Greek nation 'in the name of the Holy and Indivisible Trinity', and 'before God and man'. Its first article, devoted to religion, declared Orthodoxy to be the state religion, thus offering first and foremost a religious definition of the nation, as in Spain. Yet this religious dimension owed more to the very nature of the uprising as an anti-Ottoman revolt than to any direct influence from Spanish constitutionalism.

In Greece, not the Cádiz Constitution, but instead the French constitutions of 1791 and 1795 and the American constitution played an important role. The first Provisional Constitution included a catalogue of civil rights (applying only to those residents in Greece of the Christian faith), guaranteeing equality before the law, protection of property, personal safety and equal access to 'dignities'. It introduced an elected senate that could not be dissolved by the executive (as in the 1791 constitution) and an executive of five members appointed by a separate assembly (as in the 1795 constitution). While it introduced a separate and independent judiciary, its originality lay in the fact that legislative and executive powers were shared between the executive and the senate. In addition, while this constitution introduced for the first time some sort of centrally organised government, it left untouched the regional assemblies that governed the territories that had declared the revolution.[49] Consecutive revisions reflected the circumstances of the war and the need to find new compromises between the regional groups that led the revolution. The revision of this text, approved in Astros in 1823 and known as the Law of Epidavros, further centralised the structure of the state and at the same time reinforced the power of the senate. It abolished the regional assemblies but weakened also the veto wielded by the executive over the assemblies' decisions, which from being absolute became only temporarily suspensive. It also gave a role to

America, with the proceedings of their congresses, translated according to English and French treatises by Anastasios Polyzoidis) (Messolonghi: D. Mestheneos, 1824), p. iv.

49. A full translation in English was published as *The Provisional Constitution of Greece, Translated from the Second Edition of Corinth, Accompanied by the Original Greek; Preceded by a Letter to the Senate of the Grecian Confederation, and by a General View of the Origin and Progress of the Revolution, by a Grecian Eye-Witness; and Followed by Official Documents* (London: John Murray, 1823); the articles referred to here are at pp. 57–61. On Greek revolutionary constitutions, see Nicholas Kaltchas, *Introduction to the Constitutional History of Modern Greece* (New York: Columbia University Press, 1940), pp. 34–57; Aristovoulos Manessis, *Deux États nés en 1830: Ressemblances et dissemblances constitutionnelles entre la Belgique et la Grèce* (Brussels: Maison Ferdinand Larcier, 1959), esp. pp. 10–27.

the legislative assembly jointly with the executive in appointing all gov-ernmental officials, a provision inspired by the American constitution.[50] A third and final constitutional revision led in 1827 to the approval at Troezena of another and no longer provisional text with a more exten-sive catalogue of rights and an explicit reference, for the first time, to the principle of national sovereignty. The executive was now reduced to a sin-gle person, and the legislative powers of the elected assembly were rein-forced. The originality of the Greek constitutions lay not only in their cre-ative adaptation of a number of different models, but also in the persisting influence of local institutional and intellectual traditions. The pre-existing Ottoman administrative and territorial organisation provided a matrix for the administrative structures and electoral procedures of the newly declared state.[51] In addition, unlike the other constitutions of southern Europe, its models were republican texts. Yet, most Greek revolutionaries agreed on the need to find a monarch from a European dynasty as head of their new state, and started to look for one as early as 1823. They did so to legitimise their uprising in the eyes of the European powers, and to gain their support, but also out of sheer conviction that a monarch would be the best option to represent and bring together all the territories and people of Greece.[52] Thus, in spite of the peculiarities of the Greek case, most revolutionaries there agreed with their counterparts in Naples, Spain and Portugal that their future would require a monarch whose powers were limited, and not republican government.

The making of a constitutional order and its conflicts: plan of the book

The southern European revolutionaries' ambition to introduce constitu-tions and, in the case of Greece, to create a state as the precondition to it, demonstrate the extent to which these events belonged to 'a constitutional

---

50. The decrees amending the constitution at Astros in 1823 are available in French in *Constitution, loix, ordonnances des assemblées nationales des corps législatifs et du prési-dent de la Grèce, 1821–1832* (Athens: Imprimerie Royale, 1835), pp. 370–80.

51. Michalis Sotiropoulos and Antonis Hadjikyriacou, '*Patris, Ethnos*, and *Demos*: Representation and Political Participation in the Greek World', in Innes and Philp, *Re-imagining Democracy*, pp. 99–126. See also Michalis Sotiropoulos and Antonis Hadjikyri-acou, "'Βαδιζοντας προς τη μάχη ανάποδα": Οι πολιτικές αντιλήψεις του 1821 και η Εποχή των Επαναστάσεων'' ('Walking backwards into battle': Political concepts of 1821 and the Age of Revolutions), *Μνήμων* [*Mnimon*] 32 (2021): 77–109.

52. Michalis Sotiropoulos, "'United we stand, divided we fall": Sovereignty and Gov-ernment during the Greek Revolution (1821–28)', *Historein* 20, no. 1 (2021), DOI: https://doi.org/10.12681/historein.24928.

moment in global liberalism', in Bayly's phrase.[53] Crucially, one important effect of this historical experience was that it gave rise to a new popular constitutional culture. The claim of this book is that although relatively short-lived and enduringly successful only in Greece, these revolutions politicised new sectors of society, generated unprecedented quantities of printed material and fostered the discussion of novel ideas and experimentation with practices such as elections. They provided a crucial context for the emergence of liberalism as a popular political force in favour of constitutional government across southern Europe, and different in character from French and British liberalisms. These revolutionary experiences informed the political life of Portugal and Spain for many decades, and helped to forge a long-lasting revolutionary tradition on the Italian peninsula. They stirred considerable interest among public audiences beyond the boundaries of their states, and influenced events outside them. The Greek revolution was the most popular cause in Europe at the time, since it was construed as a defence of Christianity and European civilisation, but the revolutions in Naples, Spain and Portugal also attracted much attention. In France and Britain they were keenly followed and acclaimed by radicals and liberals advocating constitutional reform. In addition, events in Spain and Greece in particular had an important role in influencing the political culture and the objectives of the Decembrist insurrection of 1825 in Russia.[54]

The book argues that the most remarkable feature of these revolutionary events is the widespread political awareness among the populations that they produced. In fact, if we exclude the extremely short-lived Piedmontese revolutions, they all enjoyed substantial popular support, and were not elitist. Admittedly, the introduction of constitutions was divisive, led to alternative understandings of what rights should be guaranteed and produced bitter conflicts and civil wars, as well as popular movements against those same constitutions. Nonetheless, these conflicts helped to politicise the societies of the countries in which they took place, producing novel and unprecedented forms of participation and political awareness. In Spain and Portugal in particular, they gave rise, among other things, to new and to some extent popular counterrevolutionary movements.

53. Christopher Bayly, 'Rammohan Roy and the Advent of Constitutional Liberalism in India, 1800–30', *Modern Intellectual History* 4, no. 1 (2007): 25–41.

54. Derek Offord, 'The Response of the Russian Decembrists to Spanish Politics in the Age of Fernand VII', *Historia Constitucional* 13 (2012): 163–91; Richard Stites, 'Decembrists with a Spanish Accent' *Kritika: Explorations in Russian and Eurasian History* 12, no. 1 (2011): 5–23.

The book explores political participation, mobilisation and politicisation—whether in favour of or in opposition to constitutions and new institutions—thematically, as experiences that simultaneously affected Portugal, Greece, Piedmont, Naples and Sicily, adopting a comparative and transnational approach. The existence of shared features and connections facilitates the task. Such an method, if rigorously pursued, forces us to look not only at converging features, but also at differences and peculiarities, while circumventing the pitfalls of exceptionalism. With this in mind, I shift focus from one space to another, and zoom in and out, moving from country to country, province to province or city to city, comparing these with each other or disclosing connections between them. While comparisons and exchanges between national contexts remain important, they do not always provide the most fruitful unit of analysis. The existence of interactions at various levels, across state borders and across the sea, suggests the need to adopt the approach of connected and transnational or trans-local history. Comparisons are explored through a variety of perspectives that complement intellectual and cultural history with the history of institutions and political practices, and social and political history, microhistory and biography with the analysis of larger-scale events and spaces. By so doing, the book seeks to arrive at an understanding of how different social groups, from army officers to clerics, from artisans to shopkeepers and peasants, understood the constitution. Its central argument is that the distinctiveness of the popular constitutional culture produced by the societies here examined lay in its hybrid nature: it was a culture that upheld not only individual rights and the sovereignty of the people, but also the corporate privileges of professional bodies, the autonomy of local communities and territories and the cultural and religious uniformity of the nations. I also chart the circulation of printed material, information, rumours, political and military practices and individuals between different revolutionary contexts.

In order to do this, I have employed a wide range of primary sources, both printed and archival, and have also drawn on the existing secondary scholarship, both nationally and locally focused. At the same time, my book builds on existing scholarship that has adopted comparative and transnational approaches to compare and connect revolutions. However, most of the existing research has tended to focus on exchanges and connections between no more than two countries in southern Europe in this period, or on circulation from or into just one of these revolutions. Even the most ambitious of these comparative works, Richard Stites's *The Four Horsemen* treats each revolution separately. While it includes Russia—a country that I do not cover in my work—it leaves out Portugal, Piedmont and Sicily.[55]

A comparative and transnational approach is adopted throughout the book in each of its sections. Part I is devoted to the relationship between army, war and revolution. Its first and second chapters explore the military origins of these revolutions, which all started as *pronunciamientos* (public proclamations by the army) by military officers. It looks at the impact that these officers' participation in the Napoleonic wars and as members of secret societies had in moulding new forms of patriotism and in developing insurrectionary plans in favour of constitutions. By studying the content and the transnational circulation of the manifestos issued by the insurgent officers and their contact with crowds, as well as the impact of war on society, this part of the book demonstrates the influence that military experiences had on popular mobilisation, and the extent to which such experiences redefined the relationship between political and military powers. After an initial consensus, ideological cleavages within the armies (in Spain and Portugal), and resistance by irregular armed groups against submission to political authorities (in revolutionary Greece) led to multiple conflicts that divided societies and territories along with their military forces. The third chapter looks at the impact that civil wars had in polarising public opinion around specific political programmes, and explores the role that guerrilla warfare and violence played in support of military operations. The fourth chapter in this section explores wars of national liberation. It seeks to explain why armed mobilisation against foreign armies called to crush the revolutions in Spain, Piedmont and Naples failed in spite of the popular support that had existed for the constitutions. Although in Greece the national insurrection succeeded, its fate, as everywhere else, was determined by foreign intervention.

By looking at the movement of volunteers, refugees and migrants across the Mediterranean, chapter five illuminates the connectedness of the revolutionary experience, and highlights the importance of trans-Mediterranean and trans-imperial crossings. It uses the biographies of three individuals who took part in the events in Palermo in 1820—an Ottoman Greek formerly employed by the Neapolitan navy, an Irish general at the service of the Bourbon absolutism and later head of the Greek revolutionary army, and a Sicilian revolutionary—to track the variety of mobilities that existed over the area between Portugal and Greece. It

55. Stites, *Four Horsemen.*

shows that while the revolution inaugurated new international trajectories, it also intensified existing ones, some dating from previous centuries, others initiated by the Napoleonic wars. The 1820s unleashed an era of political and social instability that continued until at least the 1860s.

In order to explore how constitutions were experienced and understood by different social groups, Part II of the book focuses on petitions to parliaments, national and local elections and plans for territorial reorganisation in each state. It demonstrates the ambiguous nature of the political culture produced by the revolutionary experience. Large sectors of society supported representative government with the object of defending corporate privileges and limiting scope for competition, and protecting local communities from state interference, while only minorities were keen to dismantle any form of protection of corporate life, and strengthen central government. Thus, notions of the state as an assemblage of territories and self-ruling localities often went hand in hand with demands to protect individual rights, and support for the rule of law, for the authority of the state, and for universal male suffrage. As an analysis of territorial conflicts and requests from communities suggests, constitutions were often understood as decentralising documents that protected local self-government. Demands for local autonomy associated with the quest for constitutional freedom were to reappear across southern Europe during the revolutions of the subsequent decades.

Part III explores the birth of a revolutionary public sphere. It focuses on the new circuits of communication that came about in this period, by studying the content and the national and transnational circulation of printed material, and the relationship of this to revolutionary sociability. It then moves on to explore the activities of patriotic societies, and argues that revolutionary practices such as banquets, singing and public ceremonies played a key role in shaping support for and an understanding of the constitution. In this context, secret societies changed character, and their activities in defence of the constitution turned from secret to public. While the revolutionary public sphere was the product of an interaction between mobilisation from above and spontaneous participation, this part of the book highlights the existence of local traditions of popular protest. It shows that crowd action in defence of the constitution had striking similarities to early modern urban revolts. Finally, it gives due attention to the anti-revolutionary popular culture that emerged in this period. It argues that the new counterrevolutionary public sphere of the 1820s can only be understood in terms of having developed in response to, and in dialogue with, the pro-constitutional sphere.

Part IV, finally, discusses the relationship between constitutional culture and religion. It argues that the relationship between religion and politics was at the heart of the political conflict between supporters and enemies of the revolutions. It shows that rather than rejecting religion, liberals strove to find an accommodation between their values and 'revealed truth'. Although they argued for enlightened forms of religiosity, most of them considered the religious uniformity of their societies advantageous, and many opposed religious toleration. Through a set of microhistories and trans-local comparisons, this part of the book highlights the role played by important sections of the clergy in supporting and preaching the constitution to the faithful, but also the divisions that the revolutions created within churches, down to the level of monastic communities and cathedral chapters. It highlights the importance that eighteenth-century reform movements and Enlightenment ideals had in shaping such attitudes, and assesses the impact that the revolutions had on churches and on liberal attitudes towards religion in the following decades.

The epilogue of the book uses the biographies of four revolutionaries— a Neapolitan international freedom fighter, a Portuguese army officer, a Spanish politician and moderate liberal thinker and a Greek memorialist and former guerrilla fighter—to discuss the aftermath and legacies of the 1820s revolutions, up to the 1860s, when the age of revolutions came to an end in southern Europe. These biographies suggest that the events of the 1820s continued to represent a point of reference for subsequent revolts, and that military initiative for regime change remained a constant feature of the life of these countries in the following decades. At the same time, from the 1830s onwards, moderate liberalism emerged as a new option holding out the hope of moving beyond the revolution to stabilise the political order. While the revolutionary legacy of the 1820s and the memory of the events of those years endured, portions of the educated classes of the countries concerned became convinced that a different sort of compromise with monarchical power had to be found to stem an otherwise never-ending revolutionary cycle. It is to the origin of this cycle that the following pages are devoted.

PART I

War, Army and Revolution

{〰〰〰〰}

Introduction

In February 1821 Vincenzo Pannelli and Carlo Cicognani entered the Papal States from the Kingdom of the Two Sicilies, crossing the border that divided the Abruzzo and Marche regions on the Adriatic coast. They were at the head of a small military cohort which they had named the 'Roman Legion'. In the town squares of the towns of Ancarano and Offida, joined now by other Neapolitan volunteers crying, 'Long live Pius VII! Long live the Spanish constitution!' and waving a tricolour flag, members of this 'Roman Constitutional Army' read out a proclamation in the name of the pope, the Catholic church, and the Spanish constitution in front of small crowds to whom cockades were distributed. Their manifesto claimed that this constitution, by binding together people and sovereign, and by sparing them the evils of aristocracy and any potential abuses of power, had become the 'Codice rigeneratore de' popoli cattolici' (restorative code of the Catholic peoples), having been endorsed by four different peoples in succession. The expedition had been meant to precipitate a carefully planned insurrection that would spread across the entire Papal States from the Marche to the Romagna: the organisers had foreseen the creation of four distinct military *campi* (districts) in different regions, where army officers and soldiers would muster and elect representatives to juntas that would in their turn appoint a provisional government in the city of Spoleto, far though it was from the capital city, Rome. Moving between the Papal State and the Kingdom of Naples, where they had spent a few months as temporary refugees under the recently established constitutional government, Pannelli and Cicognani had set up a new secret society called the Unione patriottica costituzionale, and had printed some six hundred copies of the proclamation given in advance of the insurrection to individual emissaries for distribution to the villages of the Papal States. The revolutionary attempt, however, was a hopeless failure. The Neapolitan revolutionaries refused to endorse their plans, and no parallel insurrections broke out in the rest of the papal territories, where their proclamations were met with widespread indifference. Their small military contingent was soon dispersed by papal troops: some of its members were immediately arrested, while others managed to make good their escape.[1]

This forgotten revolutionary attempt was neither an isolated occurrence nor unique in the nature of its planning, organisation, initial unfolding and key political messages. In fact, it belonged to a global wave of revolts stretching from Latin America to Asia in which army officers lead a variety of rebellions, mutinies and military insurrections threatening the integrity of the Spanish, Portuguese, Russian and Ottoman empires, and demanding political change in the states of Piedmont and of Naples. As a matter of fact, the army was at the centre of any and every civil conflict that erupted in the aftermath of the Napoleonic invasions. As the authors of the Roman constitutional manifesto discussed above were fully aware, theirs was the fourth revolution demanding a constitution that had taken place within Catholic countries in Europe. The first such revolution was initiated on 1 January 1820 by Rafael Riego, who, along with his troops based in the Andalusian town of Las Cabezas de San Juan (between Seville and Cádiz), had refused to cross the Atlantic and fight against the Latin American insurgents, a decision coordinated with that of Antonio Quiroga's regiments, which were already stationed on the coast. These military initiatives sent out shock waves across the Mediterranean and southern Europe. In the first days of July 1820, the Neapolitan revolution was launched by the officers Michele Morelli and Giuseppe Salvati, based in Nola, and immediately taken up by other, more senior officers, namely Lieutenant Colonel Lorenzo De Concilj and General Guglielmo Pepe. The rebellion of the garrison based in Porto under the leadership of Lieutenant Colonel Bernardo Correia de Castro e Sepúlveda and Colonel Sebastião Drago Valente de Brito Cabreira ensued soon after, on 24 August 1820, marking the beginning of the Triénio (1820–23) in Portugal. It was at the start of the next year that the Roman *carbonari* (members of the Carboneria secret society) organised their failed military uprising, one followed on 10 March 1821 by a pronunciamiento by Captains Giacomo Garelli and

1. Domenico Spadoni, *Una trama e un tentativo rivoluzionario dello stato romano nel 1820–21* (Rome: Albrighi e Segati, 1910). On the larger context of Papal–Neapolitan diplomatic relations during the revolution of 1820–21, see Hugh Brady, *Rome and the Neapolitan Revolution of 1820–21: A Study in Papal Neutrality* (New York: Columbia University Press, 1937).

Isidoro Palma di Borgofranco in the garrison of the city of Alessandria in Piedmont, which inaugurated the short-lived Piedmontese revolution. Only two weeks before, on 24 February, Alexandros Ypsilantis, at the head of a growing army of volunteers from the Christian populations of the Ottoman Empire, had delivered his declaration to the Greeks from the city of Jassy (Iași) in Moldavia, two days after crossing the river Pruth from Russian Bessarabia into Moldavia at Sculeni.[2] While it did not succeed in the Papal States, a similar revolutionary strategy put into practice by officers in Spain, Portugal and Naples first, and later in Piedmont, swept all before it, at least for the time being, compelling the existing authorities to accept the constitution. In Greece, it was successful in triggering an insurrection that led to the creation of a new state.

Through the so-called pronunciamiento, the military took the initiative in bringing about a change of government and in facilitating the introduction of a constitution by means of a public declaration that would launch the revolution by giving all the existing social groups favourable to change a sign that they should join in the insurrection. This practice was founded on the experience of Spanish popular insurrection and military revolt against the French invasion, which led to the belief that it was possible to combine popular revolt with guerrilla warfare and the military leadership of a regular army. As a military strategy, it was justified by the Rousseauian belief in the army's capacity to represent and act on behalf of the will of the nation: the mass participation of Spaniards in the guerrilla warfare against the invader proved the strength of such a bond between people and military leadership. Although this belief was based on a romanticised and exaggerated estimation of the patriotic and military virtues of the Spanish peasantry, the effectiveness of guerrillas having turned out to be limited and their contribution more than a little controversial, it proved to have an enduring appeal beyond the initial stages of these revolutions.[3]

2. For a narrative of these events, which however excludes Portugal and Piedmont, see now Stites, *Four Horsemen*. This is the date according to the Julian calendar, still used in the Ottoman Empire until 1917 (and would be 8 March according to the Gregorian calendar used by then in most of Europe). Please note that henceforth events in the Ottoman Empire and in connection with the Greek rebellion are cited using the Julian calendar.

3. Charles J. Esdaile, *Fighting Napoleon: Guerrillas, Bandits and Adventurers in Spain, 1808–1814* (New Haven, CT: Yale University Press, 2004); Esdaile, 'Popular Mobilisation in Spain, 1808–1810: A Reassessment', in *Collaboration and Resistance in Napoleonic Europe: State Formation in an Age of Upheaval, c. 1800–1815*, ed. Michael Rowe (New York: Palgrave Macmillan, 2003), pp. 90–106; Esdaile, 'Heroes or Villains Revisited: Fresh Thoughts on *la guerrilla*', in *The Peninsular War: Aspects of the Struggle for the Iberian Peninsula*, ed. Ian Fletcher (Staplehurst: Spellmount, 1998), pp. 93–114.

I argue that through the pronunciamiento, southern European revolutionaries justified their decisions by means of the formulation of a script stipulating how to declare, ratify, implement and enforce a revolution. It thus constituted a strategy that was both military and political. I borrow here Keith Baker and Dan Edelstein's definition of a revolutionary script as a narrative or set of narratives whose plot is defined against other earlier revolutions and scripts, and which generates events as well as practices. The process of its formation is the result of a competition to impose a specific script in a given revolutionary situation.[4] The script therefore has to be understood in terms both of its key principles, claims and justifications, and of its related practices (public rituals and political acts). Both the content of its main public documents—its manifestos—and the way in which they circulated are thus relevant to the analysis of the script, along with their reception. I am therefore concerned primarily with the pronunciamiento as a communication strategy addressing at the same time both military and civilian publics, as well as local, national and international audiences.[5]

This southern European revolutionary wave shared with the Spanish case a number of similarities: the importance of secret societies, in which the military and civilians collaborated; the determination of the military to engage with and communicate to the people on whose behalf they had intervened; and the decentred geographical origin of the revolutions, which were initiated far away from the capital cities or the hearts of the countries to be revolutionised. Thus the key features of the script followed by Cicognani and Pannelli were by no means wholly original, but represented a variant upon those taking place across the European peripheries in the same period. Historiography has explored primarily the script's Spanish origin, and highlighted its transnational influence as a model that would subsequently be much imitated. My claim, however, is that insurgents beyond Spain did not one and all simply imitate this original example, but rather shaped their own individual scripts in relation to it. In other words, military officers elsewhere often took Rafael Riego and Antonio Quiroga's pronunciamiento and its unfolding, directly or indirectly, as an example against or in terms of which to explain or defend their own initiatives. At the same time, the organisers and supporters

4. Keith Michael Baker and Dan Edelstein, eds, *Scripting Revolution: A Historical Approach to the Comparative Study of Revolutions* (Stanford, CA: Stanford University Press, 2015), esp. the introduction at pp. 1–21.

5. On this crucial aspect of the pronunciamiento, see Will Fowler, ed., *Forceful Negotiations: The Origins of the Pronunciamiento in Nineteenth-Century Mexico* (Lincoln, NE: University of Nebraska Press, 2010).

of these various insurgencies all made similar claims in in justification of their actions. As I shall demonstrate, their main political manifestos tended to share a number of themes and concepts. It is also striking to note that the insurgents all rooted the legitimacy of their intervention in the peoples' insurrections against Napoleon. Moreover, the synchronicity of such events and the intra-regional circulation of their key texts gave rise to a shared belief among liberals that these revolutions constituted a single event, one that enacted a veritable 'southern European script'. Central to this script was the contention that these revolutions represented the peaceful regeneration of the South, as opposed to the aggressive and destructive nature of the French revolution, consolidating the perception that each of these revolutions was both a local-national and a European event, and furthermore one pitted against an oppressive European North.

In spite of these converging transnational features, what remained more controversial was just how to put into practice the claim to be acting on behalf of the nation. While officers considered public support for the military initiative and direct communication with crowds as necessary to justify their action in the name of the people, they oscillated between a commitment to fomenting insurrection across society at large, and concerns about containing violence out of fear of unrest and anarchy. The interpretation of this crucial aspect of the revolutionary script varied not only from country to country, but also among revolutionaries acting together in the same country or even city. Chapter one below charts the emergence of secret societies as organisations in which political opposition and conspiracies were planned jointly by civilians and members of the army. It shows that in spite of having Freemasonry as a shared source of inspiration, the secret societies used to organise these revolutions were substantially different in nature from the Masonic lodges. It then goes on to explore the transition from Napoleonic-era fighters to revolutionaries that marks the biography of the officers who organised and unleashed the revolts, and demonstrates the importance of the Napoleonic conflicts in shaping new political platforms, as well as that of the post-Napoleonic crises of demobilisation in accounting for military political activism in the years between 1815 and 1820. Historiography, and in particular the Spanish account, has rightly emphasised the importance of setting the intervention of the army in a broader social context, highlighting the extent to which officers were only one element within a larger coalition of forces willing to question the political status quo, sometimes suggesting, indeed, that the existence of such support was more important than the actual activism of the officers in accounting for the planning and success of the revolution.[6] However, as is argued in chapter two below, not only the Spanish, but also all other pronunciamientos were in fact also events that addressed concerns and problems specific to the armed forces of the countries involved. In other words, they were also military events in and of themselves. Nonetheless, the army officers always sought the engagement and support of civilian populations to legitimise their interventions. The chapter focuses on the pronunciamientos as communication campaigns: it looks at both the content and reception of their public manifestos, and discusses how they circulated and were interpreted at both the national and the international level. These documents, addressing both military and civilian audiences, give important hints about the nature of the revolutionary script, and about the existence across southern Europe of a shared language serving to explain and justify the revolution. The chapter then moves on to consider the broader social context of the revolutions. It interrogates the commitment by the army to act in the name of the nation, by looking at the ways in which the militaries engaged with crowds and, more generally, at the participation of civilians in the pronunciamientos and the officers' reaction to this. However, as the final section of the chapter demonstrates, such a claim to act in the name of the nation gave rise to different interpretations of the nature of such commitment, as officers held a variety of, and at times even conflicting, opinions on the nature, limits and desirability of popular participation. In spite of these variations both in the discourse regarding revolution and its actual practice, all the individual events discussed point alike to the fact that these revolutions enjoyed a remarkable popularity and mass following, and one that helps to explain their almost immediate success.

6. There is a discussion of the historiography in Claude Morange, *Una conspiración fallida y una Constitución nonnata (1819)* (Madrid: Centro de Estudios Políticos y Constitucionales, 2006), pp. 84–88.

CHAPTER ONE

Conspiracy and Military Careers in the Napoleonic Wars

Secret societies and the planning of revolutions

The organised political opposition and resistance to the status quo that is at the origin of the 1820s revolutions found its primary expression within secret societies. Masonic lodges in Spain, the Maçonaria and the Sinédrio in Portugal, the Carboneria in the Kingdom of the Two Sicilies, the Adelfi and the Federati in Piedmont and the Philiki Etaireia in the Ottoman and Russian empires offered the organisational means and protection needed to discuss, plan and conceive new political projects that enabled vague or conflicting initiatives and specific plans of action to coexist.

The secret societies that sprung up in the post-Napoleonic period found in the organisation and principles of European Freemasonry a common matrix and a shared source of inspiration. However, they also differed significantly from it at many levels. It is fair to say that the world of secret societies on the eve of the 1820s revolutions was radically different from that existing in Europe in the previous century, and in particular before the French revolution, and also from that which had existed during the Napoleonic era. Eighteenth-century Freemasonry represented, in the words of one of its historians, a 'practical realization of the Enlightenment': as such, it was not an organisation with radical political purposes, but simply espoused the philanthropic aspirations and values of Enlightenment culture.[1] It aimed at contributing to the improvement of society by making its members better fathers, more virtuous individuals and more

1. Margaret C. Jacob, *Living the Enlightenment: Freemasonry and Politics in Eighteenth-Century Europe* (New York: Oxford University Press, 1991), pp. 20–21.

upright and law-abiding citizens. With its emphasis on assemblies, compliance with regulations and justice (implemented by internal tribunals) it has been described as a school of government. However, while some of its principles may seem to have suggested democratic, egalitarian or pro-constitutionalist attitudes, in reality they did not translate into a set of specific and shared political aspirations, let alone into a revolutionary programme.[2] By the end of the eighteenth century Freemasonry had established itself across southern Europe, although the size of its membership and the number of lodges differed from country to country. In Spain, Portugal, the Ottoman Empire and in the communities of the Greek diaspora its presence was confined to a mere handful of lodges set up by groups of foreigners: in Spain first by the British and then by the French; while in Portugal it was imported from Britain, and the first Grande Oriente Lusitano, established in 1802, sought British protection. No doubt the condemnation of the Catholic church, marked by Benedict XIV's bull *Providas Romanorum* issued in May 1751, which identified Masonic secrecy and indifference to religion as threats to both church and state, set the tone for governmental attitudes towards the association.[3] On the Italian peninsula, however, and in the Kingdom of Naples in particular, where Freemasonry had enjoyed the protection of Queen Maria Carolina as early as the 1770s, it established itself more rapidly and more extensively than anywhere else. By 1789 there were no less than twenty-three lodges in Naples itself and twenty-seven in the rest of the kingdom.[4]

Freemasonry dramatically expanded it presence across southern Europe during and immediately after the Napoleonic wars and the occupations of the continent by British and French armies. In this context, it was itself set up first as a tool of support for the existing governments of the satellite states and occupying forces. No longer a politically neutral organisation, the Bonapartist Freemasonry that took root in occupied Spain and on the Italian peninsula was militantly pro-government, recruiting as it did the administrative and military elites of France and its satellites. It identified the ethical and philosophical values of the organisation with the reforming agenda of the Bonapartist regime, enabling it to forge an alliance with and gain the backing of local elites. As the French army advanced, so too in their wake were lodges established in Spanish

2. Ibid.

3. José A. Ferrer Benimeli, *Masonería, Iglesia e ilustración: Un conflicto ideológico-político-religioso*, 4 vols (Madrid: Fundación Universitaria Española, 1977).

4. Anna Maria Rao, 'La massoneria nel Regno di Napoli', in *Storia d'Italia, Annali 21: La massoneria*, ed. Gian Mario Cazzaniga (Turin: Einaudi, 2006), pp. 513–42.

cities. By 1809 there were two different types of Masonic association: one that recruited exclusively French military officers and citizens, was associated with the French Grande Oriente; the other, called the Gran Logia Nacional, created by the king, Napoleon's brother, who was its grand master, and by Joaquín Ferreira as grand representative of the grand master, constituted the first autonomous Spanish national organisation. It gathered together the so-called *afrancesados*, those Spanish civil servants and officers who supported the French government and French administrative reforms enacted in the country. Significantly, associated as they were with the enemy, Masonic lodges seem to have been negligible in, if not entirely absent from, liberal Cádiz, where the Spanish insurgents gathered to draft their own constitution while fighting the French invading army.[5]

By contrast with Spain and Naples, Portuguese Freemasonry actually expanded in the period thanks to its connections with British lodges.[6] In Italy, where no alternative political project comparable to that devised in Cádiz could be established, the secret societies implanted under the aegis of the French, and controlled by local civil servants, would soon develop an ambiguous attitude towards the French regime. While formally they represented an extension of the Napoleonic regime, they came to include also those individuals who, although working in the administration and the army, were increasingly critical of the lack of autonomy of the satellite states, and supported forms of Italian patriotism independent of France.[7] They also created entirely independent para-Masonic organisations hostile to the pro-governmental ones. In the Italian states the emergence of a political opposition to foreign occupation, and the rise of Italian patriotism, were associated with the birth of a set of new secret societies, and the Carboneria in particular. The use of Masonic or para-Masonic lodges to give voice to political opposition intensified in the aftermath of the restoration across southern Europe. In the absence of a public sphere independent of governments, existing and new clandestine organisations not only provided forms of sociability and opportunities for discussion that were formally forbidden and could not be enjoyed in public, but represented an ideal arena for those unhappy with the political status quo and

5. José A. Ferrer Benimeli, *Masonería española contemporánea, 1800–1868*, 2 vols (Madrid: Siglo XXI de España, 1980), 1, pp. 38–42, 82–105.

6. António Henrique de Oliveira Marques, *História da Maçonaria em Portugal*, 3 vols (Lisbon: Editorial Presença, 1990–97), 1: *Das origens ao triunfo*, pp. 74–81.

7. Zeffiro Ciuffoletti, 'La massoneria napoleonica in Italia', in *La massoneria: La storia, gli uomini, le idee*, ed. Zeffiro Ciuffoletti and Sergio Moravia (Milan: Bruno Mondadori, 2004), pp. 121–34.

determined to reverse it. The use of secret societies to advance specific revolutionary programmes constitutes the single most important novelty as regards the practices and culture of Enlightenment Freemasonry. But the world of secret organisations that thrived in the years before the 1820s revolutions was different from that of eighteenth-century Freemasonry also for other reasons. While transnational connections and exchanges across borders continued to exist (and were particularly extensive in the case of the Philiki), these organisations increasingly espoused a national outlook. Without entirely abandoning the Enlightenment principles of philanthropy and cosmopolitanism, they took on Romantic and national ideals and, in some cases (for instance, the Carboneria and the Philiki) adopted a deeply religious language that was a far cry from that of eighteenth-century Freemasonry. Finally, they represented one of the main vectors for those wishing to express their support for, and circulation of, constitutional projects.

Admittedly, any analysis of the impact and scope of clandestine activities in this period needs to take into account the fact that documentary sources and historiographical traditions have tended, for various reasons, to exaggerate the size and revolutionary potential of these organisations, and to posit a direct and univocal link between clandestine organisations and insurrections. The conspiracy theories fomented by counterrevolutionary culture, and originating in the Abbé Barruel's international best-seller *Mémoires pour servir à l'histoire du Jacobinisme*, were compounded by the tendency of European police forces to imagine actual or potential revolutionary actions to be the work of centrally controlled international organisations that coordinated plots through sects operative across several different countries.[8] As a consequence, a number of words of caution and provisos are in order here.

First of all, while the effective size of each organisation is difficult to determine with any certainty, given that the numbers cited by contemporary sources are often wildly different, the extent and importance of clandestine activities varied greatly from country to country. Second, they provided a space for people with different and even conflicting political objectives: while they intended to organise opposition, they lacked a clear direction or precise plans. In addition, the transition from the Enlightenment to the age of revolutions made it possible for both more traditional

---

8. See the important dissertation by Luca Di Mauro, 'Le Secret et Polichinelle, ou Culture et pratiques de la clandestinité politique à Naples au début du XIX siècle (1799–1821)', unpublished doctoral dissertation, Sorbonne Université, Paris, 2015.

and new understandings of the purposes of clandestine sociability to coexist, especially in an organisation such as Freemasonry. Moderate reformers, educated professionals committed to contributing to the improvement of the existing institutions and faithful to enlightened principles of gradual progress, could be found alongside radicals and individuals unabashedly advocating revolution.[9]

These provisos notwithstanding, it cannot be denied that secret societies became rapidly politicised at the end of the Napoleonic era: although the nature and extent of their politicisation varied, this radical transformation of their use and purposes was crucial in preparing the ground for revolutions. In short, it is safe to say that the revolutions were not the product of secret societies functioning as monolithic organisations. Even in this new conspiratorial context, not all existing lodges, or indeed the individuals who had joined them, were involved in revolutionary endeavours. Nonetheless, it is equally safe to say that no revolution was conceived and enacted without being sustained by some secret societies, whether already existing or created ad hoc. In all cases, they were used by those army officers (and their civilian allies) who planned the pronunciamientos of 1820 and 1821, and equally by those who had been engaged in the previous years in planning a number of different failed insurrections in Portugal, Spain and the Kingdom of the Two Sicilies. While the geographical origins of the revolutions point to the importance of specific places and groups in taking the lead, secret societies had enabled the creation of networks connecting individuals in different cities and regions, both inside and outside the states where the revolutions were organised. The polycentric nature of these organisations was an important structural element that contributed to ensuring support for, and the success of, the pronunciamientos.

The transformation undergone by Freemasonry in Spain in the first years of the restoration clearly demonstrates the increasing, although uneven, politicisation of this organisation, and the importance that the creation of ad hoc lodges and the establishment of conspiratorial networks across geographical space had between 1814 and 1820. In the Spanish Masonic lodges that were established after 1814, people with apparently conflicting ideological backgrounds and experiences, such as the Spanish 'Josefinos' (those who had collaborated with French rule under Napoleon's brother as king) and the liberals who had supported the 1812 constitution could be found side by side. Those Spanish liberals who during the

9. Paulo Henrique de Magalhães Arruda, 'Hipólito José da Costa, the Freemason', unpublished PhD dissertation, Kings College London, 2016.

Napoleonic wars had been hostile to Freemasonry—as it was associated primarily with collaboration with the French occupation—after 1814, as a result of King Fernando's persecution, took advantage of the protection offered by it to devise new forms of political resistance. It is therefore not surprising that the lodges that were established after 1814, and in particular between 1817 and 1819, overlapped with the conspiratorial network that enabled the planning of a series of failed pronunciamientos during those years. In turn, individuals who were involved in the organisation of insurrections, both civilian and military, had contacts and exchanges with secret societies in other countries. These failed revolts seem to have had different programmes and to demonstrate the adoption among insurrectionary officers of a variety of political stances that ranged from outright support for the Cádiz Constitution to preference for a more conservative charter inspired by the British political system (as was the case with the 1819 plot). As a historian of Spain has argued, '[M]asonry unquestionably offered them a space of convergence where different political tendencies could coexist [. . .] and an effective structure to organise forces otherwise geographically dispersed'.[10] The lodge called La Reunión Española, set up in La Coruña in 1814, included among its members General de Lacy, the organiser of the unsuccessful pronunciamiento in Catalonia of 1817 in favour of the Cádiz Constitution.[11] Such efforts had failed for a number of reasons, but mainly because of the isolation of their organisers from the rest of the army and the lack of broader coordination across the country. From 1817 onwards, Freemansonry provided larger, less localised networks of support for the subsequent insurrectionary bids of Evaristo San Miguel at El Palmar, near Cádiz in 1818, and of Colonel Joaquín Vidal in Valencia in 1819. The so-called Beitia plan that in 1819 had seen the gathering of a group of conspirators in favour of a moderate constitution was supported by a network of individuals who had joined Masonic lodges in Vitoria, Galicia, Madrid and Cádiz, and who sustained contacts in France too. The instructions for the plan employed a language reminiscent of Masonic culture, and to designate its subscribers used terms reminiscent of the names of lodges existing in Spain under the French occupation.[12] Also in 1819, some of the protagonists of earlier plots organised a new, complex and extensive military rising, this time on the basis of a more moderate political programme aimed at introducing a constitution inspired by the French

10. Morange, *Una conspiración fallida*, p. 50.

11. Benimeli, *Masonería española*, 1, p. 168.

12. Morange, *Una conspiración fallida*, pp. 42–43. The instructions of the plan are at pp. 374ff.

Charte of 1814.[13] These revolts failed too, however, this time because they were discovered and repressed at an early stage of their planning, or had been betrayed by some of their supporters.[14]

Plotters could take advantage of existing Masonic lodges, or could create new ad hoc clandestine organisations that imitated Freemasonry, without being formally part of it. Rafael Riego's own relationship with the secret societies demonstrates the instrumental and ad hoc, rather than structural, relationship that conspirators maintained with Freemasonry or with other clandestine associations. According to the traditional mythography of Riego, he had become a freemason while a prisoner in France; in reality, he had become involved with secret networks just before his pronunciamiento of 1 January 1820.[15] Riego's pronunciamiento was the byproduct of an earlier failed conspiracy staged at the beginning of 1819. This earlier conspiracy had involved, on the one hand, a number of wealthy merchants from Cádiz, including Juan Álvarez Mendizábal and the Valencian Mariano Bertrán de Lis, and on the other a group of young military officers stationed outside Cádiz and preparing to cross the Atlantic, protected by the captain general of Valencia, the Count of La Bisbal. These merchants used their Masonic lodge to plan their activities: thanks to the mediation of Antonio Alcalá Galiano, they also liaised with the officers they needed to organise the pronunciamiento.[16] Riego was one of these young officers, but his role was marginal, as he had only joined the plot at the last minute. The discovery of the conspiracy in early July thanks to La Bisbal's deputy, Pedro Sarsfield, acting as informer, led to the arrest of both a number of civilians and some fifteen officers. After this defeat, a smaller number of conspirators resolved to regroup and to set up new secret committees, called *juntas* or *comisiones*. The central junta, led by Mendizábal, was based in the town of Arcos, and others were established in each of the regiments supporting the plan for the pronunciamiento in

13. Morange, *Una conspiración fallida*, pp. 66–89.

14. Ibid.; Irene Castells, *La utopía insurrecional del liberalismo: Torrijos y las conspiraciones liberales de la década ominosa* (Barcelona, Editorial Crítica, 1989). On the events between 1814 and 1819, see also José Luis Comellas, *Los primeros pronunciamientos en España* (Madrid: CSIC—Escuela de Historia Moderna, 1958); Brian R. Hamnett, *La política española en una época revolucionaria, 1790–1820* (Mexico City: Fondo de Cultura Económica, 2011), pp. 238–52.

15. Víctor Sánchez Martín, 'Rafael del Riego: Símbolo de la revolución liberal', unpublished doctoral dissertation, University of Alicante, 2016, pp. 221ff.

16. Hamnett, *La política española*, pp. 250–51. Antonio Alcalá Galiano, *Apuntes para servir a la historia del origen y alzamiento del ejército destinado a Ultramar el 1 de enero de 1820* (Madrid: Aguado y Compañía, 1821), pp. 22–41.

favour of the Cádiz Constitution: from Cádiz to Villamartín and Alcalá. It is doubtful that these new clandestine organisations were fully-fledged Masonic lodges, although they imitated their structures. This time the sole key figure turned out to be Riego, although he was once again among those who joined the conspiracy late.[17] At the same time, the presence of Masonic lodges in other cities helped to guarantee support for Riego in the immediate aftermath of his pronunciamiento. In La Coruña, for instance, the officers of the artillery regiment that joined the constitutional revolt were members of the Masonic lodge called Los Amigos del Orden.[18]

Likewise in Portugal, Freemasonry acquired a new revolutionary potential at the end of the Napoleonic wars. It was reorganised when the French army left its territories for good in 1812, and a string of new lodges was opened in Lisbon, Coimbra, Porto, Setúbal and Trás-os-Montes. The conspiracy organised in 1817 which involved General Gomes Freire de Andrade bears witness to the new revolutionary role that was taken on by some Masonic lodges in Portugal, where the return of political exiles played a crucial role in revitalising the secret societies. After quitting Portugal with the French army, Andrade, whose past history of militant Freemasonry dated back to 1785, re-entered the country in 1815 with many other exiles who had temporarily settled in England or France. Appointed grand master, he initiated a programme of reform and reorganisation of Portuguese Freemasonry, advocating the creation of close ties with British lodges. Andrade played only a secondary role in the organisation of the conspiracy, which was led by army officers and men of letters belonging to a lodge called the Supremo Conselho Regenerador. These conspirators aimed at introducing a constitutional government and at putting an end to the British tutelage over the country represented by William Beresford's military leadership. However, the organisers supposed that Andrade would be willing to replace Beresford, once the latter was imprisoned, in assuming command of the army. The discovery of this military conspiracy resulted not only in the arrest and execution of Andrade, but in a general repression of the Maçonaria.[19] Soon afterwards, Dom João issued

17. Alcalá Galiano, *Apuntes*, pp. 50–53.

18. Alberto J. V Valín Fernández, 'Masonería y movimiento liberal en la sublevación coruñesa del 1820, en apoyo del pronunciamento de Rafael Riego', in *Ejército, pueblo y constitución: Homenaje al General Rafael Riego*, ed. Alberto Gil Novales (Madrid: Anejos de la Revista Trienio [Ilustración y Liberalismo], 1987), pp. 157–79.

19. On this failed plot, see Jorge Pedreira and Fernando Dores Costa, *D. João VI: O Clemente* (Lisbon: Círculo de Leitores, 2006), pp. 263–65, and more recently the essays in Miriam Halpern Pereira and Ana Cristina Araújo, eds, *Gomes Freire e as vésperas da Revolução de 1820* (Lisbon: Biblioteca Nacional de Portugal, 2018).

an *alvará* (licence) rendering all secret societies illegal, and their members liable to the death penalty for lese-majesté. While Masonic activities were substantially reduced—and a Grand Diet of the organisation, in order to prevent repression and allegations of conspiracy, had decided to reduce its structures to one lodge just before the *alvará*—they did not disappear completely between 1817 and 1820. Several new lodges were set up in Coimbra, and in Elvas, along with a number of para-Masonic clubs. These latter enabled their members to meet without being accused of illegal activities, because they were not formally part of Freemasonry. The Sinédrio, the organisation within which the promoters of the 1820 pronunciamiento of Porto planned their military intervention, was one of these lodges organised after the repression. Set up in January 1818, and originally composed of four freemasons, it was initially an independent organisation, but seems to have been recognised as Masonic by 1820. While it is not known whether its members sustained links with other lodges created after 1817, it is conceivable that contacts existed between the plotters in Porto and individuals in various Portuguese cities.[20]

Like the Portuguese Sinédrio and the Spanish lodges set up to plan Riego's pronunciamiento, the Greek Philiki Etaireia was created on a Masonic template and was set up by freemasons. In practice, however, it turned out to be an entirely new and distinct organisation that, compared to Freemasonry, had radically different aims. One of the three founding members of the Philiki, Emmanouil Xanthos, had joined a French lodge called L'Union de l'Orient, based in Lefkada (one of the Ionian islands), in 1813. The Ionian islands represented at the time a very important Masonic centre in the Mediterranean. It was in Corfu, still under Venetian rule, that a first Masonic lodge, the Loggia Beneficenza, had been established in 1782, and its activities and membership were revitalised under French occupation (1797–99; 1807–14), when a new French lodge called Saint-Napoleon was opened. Once the island had been turned into a British colony, the Beneficenza became the first Grand Orient of Greece, and the Duke of Sussex, who was then also grand master of the United Grand Lodge of England, its first grand master. In the same year that he had joined the lodge, Xanthos had drawn inspiration from its structures and beliefs to create, in the imperial-Russian city of Odessa and in collaboration with Athanasios Tsakalov and Panagiotis Anagnostopoulos, a novel organisation that was entirely dedicated to the regeneration and the liberation of the Greek nation: this was the Philiki Etaireia (i.e. Society of Friends).

20. Marques, *História da Maçonaria*, 1, pp. 107–18.

He continued to have dealings with Freemasonry after the foundation of the Philiki: during a visit to St. Petersburg in May 1820, when he unsuccessfully approached the then foreign minister of Russia, Count Ioannis Kapodistrias, who refused to join the Philiki, he became a member of a Masonic lodge called Les Amis Réunis. During the same trip, he obtained backing for his conspiratorial plans from another freemason, Prince Alexandros Ypsilantis, soon to be the military leader of the insurrection in the Danubian Principalities.[21] The symbol of the phoenix, the mythical bird serving as a metaphor of the rebirth of the Greek nation after centuries of enslavement under the Ottomans, and one of the most powerful emblems of the Philiki, was already circulating, and was employed also by Masonic lodges on the Ionian islands during this same period.[22]

Beyond the Ionian islands, the Greek communities of the diaspora across the Mediterranean had been present in the ranks of Masonic lodges since the late eighteenth century. However, as in the case of Portugal and Spain, a direct relationship between Masonic membership and support for the revolutionary or the national cause is hard to establish even for those lodges in which a substantial contingent of Greek members can be proved to have existed. In the decade before the Greek insurrection, for instance, in the city of Marseille, Ottoman Greeks and Turks shared membership in the same lodges without tensions, and early declarations of allegiance to the Greek cause were hard to detect among their Greek members. Things changed dramatically once the revolution had broken out; but by then, while many French freemasons were actively engaged in the philhellenic movement, few Greeks were still involved in Freemasonry, possibly because they had preferred other organisations, such as the Philiki.[23] The Masonic lodge on the British-ruled Ionian island of Corfu, which gathered together both the civil servants of the occupying power and the local elites, did play an important role in supporting the Greek revolution, but only once it had broken out.

In spite of the affiliation that some of the members of the Philiki had with Freemasonry, its founders did all they could to stress the differences that existed between their own organisation on the one hand and the

21. Andreas Rizopoulos, 'Activités maçonniques avec arrière-plan politique—et réciproquement—en Grèce au XIXe siècle', *Cahiers de la Méditerranée* 72 (2006): 203–24.

22. Catherine Brégianni, 'L'influence maçonnique sur l'hellénisme durant la dernière période ottomane et les symboles de l'état grec', in *Diffusions et circulations des pratiques maçonniques, XVIII–XX siècle*, ed. Pierre-Yves Beaurepaire, Kenneth Loiselle, Jean-Marie Mercier and Thierry Zarcone (Paris: Classiques Garnier, 2012), pp. 285–99 at 290–92.

23. Mathieu Grenet, 'La Loge et l'étranger: Les Grecs dans la franc-maçonnerie marseillaise au début du XIXe siècle' *Cahiers de la Méditerranée* 72 (2006): 225–43.

Masonic world and the Carboneria on the other, highlighting above all the religiously devout nature of the former.[24] Apart from the religious overtones of its principles and its unprecedented commitment to the regeneration of the Greek nation, however, what made the Philiki unique was not so much the size of its membership, but rather its remarkable extension into a wide variety of different and distant geographical spaces. Among the para-Masonic organisations operative in southern Europe on the eve of the revolutions, the Philiki stood out for the exceptional geographical range of its transnational and trans-imperial networks, stretching from the Russian to the Ottoman and Austrian empires, as well as the Mediterranean and continental Europe. The geography of the membership of the Philiki overlapped with the very extensive map of the Greek Enlightenment. In continental Greece, this map was centred around three areas: Yannina and north-western Greece, including Moschopolis and Kozani; eastern Thessaly; and the north-eastern Aegean, between Kydonies, Chios and Smyrna. Westward it stretched to the Danubian Principalities, and in particular to the cities of Jassy and Bucharest, and then covered the key centres of the Greek diaspora in the Mediterranean (Venice, Trieste, Pisa and Livorno) and in Europe (Vienna and Leipzig). The Philiki started on the margins of this map, in Odessa, Moscow, Moldavia and Bessarabia, but once it had spread it covered most of the geography of the Enlightenment, consolidating its presence also in areas that had been negligible insofar as the map of the Enlightenment was concerned: for example, the Peloponnese. It also overlapped with the geography of the Orthodox church, with its centre in Constantinople. Its rapid expansion owed much firstly to the appointment in 1818 of twelve so-called apostles: envoys charged with the recruitment of members, both in the Greek-speaking territories of the Ottoman Empire (from Olympos to Macedonia, from Thrace to the Aegean, the eastern Peloponnese, the Mani peninsula, Sterea Ellada—as continental Greece was otherwise called—and Thessaly) and on the Ionian islands and in centres of the diaspora; and secondly to the introduction of the system of ephories: administrative units made up of local members.[25]

24. Nicolas Ypsilanti, *Mémoires du prince Nicolas Ypsilanti: D'après le manuscrit no. 2144 de la Bibliothèque nationale de Grèce, publié par le Dr. D. Gr. Kambouroglous* (Athens: Librairie Française & Internationale G. Eleutheroudakis, n.d.), pp. 5–6.

25. George Dimitrios Frangos, 'The Philike Etaireia 1814–1821: A Social and Historical Analysis', PhD dissertation, Columbia University, 1971. On the geographical scope of the organisation, see Paschalis Kitromilides, Ἡ Φιλική Εταιρεία και η πολιτική γεωγραφία του Διαφωτισμού' (The Philiki Etaireia and the political geography of the Enlightenment), in Οι πόλεις των Φιλικών: Οι αστικές διαδρομές ενός επαναστατικού φαινομένου; Πρακτικά ημερίδας, Αθήνα, 14 Ιανουαρίου 2015 (The cities of the Philikoi: The urban trajectories of a

It is important to stress that the Philiki was never run from one specific place only, but remained polycentric in nature. While the cities of Odessa and Izmail, and Constantinople, were particularly important in the development of the organisation, their importance lay precisely in their being hubs connecting different people and regions. The Russian-imperial frontier city of Odessa, where the organisation was first established, was a crossroads where both merchants and Greek veterans who had fought on behalf of Russia could be recruited; the Ottoman capital Constantinople, where the Philiki's leaders gave the organisation a proper structure in 1818, was an ideal place to communicate across the empire; Izmail, in Russian Bessarabia, where in 1820 the insurrection was planned and agreed in the presence of members of the local ephories a few months before it broke out, was another frontier port city with a large Greek- speaking community, which could be reached relatively easily from the Peloponnese and also from the Danubian Principalities. The organisation's leaders had been constantly on the move to publicise their projects, connect with different groups and leaders and recruit new members.[26]

The existence of members in different parts of the Ottoman Empire and on its borders enabled the Philiki's leaders to conceive a range of different military and insurrectionary strategies, adjusting the geography and the timing of the insurrection to changing circumstances. Between May and September 1820, soon after becoming the leader of the Philiki and after consultation with members in various cities around the Black Sea, Alexandros Ypsilantis, supported by his close collaborators Georgios Leventis and Grigorios Dikaios (known as Papaflessas), completed in Bucharest a 'General Plan' which envisaged the organisation of a revolt of Serbians and Montenegrins, followed by a Greek insurrection in Moldavia-Wallachia triggered by the military intervention of the Greeks' military leaders there, Giorgakis Olympios and Savvas Fokianos; the provocation of a Russo-Turkish war; the occupation of Epirus by the local Greek

revolutionary phenomenon; Proceedings of a conference Athens, 14 January 2015), ed. Olga Katsiardi-Hering (Athens: The Hellenic Parliament Foundation, 2018), pp. 25–35.

26. On the movements of its leadership, see Ypsilanti, *Mémoires*, p. 66. On these cities, see Nassia Yakovaki, Ὀδυσσός, Κωνσταντινούπολη, Ισμαήλι: Τρεις οργανωτικοί σταθμοί ενός αχαρτογράφητου δρομολογίου' (Odessa, Constantinople, Izmail: Three organisational centres of an uncharted trajectory), in *Οι πόλεις των Φιλικών: Οι αστικές διαδρομές ενός επαναστατικού φαινομένου; Πρακτικά ημερίδας, Αθήνα, 14 Ιανουαρίου 2015* (The cities of the Philikoi: The urban trajectories of a revolutionary phenomenon; Proceedings of a conference, Athens, 14 January 2015), ed. Olga Katsiardi-Hering (Athens: The Hellenic Parliament Foundation, 2018), pp. 173–200.

captains; and the torching of the Ottoman fleet in Constantinople. The Peloponnese would be the centre of events, and Ypsilantis was supposed to go there with Papaflessas. However, later on this plan was modified, and a new, partial plan focusing on Constantinople, and including an attempt on the sultan's life, was drafted.[27]

In the end, the Danubian Principalities turned out to be more important than had originally been supposed, and no insurrectionary plans were carried out in Constantinople. The Philiki in the principalities proved crucial, as they included the military leadership in charge of recruiting mercenaries (Olympios in particular), soldiers who had fought for Russia in earlier wars and students from the educational establishments of Bucharest and Jassy who joined Ypsilantis as volunteers.[28] Likewise, the primates (dominant landholders) and clerics of the Peloponnese who had joined the ranks of the Philiki (in spite of their initial hesitation) were crucial in triggering the insurrection there. The political strategy and the objectives of the secret society were equally unclear, at least until 1820. The majority of the members of the Philiki wanted the rebellion to obtain self-government, to be supported by Russia, and an autonomous Greece to be protected by the Russian Empire, while the nature of its intended relationship with the Ottoman polity was left vague. But in 1820 as important a leader as Prince Mavrokordatos put forward a different geopolitical vision. Hostile to the assignment to Russia of a hegemonic role in the region, he argued that it was in the interests of the European powers to prevent this from happening, by supporting the oppressed peoples of the Ottoman Empire. He thus envisaged the creation of three independent principalities (Moldavia, Wallachia and Serbia), which should be placed under the protection of Austria. The Ottoman areas around the Black Sea should be handed over to Russia, while some islands, such as Cyprus and

27. Alexandros Despotopoulos, 'Ἡ Ἑλληνικὴ Ἐπανάσταση (1821–1830)' (The Greek revolution, 1821–1830), in Ἱστορία του Ελληνικού Έθνους (History of the Greek nation), ed. Giorgos Christopoulos and Ioannis Bastias, 17 vols (Athens: Ekdotiki Athinon, 1970–2000), 12: Η Ελληνική Επανάσταση και η ίδρυση του ελληνικού κράτους (The Greek revolution and the foundation of the Greek state), pp. 16–18.

28. Dimitris Kontogeorgis, 'Μεταξύ πανδούρων και βογιάρων: Οι Φιλικοί στο Βουκουρέστι και στο Ιάσιο' (Between pandouroi and boyars: The Philikoi in Bucharest and in Jassy), in Οι Πόλεις των Φιλικών: Οι αστικές διαδρομές ενός επαναστατικού φαινομένου, Πρακτικά ημερίδας, 14 Ιανουαρίου 2015 (The cities of the Philikoi: The urban trajectories of a revolutionary phenomenon; Proceedings of a conference, Athens, 14 January 2015), ed. Olga Katsiardi-Hering (Athens: The Hellenic Parliament Foundation, 2018), pp. 57–76.

Crete, should be ceded to Britain. What remained should constitute a new Greek empire.[29]

Compared to the conspiratorial activities that had developed in Spain, Portugal and the Greek world in the context of secret societies, those that took place on the Italian peninsula stand out for two reasons. First of all, secret societies there took on a politically subversive overtone and anti-governmental attitudes earlier than anywhere else in southern Europe. In Naples in the 1770s, Freemasonry had provided a space for support to enlightened despotism and for a consensus with the monarchy, but the distancing of the dynasty from a reforming agenda, signalled early on by the dismissal in 1777 of the prime minister Bernardo Tanucci, created a rift between its members and the monarchy. The outbreak of the French revolution led to Masonic lodges being used for conspiratorial activities, discovered and repressed in 1794, by local intellectuals who had for their part turned to Jacobinism.[30] At first directed against the Bourbon absolute monarchy, in the following years secret society activism came to target French rule. Once it had displayed its politically authoritarian and economically exploitative nature, French rule on the peninsula, though initially welcomed by Italian patriots attracted to the principles of the revolution and hopeful that independent republics might be established, alienated its earlier local supporters. Italian patriots thus turned to secret societies as the only available space in which to organise and express their political opposition to foreign occupation and to formulate their plans for independence. The most important and influential secret society, the Carboneria, apparently established in the Kingdom of the Two Sicilies between 1806 and 1808 by the French official Pierre-Joseph Briot, a member of the Council of State of the Kingdom of Naples who had come to support the independence of Italy from French rule, was soon filled with those members of the Neapolitan army and the civil service critical of Joachim Murat, becoming an organisational alternative to progovernmental Napoleonic Freemasonry. It absorbed and embraced the radical beliefs of pre-existing heterodox Masonic secret societies, whose members had rejected the politically neutral or pro-government stance of traditional Freemasonry as early as the late eighteenth century. In particular, it adopted ideas that had originally been elaborated by the society of the Illuminati, a secret para-Masonic organisation set up by Adam Johann

29. Alexandre Mavrocordato [Alexandros Mavrokordatos], *Coup d'œil sur la Turquie* (1820), in Anton von Prokesch-Osten, *Geschichte des Abfall der Griechen vom türkischen Reich im Jahre 1821* (Vienna: Gedold, 1867), p. 52.

30. Rao, 'La massoneria'.

Weishaupt in 1776, in Bavaria. The Illuminati advocated radical egalitarian ideals and a social revolution, without explicitly calling for a political revolution. The Carboneria's earliest structures seem to have developed out of certain lodges of the Illuminati, as well as out of the heterodox para-Masonic society of the Filadelfi, founded in 1803 by the famous Jacobin and international conspirator Filippo Buonarroti, who established its headquarters in Paris first, and later in Geneva.[31] More or less at the same time as the rise and diffusion of the Carboneria in southern Italy, the establishment of the Adelfia after 1804 ensured the further dissemination of Buonarroti's radical egalitarian and democratic ideas in northern Italy. In Piedmont, the Adelfia thus became the leading secret society until it was absorbed in 1818 by a new organisation called the Sublimi Maestri Perfetti. While the Carboneria acquired members in Piedmont also, it never became the dominant secret organisation there, as it did in the Kingdom of the Two Sicilies.[32]

An equally important peculiarity of the Italian secret societies, and especially the Carboneria, was their rapidly acquired mass membership. While conspiratorial networks in Piedmont would seem to have been more limited in size even on the eve of the 1821 revolution, in the Kingdom of the Two Sicilies the Carboneria managed to recruit widely across different social groups and in the villages of the countryside. It also displayed an ability to organise armed resistance by hiring fighters among the local peasantry and bandit groups. The popular following of the Carboneria depended on the capacity of individual *vendite* (lodges) to muster the so-called *turbe carboniche*: subaltern groups made up of members of the popular classes, often organised as confraternities. The Carboneria's ability to mobilise the lower classes, and commitment to doing so, owed much to the influence of the French *compagnonnages*, confraternities of

31. Francesco Mastroberti, *Pierre-Joseph Briot: Un giacobino tra amministrazione e politica (1771–1827)* (Naples: Jovene, 1998); Giuseppe Berti, *I democratici e l'iniziativa meridionale nel Risorgimento* (Milan: Feltrinelli, 1962), pp. 137–65. On the historiography, see Fulvio Conti, 'La massoneria e la costruzione della nazione italiana dal Risorgimento al fascismo', in *La massoneria: La storia, gli uomini, le idee*, ed. Zeffiro Ciuffoletti and Sergio Moravia, pp. 135–91, esp. 146–48. A reassessment of its origins can also be found in Cazzaniga, 'Origini ed evoluzioni dei rituali carbonari italiani', in *Storia d'Italia, Annali 21: La massoneria*, ed. Gian Mario Cazzaniga (Turin: Einaudi, 2006), pp. 559–78.

32. Renato Sòriga, *Le società segrete, l'emigrazione politica e i primi moti per l'indipendenza* (Modena: Società tipografica modenese, 1942), pp. 107–36; Arturo Bersano, *Adelfi, federati e carbonari: Contributo all storia delle società segrete* (extracted from *Atti della Reale accademia delle scienze di Torino*, vol. 45) (Turin: Vincenzo Bona, 1910); Oreste Dito, *Massoneria, Carboneria ed altre società segrete nella storia del Risorgimento italiano* (Turin: Casa editrice nazionale, Roux e Viarengo, 1905), pp. 340–43.

itinerant workers that existed in the French Jura, where the French Charbonnerie originated. Their rituals and structures were transferred into the
Carboneria by its founders, and adopted early on when recruiting armed
groups and turbe. The commitment to reaching out to all ranks of society was also retained, and groups of affiliates external to the ranks of the
organisation were created to guarantee links with the popular classes.[33]
The carbonari employed their popular turbe early on for insurrectionary
purposes. The earliest instances of insurrectionary activity organised by
the Carboneria dated to 1813, when its armed bands had clashed with the
army in Calabria. With the restoration, attempts were made to repress
its activities. In 1816 secret societies were declared to be illegal, and their
membership incompatible with public service. The Prince of Canosa,
minister of police between 1815 and 1816, was responsible for a campaign
against the Carboneria and supported a parallel counterrevolutionary
secret society, the so-called Calderari, to fight it. Those enemies of French
rule who had favoured the return of an absolute monarchy had flocked
to the Carboneria in the years of Murat's regime, but from 1813 onwards,
when the secret society of the Trinitari had been founded, and later, with
the creation of the Calderari, the Carboneria became the target not only of
governments, but also of parallel anti-revolutionary organisations.[34]

In spite of this temporary crisis, the Carboneria's membership grew
steadily, its size far outstripping that of any other similar organisation;
it became the largest secret society in southern Europe. Contemporary
sources suggest that Spanish Freemasonry was made up of no more than
a few lodges and a few hundred members by 1820. Likewise, the networks
of the Philiki Etaireia on the eve of the Greek revolution had acquired
a membership of little more than a thousand individuals.[35] According
to contemporary estimates, the Carboneria in the Kingdom of the Two
Sicilies had, as early as 1817, no less than three hundred thousand members, and this figure had more than doubled by the eve of the 1820 revolution.[36] These numbers may well be exaggerated, but they nonetheless

33. On the origins of the turbe, see Carolina Castellano, *Spazi pubblici, discorsi segreti: Istituzioni e settarismo nel Risorgimento italiano* (Trento: Tangram, 2013), pp. 82–86.

34. Castellano, *Spazi pubblici*, pp. 59–62.

35. Morange, *Una conspiración fallida*, pp. 46–56; George Dimitrios Frangos, 'The Philiki Etairia: A Premature National Coalition', in *The Struggle for Greek Independence: Essays to Mark the 150th Anniversary of the Greek War of Independence*, ed. Richard Clogg (Hamden, CT: Archon Books, 1973), pp. 83–103.

36. Domenico D'Alessandro, 'Documenti inediti su Massoneria e Carboneria nel Regno delle Due Sicilie', in *Sentieri della libertà e della fratellanza ai tempi di Silvio Pellico*, ed. Aldo Mola (Foggia: Bastogi, 1994), p. 79. Daum, *Oscillazioni*, p. 98.

suggest that it had acquired a popularity of exceptional proportions, and that it already had a capillary presence in the territories of the kingdom before 1820. Two administrative reforms contributed to this steady rise in popularity during the restoration: first, in 1817, the introduction of a new administrative organisation of the state that confirmed the central-ised system first introduced in the kingdom under French occupation, and aroused widespread hostility among the provincial middle classes nostalgic for their local autonomy; and second, in the same year, the establishment of *milizie provinciali* (provincial militias), paramilitary organisations set up to defend public order against crime and brigandage according to the French model. Rather than contributing to the defence of law and order, these became a tool to disseminate still further the Carboneria, which infiltrated them. Many of the ninety thousand small and medium landowners from the provinces, who combined hostility to the central state with support for a constitution, filled the ranks of the secret organisation.[37] By 1817 the Carboneria had already provided a locus for the planning of revolutions, and its members included individuals from all social backgrounds, both civilian and military. In May, a general meet-ing of the Carboneria, with representatives from all the provincial ven-dite, was organised in the town of Pompeii on the outskirts of Naples, on the initiative of the leaders from Salerno, where the society was par-ticularly strong. A general plan was discussed and approved by the entire organisation, based on the request, made public to the highest echelons of the state, to establish a constitutional monarchy according to the Span-ish model. But besides this early attempt at organising a national plan, there was an outbreak of independent conspiratorial activities in other provinces. In the contado of Lecce in Puglia, for instance, the Carboneria, with the support of the famous local bandit groups of Gaetano Vardarelli and Ciro Annicchiarico, planned the creation of provisional juntas and attempted an armed insurrection that was repressed only thanks to the intervention of General Sir Richard Church with his 5,500 troops.[38]

As the events of 1817 demonstrate, in spite of their early establish-ment and mass following, the secret organisations that rapidly expanded across the Italian peninsula following the restoration, like their counter-parts in other areas of southern Europe, accommodated a variety of political positions and conspiratorial projects. The Carboneria included

---

37. Luigi Minichini, *Luglio 1820: Cronaca di una rivoluzione*, ed. Mario Themelly (Rome: Bulzoni, 1979), pp. xiv, 60–64.

38. Di Mauro, 'Le Secret et Polichinelle', pp. 457–83.

crypto-republicans, supporters of the creation of an Italian federation and constitutionalists of varying tendencies. In Sicily it also harboured groups hostile to Naples and advocating full autonomy for the island. In Piedmont secret societies supported a national programme either to reconstitute the Kingdom of Italy or to create a federation of the existing states that would recognise the principle of popular sovereignty and expel the Austrians from the peninsula: the statutes and oath of the Federati explicitly referred to the liberation of Italy from the foreign oppressor. However, these objectives could be combined with differing political tendencies. The radical egalitarian, anti-aristocratic outlook of the supporters of the Cádiz Constitution who had joined the Sublimi Maestri Perfetti via the Adelfia, and who controlled the military garrison of Alessandria, clashed with the more moderate aristocratic members of the sister organisation of the Federati. These latter included figures such as Santorre di Santarosa and Moffa di Lisio, in Piedmont, and Count Federico Confalonieri in Lombardy. In addition, it should be noted that the popular appeal enjoyed by the Carboneria did not necessarily translate into a politicisation of all the individuals it managed to attract. Like Freemasonry in Spain in the same period, not all its members were equally hostile to the political status quo. For instance, the carbonari in the Papal States, and especially the turbe carboniche organised in the Romagna, treated the organisation merely as a confraternity acting in defence of their professional interests, and their affiliation was therefore devoid of any politically subversive aims.

Finally, both the Carboneria in Naples and the secret societies of Piedmont, like their Spanish, Greek and Portuguese counterparts, had established formal and informal networks connecting different provinces, cities and, in the case of the Carboneria, even the smallest villages. By infiltrating the ranks of existing armies, and by recruiting local civilian notables, such organisations had spread to all the provinces of both kingdoms. It is no surprise that the city of Alessandria, epicentre of the Piedmontese insurrection, had also hosted the meeting that in 1818 had led to the creation of this new society of the Sublimi Maestri Perfetti; it had remained a crucially important centre of conspiracy. But lodges of this organisation, called *chiese* (churches), existed also in Turin, Asti, Tortona, Voghera, Genova and, beyond Piedmont, in Lombardy, in the cities of Parma and Piacenza.[39] In the Kingdom of the Two Sicilies, the provincial centres that had recruited the largest memberships were also those where the revolution broke out and found its strongest support: the city of

---

39. Sòriga, *Le società segrete*, pp. 116–17.

Avellino and the Irpinia, along with Salerno and its outskirts, and Foggia in Puglia. At the same time communication channels had been established with the other peripheral vendite of the kingdom in view of the imminent military coup. It was the existence of widespread and well-established networks among secret society affiliates in Portugal, Spain, Piedmont, the Kingdom of the Two Sicilies and the Ottoman Empire that facilitated the planning, organisation and execution of the pronunciamientos in 1820 and 1821. These extensive networks made communication among revolutionaries based in distant places possible, and connected the epicentres of the uprisings (Porto and Cádiz, Alessandria in Piedmont, Avellino and Salerno in the Kingdom of the Two Sicilies, the principalities of Moldavia and Wallachia and the Peloponnese in the Ottoman Empire) with far-flung territories and provinces, creating the preconditions for their success and for the popular mobilisation that accompanied their enactment.

From fighting in the Napoleonic wars to declaring the revolution

The Napoleonic wars had profoundly altered the role of armies in European and extra-European societies. While the French revolutionary experience introduced a distinction and division between military and civil life that had never existed under the ancien régime, it was during these same wars that the military career acquired an unprecedented political meaning, army officers carved out a new political role for themselves and the relationship between war, army and society was radically transformed. Armies grew dramatically in size and moved across the boundaries of their countries of origin, officers acquired a novel prestige and visibility, and an unprecedented percentage of the population was affected by war, by virtue of their participating in conflicts either through forced conscription into regular armies, or as mercenaries, or by joining informal groups of fighters in guerrilla units. Wars reinforced old forms of patriotism, based on the defence of localities and traditional institutions, but also forged new ones that combined hostility against the French with new ideological principles, whether directly borrowed from the French revolution or independent of it. Enlistment in the army had guaranteed a new upward mobility in the military ranks, and the creation of a new class of officers based on meritocracy. Whether they belonged to a generation of young army officers born between the mid-1780s and early 1790s—like Guglielmo Pepe (born in 1783), Antonio Quiroga and Rafael Riego (both 1784), Michele Morelli and Giuseppe Silvati (1792 and 1791), Bernardo Correia de Castro e Sepúlveda (1791) and Alexandros Ypsilantis (1792); or to an older one, such as Sebastião Drago Valente de Brito Cabreira (born in 1763), most of the military leaders of the 1820s revolutions had direct experience of these events and had been deeply affected by them. They had all fought long campaigns in other countries and, thanks to their professional qualities, progressed rapidly up the military hierarchy. Another shared feature of their participation in these events was their direct or indirect knowledge of the political and military events that took place in Spain, where many of them were involved in the conflict between French, British, Portuguese and Spanish armies.

The Spanish insurrection and popular resistance against French occupation was by far the best known of all the uprisings triggered by Napoleonic military expansion on the southern peripheries of Europe. Echoes of these events left an enduring mark on the political and military culture of these generations of southern European soldiers, not only within but also beyond Spain, as the revolt of the Spanish people became a point of reference in later years both in terms of military strategy and as an example of popular mobilisation in defence of freedom. The French invasion of the Iberian peninsula in 1808 marked not only the end of the Bourbon dynasty (both Fernando VII and his father Carlos IV had been taken out of the country to the French city of Bayonne, where they were dethroned on 6 May 1808, and in the following days Napoleon's brother Joseph was placed on the throne of Spain), but also a crisis in, indeed the demise of, the Spanish ancien-régime army. This was a body relatively small in size, based on an unflinching loyalty to the monarchy, and aristocratic in its values and in the composition of its officer body. This army was in fact easily defeated in 1808 by a much larger force of French veterans. As a result, the invasion radically transformed its composition and warfare in general.[40] A first striking consequence of the French occupation was the explosion of guerrilla warfare. As early as 1808 the guerrilla units supplementing the regular army represented the most important feature of a generalised insurrection that continued until the end of the French military occupation. At first such groups came into being spontaneously, attracting soldiers and villagers alike, but once local and provincial juntas had been created, these latter contributed to their organisation and appointed their leaders (who as a result could be interchangeably clerics, aristocrats, bandits, wealthy farmers or army officers). Although all the members of the

---

40. Ronald Fraser, *Napoleon's Cursed War: Popular Resistance in the Spanish Peninsular War* (London: Verso, 2008).

partidas (partisan bands) would habitually invoke religion and the absent king, in fact a variety of motivations drove individuals to join the guerrilla war. The revolt against the foreigner could not be separated from an element of social revolt, from the disintegration of the Spanish army and from the existing domestic political and economic context. Guerrilla bands attracted into their ranks high numbers of deserters and soldiers evading conscription, as well as mercenaries; the French occupier, at least at first, was not the only target of the hatred of the bands, who attacked individuals associated with the very unpopular policies of Manuel Godoy's ministry, the fall of which marked the end of Carlos's reign in 1808.[41] Grievances against feudal dues, rebellion against the taxation introduced by the French administration and opposition to the sale of common land that took place during French occupation all played a role.[42] At the same time, the social composition of the partidas differed substantially from place to place, as did their respective sizes, although their presence, and therefore local activism, was widespread throughout both the war and the territories of Spain occupied by the French. It may come as a surprise that the largest guerrilla forces were concentrated in the mountains of Navarre, where there was no acute poverty, as taxation was limited, feudal obligations were absent, farmers owned their own land, and therefore the local populations had much to lose from administrative reform and military occupation. In this province only a quarter of the partida of Francisco Espoz y Mina, made up of 3,477 volunteers, came from the coast, where poverty was rife and feudalism resulted in great social inequalities.[43] In other provinces artisans predominated over peasants in guerrilla groups.

While this type of warfare never involved more than thirty to forty thousand individuals, and the partidas or bands were never sufficient or efficient enough to themselves defeat the French, guerrilla warfare did nonetheless prevent the French from controlling fully the territories they formally ruled, and forced them to maintain a large army tormented by the rapid attacks of small bands protected by local populations. In addition, guerrillas were only one aspect of a more widespread participation in forms of resistance against the invasion, that affected not only mountainous and rural areas but also most Spanish cities. The uprising of 2 May 1808 in Madrid, when the crowds trying to prevent the departure for Bayonne from the royal palace of the daughter and son of the king

41. Esdaile, *Fighting Napoleon*.
42. Fraser, *Napoleon's Cursed War*.
43. Esdaile, *Fighting Napoleon*, pp. 90–92.

revolted against Murat's army, was just the first and most famous example of insurrection and the mobilisation of urban popular classes. Unlike any other Napoleonic campaign in Europe, the war in Spain was moreover marked by a number of prolonged sieges of cities, most notably of Zaragoza (Saragossa) and Gerona (1808 and 1809), Cádiz and Badajoz between 1810 and 1812, Tarragona in 1811 and Valencia the following year: all experiences characterised by the mobilisation of these cities' populations and by forms of spontaneous and organised resistance in the name of the king, as well as in defence of their own communities.[44] Regardless of the diversity of motivations inspiring those who participated in the insurrection, and in spite of the limited numbers of individuals formally involved in guerrilla bands, the experience of war to which the Napoleonic invasion subjected most of the Spanish population had, according to one historian, the crucial effect of 'turning the doctrine of popular sovereignty into a de facto reality'.[45]

The insurrection and the fight against the French also created the preconditions for the emergence of an entirely new regular army, whose values and composition were likewise radically transformed. The unprecedented mobilisation triggered by the insurrection and the war against Napoleon, originally coordinated by the juntas, with the introduction of conscription for all men between the ages of sixteen and forty-five, led to the de facto transformation of the army into a national one, based on the notion that all citizens were obliged to contribute to the defence of the country.[46] This new model of a national army was confirmed by the text of the constitution approved in Cádiz in 1812: to this end, the constitution stated that no Spaniard could be exempt from conscription when the government called upon him, and that to complement the regular army, national militias were to be established.[47] These were to be organised at the provincial level, and represented the contribution of citizens, as citizens in arms, to the efforts of the army, in case of emergency or sudden war. The entire military career was in its turn transformed. The requirement to belong to the aristocracy to join the officer corps was abolished in 1811, and military academies trained a new body of professional and competent individuals

44. Gonzalo Butrón Prida and Pedro Rújula, eds, *Los sitios en la Guerra de la Independencia: La lucha en las ciudades* (Madrid: Silex; Cádiz: Universidad de Cádiz, 2012).

45. Charles J. Esdaile, 'El levantamiento español', in Esdaile and Javier Tusell, *Época contemporánea: 1808–2004*, vol. 6 of John Lynch, ed., *Historia de España*, 6 vols (Barcelona: Crítica, 2001), pp. 13–31.

46. Fraser, *Napoleon's Cursed War*, pp. 128–41.

47. See Articles 356, 361 and 364 in *Constitucion política de la monarquia española, promulgada en Cádiz, á 19 de marzo 1812* (Cádiz: Imprenta Real, 1812), pp. 97–98.

in support of the constitution. A new central general staff attached to the Ministry of War and answerable to the government was organised to meet the expectations of this new professional body and support organisation of the war effort. The sheer impact of the insurrection, which required a far greater number of officers than ever before, and the ethos of reforms that enabled ambitious individuals to rise through the ranks on merit alone, produced an entirely new army. By the end of the uprising the bulk of its officers, or at least the middling ranks, were no longer aristocrats, and their numbers had increased dramatically, along with those of the army a whole, which by the end of the war in 1814 amounted to no fewer than 160,000 individuals.[48] Antonio Quiroga was one of the officers who benefited from these changes to build a successful career at the heart of the new military organisation. Having left the navy in 1808, he joined the army as a sub-lieutenant but was promoted to captain the following year after fighting, like Rafael Riego, in the battle of Espinosa de los Monteros; in succeeding years he continued to be directly involved in military operations, and having temporarily been taken prisoner, in 1810 he was promoted to adjutant to the general staff. In 1812 he was elevated to the rank of lieutenant colonel, remaining attached to the general staff which defined the strategy of the war until 1814, when this body was dissolved.

As a consequence of this evolution, the army carved out not only a new social space for itself, but also an entirely novel political role. While the regular army lost the preeminence it had enjoyed under the ancien régime (with the insurrection the captain generals lost their traditional control over civil authorities), it acquired a new visibility and influence over political affairs. As early as 1808, when popular protests against the abdication of the king broke out across the country and local and provincial juntas were set up in support of the monarch, officers were appointed as members of these bodies, although their role in such committees varied from place to place. Sometimes they were simply hired as experts to advise civilian authorities, whereas in cities like Zamora and Gerona they were directly co-opted and integrated into them; in Badajoz and Cádiz, where important military garrisons were stationed, they dominated the juntas; in some others, such as Zaragoza, where General José de Palafox seized power, they went so far as to set up dictatorships that governed in place of the juntas.[49] The participation of army officers in the juntas paved

48. Esdaile, 'El levantamiento español', p. 49.
49. Richard Hocquellet, 'Elites locales y levantamiento patriótico: La composición de las juntas provinciales en 1808', *Historia y Política* 19 (2008): 129–50.

the way to a more general involvement of the army in affairs of state. The Junta Suprema that was set up with representatives from all the provincial juntas in 1808 included seven military officers out of a total of twenty-one members. A general belonged to the regency council of five grandees that replaced the Junta in 1810, and led to the summoning of the Cortes. Army officers likewise represented a very substantial proportion of the members of the Cortes of Cádiz: between 1810 and 1813: an average of fifty-five deputies (out of 270) belonged to the army.[50] This presence enabled them to contribute to an ongoing debate about the relationship between the army and government, about whether priority should be given to the war over the consolidation of the constitutional order and about the extent to which the Cortes should control both the military apparatus and the conduct of war operations, or else leave this responsibility primarily to the regency: controversies that spilled outside parliamentary debates into the public sphere.[51] What further contributed to officers' public visibility and prestige was also the sudden and unprecedented production and circulation of printed material and the birth of an independent political journalism, confirmed by the introduction of freedom of the press in 1810. Military matters featured prominently. Dialogues published in periodicals and pamphlets often stressed the difficult conditions in which soldiers and officers operated, contrasting the selflessness and abnegation of the military men, who risked their lives for the nation, with the tranquillity and security enjoyed by civil servants and, above all, by clerics. It also lamented the lack of due recognition of their sacrifice in defence of the fatherland. In an article entitled 'El militar sufrido' published in 1812, an imaginary visit to a temple dedicated to the glory of the military provided an opportunity for a resurrected fighter to complain about the neglect suffered by combatants.[52] At the same time, the press provided details of the activities of the guerrilla bands and their leaders, describing in exhaustive detail their activities against the French. By so doing, it did much to turn them into patriotic heroes of exceptional military virtue. The press highlighted the

50. Fraser, *Napoleon's Cursed War*, p. 204; José Cepeda Gómez, *El ejército español en la política (1787–1843): Conspiraciones y pronunciamientos en los comienzos de la España liberal* (Madrid: Fundación Universitaria Española, 1990), pp. 152–53.

51. Roberto L. Blanco Valdés, *Rey, Cortes y fuerza armada en los orígenes de la España liberal, 1808–1823* (Madrid: Siglo XXI de España, 1988), pp. 99–102.

52. The article, published by the *Diario Mercantil de Cádiz* in 1812, is quoted in Marieta Cantos Casaneve, Fernando Durán López and Alberto Romero Ferrer, eds, *La guerra de pluma: Estudios sobre la prensa de Cádiz en el tiempo de las Cortes (1810–1814)*, 2 vols (Cádiz: Universidad de Cádiz, 2009), 1, at p. 217. On press coverage of military issues, see also ibid., pp. 213, 250–51, 255–56, 283.

humble origins and major contribution to the defence of the fatherland of the 'invincible' and 'incomparable' Francisco Espoz y Mina, a former peasant turned head of one of the largest *bandas*, of Juan Martín Díez, called 'El Empecinado', another former farmer noteworthy for his apparent ubiquity, and of Jerónimo Merino Cob, known as 'El Cura Merino', a former parish priest who could rely on close ties with the *Gazeta de la Provincial de Burgos* to advertise his stirring deeds; all of whom acquired national fame thanks to extensive press coverage.[53]

Admittedly, not all officers welcomed the transformation that the war and the constitution had brought to the army and to the governance of the country. The military establishment resented reforms that had deprived officers of their privileges and subjected the army to the civilian authority of the Ministry of War, and some of the *realista* (royalist) officers (that is, those loyal to the absolute monarchy) were also offended by the attacks on its aristocratic tradition.[54] This experience was in fact to produce profound ideological and political cleavages within the army itself, opposing absolutist to liberal officers, and dividing along similar lines civilians and members of the bands, even if one and all had been caught up in the conflict with the French. At the same time these political polarisations, the turbulence of the period and the centrality of the role of the military class led also to a new phenomenon: the use of force by officers to determine the conduct of political affairs, a habit that gave rise to the practice of the pronunciamiento. It should not be forgotten that in 1808 it was the aristocratic Guardia Real stationed at the royal palace of Aranjuez that intervened to support Fernando's decision to remove the prime minister Godoy and replace his own father on the throne. From that date onwards, military interventions might take place both in defence of and against the constitution. During the war officials had set up dictatorships in the name of the monarch's absolute rights, but constitutional officers had likewise tried to influence political decisions. In 1811 General Francisco Ballesteros unsuccessfully attempted to lead his troops into an insurrection to prevent the appointment of Lord Wellington as head of the Spanish army: the Cortes vetoed this appointment, but Ballesteros was punished for his insubordination. In 1814, what put an end to the constitutional regime on the return of Fernando VII was the military intervention of General Francisco

---

53. Alberto Ausín Ciruelos, 'Propaganda, periodismo y pueblo en armas: Las guerillas y sus líderes según la prensa de la guerra de independencia (1808–1814)', *Aportes* 97 (2018): 7–43.

54. Blanco Valdés, *Rey, Cortes y fuerza armada*, pp. 257–59 and passim.

Xavier de Elío, who made his troops available to the monarch in Valencia to declare his absolute rights and repeal the constitution.[55]

After Fernando VII's restoration of absolutism in 1814, this novel practice was adopted by a number of former leaders of *bandas de guerrilleros* who had become staunch supporters of the constitution. In 1814 Francisco Espoz y Mina, who had led guerrilla bands in Navarre, organised an insurrection in Pamplona; in 1815, at La Coruña, it was the turn of another officer famous for his past guerrilla activities, Juan Díaz Porlier. In 1817 it was the turn of Luis de Lacy at Caldetas in Catalonia, who had led guerrilla activities in that region. Compared to these officers, Riego's involvement in the struggle against the French had been very limited: after participating with his regiment in the *motín* (tumult) of Aranjuez which in March 1808 had led to the abdication of King Carlos IV in favour of his son Fernando, he refused to participate in the battle of Espinosa de los Monteros. He was taken prisoner by the French and remained in captivity in France—in Dijon, in Autun and finally in Chalons—until 1813, when he managed to escape, return to Spain, and swear an oath of allegiance to the constitution along with General de Lacy.[56] Thus he too had learnt from his fellow liberal officers that it was legitimate to intervene militarily in defence of the constitution.

The experience of military occupation and resistance in Portugal bore some striking similarities to Spanish events, but also showed substantial differences. As in Spain, a major consequence of the conflict was the ousting of the dynasty. The French invasion and occupation of the country by General Jean-Andoche Junot between December 1807 and July 1808 determined the departure of the regent prince Dom João along with the entire royal family and the court to Brazil, under British protection. It also led to the of the disbanding of the army, the dissolution of the regency council appointed by the regent upon his departure and the deposition of the dynasty. No sooner had the British army under the command of Sir Arthur Wellesley landed in Portugal and Junot's troops been expelled from the country, with the support of a generalised popular insurrection, than Portugal became a territory of strategic importance in the fight against Napoleon, and remained so until 1814. Portugal was attacked again, first in March by the French troops of Marshal Soult, who briefly occupied the city of Porto, and again between summer 1810 and spring 1811, when the British managed to stem a French expedition led by Marshal Masséna

---

55. Ibid., pp. 110, 178, 188–95.

56. Alberto Gil Novales, 'Rafael Riego', in *Diccionario biográfico del Trienio Liberal*, ed. Alberto Gil Novales (Madrid: Ediciones El Museo Universal, 1991), pp. 562–63.

thanks to the fortified defences provided by the lines of Torres Vedras, north of Lisbon. Otherwise free from any permanent French occupation and protected by the British army, Portugal proved to be an ideal space for the British to organise and equip their expeditionary forces to mount attacks on Spain.[57] In this context the Portuguese authorities could not rule independently over the country, nor was any new political constitutional experiment akin to that developed in Cádiz conceived, attempted or experimented with in these exceptional circumstances. With the arrival of the British army, the council of the *governadores do reino* (governors of the kingdom) that ruled Portugal in the name of the regent prince Dom João was reinstated. No official regency including a member of the dynasty and acting independently was appointed in Portugal, and the regent from Brazil insisted on retaining his full authority over the governadores. In 1809 the governadores had suggested that the Cortes of Portugal be summoned to approve the extraordinary financial contributions needed for the war effort. This was not viewed by the governadores as a step towards the transformation of Portugal into a constitutional country, as would happen in Spain in years to come: in their view, in fact, the traditional bodies of the kingdom could on their own ensure the support needed for such unpopular measures. However, the government in Rio de Janeiro vehemently opposed the idea, which was immediately abandoned.[58] In practice, from then on it was not the governadores who represented the absent monarch, but rather the British army commander William Carr (later Viscount) Beresford, who wielded almost absolute power. Whereas up until 1810 two members of the council in particular, the elected patriarch Dom António de S. José de Castro and Dom José de Sousa, had endeavoured to resist British hegemony over government, formulating to that end an independent military and political strategy, albeit with scant success, from the following year Dom João put a stop to these efforts, and to conflicts between these two governadores and the occupying army, confirming British political and military leadership over the country. The governadores' authority was subsequently confined to implementing fiscal and economic policies geared to supporting British military ventures.[59]

57. José Miguel Sardica, *A Europa napoleónica e Portugal: Messianismo revolucionário, política, guerra e opinião pública* (Lisbon: Tribuna da História, 2011).

58. Fernando Dores Costa, 'O Conde de Palmela em Cádis (1810–1812)', *Ler História* 64 (2013): 87–109 at pp. 97–98.

59. Paquette, *Imperial Portugal*, p. 91; Fernando Dores Costa, 'The Peninsular War as a Diversion and the Role of the Portuguese in the British Strategy', *Portuguese Journal of Social Science* 22, no. 1 (2013): 3–24 at pp. 8–11.

Like Spain, Portugal experienced a general popular uprising against the French occupier. Inspired by Spanish events, in 1808 an insurrection broke out spontaneously across the country and led to the organisation of guerrilla units as well as of city and provincial juntas. Individual and collective acts of violence did not target the French invaders alone, however, but were often directed at foreigners, or at individuals perceived to be such, who had resided in Portugal for a long time, as well as at those accused of being collaborators, or *jacobinos*, and conspirators. Popular violence was therefore not driven exclusively by hatred for the invader: insurrection here provided opportunities to revolt against onerous taxation, or feudal obligations, as well to take personal revenge for slights best understood in the context of communal rivalries. Tradesmen, merchants and shopkeepers were also often the target of popular rage. The local elites hastened to assume the leadership of popular movements, localised tumults and uprisings, in an attempt to control the violence, but only once it had erupted and threatened to escalate. The dismantling of the army effected by the French also made possible the participation of officers in the popular insurgencies against the occupying forces, and their being co-opted by juntas created to coordinate the war against the French occupying army. Thus Portuguese revolutionaries in 1820 had no need to refer to the memory of the Spanish guerrilla conflict, as the Italians would do, but they did refer to their own guerrilla war, representing what had been a set of local revolts as a national event to justify their military intervention in the name of the people. One of the organisers of the 1820 revolution in Porto, Sebastião Drago Valente de Brito Cabreira, had been a leading figure in the anti-French revolt that broke out in 1808 in the Algarve. His published account of the insurgency in that region confirms the dynamic of these events as observed almost everywhere in the country. Cabreira had refused to cooperate with the French occupier, and his house in Faro became the centre of conspiratorial activities against them. It was simply to stem the 'confusion without order' that had affected Faro as well as the other cities of the Algarve, from Tavira to Olhão, where the popular classes had taken the lead in attacking the French, that Cabreira decided to intervene militarily and gain control over the tumults. As a consequence, a local governmental junta for which Cabreira would continue to work during the insurrection as adjutant general to his president, Francisco de Melo da Cunha Mendonça e Meneses, was set up, whose members belonged to the army, the aristocracy, the clergy and the people, including even a stonemason.[60]

---

60. Drago Valente de Brito Cabreira, *Relação histórica da revolução do Algarve contra os francezes, que dolozamente invadirão Portugal no anno de 1807* (Lisbon: Typografia

In Portugal, however, the establishment of these juntas did not represent a first step towards the creation of central representative institutions, leading potentially to the establishment of a Cortes and the approval of a new constitution. As in the Algarve, these were bodies composed of the traditional orders of the ancien régime: clergy, local aristocratic elites and the *povo* (populace).[61] The proclamations they issued, calling upon the population to take up arms, did not present a new political language. Although they justified the revolts in the name of the existence of a broader idea of national community, and although the terms *nação*, *pátria* and *povo* employed by them acquired a new currency and meaning in the light of the generalised uprising, their language was still associated with a traditional vision of society as organised by rank. The idea of defending the freedom of the *pátria* from the foreigner was geared, as was often the case also in Spain, to the re-establishment of absolute monarchical sovereignty. The juntas' *patriotismo* was further legitimised by the support of the clergy, who sanctioned it in sermons, religious services and addresses, while giving support to, as well as participating in, the armed struggle.[62]

It was only in the city of Porto, the epicentre of the insurrection against the French, that the organisation of committees to lead the revolt gave rise to explicit demands to summon the Cortes of Portugal. In June 1808, following on from Spanish events, the pronunciamiento of a Spanish general based in Porto, Domingos Bellesta, inaugurated the revolt against the French, and led to the creation of a junta chaired by the city's bishop. Immediately afterwards a Portuguese officer, João Manuel de Mariz, set up a military committee and organised a second military coup against the French, supported by his troops, whose aim was not simply to reinstate the absolute monarchy: in his manifesto Mariz declared, significantly enough, that the Portuguese nation was anxious to have its representative rights recognised, and that the decadence of the country was due to the fact that for too long the Cortes had not been summoned. Whether these officers simply wanted to reintroduce the ancient Portuguese Cortes, representing as it had done all the orders of society, or whether they had in

---

Lacerdina, 1809). On the Portuguese guerrillas, see Vasco Pulido Valente, 'O povo em armas: a revolta nacional de 1808–1809', *Análise Social* 15, no. 57 (1979): 7–48; Fernando Dores Costa, 'Franceses e "jacobinos": Movimentações "populares" e medidas de polícia em 1808 e 1809; Uma "irrupção patriótica"?', *Ler História* 54 (2008): 95–132.

61. José Viriato Capela, Henrique Matos and Rogério Borralheiro, *O heróico patriotismo das províncias do norte: Os concelhos na Restauração de Portugal de 1808* (Monção: Casa Museu, Universidade do Minho, 2008).

62. João Francisco Marques, 'O clero nortenho e as invasões francesas: Patriotismo e resistência regional', *Revista de História* 9 (1989): 165–246.

mind a new model of representation, is unclear. In any case, Mariz and his supporters were immediately imprisoned and then exiled by the junta led by the bishop. It is perhaps not by chance that the military insurrection of 1820 in favour of the constitution was perpetrated by the military garrison of this same city.[63] In 1808 the only alternative constitutional programme supported in Portugal was that demanded by a group of *afrancesado* aristocrats and jurists in a petition to Napoleon, inspired by the constitution granted by Napoleon to Warsaw and associated with the introduction of the Napoleonic code. The constitution in question was based on a bicameral system, the recognition of Catholicism as the state religion, equality before the law and administrative reform. This constitution, while representing the first instance of Napoleonic reformism in Portugal, would seem to have had only a limited impact on constitutionalism in the years to follow.[64]

Although no explicit reformist agenda issued from the Portuguese juntas, in Portugal too the militarisation of society had a profound impact, produced enduring political cleavages, and prepared the ground for the political activism of the army in the post-Napoleonic era. It should be noted that a large proportion of Portuguese soldiers and officers had experienced war not only in Portugal itself, but also on Spanish soil, where they were exposed to new ideas and came to nurse new professional and political aspirations. A small but significant number of volunteers fought on the side of the French. As soon as they occupied Portugal, the French almost immediately constituted three Lusitanian legions from three different regions that fought in defence of Napoleonic rule on the Iberian peninsula. A range of different motivations determined the decision taken by some six thousand men to fight in these legions. Some had enthusiastically embraced the egalitarian values of Napoleon's military culture, others were driven by hatred for Britain, while yet others, whether or not they were freemasons, had liberal aspirations and hoped for the creation of a future constitutional regime. One of the three commanders, Gomes

63. Vasco Pulido Valente, *Ir prò maneta: A revolta contra os franceses (1808)* (Lisbon: Aletheia Editores, 2007), pp. 50–52; António do Carmo Reis, *Invasões francesas: As revoltas do Porto contra Junot* (Lisbon: Editorial Notícias, 1991), pp. 101–19; Sérgio Campos Matos, 'Linguagem do patriotismo em Portugal: Da crise do Antigo Regime à I República', in *Linguagens e fronteiras do poder*, ed. Miriam Halpern Pereira, José Murilo de Carvalho, Maria João Vaz and Gladys Sabina Ribeiro (Lisbon: Centro de Estudos de História Contemporânea Portuguesa, 2012), pp. 35–52 at 40–43.

64. See Hespanha, *Guiando a mão invisível*, pp. 55–59. An example of a jurist influenced by these ideas was José Joaquim Ferreira de Moura.

Freire de Andrade, would in 1817 be involved in a conspiracy to expel the British and introduce a constitution.[65]

The majority of conscripts, however, fought under British leadership against the French army in Portugal as well as in Spain. From 1808 onwards the arrival of the British on to Portuguese soil under the command of Lord Beresford not only marked a new phase in the Napoleonic wars, but also led to the reconstitution of a Portuguese army, under British command, following which, in December 1808, the regency declared that the nation as a whole should arm itself, ordering that all able-bodied men between the ages of fifteen and sixty should enlist.[66] In practice this objective was not achieved, as a number of practical and financial obstacles it impossible. However, in spite of the very high numbers of deserters (25 per cent of all infantrymen), who either joined the guerrillas or, more frequently, simply returned home, this meant that almost half of the Portuguese men in the age range stipulated had served in the army in this period. Between 1809 and 1811 the army was each year composed of an average of fifty thousand individuals, amounting to an exceptionally high percentage of the adult population. Indeed, the contribution of the Portuguese troops proved crucial to British military strategy in Spain, and its success would have been unthinkable without them. Around thirty thousand Portuguese soldiers fought in Spain, and in France too. For instance, 19,250 Portuguese troops fought in the battle of Salamanca, in 1812, and in 1813 some 26,400 fought in the battle of Vitoria. In addition to no fewer than ten major battles on the peninsula itself, Portuguese soldiers were also involved in Wellington's expedition into French territory between 1813 and 1814, and were present on several crucial battlefields there.[67] The war provided opportunities for rapid promotion for a whole generation of Portuguese officers. Bernardo Sepúlveda, the youngest colonel in the Portuguese army when he initiated the revolution in Porto in August 1820 with Cabreira, belonged to a wealthy family with military traditions but only recently ennobled: he was the second son of another officer, Lieutenant General Manuel Jorge Gomes de Sepúlveda, who had led the anti-French insurrection in Trás-os-Montes in 1808, and brother

65. On this, see Joaquim Veríssimo Serrão, *A instauração do liberalismo (1807–1832)* (*História de Portugal*, vol. 7) (Lisbon: Editorial Verbo, 1984), pp. 33–37.

66. Manuel Themudo Barata, 'A subversão organiza-se a nível nacional', in *Nova história militar de Portugal*, ed. Manuel Themudo Barata and Nuno Severiano Teixeira, 5 vols (Lisbon: Círculo de Leitores, 2003–4), 3, pp. 164–74 at 165.

67. Fernando Dores Costa, 'Army Size, Military Recruitment and Financing in Portugal during the Period of the Peninsular War—1808–1811' *E-Journal of Portuguese History* 6, no. 2 (2008): 31–57; Costa, 'Peninsular War as a Diversion'.

of another officer, who in 1815 received the new title of Viscount de Erve-dosa.[68] Bernardo himself had fought against the French under the British and had distinguished himself at the battle of Albuera in 1811 and at Salamanca the following year in Wellington's army in Spain; he was in fact a much trusted aide-de-camp of Lord Beresford, who had supported his career. Being required to fight under the command of the British while the country was de facto under British military authority, however, soon came to be resented by the Portuguese officers, who were aware of their British counterparts' contempt for and lack of trust in the ability of the Portuguese army to fight effectively, at least in the earliest stages of the conflicts, and by the rank-and-file troops, who resented mass conscription. In addition, it was Britain that the military class considered responsible for the dire economic plight of their country, a sentiment they shared with the population at large. If Portugal had experienced the destruction of war, it was also suffering from an economic depression because of British trade impositions and priorities. The opening up of the ports of Brazil to foreign shipping in 1808, confirmed by a treaty with Britain in 1810 according preferential treatment to British goods, combined with the disruption caused by the war, had a considerable impact in Portugal. Between 1808 and 1813 trade with Brazil suffered a reduction of 75 per cent compared to the period between 1796 and 1806.[69] The feelings engendered by these conditions were in fact to intensify in the years immediately preceding the 1820 revolution. Thus hatred for the French invader, but also intolerance for Portuguese subordination to the British army, shaped the patriotism of this generation of officers and their troops.

Besides the participation of a substantial share of the population in the war effort at home and abroad, political journalism represented another important channel of communication of new ideas during this period. In Portugal as well as Spain, the war coincided with the explosion of the public sphere and the wider circulation of information. Portuguese officers and soldiers who fought in Spain became familiar with the debates and process that led to the proclamation of the Cádiz Constitution, but also within

68. António Monteiro Cardoso, *A revolução liberal em Trás-os-Montes (1820–1834): O povo e as elites* (Porto: Edições Afrontamento, 2007), p. 77; José Acúrsio das Neves, *História geral da invasão dos franceses em Portugal e da restauração deste reino* (Porto: Edições Afrontamento, 2008 [1810–11]), pp. 265–72.

69. Valentim Alexandre, *Os sentidos do Império: Questão nacional e questão colonial na crise do antigo regime português* (Porto: Edições Afrontamento, 1993); Paquette, *Imperial Portugal*, pp. 92–95. On British attitudes, see Gavin Daly, *The British Soldier in the Peninsular War: Encounters with Spain and Portugal, 1808–1814* (Basingstoke: Palgrave Macmillan, 2013).

the borders of Portugal voices in favour of political reform could be heard, even if public opinion and the various readerships were still limited in size. Between 1809 and 1810 in particular, in the context of the war effort against the French, the number and distribution of printed publications escalated, and political journalism saw the light for the first time. Besides featuring conservative defences of monarchical patriotism, anti-French propaganda and articles about the war translated from the Spanish and British press, periodicals might now contain critiques of the commercial treaty with Britain, calls for institutional reforms, and could even, in the case of Rocha Loureiro's *O Correio da Peninsula*, include outright support for a constitution. Even if the government hastened to limit freedom of the press from 1810, abolishing a number of periodicals and imprisoning suspected liberals, and even though the birth of new periodicals slowed down considerably, and the space devoted to political information was reduced, publication did not grind to a halt: between that year and 1819 thirty-four more titles appeared on the market. In addition, in spite of the government's attempts to prevent the circulation of foreign journalism, it could not altogether obstruct the penetration of the exile press printed in Paris or London, which provided a crucial contribution to the dissemination of liberal and reformist ideas. *O Português*, edited by Rocha Loureiro, the *Investigador Português em Londres* and *O Campeão Portuguez*, edited by José Liberato Freire de Carvalho, all of which supported the summoning of the Cortes as in Spain, circulated also within the Portuguese Empire.[70]

The almost permanent integration of the Italian peninsula into the orbit of the French Empire during the Napoleonic period made the experience of the wars and military service by its populations different from that of the rest of southern Europe. Unlike the cases of the Portuguese and Spanish armies, which fought mainly against Napoleon, Italian participation in the Napoleonic wars was almost exclusively on the side of the French, whether as conscripts or volunteers from Italian territories annexed directly to the French Empire (such as Piedmont), or from Italian satellite states (the 'sister republics' between 1796 and 1799, and the Italian Republic, which became the Kingdom of Italy in 1805), and the Kingdom of Naples—excepting of course those officers and troops who withdrew to Sicily with King Ferdinando in 1806. Admittedly in Italy, and in Naples in particular, the patriotism and liberalism associated with military careers and the experience of war had quite different political roots

70. Sardica, *A Europa napoleónica*; José Tengarrinha, *Nova história da imprensa portuguesa das origens a 1865* (Lisbon: Círculo de Leitores, 2013), pp. 161–75, 187–97, 203–10.

if compared with Portugal and Spain in particular, where the collaborators and supporters of the French, the so-called *afrancesados*, represented a minority among patriots, and were treated by the Spanish *doceañistas* who had fought against Napoleon and supported the constitution, as enemies and traitors. On the contrary, the Italian and Neapolitan revolutionary cultures that stemmed from the Napoleonic era, unlike their Spanish and Portuguese counterparts, were rooted in the political principles of the French revolution. These radical differences notwithstanding, the Italians and Neapolitans nonetheless ended up, much as their contemporaries on the Iberian peninsula had done, treating Napoleonic imperialism as their enemy. Their integration into the Napoleonic armies did not prevent local officers from developing an entirely new and autonomous brand of Italian and Neapolitan patriotism that, indebted though it undoubtedly was to the principles of the French revolution, could turn out to be equally hostile to French rule. The tension between early support for the French legal and institutional reforms on the peninsula, identification with the new values embodied by the Napoleonic armies and frustration with the exploitative and authoritarian nature of French rule were a key feature of the experience of Italian patriots in these years.

The Italian peninsula provided a very substantial contribution to the Grande Armée. French authorities started to recruit Italian soldiers as soon as they had established a presence in northern Italy through the creation of the sister republics between 1796 and 1799. However, before 1802 the officers and soldiers recruited in the Cisalpine Republic had consisted only of volunteers. The consolidation of French rule on the Italian peninsula, which led to the establishment of the Italian Republic in 1802, that of the Kingdom of Italy in 1805 and that of the Kingdom of Naples in 1806, brought with it the introduction of compulsory military service for all able-bodied male adults for a stint of four years. Between 1797 and 1814 the army recruited 164,000 conscripts and more than 44,000 volunteers from the Italian republics and the Kingdom of Italy. To these numbers, 50,000 troops from Naples and 164,000 from the departments annexed to the French Empire (including 95,000 Piedmontese, 10,000 Tuscan and 23,000 Ligurians) should be added.[71] The impact of the militarisation of Italian societies was twofold. On the one hand, compulsory conscription, never experienced before by the populations of the Italian states, gave

71. Data available in Franco Della Peruta, *Esercito e società nell'Italia napoleonica: Dalla Cisalpina al regno d'Italia* (Milan: FrancoAngeli, 1996), and also in Carlo Zaghi, *L'Italia di Napoleone* (Turin: UTET, 1989), p. 253.

rise to widespread resistance and opposition, as everywhere in territories occupied by the French. Resistance ranged from desertion, a phenomenon that deprived the French armies in Italy of tens of thousands of individuals and was treated by the Napoleonic authorities as an emergency, since it fostered further disobedience and led to crime and banditry, even to outright rebellion. Indeed, Italian territories were afflicted by *insorgenze*, the more or less exact equivalent of the guerrilla warfare that had ravaged Spain and Portugal. In Rome, for instance, in 1810, only one-third of the designated conscripts could actually be drafted. In Naples, in 1807 and 1808, attempts to organise compulsory conscription failed almost entirely. Such measures could simply not be enforced in a number of regions, and brigands and prisoners had to be drafted instead. In 1809 it was only by doubling the quotas, and introducing the compulsory conscription of two men for every thousand inhabitants, that better results were achieved, although desertion continued to be a scourge.[72] The uprising in Calabria between 1806 and 1809 represented the most dramatic example of anti-French resistance, and one that could only be suppressed through the intervention of volunteers in support of the French army. This revolt had been incited directly by Queen Maria Carolina, who had withdrawn with the king to Sicily upon the arrival of the French army, and by her emissaries. Breaking out first in the mountains of the Sila, it spread through the entire region, supported by the priests and by sections of all social classes. In practice, guerrilla warfare was waged by the *masse*, armed bands numbering from just a handful to sixty or more members, composed of peasants, shepherds and veritable bandits led by the so-called *capi masse*, brigands themselves or feudal officials in the hire of great landowners. As in Spain and Portugal, a variety of motives inspired those who rallied to these insurrectionary movements. Some rose up in the name of religion and the monarchy, chafing under French rule and its fiscal and military impositions; but others engaged also in looting, kidnapping and attacks on property. Thus members of the *masse* took advantage of the revolt to engage in vendettas and settle old scores with other members of their own or of other communities.[73]

On the other hand, however, military service attracted early on those supporters of the French revolution who had welcomed the arrival of the French, the end of absolute monarchies and ancient oligarchical

---

72. For Naples, see John A. Davis, 'The Neapolitan Army during the *decennio francese*', *Rivista Italiana di Studi Napoleonici* 25, no. 1 (1988): 161–77; Davis, *Naples and Napoleon*, pp. 219–20; Renata De Lorenzo, *Murat* (Rome: Salerno Editrice, 2011), pp. 216–17.

73. On these events, see Davis, *Naples and Napoleon*, pp. 211–19, 225–27.

republics and the dawn of a new era of regeneration of their states in the name of popular sovereignty, liberty, equality and fraternity. From the outset, therefore, joining the French army represented first and foremost a political decision rather than simply a professional one. The mottos inscribed on the flag of the Lombard legion, established in 1796, translate as 'Italian freedom' and 'Democracy or death'.[74] It is within the army and the war ministries of the Cisalpine and Italian republics that we might find different political factions existing at the time among the *patrioti*, and among French officials and administrators as well, ranging from the most radical supporters of democracy and independence, who in some cases became outspoken in their criticism of Napoleon's betrayal of their early hopes of emancipation, to the more moderate collaborators with Napoleon. The ministers of war of the Cisalpine Republic, first Pietro Teulié, and after him Francesco Melzi, vice-president of the Italian Republic, had hoped that universal military conscription would represent a first step towards the establishment of a fully-fledged Italian national army, one that would in turn lay the foundations for a future wholly independent Italian state.[75] In practice, Napoleon never sanctioned the existence of a separate Italian army, with its potentially national overtones, but considered the contribution of Italian troops to the war effort, although substantial in size, simply as a support, auxiliary to the Grande Armée. After 1802, any hopes that a degree of political autonomy from France could be achieved having by then been dashed, Napoleonic rule took on a more explicitly authoritarian tone and any form of political opposition was repressed. These thwarted aspirations were then wholly transferred to conspiratorial networks of secret societies, whose ranks were filled by army officers of varying political inclinations, from radical democrats to constitutionalists, all advocates of a Neapolitan and Italian patriotism. In this new political context many officers nonetheless continued to support Napoleonic rule, convinced as they were that the separate administrative and legal existence of the kingdom, although without any form of representation and autonomy, was for the time being all that could realistically be hoped for, a modest advance of this sort being necessary to create gradually the preconditions for self-rule in

74. Zaghi, *L'Italia di Napoleone*, p. 249.

75. Stefano Levati, 'Politica, affarismo ed esercito: La lotta per il potere nel Ministero della guerra durante la Seconda Repubblica Cisalpina e la Repubblica Italiana (giugno 1800–maggio 1805)', in *L'affaire Ceroni: Ordine militare e cospirazione politica nella Milano di Bonaparte*, ed. Stefano Levati (Milan: Guerini e Associati, 2005), pp. 65–96.

the future.[76] In addition, the career opportunities offered by the army, and the fact that its new social composition reflected the principles of merit and competence as opposed to privilege, constituted an important reason for the enduring commitment of its Italian officers to the Napoleonic project on the peninsula.

The revolutionary notion of military service was the most direct and tangible application of the principles of the revolution and its notion of citizens in arms, and the values embodied in the military career its most enduring legacy. As in Spain, the war produced an entirely new type of army compared to those existing in the Italian states before the Napoleonic conquest: one in which relations between officers and men were less hierarchical, and a stronger spirit of camaraderie bound together all members regardless of their rank. The new military schools and academies founded by the French offered new professional opportunities, and created a new military elite based on technical training and expertise, attracting almost invariably individuals committed to the cause of the political regeneration of Italy. The most famous of them, the Scuola Militare dell'Artiglieria e del Genio of Modena, established in 1797, produced highly skilled professionals, engineers whose loyalty to the regime was repaid by their receiving the best training available.[77] In Naples the military school of the Nunziatella was reopened in 1811 as the new Scuola politecnica militare, and in the same year a 'Scuola d'ingegnieria' was founded there. These new institutions reinforced the politically reformist attitudes of the Neapolitan army, leading it to offer its support to the revolution in 1820.

In the Kingdom of Naples the officers close to Joachim Murat who filled the upper echelons of the army were among the most fervent advocates of a programme of patriotic renewal and autonomy from France. Between 1808—when he replaced Napoleon's brother Joseph who was sent to Madrid—and 1815, Murat strove to guarantee a degree of autonomy for the kingdom, endeavouring to resist the onerous financial demands of Napoleon, and aspiring to create a new Italian dynasty that would in due course reign over a fully independent kingdom. The group of Neapolitan officers comprising Guglielmo Pepe, Florestano Pepe, Luigi Blanch and Pietro Colletta, all future protagonists of the 1820 revolution, who had

76. On the relationship between nationalism and war in the period, see Maria Canella, ed., *Armi e nazione: Dalla Repubblica Cisalpina al Regno d'Italia (1797–1914)* (Milan: FrancoAngeli, 2009).

77. On the military academies, see Bruno Giordano, 'La scuola militare di Modena in età napoleonica (1798–1820)', in *Istituzioni e cultura in età napoleonica*, ed. Elena Brambilla, Carlo Capra and Aurora Scotti (Milan: FrancoAngeli, 2008), pp. 295–315.

been involved in the 1799 Neapolitan revolution and embraced early on the principles of French republicanism, developed a new brand of patriotism that was both Neapolitan and Italian, accepted the ideological foundations of French rule and the new ethos of the Neapolitan Muratist army, while rejecting the radicalism of the 1799 republic. Their particular brand of nationalism thus converged with the political vision and aspirations of Murat, whose own military career embodied the new meritocratic nature of the Napoleonic army. Murat's ambitions could not be fulfilled, as the kingdom's existence and domestic policies remained geared to the financial and military needs of France. Nonetheless, his aspirations seemed to be turning into reality between 1814 and 1815, when he tried to create a 'Kingdom of Italy' in the south that included also the Papal States, first by allying himself with the Austrians to fight against Napoleon, and in 1815 when he sided once more with the emperor, in his last, short-lived attempt to regain power after exile on Elba, to defend the same political project. In 1814, during the military campaign in northern Italy in support of the allies, Neapolitan officers such as Guglielmo and Florestano Pepe, Carrascosa and Colletta put pressure on him to embrace also the constitutional cause in order to guarantee their support for his dynastic ambitions, in the midst of proliferating carbonarist conspiracies and an insurgency in favour of the constitution in the city of Teramo. Murat only very belatedly yielded to these aspirations, by issuing a constitution in March 1815, while in Rimini. This text protected freedom of the press and foresaw the establishment of a senate appointed by the monarch and an elective 'Consiglio dei notabili' made up, through a complex indirect electoral system, of deputies representing the provinces, the cities, trade and the university of Naples. However, this happened far too late, just before the loss of the kingdom to the Bourbons.[78]

What had by then further consolidated a new sense of national belonging was the participation of large numbers of soldiers from the peninsula in wars across Europe. Italian troops fought mainly in central Europe and, above all, in Russia and Spain, where three Italian divisions comprised almost thirty thousand troops. From the Kingdom of Naples, nine thousand soldiers were sent to Spain and thirteen thousand to Russia, where Murat himself had fought in 1812. Italian participation in the invasion of the Iberian peninsula was marked by high rates of desertion and

78. On Murat in 1814 and 1815, see De Lorenzo, *Murat*, pp. 284–305; Davis, *Naples and Napoleon*, pp. 259–64; on this constitution, Giuseppe Galasso, *Storia del regno di Napoli*, 5 vols (Turin: UTET, 2006–2007), 4, pp. 1299–301.

heavy casualties, as only a small percentage of those who went survived the campaigns in Spain.[79] Nonetheless, this was the campaign that would leave the deepest mark and produce the most enduring memory among the survivors, especially the officers. All the most prominent supporters of the revolution in the army in 1820 had not only supported Murat's project and helped to suppress insurgencies and banditry in Calabria and in other Neapolitan provinces, but had also taken part in military activities in the Spanish (or Russian) campaigns. Luigi Blanch, a moderate supporter of constitutionalism in 1820, had been in Calabria in 1808 and fought at Danzig in 1809; Florestano Pepe, who in 1820 led the naval expedition to put down the Sicilian revolt against constitutional Naples, had curbed brigandage in Molise and participated in the war in Spain as chief of staff between 1810 and 1812; Francesco Pignatelli di Strongoli suppressed brigandage in Salerno in 1807, fought in Catalonia in 1810 and supported the introduction of the constitution in 1820; Captain Gaetano Costa, a member of the Carboneria who led the military expedition in eastern Sicily against the independentists in 1820, had been served as lieutenant in Spain in 1809.[80]

Although fighting on the side of the French against the Spaniards, and struck by the sheer cruelty and savagery of the conflict, Italian officers developed at the same time an admiration for the resilience and bravery of the Spanish people, and ended up associating their own Italian patriotism more closely with the Spanish version than with the French. Florestano Pepe's brother Guglielmo, who had fought in Spain between 1811 and 1813, remembered with pride the contribution of the Italian regiments to the war, and the great valour of their soldiers. He further recalled the tensions and conflict with their French commanders, offended by their refusal to treat Napoleon as an idol, and their tendency to make an immoderate case for their Italian patriotism. Like other Neapolitan officers fighting in Spain, Pepe had likened the anti-French guerrilla warfare that had broken out in Calabria in 1806, and which he had helped to repress while serving in the army, to the constant threat of guerrilla bands to which he was subjected when making his way to the city of Zaragoza.[81] He also

79. Franco Della Peruta, 'War and Society in Napoleonic Italy: The Armies of the Kingdom of Italy at Home and Abroad', in *Society and Politics in the Age of the Risorgimento: Essays in Honour of Denis Mack Smith*, ed. John A. Davis and Paul Ginsborg (Cambridge: Cambridge University Press, 2002), pp. 26–47. On Murat's army, see De Lorenzo, *Murat*, pp. 242–60; Davis, *Naples and Napoleon*, pp. 251–54.

80. De Lorenzo, *Murat*, pp. 263–64.

81. Guglielmo Pepe, *Memoirs of General Pepe, Comprising the Principal Military and Political Events of Italy*, 3 vols (London: Schulze and Co., 1846), 1, pp. 287, 305–7. A comparison between the two wars can also be found in other contemporary accounts: see Nino

noted the differences between the two phenomena, later regretting that
the landowners and the elites in Calabria were at odds with the insurgents. By contrast with the situation in Spain, it was therefore clear to him
that in Calabria the war against the French could not be won.[82] This ex-
post regret for a missed opportunity, and the comparison between the two
sets of circumstances, was clearly the product of a retrospective recasting and much mythologising, but reflected also the genuine frustration, if
not intolerance, shared at the time by many Italian Napoleonic officers, at
the vagaries of French imperial rule, and resentment at the high percentage of foreigners among army officials, which limited opportunities for
native officers. This regret further reflected scepticism at the possibility
of turning Neapolitan soldiers into Muratist patriots, aware as they were of
the cultural gap then evident between the local populations and the values underpinning the new regime. In the years following, the importance
of the memory of Spanish events proved crucial to the development of a
model of national insurrection, one that bore witness to the popular foundations of freedom. This importance is demonstrated by the proliferation
of memoirs by those Italian veterans who had fought in Spain. Pepe's own
account is merely one example of what would become a distinct literary
genre, featuring a good number of posthumous publications, but also a
quantity of manuscripts that were destined to remain unpublished. Some
of these memoirs went into print long after the 1820s revolutions, but, significantly, during the 1820 revolution in Naples articles by veterans from
the Peninsular War described the rebellion as an insurrection in which
single guerrilla units made up of small numbers of partisans could, by
coordinating assaults from their strongholds in mountainous areas, defeat
regular armies and expel the enemy. Thus the pronunciamientos in Nola
and Avellino of 1820 and that in Piedmont of 1821, like their Spanish and
Portuguese equivalents, cannot be understood without taking into account
the importance of the Napoleonic military experience for that generation
of patriots from the Italian peninsula. It is no surprise that one of the
two officers to have initiated the pronunciamiento in Nola, Giuseppe Silvati, had fought in Spain between 1810 and 1812.[83] And the importance

Cortese, L'esercito napoletano e le guerre napoleoniche: Spagna, Alto Adige, Russia, Germania (Naples: Ricciardi, 1928), pp. 35–36.

82. Pepe, Memoirs, 1, pp. 227.

83. See the article in La Minerva Napoletana, Naples, 10 February 1821, pp. 59–126. For
later memoirs, see also Camillo Vacani, Storia delle campagne e degli assedj degl'Italiani
in Ispagna dal 1808 al 1813, 2 vols (Milan: Imperiale Regia Stamperia, 1823). On Silvati's
career, see at least Carmine Pinto, 'Giuseppe Silvati' in Dizionario biografico degli italiani

attributed, in their first public manifesto by the Piedmontese officers who declared the revolution in Alessandria, to the creation of an Italian federation, as well as its anti-aristocratic overtones, were likewise the direct product of their professional and political experience as Napoleonic combatants, during which they had embraced the national cause as one based on the sovereignty of the Italian people, and the egalitarian principles of the French revolution.

If we exclude the expedition to and the temporary conquest of Egypt in 1798, which gave rise to phenomena similar to the popular uprisings of southern Europe, the impact of Napoleonic expansionism on the Ottoman Empire was more limited than had been the case on the Iberian and Italian peninsulas. This difference notwithstanding, the Napoleonic conflicts substantially weakened its influence and power in the Mediterranean and Balkans, reduced its sovereignty over a number of territories, and transformed the relationship between society and army in its lands as radically as anywhere else in the southern peripheries of the continent, laying the ground for the military revolts of 1821. Between 1799 and 1806, in an attempt to stem the expansion and influence of revolutionary France in the Mediterranean, the Ottomans had first allied themselves with their traditional enemy, Russia. This alliance led to a joint protectorate by the two empires over the Ionian islands, a former Venetian territory that revolutionary France had conquered along with Venice in 1797. Between 1800 and 1806, under the name of the Septinsular Republic, these islands became a federation governed by an aristocratic and federal constitution under Ottoman sovereignty and Russian military occupation. By 1807, however, the Ottoman–Russian alliance had come to an end, and as a consequence of the peace of Tilsit between France and Russia the islands were handed over to France. The collapse of the alliance led to a new war, which was fought between 1806 and 1812, this time in the territories of the principalities of Moldavia and Wallachia, where in the previous decades the armies of the two empires had clashed during a sequence of different wars (1768–74; 1787–1792). Between 1809 and 1812 the Russians managed to occupy and, albeit temporarily, annex the principalities. Although the territories were returned to the Porte, the peace treaty of 1812 signed at Bucharest reaffirmed the role of Russia as protector of Christianity and

---

(Rome: Istituto della Enciclopedia Italiana, 2018), vol. 92, pp. 622–25. On the memory of the war in Spain, see Renata De Lorenzo, 'La costruzione di un sistema patriottico: Protagonisti e memorialisti napoletani nella Guerra Spagnola', in *Gli Italiani in Spagna nella guerra napoleonica (1807–1813): I fatti, i testimoni, l'eredità*, ed. Vittorio Scotti Douglas (Alessandria: Edizioni dell'Orso, 2006), pp. 217–53.

reinforced its prestige among the Orthodox populations of the principalities and beyond. In addition, the treaty made Russia guarantor of the autonomy of Serbia, and confirmed the cession of Bessarabia to Russia.[84]

Another consequence of such conflicts was the strengthening of the power of Ali Pasha of Yannina at the expense of the Ottomans. Taking advantage of the Ottoman war against France first, and after 1806 of Russian–Ottoman enmity, Ali Pasha managed to carve out a de facto independent state, although still formally under Ottoman sovereignty, which went well beyond the original Pashalik of Yannina. Between 1798 and 1800 he succeeded in occupying the former Venetian territories of Preveza, Vonitsa and Butrint, and by 1810 he controlled territories that stretched from what is today southern Albania and Epirus in Greece to eastern and western central Greece (known in Greek as Roumeli).[85] The Ottomans responded to the challenges posed by these military defeats and by the glaring inadequacy of their armed forces with a number of attempted military reforms. The traditional armed force of their empire, the Janissaries, had grown in size since the previous century; although nominally a salaried standing army, it had increasingly had to rely on trade to make a living, and had become semi-civilian in nature and ineffectual as a military force compared to its European counterparts. The most notable attempt at military reform was Selim III's creation of a new Western-style voluntary militia, dressed, equipped, drilled and organised according to European military principles: the so-called *nizam-ı cedid*, or 'New Order'. By 1805 this new army included no less than twenty-four thousand men, counting both rank-and-file soldiers and officers. More than anywhere else in southern Europe, however, these reforms were met with the hostility of the traditional military class of the empire, whose perceived inadequacy and inefficiency had led the sultan to establish alternative military forces. The Janissaries' bitter opposition to the creation of a regular army resulted in further turbulence and instability within the empire and triggered a number of revolts. In 1804 the Serbian uprising, which led to the first and largest outbreak of guerrilla warfare by a Christian population within the Ottoman Empire, was triggered by the Janissaries' reaction to the

84. On the wars, see Virginia Aksan, *Ottoman Wars, 1700–1870: An Empire Besieged* (Harlow: Longman Pearson, 2007), pp. 241–81. On the treaty, see also Alexander Bitis, *Russia and the Eastern Question: Army, Government, and Society, 1821–1833* (Oxford: Oxford University Press, 2006), pp. 27–30.

85. Katherine Fleming, *The Muslim Bonaparte: Diplomacy and Orientalism in Ali Pasha's Greece* (Princeton, NJ: Princeton University Press, 1999).

establishment of an independent militia of Christian Serbians, a decision the sultan had taken precisely to undermine Janissary authority in this region. In 1807 the deposition of Selim III, followed by the deposition of the new grand vizier and the abandonment of military reform by the new sultan, Mahmud, were all the result of the direct intervention of the Janissaries stationed in Constantinople.[86]

But besides these failed attempts at military reform, another major consequence of these conflicts was that they provided unprecedented opportunities for employment for the Christian populations of the empire. Thousands of their number joined the European armed forces in these same years, fighting both in and against the French Grande Armée. Regions like Himara in Albania and Souli in Epirus, characterised by strenuous defence of autonomy, had had a tradition of mercenary service with foreign armies (including the army of the Neapolitan kingdom) that dated back many centuries. During the Napoleonic wars, however, demands for these fighters increased dramatically, and in the year 1810, for instance, Himara provided the British with some ten thousand soldiers. Fighters were hired also in other parts of the empire. In 1804 agents sent to the Morea and Epirus to hire mercenaries for the Russian, French and British forces managed to recruit ten thousand from the Morea alone. They also searched for mercenary troops willing to fight for Ali Pasha, who was constantly engaged in warfare with European and Ottoman forces as well as local populations. Loyalties were temporary, troops could readily switch sides and often did so, and individuals from the same communities could be found fighting against each other. The Souliots, a nomadic population composed of independent clans living between Epirus and the Ionian islands, are a case in point. During the conflict between the French army and Ali Pasha in 1798, in the area around Preveza, they fought for both sides along with other Christian Greeks and Albanians. After entering into a temporary agreement with them, Ali turned against all of their clans alike and attacked them between 1800 and 1804. The Souliots were also employed by the powers that subsequently ruled over the Ionian islands: hired first by the Russians to defend the islands against Ali Pasha, in 1807 they joined regiments fighting for the French who were now occupying the

86. On military reform see Aksan, *Ottoman Wars*; Avigdor Levy, 'The Officer Corps in Sultan Mahmud II's New Ottoman Army, 1826–39', *International Journal of Middle East Studies* 2, no. 1 (1971): 21–39. On Janissaries and on military reform, see also Anscombe, *State, Faith, and Nation*, pp. 46–53.

islands, and later they did the same for the British.[87] The Souliots were not the only Ottoman Christian members of these 'Greek' units, thanks the efforts of agents sent out with this precise aim in mind. In the early years of the nineteenth century a surplus of fighting forces available to the European armies was also produced by the expulsion from the Ottoman Empire of bands of brigands, the so-called *klephts* from the Peloponnese (between 1802 and 1806), along with many so-called *armatoloi*—members of a Christian military class presiding over military districts in southern Roumeli, and the Souliots, expelled by Ali Pasha. The Ottoman authorities had decided to persecute those social groups that threatened the order of their provinces while building regular armies based on modern principles. During the Napoleonic wars such klephts and armatoloi (at least six thousand of them) found refuge mainly on the Ionian islands, and went to Russia seeking employment in the Neapolitan, Russian and French armies; a minority reached the Aegean islands where they engaged in piracy.[88]

Another important area for the recruitment of volunteers was the Danubian Principalities, whose Christian populations (Serbians, Greeks, Bulgars and Moldavians) had fought for the Austrian and above all the Russian imperial armies since the previous century. Although they all had a reputation for being unreliable and prone to looting and desertion, the so-called Pandours, a belligerent population of Serbian origin from southern Wallachia, were considered to be the best mercenaries. Twenty thousand Pandours, and Serbian, Bulgar and Serbian units, had offered their services to the Russian imperial army in the Russo–Ottoman wars between 1806 and 1812. In 1807, after the seizure by Russia of the principalities and the conquest of Bucharest by General Mikhail Miloradovich, they had managed to defend the whole of Wallachia with little support from the Russian army.[89] In 1821, the availability of Pandours was crucial to the organising of both Ypsilantis's army and that of Tudor Vladimirescu, who had devised his own independent uprising, and enjoyed the support of Pandour militias for that purpose.

87. Yanni Kotsonis, *Η Ελληνική Επανάσταση και οι αυτοκρατορίες: Η Γαλλία και οι Έλληνες, 1797–1830* (The Greek revolution and the empires: France and the Greeks, 1797–1830) (Athens: Alexandreia, 2020), pp. 75–94.

88. Panagiotis Stathis, 'From Klephts and Armatoloi to Revolutionaries', in *Ottoman Rule and the Balkans 1760–1850: Conflict, Transformation, Adaptation; Proceedings of an International Conference held in Rethymno, Greece, 13–14 December 2003*, ed. Antonis Anastasopoulos and Elias Kolovos (Rethymno: University of Crete, Department of History and Archaeology, 2007), pp. 167–79.

89. Bitis, *Russia*, pp. 325–331, 343–44.

FIGURE 1. Prince Alexandros Ypsilantis as
an officer in a hussar regiment of the Russian
army (portrait in oils by unidentified artist,
1814–17; Pushkin Museum, St. Petersburg).
Image: Wikimedia Commons

Service in the Russian imperial army of the Ottoman 'Greeks' was not
a new phenomenon, but built on a long-established tradition that the Russians had encouraged at least since the reign of Catherine the Great in the
1760s, when the Russian army had started to organise Greek regiments,
and its fleet included Greek sailors and officers. The members of these
units came from the Danubian Principalities, the Greek diasporic communities and the Aegean and the Ionian islands alike. Academies like the
Cadet Corps of Foreign Co-religionists in St. Petersburg had been set up
especially to train Greek and foreign Orthodox officers for the Russian
forces.[90] Prince Alexandros Ypsilantis's own integration into the highest
ranks of the Russian imperial army therefore represented a specific, but
by no means unique example, of Ottoman Christians at the service of the
European powers during the Napoleonic conflicts.

90. Nicholas Charles Pappas, *Greeks in Russian Military Service in the Late Eighteenth
and Early Nineteenth Centuries* (Thessaloniki: Institute for Balkan Studies, 1991).

What rendered Ypsilantis's case distinct was the fact that he belonged to a specific Greek aristocratic elite, the Phanariots, who worked in the service of the sultan as interpreters and diplomats, and traditionally also held positions as princes (hospodars) of the Danubian Principalities. Their role as intermediaries and their position of power in these principalities put them in privileged contact with other European powers, and with Russia in particular. Since the middle of the previous century Russia had in turn used them as a channel of influence in the principalities, and had given them protection or support. As a consequence, a number of them (for instance, members of the Mourouzis and Sturdzas families of hospodars) had lent explicit backing to Russia during the frequent wars between the two empires, and after being expelled from the principalities they entered the service of the czar, including his army. The family of Alexandros Ypsilantis had a similar story. His father Konstantinos, a former hospodar of Wallachia, had facilitated the Russian invasion of the principalities by offering military support, and had in turn tried to take advantage of the conflict to consolidate his power in the region, hoping to turn his position into a permanent one. As a result he was deposed by the Ottomans and in 1808 went into exile in St. Petersburg, where his four children had a privileged education paid for by the czar and would eventually join the Russian imperial army.[91] One and all were enrolled in the prestigious Imperial Guard Regiment of the Household Cavalry. Alexandros's military career as a Russian officer in particular stands out: he had direct experience of combat during and after the French invasion of Russia between 1812 and 1813, when he contributed to the defence of Moscow and fought in the battles of Klyastitsy and Polotsk. In 1813, participation in the battle of Dresden, where his right arm was blown off, earned him promotion to the rank of lieutenant colonel. By 1817 his services to the empire in the Russian delegation at the Congress of Vienna, and the esteem of the czar, led to his being promoted to the rank of major general.

The impact of such experiences was manifold. First, for most of these Ottoman Christian mercenaries, the Napoleonic wars may have represented the first experience leading them to entertain the notion of being Greek, or 'Macedonian', since the European armies in the region organised

---

91. On the Ypsilantis, see Bitis, *Russia*, p. 99; Theophilus C. Prousis, *Russian Society and the Greek Revolution* (DeKalb, IL: Northern Illinois University Press, 1994), pp. 8–9. On Phanariots in St. Petersburg, see also Zanou, *Transnational Patriotism*, pp. 84–89; Thomas W. Gallant, *The Edinburgh History of the Greeks, 1768 to 1913: The Long Nineteenth Century* (Edinburgh: Edinburgh University Press, 2015), pp. 19–23.

regiments labelled 'Greek' to identify their Christian members from the Ottoman Empire. More than any other group, however, Christians from Albania and from the region of Himara in its southern periphery, Souli in Epirus, the Archipelago, the Ionian islands, the Peloponnese or even more specifically the Mani peninsula, as well as the diaspora, were a collection of diverse and distinctive communities, with different traditions, habits, forms of governance and linguistic abilities. These various groups had little in common with each other, and soldiers often resented commanders who did not come from the same region as themselves. Thus, besides being Christian, their only common denominator was the label assigned to them by the various European armies that had assembled these 'Greek' fighting units. These Christian fighters from the Ottoman Empire combined temporary allegiance to those imperial powers they were fighting for with a more permanent allegiance to their ethnic or regional communities, along with the newly acquired Greek one of their individual regiments. The aforesaid Greek allegiance may have been something that they had first heard of, or that they first started to use to define themselves, precisely while they were serving as imperial mercenaries, and not before.[92] Moreover, these wars provided them with European professional military drilling and discipline, and also with exposure to the new ideas that accompanied the ideological clashes underpinning the Napoleonic wars and their propaganda. Those fighters who came from Roumeli and the Peloponnese, in particular, were often former bandits or members of the local military classes of the armatoloi and the *kapoi* (armed men in the service of the notables of the Peloponnese, otherwise known as *kapetanaioi*), and their bands of irregulars had neither the discipline nor the military technique of contemporary regular armies. Prominent military leaders of the Greek revolution such as Theodoros Kolokotronis, a former *kapos* working for the powerful Deliyannis family in the Peloponnese, after being expelled from the empire by the Ottoman troops, fled to Zante. At first he offered his services to the French army and went as far as to ask to visit Bonaparte in Paris. His plans failed, and with the arrival of the British on the islands he went on to fight for them on the island of Santa Maura. In 1810 he joined the British Duke of York's Greek Light Infantry regiment, where he received military training. It was in this period that he joined the Philiki and came to the conclusion that 'the French revolution and the doings of Napoleon had opened the eyes of the world.

92. Kotsonis, *Η Ελληνική Επανάσταση* (The Greek revolution).

The nations knew nothing before, and the people thought that kings were Gods upon the earth.'[93]

It is important to note that echoes of Spanish events also reached the distant lands of the Russian and Ottoman empires. The Russian army may not have fought on the Iberian peninsula, but political and military events there were well known to the Russian reading public thanks to extensive press coverage. Awareness of the Spanish anti-French guerrilla insurgency as well as admiration for the 1812 Spanish constitution circulated in the ranks of the Russian army during and after the Napoleonic military campaigns. In 1812 the czar had recognised the Spanish Cortes, and in the same year Napoleon's invasion of Russia did much to establish a firm link between Russian and Spanish patriotism, construed as twin instances of popular resistance to French expansionism.[94] After the wars the memory of Spanish heroism and, above all, of the Spanish constitution continued to play an important role in shaping the liberalism of Russian officers and intellectuals, who saw in the Spanish experience evidence of the extent to which the anti-Napoleonic war could lead to recognition of the legitimate rights of peoples. Thus in the capital of the Russian Empire, much as elsewhere, a Christian Greek officer of Ottoman origin such as Ypsilantis could regard the Spanish insurrection as a source of inspiration when prosecuting his own insurrectionary plans in the Danubian Principalities. Here, after all, the populations of Serbia had conducted guerrilla warfare not dissimilar from that following on from the military occupation of Spain. Ypsilantis's reference to the Spaniards' struggle against Napoleon in his first public insurrectionary manifesto, issued in Jassy in 1821, was therefore by no means casual or surprising. Thus, although the enduring memory of Iberian events was not in this case the result of direct experience, as it had been for many Italian, Portuguese or Spanish officers, it nonetheless constituted a source of inspiration also for Russian and Greek officers in the aftermath of the Napoleonic wars.

93. Theodoros Kolokotrones [Kolokotronis], *Kolokotrones the Klepht and the Warrior: Sixty Years of Peril and Daring; An Autobiography*, trans. Elizabeth Mayhew Edmonds (London: T. F. Unwin, 1892), pp. 117–27.

94. Susanna Rabow-Edling, 'The Decembrist Movement and the Spanish Constitution of 1812', *Historia Constitucional* 13 (2012): 143–61.

CHAPTER TWO

Pronunciamientos and the Military Origins of the Revolutions

After the Napoleonic wars: economic crisis and an impossible military demobilisation

The end of the Napoleonic wars and the financial crisis affecting states as that period drew to a close, as well as the ideological distance the restored governments, in particular the monarchies of Spain, Piedmont and Naples wished to establish between themselves and the preceding regimes, had a profound impact on armies and military careers. The demobilisation of armies that inevitably followed the end of the wars resulted in a substantial reduction of their size and in the purging of individuals compromised by association with the past regimes. Crucial aspects of the military reforms implemented in the previous years were abandoned completely. These factors were vital in accounting for the political activism of officers after 1815, and the widespread support among them for revolution. In Spain and Piedmont many army officers had lost their positions or had been demoted, and the size of the armies substantially reduced. In Spain, this reduction was also accompanied by a determination to revive the traditional structure of the army as an aristocratic body primarily loyal to the monarch. Returning to power in 1814, King Fernando of Spain had dismantled all the guerrilla units created during the war against the French, reduced the army with its excessive number of officers and exiled or imprisoned some of the liberals among them. The casualties of these measures were officers of middle-class or plebeian origin, either ex-guerrilla leaders, or former prisoners of the French army, or products of the reform of the army introduced after 1811, who were put on half pay, and who suffered a demotion. Significantly, the 1811 decrees that had opened up the military and naval academies to all ranks of society were revoked, the Central General Staff—the symbol of the new liberal professional army— was dismantled, and aristocratic officers with absolutist credentials were appointed. Discontent among the soldiers who supported Quiroga and Riego in 1820 was further exacerbated by their reluctance to be made to cross the Atlantic to fight in the Americas.[1] Although there were no similar purges to the armies in Piedmont and Naples, in these countries too, after 1815, those officers who had owed their careers and promotions to service in the Napoleonic armies lost all hope of advancement. The Napoleonic officers who returned to Piedmont after the battle of Waterloo were reintegrated into the Sardinian army, but were demoted to a rank lower than that they had attained during the Napoleonic era. In the upper echelons of the army, an effort was made to include both officers who had served under Napoleon and those who had remained loyal to the dynasty, but otherwise loyalty to the dynasty and enlistment prior to the French annexation of the kingdom became the criteria for promotion, and aristocratic families regained their preeminence within the military. This, not surprisingly, embittered many officers otherwise loyal to the monarchy.[2] In Naples too, the amalgamation of Murat's army with the Sicilian one that had remained loyal to the Bourbons proved difficult. Officers who had fought under the Napoleonic ruler Murat did not lose their jobs, as the Treaty of Casalanza guaranteed that they would be kept in employment and their rank maintained. However, after 1815 they forfeited any chance of promotion, and the royalist officers of the older generations who had left Naples with the monarch took precedence over the younger Muratists. In addition, the distinction between the two factions continued to matter in a number of crucial circumstances: most notably, service under Murat was not taken into account when calculating length of service and seniority, a form of discrimination that favoured Sicilians.[3] While Napoleonic officers had been promoted from being ordinary soldiers on merit,

1. Eric Christiansen, *The Origins of Military Power in Spain, 1800–1854* (Oxford: Oxford University Press, 1967), pp. 17–20; Stanley G. Payne, *Politics and the Military in Modern Spain* (Stanford, CA: Stanford University Press, 1967), pp. 8–19.

2. Ferdinando Pinelli, *Storia militare del Piemonte*, 3 vols (Turin: Degiorgis, 1854–55), 2, pp. 480–81, 511; Walter Barberis, *Le armi del principe:. La tradizione militare sabauda* (Turin: Einaudi, 1988), pp. 282–85.

3. Davis, *Naples and Napoleon*, p. 298; Luigi Blanch, 'Luigi de' Medici come uomo di stato e amministratore', in Blanch, *Scritti storici*, ed. Benedetto Croce, vol. 2: *Il regno di*

those appointed after 1815 almost invariably came from a gentlemanly background.[4]

In Portugal, what created resentment among the ranks of the Portuguese army was the fact that after the end of the war against the French the army continued to be controlled by Marshal Sir William Carr Beresford, who was the de facto ruler of the country along with the regency. British officers held the most important posts and advanced in their careers more easily than did the Portuguese. Beresford's rule was tangible proof that the kingdom was no longer independent; and his reform of the army in 1816 created additional reasons for resentment. The reform had established new hierarchies, by making careers dependent directly upon him; by so doing, it had upset traditional career paths, reduced the autonomy of the *câmaras* (local or municipal councils) in appointing local military officials (the *capitães mores*), and reduced pension privileges.[5] Last but not least, the financial crisis affecting the kingdom had made it difficult for soldiers and officers to receive their regular pay, and complaints about economic conditions in the army were common. So even in Portugal, where the army in 1820 had retained the exceptionally large size achieved during the earlier years of war, conditions for the troops became critical as payments were systematically delayed. This situation aggravated the grievances against the British, as the army along with the general population blamed them for the economic crisis, while demanding at the same time the return of the monarch to Portugal to put an end to its de facto colonial status.

The demobilisation of the armies and military fleets in the Mediterranean adversely affected the Christian populations in the Ottoman world in a particularly acute way, given that those foreign armies (Russian, Neapolitan and British) that had given employment to Ottoman Christians as mercenaries for over a decade no longer needed them. Between 1814 and 1820 such special corps made up of Christians from the Ottoman lands— namely, the French Chasseurs d'orient, the two British 'Greek' Light Infantry Regiments, the Greek Battalion of Odessa set up by the Russians, and the Neapolitan 'Macedonian' Regiment—were all disbanded.[6]

Napoli dalla restaurazione borbonica all'avvento di re Ferdinando II (1815–1830) (Bari: Laterza, 1945), pp. 1–126 at 58–60.

4. Biagio Gamboa, *Storia della rivoluzione di Napoli entrante il luglio del 1820* (n.p.: Presso il Trani, n.d.), p. 94.

5. Malyn Newitt and Martin Robson, *Lord Beresford and British Intervention in Portugal, 1807–1820* (Lisbon: ICS, 2004); Fernando Pereira Marques, *Exército e sociedade em Portugal no declínio do antigo regime e advento do liberalismo* (Lisbon: A Regra do Jogo,1981), pp. 154–66, 170–71, 186–87.

6. Stathis, 'From Klephts and Armatoloi', p. 174.

Some returned to the Ottoman Empire, while a significant proportion of those who had fought for the Russian imperial army settled in southern Russia, but many remained in the Septinsular Republic and without employment. The thousands of mercenaries from Moldavia and Wallachia no longer needed after 1812, and now in search of new opportunities to sell their services, should be added to the groups of unemployed Ottoman mercenaries. Therefore, on the eve of the revolution, the Ionian islands and the Ottoman lands were thronged with former combatants ready for action, and bristling with weapons primed for use. In the words of a historian of modern Greece, 'To say that by 1821 the Balkans were awash in guns would be going too far, but not by much.'[7]

It is not by chance that the first steps in enacting the pronunciamientos were marked by concerns directly related to the material circumstances of the armies involved. The distribution of monies and promotions would anticipate or follow on from the declaration of the revolution in some Piedmontese garrisons. The first proclamations issued by the officers in Porto directly addressed the financial condition of the Portuguese army, as a problem to be resolved urgently.[8] Requests for a promotion, for a pay rise and the recognition of past military honours were among the common demands among those who supported the revolution, and among the first measures adopted by provisional governments.

The broader appeal that the revolutionary initiative of the armies had across southern Europe and the Balkans cannot however be understood unless we take into account the impact upon the societies in question of the post-Napoleonic economic crisis. This economic depression was the result of the transition from a war economy, artificially stimulated by exceptionally high public expenditure, to a peacetime one. It was also the product of the famines and crop failures that afflicted most of the continent between 1816 and 1817. It was accompanied by a collapse in agricultural prices, a stagnation or decline in exports from Spain, Portugal, Naples and Sicily and an increase in grain imports from abroad (Russia and North America in particular). A combination of these factors resulted in the impoverishment of many social groups.

In the case of Spain and Portugal this negative trend had started already some years before. The collapse of agricultural and industrial

7. Gallant, *Edinburgh History*, p. 22.
8. In the city of Voghera in Piedmont, a pay rise was introduced just days before the revolution. See AST, Segreteria di Stato Affari Interni, Alta Polizia, Processi politici del 1821, fascio 53, no. 49: Prefettura of Voghera, April 1821.

exports from Spain and Portugal in particular dated back to the Napoleonic invasion of the Iberian peninsula, an event that dealt a mortal blow
to colonial trade. As noted earlier, the transfer of the Bragança dynasty
to Brazil in 1808 put an end to the monopoly exercised by local export-
ers and producers, and opened up the colonial trade to foreign interests.
Such trade did not resume with the cessation of hostilities: in fact, after
1816, it continued to decline steadily. Those who paid the heaviest price
were the producers of wine from the Douro region and their wholesalers
from Porto. Likewise, exports from Catalonia halved between 1815 and
1819, compared to their level in 1803. Although Catalan textile production
enjoyed a temporary boost in 1819, the importing of foreign manufacturing goods continued to grow after 1815 in Spain. In particular, commercial
interests in Cádiz were hit very hard by the wars of independence in Latin
American countries and by the curtailing of the liberalisation of trade
with them. This crisis continued after 1815. Between 1815 and 1820 some
110 trading houses closed down in the city, where many merchants started
to conspire actively against the absolute monarchy. Requests after 1814 for
protection of national industrial production in Spain were only partially
satisfied, and did not produce the expected results. At the same time, the
national authorities turned a deaf ear to demands for the reconstitution
of monopolies for the Atlantic trade in Spain and Portugal. It is by no
surprise that the revolution started in the cities of Porto and Cádiz, whose
merchants had suffered so much from the collapse of the Atlantic trade.
As one historian has written, when describing the broader social context of
Riego's pronunciamiento, 'The movement that brought down Fernando's
regime at the beginning of 1820 reflected the convergence of the interests
of the mercantile class of Cádiz and the industrial producers of the littoral
of Cataluña and Valencia.'[9]

A commercial crisis also hit the eastern Mediterranean after 1815.
The Greek merchant fleet, and in particular that from the islands of
Spetses, Hydra and Psara, had benefited from long periods of steady expansion, and had been stimulated in particular by the speculative opportunities that the continental blockade imposed by the French from 1807
had offered, encouraging the smuggling of goods and wheat in particular into French, Italian and Spanish blockaded ports. In this sector, the
post-war crisis resulting in the collapse of grain prices, further enhanced
by renewed competition from Western shipping, hit very hard. It led to

9. Hamnett, *La política española*, p. 237.

shrinking profits, the lowering of the wages of sailors and increasing maritime unemployment.[10]

This generalised commercial depression, combined with the collapse in grain prices, also adversely affected rural societies across these different countries. The decline of wine exports from Catalonia, and the drop in prices (to one tenth of those recorded in 1792), for instance, impoverished small farmers and landless peasants. At the same time, the increase in taxation introduced in 1817 to deal with the financial crisis of the Kingdom of Spain exacerbated the hostility of the rural world towards the absolutist government. In Sicily, where the prices of wheat and other grains, olive oil, wine and salt fell by between 50 and 70 per cent, the economic crisis ruined small farmers, along with many middle-class renters of estates (the so-called *gabellotti*), and led to a dramatic reduction of consumption by peasants, many of whom starved. Another unwelcome outcome of these events was the increased indebtedness of Sicilian smallholders, who between 1816 and 1817 could only afford to borrow money to buy seeds at very high rates. In these circumstances most members of rural communities simply could not pay taxes. In such times of economic depression, excessive fiscal pressure was also why peasants in the Peloponnese and Roumeli (as the continental part of contemporary Greece was called at the time) did not hesitate to join the rebellion against their Ottoman authorities in 1821.[11]

These circumstances account for the existence of many audiences sympathetic to the insurgent armies, and for the lack of all but the most modest or token resistance to their political interventions in their various countries. While a generalised insurrection took place only in the Peloponnese, across southern Europe large sectors of society had many grievances, and as many reasons to be hopeful that new governments would improve their lot. This is why they either publicly manifested their support for the

10. Kostas Kostis, *History's Spoiled Children: The Formation of the Modern Greek State* (London: Hurst, 2018), pp. 30–31; Nikolas Pissis, 'Investments in the Greek Merchant Marine (1783–1821)', in *Merchants in the Ottoman Empire*, ed. Suraiya Faroqhi and Gilles Veinstein (Leuven: Peeters, 2008), pp. 151–64, esp. 151–54.

11. Hamnett, *La política española*; Josep Fontana, *La quiebra de la monarquía absoluta, 1814–1820* (Barcelona: Crítica, 2002); Jaime Torras, *Liberalismo y rebeldía campesina, 1820–1823* (Barcelona: Ariel, 1976), pp. 39–42; Julião Soares de Azevedo, *Condições económicas da revolução portuguesa de 1820* (Lisbon: Básica Editora, 1976), esp. pp. 154–84; Francesco Renda, *Risorgimento e classi popolari in Sicilia, 1820–1821* (Milan: Feltrinelli, 1968), pp. 24–28; Ciro Rocco, 'La crisi dei prezzi nel regno di Napoli nel 1820–21', in *Il Mezzogiorno preunitario: Economia, società, istituzioni*, ed. Angelo Massafra (Bari: Edizioni Dedalo, 1988), pp. 169–79.

regiments declaring revolutions, or simply sat on the fence, hoping for some improvement in their material conditions.

Communicating the revolutionary script: nation, army and constitution

The very first act of the pronunciamiento was the reading of a proclamation in front of the regiments and soldiers supporting the revolutionary plots: this is what Riego did before his troops gathered in the square outside the military quarters of the village of Las Cabezas de San Juan, and the Portuguese officers replicated this model by addressing their troops in the large open space of the Campo de Santo Ovídio outside the military garrison in Porto; soon after the beginning of the military expedition by Morelli and Silvati from Nola, General Pepe and his chief of staff Lorenzo De Concilj addressed the troops and armed militias gathered in Avellino; likewise, the officers based in Alessandria, in Piedmont, summoned their troops to the square of the military fortress where they were stationed for the same purpose. Ypsilantis did the same, after crossing the river Pruth, and as soon as he had reached the city of Jassy in Moldavia. However, this first act was soon followed by other public readings and by the production and circulation of declarations addressing a variety of themes at the local, national and international level. Officers systematically addressed the local communities of the villages and towns they traversed in their expeditions, but these direct public events were part of a much wider and more complex strategy attempting to communicate and foment revolution across the country in order to guarantee its success. The declarations of the revolutions by the officers were in fact followed by a number of similar events, or 'copycat' pronunciamientos, often coordinated and planned in advance. In the Kingdom of the Two Sicilies, for instance, the events of Avellino were communicated across the kingdom by using the 'optical', or Chappe's, telegraph that had existed in its territories since Murat's government, and had been retained at the restoration. By means of a mobile arm, the telegraph enabled the formulation of visual messages transmitted from one station to the next across the territory. A telegraphic station based in Avellino connected both sides of the peninsula, enabling messages to travel from Naples to the heel of the peninsula and to Sicily in just a few hours.[12] It was thanks to a signal received by telegraph that, almost immediately after the events in Avellino, the cavalry officers of the city of

12. On the telegraph in the kingdom, see Daum, *Oscillazioni*, pp. 205–10.

Foggia in the region of Puglia declared the constitution, and General Rossaroll did the same in the military garrison of Capua, north of Naples.[13] In Portugal, a few weeks after the pronunciamiento of Porto, events were replicated, among other places, in the university city of Coimbra: here too, the newly elected commander of the city, General Pinto de Silveira, summoned the troops to the main square, the Campo de Santa Clara, read the proclamations produced in Porto, had the soldiers swear an oath of allegiance to the constitutional government, and was in turn acclaimed by the troops. A parade across the city then culminated in a public civil ceremony in the Câmara (town hall), where all civil and religious authorities as well as the chancellor of the University swore an oath to the constitution.[14] These events produced their own particular public documents, at times replicating the original, but as often varying from the first ones produced in Porto. Besides Coimbra, proclamations were independently issued in other cities of the kingdom such as Braga and Setúbal, and also by the military and civilian authorities in the town of Elvas, on the border with Spain, where regiments had at first disagreed as to whether or not to side with the revolution.[15] In addition to city and national audiences, addresses signed by the inhabitants of the revolutionary city of Porto targeted specific regions: namely, the populations of Beira, Alto Douro and the people and soldiers of Trás-os-Montes, to urge them not to support army leaders hostile to the revolution.[16] In Piedmont the revolution was marked by the almost simultaneous publication of proclamations in two distinct places, the garrison of Alessandria, where Guglielmo Ansaldi signed his public documents, and the town of Carmagnola, south of Turin, where Santorre di Santarosa and Gugliemo di Lisio issued their own manifestos. These two sets of documents reflected also the existence of two distinct justifications of the revolution, and different variants of the revolutionary script.

The most striking example of a communications campaign was that carried out by the Greek revolutionaries, whose production and distribution of manifestos would seem to have been planned with great care. While the events of Jassy were not replicated, and no copycat pronunciamientos took place after the launch of Ypsilantis's military campaign, a meticulous

13. Orazio De Attellis, 'L'ottimestre costituzionale delle Due Sicilie' (manuscript, 1821), in BNN, MS VA 47/2, pp. 107, 117, 119.

14. *Mnemosine Constitucional*, no. 26, 24 October 1820, p. 3.

15. On events in Elvas, see *O Liberal*, 20 November 1820, pp. 4–5; the declaration to the city of Elvas is in *O Padre Amaro, ou Sovéla, Politica, Historica, e Literaria* (London, 1820), October 1820, vol. 2, pp. 173–75.

16. *Mnemosine Constitucional*, no. 25, 23 October 1820, p. 4; no. 26, 24 October 1820, p. 3; no. 27, 25 October 1820, p. 6.

and capillary effort was undertaken to send his manifestos across the entire Ottoman Empire, so as to reach all the Greek populations. This is even more remarkable if we consider that no printed press existed in the core regions of the empire, if we except Constantinople.[17] On the eve of the insurrection, the Philiki Etaireia had managed to gain control of the two Greek printing shops of Jassy and Bucharest to produce Ypsilantis's manifestos during the residence of the revolutionary army in these cities in February and March 1821. In addition, Ypsilantis travelled with a portable printing press of his own so that he could produce additional documents during his campaign across the empire, and he made use of it in the city of Târgoviște, north of Bucharest, between April and May of that year. The networks of the Philiki Etaireia facilitated the circulation of Ypsilantis's declarations across the regions of the Ottoman Empire populated by Greek speaking inhabitants, travelling beyond the continental regions of Greece across the Aegean. It was the emissaries of the Philiki, called at the time 'apostles' and 'evangelists', who brought with them to the islands both information about the insurrection and copies of the declaration. The public reading of these texts was at the centre of ceremonies sharing similar features, which served the purpose of sacralising their messages, refounding the community in national and religious terms, and committing it to martyrdom for freedom. When the text arrived on the island of Naxos, the bishop gathered together all the priests of the island, and organised a procession in which he led thousands of people towards the main church while holding a revolutionary standard. It was in the church that he read out the declaration in front of a large crowd, and reported the news about the revolution brought by the 'apostles', encouraging all men and women to fight for the cause of liberty and religion.[18] Similarly, the public reading of Ypsilantis's manifesto represented the central element of a ceremony on the island of Samos that marked the beginning of the revolution. In April 1821 one of the leaders of the local insurrection, Georgios Dimitriadis, summoned the villagers to the church of Marathokampos, and at the end of the mass, standing on a bench, he read Ypsilantis's declaration in front of five hundred people. When he had finished, everyone cheered, 'Long live liberty, long live the nation, long live the *patris* [fatherland]!' Then

17. Konstantinos Hatzopoulos, 'Οι επαναστατικές προκηρύξεις του Αλ. Υψηλάντη: Προβλήματα σχετικά με την εκτύπωση τους' (The revolutionary declarations of Al. Ypsilantis: Problems with their publication), *Ελληνικά* [*Ellinika*] 33, no. 2 (1981): 320–73.

18. Robert Walsh, *A Residence at Constantinople during a Period including the Commencement, Progress, and Termination of the Greek and Turkish Revolutions*, 2 vols (London: Westley & Davis, 1836), 1, pp. 186–87.

everyone received a candle and a symbol with the phrase 'The fatherland is calling you', and raising their right hands to the sky they all took an oath: 'We are ready to fall into the fire and die for our liberty, our nation and our fatherland.' Then they went to the central square of the village and raised the Greek flag.[19] The likelihood is that such public readings happened also in other villages on other islands or in regions of continental Greece, since further evidence points to the declaration's wide circulation. It was reproduced in a manuscript gazette put out in the early days of the revolution.[20] A large quantity of these documents, along with other writings by Ypsilantis, hidden in a cave in a small village, were in fact found by the Ottoman authorities in the rugged region of Mount Olympos in the spring of 1822.[21] The manifesto circulated also outside the Ottoman Empire, reaching the communities of the Greek diaspora. This happened, for instance, in the port city of Odessa on the Black Sea coast of the Russian Empire, where the activities of the Philiki Etaireia had first been organised; the thriving Greek merchant community provided a receptive public for the language of nationalism, and Ypsilantis's statements were read in public.[22] Finally, Ypsilantis took great care to send it to diplomatic representatives, both to acquaint the international community with his exploits and to use their channels of communication to spread word of them further within and beyond the empire. For instance, he sent many copies to Baron Stroganov, the Russian representative in Constantinople, in the hope that he would also forward them to members of the Philiki.[23] These communication efforts were further amplified by public addresses to the European powers issued by other military leaders such as Dimitrios Ypsilantis, brother of

19. Georgios Dimitriadis, Ιστορία της Σάμου συνταχθείσα και εκδοθείσα υπό Γεωργίου Δημητριάδου, Σαμίου ανόπτου [sic] των κατά την Επανάστασιν γεγονότων προς χρήσιν της φιλομαθούς νεολαίας προς ην ο συγγραφέας την παρούσαν ανατιθήσι (History of Samos written and published by Georgios Dimitriadis, from Samos and a witness to the events of the revolution to be used by the educated youth to whom the writer dedicates this work) (Chalkis: Typ. Evripou, 1866), pp. 26–27.

20. Σάλπιγξ Ελληνική [Salpix Elliniki], August 1821, in Aikaterini Koumarianou, ed., Ο Τύπος στον Αγώνα, 1821–27 (The press in the 'Struggle', 1821–27), 3 vols (Athens: Ermis, 1971), 1, pp. 39–40.

21. Le Spectateur Oriental: Feuille Littéraire, Critique et Commerciale, no. 51, 9 May 1822, p. 3.

22. Maxime Raybaud, Mémoires sur la Grèce pour servir à l'histoire de la guerre d'indépendance (Paris: Tournachon-Molin Libraire, 1834), pp. 192–93. On the Greek community there at the time, see Evrydiki Sifneos, 'Preparing the Greek Revolution in Odessa in the 1820s: Tastes, Markets and Political Liberalism', Historical Review/La Revue Historique 11 (2014): 139–70.

23. See Stites, Four Horsemen, p. 200.

Alexandros, who wrote to the French and Germans in a public document from the city of Odessa at the beginning of April 1821, just before going to Greece as leader of the revolutionary army, and Petrobey Mavromichalis, commander of the Spartan and Messinian forces, who issued a manifesto to the European courts in March 1821.[24] By so doing, the Greek revolutionary leadership wanted not only to gain the support of foreign public authorities, but also to influence international public opinion.

It should be noted that the documents circulating during and in the immediate aftermath of the pronunciamientos varied enormously in content and nature. As should already be clear by now, they targeted a very broad range of audiences, being addressed at varying times to the nation, to central governments, to the army and soldiers or to specific regions, as well as to individual towns and villages. A single soldier wrote a public address to the inhabitants of his own village, Montoro, in the province of Avellino, to thank the 'brave soldiers of the Neapolitan nation' for being among the first to have taken up arms against ministerial despotism and in favour of a constitution.[25] As a consequence, while these were all public documents produced to justify and explain the revolutionary initiative of the army, they varied enormously in length, from a very few lines to very extensive and elaborate texts. Another important element adds complexity to the nature of such communication: one has to take into account that, while these documents were posted up outside churches and other public buildings, and read out in front of audiences, the public speeches delivered in such circumstances were often improvised, or else their content is now lost. Thus we can assume that additional variants to the themes covered by the written texts were produced. The case of the Piedmontese revolutions, for which a large body of indirect evidence is available, confirms the importance of the practice of improvising public speeches, whose content does not coincide with the manifestos read alongside them.

What added further to their diversity is the fact that the declarations reflected their specific revolutionary contexts and addressed the political crises of their own countries in particular, thus often serving very diverse objectives. The Portuguese, Spanish and Ottoman addresses related to a set of very different imperial crises, and their content can only be

24. *Archives diplomatiques pour l'histoire du tems et des états: L'année 1821*, 2 vols (Stuttgart and Tubingen: Librairie Cotta, 1822), 2, pp. 563, 564; John Lee Comstock, *History of the Greek Revolution, Compiled from Official Documents of the Greek Government* (New York: W. W. Reed & Co., 1828), p. 160.

25. BL printed collections: broadsheet, 'Ai bravi soldati della nazione napolitana! Bravi montoresi!', Naples, 8 July 1820.

understood with reference to these. In spite of the language adopted by the insurgents, who went as far as to espouse the discourse of national independence in Portugal and Greece, these revolts aimed first and foremost at reforming, rather than dismantling, the existing empires. What these disparate events had in common was a demand by their military and civilian leaders for political reform, and in particular, for new constitutional arrangements. The Portuguese pronunciamiento, for instance, aimed at addressing the structural transformation of Portugal from imperial metropole into a colony under British protection, the transfer of the monarchy from Lisbon to Brazil in 1808 having led to a radical rearrangement of the Portuguese Empire. Riego's refusal to embark for Latin America to crush the insurrection of the colonies, on the other hand, amounted also to an attempt to address the crisis of the empire by calling for the reintroduction of the constitution on both sides of the Atlantic. Riego refused to cross the Atlantic with his troops to fight for the survival of the empire, but he was not in favour of its dissolution. Although in 1819 he had been in touch with tradesmen from the Río de la Plata based in Cádiz plotting for the emancipation of the colony and offering to finance his revolt, Riego wanted to resolve the imperial crisis of the empire by reintroducing a constitution across its territories: a stance that mirrored earlier pronunciamientos.[26] Ypsilantis's rebellion, meanwhile, can only be understood in a broader Ottoman imperial context. It was not simply a Greek affair: it exhorted all Christian populations of the empire to rise up and renegotiate their relationship with Ottoman imperial rule. But nor was his rebellion an outright call for full independence. The political objectives of Ypsilantis and the other insurgents were not clear, beyond a general desire to gain a greater degree of autonomy from the Ottoman authorities for the Christian populations of Wallachia, Moldavia and the Greek-speaking regions of their empire. The example of the Serbian rebellion that had led to the creation of an autonomous principality subject to the Porte in 1817, rather than full independence, was the model available and realistically achievable in their minds.[27] Ypsilantis's insurgency coincided with another rebellion of Christian populations of the Ottoman Empire: the insurrection led by Tudor Vladimirescu, a Romanian whose social base

26. Eugenia Astur, *Riego: Estudio histórico-político de la Revolución del año veinte* (Oviedo: Escuela Tipográfica de la Residencia Provincial de Niños, 1933), pp. 143–46; Francisco Varo Montilla, 'La causa del Palmar: Conspiración y levantamiento de 1819', doctoral dissertation, UNED, Madrid, 2009, available at http://e-spacio.uned.es/fez/view/tesisuned:GeoHis-Fvaro (accessed 14 August 2022), pp. 216–19, 222–25.
27. Anscombe, 'Balkan Revolutionary Age'.

and political objectives clashed with those of Ypsilantis. At first the two fought on the same side, but soon their incompatible social and political objectives led to a clash and to the death of Vladimirescu.

The nature of these events varied also in other important respects. While they bore the character of 'forceful negotiations' that did not aim at bringing down existing authority, they could also inaugurate military action. The Piedmontese and Greek military uprisings were far from being peaceful affairs, as they were also effectively declarations of war—acts designed to launch military campaigns against the Austrian and Otto-man empires respectively. Finally, Ypsilantis's proclamations, compared to those issued in the other countries, were vague in terms of the political demands they included, and not nearly as explicit as all the other manifes-tos in putting the constitution at the centre of the army's demands.

In spite of this great variety, a set of strikingly similar concepts and arguments was advanced in documents printed in Portugal, Spain, Piedmont, Naples and the autonomous principalities of Wallachia and Moldavia. While there is no evidence of mutual influence and 'cross-contamination' from the proclamations of one revolution to another, what emerges from them is the existence of a remarkable conceptual conver-gence that invites us to discuss them in terms of variations on similar themes. A preliminary analysis of Riego's manifesto, the first in chron-ological order to be produced in this revolutionary wave, can help shed some light on the means employed by its organisers to justify the revolt. As Riego's manifesto was the first to show, these were texts saturated with nationalist ideology. They drew together into a coherent narrative of decadence and regeneration the role of the army in fulfilling national aspirations for freedom. Lynn Hunt has demonstrated the extent to which the French revolution disseminated a new idea of the army, intimately linked with the republican notion of nationhood. With the revolution, the status of the soldier came to be redefined in the context of a brotherhood of equals, a community of heroic individuals bound by familial and moral ties alike, who fought in defence of their own country. This new, egalitarian vision of the nature of the army belonged to a broader 'family romance', one which associated the idea of the nation as born out of the revolution-ary experience with its metaphorical representation as a family. In this new context, war came to be legitimised in terms of soldiers' moral duty to sacrifice their lives in defence of the fatherland, and testifies to their attachment to the nation, a notion represented in biological terms. The Napoleonic wars were thus marked by the emergence of a pan-European military culture which conceived war as the enterprise of a brotherhood of young individuals committed to the defence of their domestic sphere and households.[28] The idea of the army that Riego and Quiroga conveyed in their speeches addressing their own troops was profoundly marked by this ideological framework. In the case of Spain, it was the experience of the French invasion that provided the historical context to justify the adoption of this model, as that patriotic experience could be rethought as one of military sacrifice, male heroism and martyrdom in the defence of families. Riego opened his declaration to the troops by stating,

> Soldiers, my love for you is great. Because of this, I as your commander cannot permit you to leave your country aboard some rotten vessels to go off and wage an unjust war in the New World—nor to have you abandon your parents and siblings, leaving them sunk in abject poverty and oppression. You owe them your life, and so are duty-bound in gratitude to survive and support them in old age. Further, if necessary, you must sacrifice your own lives in order to burst the chains that have bound them in oppression since 1814.[29]

Similarly Quiroga, on 5 January, addressing his soldiers at San Fernando, employed a language of military brotherhood and family allegiance to justify their act of defiance. He reminded them that their refusal to leave for America for an unnecessary war and their rebellion had been a legitimate means to prevent '[y]our families remain[ing] in the most merciless slavery', and that their own brotherhood would be increased by the numbers of soldiers that would join them: 'in the very ranks whom the government may assemble, you will find brothers who will join us'.[30]

This notion of brotherhood was by no means merely symbolic, moreover. It was related to a quest for the democratisation of the structure and values of the army. In other words, those officers and soldiers who supported the revolution rejected the aristocratic, authoritarian foundations of military life reintroduced by the restored monarchies, pitting against them the egalitarian principles underpinning the reforms the armies

28. Lynn Hunt, *The Family Romance of the French Revolution* (Berkeley, CA: University of California Press, 1992). For Prussia, see Karen Hagemann, *Revisiting Prussia's Wars against Napoleon: History, Culture and Memory* (Cambridge: Cambrdige University Press, 2015); for Italy, see Lucy Riall, *Eroi maschili, virilità e forme della guerra*, in *Il Risorgimento*, ed. Alberto Banti and Paul Ginsborg (Turin: Einaudi, 2007), pp. 253–88.

29. 'Proclama a las tropas', Cabeza de San Juan, 1 January 1820, in Alberto Gil Novales, ed., *Rafael Riego: La Revolución de 1820, día a día* (Madrid: Tecnos, 1976), pp. 34–35 (translation: Stites, *Four Horsemen*, p. 28).

30. Quiroga, 'Address to His Soldiers', San Fernando, 5 January 1820. I quote the English translation that appeared in *The Monthly Magazine*, no. 49 (April 1820), p. 273.

FIGURES 2A AND 2B. Rafael Riego (2a) and Antonio Quiroga (2b) (lithographs by Godefroy Engelmann, after drawings by Hippolyte Lecomte, Paris, 1820). Images: Wikimedia Commons

had undergone during the Napoleonic wars. In this domain too, both the declarations of the officers and the practices surrounding the pronunciamiento converged. At least at the beginning of the rebellions, these public declarations of brotherhood were accompanied also by acts and practices that challenged military hierarchy and authority, and aimed at reconstituting them on new grounds. For instance, the elections of constitutional mayors in the towns affected by Riego's expedition were accompanied by scenes of officers 'treating soldiers like brothers': as a result soldiers would no longer doff their caps as a sign of respect and deference.[31] In one of his first speeches to the soldiers of the military citadel of Alessandria, on the inception of the Piedmontese revolution, Giacomo Garelli criticised the aristocratic presence in the ranks of the army as symbolic of its despotic nature, and advocated the principle of merit in the military career.[32]

In some cases the pronunciamientos revived the French revolutionary tradition of electing army officers, a practice associated with the notion of citizenship in arms first adopted for the national guards, and later

31. AHN, Estado, legajo 3081-II: document with no date [January 1820].
32. AST, Segreteria di Stato Affari Interni, Alta Polizia, Affari politici, report no. 26: 'Revolte de la Citadel d'Alexandrie', p. 4.

extended to voluntary militias.[33] At the very beginning of the revolts of 1820 and 1821, soldiers supporting the revolution occasionally elected their officers in army barracks or in public spaces, to give their authority a new democratic legitimacy and to mark symbolically the rebirth of the army as a constitutional body. This happened, for instance, after the seizure of the citadel of Alessandria, or in some barracks in Savoy.[34] It had also happened in Spain, just before the issuing of the pronunciamiento. Antonio Quiroga was elected general in charge of the rebellion before the pronunciamiento, through a consultation with all the officers supporting the plot organised by Antonio Alcalá Galiano.[35] During the early stages of the revolution in Naples, the Carboneria replicated this model when creating its own armed forces: in the province of Salerno the officers of the *milizie carbonare*, set up to support the existing provincial militias (*milizie provinciali*), were chosen by the members of each unit by majority voting.[36] The introduction of the constitution by the army was confirmed also through another form of direct democracy: public acclamation, a practice that likewise suggested the link between the army and popular sovereignty. In the city of La Coruña, for instance, the military leader Félix Acevedo was acclaimed in public after the declaration of the constitution by both soldiers and civilians.[37] By these means, the officers were demonstrating the popular legitimacy of their role and the extent to which their revolutionary initiative had the approval of the nation.

At the heart of these manifestos stood not only this metaphorical idea of the nation as a family and of the army as a brotherhood, but also a more explicitly political conception of the sovereign nation, the vindication of whose rights justified the main political demand of the insurrection: the reintroduction of a constitution. Riego vindicated these rights not in terms of the French revolutionary culture, but rather by invoking the specific historical context that had produced the 1812 constitution and had recast monarchical power on new foundations. He argued that the king owed his own throne 'to those who fought in the war of independence' and to their sufferings and sacrifices, and had sworn an oath to the constitution, a 'pact

---

33. Thomas Hippler, *Citizens, Soldiers and National Armies: Military Service in France and Germany* (London, 2008), p. 58.

34. Walter Bruyère-Ostells, *La Grande Armée de la liberté* (Paris: Tallandier, 2009), p. 204.

35. Alcalá Galiano, *Apuntes*, pp. 46–51.

36. ASN, Borbone, 726, f. 210.

37. AHN, Estado, legajo 3081-I: Félix Acevedo, manifesto entitled 'Soldados', 22 Febuary 1820.

between monarch and the people'.[38] Quiroga likewise associated military valour and the sacrifice of the army pitted against the French invader with the creation of the constitution in 1812. In the address of the constitutional army to the other parts of the Spanish military issued on 9 January in San Fernando, he reminded the Spanish army of the role it had played: 'Whilst you were shedding your blood in front of the enemy host, the fathers of the country were raising the sanctuary of the laws, and building [. . .] on your immortal sacrifices.'[39] These proclamations and other statements issued to the officers and the people during these and succeeding days thus contained a direct and blunt attack on King Fernando's absolutism, condemning him for his despotism and tyrannical proclivities. However, while attacking the sovereign head on, these addresses never went as far as to challenge the monarchy itself as an institution, but rather demanded that the monarchy once more become a constitutional one.

In similar terms the Portuguese, Piedmontese, Neapolitan and military insurgents justified their role as being representative of national aspirations, arguing that it was their duty to rescue the nation from despotism, tyranny and decadence. As Colonel Lorenzo De Concilj claimed in his proclamation to 'the people of Irpinia', given the public vote for the constitution announced upon the arrival of the army in Avellino, his intervention simply stemmed from recognition of the will of the people, and made reference to representative government as the form most suited to the contemporary needs of Europeans.[40] In Portugal, Cabreira, addressing the soldiers, claimed that it was the army's duty to save the fatherland.[41]

Santarosa's declaration of March 1821, which inaugurated the Piedmontese revolution, justified the army's intervention and spoke about the need for the king to recognise 'the rights and interests guaranteed by a liberal constitution'.[42] The proclamations issued from Alessandria by the revolutionary *giunta* (junta) under the presidency of Gugliemo Ansaldi

38. Riego, 'Proclama a los oficiales y al pueblo', Cabezas de San Juan, 1 January 1820, in Gil Novales, *Rafael Riego*, p. 35.

39. Quiroga, 'The Corps of the National Army to the Remainder of the Spanish Military', 9 January 1820; translation in *The Monthly Magazine*, no. 49 (April 1820), p. 273.

40. Lorenzo De Concilj, 'Ai popoli irpini' (n.d.), in Biagio Gamboa, *Documenti storici* attached to Gamboa, *Storia della rivoluzione*, pp. 8–10.

41. Cabreira and Sepúlveda to the soldiers, 24 August 1820, in Marques, *Exército e sociedade*, p. 265.

42. Santorre di Santarosa and Guglielmo di Lisio, 'Dichiarazione a nome dell'esercito piemontese', Carmagnola, 10 March 1821, in Filippo Antonio Gualterio, *Gli ultimi rivolgimenti italiani: Memorie storiche con documenti inediti*, 4 vols (Florence: Le Monnier, 1852), 1, pp. 145–46; French and German translations in *Archives diplomatiques*, 2, pp. 16–17.

SEBASTIÃO DRAGO VALENTE DE BRITO CABREIRA

CORONEL DO REGIMENTO D'ARTILHARIA N.4.

Presidente do Conselho Militar, na noite de 23 de Agosto Vice-Pre-
sidente da Junta Provisional do Supremo Governo do Reine insta-
lada no sempre memoravel dia de 24 do dito mez de 1820.

FIGURE 3. Sebastião Drago Valente de Brito Cabreira
(etching by Jose Vicente Sales, after drawing by
Francisco António Silva Oeirense, 1820–22, Lisbon).
Image: Wikimedia Commons

employed a more politically radical language: they referred explicitly to the
independence of Italy, being issued 'in the name of the Italian federation',
spoke of the Piedmontese monarch as its future king and described the
constitution of Spain as the document that would abolish any and every
privilege, promoting elections instead, and turning the people and the
king into one single family.[43] Guglielmo Pepe's proclamation as head of
the constitutional army referred to the monarch as something more than a

43. See the two proclamations issued by the giunta of Alessandria on 10 March 1821, in
Gualterio, *Gli ultimi rivolgimenti*, 1, pp. 146–48.

king, rather the 'father of his people', and to a 'monarchical representative constitution' as the text that would guarantee the freedom of the nation.[44]

The tone of manifestos produced in Portugal, Piedmont and Naples was therefore far more respectful towards the monarch than that of Riego's first documents, which had been harsh in their denunciation of Fernando's despotism. What the manifestos made explicit was that the revolutionaries did not challenge the institution of monarchy in itself, but wanted only to revise its foundations in constitutional terms. This was in fact a central element of their script and their revolutionary culture, and one worth highlighting. In the case of Portugal, this is not surprising, given the fact that the Portuguese army had intervened to demand the return of the sovereign from Brazil to Portugal. But the other revolutions, on the Italian peninsula, were equally monarchically oriented. The Piedmontese revolution represented the only case in which the plotters had tried to negotiate their intervention with the heir to the throne, and had counted on the support of Prince Carlo Alberto as a precondition for its success. A few days before proclaiming the constitution, a group of aristocratic officers, Santorre di Santarosa, Carlo Asinari di San Marzano, Gugliemo Moffa di Lisio and Giacinto Provana di Collegno, met with the heir to the throne, requesting his support for and consent to their plans. While the extent to which Carlo Alberto gave his approval is unclear, what is certain is that the revolutionaries considered the prince's backing as key, and were convinced he had compromised himself.[45] At all events, from the earliest stages of these revolts the revolutionaries highlighted the constitutional credentials of the monarchs, advancing the idea that they had granted their approval spontaneously and willingly. In Naples this more than dubious claim was supported by the publication of forged historical documents, purportedly dating from 1815, when Ferdinando was still in Sicily and under British protection. According to these, Ferdinando had promised to grant a constitution once restored to his throne in Naples. This proclamation appeared as early as July 1820 in the constitutional press, and was mentioned in parliamentary debates as evidence of the royal commitment to the constitution.[46] In reality not only was the document false, but Ferdinando was

44. Guglielmo Pepe, 'Il comandante in capo dell'esercito costituzionale ai popoli del regno delle due Sicilie', Avellino, 7 July 1820, in Gamboa, *Documenti storici*, pp. 29–30.

45. On the debate about the prince's support and conduct, see Giorgio Candeloro, *Storia dell'Italia moderna*, vol. 2: *Dalla restaurazione alla rivoluzione nazionale*, 2nd edn (Milan: Feltrinelli, 1988), pp. 111–19.

46. See *L'Imparziale*, no. 1, 28 July 1820, pp. 2ff. On the circulation of these false documents, see Daum, *Oscillazioni*, pp. 405–8.

far from being an enthusiastic supporter of the charter. In the early days of the revolution, the monarch's decision to give up any governmental responsibility in favour of his son Francesco, appointed as 'vicar of the kingdom', on grounds of ill health, represented a clear sign of the distance he wished to keep from the constitutional regime.[47] Yet the revolutionary press redefined him and the heir to the throne, Francesco, as 'citizen princes', who had introduced the constitutional system.[48]

In Spain too, the constitutional credentials of the king became central to the communication of the revolution. No sooner had the king of Spain accepted the constitution, than Riego abandoned his earlier confrontational language, praising the monarch in his public communications. As in Naples, celebrating the king as a constitutional monarch required some rewriting of recent history, given Fernando's direct role in bringing about the restoration and in abolishing the constitution in 1814 upon his return to Spain. The argument most commonly used, as in the case of the proclamation issued by the junta of Asturias, was that of the innocence of the king, who had been badly advised, surrounded as he had been by evil people. Again, as in Naples, the revolutionary press went so far as to praise him as a citizen king, or as the father of the constitution.[49]

All revolutionaries agreed that what had lent legitimacy to the people's demands for new rights and for a new relationship between them and the monarchs had been the Napoleonic wars. The proclamations made it clear that it was the people who had saved the thrones of their kings from French despotism and usurpation. References to the uprisings, guerrilla warfare, and to all forms of popular resistance that had erupted across the territories occupied by the French army were offered as evidence of the sacrifice of the people, for which the proper reward would be the granting of constitutional rights. Thus all the pronunciamientos assumed an explicitly anti-Napoleonic tone. As the officers and soldiers of Porto reminded the governadores in Lisbon, who were reluctant to accept the constitution, it had been 'the people and the army who restored the

47. Galasso, *Storia*, 5, p. 181.

48. See for instance, *La Voce del Secolo*, no. 1, 25 July 1820, p. 1.

49. Víctor Sánchez Martín, 'Creación, construcción y dudas sobre la imagen del héroe revolucionario y del monarca constitucional en 1820', in *Culturas políticas monárquicas en la España liberal. Discursos, representaciones y prácticas (1808–1902)*, ed. Encarna García Monerris, Mónica Moreno Seco and Juan Ignacio Benedicto (Valencia: Universitat de València, 2013), pp. 59–88 at 63–70; Emilio La Parra López, 'La metamorfosis de la imagen del rey Fernando VII entre los primeros liberales', in *Cortes y revolución en el primer liberalismo español*, ed. Francisco Acosta Ramírez (Jaén: Publicaciones de la Universidad de Jaén, 2006), pp. 73–96.

kingdom, occupied by the French, and therefore they represented again a legitimate source of authority'.[50] Reference to the Spanish rising against the French invader can be found also in Ypsilantis's proclamation, which made an explicit reference to Spain, 'who first by herself put to rout the invincible phalanxes of a tyrant'.[51] On assuming the title of head of the constitutional army, Guglielmo Pepe stressed how the peoples of the Neapolitan kingdom had already shown their valour, as they had been the first to mount a resistance against the French army.[52] Santarosa justified the exceptional powers assumed by the army in defence of the nation by making reference to the war waged by the Prussian army against Napoleon in 1813.[53] The historical narratives emerging from these proclamations did not only refer to the recent Napoleonic conflicts as sources of legitimacy for the revolutions, but also to the antiquity of the nation and its freedom when justifying either claims to self-rule or requests for constitutional freedoms. Thus the pronunciamientos were presented, among other things, also as 'restorations' of ancient liberties, inventing a tradition on the basis of which older instances of constitutional liberties needed to be rescued. For Riego, the Spanish people had always ruled over themselves, as the Spaniards were an 'ancient and sovereign people, that always dictated their own laws and appointed their kings'.[54]

When addressing publicly the governadores of the kingdom based in Lisbon, the military officers writing from Porto referred to the creation of a provisional junta of government, and to the right to call for the introduction of representation as a reconstitution of the ancient Cortes in 1641, after the Portuguese revolution and war against Spain that had reinstated the rights of the Portuguese monarchy.[55] History was also employed to highlight the continuity between ancient and modern rebellions, and justify the cause of national emancipation and the historicity of the nation itself. This was even more powerfully argued in the case of Ypsilantis's rebellion, one that aimed at creating a new political community. In his speech, all the

50. 'Os officiaeis e soldados da guarnição do Porto aos governadores de Lisboa', 3 September 1820, in *Mnemosine Constitucional*, no. 4, 28 September 1820, p. 2.

51. Alexandros Ypsilantis, 24 February–8 March 1821, Jassy, in Richard Clogg, *The Movement for Greek Independence, 1770–1821: A Collection of Documents* (London: Macmillan, 1976), pp. 201–2.

52. Pepe, 'Il comandante in capo dell'esercito costituzionale ai popoli del regno delle due Sicilie', Avellino, 7 July 1820, in Gamboa, *Storia della rivoluzione*, p. 30.

53. Gualterio, *Gli ultimi rivolgimenti*, 1, p. 145, and *Archives diplomatiques*, 2, p. 17.

54. Riego, Puerto de Santa María, 1 January 1820, in Gil Novales, *Rafael Riego*, p. 39.

55. 'Os Oficiais da cidade do Porto aos Governadores de Lisboa', 1 September 1820, in Marques, *Exército e sociedade*, pp. 229–30.

tropes of Greek historical narrative, that rooted contemporary claims in classical antiquity, and in the struggle against the Persians as forerunners of contemporary Oriental despotism, could be detected:

> Let us then once again, O brave and magnanimous Greeks, invite Liberty to the classical land of Greece! Let us do battle between Marathon and Thermopylae! Let us fight on the tombs of our fathers, who, so as to leave us free, fought and died there![56]

The call for a constitution additionally projected the language of the proclamations into the future, as they tended to foresee a time of regeneration and, above all, of happiness. Happiness was in fact another key concept in these texts, a public condition that could now be achieved with the reintroduction of freedom. Thus Riego, when addressing the crowd in Algeciras, claimed that '[t]he generous cry pronounced by the National Army has been the dawn of the happiness of the fatherland', while De Concilj confidently claimed that, following the introduction of the constitution, 'We shall be happy.'[57] Happiness continued to be a central theme of early revolutionary printed material. The proclamations thereby produced historical accounts that justified the revolutions in terms of the distant and the recent past, and promised a future of progress and wellbeing on the basis of their immediate achievements.

The awareness of these events resulting from the circulation of news and of texts across southern Europe in turn fed into another important element of the shared features of these revolutionary scripts: the description of such events as the regeneration of the South. The key national revolutionary manifestos in fact not only shared a number of central themes with the others, but were circulated widely across the Mediterranean. Whether reprinted in newspapers or as leaflets, copies of foreign proclamations were reproduced in other revolutionary contexts, and accompanied by detailed information about the events that had produced them. The manifestos issued by Ypsilantis were published by the Neapolitan, Spanish and Portuguese press, along with regular news about his military campaigns. The Neapolitan and Sicilian press, for instance, made available to their publics a translated version of Colonels Sepúlveda and Cabreira's proclamation to the soldiers read in Porto on 24 August, and also the address of the Porto provisional junta to the Portuguese people, thanks

56. Ypsilantis, 24 February–8 March 1821, Jassy, in Clogg, *Movement for Greek Independence*, p. 203.

57. Riego, at Algeciras, 1 February 1820, in Gil Novales, *Rafael Riego*, p. 46; De Concilj, 'Proclama', 5 July 1820, in Minichini, *Luglio 1820*, p. 207.

FIGURE 4. Documents on the Neapolitan and Greek revolutions reproduced in the Portuguese press: *Astro da Lusitania*, no. 131, 28 April 1821; Biblioteca Nacional de Portugal, Lisbon). Image: Biblioteca Nacional de Portugal, with permission

to reproductions in the Spanish press.[58] Likewise, the Portuguese and Spanish press published the public documents of the Piedmontese and Neapolitan revolutions. While some awareness of the Portuguese, Spanish, Piedmontese and Neapolitan proclamations among the Greek leadership cannot be ruled out, the Greek press, which came into being only when these other parallel revolutions had either come to an end or were well under way, does not seem to have contributed to this trans-regional exchange of published documents. Thus documents flowed from east to west, but their circulation in the opposite direction cannot be attested beyond the Kingdom of the Two Sicilies and Sicily itself, where it seemed to stop.

Thanks to this circulation, liberals in Portugal, Spain and Naples not only became aware of all the revolutions taking place simultaneously, but

58. *L'Imparziale Siciliano*, 16 October 1820, p. 1. See also the broadsheet 'Rivoluzione del Portogallo: Proclama della Giunta provvisoria del governo supremo del regno; Ai portoghesi', Naples, 6 October 1820, in SNSP, broadsheet collections. It seems that the source was the Spanish press, as *El Universal* was mentioned. See also the publication of Ypsilantis's proclamations to the Moldavians and Wallachians in the *Astro da Lusitania*, 25 April 1821, no. 128, p. 2, and 28 April 1821, no. 131, p. 2.

ended up producing remarkably homogeneous and strikingly similar accounts of what made this revolutionary wave unique and superior to any others that had taken place before. In all three locations, observers saw the role of the army in bringing about constitutional government peacefully as a peculiarity that marked the revolutions of this specific revolutionary wave. For them the uprisings of the South were in marked contrast to the aggressive and destructive nature of the French revolution. This distinction served the purpose of turning the southern margins of Europe into the centre insofar as initiatives for the regeneration of the continent were concerned. In the words of an anonymous journalist writing in the Portuguese *Genio Constitucional*, what the events of the Isla de León, Porto and Nola in Naples had demonstrated was the extent to which the armed forces could be transformed from a tool of despotism and oppression into one of freedom and glory, as armies belonged now to the nation. He concluded that the recent military events could not be described as rebellions, since rebellions were acts against the will of the nation, not interventions on its behalf. As a matter of fact, it was the duty of the army to intervene and resist oppression and injustice.[59] For the Portuguese *Mnemosine Constitucional*, Spain, Naples, Sicily and Portugal were now at the head of a great European revolution. France would soon follow, and all the nations of the north of Europe would be given an opportunity to break away from despotism.[60] The explosion of the rebellion in the Ottoman Empire broadened this notion of southern freedom to include Greece. Commenting on the most recent events, the opening article of the first issue of the exaltado newspaper *El Eco de Padilla*, in August 1821, after the repression of the Piedmontese and Neapolitan revolts and the reappearance of the 'genius of liberty' among the Greeks thanks to Ypsilantis's declaration of independence, referred to the need to re-establish and defend the freedom of the 'southern part of Europe' against the despotism of northern Europe.[61]

What was therefore often stressed was the degree to which the military introduced an element of stability and order into the revolutionary process, without thereby betraying the principles of liberty the revolution wished to fulfil. In southern Europe, the prominent Portuguese liberal João Baptista da Silva Leitão de Almeida Garrett argued, 'the armed forces

59. 'Nota del redactor', *Genio Constitucional*, Porto, 17 October 1820, pp. 2 and 3.

60. *Mnemosine Constitucional*, no. 8, 3 October 1820, p. 1. See also the original in *El Conservador*, 2 September 1820.

61. *El Eco de Padilla*, 1 August 1821, pp. 3–4.

avoided tumults, suppressed disorders, and the altars of freedom were not stained with blood'.[62] For Almeida Garrett, the army was the only force that could legitimately have taken the lead in initiating a peaceful revolution in August 1820. The military had in fact the unique advantage of representing the interests and will of the entire nation better than any single social group: neither the clergy, hostile to reform, nor the aristocracy, nor the people (povo), with its insurrectionary proclivities, was suited to this task. This interpretation was shared by Neapolitan revolutionaries, who praised the extent to which the Spaniards had subordinated passions to reason in their revolution, and in a similar vein argued that 'the cordial union between people and army' in Portugal and Naples demonstrated the possibility of reconciling legislative reform with justice.[63] In dedicating a historical account of the ancient Portuguese Cortes to the army, a military officer noted that the recent events demonstrated how the troops had given the notion of military victory a new meaning, one associated not with blood, but with reclaiming lost public rights.[64] Clearly, the memory of the revolutionary wars and the Napoleonic expansion across the continent, with its glories, but also with its excesses and bouts of wanton destruction, was one that southern European liberals wished to keep at arm's length.

The Greek revolutionaries, on the contrary, did not endorse this narrative and did not publicly espouse the idea of a southern regeneration adopted by their Portuguese, Spanish and Neapolitan counterparts. References to southern Europe were absent from the Greek revolutionary press and from their public manifestos. This is not just because the nature of their rebellion did not readily fit into a narrative highlighting the peaceful intervention of the army. More importantly, it was incompatible with the importance the Greek revolutionaries attributed to winning over European audiences and diplomatic circles to their cause, an objective that required taking a distance from the uprisings that were being condemned by those very states whose support the Greek revolutionary leadership was seeking. It is therefore not surprising that Ypsilantis was immediately criticised by members of his circle for mentioning the Spanish

62. João Baptista da Silva Leitão de Almeida Garrett, *O dia vinte e quatro de Agosto* (Lisbon: Typ. Rollandiana, 1821), p. 51. Similar ideas were advanced in 'Anno primeiro da restauração de nossa libertade: Portugal', in José Liberato Freire de Carvalho's *O Campeão Portuguez, ou O Amigo do Rei e do Povo*, 1821, p. 356.

63. *Il Censore*, 5 January 1821, no. 13, pp. 50–51.

64. Cypriano José Rodrigues das Chagas, *As cortes ou os direitos do povo portuguez que dedica ao exercito* (Lisbon: Officina de António Rodrigues Galhardo, 1820), p. 1.

anti-Napoleonic rebellion in his manifesto, as any association with Spain risked giving excessively radical connotations to a rebellion that in their view ought to be justified only as a cause of civilisation against Turkish despotism.[65] Some of his close supporters warned him against any association with the constitutional risings in Spain, Piedmont and Naples, inviting him to stress instead the extent to which theirs was primarily a fight for religion against despotism.[66] This view sometimes owed a debt to a conservative interpretation of the Greek national movement that was incompatible with political radicalism, highlighted the religious bond with the Russian Empire and prioritised the defence of Orthodoxy and need for Russian protection over full emancipation, or a general insurrection.[67] Whether directly influenced by this strand of Orthodox pro-Russian nationalism or not, the early public addresses to an international audience produced by the revolutionaries made appeals to notions of European civilisation and Christianity, rather than to the regeneration of the South, to justify their action. In a proclamation of the Greeks to the Europeans, Ypsilantis defended the Greek cause as one that would re-establish the place of the Greeks among civilised peoples. Ypsilantis made clear that the Greeks did not seek to foment revolution among peoples who already enjoyed civic freedom, stating that 'our insurrection is different from the others'.[68] The declaration of independence approved at Epidavros on 15 January 1822 endorsed the anti-French rhetoric adopted by southern revolutionaries, stating that the Greeks' fight was not the effect of a 'seditious and jacobinical movement', but made not mention of 'southern Europe'. Rather, it referred to the desire of the Greeks to 'advance as the equals of

65. Emmanuel G. Protopsaltis, ed., Ιστορικόν αρχείον Αλέξανδρου Μαυροκορδάτου (Historical archive of Alexandros Mavrokordatos), 6 vols (Athens: Academy of Athens, 1963), 1, p. 302.

66. Georgios Katakouzinos, Υπόμνημα του Πρίγκηπα Γεωργίου Κατακουζηνού' (Memorandum of Prince Georgios Katakouzinos), Kishinev, 28 October 1821, in Δύο πρίγκηπες στην Ελληνική Επανάσταση: Επιστολές αυτόπτη μάρτυρα και ένα υπόμνημα του Πρίγκηπα Γεωργίου Κατακουζηνού (Two princes in the Greek revolution: Letters of an eye witness and a memorandum by Prince Georgios Katakouzinos), ed. Vasilis Panayiotopoulos (Athens: Asini, 2015), pp. 259–96.

67. Konstantina Zanou, 'Imperial Nationalism and Orthodox Enlightenment: A Diasporic Story between the Ionian Islands, Russia and Greece, ca. 1800–1830', in Isabella and Zanou, Mediterranean Diasporas, pp. 111–34; Ada Dialla, 'Imperial Rhetoric and Revolutionary Practice: The Greek 1821', Historein 20, no. 1 (2021), DOI: https://doi.org/10.12681/historein.27480; Stella Ghervas, Reinventer la tradition: Alexandre Stourdza et l'Europe de la Sainte Alliance (Paris: Honoré Champion, 2008).

68. Proclamation of the Greeks to the Europeans, 12 June 1821, in Archives diplomatiques, 2, pp. 597–602, quotation (in French) at p. 599.

the Christians of Europe'.[69] Thus even in their geographical imagination, the revolutionary scripts produced in the 1820s had striking similarities, but also remarkable asymmetries.

The army and popular mobilisation

As the audiences targeted by the manifestos issued by the officers demonstrate, the armies were committed to communicating not only with their own soldiers, but also with civilians. In fact, officers were convinced that the legitimacy of their revolutionary acts required visible proofs that the populations were supporting their intervention. As a military strategy, the pronunciamiento required the support of civilians and troops alike. This is why the insurgent troops did all they could to encourage public demonstrations of support for their declarations of the revolution by civilians in the earliest stages of the pronunciamiento. In Portugal, Spain Naples, Piedmont and the Danubian Principalities, civilians were present from the earliest stages of the pronunciamientos, alongside military audiences. On the 1 January 1820, Riego timed his public declaration to the soldiers with the end of mass, so that the population of Las Cabezas leaving the church of San Juan Bautista could be present at his public speech.[70] Admittedly, efforts by the army to mobilise crowds in public demonstrations in favour of the revolutions were often not successful. Riego's ride from Las Cabezas through a succession of villages, and his army's public attempts to attract the attention of the local population, were often met with indifference: public squares remained empty or at best a few curious bystanders might attend the declarations of the constitution and the reading of the manifestos. In addition, some municipal authorities responded to Riego's attempts at winning recognition for his declaration of the constitution with public demonstrations of allegiance to the king. In Cádiz, for instance, at the end of January, the municipal authorities addressed the crowds from the balcony of the town hall, vowed allegiance to the monarch and organised military parades in the public square.[71] In Portugal too, not all urban centres responded to the army's decision to mount

69. The National Assembly to the Greeks, 'Declaration of Independence', 15 January 1822, in Edward Blaquiere, *The Greek Revolution: Its Origin and Progress* (London: G. & W. B. Whittaker, 1824), pp. 327–29.

70. Eugenio Antonio del Riego Núñez, *Obras póstumas poéticas de Don Eugenio Antonio del Riego Núñez* (London: Charles Wood, 1843), pp. 10–14.

71. AHN, Estado, legajo 3081-II: letters to the Duke of San Fernando, Seville, 12 January 1820, and Cádiz, 28 January 1820.

public demonstrations of allegiance to the new revolutionary provisional governmental junta established to replace the governadores in Lisbon. The city of Braga in the north-western province of Minho, for instance, responded grudgingly to the request for public displays of support for the new government. Here the proclamation of the new constitutional regime in the Câmara of the city "felt more like a funeral than an acclamation", and neither the clergy, nor the employees of the law courts, attended the public ceremony to take an oath to the constitutional monarchy. The public square outside the Câmara was deserted and the local population entirely absent from these ceremonies. Local liberal sources highlighted the responsibility of the bishopric in boycotting these celebrations.[72]

In spite of occasionally being met with indifference, however, in general the pronunciamientos succeeded precisely because the populations were not indifferent, but actively involved. Yet the extent of this involvement, as well as the nature of the interaction varied from place to place, since in some locations civilian initiative played a more important part than in others. The following pages explore the role played by civilian populations in the early stages of the revolutions, and look at the ways in which they responded to military revolutionary intervention, or took their own independent initiative. In Spain, what guaranteed the success of Riego's pronunciamiento was the support offered by the populations of all the major urban centres of the country; and although his expedition was a failure from a military point of view, it triggered a domino effect in the major cities of Spain and the combining of civilian initiatives with local garrisons' interventions in support of the constitution. Local circumstances dictated the terms of the interaction between each city garrison and the population, as well as the intensity of popular mobilisation. These urban pronunciamientos thus were the outcome of local political struggles, and took place in communities where there existed a past history of genuine commitment to the constitution, and a memory of recent failed pronunciamientos that had produced deep political divisions among civilians and within military garrisons. It should therefore come as no surprise that the first important city to respond to Riego was La Coruña. It was in this city that the first military revolt of the restoration, led by General Juan Díaz Porlier, had taken place in 1815, there being links there also with other cities.[73] In February 1820 a group of civilians attacked the Capitanía general

72. BNP, Manuscritos Reservados, 10706, f. 1: report sent to José Borges Carneiro, 11 September 1820.

73. Cepeda Gómez, *El ejército español*; Hamnett, *La política española*, pp. 240–41.

with the support of military officers and arrested the military leader of the city, General Venegas. The *pronunciados* had contributed to the arming of the civilians so as to guarantee the success of their plans. From La Coruña the revolution spread to the surrounding cities of Galicia such as Vigo, Ferrol and Lugo, where juntas were established and the local populations lent their support to the constitutional movement.[74]

From Galicia the insurrection moved to Zaragoza, the capital of Aragon. This city too had a significant history of popular mobilisation. Its inhabitants had already demonstrated their activism during the Peninsular War. In the aftermath of the Madrid revolt of 2 May 1808, the crowds had taken to the streets of Zaragoza, and under the leadership of General Palafox the city had endured two brutal sieges at the hands of the French army and contributed to its own defence: it had successfully resisted the enemy in the first engagement, and only succumbed after bloody street fighting to the second assault, in February 1809.[75] Nor did it remain passive in 1820. In fact, it enthusiastically supported the declaration of the constitution: large crowds attended the public oath sworn by the military and civil authorities of the city on 5 March, and also forced the captain general of Aragon, the reactionary Marquis of Lazán, to side with the revolution. When a new captain general, hostile to the constitution, General Haro, was sent by the government to the city to regain control, a popular revolt erupted, and Haro was arrested.[76]

The city of Barcelona, meanwhile, confirmed in 1820 the reputation as a centre of popular liberalism that it had earned during the war against the French. The Bourbon restoration had not succeeded in suppressing its liberal leanings, and political opposition persisted through the development and growth of Masonic lodges. In 1817 the capital of Catalonia had been the scene of a failed pronunciamiento led by General de Lacy, followed by the imprisonment of hundreds of military men compromised in this plot. The captain general who had been responsible for the execution of de Lacy, General Francisco Javier Castaños, was still in place in 1820. Thus support for Riego's pronunciamiento coincided with a city insurrection against Castaños, who became the target of revenge by both military

74. Antonio Moliner Prada, *Revolución burguesa y movimiento juntero en España* (Lleida: Milenio,1997), pp. 96–102.

75. Charles J. Esdaile, *The Spanish Army in the Peninsular War* (Manchester: Manchester University Press, 1988), pp. 67–68, 75–77, 159–63; Raymond Rudorff, *War to the Death: The Sieges of Saragossa, 1808–1809* (London: Purnell Book Services Ltd, 1974).

76. Manuel Pando Fernández de Pinedo, marqués de Miraflores, *Apuntes histórico-críticos para escribir la historia de la revolución de España desde el año1820 hasta 1823* (London: Richard Taylor, 1834), p. 32; Moliner Prada, *Revolución burguesa*, p. 105.

and civilians. On 5 March Castaños succeeded in suppressing a military plot organised by a number of officers, but in the following days opposition to him mounted, and culminated in a mass demonstration in the main square of the city, the Plaza de Palau. On 10 March both civilians and soldiers gathering outside his palace demanded his resignation and his replacement with a constitutional general, Pedro de Villacampa, who was soon acclaimed as the new captain general of the city. Even the owners of the factories in the city had closed down on that day to encourage their workers, who included shoemakers and carpenters, to participate in the demonstration. The crowd attacked and looted the palace of the Holy Inquisition.[77]

While the involvement of local lodges of secret societies in preparing these local uprisings can be assumed in many cases, evidence of earlier planning of civilian and military engagement within conspiratorial networks is best shown by events in Piedmont and Naples. Here, organisers succeeded in employing directly or indirectly the secret societies to which they belonged to guarantee public support for the revolutions from their earliest stages. The mutiny of the military citadel of the city of Alessandria, the event that inaugurated the Piedmontese revolution, took place in the presence of a large number of civilians who had been informed of the imminent insurrection. As soon as the officers had raised the tricolour flag, cannon were fired, and the cavalry entered the garrison accompanied by a military band; a crowd waiting outside the gates was allowed into the citadel to attend the declaration of the constitution and listen to the speeches made by the officers.[78] This early presence of a public reflected the organisational efforts of the officers and civilians plotting together in the secret societies of the city to alert their membership to the event: the meeting that planned the mutiny of 9 March 1821 included a medical doctor, a lawyer, a contractor and a judge.[79] The two separate events that marked the insurrection in the capital city of Turin, shortly after those in

77. Josep Fontana, *La revolució de 1820 a Catalunya* (Barcelona: Rafael Dalmau, 1961), pp. 21–25; Jordi Roca Vernet, *La Barcelona revolucionària i liberal: Exaltats, milicians i conspiradors* (Barcelona: Pagès Editors, 2011), pp. 31–46.

78. See documents published in *La rivoluzione piemontese dell'anno 1821: Nuovi documenti*, in *Biblioteca di storia italiana recente (1800–1870)*, vol. 11 (Turin: Bocca, 1923); and also AST, Segreteria di Stato Affari Interni, Alta Polizia, Affari politici, Moti del 1821, mazzo 11, no. 25.

79. Francesco Gasparolo, 'Il primo moto rivoluzionario del 21 in Alessandria', *Rivista di Storia, Arte, Archeologia per la Provincia di Alessandria* 30 (1921): 3–31; Adolfo Colombo, 'I moti di Alessandria nel 1821 secondo nuovi documenti', *Rivista di Storia, Arte, Archeologia per la Provincia di Alessandria* 31 (1922): 291–336.

Alessandria, likewise confirmed this pattern. The first was led by Captain Vittorio Ferrero, a thirty-one-year-old officer from the Legione Reale Leggiera, who, following the orders of his superiors, moved back into the capital city. Passing through the gates of Turin, and pausing outside a hotel not far from the church of San Salvario, Ferrero publicly affirmed his commitment to the revolution, declaring his support for the constitution in front of eighty soldiers and more than a hundred civilians.[80] These civilians, alerted to the organisation of such public demonstrations by secret society activists, included several teachers and thirty-four students from the local Collegio delle Provincie, many of whom had been involved in the conspiracy through the Carboneria. Thus it was a combination of troops and civilians that left the capital city under Ferrero's orders and proved willing to join forces with those at the centre of the insurrection, the citadel of Alessandria. By the time they had reached the town of Chieri on their way to Alessandria, the combined number of civilians and soldiers entering the town would seem to have risen to four hundred. In Chieri, Ferrero also addressed the crowds of local inhabitants on the need to fight the Austrians and promulgate a constitution.[81] The second event, taking place in Turin the day after the insurrection of San Salvario, was the storming of the citadel. While this was a strictly military event, in which the insurgents seized control of the fortress, in this case too a number of army officers, soon after declaring the constitution and raising the tricolour flag, harangued the crowds gathered under the walls of the citadel, shouting 'Death to the Germans!' and 'Hurrah for the constitution!'[82]

In the provinces outside Naples, widespread support for the revolution among civilians had been the result of the capillary dissemination of the Carboneria in previous years. In the Irpinia, an area in which the revolution had been spearheaded by the officers Michele Morelli and Giuseppe Silvati, the Carboneria had spread among the members of the provincial militia thanks to the efforts of General Pepe, allied as he was with these two officers. These militias, first set up during the Napoleonic era, had been maintained by the Bourbon king after the restoration of his rule, with the hope of being able to use them to guarantee order against crime

80. Arturo Segre, 'L'episodio di S. Salvario', in *La rivoluzione piemontese dell'anno 1821*, pp. 251–319; AST, Segreteria di Stato Affari Interni, Alta Polizia, Affari politici, Moti del 1821, mazzo 11, no. 30.

81. See AST, Segreteria di Stato Affari Interni, Alta Polizia, Processi politici del 1821, fascio 53, no. 108.

82. 'Morte ai tedeschi!' and 'Viva la costituzione!': as quoted in Adolfo Colombo, 'La rivolta della cittadella di Torino (12 Marzo 1821)', in *La rivoluzione piemontese dell'anno 1821*, pp. 527–46.

FIGURE 5. Student protest at San
Salvario, Turin, March 1821 (lithograph
after drawing by Antonio Masutti, n.d;
MuseoTorino, Turin: Risorgimento
exhibition, 'I moti: gli studenti del 1821').
Image: https://www.museotorino.it

and brigandage. Pepe's own role in reorganising the militias in Puglia and
Avellino had given him the opportunity to exert his political influence over
them.[83] In the days immediately preceding the mutiny, another member of
the Carboneria, the priest Luigi Minichini, had tried to impose his authority over Morelli and Salvati, and had created his own army of civilians, or
paesani, to support the military operations.[84] In the days leading up to
the pronunciamiento, his constant interaction with other leaders of the
Carboneria, and with local dignitaries from the neighbouring villages and
towns who had lent their support, demonstrates the importance of the
broader social context of such a revolutionary project. These preparations
laid the ground for substantial mobilisation around the troops stationed

83. On this, see Ruggero Moscati, ed., *Guglielmo Pepe, 1797–1831*, vol. 1 (one vol. published) (Rome: Istituto per la storia del Risorgimento italiano, 1938), pp. lxxx–lxxxi, 112.
84. Minichini, *Luglio 1820*, pp. 90–125.

in Capua and then those in Avellino. The troops led by the two officers, flanked by Minichini, approached and entered the city of Avellino at the head of over a thousand individuals, including armed civilians recruited by the Carboneria leaders in the surrounding villages. Armed villagers intervened also to force reluctant regiments to support the constitution in Avellino, where its declaration took place along with the acclamation of another officer, Lorenzo De Concilj, as leader of the constitutional army, in front of troops from all parts of the province and the inhabitants of the city. Given the number of people gathering around the palace of the *inten-dente* (the representative of the central government), De Concilj had first to show himself from the balcony, and then on horseback, before swearing an oath of allegiance to the constitution alongside the troops.[85]

The Carboneria's popularity and the extensive nature of their networks explain also the enthusiasm directed at the constitutional army in Salerno and its province upon its arrival, once the troops loyal to the king had been driven from the outskirts of the city.[86] When news of the events of Nola and of the departure of the anti-constitutional troops led by General Campana arrived in the village of San Severo, only a few miles from Salerno, five hundred carbonari took up arms and gathered in the public square, disbanding again when it had become clear that the outcome of the conflict was uncertain, and reorganising themselves again in public on the arrival of the constitutional troops.[87] As had been the case in the previous days in Avellino, and once again in Salerno, the entry of the constitutional army into the city was followed by that of the provincial militias and the armed carbonari similarly organised in military units. Two thousand of them came from the district of Sala alone.[88] On 8 July a provincial 'Giunta governativa provvisoria' controlled by carbonaro leaders such as Rosario Macchiaroli and Gerardo Mazziotti, was appointed by acclamation by civilians and soldiers alike gathering in public.[89] A few days later, once news broke that the constitutional troops had entered Naples and that Francesco, the heir to the throne, had accepted the constitution, public demonstrations of support for the revolution spontaneously and

85. Gamboa, *Storia della rivoluzione*, pp. 13, 33–34; ASN, Borbone, 275, ff. 57–58, 97–98.

86. Gamboa, *Storia della rivoluzione*, pp. 61–62.

87. Antonio Stassano, *Cronaca: Memorie storiche del Regno di Napoli dal 1798 al 1821*, ed. Roberto Marino and Mario Themelly (Naples: Istituto italiano per gli studi filosofici, 1996), p. 359.

88. Stassano, *Cronaca*, pp. 360–61, 65–66; ASN, Borbone, 726, ff. 209–11: note on the 'armata costituzionale'.

89. ASN, Borbone, Carte Canosa, 724, ff. 89–91.

peacefully erupted also in the cities of eastern Sicily. The civilian populations of Messina and Catania took to the streets to demonstrate their
support. In Messina civilians mingled with soldiers in the square in front
of the cathedral to toast the constitution; in Catania, in particular, the
mass presence of women in these public gatherings was noted, and all the
houses were illuminated at night as a sign of rejoicing at these events.[90]

While the interaction between the military and civilians was a common
feature of the first steps in the pronunciamientos, in some circumstances
it was the spontaneous and uncontrolled mobilisation of civilians that
prevailed and determined the success of the insurrection, either pushing
those sectors of the army that had remained at the margins of events to
join the uprising, or forcing hesitant authorities to declare their allegiance
to the constitution. This happened far away from the military epicentres
of the revolution, in the capital cities of Madrid and Lisbon, where the
initiative taken by local populations proved of fundamental importance in
forcing the Spanish monarch to accept the constitution, and in convincing
the Portuguese governadores to resign and permit the establishment of a
provisional government. In this respect, the contrast between events in
Porto and Lisbon could not be more striking. After 24 August 1820, public
demonstrations of support for the revolution in Porto had been orderly
and had been prompted by the military and the provisional government;
in the capital of Portugal the popular initiative anticipated the military.
In Lisbon the governors representing the king based in Brazil had been
reluctant to yield to the demands of the revolutionary army of Porto, and
to accept their request to establish a new provisional government poised
to introduce a constitution. The army in the capital decided to proclaim its
support for the revolution only when popular protests and rallying cries in
favour of a new government erupted in the Rossio square, making it clear
where public opinion stood, in mid-September 1820, three weeks after
the events of Porto.[91] Information about Spanish events had prepared the
ground for popular mobilisation in support of the revolution in the capital
since the beginning of the year. According to diplomatic correspondence,
news of Riego's pronunciamiento had fostered a 'spirit of insurrection' in

90. Gerardo Bianco, *La rivoluzione siciliana del 1820 con documenti e carteggi inediti*
(Florence: Bernardo Seeber Editore, 1905), pp. 32ff; *Giornale Costituzionale del Regno
delle Due Sicilie*, no. 18, 28 July 1820, p. 73.

91. Clemente José dos Santos, *Documentos para a história das Cortes gerais da nação
portuguesa*, 8 vols (Lisbon: Imprensa Nacional, 1883–1891), 1, pp. 65–68. On this, see Vasco
Pulido Valente, *Os militares e a política (1820–1856)* (Lisbon: Imprensa Nacional, 2005),
p. 63.

FIGURE 6. Meeting of the Provisional Junta at the Regency Palace in Rossio Square, Lisbon, 1 October 1820 (aquatint by António Cândido Cordeiro Pinheiro Furtado, c. 1820; Museu de Lisboa, Lisbon). Image: Wikimedia Commons

Lisbon, where the population was frustrated and exasperated by the fact that Portugal was now de facto a colony of Brazil.[92]

In the capital of Spain likewise, impatient crowds played an important part in forcing the king to take an oath to the constitution and in determining the replacement of absolutist municipal government with a constitutional dispensation. Once the 7 March decree of the monarch to reinstate the constitution and swear an oath to it became known, public demonstrations broke out cross the city: the crowds freed the prisoners of the Holy Inquisition and raised a temporary constitutional stone in Plaza Mayor. But the hesitation of the king to act on his promise led to further disturbances two days later, when a protest was organised in front of the royal palace, and the demonstrators entered the building and tried to reach the royal apartments. At the same time, a large crowd gathering outside the Casas Consistoriales (city hall) demanded the appointment of a constitutional *ayuntamiento* (city council). Refusing to accept the constitutional *alcaldes* (mayors) chosen by the king, who had appointed those of 1813 and 1814, they elected by acclamation individuals of their

92. AHN, Estado, legajo 3081-II: Manuel de Lardizábal y Montoya to the Duke of San Fernando, Lisbon, 15 January 1820.

own choosing. The multitude then accompanied the new members of the ayuntamiento to the royal palace, forcing them to meet the king, and compelled the monarch himself to take an oath to the constitution, there and then, in front of the new municipal authorities. Whether these events took place in an entirely spontaneous way or otherwise is not certain. However, most sources agree about the interclass nature of the popular participation, from 'respectable individuals' to artisans and the populace at large.[93]

An even more widespread mobilisation in favour of the pronunciamiento can be identified in the city of Cádiz, whose urban population displayed an enthusiasm for the revolution that would seem to have had no match elsewhere in Spain. The strong liberal tradition and the intense politicisation of the population of the city, where the Cortes had gathered between 1810 and 1812 to draft the constitution though under siege from the French army, accounts for the mass displays there of support for Riego and Quiroga soon after their pronunciamiento, and the determination of the city's population to force its reluctant military garrison to accept the constitution. On 9 March 1820 an immense crowd gathered in the Plaza de San Antonio to welcome the head of the army in Cádiz, General Manuel Freyre, shouting '¡Viva la constitución!', whereupon a copy of the constitution was thrust into his hands. The general felt he had no choice but to promise that the following day a ceremony would take place to swear an oath to the constitution. On that day, however, a number of officers and soldiers attacked the crowds gathering to celebrate the revolution in the same square, unleashing a three-day long conflict between these and the troops that resulted in a high number of casualties. While it was only when the king's consent to the reintroduction of the constitution was officially confirmed that these bloody clashes came to an end and calm was restored, the intensity and duration of these street fights pointed to the determination of the population to defend the constitution.[94]

In Genoa, the capital of Liguria, the coastal province of Piedmont-Sardinia, a popular insurrection in defence of the revolution and the

93. Estanislao de Kostka Bayo, *Historia de la vida y reinado de Fernando VII de España*, 3 vols (Madrid: Imprenta de Repullés, 1842,) 2, p. 159; Miraflores, *Apuntes histórico-críticos*, pp. 43–46. On these events, see also Álvaro París Martín, 'Artesanos y política en Madrid durante el resistible ascenso del liberalismo (1808–1833)', *Theomai* 31 (2015): 43–62 at pp. 52–53.

94. *Manifiesto que da al público el teniente general Do Manuel Freyre para hacer conocer su conducta en le tiempo que tuvo el mando del egército reunido de Andalucía [. . .]* (Seville: Imprenta Mayor, 1820); Miraflores, *Apuntes histórico-críticos*, pp. 34–37; Miraflores, *Documentos a los que se hace referencia en los apuntes histórico-críticos sobre la revolucion de España*, vol. 1 (one vol. published) (London: Richard Taylor, 1834), pp. 81–84.

FIGURE 7. Arrival of General Quiroga in Cádiz, 1820 (engraving by Charles François Gabriel Levanchez *et fils*, after drawing by Pierre Martinet, Paris, 1820; San Telmo Museoa San Sebastián). Image: San Telmo Museoa San Sebastián, with permission

constitution preceded, rather than followed, any military declaration of support for it in the city. Here, what determined popular activism was the enthusiasm of university students for the constitutional government, along with widespread popular frustration at the loss of independence of the former republic of Genoa, annexed to Piedmont in 1814, combined with strongly anti-aristocratic sentiments directed at the city's ancient oligarchical elite. In March 1821 the decision by the governor of Genoa, Admiral Giorgio de Geneys, to publish King Carlo Felice's rejection of the constitution and his reaffirmation of the principles of absolutism resulted in public disorder. The governor's palace came under attack at the hands of angry crowds, in which university students, shopkeepers and tradesmen, but also coal porters, sailors and dockworkers, had a prominent role. While on 21 March such an assault was successfully repulsed by the troops, an insurrection two days later led to the arrest of the governor, the occupation of the police headquarters and the establishment of a 'Commissione amministrativa di governo'. On that same day, in the face of sustained popular mobilisation, two regiments that were supposed to maintain law and order and defend the governor defected and fraternised with the crowds protesting in the streets, contributing to the success of the protests and the governor's arrest.[95]

In other places, popular initiative can only be understood in the context of ongoing conflicts between authorities and local communities or specific social groups. In the province of the Capitanata of the Kingdom of the Two Sicilies (corresponding to modern Puglia), the revolution resulted in a direct popular attack against the local intendente, one Nicola Intonti, an attack led by his own deputy, the sottintendente Rodinò, with the support of the Carboneria. Intonti had been relentlessly persecuting the members of the local Carboneria ever since his appointment as intendente in late 1817; when news of the declaration of the constitution by the army reached the province on 5 July 1820, Rodinò along with a number of prominent carbonaro leaders led hundreds of supporters from the villages of Sansevero and San Nicandro on an expedition to the city of Foggia, in an attempt to arrest and compel the resignation of the intendente, who barely escaped with his life. He was replaced by his deputy, who thereupon set up an autonomous administration called the 'Supreme Magistracy of the United Provinces of Daunia'.[96]

The cases of spontaneous and at times violent mobilisation described above often turned out to be decisive in determining the fate of the revolutions. However, it should be emphasised that while the pronunciamiento's aim was to encourage popular support to force revolutionary change, the ultimate objective of the officers themselves was to channel, direct and control popular enthusiasm, rather than unleash it in an uncontrolled and unplanned manner. In spite of these cases of spontaneous civilian intervention in Portugal, Spain, Piedmont and Naples, the armies considered popular mobilisation as merely part of what they expected and wished to be a fundamentally peaceful strategy, one in which the display of force was meant to invite the authorities to declare a constitutional

95. AST, Segreteria di Stato Affari Interni, Alta Polizia, Affari politici, Moti del 1821, mazzo 11, nos 60 and 63; Carlo Bornate, 'La partecipazione degli studenti liguri ai moti del 1821 e la chiusura dell'università', in *Giovanni Ruffini e i suoi tempi: Studi e ricerche* (Genoa: Comitato regionale ligure della Società nazionale per la storia del Risorgimento, 1931), pp. 95–161; Bornate, 'L'insurrezione di Genova nel marzo 1821', in *La rivoluzione piemontese dell'anno 1821*, pp. 331–468.

96. Giuseppe Clemente, 'Nicola Intonti e i moti del 1820–21 in Capitanata', *La Capitanata* 22 (1984–85): 195–203.

government without any use of excessive violence. They hoped and trusted that the army would prove able to control and guide civilians, with armed conflicts being kept to a minimum. In most cases, therefore, references to the Spanish insurrection against Napoleon were not to be taken at face value. Even as a military strategy, the pronunciamiento was meant to be relatively peaceful, in that it aimed at forcing authorities to concede the political demands of the officers without resorting, except when unavoidable, to armed conflict. Adopting a strategy criticised by some of his officers, Riego chose from the very outset of his pronunciamiento not to deploy violence against those soldiers and officers who refused to join the revolution. Taking his battalion out of Las Cabezas de San Juan, where he had inaugurated the pronunciamiento, he did not compel the troops to take an oath to the constitution, and allowed those individuals who did not wish to do so to leave, convinced that force was the tool of despotism and that his show of leniency would pay off.[97] Even without explicit adoption of this specific policy, in practice, as the contemporary press in Portugal, Spain, Piedmont and Naples had highlighted, military confrontation between regiments and battalions supportive of the constitution and those loyal to the absolute sovereigns was minimal: for regiments and officers hostile to the insurrection lost little time in acquiescing to the demands of the constitutional troops. In Portugal, General Manuel da Silveira Pinto da Fonseca Teixeira, Count of Amarante, based in Chaves in the north of the country, and the military governor of Beira, António Marcelino da Vitória, at first succeeded in organising some resistance, refused to recognise the authority of the junta in Porto and published manifestos against the revolutionaries. However, they soon found themselves isolated, and Amarante, having lost the support of all the regiments that had originally sided with him, decided to flee to Spanish Galicia.[98] In Piedmont (and Savoy) most of the violence was confined to the actual garrisons, where officers hostile to the revolution were imprisoned, either just before or just after declarations in favour of the constitution, by the local military garrisons.[99]

To this general pattern the Greek case constituted the only real and egregious exception, and one that, given its peculiarity, requires some elaboration. The Greek revolution consisted of two loosely coordinated and very different events: a military venture in the Danubian Principalities, and a popular and mass insurrection in the distant provinces of

97. Astur, *Riego*, pp. 175–76.
98. Cardoso, *A revolução liberal*, pp. 71–72.
99. AST, Segreteria di Stato Affari Interni, Alta Polizia, Affari politici, Moti del 1821, mazzo 11, no. 71: Rivolta Brigata Alessandria, Chambery.

mainland Greece (Roumeli) and the Peloponnese. Ypsilantis's intervention was therefore not designed to be peaceful, nor was it confined to speaking to crowds in public. It was a direct incitement to an armed rebellion,
addressed to various Christian populations across the Ottoman Empire.
Ypsilantis's military expedition in the Principalities, initiated by crossing
the river Pruth at the border between the Russian Empire and Moldavia
with the support of its prince, Michail Soutsos, precipitated a full-scale
war. The intent was in no wise peaceful. Unlike any other revolutionary
army, the force's core was made up of mercenaries who would fight only
if properly remunerated. On 24 March 1821 Ypsilantis crossed the border
with two hundred Albanian fighters. In Wallachia the insurrection's other
collaborators, such as Giorgakis Olympios, formerly responsible for the
militias of the (latest) hospodar of the province, had managed to recruit a
great number of Albanian irregulars, the so-called Arnauts or Pandours,
who would however down arms if not promptly and regularly paid. Yet
broader support for Ypsilantis's insurrection was provided by the volunteers who joined his army and those of his allies and military leaders after
the inception of their campaigns.[100] The special corps of the so-called
Sacred Band, or Holy Legion, composed mainly of students from the
Greek college of Jassy, whose numbers swelled from the original ninety to
around 450, joined him as he was leaving Moldavia for Wallachia. Aside
from this battalion, more Greeks from other parts of the empire and the
Greek diaspora on the Black Sea rallied to the revolts and flocked into
the cities of the Principalities. However, Ypsilantis's army was not simply made up of Greeks, who accounted for only a small percentage of his
fighters, but was pan–Christian-imperial in composition. In Jassy his two
thousand troops included Serbians, Bulgarians and Montenegrins, along
with the Holy Legion and guards of Prince Soutsos. By the end of the campaign his army of 6,500 soldiers reportedly contained only two hundred
Greeks, while the others included Moldavians, Albanians and the aforementioned ethnic groups. Other armies led by allied military leaders were
mainly made up of Bulgarian troops.[101]

100. Raybaud, *Mémoires*, 1, p. 190; Nikolai Todorov, 'Quelques renseignements sur
les insurgés grecs dans les Principautés danubiennes en 1821', in *Μελετήματα στη μνήμη
Βασιλείου Λαούρδα/Essays in Memory of Basil Laourdas* (Thessaloniki, 1975), pp. 471–77.

101. Despotopoulos, 'Η Ελληνική Επανάσταση' (The Greek revolution), pp. 20–69 at 25;
Veselin Trajkov, 'La coopération bulgaro-grecque dans les luttes de libération nationale', in
*Πνευματικές και πολιτιστικές σχέσεις Ελλήνων και Βουλγάρων από τα μέσα του ΙΕ΄ αιώνα έως
τα μέσα του ΙΘ΄ αιώνα* (Spiritual and cultural relationships between Greeks and Bulgarians
from the middle of the 15th to the 19th century) (Thessaloniki: Institute for Balkan Studies, 1980), pp. 47–53.

Kampf der heiligen Schaar für Griechenlands Befreyung.

Fünf Hundert griechische Jünglinge der edelsten Art, gebildet auf Deutschlands Hochschulen, folgten freiwillig dem ersten Rufe Hypsilanti's zur Rettung des unterjochten Vaterlandes, ål, ten fröhlich zur Schlacht und fielen, wardig ihrer großen Ahnen, im heiligen Kampfe für das Aälire der Menschen, für Freiheit und Vaterland, gleich Leoniåas und seine unsterblichen Schaar. Wenn, im heiligen deutschen Kriege gegen die Zwingherrschaft, die Phalanx in der ersten Schlacht, bei Lützen, nicht siegten; so auch die tapfern Griechen hier nicht gegen die Über, zahl; allein, sie bewährten ihre Würdigkeit zur Freiheit, und aus dem Heldenblute hier, wie aus jenen dort, erwuchs das Vertrauen —— und später der Sieg !

FIGURE 8. Prince Ypsilantis's 'Sacred Band' of students at the battle of Drăgășani, 19 June 1821 (etching, printed by 'O.O.', 1822; Gennadius Library Catalogue at Gennadeios Search [https://ascsa.edu.gr]). Note the symbols of the Philiki Etaireia on the Greek flags. Image: Gennadius Library, with permission

In spite of being the only organiser of a fully-fledged military campaign, however, Ypsilantis still looked for a public audience to legitimise his revolutionary expedition, much as the army officers in the rest of southern Europe were doing. In the cities of Jassy in Moldavia and Bucharest in Wallachia, where he arrived at the end of March, public ceremonies celebrating the expedition drew local crowds and attracted Greek volunteers. In Jassy, the metropolitan blessed Ypsilantis's revolutionary flag, which featured the cross with the icons of Saints Constantine and Helen on one side, and the phoenix on the other; and during a religious ceremony attended by large numbers of both clerics and civilians, at which all present swore an oath to the fatherland, he touched the general's head with the side of a sword. In Bucharest likewise, a religious blessing of the flag by two bishops took place in the private residence of the local army leader Yannis Pharmakis, not in a church as in Jassy, but the ceremony was followed by a public procession through the city streets with the enthusiastic singing of patriotic hymns.[102] While in these cities the presence of a revolutionary army attracted attention and won public support, however, the peasants of the Danubian Principalities remained indifferent or hostile to this military initiative. Moreover, Ypsilantis's expedition ended in failure. In May, Ottoman troops entered the Principalities, forcing Ypsilantis and his allies to abandon Bucharest and withdraw to Târgoviște. Ypsilantis was defeated on 7 June at Drăgășani, where his Sacred Band was wiped out. He withdrew into the Habsburg Empire, while his ally Giorgakis Olympios died and Pharmakis was taken prisoner and subsequently executed.[103]

Military events in Moldavia and Wallachia had, however, an impact on surrounding territories similar to that of Riego's pronunciamiento on the rest of Spain: they provided a signal to the existing networks of the Philiki Etaireia in the Peloponnese and beyond, successfully inciting action there. The general insurrection that took place in the distant provinces of Roumeli and Peloponnese represented the only example between 1820 and 1821 of violent and generalised popular revolt. These generalised popular revolts were noteworthy for another reason, too. Besides being by and large peaceful, the uprisings associated with the military revolutions of Portugal, Spain and Piedmont had been mainly urban events. In the Kingdom of the Two Sicilies, in the provinces surrounding Naples and in Sicily, the peasantry had also been involved. Even more than the Neapolitan revolt, the Greek insurrection for its part affected not only urban but also rural populations. Thus the rebellion coordinated by the Philiki represented the closest parallel to what the Spanish population had done during the guerrilla war against the French after 1808. The network of the Philiki Etaireia established in the previous years and connecting its leadership with prominent notables of the Morea (the Peloponnese) had laid the ground for discussions and the planning of a future general insurrection that broke out in March 1821 and mobilised most of the local populations. The reasons for the mass uprising here were partly independent from Ypsilantis's initiative, and local circumstances dictated the decision of the local leaders to intervene. Even more than in the case of the Neapolitan revolution, this was a set of only loosely connected or coordinated events. When contacted by the Philiki Etaireia's emissaries, the primates

102. Despotopoulos, 'Ή Ελληνική Επανάσταση' (The Greek revolution), pp. 25, 30; Ilias Foteinos, Οι άθλοι της εν Βλαχία Ελληνικής Επαναστάσεως το 1821 έτος (The feats of the Greek revolution of the year 1821 in Wallachia) (Leipzig, 1846), pp. 66–68.

103. George Finlay, *History of the Greek Revolution*, 2 vols (London: W. Blackwood, 1861), 1, pp. 162–68; Despotopoulos, 'Ή Ελληνική Επανάσταση' (The Greek revolution), pp. 43–56.

of the Morea had been reluctant to commit themselves to an immediate insurrection in early 1821. However, their initiative was hastened by awareness that the Ottoman authorities had knowledge of their plots and of the arming of Christian subjects, and were therefore ready to conduct repression. In fact, in late March 1821 the Ottoman authorities had started to summon the primates to the capital of the region, Tripolitsa, and those who complied were imprisoned. At the same time, vague reports from Moldavia and hopes of a Russian intervention intensified, and further encouraged the rebellion.

Almost immediately a number of informal armies of considerable size, including peasant fighters, were organised to attack the main Ottoman military strongholds. Five thousand armed peasants descended towards Patras accompanied by the city's Bishop, Palaion Patron Germanos (Georgios Iannou Kozias). The Christian Albanian tribes living just to the north of the Isthmus of Corinth organised an attack on the acropolis of Corinth against the Ottoman troops, in armed groups comprising some two thousand musketeers. Soon after the arrival of Ypsilantis's emissaries on the peninsula of Mani in the Peloponnese, its population rose under the leadership of Petrobey Mavromichalis. Here, Greek and Albanian insurgents organised in units of armed civilians succeeded in seizing control of most of the fortresses. But besides these instances of irregular warfare, everywhere individual peasants or very small groups of them organised attacks on Ottoman properties and communities in what came to be a systematic ethnic cleansing. Indeed, the elimination of the Muslim populations in areas inhabited largely by Christians was more the result of these initiatives than the effect of organised warfare. Entire villages rose, not only in the Peloponnese, but also in Roumeli, and specifically in Attica. It is said that over 1,500 armed peasants attacked the city of Athens, occupied by an Ottoman garrison, placing it under siege.[104]

Another peculiarity of the Greek insurrection was its maritime and insular dimension. The enthusiastic support lent by a number of the leaders of the key islands to the revolt resulted in the almost immediate transformation of their commercial fleet into a military one dedicated to the defence of the revolution. On the islands popular initiative was crucial: in some cases, the revolution coincided with popular revolts. Since the local grandees of Hydra, the so-called *noikokyraioi*, were initially reluctant to rally to the cause and lend support to the Greek rebels besieging the

104. See Douglas Dakin, *The Greek Struggle for Independence, 1821–1833* (Berkeley, CA: University of California Press, 1973), p. 59; Thomas Gordon, *History of the Greek Revolution*, 2 vols (London: William Blackwood & T. Cadell, 1832), 1, pp. 143–74.

Ottoman fortress of Corinth, in March 1821 a local ship's captain, Antonis Oikonomou, led a popular rebellion and managed to rule the island for forty days, during which time he forced the wealthy citizens of the island to fund the creation of a military fleet.[105] Between April and June 1821 the islands of Hydra, Spetses and Psara armed vessels and appointed admirals who took to sea, plundering foreign vessels and engaging in battle with the Ottoman fleet. In June Admiral Tombazis from Hydra had the first confrontations with Ottoman vessels from the Dardanelles, north of the island of Chios. While not immediately successful, these maritime activities led to other regions opting to participate in the revolution. It was the arrival of another squadron, led by Admiral Miaoulis from Hydra, that in June convinced the cities of Messolonghi and Vrachori on the western coast of Greece to join the uprising.[106] Initiated on the western coast of the Mediterranean by an army refusing to cross the Atlantic, the revolution had thus spread from the Iberian peninsula both eastward and westward to its Atlantic coasts, mobilising urban populations. However, it found its fullest maritime and popular dimension on the eastern side of the Mediterranean, from the Peloponnese to the islands of the Aegean.

In the name of what nation?

Although the extent to which local populations had lent their support to the armies had varied enormously, and solidarity had manifested itself both as spontaneous protests and as pre-organised demonstrations, civilian participation was certainly a common feature of the pronunciamientos. What made it controversial among the military leaders of the revolutions however, was not only the fact that sometimes, as events in Cádiz, Genoa or Hydra show, popular initiative was uncontrolled and unpredictable. The military officers' claim to act in the name of the nation gave rise to different and even conflicting interpretations of the nature of such commitment, and therefore created different expectations and plans regarding subsequent actions. Competing, not to say diverging, views among the revolutionaries on the timing, extent and desirability of such popular mobilisation not only existed, but resulted in disagreements and even in clashes. The various national armies and the military ranks supportive of the revolution entertained a variety of political positions and a variety

---

105. Spyridon Trikoupis, *Ιστορία της Ελληνικής Επαναστάσεως* (History of the Greek revolution), 2nd edn, 4 vols (London: Taylor and Francis, 1860–62), 1, 143–45, 151–54 (for the islands in general, 143–65); Gordon, *History*, 1, pp. 165ff.

106. Dakin, *Greek Struggle*, pp. 75–77.

of attitudes towards popular mobilisation. These different opinions point in turn to different ways in which the revolutionary script could be interpreted. While some preferred a minimal engagement of the populace, or one that was supposed to take place only at the outset and solely to guarantee the ultimate success of the revolution, others were keen on repeated and constant displays of popular support, and may even have considered joint military and civilian mobilisation a permanent feature of the revolution.

The tensions between the Muratist leadership and different factions of the Carboneria at the beginning of the Neapolitan revolutionary events are a case in point. In 1820 the revolutionary army entered Naples triumphantly in what looked like a public display of concord between the various military leaders, and between army and civilians. After first gathering on the Campo di Marte, the open space on the outskirts of the capital created under Murat for military training and military parades, more than twenty thousand individuals, including fourteen thousand soldiers, the provincial militias and thousands of armed and unarmed *paesani*, entered the city on 9 July 1820, parading down the Via Toledo, thronged with cheering crowds of onlookers. At their head was the 'Sacred Squadron' led by Morelli, followed, after the corps of armed civilians, by Luigi Minichini and General Guglielmo Pepe.[107] The only act that disturbed this otherwise peaceful display of unity was the abrupt intervention of a military officer, Orazio De Attellis, who shouted 'Viva la repubblica!' in front of the heir to the throne and the revolutionary leadership.

In fact this apparently harmonious final act of the revolution, which aimed at demonstrating the concord existing between the people and the military, concealed deep ideological and strategic divisions. While all the main military actors of the revolution had praised popular participation and declared at the same time their commitment to avoiding violence and anarchy, in practice they also held different opinions about the desirability of maintaining civilian mobilisation. The more radical army officers connected to lodges of the Carboneria in Naples—such as Orazio De Attellis, who had dared to disturb the public ceremony in front of the royal palace—had not wanted the army to enter Naples, as they feared that Pepe would betray the revolution. On the night before the mass gathering on the Campo di Marte, De Attellis, a provincial nobleman of radical political

---

107. Antonio Morelli, *Michele Morelli e la rivoluzione napoletana*, 2nd edn (Bologna: Cappelli, 1969); Pepe, *Memoirs*, 2, pp. 251–53; De Attellis, *L'ottimestre costituzionale*, pp. 163ff.

FIGURE 9. The entry of General Guglielmo Pepe into Naples, 9 July 1820 (lithograph by Johann Moritz Rugendas, Augsburg, 1820; Museo di San Martino, Naples). Image: Brown Digital Repository, https://repository.library.brown.edu/studio/item /bdr:244506, with permission

opinions and a member of the Carboneria in Naples, tried to prevent the entry of the army by gathering on the same Campo with three hundred other members of the carbonaro lodges of the capital, including many students and members of the national guard. There they issued a manifesto asking Pepe to remain in the city of Gaeta, set up a provisional government there, and maintain his temporary dictatorship until such time as the constitution had been fully implemented. The manifesto demanded also the immediate and free distribution of copies of the constitution to the population, the abolition of the Bourbon police and the reinstatement of the army officers who had been made redundant after 1815.[108] For them, the concentration of civilians alongside the army and on the outskirts of the city was required to preempt any counterrevolutionary moves. Pepe, on the contrary, had decided to hasten the transfer of the army into the city not only to forestall negotiations with the carbonaro lodges, which might have undermined his authority, but also because he feared popular disturbances and disorders in the capital. The Muratist general therefore sought to exert a far tighter control over popular mobilisation than the radical wings of the army would for their part have wished. According to De Attellis, such a large presence of *paesani* at the mass gathering on the Campo di Marte preceding the entry into Naples had been resented by Pepe, who had indeed tried to prevent it, as 'he perhaps preferred this to be considered not a national movement but only a sectarian and military revolt'.[109]

Disagreements about the nature of popular participation therefore were linked to disagreements about the actual objectives of the revolution. Whereas in Naples the tensions between carbonari and Muratists did not result in open confrontation, in Portugal political conflicts within the army gave rise to subsequent pronunciamientos. In Portugal too, popular mobilisation and civilian participation were used to justify further military intervention and, as had happened in Naples, their desirability and legitimacy became a bone of contention. Political disagreements account for the organisation of a second, failed military pronunciamiento in November 1820, the so-called Martinhada, in which an unlikely alliance was forged between radical officers led by Captain Bernardo de Sá Nogueira and anti-revolutionary military forces who wanted the end of the constitutional experiment, *against* the existing revolutionary government led by Marshal Gaspar Teixeira de Magalhães e Lacerda, general-in-chief of

108. De Attellis, *L'ottimestre costituzionale*, pp. 150–51, 153–56.
109. Ibid., p. 163.

the Army of the North. The radical elements within the army, supported by the artisans' corporations of the city of Lisbon, their institution, the Casa dos Vinte e Quatro, and its leading official the *juíz do povo* (people's judge), were not satisfied with the political conduct of events after the creation of a provisional government, fearing first that what would be summoned was the old traditional Cortes assembling the three estates, and then resenting the call for the election of a constituent assembly, which they saw as a dilatory tactic to prevent the immediate introduction of the Spanish constitution.[110] On 11 November the troops and cavalry of the *pronunciados* occupied the Rossio square, and soon after the army officers and the juíz do povo, gathering in the Casa do governo, swore an oath to the Spanish constitution, committed themselves to its immediate implementation and demanded the co-optation of their representatives into the government. The government and army responded swiftly, however: by the 17th, the coup had been defeated and its leader arrested. The justification for his actions provided by Nogueira during the trial that followed his incarceration on the one hand, and the attacks levelled at him by the constitutional and pro-government press on the other, demonstrate the extent to which the legitimacy of military interventions depended on proving that they had had the endorsement of the entire and sovereign people, and also the existence of conflicting opinions about the legitimacy of such claims. Once arrested, Nogueira defended his attempted coup by arguing that the support given by the Casa dos Vinte e Quatro, that is to say the institution representing all the artisans of the city of Lisbon, and the city garrison, as well as the people of the capital, justified his decision. The public demonstration of the citizens of Lisbon who on the night of 17 November had gathered in great numbers in the main square of Rossio shouting 'Long live the Spanish constitution!' demonstrated the full popular support there was for demands for the immediate implementation of the Cádiz Constitution. Nogueira also justified military intervention by arguing that, as the events of Spain, Naples and Portugal had already shown, since sovereignty belonged only and exclusively to the nation, the army could act on its behalf only temporarily and during the time needed to set up a full representative government.[111] The revolutionary press, siding with the provisional government, on the contrary criticised such intervention unreservedly, rejecting the claim that the nation supported it. For the

110. Valente, *Os militares*, pp. 64–69. See details also in *Mnemosine Constitucional*, no. 43, 13 November 1820, p. 3.
111. AHM, Arquivo Particular de Sá da Bandeira, 3/18/02, 4 December 1820.

moderate liberal *Astro da Lusitania*, the juíz do povo—the leading official of
the Casa dos Vinte e Quatro, elected by the artisans—and the army officials
involved in the Martinhada were individuals who could properly claim to
represent neither the entire Portuguese nation nor the city of Lisbon. As a
consequence, their initiative represented only an act of despotism carried
out by a faction, enforced with violence upon the capital.[112]

What often remained controversial among the army officers was not
only the extent of popular participation, but also the relationship to be
established between the revolutionary army and the civil authorities
in the transition from provisional juntas to the establishment of a fully
autonomous constitutional government. Following the script inaugurated
by the anti-Napoleonic rebellion after 1808, these insurrections were
marked by the creation of temporary juntas which included a combination
of army officers and civilians who claimed to act on behalf of the nation.
As discussed earlier, it was in Spain that this phenomenon was replicated
most promptly, and in most cities across the country, but following military intervention provisional juntas were set up widely across southern
Europe: in Porto, as well as in the cities of the Kingdom of Two Sicilies, in
the Piedmontese cities of Alessandria and Asti, and across the Peloponnese as well.

Members of the army were divided over the question of whether to
keep the population and the army in a state of constant mobilisation in
order to protect the revolution, or to disband it once a provisional government had declared its allegiance to the constitution. They were also
divided over whether and when these temporary juntas, giunte or committees should be disbanded. In Spain, although a provisional revolutionary
government (Junta de Gobierno) had been established in March, and the
king had sworn an oath of allegiance to the constitution in July during a
session of the newly elected Cortes, the revolutionary army of Quiroga and
Riego had continued to remain stationed on the outskirts of Cádiz, at Isla
de León. The officers considered its presence there a guarantee of the survival of the revolution and a necessary precaution to protect the constitution. However, the government demanded that the constitutional army be
disbanded. As a sweetener, Riego was offered the post of captain general
of Galicia, but rather than assuming it immediately, he went to Madrid to
negotiate with the monarch and the government regarding the survival
of his battalions. Once in the capital, he made an impassioned defence of
the role the army had played and would have wished to continue to play,

---

112. *Astro da Lusitania*, no. 8, 15 November 1820.

challenging allegations that its survival would have represented a threat to the Cortes and a potential source of political interference.[113]

Although Riego's and Quiroga's demands were ultimately ignored and their army disbanded, their conduct during the first nine months of the revolution was taken as a point of reference by the Neapolitan and Piedmontese revolutionaries when arguing over the need to maintain the revolutionary army in defence of the constitution. The Spanish script was therefore present in the mind of the Spaniards' Italian counterparts when discussing the benefits of maintaining a constitutional army in defence of the constitution far from the capital city. Orazio De Attellis had argued against the constitutional army entering Naples, and in favour of relocating it to the city of Gaeta in order to guarantee the smooth implementation of the constitution, with reference to Riego's army. Gugliemo Pepe, too, although hostile to this opinion, when addressing the Neapolitan parliament in October, justified his decision to take the army into the capital and to renounce his title as head of the constitutional army with reference to Spanish events. For Pepe, the equivalent of the army of the Isla the León was not needed in the Kingdom of the Two Sicilies, as the constitution enjoyed the support of the monarchy and the parliament, and no longer needed protection.[114] Riego's address to the nation and the Cortes of October 1820, in which he asserted the allegiance of his army to the constitution against allegations of his own authoritarian tendencies, was republished by the press in Naples, where it was taken as evidence of his selfless dedication to the nation.[115]

Piedmontese revolutionaries for their part embraced the same revolutionary script, whereby army officers were viewed as guardians of the constitution, insofar as its survival needed to be safeguarded. In two long articles appearing in the only periodical published during the Piedomontese revolution, *La Sentinella Subalpina*, Giuseppe Crivelli praised the conduct of Guglielmo Ansaldi, the military governor of Alessandria, who had consistently acted in defence of the constitutional order, in this regard following in the footsteps of Riego and Quiroga's army at the Isla de León. In his view, the decisions to maintain the defence of the garrison in Alessandria and strengthen it with the aid of civilian forces were taken in the name of moderation and stability, to prevent a civil war and defend

113. Alberto Gil Novales, *El Trienio Liberal* (Madrid: Siglo XXI España, 1980), pp. 18–20.

114. Moscati, *Guglielmo Pepe*, 1, pp. 112–14.

115. *L'Imparziale*, 14 November 1820, p. 1.

the constitutional regime, as Quiroga, Riego, Pepe, Filangieri, Carrascosa and the Portuguese officers had done.[116]

Conflicts and debates that emerged around the organisation and the consolidation of the revolutionary order therefore demonstrate that the claim to be acting on behalf of popular sovereignty was universally asserted, but the meaning of national sovereignty was ambiguous, and its interpretation could lead to a multiplicity of behaviours. What the various ways in which the armies interacted with local and national authorities, as well as with the civilian population, show is the flexibility and adaptability of their military strategies, and the plurality of possible interpretations of a revolutionary script based on an otherwise shared template.

Conclusions

The surprising success of the pronunciamientos lay not so much in well-organised military campaigns, or in victories on the battlefield against hostile troops, which in fact were few and far between, but rather in the ability of their organisers to build a consensus and coordinate public demands for change both in the ranks and among civilians, across the territories of their respective states. This was possible also thanks to the support of well-planned communications campaigns. In spite of differences of opinion about the desirability or otherwise of mobilising the people, all the organisers implemented a strategy of 'forceful negotiations' that combined public calls for change with displays of loyalty to the existing authorities. Admittedly, compared to its Portuguese, Spanish, Piedmontese and Neapolitan equivalents, Ypsilantis's revolt represented a much more radical challenge to authority. However, like any of the other southern European pronunciamientos, its force lay primarily in its capacity to mobilise opposition in the Greek lands of the Ottoman Empire with the aim of renegotiating the terms of imperial rule and allowing a higher degree of autonomy, rather than acquiring fully-fledged independence. Like Riego's expedition, Ypsilantis's military campaign failed in itself; but as I hope this chapter has demonstrated, although popular participation varied from place to place, and from region to region, in intensity and scale, it is impossible to dismiss these revolutionary events as solely military revolts devoid of any larger support. The local populations did in fact rally to these revolts in urban centres and, in many regions, in small villages also (for instance, in the provinces surrounding Naples) and among the peasantry

---

116. *La Sentinella Subalpina*, 21 March 1821, p. 11.

(in the Peloponnese and Roumeli). This support arose from a wide variety of political and material circumstances, related to a crisis of legitimacy suffered by the existing governments, but was facilitated by pre-existing secret society networks. In all cases, however, armed officers sought to capitalise on the language of national liberation, producing a script that justified their intervention in the name of popular sovereignty—a sovereignty legitimised by the popular revolts against French expansionism and in defence of the existing monarchies—and by making explicit reference to contemporary Spanish revolutionary events. They did so primarily in the name of nations as communities, without putting much emphasis on the need to defend individual rights. As the next chapter will discuss, beyond this veneer of unanimity and in spite of their success, the pronunciamientos would soon uncover pre-existing tensions and disagreements among the military and civilian elites of each of their societies that would ignite new and violent conflicts and lead to widespread civil strife.

CHAPTER THREE

Civil Wars

ARMIES, GUERRILLA WARFARE AND MOBILISATION IN THE RURAL WORLD

THE EXISTENCE OF BROAD coalitions in favour of political change in the ranks of the various armies had guaranteed the success of the revolution in Portugal, Spain, Piedmont and Naples, and had precipitated the anti-Ottoman uprising in Greece. However, changing political circumstances, notably the alliance between anti-revolutionary elites and monarchical institutions, would soon shake such a consensus. The temporary rapprochements between different groups and factions within the armies created on the eve of the revolutions was not slow to collapse. While the revolutions had prompted military reforms on the basis of the principle of the nation in arms, they also gave rise to discontent and hostility among some sectors of the military classes, for such reforms undermined privileges, disrupted careers and affected the existing make-up of the armies. The desire felt by monarchs to get rid of the constitutional guarantees they had earlier been forced to accept sowed division within the armies themselves. In Greece too, the enthusiasm for Ypsilantis's military intervention, which had fuelled the insurrection, was soon replaced by divisions and clashes between warlords and chieftains primarily concerned with the shoring up of their own local power. In spite of the much-mythologised eirenic nature of the military interventions, in most countries—the case of the Greek insurrections being an exception—the armies became entangled in conflicts in which regular and irregular forces interacted constantly. In their most acute form, such conflicts led to fully-fledged civil wars. As a consequence, armed forces continued to be protagonists also during the revolutions, and army officers continued to play a crucial role as political actors until the end of the revolutionary experiments.

In the section that follows, I highlight the various ways in which army leaders continued to be at the centre of politics, propounded competing notions of national interest and popular sovereignty and became entangled in political tussles that soon escalated into civil strife. While the outbreak of civil wars is only explicable in relation to specific local as well as national contexts, in all countries the pronunciamientos became the catalyst for a set of political and regional crises that undermined the revolutions from within. The conflict between Sicily and Naples and within Sicily itself, the civil wars between the northern regions of Portugal (Trás-os-Montes in particular) and the rest of the country, between Navarre and the Basque countries and the Spanish constitutional government, and between the Peloponnese, continental Greece and the islands, opposed supporters of the constitutional orders to their enemies, but also divided advocates of different models of state organisation. The territorial and local basis of these civil conflicts encouraged popular participation in them: all of these armed disputes were associated with considerable degrees of civilian mobilisation and guerrilla warfare. This phenomenon had much to do with the peculiar features of each of these countries' agrarian societies. From Portugal to Greece, the revolutionary or counterrevolutionary movements did in fact capitalise on the traditional bonds of allegiance existing at a local level between landowners, village leaders, religious classes and the peasantry in rural societies, whereby armed groups were recruited. Their existence often overlapped with that of banditry and of other forms of rural violence. Admittedly, these were not entirely new phenomena. In some regions (in particular in Sicily with the so-called *bande*, and in the Ottoman lands with the klephts and armatoloi), armed groups had been a traditional feature of society, closely linked to the defence of land owner-ship or local communities, or to the administration of border regions. In the previous two decades or so, administrative reforms from the centre had exacerbated the existing conflicts in these rural societies, and prepared the ground for further violence. In other areas (Spain and Portugal in partic-ular), it was the Napoleonic wars that had led to an unprecedented escala-tion of new types of violence and the organisation of partidas—partisan units that would either be acting independently, or else would be deployed to support regular armies.[1] Yet during the 1820s these informal armed

1. For Spain and the Ottoman lands, see the previous chapter; for Portugal, see also Valente, 'O povo em armas'.

units served new political purposes in the context of the cleavages and conflicts created by the revolutions.

In particular, civil wars stimulated the mobilisation of rural populations and above all of the peasantry, leading many of them to take up arms. As I suggested earlier, the rural world had not been in principle hostile to the revolutions. Although peasants did not rise up in support of the revolution in Spain and Portugal, they did not oppose it either. In Sicily and the Peloponnese, their mobilisation coincided with the very beginning of the insurrections, and intensified during the civil war. The active participation of the peasantry in these civil conflicts needs to be understood in relation not only to the new ideological, territorial and political conflicts occasioned by the establishment of the new regimes, but also to the pre-existing conditions prevailing in the rural world and to the nature of its property relations. From Portugal to Greece, the rural world was indeed in crisis. The short-term economic reasons for this crisis have been briefly sketched above. What needs to be added here is the fact that, in the previous two decades, the adverse effect of the Napoleonic wars, and the legal measures implemented to abolish seigneurial jurisdiction in Spain, Naples and Sicily, had left the rural world in turmoil, intensified rural unrest and exacerbated conflicts within local communities. In Spain, what intensified pre-existing tensions between peasant communities and their landlords was the abolition by the Cortes in 1811 of seigneurial jurisdiction, a reform whereby landlords became simply landowning proprietors, and the decision, approved in 1813, to sell and privatise communal lands owned by villages and municipal authorities (*tierras baldías y propias*). These measures affected a large proportion of the kingdom's rural inhabitants. At the beginning of the century in Spain, the extent of seigneurial jurisdiction varied from province to province, but only just over half of the land was in private hands. In the provinces of Galicia and Valencia, for instance, the overwhelming majority of communities were subject to seigneurial jurisdiction: in Galicia, only twenty-eight communities were under direct royal administration, as against 380 under seigneurial jurisdiction, and 290 under ecclesiastical jurisdiction.[2] Following the reform of 1811, the fact that landlords from then on had to have their property rights validated by local authorities led to the contestation of such rights by communities, land occupations and refusals by peasants to pay their landlords those dues they still owed them as their tenants. At the same time, the sale of communal lands reinforced the local rural

2. Hamnett, *La política española*, p. 149.

middle classes only, and frustrated peasants' hopes and expectations of acquiring their own plots of land. The return of absolutism aggravated further social tensions in the countryside. The partial reintroduction of seigneurial rights in 1814, with the exclusion of monopolies and exclusive privileges, was interpreted all too broadly by many feudal lords, who seized the opportunity to reclaim illegally old impositions over their tenants. Reasons for resentment therefore grew and festered in rural communities, which submitted complaints to local authorities. The land occupations started by the abolition of feudalism of 1813 continued.[3] Something similar took place in the same period in Naples. At the beginning of the century in the Kingdom of the Two Sicilies, a much higher proportion of land was under seigneurial jurisdiction, amounting to 80 or 90 per cent of the total. Although tensions between villages and feudal lords over rights and duties had always existed, these were intensified dramatically by the the decision taken in 1806 by Joseph Bonaparte, then king of Napoleonic Naples, to abolish feudalism. This law privatised the former feudal lands, converting privileges and revenues of non-feudal origin into rent and private properties, and abolishing the remaining seigneurial rights. It envisaged the privatisation and distribution of the *terre demaniali*, the common land owned by communities, among their members. The customary rights (*usi civici*) formerly enjoyed by these would be abolished, and compensated with the distribution of former feudal lands.[4] In practice, however, the application of this principle proved difficult. The division of the land between former feudal lords and communities required to start the process of their privatisation and distribution was almost invariably contentious. What prevented the distribution of commons was their illegal occupation, not only by former feudal lords but also by private owners who took the opportunity of privatisations to acquire yet more land. As the following pages make plain, while the conflicts arising from these reforms were widespread, it was not in the Neapolitan provinces, but rather in Sicily that the eruption of a civil war coincided with a generalised peasant mobilisation. On the island itself the introduction of anti-feudal legislation coincided with British occupation and the introduction of a Sicilian constitution in 1812. It was here that the collapse of the feudal system and the dismantling of feudal militias paved the way to the emergence of powerful middlemen, a sort of agrarian middle-class, the *gabellotti*, who

3. Ibid., pp. 152–55, 158–59, 221–23; Fontana, *La quiebra*, pp. 197–202.

4. On Naples, see Davis, *Naples and Napoleon*, pp. 234–36; on Sicily, see also Orazio Cancila, *L'economia della Sicilia: Aspetti storici* (Milan: Il Saggiatore, 1992), pp. 107–20.

owned properties and organised armed groups in defence of large landed interests. The violence associated with the protection of these interests in the Sicilian countryside, a violence long predating the 1812 reforms, increased and exploded between 1820 and 1821.

In Portugal too, most of the land was under seigneurial jurisdiction, and by the end of the eighteenth century only 40 per cent of it was directly controlled by the crown. Although in Portugal—in contrast to Spain, Naples and Sicily—no substantial attempt to reform the feudal jurisdiction had been attempted by 1820, pre-existing conflicts and anti-seigneurial movements in its rural society intensified as much as anywhere else in the decade before the revolution. In order to tackle the economic crisis that afflicted the kingdom at the end of the Napoleonic wars, the government tried to stimulate agriculture through a set of measures whose consequences proved controversial, especially for the poorest strata of the agricultural world and for villages. The government attempted with little success to raise money by selling properties owned by the crown, in the hope that this measure might stimulate the emergence of a new propertied class committed to increasing the productivity of the countryside. It was more successful, however, in encouraging and facilitating the occupation, sale and permanent lease (*aforamento*) of unexploited *baldios* (communal lands), all measures it thought would contribute to the same goal of increasing agricultural profits. In 1815 it decreed that such lands would be exempted from taxation, along with the hitherto uncultivated lands owned by *donatários* (as the holders of seigneurial rights were called), which were finally put to profitable use by tenants. Admittedly, some attempts had been made since 1800 to distribute the baldios also among landless peasants. However, lack of liquidity and of access to credit forced most of them to sell whatever small properties they had recently acquired. These measures therefore benefited first and foremost wealthier farmers and middle-range property owners. They created a great deal of resentment in rural communities, whose access to village lands was reduced, while their chances to supplement their income by cattle farming were likewise eroded. The economic depression acted as a trigger for yet more conflicts and turmoil. In the years before the revolution it intensified tensions between different communities competing for access to land, but led above all to an increase in anti-seigneurial protests. Communities, groups of rural labourers and villagers refused to honour their fiscal obligations, or questioned the rates that had been set. Hostility and protests against the leasing of common land and feudal dues therefore set small farmers, villagers and village authorities (who benefited from the income produced by the communal lands) at odds with large cattle ranchers and landowners, and rural communities at loggerheads with the rural middlemen representing the holders of seigneurial rights.[5]

As in Portugal, so too in the territories of the Ottoman Empire where the revolution broke out in 1821, no radical reform of land ownership had been attempted in the previous decades. Unlike its Portuguese, Spanish or Neapolitan and Sicilian counterparts, the Greek peasantry did not seem to have any specific aspirations as regards any 'land question'. Greek peasants worked as sharecroppers or as farmers at fixed rents on large, privately owned estates (*çiftliks*) and, to a lesser extent on semi-public estates such as the timars, as hereditary tenants. Timars were by origin military fiefs granted by the sultan to his cavalry officers or officials, a type of property in decline by the early nineteenth century. In the areas with the highest concentration of Christian populations, the largest landed properties tended to be in the hands of a few Muslim families. Christian notables in the Peloponnese and the Morea also owned substantial estates, but these were smaller in size than those owned by Muslims, and rarely amounted to more than 200–400 hectares. While many peasants owned privately their houses and gardens, and had access to village communal properties, as in the rest of southern Europe, a section of the rural workforce was made up of landless (and often itinerant) peasants.

Those agricultural workers who were lucky enough to lease land not only owed a share of their produce to the landlord, but had to pay taxes (tithes) on the rest of their harvests. What peasants bitterly resented was precisely the fiscal regime associated with the existing landed property system. The increase in taxation in the decades before the revolution intensified a pre-existing tendency on the part of the peasantry to abandon lowlands and agriculture and move to mountainous areas and villages where conditions of living were hard and estates much smaller, but governmental controls and tax burdens could be avoided. This trend in turn increased pressure on those who remained behind to work in agricultural areas of the lowlands, as village taxes were based on population size but were rarely revised to take demographic change into account.[6] As a consequence, the

5. José Tengarrinha, *Movimentos populares agrários em Portugal (1751–1825)*, 2 vols (Lisbon: Publicações Europa-América, 1994), 2, pp. 67–72, 122–25.

6. William W. McGrew, *Land and Revolution in Modern Greece 1800–1881: The Transition in the Tenure and Exploitation of Land from Ottoman Rule to Independence* (Kent, OH: The Kent State University Press, 1985), pp. 10–12; Socrates D. Petmezas, 'The Land Issue in the Greek War of Independence: A Reappraisal', working paper, presented at conference '1821: What Made It Greek and Revolutionary?', organised by Yannis Kotsonis and Ada Dialla, Athens, July 2018.

rural world in the Greek-speaking provinces of the Ottoman Empire, as much as that of the rest of southern Europe, was far from free of tensions.

Admittedly, no simple relationship can be established between the material conditions and exploitation of farmers and peasants and their participation in the civil strife that erupted during the revolutions. However, it is undeniable that the nature of the organisation of rural communities, and the way in which property relations and taxation had affected the countryside in the previous two decades, shaped peasants' expectations on the eve of the revolutions. These factors help us understand what the demands of the rural world during the revolutions were, and the extent to which the revolutionary regimes managed to meet them or not. They also represent the background against which their armed mobilisation came about during the civil conflicts that broke out soon afterwards.

In the pages that follow, I will explore the different ways in which civil wars undermined the initial support for revolution, in the armies and in the population (both urban and rural) at large, and polarised public opinion for or against it. Notwithstanding their regional peculiarities and differences, these conflicts displayed some shared features. First of all, they rendered relations between military and civilian classes at best fluid, controversial and contentious. Military leaders acted in favour of or against constitutional government, or sought to revise it; but by so doing they took on a visibility and influence that went beyond that of the army. Second, such conflicts politicised society to unprecedented degrees, as direct experience of war or violence, along with propaganda, forced communities and individuals to take sides, if not to engage in military activities. As a consequence, it was around a number of prominent army officers and guerrilla leaders that political affiliations were defined. The first section below looks at Portugal. It shows the extent to which in this country, military pronunciamientos became an effective tool of political intervention, marking each stage of the cycle between revolution, counterrevolution and constitutional reform during the entire decade. In Spain, the subject of the second section below, escalation of a civil war divided society and the armed forces, just as it did in Portugal. But there more than anywhere else, it was the appointment of military leaders as captains general of each province that proved politically critical, triggering popular reactions across the country. The third section goes on to discuss the civil war in Sicily. It looks at the impact that the movement for independence had in dividing public opinion on the island itself, and in producing new military heroes with large followings which, as their participation in the separatist guerrilla warfare demonstrated, reflected traditional social hierarchies. As elsewhere, the civil war in Sicily lent the constitutional army renewed visibility and political influence, but its conduct in the war also gave rise to political controversy. Finally, the chapter goes on to consider the Greek revolution. It explores the difficult integration into the new revolutionary order of the Ottoman military classes, which strove to retain their autonomy against any administrative control, whether old or new. While the success of the revolution depended upon the support of these military chieftains in the fight against the Ottomans, the civilian revolutionary leadership struggled to guarantee their allegiance and subordination. Thus in Greece the military classes, while essential to the fight for emancipation, were also the most reluctant across all of southern Europe to subject themselves to civilian authorities. It was this reluctance that produced divisions among them and led to civil wars.

Portugal and political change through military pronunciamientos

In Portugal, more than anywhere else, the pronunciamiento became the main instrument of political intervention on behalf of or against the constitution. While military pronunciamientos were organised in Spain at the end of the Trienio by constitutional officers exiled abroad on account of their failed attempts to put an end to Fernando's absolutism, it was in Portugal more than elsewhere that army officers continued to intervene after 1820 by determining the end or the introduction of a new constitution by military intervention. The constant resort to this practice triggered a continuous cycle of civil wars and divided the country and its population for over a decade. In 1820 the army's desire to recall the monarch from Brazil and free itself from British tutelage had united liberal and conservative army officers around a common goal. But disputes between supporters and enemies of the constitution would soon arise. While such divisions had existed already in 1820, the dynastic crisis arising from 1823 onwards catalysed them by offering conflicting sources of legitimacy. This dynastic crisis produced deep political divisions that cut across the entirety of Portuguese society, and military intervention gave a voice to them. In Portugal military activism therefore interacted with, and became the main trigger for, a remarkable degree of popular mobilisation both in favour of and against the revolution, although its intensity varied from case to case. In the years between 1823 and 1834 military officers were successful in gaining the support of substantial sectors of the urban populations of the cities, from where they launched their military and political challenge to the enemy. What the turbulent history of Portugal in the 1820s shows is the extent to which the pronunciamiento itself became a 'bipartisan' device of military intervention. Military initiatives in the name of the nation could also be deployed by the enemies of the revolution and of the constitution. Between 1823 and 1827 all the military interventions that took place either aimed at dismantling the constitutional order, or at establishing more moderate versions of it. In 1828, when Dom Miguel seized power and withdrew the constitution granted by his brother in 1826, a new wave of pronunciamientos in favour of the constitution was released. Between 1823 and 1824 three attempts (the first and the third failed, while the second proved successful) were made to dismantle the liberal order by military means. All of them enjoyed a degree of popular support. The peculiarity of the second and third attempts was that the challenge to the political status quo was no longer coming from sectors of the army or the elites alone. Indeed, they had been organised with the full support and under the leadership of a key member of the royal family, the heir to the throne, Dom Miguel. These events demonstrate how the role of the monarchy was crucial to guaranteeing eventual success. Royal leadership was key to the fate of these military initiatives, as it could ensure sufficient support among the army and the population.

The rebellion led by the Count of Amarante in the Portuguese region of Trás-os-Montes in February 1823 can help us to understand both the complex nature of the military counterrevolutionary movement, its professional, class and regional origins and its relationship with its broader social context.[7] This was primarily an aristocratic affair, led by a clan which had considered the constitutional experiment to be an attack upon its rank and class interests. In the case of the Count of Amarante, family connections also played an important role.[8] The leaders of the rebellions were, alongside Amarante, two of his uncles, Gaspar Teixeira de Magalhães and António da Silveira, who had been nothing less than the president of the former provisional junta of governing the kingdom, and his cousins Luís and José Vaz Pereira Pinto Guedes. Yet behind this aristocratic military leadership there was broader support from the army stationed in the region. The core group of the military officers loyal to Amarante had refused to join the constitutional rebellion from the very outset because of their loyalty to the absolute monarchy, while others had changed sides later on, as a result of their disappointment with the revolutionary policies

7. A thorough discussion of these events is in Cardoso, *A revolução liberal*, pp. 138–62.
8. Cardoso, *A revolução liberal*, pp. 146–47.

towards the army. In 1821 the ancient system of the *ordenanças*, the territorial organisation of the army that had attributed to each *capitão mor*, generally chosen from among the local aristocracy by the câmaras, the power to draft soldiers, was abolished, along with a separate military judicial system, the *foro pessoal*. This decision was not only designed to reinforce the central authorities' control over the territories (the office of *capitão* was abolished in times of peace, and provincial militias were created), but was also aimed at weakening social and professional privileges. Aristocratic officers, however, had considered the abolition of the ordenanças and of the *foro* as a direct attack on themselves, and resented them bitterly.[9] Support for Amarante's revolt therefore benefited from the frustration of aristocratic officers with the new military reforms.

Significantly, these counterrevolutionary pronunciamientos employed rituals and communication strategies strikingly similar to those adopted by the officers who had rebelled in the name of the constitution. Like their revolutionary counterparts, counterrevolutionary officers sought popular support, issued proclamations addressing various audiences, from the army to local communities, regions and the entire nation, and tried to distribute these as broadly as possible to justify and legitimise their actions. The military insurgency was timed to coincide with the start of a religious procession setting out from the church of the Misericórdia in the city of Vila Real, when Amarante, surrounded by a number of local landowners and followed by a throng of civilians and shouting 'Viva o rei absoluto, morra a constituição!' (Long live the absolute king, death to the constitution) proceeded on horseback to the town hall. There, along with the army officers and the civilian authorities, he took an oath of allegiance to the monarch. A Te Deum followed to celebrate the return to absolute rule. The cavalry invited the inhabitants of Vila Real to appear at the windows of their homes and demonstrate their support.[10] The troops then proceeded to the city of Chaves where similar public ceremonies and displays of popular enthusiasm took place. Here Amarante, in front of members of the câmara, divided into nobility, clergy and people, as tradition dictated,

9. See Arnaldo da Silva Marques Pata, *Revolução e cidadania: Organização, funcionamento e ideologia da Guarda Nacional (1820–39)* (Lisbon: Colibri, 2004), pp. 23–25; Fernando Pereira Marques, *Exército, mudança e modernização na primeira metade do século XIX* (Lisbon: Cosmos, Instituto de Defesa Nacional, 1999), pp. 25–48. See also the decree of abolition and the debate around it in *Diário das cortes geraes e extraordinárias da nação portugueza*, 7 vols (Lisbon: Imprensa Nacional, 1821–22), 3, no. 144, 4 August 1821, p. 176.

10. Santos, *Documentos*, 1, pp. 596–97.

declared the creation of a provisional regency in the name of the monarch, and was acclaimed by all those present.[11]

His revolt enjoyed some support among the local peasantry. In this province, what prevailed was the direct cultivation of small properties, with rye, maize and potato featuring prominently. Besides the cultivation of these crops, farmers typically engaged in cattle farming, an activity for which they took due advantage of common land. Most of the land they cultivated was subjected to multiple fiscal obligations and impositions. Farmers owed a rent to their feudal lord, depending on the type of contract to which they were subject—most commonly contracts of emphyteusis (*enfiteuse*), or lease (*arrendamento*). They also paid the tithe to the Church. As dwellers in villages subject either to royal or to feudal jurisdiction, they moreover paid as a community the so-called foral rights (*direitos de foral*), to the donatários or to the crown. In Trás-os-Montes these dues were much lower than in other parts of Portugal; consequently there it was rent that represented the heaviest financial burden for farmers.[12] During and after the constitutional period, intermittently, protests, some even violent in nature, erupted to contest decisions taken by the câmaras to demand that the community contribute to public works, or to crack down on smuggling; but these often did not take on explicit ideological overtones in favour of or against the constitution, and remained localised in nature and in the aspirations they expressed.[13] In 1823, however, what mobilised peasants against the constitutional regime was the fact that the reforms enacted by it were at the same time insufficient and detrimental to their interests. In 1821 the government decided to protect by its *lei dos cereais* (grain law) the interests of Portuguese grain producers against Spanish competition, in the hope that this would encourage the cultivation of waste lands and the development of agriculture. The immediate effect, much resented by peasants, was a sudden and steep increase in the price of their staple foods (bread in particular). At the same time the partial abolition of seigneurial rights put into effect in 1822, when the *direitos de foral* were cut by half, had only a limited impact on most rural communities in Trás-os-Montes, where their rate was modest. Conversely, the heaviest burdens for the farmers, namely, the rates set by their lease, and other obligations stipulated in their contracts, which had often increased

11. Cardoso, *A revolução liberal*, pp. 140–41.

12. Ibid., pp. 43–47.

13. See, for instance, the cases discussed in Tengarrinha, *Movimentos populares*, 2, pp. 196–200.

steadily in the previous decades, were left untouched.[14] In 1823, therefore, it was precisely the hostility towards the new law protecting grain production that encouraged the mobilisation of rural communities in support of the Count of Amarante, to cries of 'Viva o rei!' and 'Morra a constituição!'[15]

A few guerrilla groups were organised by local landowners, and groups of villagers assaulted constitutional troops coming into the province. In retaliation for this vocal backing given to the rebellion and for its open hostility to the constitutional troops, the village of Trindade was torched, in execution of martial law under the orders of the constitutional General Pego.[16] Yet these acts of defiance did not spill over into a general rebellion of the province. Likewise, the support of the army was not unanimous, and some of the regiments that had been expected to lend their support in the end did not. In Chaves, the troops joined the rebels, and so did the majority of the regiments stationed in Bragança. The troops in Minho and Beira, however, opted to remain loyal to the government, took the opportunity to renew their allegiance to the constitution and had a hand in the suppression of the revolt. To understand the limited support for this intervention, we need to take into account the role of the king. In spite of Amarante's public declarations that the king had to be freed, the monarch in fact did not support his rebellion, and this did much to undermine it. In the end, the excessively reactionary nature of the pronunciamiento, along with monarchical hostility, determined its failure. If many army officers beyond those closely associated with Amarante were critical of the constitutional regime, they may not all have been ready to revert to absolutism. Therefore, in spite of an early and unexpected victory against the constitutional troops in Santa Bárbara on 13 March, the revolt was soon crushed, the introduction of martial law preventing any further popular unrest.[17]

Only three months later, however, a new military intervention, the so-called Vilafrancada, was successful in putting an end to the Portuguese Triénio. A number of factors determined this outcome. Although the Vilafrancada reflected mounting dissatisfaction with the constitutional regime,

14. Cardoso, *A revolução liberal*, pp. 109, 110, 121–22.

15. Ibid., pp. 143–44.

16. José Sebastião de Saldanha Oliveira e Daun, *Diorama de Portugal nos 33 mezes constitucionaes, ou Golpe de vista sobre a revolução de 1820, a Constituição de 1822, a Restauração de 1823* [. . .] (Lisbon: Impressão Regia, 1823), p. 161.

17. On this battle and the final defeat, see Cardoso, *A revolução liberal*, pp. 149–50, 151–54.

and occurred in the context of a public opinion increasingly hostile to it, what accounted for the success of this second royalist pronunciamiento was in fact the support of the crown, as well as the favourable international context, that had further isolated the Portuguese constitutional government. It took place at the end of May, on the 27th, just three days after the military occupation of Madrid by the French army.

Its leader was a member of the royal family, the young son of the Dom João VI, Dom Miguel, who acted with the support of some sectors of the army, and in particular with the army regiments based in Lisbon. What rendered this new initiative more appealing than the one that had failed three months before was an ideological distancing from Amarante's nostalgia for absolutism. Admittedly, in his public announcement of 27 May 1823 from the town of Vila Franca, Dom Miguel was at some pains to recall the valorous attempts of Amarante. He thus referred to the 'generous transmontanos', who, he said, had begun the fightback against the revolutionaries. He even made so bold as to repudiate the events of 24 August 1820 which, instead of effecting the restoration of ancient national rights, had in fact, he claimed, brought about the nation's ruin, the transformation of monarchical power to a mere shadow of itself. Crucially, however, Dom Miguel's political language was different, representing as it did an attempt to reconcile liberalism with the rights of the monarchy. He in no way intended, he thus declared, to 'restore despotism [. . .] or take revenge', and called for the liberation of the king from his servitude, so that he might be free to grant a constitution tainted neither by despotism nor by licence.[18]

This moderate political stance encouraged support from broader sectors of the army, as it could appeal both to staunch absolutists and former revolutionaries. First conceived in Lisbon, the coup started when the twenty-third regiment, stationed in the castle, agreed to join the cavalry led by Dom Miguel himself outside the city on the early morning of 27 May, to proceed to the town of Vila Franca. Soon after the outbreak of the rebellion, however, the majority of the troops garrisoned in Lisbon declared their allegiance to Dom Miguel, who was reached in Vila Franca by other senior army figures.[19] Even a number of prominent radical officers were now ready to endorse this more moderate brand of constitutionalism. This group included Bernardo de Sá Nogueira, who returned now from France,

18. Santos, *Documentos*, 1, pp. 698–99.
19. Maria Alexandre Lousada and Maria de Fátima Sá e Melo Ferreira, *D. Miguel* (Lisbon: Círculo de Leitores, 2009), p. 49.

having gone into exile there after the failed attempt to introduce the Cádiz Constitution in 1820—the so-called Martinhada—to join Dom Miguel's conspiracy. Bernardo Correia de Castro e Sepúlveda, who had been one of the military leaders of the pronunciamiento in Porto in 1820, belonged to this same group. At the beginning of the coup Sepúlveda had remained in Lisbon with his regiment in order to protect the monarch and out of loyalty to the constitutional government. On 30 April he had been forced by the crowds of Lisbon to take an oath to the constitution. Shortly afterwards, however, he defected and left the capital to declare his allegiance to Dom Miguel.[20]

Yet the initiative of Dom Miguel alone, against his father's wishes, might not have been sufficient to guarantee a favourable outcome to his military coup. What determined its ultimate success was, in the end, the attitude of the king himself. João was well known for his indecisiveness. Although he may have been willing to abolish the constitution and introduce a more moderate document in order to curtail Dom Miguel's rebellion, on 30 May he did nonetheless make a public declaration of allegiance to the constitution, condemned his son's conduct, and appointed a new government. In a sudden volte-face that same night, however, he left the capital with a regiment in attendance, whereupon he joined his son in Vila Franca, and there declared, in a public address to the inhabitants of Lisbon, that the current constitution was contrary to 'the will, customs and beliefs of the monarchy', as the violence of the civil war had already demonstrated, and that a new one better suited to the monarchy was needed.[21] This message was reiterated soon after, in a second declaration, issued on 3 June, which represented the events of those days as necessary to rescue 'monarchical dignity' as the only viable and solid foundation of a constitution. While the king dismissed the constitutional experiment as one based on 'subversive and unsubstantiated principles', whose ultimate goal was to 'bury the Portuguese monarchy', he at the same time promised a new constitution that would guarantee the peace. The proclamation shared with the revolutionary ones a promise that the order inaugurated with it would bring public happiness, in this specific case as a royal promise to the Portuguese people.[22]

20. Marianne Baillie, *Lisbon in the Years 1821, 1822, and 1823*, 2 vols (London: John Murray, 1825), 2, p. 175; Victor de Sá, *A crise do liberalismo e as primeiras manifestações das ideias socialistas em Portugal (1820-1852)* (Lisbon: Seara Nova, 1969), pp. 80-81.

21. Santos, *Documentos*, 1, pp. 706, 712.

22. Ibid., pp. 748-49.

This final act not only convinced those sectors of the army that had remained loyal to the constitution to side with the king, but put an end to any popular resistance. The initial popular mobilisation in defence of the constitutional regime in evidence in Lisbon disappeared in the face of the agreement between Miguel and João. As a foreign observer noted, following Dom Miguel's pronunciamiento, the city 'was in tumults from one end to the other', and Dom Miguel's declaration in favour of a new constitution was initially received with hostility.[23] In the capital, in fact, the national guard had at first responded en masse to the call by the municipality to take up arms and assemble in the Praça do Comércio and the Rossio square.[24] Yet such displays of loyalty to the constitution soon evaporated, and popular opinion 'seemed to be rapidly turning in an opposite direction'.[25] When on 5 June the king came back into the capital accompanied by Dom Miguel and by the troops led by Brigadier João Francisco de Saldanha Oliveira e Daun, they were universally acclaimed and the crowds were such that the procession of civil authorities could not reach him to pay their homage before the Te Deum.[26]

In April the following year Dom Miguel intervened militarily once again, but this time his attempt to restore the absolute monarchy failed precisely because of the hostility of his father, pressure from foreign powers and lack of support from large sectors of the army (although Dom Miguel himself was its commander-in-chief). The so-called Abrilada, like the attempted revolt of Amarante, was another ultra-royalist attempt to reintroduce absolute rule that was opposed to any political compromise and driven by hatred for those moderate politicians such as the Counts of Vila Flor and Palmela who were in office at the time. Dom Miguel's bid was supported by Queen Carlota Joaquina, hopeful of becoming regent after deposing the king during Dom Miguel's minority, by the patriarch of Lisbon and by a number of aristocrats who were uncompromising in their royalist beliefs, the Marquis of Abrantes among them, along with most of the officers and troops of the Lisbon garrison. Dom Miguel's justification for this military intervention was his—probably genuine—fear that the life of the monarch was under threat as the freemasons were plotting his death.[27] On 30 April he assembled the troops in the Rossio square, in the heart of Lisbon, where many other military episodes had taken place

23. Baillie, *Lisbon*, 2, p. 171.
24. Santos, *Documentos*, 1, p. 715.
25. Baillie, *Lisbon*, 2, p. 171.
26. Santos, *Documentos*, 1, p. 751.
27. Lousada and Ferreira, *D. Miguel*, pp. 75–84.

FIGURE 10. Dom Miguel as commander-in-chief of the army, 1823 (engraving by António José Quinto, c. 1823; Biblioteca Nacional de Portugal, Lisbon). Image: Wikimedia Commons

in the previous years, and went to see the monarch at the Bemposta Palace to justify his action. The monarch at first justified his son's actions publicly and left him at the head of the army. In line with the script of the earlier, liberal, pronunciamientos, Dom Miguel felt it incumbent upon himself to address both the Portuguese people and the army, and did so on 3 May, pointing to the threat to the country's safety represented by the secret societies. In his manifestos the 'Masonic clubs' were accused of being responsible also for the collapse of the empire and the independence of Brazil.[28] While conceived and enacted in the capital city, the coup gained popular support in the absolutist northern province of Trás-os-Montes, where public displays of rejoicing spontaneously erupted in several villages and towns, and in Vila Real a number of supporters of the

28. Santos, *Documentos*, 1, pp. 861–62.

constitution were arrested.[29] Yet just a week later the swift decision of the king, advised accordingly by European diplomats, to reject his son's initiative, resulted in the collapse of the coup. On 13 May the king summoned his son, who immediately left the country. The regiments involved were disbanded and officers sent back to their regions of origin, while Miguel himself subsequently went into exile in Paris.

The following two years, during which the king in fact failed to introduce a constitution and ended up summoning the traditional Cortes, were relatively calm. Yet the death of João in March 1826 precipitated a new dynastic crisis and created the preconditions for a further wave of absolutist revolts and military pronunciamientos, leading to a fully-fledged civil war. Soon after Dom João's death, his son and successor Dom Pedro IV introduced a new constitutional charter and immediately abdicated the throne of Portugal in favour of his daughter. It was his solemn wish that Dona Maria, the legitimate heir, would marry her uncle, Dom Miguel, who was then living in exile in Vienna. In the absence of both Dona Maria and Dom Miguel from Portugal, another of Dom Pedro's sisters, Dona Isabel Maria, acted as regent in Lisbon. In spite of the oath of allegiance Dom Miguel had sworn to the charter in Vienna in October 1826, between 1826 and 1827 military rebellions against the constitution were mounted in his name. Although in early 1827 the absolutist troops had been defeated, this phase of Portuguese history was marked by the determination of many garrisons and regiments to reject the constitutional regime, and by an unprecedented intensification of informal warfare and popular violence erupting across the country, and especially in the north. These pronunciamientos lacked any form of coordination, and took place simultaneously in different provinces and cities, especially in the peripheries of the country, in the Algarve in the south in July 1826, and subsequently on the Spanish border at Elvas and in the north in Beira and Trás-os-Montes. Regular troops and substantial guerrilla units commanded by the Count of Amarante (by this time Marquis of Chaves), who had led the failed pronunciamiento in 1823 and retreated into Spain to flee the constitutional troops and reorganise themselves, were now ready to cross the borders again.[30]

The widespread guerrilla warfare that exploded between 1826 and 1827 was much more widespread than in 1823, but did not constitute a generalised peasant rebellion against liberalism, nor was it triggered by

29. Cardoso, *A revolução liberal*, p. 181.

30. Vasco Pulido Valente, 'Os levantamentos "Miguelistas" contra a Carta Constitucional (1826–27)', *Análise Social* 30, no. 133 (1995): 631–51; Valente, *Os militares*, pp. 75–97.

demands to abolish feudal rights and dues (the *forais*) and to implement constitutional reforms. In fact, counterrevolutionary guerrilla actions thrived in specific regions only, and in particular in those of Trás-os-Montes and Beira, where the petitionary movement against the *forais* was almost entirely lacking, and the burden of feudalism was not felt.[31] Thus it is difficult to relate rural guerrillas directly to specific economic grievances. As had happened in Sicily and Spain, rural mobilisation reflected a range of different social conflicts and also divided rural communities, whose members did not all side with the counterrevolution. Mobilisation against the constitutional government occurred at the local level. It relied on local aristocratic holders of the post of capitão mor, who availed themselves of their personal prestige and authority to create armed groups. Crucially the system of the ordenanças that provided them with authority to draft soldiers, abolished in 1821, had been reintroduced after the pronunciamiento of Vila Franca. Mostly composed of the poorest, the youngest and the unmarried members of these communities, the *partidas realistas* were predominantly small armed units that attacked individuals and the properties of those known to be liberals and considered to be a threat to the existing hierarchies.[32] In other circumstances, the inhabitants of different villages boasting opposed guerrilla units fought either in favour of or against the constitution. This circumstance suggests that, as in Sicily, local rivalries were an important factor in determining political allegiances.[33] While this movement had a strong rural dimension, meanwhile, it must not be forgotten that volunteers fighting for Dom Miguel came also from cities. For instance, between 1826 and 1827 the university of Coimbra furnished six different companies comprising 411 students, who were organised to join the counterrevolutionary efforts in the north.[34] What kept this heterogeneous counterrevolutionary movement together was therefore a

31. On this movement against feudal dues, see chapter eight below, on petitions.

32. Nuno Gonçalo Monteiro, 'Societat rural i actituds polítiques a Portugal (1820–1834)', in *Carlisme i moviments absolutistes*, ed. Josep Maria Fradera, Jesús Millán and Ramón Garrabou (Girona: Editorial Eumo, 1990), pp. 127–50; Maria Alexandre Lousada and Nuno Gonçalo Monteiro, 'Revoltas absolutistas e movimentação camponesa no Norte, 1826–1827 (algumas notas)', in *O liberalismo na Península Ibérica na primeira metade do século XIX*, ed. Miriam Halpern Pereira, Maria de Fátima Sá e Melo Ferreira and João B. Serra, 2 vols (Lisbon: Sá da Costa Editora, 1982), 2, pp. 169–82.

33. Cardoso, *A revolução liberal*, pp. 203–6.

34. F. A. Fernandes da Silva Ferrão, *Apologia dirigida à nação portuguesa para plena justificação do corpo dos Voluntarios Academicos do anno de 1826* (Coimbra: Imprensa de Trovão e Companhia, 1827); *Relação de todos os individuos, que compozerão o Batalhão dos Voluntarios Academicos, organizado e armado no anno lectivo de 1826 para 1827* [. . .] *agora fielmente reimpressa, e accrescentada com algumas notas correctivas e illustrativas*

common culture based on allegiance to Dom Miguel, religion and the celebration by the royalist insurgents of heroes such as Amarante.

This wave of formal and informal military interventions had not been
strong enough, however, to put an end to the constitutional regime. Their
failure to prevail was once more in large part due to the lack of a credible
royal pretender. It was only the return of Dom Miguel to Portugal from
his exile in 1828, his decision to abrogate the constitution, to dissolve the
constitutional Cortes in March and to reopen the ancient Cortes in early
May that marked the return of absolutism. Dom Miguel's success in turn
triggered a new wave of military interventions, this time in defence of liberalism and the dynastic rights of Dona Maria (or Dom Pedro) against the
usurper. The army revolts in defence of the constitution of 1828 against Dom
Miguel did not succeed, yet they were important, for two reasons. First,
the return of absolutism split the army irredeemably into two opposing
camps, and society more broadly along with it. In spite of the repression
of the pro-constitutional revolts on the mainland, the pronunciamiento
on the island of Terceira in the Azores led to the establishment of a mixed
military and civilian junta, from which constitutional resistance was reorganised and directed in the following years against Dom Miguel. This military response broadly followed the script inaugurated in Porto in 1820.
Second, the mobilisation associated with this wave of pronunciamientos
in defence of the constitution showed the extent to which constitutionalism, and not absolutism alone, had taken root in Portuguese society, and
was far more pronounced than in 1820. More generally, such widespread
participation points to the remarkable degree of political awareness resulting from years of political conflict. In many circumstances, public displays
of support for one side or the other erupted in a spontaneous way, anticipating political and military intervention, and popular participation was
far more intense than it had been eight years before. This observation is
borne out by accounts of crowd activity and conflict in all the main centres
of military insurrection.

Popular displays of support for the constitution had first erupted in
July 1827, when the resignation of the liberal hero General Saldanha
from the Ministry of War provoked fears of an imminent absolutist coup.
Between 25 and 27 July demonstrations erupted in the main squares of
the city of Lisbon, where thousands marched in the streets and addressed
the juíz do povo. In Porto citizens organised processions at night with

(Coimbra: Real Imprensa da Universidade, 1828). See also ANTT, Intendência Geral de
Polícia [hereafter IGP], Coimbra 286, f. 175: April 1826.

torches and the singing of the 'Hymno nacional'.[35] In 1828 Porto confirmed itself to be the centre of military and civilian opposition to Dom Miguel, and the example set by its population triggered similar responses in the rest of the country. Admittedly the câmara of Porto had initially responded to his dissolution of the constitutional Cortes in March and the request by the senate of the city in Lisbon to reinstate absolutism by acclaiming Dom Miguel as king, on 29 April. This acclamation was accompanied by public demonstrations of loyalty to him.[36] However, a strongly constitutionalist sector of public opinion, capable of organising itself, immediately became evident. The day after the acclamation of Dom Miguel, over six thousand people gathered in the Campo de Santo Ovídio, where the revolution had been declared in 1820, shouting 'Viva Dom Pedro IV!', 'Viva Rainha Senhora Dona Maria!' and 'Viva a constituição!'[37] This public demonstration reassured the constitutional troops that the population would be on their side should they decide to intervene.

Just over two weeks later in fact, the tenth battalion of the Caçadores, coming from Aveiro, and sixth infantry regiment converged with the local population in the Campo de Santo Ovídio to declare the constitution. Crucially, this demonstration, six thousand-strong, also provided the military with justifications for their intervention in the name of the entire city. Once more in line with the script established in 1820, the manifesto of the military council that took power on 18 May made reference precisely to the popular demonstrations of 29 and 30 April to legitimise its authority and account for its actions. For the signatories of the proclamation, those citizens of the city who had rallied to Dom Miguel had been merely a 'prostituted rabble' and 'filthy paupers'. Conversely, the following day, 'the respectable name of D. Pedro IV' attracted a vast, docile crowd. The manifesto suggested that Dom Miguel had unduly assumed the royal prerogatives, in breach of his own oath of allegiance to the constitution, while claiming to intervene in the name of the sovereign powers of Pedro IV.[38] In order to create a new and legitimate constitutional authority, arrangements were made for the election of a new governmental commission. With this end in mind, some fifty electors were selected, including in their number landed proprietors, the clergy, representatives of the judiciary,

35. Santos, *Documentos*, 3, pp. 815–25, 829.

36. Pedro Augusto Dias, *Subsidios para a história politica do Porto* (Porto: Typographia Central, 1896), pp. 58–60.

37. Joaquim José da Silva Maia, *Memorias historicas, politicas e filosoficas da revolução do Porto em maio 1828* (Rio de Janeiro: Typographia de Laemmert, 1841), pp. 17–18.

38. 'Manifesto', 18 May 1828, in Santos, *Documentos*, 4, 558–61.

men of letters and workers, as well as the members of the military council that had taken control of the city. The result of this election was a junta presided over by a general, and comprising seven members and four secretaries, among them four army officers, five *desembargadores* (judges) and two tradesmen. The junta immediately recruited twenty-eight battalions of volunteers in support of the army.

When news of the rebellion of Porto spawned copycat pronunciamientos in Penafiel, Braga, Chaves, Bragança and Coimbra, among many other places, the local populations did not remain passive. In the university city of Coimbra, the announcement of the return to the country of Dom Miguel thus led as early as the end of February and the beginning of March to various episodes of rioting and public disorder and to clashes between enemies and supporters of absolutism. News of Dom Miguel's arrival produced conflicting public reactions among students, who either shouted 'Viva Dom Miguel!', or 'Viva Dom Pedro IV!' and 'Viva a Carta!'[39] Further demonstrations in favour of Dom Pedro IV and the Carta erupted as soon as news of the rising of Porto reached the same city on 21 May. When constitutional militias and civilians from the town of Figueira da Foz entered the city, their commanding officer read out the manifestos issued by the Porto junta in front of cheering crowds consisting of students and members of the local populace.[40] Joint military and civilian action in favour of the constitution soon followed in the Algarve, the southern coastal region bordering Spain. In the city of Lagos the first battalion of the second infantry regiment rose up with the support of the city militias on 25 May, and also forced the city of Tavira, where the governor of the army of the province resided, to do the same.[41] In these two cities, the municipalities declared their allegiance to the constitution in the name of Dom Pedro. Only three days later troops loyal to Dom Miguel defeated the constitutional forces—not least because the military governor of Faro had been quick to renege on his earlier oath. Yet what is remarkable about these events is the participation of civilians. The constitutional regiment marching towards Faro, accompanied by hundreds of armed villagers, thus clashed with the town's inhabitants, who had themselves taken up arms upon sighting the fast-approaching troops. Civilian action continued in the succeeding days, when attacks were directed against supporters of the constitution in the town of Olhão and in Faro itself.[42]

39. ANTT, IGP, Coimbra 286, ff. 288, 289.
40. Ibid., ff. 361–64; Maia, *Memorias*, pp. 38–39.
41. Santos, *Documentos*, 4, pp. 600–601, 606.
42. ANTT, IGP, Algarve 244, ff. 177, 180, 186.

The countryside was not immune to this popular reaction against absolutism. Partidas in support of the constitutionalists were organised also in the otherwise royalist region of Trás-os-Montes, where the army had sided with the constitution. Here a constitutionalist guerrilla unit of five hundred volunteers from villages east of Vila Real that had remained loyal to the constitution since 1823 forced the local authorities to recruit new volunteer units fighting in the name of Dom Miguel.[43]

In the end, this wave of military risings in defence of the constitution was defeated. Although support for the constitution emerged in garrisons and military units across the country, they remained for the most part isolated from each other. While a large number of constitutional regiments had converged upon Coimbra to organise defence against the realistas, guaranteeing an important military victory against them at the end of June, their early withdrawal towards Porto gave Dom Miguel's troops an unexpected and crucial advantage, facilitating the brutal revenge of Dom Miguel's troops upon the unprotected population of the city.[44] Dom Miguel was successful in organising a guerrilla war that prevented the various constitutional garrisons and army units from taking control over larger territories and coordinating their actions. The government of Porto armed volunteers, but failed to hold sway over the countryside.[45] The constitutionalist pronunciamientos of 1828 nonetheless demonstrate the loyalty to the constitution evinced by large sectors of the army, and the existence of urban audiences willing to be mobilised at each and every one of these military interventions. A mass gathering marked the end of the revolution in Porto: it was precisely in the Campo de Santo Ovídio, where supporters of the constitution had spontaneously flocked on 30 April to protest against the acclamation of Dom Miguel, that on 3 July an even larger crowd of over twelve thousand staunch constitutionalists, comprising both civilians and army officers and soldiers, gathered before leaving the city. By the time they reached the border with Spanish Galicia, and having been attacked by their enemies, there were still nine thousand of them.[46] The data available about the social background and occupations of those arrested in Porto, Coimbra and the Algarve in 1828 show that by then constitutionalism had acquired a substantial social basis, which, while predominantly urban in nature, cannot be defined as merely either elitist or marginal. In Coimbra it comprised mainly students

43. Cardoso, *A revolução liberal*, pp. 218–19.
44. Maia, *Memorias*, pp. 63–64.
45. Cardoso, *A revolução liberal*, pp. 216–20.
46. Maia, *Memorias*, pp. 104–8.

(34.4 per cent), but the next largest category, before that of military and civil servants, was that of artisans (15 per cent).[47] Supporters of the constitution therefore often went beyond the wealthier middle classes to include the petty bourgeoisie. Of the 263 arrested and found guilty of participating in the liberal pronunciamiento in the province of Faro in the Algarve in 1828, only 116 belonged to the army. The rest were priests, property owners and tradesmen, but also shopkeepers, tailors, barbers, sailors, bricklayers and a number of individuals simply identified as 'workers'.[48] The civil war had thus split Portuguese society, and engendered a veritable popular constitutionalism on a large scale in some of the most important centres of the country, along with a resilient popular royalist movement.

Fighting in the name of a prisoner king: counterrevolution in Spain

As in Portugal, so also in Spain during the Trienio popular participation and political awareness increased both in cities and in the countryside, thanks to the ideological polarisation brought about by civil strife. In Spain too, monarchical hostility to the constitutional order led to royalist military interventions and guerrilla warfare, supported by some members of the military and civilian elites as well as of the local populations. This assault on the constitutional order produced a substantial response that confirmed the loyalty of part of the army and of public opinion to the revolution, and benefited from the support offered by a newly established type of paramilitary organisation: namely, the national militias. Most of the latter remained voluntary organisations whose ranks were chiefly filled by citizens with sufficient means to afford the expensive uniform, although sometimes 'patriotic' philanthropy also enabled poorer artisans and day-labourers to join. Organised locally by the constitutional councils to maintain public order and defend the new political system against its enemies, national militias became one of the pillars of the constitutional system.[49] The civil strife in Spain differed substantially, however, from its

---

47. William Young, *Portugal in 1828, Comprising Sketches on the State of Private Society, and of Religion in that Kingdom under Dom Miguel* (London: Henry Colburn, 1828); Rui Cascão, 'A revolta de maio de 1828 na Comarca de Coimbra: Contribuição para uma sociologia da revolução liberal', *Revista de História das Ideias* 7 (1985): 111–53.

48. ANTT, IGP, Algarve 244, ff. 532–33.

49. Álvaro París Martín, 'Milicia nacional', in *El Trienio Liberal (1820–1823): Una mirada política*, ed. Pedro Rújula and Ivana Frasquet (Granada: Editorial Comares, 2020), pp. 213–38.

Portuguese equivalent, and for one reason in particular. In Spain, there was no dynastic crisis comparable to that afflicting Portugal and bestowing added public legitimacy upon the counterrevolution. Although he secretly worked against the constitution, his hostility towards it being known and resented by the exaltados in particular, King Fernando VII in fact remained formally and officially a constitutional monarch. While during the Trienio some counterrevolutionary leaders started to see his younger brother Carlos, the heir to the throne, as a possible alternative candidate, the prince did not act independently to undermine his brother's occupation of the throne. This helps to explain why, although counterrevolution had become a popular movement by 1822, it failed to bring down the constitutional regime. Only with the French military invasion of 1823 was the revolution brought to a halt. The fact that the king was never given the opportunity to denounce the constitution publicly—although he was secretly working against it—limited the chances of success of counterrevolutionary efforts attempted during the Trienio itself. Contemporaries immediately defined the fight against the counterrevolution as a civil war. However, another peculiarity lay in the way Spanish revolutionaries conceived of it. Unlike their Portuguese, Neapolitan and Greek counterparts, who referred to civil war as a shameful event, in Spain many supporters of the constitution, and the exaltados in particular, extolled it. To the counterrevolutionaries' argument that civil war was the inevitable by-product of the revolution, a source of 'disorder and anarchy', Spanish radicals responded that at times 'civil war is a gift from heaven'. Drawing on the ideas of Mably, they maintained that civil war was necessary and beneficial, insofar as it aimed at defeating despotism. In such circumstances a civil war, carried out by free men, was 'an open war against those who want [only] to be vassals'.[50]

The hostility to the constitution of a substantial section of the army, and the latter's willingness to intervene in defence of absolutism whenever possible, rendered the political life of the constitutional period highly unstable and intensely contested from its very outset. Well before the outbreak of a fully-fledged civil war, what put the army at the centre of all the political conflicts of the Spanish Trienio were appointments to the important offices of captain general in the provinces and military commander of major cities. Since the political leanings of military leaders in favour of or against the constitution were well known to the public, such appointments

---

50. See, for instance, *El Zurriago*, no. 5, 1821, in *Textos exaltados del Trienio Liberal*, ed. Alberto Gil Novales (Madrid: Ediciones Júcar, 1978), pp. 101–3.

became the object of political controversy, dividing not only supporters of the constitution and their enemies, but also moderados and the exaltados. It was by replacing officers loyal to the constitution with military leaders of conservative or absolutist leanings that the monarch endeavoured to weaken the power of the constitutional regime. Instances of mass mobilisation and public protest that often succeeded in influencing or even reversing governmental decrees occurred every time a commander was demoted, replaced or appointed. The most high-profile and controversial military career of the Trienio was that of Rafael Riego, whose demotion from the captaincy-general of Aragon in 1821 provoked an uproar across the entire country.[51] But his was not the only case of an officer whose promotion or demotion occasioned public controversy. In November 1820 the king decided to appoint José Carvajal as the new captain general of Castilla la Nueva, replacing General Gaspar Vigodet.[52] Once the decision to appoint Carvajal was made public, crowds started to fill the Plazuela, the square outside the Ayuntamiento (city hall) of Madrid, where they called for the reopening of the Cortes in defence of the constitution.[53] Similar events took place in Cádiz on the appointment of an absolutist commander general.[54]

By 1821, however, military leaders were also ready to put an end to the constitution by lending their support to conspiracies organised in royal circles. At the end of January 1821 the imprisonment of an honorary chaplain at the court, the Cura Vinuesa, accused of plotting against the constitution, revealed the existence of counterrevolutionary plans to arrest the leading authorities of the regime, stir up popular protest in favour of absolutism, withdraw the constitution and imprison the most prominent liberals. In an atmosphere of growing fear and near-paranoia about impending threats of a coup, a violent clash between the guards of the royal palace and some demonstrators led to public outrage and the gathering of yet more hostile crowds. While the incident was in itself quite minor, the public reactions were not. The guards were in fact disbanded. As had happened a couple of months before, upon the appointment of the unpopular royalist captain general, this time too popular mobilisation

51. On the public reactions to Riego's demotion, see the relevant pages of chapters eight and nine below, on petitions and public opinion.

52. Blanco Valdés, *Rey, Cortes y fuerza armada*, pp. 324–28.

53. AAM, Secretaría, Acontecimientos Políticos, 2–229, no. 28.

54. José M. García León, *La milicia nacional en Cádiz durante el Trienio Liberal 1820–1823* (Cádiz: Caja de Ahorros de Cádiz, 1983), pp. 72–75. See also the relevant pages in chapter eight below, on petitions.

in defence of the constitution ensued.[55] Crowds gathered in front of the Ayuntamiento of Madrid calling for measures to protect the constitution; groups of volunteers were organised, and neighbourhoods wrote to the town administration invoking 'constitution or death', declaring their commitment to the defence of the city.[56]

The events of January 1821 were merely the prelude, however, to a far more dramatic crisis in the summer of the following year, when military interventions against the revolution, supported by King Fernando's entourage, were planned and put into practice. The hope then was to deal the constitutional regime a mortal blow. As in Portugal, so too in Spain, counterrevolutionary pronunciamientos seeking to establish their legitimacy stood in as great a need of public displays of popular support as did their revolutionary counterparts. In 1822, therefore, conspirators organised public demonstrations against the constitution, and the arrest of key politicians.[57] While these military conspiracies did not succeed, they resulted in popular mobilisation across the country, if not to any great extent in the capital itself. The first episode of this crisis unfolded in May 1822 in the city of Valencia, where eighty soldiers from the local garrison revolted, crying 'Death to the constitution, long live the absolute king, long live our General Elío, death to Riego!' The rebels' principal demand was the appointment of General Francisco Elío, under arrest since 1820 for his royalist sympathies and his responsibility for having reinstated absolutism in 1814, as the new commander of the city.[58] This coup was immediately suppressed, but further attempts at military coups erupted in Madrid and its environs between 30 May and early July. On the same day as the military pronunciamiento of Valencia, other demonstrations in support of the absolute king—the demonstrators apparently being paid for their pains—erupted just outside the royal residence in Aranjuez, about forty kilometres from Madrid. This popular protest was immediately repressed by the national militia, but still more disturbances broke out in early July, this time at the instigation of the royal guards. On 1 July four battalions of the king's guards mutinied and left the royal palace in Madrid for another royal residence located in the northern suburb of the capital,

55. Miraflores, *Apuntes historicós-criticos*, pp. 84–87.

56. AAM, Secretaría, Acontecimientos Políticos, 2-230, no. 9.

57. On the plot, see Emilio La Parra López, *Los Cien Mil Hijos de San Luis: El ocaso del primer impulso liberal en España* (Madrid: Síntesis, 2007), pp. 96–98. On the military events, see also Sophie Bustos, 'El 7 de julio de 1822: La contrarrevolución en marcha', *Revista Historia Autónoma* 4 (2014): 129–43.

58. Miraflores, *Apuntes histórico-críticos*, pp. 136, 137.

El Pardo, following clashes with the crowds. The king took advantage of the turmoil, and in the following days attempted to repeal the constitution. Some six days after their departure, the same battalions re-entered Madrid, planning to take control of the capital and implement the plot, but they were defeated after a day-long battle in the streets.[59] Although this time the inhabitants of Madrid were involved only as terrified bystanders, the national militia played an important role in this victory, along with the constitutional troops led by General Francisco Ballesteros. Alongside three battalions of the militia, additional groups of volunteers were recruited on an impromptu basis to fight in this battle. While some, certainly, were lawyers or property owners, around half of their number were artisans and lowly civil servants. These events turned the militias into the symbol of popular resistance in defence of the constitution.[60]

These events echoed vastly across the country, and had considerable political repercussions. The insurrection of the royal guards provided opportunities, at least until it came to be known that the it had been suppressed, for public displays of support for the re-establishment of the absolute monarchy. In the town of Catalayud in Aragon, for instance, the news of the events of 7 July resulted in attacks upon the national militia by the *serviles* (royalists, in liberal parlance), and in one casualty.[61] Similar episodes unfolded in other cities: public demonstrations calling for the reintroduction of the absolute monarchy erupted across the country, from Cádiz to Córdoba, Cartagena, Murcia and many other towns.[62] At the same time, once the suppression of the military coup and the appointment of a new government led by the exaltado Evaristo San Miguel had become common knowledge, demonstrations in favour of the constitution broke out in many Spanish cities. In accordance with a new regulation approved at the end of that same June, new volunteers joined the ranks of the national militias, and popular mobilisation supportive of the revolution intensified. In the aftermath of the failed coup, for instance, a new *tertulia patriótica* (patriotic society) was set up in San Sebastián, and on 19 July its members toasted the recent events in Madrid at a patriotic dinner.[63] In general, the defeat of the military coup and the appointment of San

59. Ibid., pp. 142–50.

60. AAM, Secretaría, Acontecimientos Políticos, 2–231, no. 11.

61. Pedro Rújula, *Contrarrevolución, realismo y Carlismo en Aragón y el Maestrazgo, 1820–1840* (Zaragoza: Prensas de la Universidad de Zaragoza, 1998), p. 73.

62. Gil Novales, *El Trienio Liberal*, p. 51.

63. Félix Llanos Aramburu, *El Trienio Liberal en Guipúzcoa (1820–1823)* (San Sebastián: Facultad de Filosofía y Letras, Universidad de Deusto, 1998), p. 393.

Miguel coincided with the consolidation of the power of exaltados at the local level and the defeat of the moderados. In Cádiz the events of 8 July provided opportunities for popular protest, with those involved demanding the resignation of the *jefe político* (the local representative of the central government) and the appointment of a new military commander. Crowds gathering in front of the Ayuntamiento called for the national militia to protect it against possible attacks, and a *junta de seguridad* was set up to coordinate the defence of the constitutional administration in the city.[64]

Far from putting an end to the counterrevolutionary threat, the defeat of the royalist coup in Madrid led also to the intensification of counterrevolutionary guerrilla warfare across the country in what became an outright civil war. Guerrilla warfare against the constitutional regime had already started in 1821, mainly in the Basque country, Aragon and Catalonia. In the summer of 1822, however, it spread to Galicia, to the regions of Valencia and Castile, and swept across most of the rural parts of Navarre, turning its cities of Pamplona and Estella into the main bulwarks of constitutionalism.[65] Before these events, the royalist guerrilla war had amounted to little more than a series of local and regional movements. Although its expansion had often been in response to governmental decisions and to widespread hostility to the military draft, guerrilla flare-ups were rooted in specific social and economic contexts. Royalist partidas in fact mostly relied on local recruits. Army officers, priests and local aristocrats tended in the main to recruit landless peasants and small landholders—these latter joining the guerrilla campaign only seasonally, when free from agricultural duties—in units that were small in size. The majority of them, organised locally, were made up of no more than fifty individuals, while those organised at regional level (and including either mercenaries or volunteers) could call upon between a hundred and two hundred members. As in Portugal, the partidas enjoyed the support of the traditional village paramilitary organisations, the so-called *sometents*. First created in the Middle Ages and revived during the French military occupation, these were temporary armed militias, traditionally summoned in villages by the ringing of the church bell. These militias elected their own leaders and provided support for various policing and military activities. Once more as in Portugal, there were also constitutionalist sometents, although more limited in size and geographical spread than the royalist ones. In the

64. García León, *La milicia nacional*, pp. 91–94.

65. Ramón del Río Aldaz, *Orígenes de la guerra carlista en Navarra (1820–1824)* (Pamplona: Gobierno de Navarra, Institución Príncipe de Viana, 1987).

coastal areas of Catalonia, for instance, sometents in favour of the consti-tution were more numerous than those against it, and local revolutionary leaders were able to mobilise them in defence of the revolution.[66]

Such mobilisation of rural societies at the local level was also a response to a set of decisions taken by the constitutional regime that directly affected the countryside. It was at the same time the consequence of frustrated rural expectations in the aftermath of regime change. In 1820 the constitutional government had relaxed fiscal pressure, and halved the tithe (*diezmo*) due to the clergy. The rural world had welcomed these measures. Indeed, these initiatives created the popular perception that the advent of constitutional government would mean first and foremost the overturning of the previous fiscal system. By 1822, however, fiscal pressure had risen again almost to the same levels as before the revolution, due to the increase in taxes on consumption (on tobacco, salt, wine, vinegar, spirits, meat), which represented a heavier burden than tithes (paid in kind). In addition, although in 1821 the government decided to implement provisions stipulated earlier for the sale of communal lands owned by vil-lages and municipal authorities (the *tierras baldías y propias*), and of the national properties created through the sale of ecclesiastical lands and buildings, most of the time local authorities did not put such these deci-sions into practice. When sales took place, they benefited not the poorest sectors of the peasantry, but exclusively wealthy urban proprietors. It is no surprise to find that great numbers of landless peasants hastened to join the anti-revolutionary guerrilla groups. The conditions endured by the land-less were dire indeed, not only because of the fiscal policies of the previous and new regimes, but also on account of the loss of the benefits the feudal system used to offer them in its granting of access to common land and its related resources (from access to wood to that of cheap milling).[67]

The increased hostility towards the constitutional regime produced by these circumstances, however, neither simply created a rupture between cities and countryside nor produced a generalised peasant rebellion. Some rural centres sided with the counterrevolution, but others did in fact remain loyal to the constitution. In addition, as in Portugal, not all anti-seigneurial conflicts resulted in support for the absolutist cause. In Navarre, for

66. Ramon Arnabat Mata, *Visca el rei i la religió! La primera guerra civil de la Cata-lunya contemporània* (Lleida: Pagès Editors, 2006), pp. 441–42; Arnabat Mata, 'La con-trarrevolución y la antirevolución', in *El Trienio Liberal (1820–1823)*, ed. Pedro Rújula and Ivana Frasquet (Granada: Comares Historia, 2020), pp. 285–307, esp. 302–5. On somet-ents, see also Torras, *Liberalismo*, pp. 97–98.

67. Torras, *Liberalismo*, pp. 43–49, 52, 90–93, 151–59.

instance, some peasants sided with the counterrevolution, taking up arms against proprietors accused of being liberals, but in other circumstances they were in conflict with absolutist landowners, and refused to join the armed struggle against the constitution.[68]

What made the civil war an essentially local phenomenon was the fact that villages, more often than not, were divided internally. This is why common forms of violence involved the targeting of specific individuals: for instance, prominent local constitutionalists, whose houses were torched or who were assaulted by members of the same community. It was therefore only the establishment of a royalist government, the so-called *regencia* in La Seu d'Urgell in Catalonia, in a valley on the border with France, that created the precondition for some overall coordination of this movement. Its members, who included the exiled former Marquis of Mataflorida as president, as well as the bishop of Mallorca and General Ibáñez, the Baron de Eroles, acted on behalf of a king whose liberty had allegedly been curtailed.[69] The existence of a web of informants and delegates facilitated contacts between this royalist government, the king and individual counterrevolutionary leaders across the country. The most important military achievement of the regencia was the organisation of a proper royalist army, made up of large partidas, disciplined like professional armies, and comprising more than four hundred individuals.[70] Taking orders from the regencia, the royalist junta of Navarre enrolled more than four thousand men to fight under the leadership of the Baron de Eroles in Catalonia, with a view to restoring the absolute monarchy.

In spite of this substantial reorganisation, the counterrevolutionary movement was never strong enough from a military point of view, even at the height of its popularity and might, to constitute a serious threat to the constitutional regime. In fact, before the invasion of the French army led by the Duke of Angoulême in April 1823, the constitutional army had succeeded in undermining the royalist efforts to wage a national counterattack by recruiting sixty thousand more soldiers. From autumn 1822 some city councils, including Madrid, Oviedo, Cádiz and Cuenca, recruited so-called *cazadores constitucionales* to reinforce locally the defence

68. Joseba de la Torre, 'Nekazal klaseak, antzinako erregimenaren krisia eta iraultza burgesa nafarroan'/'Clases campesinas, crisis del Antiguo Régimen y revolución burguesa en Navarra', in *Zumalakarregi Museoa: Azterketa historikoak/Museo Zumalakarregi: Estudios históricos*, 2 vols (San Sebastián: Diputación Foral de Gipuzkoa, 1992), 2, pp. 189–208; Ramón del Río Aldaz, 'Camperols foralistes i contraris a la revolució burgesa? Un mite que s'esfondra a Navarra' *Recerques: Història, Economia, Cultura* 22 (1989): 25–44.

69. On the regency, see Arnabat Mata, *Visca el rei*, pp. 251ff.

70. Ibid., pp. 189–222, 429–30.

of the constitutional regime against the guerrillas and banditry. Unlike the national militias, the cazadores were fully paid and therefore did not include only members of the propertied classes.[71] Thus, between the end of 1822 and the beginning of 1823, the regime experienced the gravest military threats to its survival, but enjoyed also important victories that dealt a mortal blow to the counterrevolution. By November 1822 General Francisco Espoz y Mina's military expedition to Catalonia had effectively crushed the counterrevolutionary movement in the region, driving the troops led by the Baron de Eroles across the border into France.[72] In January 1823 the commander of Castile defeated the very large royalist partida of five thousand men led by Jorge Bessières one hundred kilometres from the capital, not far from Guadalajara, and the royalist troops were thereafter dispersed away from Madrid, between Aragon and Valencia.[73] By February 1823 these military successes had led to the expulsion of the regencia, whose members quit La Seu d'Urgell and likewise retreated into France. The activities of the counterrevolutionary partidas in Catalonia, as well as in the other major centre of royalist guerrilla activity, Navarre, had been reduced to a bare minimum, and most of the royalist troops from Navarre had fled into French territory. In Valencia and Aragon the guerrillas were still active, but not on sufficiently large a scale to pose any serious threat to the constitutional regime.[74] In these regions, what the constitutional authorities achieved was containment, rather than complete eradication of the phenomenon. As one historian has claimed with regard to the province of Aragon, royalist insurrection there had become 'chronic but not lethal'.[75]

In the final analysis, prior to the French invasion, the impact of the civil war on Spanish society bears comparison with the repercussions of civil strife for the Portuguese population in these same years. What the counterrevolutionary movement both at the centre of the country and in each province had done between the end of 1821 and early 1823 was not to put an end to the constitutional regime. Instead, it contributed to the mobilisation of sections of society in each province, city and village, be it on one side or the other, including the rural world. The widespread

71. On the Cazadores, see *Diario de Madrid*, no. 295, 24 October 1822, p. 2; Juan Sisinio Pérez Garzón, *Milicia nacional y revolución burguesa: El prototipo madrileño, 1808–1874* (Madrid: Consejo Superior de Investigaciones Científicas, 1978), pp. 325–26.

72. La Parra López, *Los Cien Mil Hijos*, p. 29.

73. Arnabat Mata, *Visca el rei*, pp. 330–47.

74. Ibid., pp. 348–55.

75. Rújula, *Contrarrevolución*, p. 82.

violence experienced at different levels of intensity in most parts of the country reinforced ideological divisions at the national, regional and local level across all social classes. But in the case of Spain, the mutual hostility between the moderados, who controlled the government up until the summer of 1822, and the exaltados, influential in most of the cities, each party being determined to deny the other all legitimacy, was also crucial in stirring up public opinion and in creating a new front of internal popular opposition.

Civil war as a war of independence: Sicily against Naples

Soon after General Pepe's pronunciamiento, a revolution broke out in Sicily. This revolt forced the constitutional army to intervene in defence of the unity of the state. The Sicilian revolution was in fact a short but rather complex military event that reflected a number of overlapping territorial conflicts, both between the aristocratic leadership of the island based in Palermo and the capital of the kingdom, and within the island itself. The beginning of the pro-independence movement in Palermo coincided with a generalised insurrection of peasants who, organised in small gangs, joined the popular mobilisation in the capital, but also looted public buildings, attacked revenue offices and murdered notables in rural villages across the island. This Sicilian civil war opposed the southern and eastern coastal cities of Catania and Messina, and a number of smaller urban centres inland, like Caltanissetta, that sided with Naples, to the capital city of Palermo and its allied towns and cities in western Sicily, including Trapani, Marsala and Agrigento. Under the banner of the Cádiz Constitution, the revolutionary government of Palermo assembled a number of different social groups and political tendencies, united by hatred against Naples, and by a desire to recover the privileges of self-government lost in the previous years. It was dominated primarily by the great aristocracy of the island, along with the corporations of the capital city. Conversely, cities like Catania or Messina on the eastern coast remained loyal to the constitutional regime and to Naples precisely because they resented Palermo's attempt to reimpose its political and administrative hegemony over the rest of the island.

As in Portugal, Greece and Spain, the civil war in Sicily combined military action by regular troops with guerrilla warfare and a high degree of civilian participation. Unlike the civil strife that flared up in Piedmont, Spain, Portugal and Greece, however, the Sicilian conflict did not divide the existing army of the kingdom. The Sicilian revolution had been made possible by an urban insurrection against the army stationed in the island's capital, Palermo, which was quickly and easily driven out of the city. With the exception of the troops in the garrison of Siracusa, a city on the eastern coast of the island, who temporarily mutinied—and were soon arrested— the army stationed on the island remained loyal to Naples. It was therefore up to the newly established provisional government of Palermo not only to organise the defence of the city, but also to create an army that would impose the city's supremacy over the rest of Sicily, with the support of the towns and villages of western Sicily that had sided with the island's capital. The army set up in Palermo, though under aristocratic leadership, consisted of informal guerrilla units. In 1820 various decrees in fact marked the appointment of a number of commanders—*gran colonnelli*— from among the most prominent aristocrats supporting the provisional government. According to the regulation approved by the government on 22 August 1820, the gran colonnelli would own their own regiments and provide some financial support for their upkeep.[76] No such army would ever come into being, however, most probably for financial reasons. Nonetheless, the provisional government of Palermo did manage to create three main guerrilla groups, led respectively by the Prince of San Cataldo, Emmanuele Requesens (son of the Prince of Pantelleria) and Gaetano Abela. Having no regular army at its disposal, guerrilla groups were the only viable solution by which the Palermitan government might meet its urgent military needs. What rendered this a credible approach to organising a successful military strategy was the memory of the Spanish popular revolt against the French. During the Sicilian revolution two prominent members of the provisional government in particular, Count Giovanni Aceto and Colonel Requesens, the new captain general of the armed wing of the revolutionary government, made explicit reference to these events in their defence of it. In his 'Proclama di un siciliano ai suoi compatrioti siciliani', Count Aceto for his part argued that the Spanish nation should serve as an example to the Sicilians: for the Sicilians, like the Spaniards, had adopted a constitution and were set to fight for their independence with their blood and valour.[77]

In practice, the Sicilian pro-independence guerrilla war resulted from the combination of these three main units and the local organisation of *bande* in individual villages. These armed groups were neither a novelty of the revolution nor the product of an imitation of Spanish events. In fact

76. ASP, Real Segreteria, Incartamenti, 5035.
77. *Giornale Patriottico di Sicilia*, no. 200, 10 August 1820.

they represented a pre-existing feature of Sicily's agrarian society. Great feudal lords had used them to defend their power and interests against competitors, hiring for this purpose bandits or villagers from the communities they controlled. Armed groups of bandits at the service of great landowners continued to proliferate also after 1812, by which time the process of the abolition of feudal rights had been set in motion.[78] In 1820 several such groups were levied to oppose the common Neapolitan enemy.

The most successful of the three guerrilla groups set up in Palermo, the one led by the Prince of San Cataldo, succeeded in conquering temporarily Caltanissetta, a city in the heart of the island that had remained loyal to Naples, albeit with the support of several 'bande'. During his expedition from Palermo towards Caltanissetta by way of his own fiefdom, and through several villages, San Cataldo had managed to muster new bande. The success of this campaign was only temporary. Far from holding on permanently to the city of Caltanissetta through a formal occupation, its participants took revenge upon the city's inhabitants, whose dwellings were burnt, looted and destroyed by the bands of villagers no longer controlled by their leaders. As a result, San Cataldo left the city rather than holding on to it, and the guerrilla formations dispersed.[79] The government in Palermo supported San Cataldo's expedition with a communications campaign based on the capillary distribution of manifestos. These leaflets called upon the entire population, including women, children and the elderly to take up arms for the cause of Sicily's independence and to defend their villages from the enemy.[80] Villagers responded enthusiastically: in the town of Troina women, children and men raised the flag of independent Sicily, while in Castrogiovanni women and children helped build barricades in defence of their village against the Neapolitan army.[81]

In the end, San Cataldo's army was little more than a motley collection of independent guerrilla groups, headed by local village leaders. Its

78. Giovanna Fiume, *Le bande armate in Sicilia, 1819–1849: Violenza e organizzazione del potere* (Palermo: Annali della Facoltà di lettere e filosofia di Palermo, 1984); Fiume, 'Bandits, Violence, and the Organization of Power in Sicily in the Early Nineteenth Century', in *Society and Politics in the Age of the Risorgimento: Essays in Honour of Denis Mack Smith*, ed. John A. Davis and Paul Ginsborg (Cambridge: Cambridge University Press, 1991), pp. 70–91.

79. Antonino De Francesco, *La guerra di Sicilia: Il distretto di Caltagirone nella rivoluzione del 1820–21* (Catania: Bonanno Editore, 1992), pp. 142–64.

80. ASP, Real Segreteria, Incartamenti, 5034: Giunta di governo, Palermo, 31 August 1820.

81. Ibid., 5035: reports from Troina and Castrogiovanni, 14 and 18 August 1820.

composition accurately reflected the social make-up of the countryside, including as it did peasants and smallholders, artisans, deserters, criminals, members of the former feudal militias now turned into private armies, the local elites and individuals who took advantage of the war to rise in prominence and outdo village rivals. In their composition, these bande often reflected that of the various rival factions within the same communities. Thus the participation of individuals in guerrilla warfare was due to a combination of differing motivations. The events in the town of Bronte on the slopes of Mount Etna exemplify the complex nature and origins of this mobilisation. The village's politics were dominated by the conflictual relations of this community with the Duchy of Bronte, a large estate given to the Nelson family by the Bourbons as a reward for Admiral Horatio Nelson's services in defence of the monarchy during the Napoleonic wars, in 1799. The centuries-long disputes between the village and the Duchy over land rights had subsequently been exacerbated by the abolition of feudalism after 1812, an event that created competition between local notables and peasants for the purchase of quotas of the common land. It also divided the community and the ducal administration over property claims and the compensation of the recently abolished *usi civici*, the customary rights enjoyed by the former. On the eve of the revolution, the municipal authorities were controlled by a group close to the interests of the duke and his administration. However, when the revolution broke out, a rival faction hostile to the Duchy mobilised the population against the local authorities, who had to flee the village, and declared its allegiance to the Sicilian independentist revolution. Having organised an armed band of five hundred villagers, the winning faction attacked the neighbouring villages, looting communal offices and distributing the contents of their public purses, and giving support to those local groups who had sided with Palermo against Naples.[82]

The Neapolitan regular army led by Colonel Gaetano Costa—himself a veteran of the Peninsular War—easily defeated the guerrilla units made up of 1,200 individuals led by a Captain Orlando outside Caltanissetta, killing two hundred of them and taking sixty prisoner. Although irregular armed groups also accompanied Costa's Neapolitan army, it was the discipline

82. On the Duchy, see Lucy Riall, *Under the Volcano: Empire and Revolution in a Sicilian Town* (Oxford: Oxford University Press, 2013), and on these events in particular, pp. 64–67, 64–87. See also Sebastiano Angelo Granata, "'L'empia masnada': Bande armate e conflitti civili nella zona etnea', in *Una rivoluzione 'globale': Mobilitazione politica, conflitti civili e bande armate nel Mezzogiorno del 1820*, ed. Sebastiano Angelo Granata (Milan: FrancoAngeli, 2021), pp. 157–89.

and strategy of his regular troops that determined the success of the campaign.[83] At the same time, his military intervention received as much popular support in eastern Sicily as the pro-independence initiative had received in the villages supporting Palermo. On 20 August 1820 the city of Catania, the capital of eastern Sicily, enthusiastically welcomed Costa, who was hailed as a hero in a flurry of poems and songs celebrating his military virtues. Its civilian population, including groups of women, spontaneously organised a legion armed with pikes to protect the city against a possible incursion by the pro-independence forces.[84] What boosted popular support for the Neapolitan constitutional government in eastern Sicily was the arrival on the island of Luigi Minichini, one of the protagonists of the pronunciamiento, sent there in September to support the military campaign. His popularity and charisma reinforced the allegiance of this part of the island to the Neapolitans, and deepened their mistrust of Palermo.[85] A crowd three or four thousand-strong met Minichini outside Catania and accompanied him into the city, where he was welcomed by the local authorities and the entire population. Similar mass demonstrations took place also in the city of Caltanissetta and in a number of other, smaller towns, Acireale among them.[86]

In the end, the conflict showed remarkable levels of involvement on the part of the population of the entire island, whether in favour of or against independence under constitutional government. While adopted by both armies, guerrilla warfare meanwhile betrayed all its limits as a military strategy. Embraced partly out of necessity and partly out of conviction, this approach was soon abandoned by the aristocratic elites of Palermo, so horrified were they by the destruction wreaked by the bande that had looted Caltanissetta. Keen to find a compromise with Naples without relying too much on unruly and unpredictable popular forces, these aristocratic revolutionaries decided to negotiate with General Florestano Pepe, whose army was already at the gates of the island's capital by September. An agreement reached with another representative of the Neapolitan government, General Carlo Filangieri, in Palermo on September, although later

83. ASC, Intendenza Borbonica, 3146, no. 170: Costa to the city of Caltagirone, 7 September 1820.

84. See BCUC, Raccolta di Fogli Sciolti: broadsheets, 'Inno Patrio per l'arrivo a Catania del Colonnello Costa nell'agosto del 1820' and 'Inno Saffico per lo disbarco a Catania del Colonnello Costa col reggimento Principessa nell'agosto 1820'; also 'Le Femmine di Catania' (Catania, 1820; a eulogy to the women of Catania for their conduct in the political struggle), broadsheet held at BL.

85. Minichini, *Luglio 1820*, p. 322.

86. Ibid., pp. 331, 332, 337.

withdrawn, seemed to appease the aspirations of some of the insurgents, as it offered separate parliamentary representation for the island. On their side, many Neapolitan revolutionaries believed that there was little to celebrate about their victory in Sicily. The common view among them was that as a civil conflict this was bound to have produced a war with no honour, an event that should be consigned to oblivion as soon as possible. Commenting upon the decision taken by the Neapolitan parliament not to issue any official congratulation for the army upon regaining control of Palermo, a journalist wrote,

> In civil wars any triumph whatsoever costs bitter tears and it is better to destroy every memory of it than perpetuate it with praises that the defeated will too much regret. The citizens of one and the same Kingdom are all brothers, and we should respect also those gone astray who have returned to order.[87]

For the same reasons, the heir to the throne, vicar of the kingdom and Duke of Calabria decreed the destruction of the flags of the pro-independence army seized in Caltanissetta, as these could not be considered 'military trophies', but only 'insignia of a temporary aberration'.[88] All such attempts to undermine the territorial integrity of the monarchy had perforce to be forgotten.

Civil war as a crisis of the Ottoman order: the Greek revolution

Like its Portuguese, Spanish and Neapolitan equivalents, the Greek revolution too became what its protagonists immediately defined as a war among brothers (*emfylios polemos*), that is to say, a conflict pitting insurgents from different regions against each other. The peculiarity of the Greek case lay in the fact that the revolution provided an opportunity for the Christian military elites to assert their independence and autonomy against the Ottoman authorities, who had traditionally accorded them substantial administrative and policing powers. By so doing, they entered into competition with other regional and social groups involved in the war. The renewed power and prestige of this military class owed much to the fact that the revolutionary struggle coincided with a bitter and prolonged

---

87. *L'Imparziale*, 14 November 1820, p. 2.

88. Nino Cortese, *La prima rivoluzione separatista siciliana: 1820–1821* (Naples: Libreria Scientifica, 1951), p. 197.

war in which their role proved to be crucial and necessary. In these circumstances, defining the boundaries and limits of military vis-à-vis civil power was more difficult than in any other southern European revolution. Given the priority that winning the war against the Ottomans had over any other consideration, these military classes were reluctant to subject themselves to civil authorities. The debates about how to organise the new political community and the attempts made to build a new state during the revolution reflected the political tensions between the military classes and other social groups, and the competition existing between the various leaders of the irregular troops themselves. It was these tensions that led to prolonged conflicts and civil wars.

In the Peloponnese the revolution represented an opportunity for the local military class, that of the kapoi, to assert itself not only against the Ottomans, but also against the hegemonic class of the region, the primates. The kapoi worked under the authority of the political and social elite of the region, the Christian primates, a social group whose power was based on landholding, tax-farming on behalf of the Ottoman authorities and control over the municipal and provincial assemblies. The role of the kapoi was to maintain internal order, and in particular to fight brigands, the armed bands of the so-called klephts, who operated across the region. The klephts defied the Ottoman authorities, holding sway over independent communities in the mountains, and organising incursions to attack and loot villages or extract money from wealthy individuals.

In the mainland Christian provinces of the empire, the revolution was likewise marked by the consolidation of the power of a military class. The so-called armatoloi, especially in the domains of Ali Pasha in Epirus and Roumeli, were much more powerful than the kapoi of the Peloponnese. While the kapoi in the Peloponnese were employed by the local Christian primates, the armatoloi were appointed by the Ottoman state to rule directly over military districts. These *armatolikia* had been created across the centuries by Ottoman authorities to police their territories and enforce law and order in exchange for properties, privileges and the right to levy taxes. Banditry also represented an endemic feature of these traditional agrarian and pastoral societies, in which law and order was difficult to enforce, and authorities often employed former brigands (klephts) to patrol frontiers, govern districts and collect taxes. Brigandage thrived in the regions controlled by Ali Pasha, in the mountains of Thessaly and Epirus, whose economy was based on seasonal migration and animal husbandry, activities that produced tensions between those coming down periodically from the mountains and farmers living on the plains. Incursions into villages for looting and theft, and the rustling of sheep flocks were their characteristic activities.[89] Although both kapoi and armatoloi were charged with the policing of the Ottoman territories against the brigandage of the klephts, in reality the distinction between them and the brigands was not always very clear. Former klephts could be invested with authority and be employed by the Ottomans or by pashas like Ali, to whom they offered their services. In fact, armatoloi and kapoi were often former brigands hired by the Ottoman elites. At the same time, the kapoi often allied themselves with bands of klephts, to challenge the existing authorities or to oppress local populations with violence and abuses.

Besides shepherds and brigands, peasants made up the rank and file of guerrilla groups. The close relationship of the military classes with their social milieux (mainly made up of peasants) accounts for their crucial role in mobilising their communities to resist the Ottoman authorities. The armatoloi were very much connected to their particular places—the villages and the peripheries they controlled (the armatolikia) and inherited from one generation to the next (because the 'office' of armatolos gradually became hereditary). Traditionally they would recruit their bands from their villages of origin, with which they maintained close family ties. The principal preoccupation of the armatoloi upon first joining the revolution was therefore to protect their domains.[90] The more powerful the chieftain, the more extensive was his patronage network and the greater his ability to recruit for military activities, even when only for a brief period. But the close links peasants had with their villages in turn meant that they considered warfare as essentially a temporary activity. Even during the revolution, peasants tended to fight for a short spell only, in order to complement the practice of agriculture with the financial rewards of looting.[91]

The outbreak of the revolution dramatically altered the lives of the peasantry. With the death and expulsion of their Muslim owners, large estates became vacant and were turned into national properties. The first national constitution, approved in January 1822, declared these lands to be national estates, along with those of the former Ottoman authorities

89. John F. Koliopoulos, *Brigands with a Cause: Brigandage and Irredentism in Modern Greece, 1821–1912* (Oxford: Oxford University Press, 1987), pp. 20–31.

90. Koliopoulos, *Brigands*; Kostis Papagiorgis, *Τα καπάκια: Βαρνακιώτης, Καραϊσκάκης, Ανδρούτσος* (*Kapakia*: Varnakiotis, Karaiskakis, Androutsos) (Athens: Kastaniotis 2003), pp. 79, 89–90, 101.

91. Dimitris Dimitropoulos, *Θεόδωρος Κολοκοτρώνης* (Theodoros Kolokotronis) (Athens: Ta Nea Istoriki Vivliothiki, 2009), p. 57.

and pious endowments. With the exception of those estates that were immediately reclaimed or occupied, their fate was left to be decided at a later date. What improved the living conditions of Greek peasants and farmers was therefore not an immediate distribution of land, for such measures were deferred, but the radical reduction in taxation and the reorganisation of the fiscal system associated with landed property. This was by far the most evident benefit farmers earned from the insurrection. Tithes paid by owners of the land were reduced to one tenth of their yield. Only leaseholders had to pay an additional ground rent, but this too was reduced, in comparison with pre-revolutionary rates.[92] At the same time, the new revolutionary authorities soon made promises to fighters that they would be given land as a form of payment and reward for their services to the nation. In May 1822 the government decided that each soldier would be paid with a *stremma* of land (the equivalent of a tenth of a hectare) for every month of fighting, but only as a reward for full military service, and similar promises were reiterated in the following years in different circumstances (for instance, on the islands of Spetses and Hydra, and in Athens). These measures seem to have by and large satisfied the peasantry. No widespread demands were made for an immediate distribution of land during the war. The only recorded protest related to access to land dates to April 1823, when a group of armed peasants protested at the Congress of Astros against attempts to sell the national estates, a measure they feared would benefit only a small oligarchy. Similar protests occurred also in Athens in 1826, when crowds halted an auction of national estates by a governmental commission.[93]

The behaviour and expectations of the revolutionary military leadership and their guerrilla groups were profoundly marked by the Ottoman administrative system, which had guaranteed them a high degree of autonomy. Varnakiotis, Karaiskakis, Diakos, Botsaris, Tzavelas and Androutsos, the great military men of the revolution, were all former armatoloi, who had been recognised as such by the Ottoman authorities or by provincial notables such as Ali Pasha. Most of them had learned their military art among the Souliots (Christian Albanians who were often at odds with Ali Pasha) and other Albanian groups with a venerable tradition in irregular warfare. In the years preceding the revolution these leaders had played a key role in the conflicts ravaging the mainland provinces of Greece. Ali Pasha's ascent to power and his carving out of a temporarily independent

92. McGrew, *Land and Revolution*, pp. 59–64; Petmezas, 'Land Issue', pp. 15–16.
93. Petmezas, 'Land Issue', pp. 15–18; McGrew, *Land and Revolution*, p. 65.

state had led to the appointment under his direct authority of a number of new klephts and the armatoloi, in whose loyalty he trusted, thus creating a new generation of armatoloi who answered to him. These armatoloi served also in his own military corps in Yannina and elsewhere. However, the defeat of Ali Pasha by the Ottoman army in 1820, and the subsequent outbreak of the Greek rebellion, created a power vacuum in the region, especially during the first years of the revolution, that lasted at least until 1823. The armatoloi formerly fighting for Ali Pasha tried to safeguard their independence and were thus reluctant to recognise the authority either of the empire or of the Greek revolutionary leadership. Things changed with the intensification of the conflict: the armatoloi were forced to choose sides as their areas of control came under the jurisdiction of the Greek administration. This military leadership therefore tried to retain its power in the new context.[94] The foremost military leader of the revolution, and a key deal-broker in all of the institutional and political negotiations of the revolution, Theodoros Kolokotronis, came from a family of kapoi from the Peloponnese. Before rising to preeminence during the revolution, he had associated himself with a powerful clan of primates, the Deliyannis. Expelled from the Peloponnese in 1806, when the Ottoman authorities had decided to destroy the powerful and unruly networks of kapoi and klephts of the Peloponnese, he settled in the Ionian islands for the following fifteen years, joining first the Russian army in their expeditions against the Ottomans and later the British forces fighting the French.[95] Although Kolokotronis, like many other military leaders, had received a formal military training serving in European armies during the Napoleonic wars, he continued to act as the leader of guerrilla units loyal first and foremost to himself.

With the creation of the first regional assemblies and authorities in 1821, attempts were made to curb the power of this military class, without however completely abolishing its structure. For instance, in 1821, in western mainland Greece, Prince Mavrokordatos temporarily maintained the system of armatoloi, but subjected them, at least formally, to the political authority of the senate of the region. Likewise the Areios Pagos, the assembly of eastern mainland Greece, transformed the armatoloi into colonels under its authority, but maintained the hereditary status of their office, allowing for their substitution by new military leaders when

94. Stathis, 'From Klephts and Armatoloi', pp. 167–79, esp. 177–78; Dionysis Tzakis, Γεώργιος Καραϊσκάκης (Georgios Karaiskakis) (Athens: Ta Nea, Istoriki Vivliothiki, 2009), pp. 30, 50, 55.

95. Dimitropoulos, Θεόδωρος Κολοκοτρώνης (Theodoros Kolokotronis), pp. 17–30; Kolokotrones, Kolokotrones, pp. 83–128.

deemed necessary. In the Peloponnese the first regional assembly established there recognised the power and influence of the kapoi by creating a military hierarchy which, while formally under the scrutiny of the senate, would legitimise their local power.[96] In practice, the integration of such preeminent men into the new institutions of the revolution proved difficult. These powerful military leaders were not only at loggerheads with each other, but were also in competition with other leading revolutionary groups, and in particular with the westernised Greeks of the diaspora who supported Ypsilantis's pronunciamiento. Mavrokordatos's attempt at Zarakova, in the heart of the Peloponnese, to convince the local military and civil elites to create a national government that would include representatives from other regions was met with the insuperable hostility of the kapoi, who threatened to murder any primates rash enough to back the project.[97] In general, in all regions, the military classes took little notice of governments, and tended to act autonomously.

Another crucial factor that prevented the integration of the military classes into the structure of the new state was their ability and propensity to negotiate a truce with the Ottomans in exchange for recognition of their authority over their territories of origin, an arrangement to which the klephts had been accustomed before the revolution. During the Greek revolution, the Ottoman tradition of seeking, whenever appropriate, negotiations with the enemy, and even of switching sides whenever convenient, according to the practice known as *kapakia*, remained common. Kapakia entailed an act of submission to the Ottomans, but also an agreement of mutual protection.[98] A number of very prominent revolutionary chieftains engaged in such practices from 1821 onwards. The foremost military leader of eastern Greece, Odysseas Androutsos, for instance, carved out his power by challenging alternately the Ottoman and the Greek authorities. Having worked for Ali Pasha first, he then joined the Philiki and rallied to the revolution, but before long entered into conflict with the Areios Pagos. Refusing to follow its military orders, he set up his own independent assembly with a view to being appointed commander-in-chief of eastern Greece. However, when the military fortunes of the revolution seemed to decline, he had no qualms about making kapakia with the Ottomans. He did this in order to reorganise his army, initially

96. Apostolos Vakalopoulos, *Τα ελληνικά στρατεύματα του 1821: Οργάνωση, ηγεσία, τακτική, ήθη, ψυχολογία* (The Greek troops of 1821: Leadership, organisation, tactics, customs, psychology) (Thessaloniki: Politeia, 1948), pp. 71–75.

97. Dakin, *Greek Struggle*, p. 83.

98. Papagiorgis, *Τα καπάκια (Kapakia).*

with the support of Mavrokordatos. While this was a temporary measure or a truce, in 1824 Androutsos decided not to take sides in the civil war, switched allegiances permanently, and joined the army of Omer Vryonis, pasha of Yannina. It was at this stage that he was arrested and murdered in mysterious circumstances by a former ally, Gouras. An equally high-profile example of a military leader whose allegiance oscillated between the Ottomans and the revolutionaries is that of Georgios Karaiskakis. An allegedly illegitimate son of an armatolos, Karaiskakis had been in the service of Ali Pasha before getting involved in the revolutionary struggle. In the early years of the revolution Karaiskakis's behaviour was dictated by his desire to keep control over Agrafa, the armatolikion where he had first risen in the military ranks.[99] While fighting the Ottomans, he would often enter into negotiations with them: for instance, in late 1822, after the military defeat of Peta and the weakening of the political power of Mavrokordatos, he made kapakia with Omer Vryonis. In 1824 he entered into direct conflict with Mavrokordatos, who had chosen a rival, Giannakis Ragkos, as leader for western Greece. Mavrokordatos then took revenge upon Karaiskakis, accusing him of treason and putting him on trial.[100] In a particularly difficult moment for the revolutionary struggle, at the end of 1826 and in the aftermath of the siege of Messolonghi, when the Ottomans were trying to regain control over western Greece, a great number of chieftains, including Ragkos and Mitsos Kontoyannis, took the decision to make kapakia so as to regain the power they had previously enjoyed in their own armatolikia.[101]

Reluctance to recognise a superior authority likewise undermined the attempts that were made to organise centralised military authorities at the national level. For this reason, the attempts made by Alexandros Ypsilantis in the early stages of the revolution, for instance, to impose a central military leadership not only in the Danubian Principalities, where he was fighting, but also in the Morea, were doomed to fail. Before being defeated himself, Ypsilantis appointed as general-in-chief of all the armed forces of Greece his brother Dimitrios, who arrived on the island of Hydra soon after the outbreak of the revolution in June 1821, after travelling from Bessarabia and the Habsburg Adriatic port of Trieste. In spite of being welcomed enthusiastically by the populations of Hydra and of the

99. Tzakis, Γεώργιος Καραϊσκάκης (Georgios Karaiskakis), pp. 32–43.

100. Papagiorgis, Τα καπάκια (Kapakia), pp. 143ff; Christos Loukos, Αλέξανδρος Μαυροκορδάτος (Alexandros Mavrokordatos) (Athens: Ta Nea Istoriki Vivliothiki, 2010), p. 33.

101. Dakin, Greek Struggle, p. 187.

FIGURE 11. *The Army-Camp of Karaiskakis* (oil painting by Theodoros Vryzakis, 1855; The National Gallery of Greece, Alexandros Soutsos Museum, Athens). Image: https://www.nationalgallery.gr, with permission

Peloponnese, his early efforts to create a national civilian and military organisation immediately collapsed. In the village of Vervena, where he tried to set up a national authority that would be above the regional one, he became entangled in the conflicts between primates and kapoi, the latter threatening to massacre the former, and was forced to abandon his plans. Likewise, his national military leadership remained nominal, and his efforts to organise a regular army failed. In Trieste, aided by a French officer, Dimitrios had put together a small regular army on the model of the Sacred Band set up by his brother in Jassy, in the hope that this would represent a first step towards imposing Western standards on Greek forces. In practice, his military authority remained confined to the troops engaged in the siege of the city of Tripolitsa, controlled by the Ottoman troops, which he joined soon after leaving Vervena. Here too, however, both the local chieftains and the soldiers involved in the siege refused to abide by the strategy for siege warfare that had been recommended, and as a consequence many of the soldiers who had been recruited started to desert. In the end, the siege was carried through to a successful conclusion not by Dimitrios Ypsilantis, who was ousted and sent far away on some pretext or other, but by the powerful chieftain Kolokotronis.[102]

The participation since the early stages of the revolution of European volunteers inflamed by philhellenic sentiments was yet another source of tension and conflict. European volunteers brought with them Western practices in the organisation and drilling of military units, as well as in military strategy. The leaders of the diaspora saw their contribution as entailing the creation of a regular army controlled by the government, which would, they firmly believed, render the fight against the Ottomans more effective. The French and British philhellenes for their part wished to make their financial contribution to the war effort conditional upon the appointment of an officer of their own choosing. This gave rise to a debate in which foreign commentators and foreign volunteers participated to an extent that had no parallel in any other revolutionary conflict in southern Europe. Small units of European volunteers had been set up as early as 1822, when the Italian officer Pietro Tarella had created a regiment of Greek fighters trained according to Western standards. In the summer of 1825 the first regular army was in fact created by a French military officer, Colonel Charles-Nicolas Fabvier, who led three thousand soldiers.[103] European philhellenes tended to dismiss guerrilla warfare and the military skills of the local chieftains as inadequate to conduct an effective campaign against the Ottomans. They considered that their lack of discipline, haphazard organisation and the absence of an effective central command amounted to structural weaknesses that prevented the Greeks from winning the war. As a philhellene wrote in 1823, 'the Greeks owe their success by sea, as well as by land, to the unexampled stupidity of the Turks'.[104]

The warlords, however, bitterly resented the intervention of European officers. In July 1822 the defeat of the Greek forces led by Mavrokordatos, and the death of Tarella along with the other European officers leading philhellenic units, at the battle of Peta in Epirus served to confirm the prejudices of the kapoi regarding the shortcomings of European, and

102. Comstock, *History*, pp. 159, 170, 181–82; Vakalopoulos, *Τα ελληνικά στρατεύματα* (The Greek troops), pp. 54–58.

103. On the creation of the regular army and on volunteers, see Thanos Veremis, *The Military in Greek Politics: From Independence to Democracy* (London: Hurst & Co., 1997); Bruyère-Ostells, *La Grande Armée*, pp. 115–23; Dakin, *Greek Struggle*, pp. 166–68.

104. BSA, Finlay Papers, H.3, no. 1: Frank Abney Hastings to Lord Byron, Hydra, 1 December 1823.

the merits of guerrilla, warfare.[105] Whenever opportunities for cooperation between the regular forces under European leadership and semi-
regular forces presented themselves subsequently, tensions arose. These
tensions stemmed not only from differences in conceiving and waging war,
but also from personal rivalries between European officers and local chieftains. These were often fuelled also by competition over access to resources.
For instance, in May 1826, soon after the occupation of Messolonghi by the
Ottoman troops of Reshid Pasha, and just before their siege of Athens,
the local chieftain in this town, Gouras, prevailed upon a part of the
population to demand and obtain the expulsion of Fabvier's troops, on
the grounds that there were not sufficient resources for their upkeep, at the
same time refusing the latter's offer to fortify the port of Piraeus.[106]

The civil wars that broke out between 1823 and 1825 show the complex
nature of the tensions unleashed by the revolution and the anti-Ottoman
war. By then Kolokotronis had become the most prominent military figure of the revolution, and led the so-called 'military party'. However, as
these events show, the conflicts that arose did not simply oppose primates,
westernised leaders and military classes. This was firstly because each of
these factions had its own military forces. In April 1823 both Kolokotronis
and the primates supporting Mavrokordatos, when attending the second
national assembly at Astros in the Peloponnese, set up separate military
camps close by. The mere presence of such troops exerted pressure on the
opposing faction and served as a provocative display of their power. As
Kolokotronis wrote in his own memoirs, the party of the primates had
'brought soldiers to support their opinions by force, and I also made use of
force to overturn their opinions'.[107] Secondly, regional rivalries and other
strategic considerations played an equally important role in determining
alliances between and across these groups, and such alliances kept shifting
according to changing circumstances. At Astros some westernised leaders such as Dimitrios Ypsilantis were now siding with the military faction
led by Kolokotronis, while some kapoi from western Greece, given their
regional allegiances, were backing Mavrokordatos.

What led to the first civil war was the fact that the modifications to the
constitutions decided at Astros and supported by the majority party of
the primates had substantially weakened Kolokotronis. The composition
of the new government was equally unfavourable to him, first because the

105. Dakin, *Greek Struggle*, pp. 93–94.
106. GSA, Vlachoyannis Collection, Karaiskakis Archive, box 5, folder 11, ff. 616–17. On
the siege of Athens, see Dakin, *Greek Struggle*, pp. 186–89.
107. Kolokotrones, *Kolokotrones*, pp. 198–99.

position of chief of the army, once held by Kolokotronis, was abolished, and the power of the assembly, whose members now included fifty-six kapoi, was reduced, with the senate now being responsible for appointing the executive; and second, because Kolokotronis was appointed vice-president of the executive, in effect a ploy to keep him in check. He was also excluded from the senate, which was controlled by representatives of the islands and by Mavrokordatos. By the end of the year, therefore, the two bodies had moved to different cities, the executive controlled by Kolokotronis in Nafplion and the senate in Salamis: an unbridgeable rift between them had been created. When the senate appointed new members of the executive, replacing Kolokotronis's ally Metaxas with Ioannis Kolettis, the old executive dominated by Kolokotronis refused to recognise them. In fact, he threatened to set up a military government or—and he used precisely these Italian words—a 'governo militare', a dictatorship.[108] The result of these unresolved tensions was a fully-fledged civil conflict. Between December 1823 and June 1824 a civil war raged, dividing the supporters of Kolokotronis, who included some very powerful clans from the Peloponnese, aided by mercenaries, from their enemies, and opposing two competing governments. The conflict was inaugurated by Panos, the son of Kolokotronis, who attacked the senate gathering in Argos, speaking then on behalf of his father, and came to an end with his surrender in Nafplion in June.

By the end of 1824 alliances had shifted again, and this time civil strife took on a more explicit regional dimension. Koloktronis and the whole of the military class of the Peloponnese with him entered into an alliance with the primates of the same region, whose position in the national government had been weakened substantially in favour of the islanders. The latter had in fact gained control over the first Greek loan sent from Britain, and had sent the Peloponnese primates to fight at a distance from the seat of government. When the province of Arcadia, in the south-west of the Peloponnese, rebelled against taxation imposed by the central administration, the executive reacted by sending an army to the region. In November 1824 Kolokotronis and his allies rallied in defence of the Arcadians. After an initial victory they were, however, defeated: in January 1825 Kolokotronis was arrested and imprisoned on the island of Hydra. His son Panos lost his life in the conflict, while Roumeliot troops flooded into the Peloponnese, indulging in looting and despoliation.[109]

108. Dimitropoulos, Θεόδωρος Κολοκοτρώνης (Theodoros Kolokotronis), p. 78.

109. On the wars, see Dakin, *Greek Struggle*, pp. 123–30; David Brewer, *The Greek War of Independence* (New York: Duckworth, 2001), pp. 226–33.

It was during these two civil wars that notions of betrayal came to be adopted to stigmatise the rebellion of the military leaders. In this period, Greek revolutionary language therefore converged with that of Portuguese and Neapolitan revolutionaries in condemning civil wars as a threat to the unity of the nation. For the *Ellinika Chronika*, published in Messolonghi at the time of the two civil wars, the rebel military leaders involved in them had sought recognition from their fatherland 'by using their sword', or 'via fraud and secrecy'. As a consequence, the war had marked the prevalence of private over public interests. Greece needed instead military leaders like George Washington or Simón Bolívar. The *Ellinika Chronika*, which quoted extensively from Bolívar's Angostura speech, praised his decision to lay down arms and, in recognition of the people's sovereignty, to become a simple citizen once again.[110] At the beginning of the second civil war, the same newspaper explicitly likened leaders such as Andreas Lontos, the Peloponnesian primate who was now challenging the central administration, to Napoleon, described as a rebel and an *apostatis* who had 'turned against the administration of his nation with arms, without having the right to do so'. Like Napoleon, Londos 'complained to the representatives of the nation [. . .] with weapons in his hands', rather than defending his opinions legally and abiding by the law.[111] In addition, the press compared the military rebels to the Ottomans: as traitors they no longer belonged to the national community. Commenting on Kolokotronis's behaviour, Georgios Koundouriotis, president of the executive at the time of the second civil war, wrote that 'traitors should be considered and be treated as Turks'.[112]

Besides the victory of the Roumeliots over the Peloponnesians, what put an end to these civil conflicts was the emergency precipitated by Egyptian invasion in 1825. Those arrested at the end of the civil war, like Kolokotronis, were released in May 1825. Since everybody's military

110. *Ελληνικά Χρονικά* [*Ellinika Chronika*], no. 58, 16 July 1824, in Koumarianou, *Ο Τύπος στον Αγώνα* (The press in the 'Struggle'), 2, pp. 116–19.

111. *Ελληνικά Χρονικά* [*Ellinika Chronika*], no. 94, 19 November 1824, in Koumarianou, *Ο Τύπος στον Αγώνα* (The press in the 'Struggle'), 2, pp. 169–71.

112. Koundouriotis to his brother, 24 December 1824, in Antonios Lignos, ed., *Αρχείον της Κοινότητος Ύδρας, 1778–1832* (Archive of the Community of Hydra, 1778–1832), 16 vols (Piraeus: Typois 'Sphairas', 1921–31), 10, p. 572. Treason still wavered between being an act against one's region of origin or against the nation, or could refer to both at the same time. In Hydra the primates invited the admirals of the navy to treat any sailor 'who acts with malice, attempts to profiteer or deserts the ship', as a traitor, as on their island of origin they would never be considered patriots: 'The Primates of Hydra to Admiral Giorgi Sachtouri and Other Captains and Sailors', 26 August 1824, in Lignos, *Αρχείον* (Archive), 10, pp. 428–29.

contribution was urgently needed, all regional groups and factions had to find a compromise. Military chieftains, in spite of their distrust for island-ers, had to learn to cooperate. The invasion by Ibrahim Pasha and the reconquest by the Egyptians led to the decision that the task of govern-ment would be undertaken by the executive and that the assembly would, at least temporarily, not be consulted. Military leaders therefore acquired novel power and visibility. Admittedly, civil strife re-emerged also after the Egyptian invasion, and remained a constant feature of the anti-Ottoman war. As Thomas Gordon observed, 'No country in the jaws of ruin ever offered a more deplorable spectacle of internal discord, than did Greece at the beginning of 1827, when her notables were divided into three fac-tions, not less opposed on grounds of general policy, than animated by personal rancour.'[113] Divisions in anticipation of the convening of the third national assembly led to the creation of two competing gatherings, one on the island of Aegina, controlled by the governmental commissions appointed in April 1826 to run the country and led by Andreas Zaimis, and one in Ermioni, dominated by Kolokotronis and supported by some of the islanders. Localised conflicts arose both in Hydra, where sailors rioted against certain primates and asked for a share of the booty from naval victories, and outside the capital city of Nafplion, where two rival military leaders bombarded each other from the forts they controlled.[114]

However, as a result of Ibrahim's invasion and the need to fight the common enemy, a consensus was reached among the chieftains that unity had to be found and compromises had to be reached. While the submis-sion of the military class to a central government remained controversial for the entire duration of the revolution, after 1825 disagreements and local conflicts no longer led to full-scale civil war. In Greece after this date, then, pressures deriving from the fight against the Ottomans ended up taking precedence over any other institutional or factional consideration.

Conclusions

The civil wars that broke out in Portugal, Spain, Sicily and Greece put an end to the revolutionary experience in Portugal alone. In this country, the intervention of Dom Miguel was crucial in shifting the military balance towards absolutism and in defeating the constitutional army. However, the re-establishment of absolutism would shortly trigger a new cycle of

113. Gordon, *History*, 2, p. 355.
114. Ibid., pp. 356–58.

civil strife that came to an end only in 1834. With the exception of Portugal, civil wars represented only temporary disturbances, which did not bring down the constitutional regimes. In the Kingdom of the Two Sicilies and in Greece, agreement between the military and civilian elites terminated the civil conflicts between Naples and Sicily, and between the Peloponnese, Roumeli and the islands. In Spain, the counterrevolutionary movement had been substantially weakened by 1823, although anti-revolutionary guerrilla activities remained disruptive at the local level. Rather than treating these as evidence of the weakness of the revolutionary experiments, this chapter has highlighted a series of consequences that these experiences had for the nature of the revolutions. First of all, they had a profound impact on popular participation. Populations in most regions were exposed to conflicting ideas of national community, national independence and regional patriotism, and had to decide whether to support the constitution or side with monarchical absolutism. Civil wars created cleavages within the same social groups, but also inside single communities down to the level of villages. In these circumstances, revolutionaries and counterrevolutionaries needed and looked for popular support in their military efforts. Admittedly, they did not always welcome the consequences of such military engagements. Portuguese liberals resented the popular mobilisation stirred up by the absolutists and dismissed peasants as uncivilised. Sicilian aristocrats, horrified by the destructive effects of the bande, hastened to find a compromise with the Neapolitan authorities in order to forestall further destruction. Even in Greece, military leaders such as Yannis Macriyannis rebuked his troops for having resorted to pillaging, looting and wholesale destruction during the civil war in the Peloponnese, while European military leaders lamented the ineffective and brutal nature of klephtic warfare. Nonetheless, popular mobilisation represented a shared feature of these events. The military participation of peasants in these civil wars was not so much the product of a generalised revolt championing the redistribution of land, but rather a reaction to, and resistance against, some revolutionary policies (in Spain and Portugal) as well as longer term transformations of property rights, and in particular of the erosion of communities' privileges (in Sicily, Portugal and Spain). These circumstances, combined with other ideological and political factors, contributed to the mobilisation of a part of the poorest in rural society.

Second, civil conflicts not only confirmed, but also enhanced, the role of military leadership. Military officers proved indispensable to the survival of the constitutional order, while at the same time some did all they could to undermine it. As a result, army leaders came to stand centre-stage in the political arena and public sphere, becoming political icons capable of mobilising public opinion, gaining substantial political influence in the name of the constitution and of representative institutions, but also on occasion undermining them. In circumstances marked by harsh political divisions and civil tumult, the army could not and did not remain disengaged: it intervened to defend or bring down governments. The roles played in civil and armed conflicts, as well as in the political arena at national level, by Theodoros Kolokotronis, Georgios Karaiskakis, Rafael Riego, Florestano Pepe, João Francisco de Saldanha and Bernardo Correia de Castro e Sepúlveda discussed in this chapter are cases in point. The nature and objectives of military interventions varied greatly. They ranged from Kolokotronis's repeated attempts to guarantee his own influence in national politics at the expense of the central authority to Riego's defence of representative institutions and his posing as a bipartisan supporter of the revolution. But in spite of claims of loyalty to the constitution, the conflictual nature of politics forced army officers constantly to take sides, and to intervene in controversies that divided public opinion and the revolutionary elites. Ultimately, civil strife and war confirmed the eminently military nature of these revolutions: events in which the army was from the outset the main political actor and the agent of a divided popular will.

CHAPTER FOUR

National Wars of Liberation and the End of the Revolutionary Experiences

Introduction

At the core of the justification for the pronunciamientos was the fact that the army acted in defence of the people's sovereignty. It was on behalf of the nation and the constitution that army officers had taken up arms across southern Europe. This led to the belief shared by all southern European revolutionaries that war was legitimate and justified when it served the purpose of defending the rights of the sovereign nation. In March 1821, the Austrians first invaded the Kingdom of the Two Sicilies, and the following April intervened militarily in Piedmont with two very brief and successful military campaigns. The Austrian military interventions in Naples and Piedmont respectively alerted also the Spanish and Portuguese liberals to the risks they were running. Threats of foreign military intervention triggered debates about the legality of such actions and about the defensive or offensive nature of the wars revolutionaries judged themselves entitled to wage. In April 1823, it was the French army that crossed the Pyrenees to reinstate the absolute monarchy. Faced with foreign military interventions, revolutionaries in Naples, Piedmont and Spain reacted with declarations of war in defence of constitutions. The constitutional governments of Naples and Spain called for national insurrections, hoping that the uprisings that had taken place against Napoleon could be replicated. The Greek war differed from all the others in two respects. First, while in Spain, Piedmont and Naples national wars broke out as a result of foreign invasions, in Greece the anti-Ottoman revolt, almost as soon as it broke out, transformed a former ruling ethnic community into the foreign enemy to be defeated and expelled. Nonetheless, Greek revolutionaries immediately labelled the conflict as a war of national liberation. Second, the anti-Ottoman revolt succeeded in its aims, as it led to the creation of a new state, while the national wars in Piedmont, Naples and Spain resulted in defeat. In spite of these differences, the fate of the Greek revolution, like that of the others, was determined primarily by foreign diplomatic and military interventions.

These national wars in fact put to a final test the effectiveness of the revolutionary script employed to accomplish evolutionary change, and revealed the limitations of this strategy. All constitutional governments appealed to their populations to rise up against the enemy, as if invoking the Spanish anti-Napoleonic uprising that was so central to their shared revolutionary script. As this chapter will demonstrate, a variety of factors determined the extent of—and imposed constraints upon—military and civilian mobilisation in defence of the constitutional regimes faced with foreign invasions. Once war was declared, popular support for the diverse constitutions varied enormously, from region to region, and from country to country, and fluctuated as time went on. The fact that the economic crisis and the civil war had made the constitution less popular in 1823 than it had been in 1820 certainly help explain the lack of mobilisation in Spain in the face of a French invasion. However, efforts to stir up a mass revolt failed for two main reasons. First, a generalised uprising could not take place in the absence of a full royal endorsement. These revolutions, declared in the name of the kings, not against them, could not survive without their explicit support. Second, faced with foreign military intervention by a superior force, armies and civilians, rather sensibly, laid down their arms.

The combination of these two factors represented an insuperable obstacle to overcome, and rendered the survival of the revolutionary order impossible. Thus the collapse of the revolutions cannot be attributed to their inherent weakness, or to the limitations of their social basis alone, but rather to these 'external' constraints. Mass mobilisation against an external threat could take place only with the explicit support of a monarch. The existence of a royal candidate willing to endorse the constitution was a condition that did not exist in Spain, Piedmont and Naples. It did exist in Portugal, where it created the preconditions for a prolonged civil war. Here too, however, diplomatic interference did not operate in favour of the survival of the constitution. Although in late 1826 the British sent an expeditionary force to Portugal, they did so more to prevent Spanish interference than to defend the constitution.[1]

A popular uprising, after all, could not guarantee a permanent victory, even in Greece, where it had been so widespread. Here too the European powers determined the fate of the revolution. However, as the section below on 'Greece and the nationalisation of the anti-Ottoman conflict' shows, in spite of the unstable and conflictual nature of Greek revolution, the shared experience of war against the Ottomans played a central role in turning the Greek rebels into a national community. It was the war that transformed Ypsilantis's original claim, when he had crossed the river Pruth, that the Greeks were a national community deserving to be liberated, into a widely accepted belief. The section will account for the reasons why, if most Greeks did not believe themselves to belong to a national community in 1821, they probably did so six years later, by virtue of the war. This same section also considers the foreign diplomatic and military pressures that determined its outcome.

The failure of the revolutionary script in Naples, Piedmont and Spain

The Neapolitan revolution collapsed in the face of foreign invasion as swiftly as it had prevailed, and with hardly any resistance, less than nine months before. In spite of the existence of some popular support for a national war, what proved fatal to its survival once this had been declared was the combination of the monarch's own conduct and the overwhelming impact of foreign invading armies. But equally striking was the evident determination of the revolutionaries, at least in public, to stand by the monarch in spite of his treacherous behaviour. When King Ferdinando was invited by the European powers to the Congress of Troppau (which was being transferred to Laibach [Ljubljana]) in early December 1820, the Neapolitan parliament gave its approval, on condition that the monarch defend the constitutional regime. This decision would prove fatal. The Austrian foreign minister Metternich had pushed already for intervention, but a request by the monarch was required. Having obtained it, on 19 January 1820 the representatives of Austria, Russia and Prussia issued an ultimatum to the Neapolitan government. Declaring the revolution to be illegal, and defining it as an act against the legitimate sovereign that

---

1. On the diplomatic context of the civil war see Paquette, *Imperial Portugal*, pp. 232–34, 300–303.

had only produced anarchy and military despotism, they demanded the immediate withdrawal of the constitution, failing which they would issue a declaration of war.[2]

Faced with this ultimatum, the Neapolitan parliament decided to reject it and to vote for a war in defence of the constitution. In the face of the Austrian threat, the Spanish slogans 'Constitution of Spain or death' and 'Long live the constitution' became the rallying cries of the carbonari demonstrating in the streets of Naples, but this language was also adopted by the parliament and the army.[3] In a proclamation to the 'warriors' of the country, the parliament called upon the army to defend it from the threat of servitude, for the sake of 'the constitution or death'.[4] Colonel Gabriele Pepe, a cousin of the more famous Guglielmo, had a copy of the constitution stitched to the flag of his regiment when leaving Naples for the front line.[5] Against this background, the press rallied in support of the national call for rearmament and mass mobilisation, but emphasised at the same time its defensive nature. As a Neapolitan dialogue argued, the Neapolitan revolutionary army, unlike that of France in 1792, was not a threat to the international order, since for its part it was not defending 'a tyrannical democracy, but a temperate monarchy based on holy laws'.[6] Crucially, in spite of disappointment with the king's conduct and rumours about his betrayal of the constitution, both the parliament and the press chose to describe their monarch as a prisoner of the Congress. Consequently they never criticised him and never attacked him publicly.

At first, the (rumoured, but undeclared) hostility of the sovereign did not seem to undermine the determination of the army to defend the constitutional regime. The imminence of a foreign invasion did not split the army into two opposing camps fighting against each other, as it was to do in Piedmont and Spain. In addition, at least at the beginning of the conflict, popular support in defence of the constitutional regime was not wanting. Indeed, it emerged spontaneously in various parts of the kingdom. As early as the end of October, the city of Catanzaro in Calabria

2. Annibale Alberti, ed., *Atti del parlamento delle Due Sicilie, 1820–1821*, 6 vols (Bologna: Zanichelli, 1926–41), 3, pp. 378–85; Schroeder, *Transformation*, pp. 610–12.

3. Carlo De Nicola, *Diario napoletano 1798–1825*, ed. Renata De Lorenzo, 3 vols (Naples: Società napoletana di storia patria, repr. 1999 [1906]), 3, p. 228; Pietro Calà Ulloa, 'Sulle rivoluzioni del reame di Napoli: Ricordi' (manuscript, Naples, 1872), vol. 2, f. 288, in BNN, MS XI F 42–43.

4. SNSP, Opuscoli 1820–21, SDX.C.11: 'Dichiarazione del Parlamento Nazionale all'armata napoletana sopra la costituzione o morte'.

5. Ulloa, *Sulla rivoluzione*, f. 298.

6. *Discorso di tre studenti sulle circostanze attuali* (Naples, 1820), p. 23.

offered to fund the organisation of a battalion of 110 volunteers, called the Compagnia franca di militi di Calabria Ultra, in defence of national independence, the constitution and the monarchy, to be sent to the capital city of Naples.[7] Such offers to support the constitutional government militarily intensified when the decision by Austria to intervene became official, in spite of the fact that the king's position had by then become known. During the month of February 1821 private citizens submitted petitions to the parliament requesting that it approve the organisation of regiments of volunteers from Catania and Messina, the cities in Sicily that had most enthusiastically rallied to the constitutional regime. As had been the case in Piedmont and in Moldavia at the beginning of the revolutions, in Naples too students volunteered to join the national war: the veterinary school wanted to organise its own regiment. Similar requests to be permitted to recruit battalions of volunteers came from the towns of Sora and Arpino in the Papal States, not far from the border with the kingdom. In the region of Calabria Citeriore, the Albanian community also wrote to offer their own battalion.[8] In those provinces that were to the fore in organising and supporting the uprising of July 1820, local communities were keen to defend the constitution. In the area of Avellino, for instance, where the revolution had begun back in July, in early March 1821 representatives of the parliament had been welcomed with hurrahs for 'the constitution, the parliament and the prince'. At night members of the militias, flanked by women, all sang together in the streets songs calling for national independence. In the district of Campagna, just outside the city of Salerno, a stronghold of the Carboneria, all were eager to contribute to the war effort: eight militia battalions had been recruited and equipped, but four more could have been set up, had there been the funds to arm them.[9] In other provinces, however, the situation was less favourable, and the response to calls for mobilisation somewhat patchy. Efforts to organise legions failed altogether in Basilicata: no sooner had they been set up than their members deserted. Likewise in the province of Abruzzo Ultra, the organising of provincial militias was weakened systematically by those well-off enough opting to buy their way out of conscription through 'offers'.[10]

Hopes that widespread mobilisation would guarantee the survival of the constitutional regime were boosted by faith in guerrilla warfare, a key

7. Alberti, *Atti del parlamento*, 1, p. 579.

8. Alberti, *Atti del parlamento*, 3, pp. 393, 433, 477.

9. Ibid., pp. 609–10; ASN, Polizia Generale II, ff. 40–45: Macchiaroli to the parliament, 5 March 1821.

10. Alberti, *Atti del parlamento*, 3, pp. 469, 566.

element of the Spanish script and based on the memory of the anti-French wars. In the words of a contemporary observer, on the eve of the Austrian invasion everybody was convinced that 'the people wanted desperately to defend itself [. . .]. Everybody looked to the example of Spain'.[11] The conviction that guerrilla warfare along Spanish lines was the most effective response to the military threat was at the basis of the decision by the Ministry of War taken belatedly in February, and then backed by the parliament in March, when the war had already been lost, to organise guerrilla units throughout the kingdom to support the regular army with *corpi franchi* (free units) of armed civilians.[12]

What most limited popular mobilisation against the foreign army, however, was the tardiness shown in setting up the provincial militias. Soon after the events of July 1820, responsibility for these had fallen to General Guglielmo Pepe. Immediately after his resignation from the leadership of the constitutional army, Pepe had been appointed head of the provincial militias of the kingdom, and asked to reorganise and reform them, a task he had already accomplished before the revolution in two specific areas, Avellino and Puglia. In line with his own vision of the nation-in-arms, Pepe set out to incorporate the majority of the population into militias. Artisans and those who were not landowners would also be included, as 'legioni' in support of the existing militias were immediately raised. In line with this policy, Pepe insisted on calling up all military men below the age of forty who had previously been discharged, introducing a system of subsidies for the neediest families affected. Pepe's commitment to the extensive participation of the population in the military defence of the country rested upon his belief that, without an army, the nation could not be formed. His stance was thus in marked contrast to General Michele Carrascosa's preferred option, which was to limit the size of the militias and recruit into them only those who were strictly needed.[13] However, not enough progress had been made in organising a national defence by the time the risk of an Austrian intervention had become tangible. Therefore, while on paper the militias could muster two hundred thousand men, in reality only a much smaller number were ready by February, on the eve of the Austrian attack. Moreover, most of these were poorly organised and armed.[14]

What affected mobilisation was not only the tardiness of decisions to organise the militias and the last-minute efforts to create guerrilla bands,

11. Ulloa, *Sulla rivoluzione*, f. 297.
12. Alberti, *Atti del parlamento*, 3, pp. 433, 629.
13. On this see Moscati, *Guglielmo Pepe*, 1, pp. lxxx–lxxxi, 112.
14. Piero Pieri, *Storia militare del Risorgimento* (Turin: Einaudi, 1962), p. 76.

but also divisions between the different military groups involved in the preparation of the defence. The Carboneria in fact set up its own *corpi franchi*, dressed in special uniforms and badges in Salerno and Capua, in an effort to stiffen the national resistance. In an attempt to demonstrate unity in the face of the external threat, the Alta Vendita (Grand Lodge) of the Carboneria in Naples had organised a banquet and invited the army leaders, Carrascosa and Colletta among them, whose military abilities they doubted, to express their support for the constitutional army.[15] However, the hostility among some sectors of the army towards the Carboneria, and their suspicions of popular mobilisation, evident already at the beginning of the revolution, re-emerged at this juncture. In the city of Capua, where resistance against the Austrian invasion was to be organised in early March, the army seemed to be more concerned with preventing the planting of the tree of liberty by the newly organised *corpi franchi* of the Carboneria than with the coordination of the war effort. Accused of taking advantage of the imminent war to organise republican insurrections, carbonaro leaders of the militias were arrested or isolated by army officers.[16] What further undermined mobilisation was the inadequate preparation of the militias and legions raised in the provinces. Those who did converge towards defensive positions in support of the regular army found themselves badly armed and equipped, with no pay, and with no suitable shelter. It was no wonder, then, that they often deserted before they had even arrived at their destination.[17] Thus the regime found itself with a more limited defence capacity than it had hoped to muster. When General Pepe decided to engage battle with the Austrian troops of General Frimont near the city of Rieti at Antrodoco, he had at his disposal 5,500 inadequately armed militiamen along with six thousand regular troops against General Frimont's nine thousand soldiers and 2,500 cavalry.

In the end, King Ferdinando's hostility to the regime, combined with Austrian military might, sealed the fate of the constitutional government. No generalised popular uprising broke out in the face of the Austrian campaign. The parliament until the very end continued to defend the monarch, arguing that he was a prisoner of the European powers and that the war had been waged against his will. Yet neither this argument nor the formal support for the constitution given by his son Prince Francesco, heir to the throne and vicar of the kingdom, were sufficient to sustain the

15. Pepe, *Memoirs*, 3, pp. 118–19.
16. Stassano, *Cronaca*, pp. 416–17.
17. Ibid., pp. 390–91.

morale of the army and the militias. In fact, the heir to the throne failed to provide a credible point of reference for the defence of the regime. Already before the start of the military operations, one of the three divisions under General Carrascosa's command made it known that they would not fight against the monarch.[18] When the Neapolitan army led by Pepe was defeated at Antrodoco, it became impossible to reorganise the troops that were retreating. Rumours about royal revenge as well as about betrayals, along with intimations that the Austrians would not take revenge upon the militias, led to the disintegration of Pepe's army. Carrascosa's own troops returned to Naples and dispersed soon afterwards.[19]

The Austrian military campaign against the constitutional regime in Naples coincided with the beginning of the Piedmontese revolution, and contributed to the anti-Austrian, nationalist nature of that pronunciamiento. Indeed, in this case, the declaration of a war of national liberation to create an Italian federation coincided with the introduction of the constitution. In communicating to the public the reasons for the revolution, army officers were positing a direct link between the two, since they considered the constitution to be a tool necessary to defeat the Austrians.[20] As had been the case in Naples, however, so too in Piedmont the behaviour of the monarch would prove fatal to the revolution. Much as in Portugal and Spain, division between those regiments loyal to the constitution and those against it led to military conflict; and this conflict between various Piedmontese forces, combined with Austrian military intervention, put an end to the Piedmontese revolution just over a month from its inception.

Besides their brief duration, the Piedmontese events were peculiar in two important respects. First, while the outbreak of revolution had been accompanied initially by some degree of popular support in Turin and Alessandria, and by a full-scale insurrection of Genoa in defence of the constitution, the war against Austria was a rapid military event isolated from any form of popular participation, Second, as discussed earlier, the revolution here had been negotiated with a member of the royal family, from a cadet branch, but heir apparent: Carlo Alberto, Prince of Carignano. Although the extent of his involvement and commitment had been unclear, his ambiguous stance nonetheless gave the organisers of the revolution a degree of confidence that he would not oppose it. In fact, a few days after the outbreak of the revolution, King Vittorio Emanuele

18. Pieri, *Storia*, p. 79.

19. Ibid., pp. 80–81, Galasso, *Storia*, 5, p. 220.

20. AST, Segreteria di Stato Affari Interni, Alta Polizia, Processi politici del 1821, fascio 53, no. 108, ff. 73, 160.

abdicated, fleeing Piedmont for Nice. In the absence of the heir apparent—his brother Carlo Felice, who was then in the Duchy of Modena—Vittorio Emmanuele appointed Carlo Alberto as regent of the kingdom. The new King Carlo Felice immediately made it clear that he was opposed to the revolution and indeed to any institutional change whatsoever; whereas Carlo Alberto, after some hesitation, on 13 March swore an oath of allegiance to the Spanish constitution. In the days following, he agreed to mobilise the army, in view of the prospect of war against the Austrians, and appointed Santorre di Santarosa as minister of war. While this decision temporarily saved the revolution, the regent's loyalty to his oath did not last long. He soon changed his mind and, following orders received from the king, 21 March he decided to abandon Turin and join the troops that had remained loyal to the monarch under the command of General Latour in Novara. This decision put an end to any hopes that the revolution might survive, its fate being sealed when Austria accepted Carlo Felice's request for military intervention to take place at the end of the same month, a request approved by the Holy Alliance gathering at Laibach.[21]

Exactly as the Neapolitan revolutionaries had done just a few weeks before, the Piedmontese revolutionaries continued to defend the monarchy and to absolve the monarch of any responsibility for what had occurred until the very end. They argued that, being in the hands of the Austrians, King Carlo Felice's declarations did not reflect his will. Once Carlo Alberto's decision to move to Novara had demonstrated beyond all doubt that the prince had completely abandoned the revolution, and the Piedmontese army led by General Latour was ready to wage a war with the support of the Austrians, the minister of war Count Santarosa issued an appeal to the soldiers in Novara to avoid a civil war, spare Piedmont a foreign invasion and unite against the Austrians by crossing the frontier into Lombardy to save the throne. The prince was spared direct criticism, Santarosa describing him as a victim of traitors but a hero of the national cause, while King Carlo Felice was described as a prisoner of the Austrians.[22] Local constitutional leaders made last minute appeals to the population to stay united against treason in order to defend the constitution, isolate the few traitors and liberate Italy from the foreigner, in proclamations which declared 'Viva l'Italia, viva il re, viva l'Italia!' and 'Viva la costituzione di Spagna! Indipendenza, o morte!' The former president of the giunta of

21. Candeloro, *Storia*, pp. 111–19.
22. Santorre di Santarosa, 23 March 1821, in Gualterio, *Gli ultimi rivolgimenti*, 1, pp. 164–66.

Alessandria addressed the soldiers in Novara as brothers, and, calling upon them to avoid infamy and betrayal, asked them to march together against the enemy.[23]

Yet neither these appeals to avoid foreign invasion nor those made to stir up popular support succeeded. The four thousand constitutional troops led by San Marzano and Morozzo di Magliano that moved towards Novara, on the Piedmontese side of the border with Austrian Lombardy, were not welcomed by the eight thousand soldiers led by General Latour and Carlo Alberto, supported by a cohort of eight thousand Austrian troops and an additional seven thousand ready to cross the border if the need arose. As had happened in Naples a month before, the war was a quick and all but bloodless event, and the battle that took place on the outskirts of Novara produced no more than thirty casualties. This was due not only to the preponderance of the forces hostile to the constitutional army, but quite simply to the fact that after this battle there was hardly any resistance shown to the invading army. With the exception of a very minor attempt on the outskirts of Vercelli by one regiment, the constitutional troops in Alessandria, Vercelli and Turin put up no resistance to the entrance of the Austrians into those cities.[24]

In Spain too, widespread mobilisation against the invasion failed to occur, and explicit calls to repeat the resistance shown to the Napoleonic troops fell on deaf ears. With the exception of Catalonia, which became the last constitutional stronghold to yield to the foreign army, the constitutional troops put up even less resistance to the French invasion than did the Piedmontese and Neapolitan armies. On 7 April 1823 the French army led by the Duke of Angoulême crossed the Pyrenees, and succeeded in conquering most of the country in three months. In the face of the invasion, the constitutional government took refuge first in Seville, and finally in Cádiz, where it capitulated at the end of September; General Mina's army negotiated the entrance of the French army into Barcelona at the beginning of November.[25] By seizing the military initiative and occupying

23. AST, Segreteria di Stato Affari Interni, Alta Polizia, Processi politici del 1821, fascio 53: broadsheet, 'Ai cittadini monregalesi ed agli abitanti della provincia', 7 April 1821; MRM, Bertarelli, Proclami di Alessandria, 05946: broadsheet, Guglielmo Ansaldi, 'Popolo! Soldati!', 26 March 1821; Ansaldi, 'Alle truppe concentrate a Novara', 3 April 1821, in Gualterio, *Gli ultimi rivolgimenti*, 1, pp. 168–70.

24. Pieri, *Storia*, pp. 99–103.

25. Josep Fontana, *De en medio del tiempo: La segunda restauración española 1823–1834*, 2nd edn (Barcelona: Crítica, 2013), pp. 39–61; Rafael Sánchez Mantero, *Los Cien Mil Hijos de San Luis y las relaciones franco-españolas* (Seville: Editorial Universidad de Sevilla, 1981).

the country, France re-established Spain as within its sphere of influence, and strengthened its position in Europe, with the support of the other powers. Military intervention had already been requested by Fernando in the summer of 1822, when he had asked the czar for assistance in regaining his absolute throne.[26] The possibility of a French intervention had been discussed by the European powers in Verona at the end of 1822, but Prime Minister Villèle was still reluctant to take that route, preferring to convince Fernando to modify the constitution by adding an upper chamber, in accordance with the French example. At the beginning of 1823 the appointment of a new foreign minister, Chateaubriand, keener on the idea of a war, persuaded the ministry to declare it, with the encouragement of Russia, the hesitant support of Austria, and the hostility of Britain alone.[27]

Historians have used terms such as 'betrayal' when describing the ease with which the constitutional army capitulated, focusing on the money used by the French to buy its consent to stop fighting. Yet Spanish events had obvious parallels with the conduct of constitutional armies in Naples and Piedmont, which disintegrated after a few desultory skirmishes against overwhelmingly larger numbers of enemy troops. The Spanish constitutional army with its fifty thousand troops had to confront the ninety thousand French soldiers who crossed the Pyrenees in April 1823, followed by an additional thirty thousand, not to mention the irregular royalist guerrillas supporting them, these amounting to between twelve and thirty-five thousand. Given such impossible odds, continuing to fight seemed hardly reasonable. Mounting a defence of the constitution in such unfavourable circumstances had to be weighed against the attraction of accepting the generous terms of the capitulation offered by the French, together with the hopes of salvaging military careers. More importantly perhaps, the leaders of the constitutional army were aware that the French government would act as a guarantor against the extremism and violence displayed during the civil war by the realistas, whose alliance with the monarch seemed indeed to be a greater threat than French occupation. The French invading army's calls to embrace the 'true fatherland', which was not the constitutional one, to desert the leaders of a 'liberticide faction' and join the majority of Spaniards in defence of the monarch, may not have been convincing, but the appeal of laying down one's arms was too strong. Advantages and opportunities for a career in the army were promised to those willing to set

26. La Parra López, *Los Cien Mil Hijos*, pp. 106–8.
27. Schroeder, *Transformation*, pp. 623–27.

aside rebellion and join the king in Córdoba.[28] Indeed, although General Mina continued to lead the resistance in Catalonia, Generals Ballesteros, General Morillo and the Count of La Bisbal, in charge respectively of the defence of Aragon, Asturias and Galicia and Castilla la Nueva, capitulated after negotiating with the French. Ballesteros avoided any military confrontation, withdrawing with his army in front of the French, while Morillo changed sides and assisted the French at the siege of La Coruña, a city that resisted for twenty-four days before capitulating; La Bisbal, a general known to be in a political sense something of a turncoat, was among the earliest advocates of an agreement with the enemy, and abandoned his troops and generals to join the French.[29]

Along with scant military opposition, little popular resistance was put up against the invading army. Most of the popular uprisings that erupted in the context of the French invasion were in fact against the constitutional regime, and in favour of the reintroduction of the absolute monarchy: the invasion was occasionally even cheered as a liberation from constitutionalism. In Zaragoza, for instance, a junta of notables was set up to guarantee law and order, prior to handing the city over to the French. The local constitutional leadership would seem to have made little attempt to stir up popular resistance, of which there is no evidence. On the contrary, upon the arrival of the French army on 24 April, the constitutional authorities left the city along with the militias, and crowds gathered to celebrate the absolute monarch. The invasion provided opportunities to vent anger at the liberals, in a combination of instances of individual violence that flared up across Spain with more substantial popular uprisings. These uprisings demonstrate the extent to which the constitutional regime had lost legitimacy and forfeited the original goodwill of sectors of the popular classes, grievously affected as they had been by the economic crisis. Major royalist insurrections broke out during the following months, in Madrid first and then in Seville. In May 1823, on their arrival at the gates of Madrid, royalist troops led by Jorge Bessières were welcomed by hundreds of individuals from the popular *barrios* (neighbourhoods), including women and children who, incited by friars, had armed themselves to loot the city and attack the liberals. Bessières's guerrillas were driven out of the city, and the insurgency was brutally repressed, but similar displays of support for absolutism, and violence against the liberals, recurred

---

28. APR, Papeles Reservados de Fernando VII, 71, ff. 107–8: 'A los soldados del exercito de Ballesteros', n.d.

29. Fontana, *De en medio del tiempo*, pp. 47–49.

a few days later upon the arrival of the French army in the capital.[30] In Seville, the departure of the constitutional government and the Cortes on 12 June 1823 resulted in an uprising in which the urban population from the poorest neighbourhoods attacked entire property-owning families and looted the luggage and belongings of those preparing to leave the city from the port. They then directed their anger and violence at the *sociedades patrióticas* (associations of supporters of the constitution) and the café where constitutionalists were accustomed to gather. Several cases of murder resulted from this uprising.[31] In these cities resentment against liberalism thus coincided with the social war of the poorest, and often unemployed, strata of the urban populations against the rich liberals, many of whom were merchants: the so-called *negros*.

Attempts to revive the memory of the Napoleonic invasion of the fatherland to stir up a similar popular resistance against the French army failed. In April 1823 the government and the Cortes decamped to Seville, from where they issued a manifesto in the name of the king that invited all Spaniards to take up arms. The manifesto claimed that the Spanish nation the king was addressing had been able to 'glorify and ensure [its] own independence' fighting against Napoleon, and the territory now to be defended against the French soldiers was the self-same earth steeped in the blood of their predecessors. It dismissed allegations that the French invasion had been carried out in defence of monarchical freedom, and argued instead that the French were seeking once more to turn Spain into a province of their empire. Thus the text defended the freedoms guaranteed by the constitution along with freedom from foreign oppression and domination.[32] Yet the lack of popular opposition to French intervention shows the extent to which these circumstances were radically different from those that had produced the legendary popular insurrection against the French twelve years before. Then, a determination to defend the monarchy in the absence of the king had stimulated the insurgency across the country against an atheistical enemy. This time, however, the monarch was on Spanish soil and, as the realistas argued, the French had come to liberate him from his captivity at the hands of the constitutionalists.

30. Álvaro París Martín, 'El fin del Trienio: Contrarrevolución popular y terror blanco en el Madrid de 1823', *Ayer*, forthcoming (2022), DOI: https://doi.org/10.55509/ayer/902. Details can be found in Bayo, *Historia*, 3, pp. 86–89; Miraflores, *Apuntes histórico-críticos*, p. 204.

31. On Zaragoza, see Rújula, *Contrarrevolución*, p. 84.; On Seville, see Fontana, *De en medio del tiempo*, pp. 52–53.

32. 'Manifiesto del rey a la Nacion', 23 April 1823, in *Suplemento à la Gazeta Española del martes 29 de abril de 1823*, pp. 81–82.

In addition, the enemy army was patently not a threat to religion, nor did it engage, as it had done under the Napoleonic banners, in gratuitous acts of violence and looting against the local populations.

In this situation, King Fernando did all he could to prevent the revolutionary government from defending itself against the invading army, and never stopped conspiring to bring down the regime. The monarch's hostility towards the constitution was now common knowledge, and members of the militias, along with the exaltados, now at long last began to advocate the end of the monarchy and the arrest of the king. Like their Neapolitan and Piedmontese counterparts, however, even at the height of the crisis of the revolution, the overwhelming majority of Spanish revolutionaries were very reluctant to question royal authority. In Seville, Fernando had done all he could to delay the departure for Cádiz, in the hope that a conspiracy would put an end to the constitutional regime.[33] When the king refused to give his consent to the departure to Cádiz required to save the constitutional government, the Cortes, after some debate, suspended his powers on the basis of Article 187 of the constitution, which allowed the establishment of a regency whenever moral or physical impediments prevented the ruling sovereign from exercising his authority. While nineteen deputies refused to vote on this matter, eighty-three approved the decision, with only one contrary vote, and a temporary regency composed of a member of the Cortes and two councillors of state was appointed. Yet this was a temporary measure, and in Cádiz the monarch was reinstated fully in his authority.[34]

While no generalised anti-French insurrection took place, it is worth noting that pro-constitutional public opinion had not simply evaporated. A lack of mobilisation did not mean that enthusiasm for the restoration of absolutism was widespread, either. Although isolated, some cases of resistance or refusal to demobilise occurred. For instance, at the end of May an attempt was made by a column of one hundred villagers led by fifteen horsemen from the constitutional army to enter and occupy the town of Tembleque near Toledo, but this column was kept out of the village by armed forces greatly outnumbering it and by the town's own population, and was eventually chased away by the French invading army.[35] When travelling from Madrid to Seville, the Cortes had been cheered by crowds gathering in each of the villages through which it passed, whereas the

33. La Parra López, *Los Cien Mil Hijos*, pp. 203–4.
34. Fontana, *De en medio del tiempo*, p. 51.
35. AHN, Consejos Suprimidos, legajo 12269, f. 94: Ayuntamiento of Tembleque to the Ministerio del Interior, June 1823.

monarch for his part had not been welcomed with similar demonstrations of support.[36] Barcelona and Cádiz confirmed their reputation as constitutional bulwarks. In Cádiz the population did not greet the monarch with any display of enthusiasm on his arrival, and remained loyal to its government until the handing over of the city to the French army by its military commander.

Besides Cádiz, it was Catalonia, and the cities of Barcelona, Tarragona and Hostalric in particular, that put up the most lasting resistance to the French army. In this region, General Francisco Espoz y Mina's troops, already engaged in fighting counterrevolutionary guerrillas since the summer of 1822, enjoyed the support of voluntary militias organised by the exaltado municipality of Barcelona. On 9 July 1823 General Mina declared martial law over the city, thus concentrating all powers in the hands of the military. Although his defence was welcomed by the radicals then governing the city, the period of the siege was marked by tensions between army and exaltados. These latter remained reluctant to accept surrender until the very last moment, despite Mina's early attempts to negotiate with the French army. They called upon people and soldiers alike to resist the invasion in the name of the oath sworn in defence of the constitution, and of the rights and freedom acquired with it, and invited militias from neighbouring cities to assist with the defence of Barcelona. They spoke of the war as an act in defence of citizens' sovereignty. It was only at the end of October, in the face of the declining support offered by the population, unemployed in spite of the promises of work given to them, that the exaltados accepted the inevitability of surrender. In the end, it was also the very generous terms of the surrender negotiated between Mina and the French that facilitated this decision: the militias had been promised that no harm would come to them after demobilisation, and the army was to be kept in employment, while civilians who wished to do so could go into exile. Thus, the exaltados' determination to resist was defeated by circumstances. The minority who refused to accept the deal, including the commander of the militias, were first arrested and then expelled from the city.[37] Like the carbonari in Naples, the exaltados in Catalonia remained loyal to their vision of a popular defence, and did all they could to mobilise some form of resistance, even in the face of a foreign invasion. In Spain, therefore, the constitutional government may have lost some of

36. Bayo, *Historia*, 3, p. 72.

37. Francisco Dueñas García, 'El sitio de Barcelona de 1823', in *El municipi de Barcelona i els combats pel govern de la ciutat*, ed Joan Roca Albert (Barcelona: Proa, 1997), pp. 123–33.

its original appeal after three years, but what dealt it the fatal blow was a military invasion against which it seemed pointless to resist.

Greece and the nationalisation of the anti-Ottoman conflict

During the anti-Ottoman uprising it was notions of honour and loyalty that first and foremost bound military warlords to the fighters of their own bands, their individual allies and the members of the local community they came from. While the practice of war continued to support such notions, and allegiance to individual leaders remained of paramount importance, during the revolution chieftains started to recognise that their military activities belonged to a larger conflict opposing Christians and infidels. Thus, in spite of the constant infighting and regardless of the frequently local nature of the conflict, many of them came to treat their fight also as a war waged on behalf of a community in a much wider sense, not just that of their own region or village. Karaiskakis, for instance, when addressing the enemy, systematically employed obscenities, dismissing them as 'shitty Turks' and making abusive comments against their faith. This was a language of rebellion through which a previously subject religious community was able symbolically to challenge its former lords and masters, who were now simply 'the Turks'.[38]

An important consequence of the uprising was the growing propensity of its protagonists to see it as a national event. It was the Philiki Etaireia that first introduced notions of brotherhood and loyalty previously unknown to Greek informal fighting practices. Dimitrios and Alexandros Ypsilantis thus invited everyone they had recruited to swear an oath of allegiance to the cause of national liberation, a breach on occasion being punished by death. Efforts to create a central administration went hand in hand with public declarations that the war of independence was a war of national liberation, and that the emancipation of Greece was in fact something that the Greeks themselves were earning through their own sacrifice. In April 1823 at Astros, the assembly that had been called to draft and approve a new constitution sent out a proclamation to the Greeks stating that 'the national war of the Greeks continues for the third

38. Nikolaos Kasomoulis, Ενθυμήματα στρατιωτικά της Επαναστάσεως των Ελλήνων, 1821–1833 (Military memoirs of the revolution of the Greeks, 1821–1833), ed. Yannis Vlachoyannis, 3 vols (Athens: Chorigia Pagkeiou Epitropis, 1939–42), 1, p. 308, quoted in Maroula Efthymiou, 'Cursing with a Message: The Case of Georgios Karaiskakis in 1823', Historein 2 (2000): 173–82 at p. 174.

year', and that 'the nation had shed torrents of blood' in order to realise its independence. The proclamation went on to declare also 'the justice of the war', one that had been fought to defend 'the rights of nature and the religion they defend'.[39]

'Nationalising' the war rendered all cooperation or compromise with the enemy utterly unacceptable. Consequently, the leaders of the revolutions came to stigmatise the practice of kapakia as unpatriotic. From the second year of the revolution, Mavrokordatos, who had himself previously approved of this practice, began to consider the act of negotiating with the enemy and resubmitting temporarily to his authority to be an act of treachery. Although the condemnation of this practice was designed to curb the power of great military leaders, it also transformed perceptions of the war and understandings of what was or was not legitimate. The trial of so prominent a chieftain as Georgios Karaiskakis contributed to the stigmatisation of these forms of betrayal of the national cause. Its coverage by the press turned it into a public event, discussed extensively among civilians and fighters alike. From the onset of the revolution Karaiskakis had refused to recognise the authority of Mavrokordatos in western Greece. In January 1824 Mavrokordatos organised a meeting with the military chieftains of his region with the aim of gaining control over their military activities. During that meeting, it was decided to centralise the recruitment and payment of the troops, make kapakia illegal, appoint a war committee of three people to direct military affairs and set up a military court. Karaiskakis, however, was unhappy about the reforms, considering them to be an intolerable attempt at undermining his authority within his own power base, the former armatolikion of Agrafa. As a consequence, he was accused of undermining the defence of Messolonghi by negotiating with the enemy in order to regain control over Agrafa. Once arrested, he was tried in the church of Anatoliko by a court made up of chieftains allied to Mavrokordatos, and presided over by the bishop of Artas.[40] Although the evidence collected against him was scant and contradictory, in the end the court condemned him to exile, stating that if evidence of his repentance were to be furnished it might see fit to revise its sentence. The public sentence of the court, published in the press and posted in the public spaces of the city, stated that Karaiskakis 'did not behave as a patriot and a Christian', and 'he offended us by taking arms

39. Comstock, *History*, pp. 267–68.

40. Trikoupis, *Ιστορία* (History), 3, pp. 118–20; Kasomoulis, *Ενθυμήματα στρατιωτικά* (Military memoirs), 1, pp. 354–90.

against the *patris* [fatherland]' and concluded that he was 'a usurper of the patris and a traitor'.[41] Nikolaos Kasomoulis, who attended the trial, wrote that this condemnation 'drew everyone away from Karaiskakis, and no one dared to take his side, not even to go near him, fearing that they could be infected'.[42]

Besides the circulation of proclamations from the central authorities, the prolonged experience of war against a common enemy paved the way to the perception of the conflict as a national one. The conflict enhanced the mobility and interaction of fighters with each other. Fighters from different regions of Greece had already entered into contact when in exile, after being expelled from the Peloponnese and from Roumeli in 1807 and fighting for the European armies. This interaction increased further during the revolution. Although the civil wars had enhanced existing regional hostilities, they also paved the way for future cooperation. As Kasomoulis noted in his memoirs, it was only during the second civil war, when the Roumeliots invaded the Peloponnese, that the populations of the Peloponnese and the islands came to see them as part of the nation (on this occasion Georgios Koundouriotis, who came from Hydra, wished to become commander-in-chief of all Greek forces).[43] As was noted earlier, an important factor determining military cooperation was the emergency created by the invasion of the Peloponnese by the Egyptian forces led by Ibrahim Pasha in February 1825, when he landed in Methoni with four thousand infantry and four thousand cavalry. The Greek factions had to put behind them the recent hatreds and divisions further exacerbated by two consecutive civil wars, and make common cause in confronting what assuredly represented the greatest threat to the revolution to date, combined as it was with campaigns from the north and the east by other Ottoman armies. In order to prevent Ibrahim from reaching Navarino, the troops gathered at Kranidi under Mavrokordatos's leadership included Roumeliots led by Karaiskakis—whose ostensible treason had by then been forgiven—and Peloponnesians as well as Souliots, but also cavalry made up of Serbian and Hungarian volunteers.[44] Kolokotronis and other Peloponnesian leaders had also been released from imprisonment to join the military campaign. Papaflessas, who only a few months earlier had crushed the anti-tax

41. The verdict is in *Ελληνικά Χρονικά* [*Ellinika Chronika*], no. 27, 12 April 1824, in Koumarianou, *Ο Τύπος στον Αγώνα* (The press in the 'Struggle'), 2, pp. 71–72.

42. Kasomoulis, *Ενθυμήματα στρατιωτικά* (Military memoirs), 1, pp. 385–89 (quotation at 389).

43. Kasomoulis, *Ενθυμήματα στρατιωτικά* (Military memoirs), 2, p. 15.

44. Dakin, *Greek Struggle*, p. 133; Brewer, *Greek War*, pp. 239–240.

rebellion of Arcadia during the second civil war, likewise contributed to the defence of the Peloponnese, mustering for this purpose some three thousand troops. Although he lost his life on the battlefield, his army inflicted heavy losses on Ibrahim's own irregular forces. Support came also from the islands, with the contribution of the navy led by Admiral Miaoulis. It was in the context of the Egyptian invasion that the central authorities issued an address to all Greeks calling for a general insurrection in support of the military efforts against the invaders. While still retaining regional distinctions, and addressing inhabitants as 'Peloponnesians, the Stereoelladitai [inhabitants of continental Greece, or Roumeli], and the islanders', it called upon all Greeks alike to abandon their ordinary activities, and take up arms, as this was 'the time for Greeks to run not behind Hermes but behind Ares'.[45] By the end of the year Ibrahim had managed to conquer most of the Peloponnesian cities and fortresses with the exception of Nafplion, and enslave thousands of civilians and damage buildings as well as crops, yet Greek military activities nonetheless prevented him from maintaining permanent control over the Peloponnese.

During the war, matrimonial arrangements played a role in forging political alliances and in creating a new national elite. While using women to extend family networks on the basis of wealth and rank was not a new phenomenon among the Christian elites of the Ottoman Empire, in the circumstances of the national insurrection this practice became a novel negotiating tool between revolutionary leaders and regional groups, exemplified by the marriages that Kolokotronis arranged for his own sons. The great Peloponnesian chief married off his eldest son Panos to Eleni, the daughter of Bouboulina, the most famous of all Greek women fighters, and a member of a prominent and wealthy shipowning family from the island of Spetses. This marriage extended the influence of both families beyond their own places of origin, guaranteeing the support of Spetses for Kolokotronis at the national level. The general married off his other son Gennaios to Photeini, the daughter of another prominent military figure, the Souliot leader Tzavelas. By this match, Kolokotronis enabled Tzavelas to switch alliances and join him in the front against other members of the government. The matrimonial history of his son Kollinos can also be understood in the light of his father's political ambitions. He had first promised him, when only twelve years old, to the daughter of a prominent Peloponnesian notable, Deliyannis, in the hope that this would mitigate

---

45. 'Proclamation of the Executive to all Greeks', 2 May 1825, in Lignos, Αρχείον (Archive), 11, pp. 220–21.

their enmity. In the end, however, the promise was not honoured, and Kollinos married into another powerful family, that of the Phanariot Ioannis Karatzas.[46]

The war had an equally profound impact on civilians, who were subjected to looting, siege and violence. While a large proportion of the population was wiped out by the war, the invasions and the wholesale destruction and slaughter, attacks on villages and towns also resulted in mass dislocation across the territories of the revolution. War and displacement had an incomparably greater impact on society in Greece than it did on any other countries involved in the southern European revolutions. The enforced displacement of civilians who, as refugees, ended up living alongside communities from other regions turned the notion of belonging to a wider community into something very concrete. During the massacre of the population of the island of Chios that took place in spring 1822, the troops brought to the island by the fleet of the *kapudan pasha* (grand admiral of the Ottoman navy) reduced a population of over a hundred thousand inhabitants to something like twenty thousand. Some forty-five thousand were enslaved, and around twenty-five thousand killed. But perhaps half of those who survived—say twenty thousand all told—fled to other Aegean islands or to the mainland.[47] Refugees had not always been welcome in other regions, and in fact they had often been treated with hostility, even attacked, by armed groups or populations from other areas. But during the important meeting of military chieftains organised by Mavrokordatos in western Greece in January 1824 to reform military discipline, the signatories agreed to guarantee the protection of refugees and to avoid the looting of Greek properties.[48]

The majority of refugees turned out to be women with their own children. Most of them were living in destitution and relied on alimony or on the scant support provided by religious and state authorities, or on private philanthropy. They were often the widows of fighters who had lost their lives on the battlefield. Fourth-fifths of the twenty thousand or so refugees to be found in Athens, Salamis, Aegina and Syros were women from other parts of Greece. This does not mean, however, that it was only as victims of the war that women paid the heaviest toll. In fact, they often gave active support to men during warfare, or themselves entered the fray.

46. Eleni Angelomatis-Tsougarakis, 'Women in the Greek War of Independence', in *Networks of Power in Modern Greece: Essays in Honour of John Campbell*, ed. Mark Mazower (London: Hurst Publishers, 2008), pp. 45–68.

47. Brewer, *Greek War*, p. 165.

48. Vakalopoulos, *Τα ελληνικά στρατεύματα* (The Greek troops), pp. 110ff.

This was particularly the case with women from Crete, and above all from Mani and Souli, who often fought with makeshift weapons and occasionally appeared on the battlefield. A handful of very prominent women, such as Bouboulina and Manto Mavroyenous, stood out as military leaders. Bouboulina, the widow of a prominent shipowner from Hydra, used her private means to arm warships and took part in naval operations. Manto, who came from a wealthy merchant family from Smyrna, also devoted some of her own funds to arming fighters in the Morea, and helped to organise the defence of the island Mykonos against Algerian pirates. At the same time, women represented by far the largest share of the displaced population, along with children and the elderly.[49] The arrival of Ibrahim in the Peloponnese resulted in more than twenty thousand children, women and old men fleeing to the Strophades islands in the Ionian archipelago.[50] Ibrahim's conquest of the cities of Argos and Tripolitsa turned several thousand of their inhabitants into refugees, who by the end of June 1825 were temporarily sheltered in tents on the outskirts of Nafplion.[51] Two articles published in the *Ellinika Chronika* in April 1824 point to the shift in the meaning of the term *patris*, or 'fatherland' that these displacements had produced among Greeks. For the newspapers, the patris was first and foremost the place or the city where one was born and one's parents resided, and it therefore never changed. Yet, since during a single lifetime and individual might settle somewhere else, it was important to understand the fatherland as an entire territory 'which [one] prefers to all other places'.[52]

Sieges of cities themselves served to forge new bonds between people. Cohabitation between regular and irregular troops perforce occurred, as did cooperation with civilians hailing from other places. In the city of Messolonghi, besieged by Rashid Pasha first and then by the Arab army of Ibrahim from April 1825 to April 1826, a population of around nine thousand individuals included local civilians, Souliots, and also fighters from several parts of Roumeli, all forced to cooperate, while outside the city the revolutionary navy and other Roumeli irregulars had rallied to its defence. These separate groups retained their identities when a delegation was organised from the city to visit the government, and the hardship of the siege

49. Eleni Angelomatis-Tsougarakis, 'Women', in *The Greek Revolution: A Critical Dictionary*, ed. Paschalis M. Kitromilides and Constantinos Tsoukalas (Cambridge, MA: Harvard University Press, 2021), pp. 420–36.

50. Comstock, *History*, p. 381.

51. James Emerson, Giuseppe Pecchio and William H. Humphreys, *A Picture of Greece in 1825*, 2 vols (London: Henry Colburn, 1826), 1, p. 261.

52. Ελληνικά Χρονικά [*Ellinika Chronika*], nos 29–30, 11 and 15 April 1824, in Koumarianou, Ο Τύπος στον Αγώνα (The press in the 'Struggle'), 2, pp. 236–39.

exacerbated conflicts.[53] When organising the exodus of the population from the city, the guards were faced with difficult decisions, so dire were the circumstances. People were starving, cases of cannibalism were recorded, and the option of killing all the city's women and children, in order to prevent the Ottomans from taking hostages, was discussed, although not implemented. The guards involved in planning the exodus justified their efforts as a duty towards the nation and the administration, as well as to the local primate leaders, and their own possible death as a 'debt owed to the nation'.[54] Those very few survivors (around two thousand) who succeeded in leaving the city, and were neither massacred by the Ottoman army nor captured by it during the exodus, became refugees. The surviving guards, for instance, fled to the city of Salona (Amfissa) in central Greece.[55] After the conquest of Messolonghi, the most important city where inter-regional collaboration was put to the test was the capital, Nafplion. Here too, the presence of military men and civilians from different regions was far from unproblematic: the fact that the military defence of the city's main fortress was in the hands of Roumeliots was resented by other groups. However, in June 1826, on the verge of another division in government that led to the setting up of a rival assembly in Kranidi, the administration reached an agreement with all forces such that the defence of the fortress would be shared equally by Roumeliots, Epirots and Peloponnesians.[56]

As a consequence of all of these experiences, not only state and regional authorities, but also local communities started to adopt new notions in public documents addressed to the enemy. An exceptionally interesting document issued by the leaders and inhabitants of Salona in November 1826 offers evidence of the impact the war had in redefining communities. Salona had been at the forefront of the anti-Ottoman rebellion since spring 1821. It was in this town that the first Areios Pagos, or assembly, of eastern Greece had been held in the same year. Given its strategic importance in connecting Thessaly to the Gulf of Corinth, it was the object of repeated attacks by the Ottoman armies in the succeeding years. Between 1825 and 1826 Ottoman troops conquered it temporarily, and in late 1826 they waged a further campaign against it. On that occasion Mehmet Pasha, vizier of Roumeli, Yannina, Arlona and Mutesaritsi, asked the local authorities of Salona to send representatives as a sign of submission to the

53. Kasomoulis, Ενθυμήματα στρατιωτικά (Military memoirs), 2, p. 161.

54. Ibid., p. 257. On the siege see also Mark Mazower, *The Greek Revolution: 1821 and the Making of Modern Europe* (London: Penguin Books, 2021), pp. 303–25.

55. Ibid., pp. 290–94; Brewer, *Greek War*, p. 281.

56. Kasomoulis, Ενθυμήματα στρατιωτικά (Military memoirs), 2, pp. 322–23.

FIGURE 12. *The Exodus from Messolonghi* (oil painting by Theodoros Vryzakis, 1853; The National Gallery of Greece, Alexandros Soutsos Museum, Athens). Image: https://www.nationalgallery.gr, with permission

Ottoman authorities, failing which they would be subjected to an assault by ten thousand troops. In his address, Mehmet defined the population as rebel *reyes*—a term which defined the status of Christian inhabitants of the empire as subjects without the same rights as the Muslims. In their public response to this ultimatum, the local authorities of Salona refused to comply with the request, and vindicated their status as free men. They claimed that they had gained their freedom through blood and the decision they had taken to the effect that death while bearing arms would be preferable to living under tyranny. This public response included a refusal to engage in any future correspondence with the Ottoman authorities, an act that, as they argued, would represent a betrayal of the national community. This public response ended with a strongly worded plea to 'address your requests to our government, as by maintaining a correspondence with your highness we could be seen as disloyal to our nation, and we fear more the curse of our nation than that of thousands of Turks'.[57] Thus, it is safe to say that in spite of the constant internal conflicts and frequent negotiations with the enemy, it was the material and direct experience of the war that made the idea of a national community, shared originally only by a minority of educated Greeks belonging to the networks of the Philiki, more widely accepted, and turned this abstract notion into a tangible reality.

This war against a common enemy lasted longer and had a more profound effect in Greece than in any other southern European country during that decade. It also showed the Ottomans that permanent subjection of the Greeks to their authority had become an impossibility. However, the combination of irregular warfare with the activities of a small regular army did not guarantee a Greek victory over the enemy. Indeed, the year 1826 was marked by another bitter defeat for the Greeks, who lost Athens to the Ottomans. The fate of the revolution, as in Spain, Piedmont and Naples, was therefore decided by foreign powers. In the end, it was the diplomatic and military intervention of European countries that encouraged the Greek leaderships to reach a compromise, and forced the Ottomans to recognise the Greek state. By contrast with the European interference in the other southern European revolutions, the peculiarity of the Greek revolution lay in the fact that in the end, diplomacy worked in its favour, and not against it. Nor was this intervention formally determined by the Congress system. The religious nature of the struggle enabled the European powers to justify their involvement in terms of the defence of European civilisation against Islamic barbarism, in accordance with a central tenet of European philhellenism. Thus they managed to legitimise their interference in the political

57. On Salona's strategic importance during the war, see William Martin Leake, *A Historical Outline of the Greek Revolution, with a Few Remarks on the Present State of Affairs in That Country* (London: John Murray, 1826), pp. 146–47; a manuscript translation of the document is held in GSA, Vlachoyannis Collection, Karaiskakis Archive, box 5, folder 11, ff. 608–10.

life of the Ottoman Empire in the name of the most popular international cause in Europe at that time. Meanwhile, the need to guarantee European diplomatic support in turn led a majority of the Greek revolutionaries to entertain a belief in the desirability of monarchical power, and to look for a potential candidate for the throne of Greece.

In particular, it was Russia, and more specifically Czar Alexander's change in attitude towards the Greek question, that paved the way to a European intervention in support of the Greek cause. Russia's right to protect the Christians in the Ottoman Empire, guaranteed by the Treaty of Küçük Kaynarca, signed in 1774 with the Porte, had not been invoked at the beginning of the Greek revolution, an event initially condemned by the czar. By 1824, however, the czar had changed his mind. To guarantee the autonomy of a Greek state, he put forward a proposal whose content replicated the power relations existing between the Danubian Principalities and the Ottomans, and also confirmed his role as protector of the Christian populations in the Ottoman Empire. In Alexander's vision, the territories liberated during the revolution should be divided into three autonomous principalities (the Peloponnese, Western Roumeli and Eastern Roumeli) under the nominal sovereignty of the Ottomans. This proposal, however, was rejected by the British foreign secretary George Canning, who feared Russia's hegemonic ambitions and mistrusted Congress diplomacy. The Greeks and Ottomans were not slow to reject it either.[58] But in spring 1826 a similar project was revived by the new czar, Nicholas (Alexander had unexpectedly died in December 1825) with the support now of the British, who had rejected a Greek request for a British protectorate during the previous year. The publication of Ibrahim Pasha's so-called 'barbarisation project' the year before—the Egyptian leader's alleged intention to clear those parts of Greece he hoped to conquer of the Christian populations, and to enslave them—and the Greek requests for intervention the year before, provided Russia and Britain with plausible pretexts to justify an initiative on strictly humanitarian grounds, and to offer to mediate between the Greeks and the Ottomans. The St. Petersburg protocol signed by the two northern powers in April 1826 proposed the creation of a Greek state that was formally tributary to the Ottomans but that would otherwise enjoy full self-government. It also legitimised Russian and British intervention (jointly or independently) in the event of Turkey's refusal to accept their mediation with the Greeks. Fourteen months later France too

58. Lucien J. Frary, *Russia and the Making of Modern Greek Identity, 1821–1844* (Oxford: Oxford University Press, 2015).

joined Russia and Britain in what became the Treaty of London, an agreement signed by the three powers on 6 July 1827. This time, the protocol went further than that agreed the year before, in that, besides confirming the proposal to create an autonomous tributary state, its secret articles granted Greece de facto recognition of independence, by authorising trade relations with it. The three countries' agreement also envisaged their joint intervention if Turkey and Greece refused to accept an armistice, to be carried out by their navies.[59] It was in fact the fleets, and not the armies, of these powers that determined the fate of the revolution and the recognition of the new state. On 20 October 1827, the British, French and Russian fleets led respectively by Admiral Sir Edward Codrington, the Count de Rigny and Count Heiden attacked the much larger fleet of Ibrahim Pasha, who had refused to abide by the terms of the protocol and to respect an armistice, in the bay of Navarino on the western coast of the Peloponnese. It was an easily won battle that lasted only four hours, resulting in a very high number of casualties among the Ottoman crews (at least six thousand), and in the sinking of the majority of the Ottoman ships, while the European fleets were left almost unscathed and their casualties were very limited. While the Ottomans refused to recognise Greece's independence, and called for a jihad, and while the war between the Greeks and their enemies continued, this victory marked the recognition of the existence of the new state, and protected its existence from then onwards.[60]

Conclusions

The southern European revolutions started and came to an end as military events. The fact that these revolutions easily succeeded but, at least in the case of Spain, Piedmont and Naples, equally easily collapsed, is at first sight paradoxical, and requires a few final words. The revolutionary strategy that combined popular mobilisation and military initiative in the name jointly of the people and the monarch was a recipe that, for different reasons, had been successful in forcing regime change. However, this revolutionary script, which was adopted across southern Europe, proved inadequate when revolutions had to be defended against a substantially larger foreign army. In Spain, the volte-face of some key military leaders in the

59. Charles W. Crawley, *The Question of Greek Independence: A Study of British Policy in the Near East, 1821–1833* (Cambridge: Cambridge University Press, 1930), pp. 43–62, 63–78.

60. Cristopher Montague Woodhouse, *The Battle of Navarino* (London: Hoddler & Stoughton, 1965).

face of foreign invasion and monarchical hostility, along with the willingness of the more moderate sectors of the revolutionary elite to seek compromise, were crucial in hastening the end of the revolutions. As much as
in Piedmont and Naples, the hostility of the monarchy to the revolution
was a key factor in undermining support for the constitution both in the
army and in the population at large. Even when it became obvious that
the support of the monarch was lacking, it was neither practically feasible
nor conceivable that the constitutional regime might survive outside the
framework of the monarchy. The loyalty of Piedmontese revolutionaries to
the monarchy was unquestioned. In Naples, memories of 1799 still loomed
large, since in that year a popular movement led by Cardinal Fabrizio
Ruffo, the so-called Esercito della Santa Fede (army of the holy faith), or
'Armata sanfedista', had marched against the Neapolitan republic, which
owed its very existence to the protection of the French army. Ruffo and his
followers had taught the revolutionaries a key lesson and had reduced the
republican option to being no more than a theoretical possibility, and an
undesirable one at that time.

In Spain, the entire revolutionary script hinged on the argument
that the Spanish people had acquired their new political rights in order
to save King Fernando's throne from the French, and that the only hope
for the survival of popular support for the constitution lay in confirming
the monarchical and anti-French nature of the revolution. In Portugal, the
same script had applied, but then civil war in the guise of a dynastic crisis
turned the defence of the constitution into a manifestation of loyalty to a
royal candidate. In Greece too, the outcome of the revolution remained
uncertain, in spite of the commitment of foreign philhellenes, and the
presence of larger irregular forces along with a small regular army, this
uncertainty leading many fighters to negotiate with the enemy. It was only
when diplomacy and foreign armies took and held the initiative against
the Ottomans that a successful outcome to the revolution was guaranteed.
Monarchs proceeded to avenge the revolutionary attempts to curb their
powers with a very few, but exemplary, executions. In Naples, Michele
Morelli and Giuseppe Salvati, captured in the Habsburg port of Ragusa
(Dubrovnik), were taken back to Naples, tried for treason and executed
in the large Piazza Mercato of the capital of the kingdom in September 1822. In Piedmont, twenty revolutionaries were condemned to death
in absentia. In Spain, Rafael Riego was condemned to be dragged to the
place of execution, hanged and quartered, and from there the various pieces
of his mutilated body would be dispatched to the different places in the
kingdom associated with his crimes. On 2 October 1823, as a sign of his

ultimate humiliation, he was hauled in a basket by a donkey to the Plaza de la Cebada in Madrid, where he was executed in front of large but silent crowds. In Portugal, repression was exceptionally harsh. In this country the return of absolutism in 1828 was marked by thirty-nine executions, and by the imprisonment of some fourteen thousand individuals.[61] Many prominent revolutionaries managed to flee their countries, however, and therefore some of the death penalties decreed after the revolutions (for instance, those of Guglielmo Pepe and Luigi Minichini) were not carried out. No fewer than 13,700 exiles left Portugal after 1828.

Therefore, in spite of repression, these final acts in the revolutionary dramas and associated wars fostered new forms of mobility and displacement, including international military volunteerism, which in turn forged new connections, entanglements and forms of solidarity. It is to the movements of people caused by the revolutions that I turn in the final chapter of this part of the book.

61. On the execution of Riego, Morelli and Salvati, see Stites, *Four Horsemen*, pp. 115–20, 176–77. On Piedmont, see Giorgio Marsengo and Giuseppe Parlato, *Dizionario dei piemontesi compromessi nei moti del 1821*, 2 vols (Turin: Istituto per la storia del Risorgimento italiano, 1982), 1, p. 190. On Portuguese prisoners, see Joel Serrão, 'D. Miguel' in *Dicionário de história de Portugal*, ed. Joel Serrão, 4 vols (Lisbon: Iniciativas Editoriais, 1971), 3, pp. 55–58, esp. 56.

CHAPTER FIVE

Crossing the Mediterranean

VOLUNTEERS, MERCENARIES, REFUGEES

Introduction: Palermo as a Mediterranean revolutionary hub

What do the lives of a Cretan naval officer, an Irish general and a Palermitan carbonaro turned international freedom fighter have in common? Taking as a starting point the lives of these three individuals, who were all involved in the revolution in Sicily between 1820 and 1821, and whose destiny after that year took them to different places, this chapter explores the ways in which mobility and conflict interacted in the post-Napoleonic period across the Mediterranean, and connected revolution and counter-revolution in North Africa, Sicily, Naples, Spain, Portugal and the Aegean Sea. It therefore considers the types of voluntary and involuntary displacement triggered by revolution, and their different directions.

An increasing body of literature has greatly expanded our understanding of the nature and direction of the flows of sympathisers and volunteers drawn to the Mediterranean revolutions. This work has unveiled the multiplicity of motives underpinning internationalism, as well as the existence of exchanges, across the Mediterranean itself, and even from extra-European countries.[1] However, one aspect of this phenomenon

---

1. Anna Karakatsouli, *'Μαχητές της ελευθερίας' και 1821: Η Ελληνική Επανάσταση στη διεθνική της διάσταση* ('Freedom fighters' and 1821: The Greek war of independence in its transnational dimension) (Athens: Pedio, 2016); Juan Luis Simal, *Emigrados: España y el exilio internacional, 1814–1834* (Madrid: Centro de Estudios Políticos y Constitucionales, 2013); Gilles Pécout, 'International Volunteers and the Risorgimento', *Journal of Modern*

still remains the primary focus of existing explanatory frameworks. What dominates current narratives is the idea that western European philhellenic volunteers driven by romanticism and revolutionary internationalism represented the majority of those who traversed the Mediterranean towards Greece after 1821. The implicit or explicit assumption of these narratives is that these revolutionaries were liberals inspired by national emancipation.[2] In addition, migration patterns and revolutionary volunteerism tend to be studied and addressed separately.

This chapter adopts a viewpoint 'from the periphery' in surveying the period and treating the theme of displacement. It takes Palermo, the capital of Sicily, as its starting point—a place rarely mentioned, if not completely neglected, in the standard narratives about exile and revolutionary activity in the post-Napoleonic era—in an endeavour to understand the ways in which individuals during the 1820s moved from one armed conflict to another, and from one country to another. By taking a decentred approach to the period and of the theme of displacement, the chapter shows that from the viewpoint of Palermo, philhellenism was not simply a novel movement committed to constitutional, liberal and national values. It was also associated with the defence of imperial interests in an age of imperial rivalry and expansion (in the case of Sir Richard Church) and with pre-existing Mediterranean professional traditions and identities (in the case of Emmanuele Scordili). It also demonstrates that revolutionary mobility and labour migration were interrelated phenomena (as in the case of Andrea Mangiaruva). Thus scrutiny of the lives of Sir Richard Church, Emmanuele Scordili and Andrea Mangiaruva serves to broaden our understanding of the causes of displacement in the age of revolution, and offers precious insights regarding the ways in which these displacements provided opportunities to renegotiate identities.

Italian Studies 14, no. 4 (special issue) (2009): 395–522; Pécout, 'Philhellenism in Italy: Political Friendship and the Italian Volunteers in the Mediterranean in the Nineteenth Century', *Journal of Modern Italian Studies* 9, no. 4 (2004): 405–27; Maurizio Isabella and Konstantina Zanou, eds, *Mediterranean Diasporas: Ideas and Politics in the Long Nineteenth Century* (London: Bloomsbury, 2015); Maurizio Isabella, *Risorgimento in Exile: Italian Émigrés in the Post-Napoleonic Era* (Oxford: Oxford University Press, 2009).

2. Roderick Beaton, *Byron's War: Romantic Rebellion, Greek Revolution* (Cambridge: Cambridge University Press, 2013); Frederick Rosen, *Bentham, Byron and Greece: Constitutionalism, Nationalism, and Early Liberal Political Thought* (Oxford: Oxford University Press, 1992); David Roessel, *In Byron's Shadow: Modern Greece in the English and American Imagination* (Oxford: Oxford University Press, 2001); Douglas Dakin, *British and American Philhellenes during the Greek War of Independence, 1821–1833* (Thessaloniki: Institute for Balkan Studies, 1955).

More generally, these case studies point to the very different ways in which one could join a revolution and become a revolutionary, emphasising the plurality of motivations involved. In other words, this chapter also discusses how people became revolutionaries, and why. Finally, these biographies suggest that the category of revolutionary volunteer overlapped, and was entangled, with that of mercenary, or of refugee, and retained strong elements of continuity with pre-existing forms of mobility across the Mediterranean.

Sir Richard Church: bridging empire, counterrevolution and revolution

What determined the success of the Sicilian revolution against Naples was the insurrection of the population of its capital, Palermo. Indeed, it was the success of this popular uprising that enabled the creation of a provisional government, the expulsion of the Bourbon army from the city and the declaration of independence. The arrival in the city of news about the Neapolitan revolution had coincided with its most important religious festival, dedicated to its patron, Santa Rosalia, and held on 15 July. The entire population would take part in the public celebrations, which culminated in a procession of the statue of the saint on a cart along the main thoroughfare, known then as the Cassaro, and around the rest of the city. This time, however, a number of individuals, wearing yellow and tricolour cockades to demonstrate their support for both the constitution and the independence of the island, no doubt prompted to do so by the aristocrats of the city, were crying 'Viva l'indipendenza!' and 'Viva la costituzione!' The festivities thus escalated into a violent confrontation with the Neapolitan troops quartered in the city and charged with keeping the peace. Refusing to declare himself in favour of the independence of the island, General Richard Church, chief of the Neapolitan army, sitting in an open landau along with some other Neapolitan officers, was attacked by the crowds and barely escaped with his life. The following day the crowds, with the support of the city guilds, seized control of the castle, along with its armoury, and drove the Neapolitan army out of the city.[3] Church immedi-

3. On these events, see Niccolò Palmieri, *Saggio storico e politico sulla costituzione del Regno di Sicilia infino al 1816 con un'appendice sulla rivoluzione del 1820*, with an introduction by Enzo Sciacca (Palermo: Edizioni della Regione Sicilia, 1972 [1847]), pp. 312–15. The general's own reconstruction is in Richard Church, *Relazione dei fatti accaduti al tenente generale Riccardo Church in Palermo la notte del 15 luglio 1820* (Naples: Tipografia Francese, 1820).

FIGURE 13. Sir Richard Church attacked by the crowds during the revolution
in Palermo, 15 July 1820 (etching by Calogero De Bernardis, in *Raccolta di
20 stampe, che rappresentano al naturale li fatti più rimarchevoli successi
in Palermo dal giorno 15 luglio sino li 5 ottobre 1820*, Palermo[?], 1820).
Image: Museo centrale del Risorgimento, Rome, www.risorgimento.it, with
permission

ately fled Sicily for Naples, where he was arrested and charged with having
triggered the revolt of Palermo.

Central to the narrative of the events both in Sicily and in Naples
was the fact that the general himself had supposedly torn the pro-
independence yellow cockade from a Palermitan citizen, a public insult
that resulted in the escalation of the revolt. This anecdote was probably
fabricated, but it served well the purposes both of those Sicilian patriots
who sought to justify the insurrection by describing Church as the symbol of Neapolitan oppression on the island, and of the Neapolitan revolutionaries in search of a scapegoat for the Sicilian rebellion. The fact that
Church was a foreigner also played an important role in these narratives.
Sicilians had from the outset resented his appointment instead of that
of a local army officer. In addition, his presence in Palermo brought back
unpleasant memories of British rule over the island during the Napoleonic wars, when he had been a member of the foreign occupying army. For
the Neapolitan revolutionaries he was a foreign traitor, or at least someone
who irresponsibly and carelessly, albeit unwittingly, had triggered a major

revolution.[4] While Church had just arrived in Palermo to assume his new responsibilities, his connection with Sicily and the Mediterranean was not new.

In order to understand Church's responsibilities in Palermo we need to go back to the Napoleonic period and to the expansion of the Napoleonic empire in the Mediterranean and across southern Europe that took place in those years. While the occupation of Sicily would prove to be temporary (1806–15), Britain acquired Malta in 1800, and Corfu and the rest of Ionian islands in 1815. Portugal, for its part, was not directly annexed, but the presence of the British army there, poised to fight the French on the Iberian peninsula, continued for some years after 1815. This military and colonial expansion brought a wave of army officers, soldiers and mercenaries, as well as imperial agents, merchants, diplomats and administrators to the Mediterranean. It also gave rise to a lively debate about the place and the strategic goals the Mediterranean should have in the British Empire. In the context of the Napoleonic wars in this sea, British agents tended to describe it as a maritime empire serving as a bulwark of freedom as against a French one based, they argued, on despotism and conquest. Inspired to a great extent by the writings of Edmund Burke, its advocates defined the British Empire in that sea as a community of free polities based on free trade and enjoying relative autonomy. A few of their number passionately believed in the need for Britain to export its constitution to the Mediterranean islands. This idea was first put into practice in Corsica between 1794 and 1796, but its most important application was in Sicily, where a constitution inspired by British institutions was introduced in 1812 under the aegis of Sir William Bentinck. However, the perceived failure of the constitutional experiment in Sicily (whose aristocracy resisted the reform of feudalism advocated by the British) led to the prevalence of an alternative imperial model in the region. This form of imperial rule, otherwise known as proconsular despotism, was based on the belief that neither the local elites nor the populace at large were suited to self-rule and representative government. Imperial government had a duty, it was argued, to civilise and reform them through sound administration, and through order rather than rights. Hence the lack of any form of autonomy granted to the populations of Malta and of the Ionian islands, when they became British after 1817.[5]

4. For a reconstruction of the origin and enduring fortune of this legend, see Antonino De Francesco, 'Church e il nastro giallo: L'immagine del 1820 in Sicilia nella storiografia del XIX secolo', *Rivista Italiana di Studi Napoleonici* 28 (1991): 23–90.

5. Bayly, *Imperial Meridian*; on debates about the British Empire in the Mediterranean, see Grieco, 'British Empire and the Two Sicilies'.

The son of a Quaker merchant from Cork, Richard Church had run away from 'school and quakerdom' to join the army at the tender age of sixteen: turning seventeen, in 1801, he was sent to fight the French in Egypt.[6] This first experience outside Europe and his encounter with the Eastern populations in Alexandria immediately convinced him of the barbarity of the Ottomans and led to his enduring sympathy for those people he already defined in 1801 as 'slaves to the Turks': the Greeks.[7]

In the following years, up to his posting to Palermo in the spring of 1820, Church traversed the Mediterranean fighting for the British Empire against the Napoleonic armies and brigandage, and specialising in the training of native troops. In 1805 he took part in the British military expedition in defence of the Bourbons of Naples, and was associated with the military occupation of Sicily. It was after taking part in the battle of Maida against the French in Calabria that he was appointed officer of a battalion of Corsican rangers and fought brigandage in that region, so as to re-establish law and order after the French invasion. But it was only once stationed on the Ionian islands, during the British occupation between 1809 and 1812, that Church would perfect his skills in the training and leading of Mediterranean fighters.[8] Here in fact he created a regiment of volunteers from the Greek lands of the Ottoman Empire, called the Duke of York's Greek Light Infantry, and employed it to conquer the island of Lefkada, then controlled by the French, in 1810. Church became hugely popular among the members of his regiment, who included some of the future military leaders of the Greek revolution, such as Kolokotronis, and many former brigands (klephts) expelled from the Ottoman Empire for their unruliness. The Greek troops under Church's command thanked him in a letter, acknowledging that through his training he had refuted 'those ingrained prejudices among Europeans who believed the Greeks to be hardly susceptible to discipline and education'.[9] Having created a first regiment of Greek light infantry in 1812, in recognition of his success he was invited in 1813 to create a second. Church's own experience in the Ionian islands left him with the belief that it was indeed possible to impose

6. E. M. Church, *Sir Richard Church in Italy and Greece* (Edinburgh: William Blackwood, 1895), p. 1.

7. On Church's promotion, see Nino Cortese, 'Il governo napoletano e la rivoluzione siciliana del MDCCCXX–XX1', *Archivio Storico Messinese* NS 28–35, no. 1 (1934): 3–245 at p. 27.

8. Stanley Lane Poole, *Sir Richard Church* (London: Longmans, Green & Co., 1890), pp. 24–30.

9. BL, Church Papers, Add MS 36543, ff. 23–24: Duke of York's Infantry troops to Church, 24 July 1812.

military discipline upon and thereby to civilise southern populations, but unlike Bentinck or other British administrators, he never believed in the usefulness of exporting constitutions and rights to the region.

After 1815, and by virtue of their permanent acquisition of the Ionian islands, the British consolidated their presence in the Mediterranean, and revived debates regarding their imperial role across this sea. Church's experience in the previous years had convinced him that the islands' self-government under a British protectorate could better serve the commercial and geopolitical interests of the British Empire in the east than would direct colonial rule. He elaborated on this vision in a memorandum drafted for the British representative at the Congress of Vienna, the Duke of Wellington, in 1815, when the future of the Ionian islands was to be decided. In this memorandum Church argued that the islands, along with the continental dependencies traditionally associated with them, deserved to enjoy self-government under British protection, and that under these circumstances the Ionian islands could become the arbiters of the Christian territories of the Morea, Roumeli, the Archipelago and Alexandria, thus winning the sympathy of their populations for Britain and increasing its influence in the region without unnecessary expense.[10]

With the restoration, Church's activities in the Mediterranean continued to be driven by a determination to civilise the local populations through military discipline alone, without encouraging aspirations for freedom and self-government. He went on to employ his skills in the service of the king of the Two Sicilies, Ferdinando I, training Greek mercenary regiments for the Neapolitan monarch and deploying them to fight brigandage. He had now decided to work for the dynasty he had already defended during the British occupation of Sicily, without disregarding at the same time the interests of Britain in the area. In the new political context set by the consolidation of a British colonial presence in the Adriatic, the recruitment of Greek fighters was of crucial importance in the contest between the imperial powers for influence over this sea. By recruiting Greek mercenaries who had previously fought for the British, Church was also trying to stymie efforts by Russian agents to attract Greek officers into Russian service.[11] At the same time, he served the Bourbon king by using these Greek mercenaries to fight against brigandage in the course of a military mission to Puglia in 1817. Here brigandage was

10. Ibid., ff. 142–46: Richard Church, report on the Ionian islands to the Duke of Wellington, December 1814.

11. BL, Church Papers, Add MS 41528, ff. 114–20, Church to William à Court, 24 July 1818.

associated with the proliferation of secret societies belonging to the world of the Carboneria, organisations that had both criminal propensities (murdering political enemies; burning crops) and political objectives (popular revolts to introduce the constitution, or even the establishment of a republic). Church succeeded in curtailing such practices and in re-establishing law and order: he hanged the leader, the famous bandit Ciro Annicchiarico, arrested 217 followers, and executed half of them.[12]

The anger levelled at the general in Palermo on 15 July 1820 was therefore fuelled not only by popular resentment at the British military occupation of the island between 1806 and 1815, but also by the memory of his role in brutally suppressing the Carboneria in Puglia. Members of the Carboneria had played an important role in fomenting the popular insurrection of the capital of Sicily. As subsequent events would show, Church's loyalty to the monarchy took precedence over that to the constitution. Released from prison after a few months in 1821, for want of any evidence of his direct responsibility for the Sicilian insurrection, the general reached the sovereign at the Congress of Laibach, where the latter had given his approval for an Austrian military intervention, and joined the Austrian invasion that put an end that year to the constitutional experiment. Church remained in the king's service as an officer until 1826. However, in an abrupt new turn in his career, after some hesitations and earlier rejections of offers by the London Greek Committee, in 1827 he agreed, on condition that the Greek factions settle their differences, to assume command of the Greek revolutionary army. Having left Naples, he was given a rapturous welcome by Kolokotronis and his soldiers, arriving on the coast of the Peloponnese, off the town of Ermioni, on 9 March of that same year.

At first sight, Church's decision to leave Naples and fight for Greek independence looks like the beginning of a radically new phase in his career. Not only did it offer him the chance for an exceptional promotion, transforming him into the chief of a national army; it also, and at one blow, turned the former defender of the political status quo and the enemy of insubordination, insurrection and revolutionary principles, into a revolutionary. Having informed the king of the Two Sicilies of his decision, he was asked to give up the uniform of a Neapolitan military officer, as the monarch did not want to be seen to interfere in a rebellion against the Porte. In Greece, Church found himself at the centre of a dense network of

12. Jakob Salomon Bartholdy, *Memoirs of the Secret Societies of the South of Italy, Particularly the Carbonari* (London: John Murray, 1821), pp. 134–48. Church, *Sir Richard Church*, pp. 139ff.

philhellenes fighting for the emancipation of the Greek nation. He had not only to negotiate between competing national groups of fighters, but also to navigate in the tricky politics of the Greek factions. In fact, he played a crucial role in pacifying them and in forging a consensus around the election of Ioannis Kapodistrias as the new governor of Greece.[13] The former enemy of the Carboneria, whose networks he had dismantled in Puglia in 1817, was now rumoured to be an active member of one of the lodges of the Grande società rigeneratrice, a secret society that connected Italian carbonari, French and British volunteers and Greek patriots. The society, whose clubs sprang up across the territories of liberated Greece, provided a space for political discussion among the different parties that divided Greek politics, and a channel of communication between them and the national assembly.[14] After meeting with success in the task of pacifying the Greek factions, Church took up his new role as leader of the army, only to suffer a bitter defeat in a battle outside Athens that led to the capitulation of the Acropolis in May 1827. He devoted the following two years to the reconquest of western Greece, but the deterioration of his relationship with Kapodistrias led to his dismissal from the army in 1829. Nonetheless, he went back to serve the Greek army in the following decades, and was appointed general and a senator of the kingdom. When he died in 1873, Church was celebrated as a national hero.

Notwithstanding the major role played by Church in the Greek revolution, it would in fact be hard to consider his activities in Greece as representing a radical break from his past professional and political experiences. If one looks at the nature of his commitment to the Greek cause, what is striking is a continuity over time in his language and motivations. When informing King Francesco I of the Two Sicilies of his decision to go to Greece, he wrote that what motivated him was the hope that he might 'limit the disaster of the Turks' exterminating war against a Christian population'.[15] This was the language employed by European philhellenes at the time.

However, the European philhellenes who were flocking to Greece to fight the Ottomans disagreed on the nature and objectives of their commitment to the Greek war of liberation. Some wanted freedom of the press

13. Dakin, *British and American Philhellenes*, pp. 144–46.

14. On Church's participation and the Society in general, see Gianni Korinthios, *I liberali napoletani e la rivoluzione greca (1821–1830)* (Rome: IISF, 1990), pp. 63–64.

15. Church to Francesco I, 1 January 1827, in Ruggero Moscati, 'La questione greca e il governo napoletano', *Rassegna Storica del Risorgimento* 20, no. 1 (1933): 21–49 at pp. 39–41.

and constitutional liberties to be introduced immediately in Greece during the war. For an important group of British philhellenes involved in the London Greek Committee, the priority of the war was not the introduction of constitutional guarantees in Greece, but rather the gradual education of the Greeks to higher civilisational standards, according to the principles they had applied when working in the Asian dependencies of the British Empire.[16]

Church was not interested in advancing a liberal agenda in Greece in either the immediate or the distant future. Indeed, in Greece he continued to pursue the civilising project he had championed in the previous years across the Mediterranean as a professional fighter, without necessarily embracing the principles of constitutionalism along with those of national emancipation. As a matter of fact, he was disliked by many European philhellenes. They considered him to be a professional with no idealism or specific ideological motivations, and reproached him for the brutality of his military strategy. It is therefore not surprising that Church would not have seen any contradiction or shift in ideological allegiances between first fighting secret societies in Puglia and attempting to crush (albeit unsuccessfully) the Sicilian insurrection, and then assuming a prominent military role in the Greek revolution. As the narrative of the war of liberation that he penned makes plain, his main priorities as a military leader had been to reorganise the army according to European standards (he complained that his troops, when taken too far from home, would desert and return to their villages of origin). He also wanted to 'civilise' the war and make warfare less ferocious by persuading his troops through financial rewards to spare the lives of their Turkish prisoners, In Greece he was confronted again, as earlier on in his career in Calabria and Puglia, with the problem of brigandage, a phenomenon that, in the context of the revolution, shifted between support for the anti-Ottoman rebellion to warfare against any and every authority, including that of the Greek military leaders.[17]

Finally, Church's commitment to the emancipation of Greece was not in contradiction with his status as a former British imperial officer, but was in fact facilitated by it. The Greek revolution in fact represented merely a novel chapter in the familiar history of European interference in Ottoman affairs, during which the British and Russian empires and the French

16. Rosen, *Bentham, Byron*.

17. Richard Church, 'Narrative by Sir R. Church of the War in Greece during his Tenure of the Command, 1827–29', at BL, Church Papers, Add MS 36563–65 (manuscript, 3 vols), 3, ff. 58–60, 364–65, 414ff and passim.

government each tried to influence the conduct and outcome of the war and compete with the other European powers not only through diplomatic channels, but also under the guise of the volunteers hailing from their various countries. While the widespread perception, among Greeks and foreigners in Greece alike, that Church was a British agent may have been incorrect, it nevertheless helped him play an important role in pacifying Greek factions and in forging a consensus around the appointment of Kapodistrias as president in 1827. In the previous three years or so the various Greek factions had organised themselves into so-called Russian, French and English parties, whose members sought to advance their own specific interests, with the support of the different European powers and philhellenes. The members of the so-called English party among the Greek revolutionaries, Church's former officer Kolokotronis among them, were initially hostile to Kapodistrias's candidature. However, after consultation with Church they decided to back him. At the same time, European philhellenes such as Church were used by Western powers to compete against rival powers within Greece. It is significant that Church himself opted for the candidature of Kapodistrias only after consultation with the British cabinet and the newly appointed governor of the Ionian Islands, Stratford Canning.[18] It would therefore be appropriate to see his activities, along with those of other prominent British military men such as Thomas Cochrane, as evidence of the expansion of the ties and webs of informal empire that through the Greek insurrection was advancing British influence into the Ottoman lands in competition with other European powers.[19] Nor was Church's support for the creation of a Greek state in contradiction with the liberal imperialist vision of the Mediterranean put forward at the Congress of Vienna in 1815, according to which support for the self-government of Greek territories would be beneficial to British commercial and geopolitical interests in the east.

The differing motivations and political stances dividing philhellenes in Greece could be found also among those British imperial officers who, after fighting in the Napoleonic wars, remained entangled in the political and military events of other southern European countries after 1815. Some of them closely identified with the cause of liberalism in southern Europe,

18. Dakin, *British and American Philhellenes*, pp. 146–47.

19. I take Gregory A. Barton's definition of 'informal empire' as 'a relationship in which a national or regional imperial elite intentionally or unintentionally exercises a dominant influence over the elite formation [. . .] in another nation or region with none of the formal structures of empire': Barton, *Informal Empire and the Rise of One World Culture* (London: Palgrave Macmillan, 2014), p. 17.

and were convinced that Britain had a duty to support freedom and civil rights abroad as at home. Indeed, a number of British officers involved in the war against Napoleon in Spain as volunteers ended up supporting the constitution during the Trienio in Spain, and a few of them became passionately committed to the defence of revolutions across the Mediterranean. Sir Robert Wilson, a man who combined military experience across Europe with political radicalism, was undoubtedly the most famous of their number. Having fought the French in Egypt, Portugal (where he commanded the Loyal Lusitanian Legion of local volunteers) and Russia, in 1818 he was elected to the House of Commons, and soon rallied to all the revolutions of the south, criticising foreign interventions to crush them, condemning the Alien Bill and advocating the right of political refugees to seek shelter in Britain. In 1823 he planned to gather together ten thousand volunteers to rescue the Spanish constitutional government in the face of the French invasion: he succeeded in leading a much smaller number of them in the temporary defence of Cádiz against the French army. This failed attempt marked the end of his career as a freedom fighter, as although he was considered for the position of chief of the Greek revolutionary army eventually offered to Richard Church, in the end his candidacy was turned down. Wilson continued nevertheless to contribute to revolutionary politics in southern Europe by lending support to international conspiracies involving exiled constitutionalists.[20]

For some British fighters, however, it would be hard to detect any ideological coherence between the various phases of their professional military careers, or a direct relationship between their defence of southern European populations against Napoleon and subsequent liberal tendencies. What seemed to mark the careers of the former British volunteers in the Peninsular War was a constant search for the professional opportunities offered by mercenary fighting. Most of them were prepared to continue in Fernando VII's service after 1814, when the monarch abolished the constitution and turned his back on liberalism, while some supported the revolution in 1820, and others went on to fight for the emancipation of the Spanish colonies against Fernando.[21]

20. On Wilson's career, see Michael Glover, *A Very Slippery Fellow: The Life of Sir Robert Wilson, 1777–1849* (Oxford: Oxford University Press, 1978); and Christiana Brennecke, 'Internacionalismo liberal, romanticismo y sed de aventuras: La oposición inglesa y la causa de España en los años veinte del s. XIX', in *Segon Congrés Recerques: Enfrontaments civils; Postguerres i reconstruccions*, vol. 1 (Lleida: Associació Recerques, Pagès, 2002), pp. 459–74.

21. Graciela Iglesias Rogers, *British Liberators in the Age of Napoleon: Volunteering under the Spanish Flag in the Peninsular War* (London: Bloomsbury, 2013), pp. 151–65.

Such men were first and foremost mercenaries, not freedom fighters. Others considered, however, that that it was in the best interests of the British Empire to defend the political status quo in southern Europe and the Mediterranean, and to stem the influence of Austria, Russia and France in this space, by preventing revolutions and constitutional reforms. It was in Portugal in particular—a de facto British protectorate—that this policy was implemented. Occupied by the British army during the Napoleonic wars, it remained a British satellite state after 1815. Lord William Carr Beresford, Irish by origin, like Church, was the commander of the Portuguese army between 1809 and 1820, first as Wellington's deputy during the Peninsular War, and later as marshal-general of all Portuguese troops, who continued to be dominated by British officers until 1820. In 1817, when Church was defeating brigandage and the secret societies' activities in Puglia, Beresford was suppressing similar clandestine activities and the conspiracy led by Gomes Freire de Andrade that aimed at introducing a constitution and freeing Portugal from the British presence. Admittedly, Beresford's political power in Portugal was much greater than that of Church in Sicily. Portugal was a satellite of the British Empire, and Beresford was in constant touch with British diplomats and Lord Castlereagh himself back at home. As head of the Portuguese army, his political influence was in direct competition only with the board of governadores ruling over Portugal in the absence of the monarch. However, the dismissals of Beresford and Church were among the first of all revolutionary acts in Portugal and Sicily respectively. As symbols of despotism and foreign occupation, Church was physically attacked by the Palermitan crowds, while Beresford was prevented from disembarking upon his return to Portugal from Brazil. While Church continued to serve in the Neapolitan army, prior to offering his professional services in Greece, Beresford moved back to England. A Tory at heart, Beresford, like Church, had no sympathy for constitutions.[22]

Richard Church, then, shared with many other British fighters an extraordinary ability to seize the opportunities offered by the rapidly changing political circumstances of his life, without being consistently committed to a specific political agenda, let alone to the spreading of liberalism across the southern peripheries of the continent. Protection of the interests of the British Empire, and the civilising of Mediterranean populations through military discipline and war, represented the constant and

22. Malyn Newitt, 'Lord Beresford and the *governadores* of Portugal', and 'Lord Beresford and the Gomes Freire Conspiracy', in Newitt and Robson, *Lord Beresford*, pp. 89–109, and 111–34.

perhaps only ideological feature of his remarkable career: one that bridged the age of revolutions from the Napoleonic era to the creation of the new— illiberal—Greek monarchy in the 1830s and beyond.

Emmanuele Scordili and the Greek diasporas

The economic depression that afflicted Sicily in the post-Napoleonic period was a crucial factor in encouraging the island's insurrection. The artisans' guilds of Palermo assumed the leadership of the revolution in response both to the erosion of their privileges and the impoverishment of their members. Thus the citizens of Palermo looked to the new provisional government with hopes not only that it might guarantee the autonomy of the islands and introduce a constitution, but also that it would improve their material circumstances. This is why, as soon as it was established, the provisional revolutionary authority of the city was flooded with hundreds of petitions by individuals asking for employment. Among them one request stands out because of the peculiar professional background of its author. It was the offer by a former Greek officer, Emmanuele Scordili, born on the Ottoman island of Crete, to work for the Sicilian revolutionary army as an interpreter. In order to back up his credentials, Scordili noted in his petition that 'since the age of twenty [he had] worked for the Russian imperial fleet, and was later enrolled in the Albanian regiment of the Kingdom of the Two Sicilies as a second lieutenant'. Since 1812, when the regiment had been finally disbanded, Scordili continued, he had received a pension, but the outbreak of the revolution that year had stopped its regular payment. In exchange for a salary, Scordili offered his services to the new government as an interpreter. His knowledge of 'the oriental languages, and especially of the Muscovite and Turkish ones', continued the former officer, would prove useful to the government, 'since the Sicilian nation would now need to establish commercial relations with the oriental nations'. In order to lend more credibility to his assurances, Scordili added that 'the Greeks and Sicilians have been, and still are, one single nation; moreover, my residence in Sicily for almost twenty years has made me a veritable Sicilian'.[23]

Submitted on 13 August 1820, this request was rejected by the provisional government: we have no evidence as to what became of Scordili after the end of the Sicilian revolution. He belonged to a professional category, the Ottoman Christian mercenary fighting for the Christian monarchs, which had existed since the sixteenth century, when the Neapolitan

23. ASP, Real Segreteria, Incartamenti, 5032, f. 85.

FIGURE 14. A soldier from the Reggimento Real Macedone (watercolour by Michela de Vito, 1820; Museo di San Martino, Naples). Image: Wikimedia Commons

kings had started to employ Christians from the Ottoman lands, and from Albania and Epirus in particular. The Reggimento Albanese Real Macedone, founded in 1736, was further strengthened at the time of the wars against the French, when, between 1797 and 1798, a new battalion of 'Cacciatori albanesi', to which Scordili had belonged, was formed The Greek regiments raised by Richard Church in the Ionian islands therefore did not represent a novel phenomenon. Nor was Scordili's past service in the Russian fleet unusual: since Catherine the Great's wars against the Ottomans from 1769 to 1774 and 1787 to 1791 the Russian imperial army too had recruited Greek regiments and had started to employ Greeks in its military fleet, or to hire Greek corsair ships in the Mediterranean.

The Napoleonic wars, meanwhile, offered novel opportunities of employment for these Ottoman Christian fighters, as all the imperial powers, including Britain, required and hired local mercenaries to fight in the Mediterranean. Scordili's biography and that of Richard Church, who had created new Greek regiments in the Ionian islands, were therefore intertwined by their participation in the same military events.

When the Albanian regiments were disbanded in 1812, some of their members were hired by the Neapolitan consular service in the Levant, and others, like Richard Church, immediately went on to join other foreign armies.[24] Like Scordili, many Greeks offered their linguistic skills to the various empires with a presence in the Levant, for the European consular services were glad to take advantage of their unique knowledge in this period, in order to advance their own commercial and diplomatic interests.[25]

24. Attanasio Lehasca, *Cenno storico dei servigi prestati nel regno delle Due Sicilie dai greci epiroti albanesi e macedoni in epoche diverse* (Corfu, 1843), pp. 55–56; Pappas, *Greeks in Russian Military Service.*

25. Theophilus C. Prousis, *British Consular Reports from the Ottoman Levant in an Age of Upheaval, 1815–1830* (Istanbul: ISIS, 2008), pp. 17–21.

In one way, however, the two biographies differ substantially. While Church's helps us understand the complex nature of European philhellenism, Scordili for his part invites us to reflect upon the impact that the Greek war of independence had on the transition from being a Christian Ottoman to becoming a Greek national. Although both Church and Scordili moved between and across different empires and states, Scordili's life belonged first and foremost to the polycentric world of the Greek Mediterranean, between its diaspora and the Greek-speaking territories of the Ottoman Empire, and can only be understood from inside it. Scordili was not just a mercenary, but also a member of one of the very many Greek communities that flourished on the shores of the Mediterranean, from Messina in Sicily to Marseilles, from Livorno to Naples, from Taranto and the Salento in Puglia to Venice and Trieste in the Habsburg Empire. Their permanently settled populations were cyclically reinvigorated by the arrival of new individuals such as himself, and their members remained in contact with their Ottoman Christian communities of origin thanks to commercial and family ties.[26] Thus Scordili's petition invites us to explore how the transition to a revolutionary context affected mobilities, and offered new possibilities for the renegotiation of cultural and political affiliations among the members of the Greek diaspora. It does so by offering insights into how this transition was affecting Greeks just before the outbreak of the Greek revolution. What did it mean to be Greek, and how did the Greek revolution change this? How did the revolution alter pre-existing mobilities between Greek communities inside and outside the Ottoman Empire?

For centuries the members of these communities had organised themselves in self-governing associations called *fratie*, or *universitas*, or *confraternità*, linked to churches belonging to the Greek Oriental rite and appointing their own priests. These communities defined themselves (using Italian terms) as a 'nazione greca', and their members as 'nazionali'. In spite of this definition referring to their religious and linguistic affiliation, the identities of their members were often fluid from both a religious and a cultural point of view, as well as that of their legal status.[27] With

26. Olga Katsiardi-Hering, 'Greek Merchant Colonies in Central and South-Eastern Europe in the Eighteenth and Early Nineteenth Centuries', in *Merchant Colonies in the Early Modern Period*, ed. Victor Zakharov, Gelina Harlaftis and Olga Katsiardi-Hering (London: Pickering & Chatto, 2012), pp. 127–80.

27. Olga Katsiardi-Hering, 'Diaspora and Self-Representation: The Case Study of Greek People's Identity, Fifteenth–Nineteenth Centuries', in *Human Diversity in Context*, ed. Cinzia Ferrini (Trieste: EUT, 2020), pp. 239–65.

the exception of those Greeks living in Venice, who had their religious rights guaranteed and could safely practise their Orthodox faith, in the Kingdom of the Two Sicilies the *confraternità* were subject, as members of the Oriental church loyal to the papacy, to the authority of the Catholic church. However, it was not uncommon for them to choose clerics from the east, professing Orthodoxy, and thus entering into conflict with the Catholic authorities.[28] From a legal point of view, and depending on their actual origins, Greeks defined themselves as Ottoman, Habsburg or Venetian, and belonged to separate congregations (in Naples, for instance, Ottoman and Venetian Greeks frequented separate churches). But these definitions were always negotiable. During the Napoleonic period in Venice, for example, a number of *nazionali* had decided to become Ottoman in order to avoid the taxation imposed on Venetian citizens.[29]

Scordili's own use of the terms *nazione greca* and *nazione siciliana* demonstrated elements of a strong continuity with the idiom that the Greek diaspora had employed for centuries, and with eighteenth-century understandings of the *nazione siciliana* as a state. While many petitions sent by individuals or communities to the Neapolitan provisional government in the same period contained references to the Cádiz Constitution of 1812 and to its definition of the *nazione* as a sovereign community of people, such references were absent from Scordili's own appeal. His cosmopolitan claim that Sicilians and Greeks were of a single nation could well have been voiced a full century before, or even earlier. However, the language of other members of the Christian Ottoman diaspora was now starting to shift in new directions, and might be taken to reflect more explicitly the new values of the age of revolutions. On the other side of the Mediterranean, on the Spanish island of Mallorca, only three months before Scordili petitioned the Sicilian government, two Greek expatriates spoke in an assembly of the patriotic society of the town of Palma de Mallorca, an association set up immediately after Riego's pronunciamiento and the declaration of the Cádiz Constitution in 1820. In the face of the hostility shown by some of its members to the presence of foreigners, the two Greek merchants made an impassioned case for their right to join the patriotic association, offering at the same time to resign, should

28. Angela Falcetta, *Ortodossi nel Mediterraneo cattolico: Frontiere, reti, comunità nel Regno di Napoli (1700–1821)* (Rome: Viella, 2016), pp. 126–32, 248–51.

29. Mathieu Grenet, '"Grecs de nation", sujets ottomans: Expérience diasporique et entre-deux identitaires, 1770–1830', in *Les Musulmans dans l'histoire de l'Europe: Passages, et contacts en Méditerranée*, ed. Jocelyne Dakhlia and Wolfgang Kaiser, 2 vols (Paris: Albin Michel, 2013), 2, pp. 311–44.

they be called upon to do so. Having lived in Mallorca, from where they had been engaged in trade between the Ottoman Empire and Spain, for ten years, Nicholas Francopulo and Yanni Papadopulo claimed to consider themselves friends of all Spaniards. Their determination to play their part in the Sociedad Patriótica Mallorquina, one of the very many similar institutions that sprang up across Spain and southern Europe during the 1820s, the two Greek merchants observed, did not seem to them to be incompatible with its nationalist aspirations, since they were both committed to the values of the revolution, and to the defence of the constitutional order that constituted the main aim of its existence. In their view, indeed, constitutional Spain, a country that had defeated tyranny and the persecution of the Holy Inquisition, was best placed to provide guidance and leadership to Greece in its own aspirations for freedom against an oppressive government.[30]

The outbreak of the Greek revolution in spring 1821, immediately after the Austrian invasion of Naples had put an end to its constitutional regime, had a profound impact on the Greek Mediterranean, stirring up new patriotic sentiments, and creating new movements across the region. Movements from and into the Greek diasporic communities before the revolution were determined both by commercial routes and by enduring links with their members' places of origin inside the Ottoman Empire. But the war moved populations to new destinations, both near and far. Besides offering their moral and financial support, thousands of Greek ex-combatants from the Russian, British and Neapolitan armies would travel to the territories of the Ottoman Empire as volunteers. A number of Greek officers asked for, and obtained, financial support from their confraternity in Naples. Members of this very *nazione* were reported to have exulted when Russia declared war on the Ottoman Empire in 1829.[31] Greek volunteers from the diaspora and from the shores of the Mediterranean included also people without any previous military experience. The city of Trieste in the Adriatic provides a case in point: on the eve of the Greek revolution, this main port of the Habsburg Empire hosted a large Greek community, or *parikia*, of around 1,500 individuals. Its existence had been formally

30. 'Actas de la Sociedad', *Sociedad Patriótica Mallorquina*, no. 1, 25 May 1820, pp. 2–4. On patriotic societies in the Spanish revolution, and that on Mallorca in particular, see Alberto Gil Novales, *Las sociedades patrióticas (1820–1823): Las libertades de expresión y de reunión en el origen de los partidos políticos*, 2 vols (Madrid: Tecnos, 1975), 1, pp. 289–300, 304–7.

31. Moscati, 'La questione greca', p. 24. Gianni Korinthios, *I greci di Napoli del meridione d'Italia dal XV al XX secolo* (Cagliari: AMED, 2012), pp. 294–300.

institutionalised in 1751, when an Orthodox church was inaugurated. The city, an important commercial and information hub between the Ottoman and Habsburg empires, had played an important role in the history of Greek patriotism early on. While its economy suffered from the setbacks of the Napoleonic period and the French occupation, which dealt a heavy blow to the role played by the city in international trade, there was an impact too upon the political and cultural life of the community. While in Vienna between 1797 and 1798, Rigas Velestinlis, who had developed the earliest plans to 'liberate' Greece from the Ottomans on the basis of the principles of the French revolution, forged links with Trieste, where he recruited a small circle of supporters among the Greek merchants. His famous poem 'Thourios' was well known in the city and sung by a number of supporters; and in the years that followed the Philiki Etaireia acquired a number of members there.[32] A turning point came in 1821, however, when Greek patriotism rapidly evolved into a more socially substantial movement. As soon as news about events in the Danubian Principalities and the Peloponnese had reached them, various local volunteers, mostly from a humble social background, left for Greece bearing passports issued by the Russian and Ottoman consuls of Trieste. In addition, the port was used by Greek students coming from European universities as a point of departure to go to Greece. This flow had been encouraged by the arrival of the Ypsilantis brothers Alexandros and Dimitris, who used the city to raise funds and organise these groups of fighters—although in July 1821 the Austrian authorities made it illegal for volunteers to gather and depart for Greece from Trieste, so the flow of fighters continued thereafter by land rather than by sea. Financial support for the revolution was provided by a number of wealthy city merchants, who offered substantial sums of money for military purposes.[33]

A greater number of volunteers came from the Ionian islands. Partly as a spontaneous reaction to the revolution, and partly thanks to the activism of local members of the Philiki who moved across frontiers, hundreds of fighters left the islands, with those from Zante and Cephalonia in particular joining the conflict in the Peloponnese as early as April 1821. Ionian volunteers had also taken part in Ypsilantis's expedition in the Danubian Principalities.[34]

32. Olga Katsiardi-Hering, *Η ελληνική παροικία της Τεργέστης (1751–1830)* (The Greek community of Trieste (1751–1830)), 2 vols (Athens: University of Athens, 1986), 1, pp. 322–23.

33. Katsiardi-Hering, *Η ελληνική παροικία* (The Greek community), 1, pp. 335–39.

34. Gekas, *Xenocracy*, pp. 62–65, 69–73; Panayotis Hiotis, *Ιστορία του Ιονίου Κράτους από συστάσεως αυτού μέχρις ενώσεως (έτη 1815–1864)* (History of the Ionian State from

New opportunities would therefore open up for individuals like Scordili in 1821. Since his name does not appear on the list of the forty veterans who by 1830 had died and had their funerals in the Orthodox church of Palermo, it is not inconceivable that he was among those who reached the Peloponnese or Roumeli at the outbreak of the rebellion from the port cities of the Mediterranean and Adriatic.[35] At the same time, not all the members of these 'Greek nations' were seduced by the call to join in the war of national liberation or responded with such alacrity to the patriotic feelings aroused by the Greek insurrection. Some in fact remained loyal to their traditional affiliations. Since this period coincided with the creation of an Ottoman consular system, a number of diasporic Greeks remained faithful to the empire even after the revolution: the Ottoman consul in Marseilles was such a Greek and—while the deputy consul there became a representative of the new Greek state—he continued to work for the Ottoman Empire and condemned the revolution.[36]

The migration flows precipitated by the revolution were not confined to a sudden increase in the movements from the Mediterranean Greek communities back into Greece. It also resulted in human displacement in territories where the revolution had broken out: a forced migration occasioned by war and the invasion of the Ottoman armies. Thus another novel form of movement produced by the revolution was that of refugees. Between 1821 and 1828 displacement caused by the revolution, along with ethnic cleansing and war casualties, resulted in a decrease of the population of the territories of the revolution by 185,000, some fifty thousand of whom must have been Muslims.[37] Scordili may well have decided to go to the Peloponnese or to Roumeli to fight, but it is unlikely that he moved back to the island of his birth, Crete, for more than a very short spell. Southern Crete had joined the insurrection immediately, in 1821, but attacks against the insurgents by the Ottoman army and fleet, culminating in the invasion of the south-west of the island by the Turko-Egyptian forces of Hussein Bey in March 1824, condemned more than ten thousand to becoming

its establishment to unification (the years 1815–1864)), 2 vols (Zakynthos: Typografeion Eptanisos, 1874), 1, pp. 409–11, 426.

35. M. Sciambra, 'Prime vicende della comunità greco-albanese di Palermo e suoi rapporti con l'oriente bizantino', *Bollettino della Badia Greca di Grottaferrata* 16, no. 5 (1962): 102–4; Vittorio Buti, 'Albanesi al servizio del regno delle due Sicilie', *La Rassegna Italiana: Politica letteraria e artistica* 39 (1939): 151–57.

36. Grenet, '"Grecs de nation"', pp. 341–43.

37. Nikolai Todorov, *The Balkan City, 1400–1900* (Seattle: University of Washington Press, 1983), p. 328.

refugees, most of whom fled to the Peloponnese.[38] While such displacement encouraged a new sense of national belonging, it also resulted in violence and intolerance among Greeks themselves. Greek refugees fleeing their province, city or island were often killed by other Greeks, who treated them as enemies, so much so that agreements had to be made in revolutionary assemblies to put a halt to such atrocities, and also to render forced displacement illegal.

Such displacements also produced a flow of refugees towards other Mediterranean countries. Other states, such as the Ionian Islands or the Kingdom of the Two Sicilies, along with the Adriatic coasts of the Habsburg Empire, started to receive refugees from the war in Greece. In the British colony of the Ionian Islands, Governor-General Maitland's immediate reaction to the outbreak of the revolution was to decree the strict neutrality of the Ionian Islands, a status that allowed the protection of refugees from the war, but that otherwise kept the territory outside the conflict. The very first refugees of the Greek revolution were probably the seven thousand individuals, mostly women and children, who because of its vicinity and safety fled to the island of Zante from the area of Patras, in the northern Peloponnese, in the very early stages of the revolt. On Zante, they enjoyed the financial support of wealthy citizens.[39]

Although these flows of refugees represented an unprecedented phenomenon, their patterns of movement remained indebted, at least initially, to pre-existing links between given localities and the Greek diaspora. Soon, refugees started to cross the sea not only to reach the Peloponnese or the islands not affected by the war, but also the communities on the Mediterranean and Adriatic shores. More than twenty thousand people left the island of Cyprus, and some of them ended up as far away as Venice or Trieste, where they could take advantage of family or commercial ties to obtain assistance. The *nazione greca* in Venice, for instance, raised money to help the refugees, to subsidise the education of their children and to send girls to learn to read and write in the convents of the city.[40]

A more substantial number of refugees reached the city of Trieste, which received three thousand migrants in 1821. One thousand of them left immediately, one thousand spent just a few days, and another thousand

38. George Dalidakis and Peter Trudgill, *Sfakia: A History of the Region in its Cretan Context* (Heraklion: Mystis, 2015), p. 187.

39. Hiotis, *Ιστορία* (History), 1, p. 388.

40. Konstantina Zanou, 'Profughi Ciprioti a Venezia e Trieste dopo il 1821 (nuovi elementi provenienti dalle carte Mustoxidi a Corfú)', in *Giornate per Cipro* (Padua: Garangola, 2007) pp. 39–62.

settled. By early 1823 the Greek community had swollen from 1,500 to 3,200 individuals. At first most of the refugees were civilians from Constantinople, Kidonies, Smyrna, Cyprus, Yannina and Arta, along with former combatants who had fought with Ypsilantis in the Danubian Principalities. In 1822 a large wave of refugees came also from the island of Chios, after the massacres there. The reason for the popularity of Trieste as a destination for refugees was twofold: they chose it first thanks to existing contacts with relatives or fellow citizens who were doing business in the city; and second, because of the importance of the existing trade links between the city, the Adriatic and the Aegean. Given the sudden number of arrivals, the community soon found it difficult to provide support for everybody. Those with family connections could more readily obtain employment and financial help, while for the rest it was the community itself that helped in providing shelter and distributed money from its own funds and from those offered by European philhellenic organisations. Still, by 1823 the community was having trouble in continuing to after the new arrivals, and the members of the community board decided to stop raising funds. Given that the Austrian government rejected any refugees who had actively participated in the Greek revolution, and allowed the others to stay in Trieste only if the community, their friends or relatives could support them, many had no alternative but to leave. As a consequence, by spring 1823 the majority of them had left for Alexandria, Odessa, Marseilles and, above all, for the Ionian Islands.[41]

While the flow of refugees stirred patriotic responses and reinforced feelings of belonging to a shared national community, it did not necessarily result in the adoption by the refugees of one specific national affiliation at the expense of others. As in previous centuries, Ottoman Christians moving across the Mediterranean were willing to renegotiate their cultural identities and affiliations. In the absence of a Greek consular service, and given that a Greek state was not recognised by foreign powers until after 1827, Greek refugees, whenever they could, sought protection from the authorities of other European countries, whether by requesting consular protection or obtaining citizenship status in these states. Greeks fleeing to North Africa during the revolution, for instance, often acquired Italian, French or British documents in Alexandria or Tunis.[42]

41. Katsiardi-Hering, *Η ελληνική παροικία* (The Greek community), 1, pp. 342–63.

42. Julia Clancy Smith, *Mediterraneans: North Africa and Europe in an Age of Migration, c. 1800–1900* (Berkeley, CA: University of California Press, 2011), pp. 86, 219.

Besides refugees and volunteers, the Greek revolution provoked another, less well known and less dramatic, type of displacement, and one that led to an even more radical juridical and religious transformation: the enslavement of Greek prisoners. As a result of the war, the slave markets of Smyrna, Constantinople, Alexandria (in Egypt) and the Barbary States were suddenly flooded by an exceptionally high number of slaves (forty-five thousand Greeks, mostly women and children, were taken from the island of Chios alone, in spring 1822), to the extent that their prices fell dramatically. This form of displacement was not new, but belonged to a centuries-long history of Christian enslavement in the Ottoman world.[43] What was new was its sudden intensification, and also the new meaning that the philhellenic movement had attributed to it, as a marker of Ottoman barbarity.

Liberating enslaved Greeks became a humanitarian cause, financed by Russian and Greek merchants and supported by committees which included diplomats, consuls and donors. Yet while these efforts led to the liberation of some enslaved Christians (for instance, in summer 1827 Russia managed to free 360 Greek slaves), they also brought to light another, unexpected phenomenon: apostasy. Not only children, but also many adults, apparently spontaneously, had converted to Islam. Some of them, when offered the opportunity to be ransomed, refused it and retained their new Muslim faith, satisfied with the professional opportunities they had found in Ottoman society.[44] Therefore, rather than simply nationalising both the Greek Mediterranean diaspora and the populations of the Greek territories, the age of revolution, by encouraging new forms of voluntary mobility and by triggering new enforced ones, led to a variety of professional, religious and political renegotiations. Among the surprising and unexpected cultural crossings of this period there featured not only the request of a Cretan member of the *nazione greca* to become a Sicilian revolutionary and to work as an interpreter, but also the decision of former Ottoman Greek subjects, the so-called *reyes* or *reyedes*, captured and enslaved during the war, to retain their new status and their faith as Muslims.

43. Robert C. Davis, *Christian Slaves, Muslim Masters: White Slavery in the Mediterranean, the Barbary Coast, and Italy, 1500–1800* (New York: Palgrave Macmillan, 2003).

44. Lucien J. Frary, 'Slaves of the Sultan: Russian Ransoming of Christian Captives during the Greek Revolution, 1821–1830', in *Russian–Ottoman Borderlands: The Eastern Question Reconsidered*, ed. Lucien J. Frary and Mara Kozelsky (Madison, WI: University of Wisconsin Press, 2014), pp. 101–30.

Andrea Mangiaruva: volunteer for
freedom and economic migrant?

With the end of the Sicilian and Neapolitan revolutions came first the occupation by the Austrian army of both the continental and the insular parts of the Kingdom of the Two Sicilies, and soon afterwards police investigations and retaliation against former revolutionaries. A number of 'giunte di scrutinio' were created to purge the civil service, the clergy and the army of conspirators, and military commissions were set up to sentence those found guilty of participation in secret societies. While a small number of leading revolutionaries were sentenced to death, and others received lengthy prison terms, a larger number were expelled from the kingdom. Yet conspiracy and secret society activities did not come to an end with foreign occupation, but revived very rapidly. An extensive revolutionary plan was organised with the support of thirty newly established secret society lodges at the end of 1821, the so-called conspiracy of Salvatore Meccio, after the name of its principal coordinator and guiding light.[45] The aim of the plot was to expel the Austrian troops occupying the island and stationed in its capital, proclaim the revolution and reintroduce the Cádiz Constitution with the support of the Neapolitan members of the Carboneria. Contemporaries described the political attitudes of these conspirators who supported the Cádiz Constitution as 'democratic', in contrast to those Palermitan aristocrats who the previous year had championed the more conservative Sicilian constitution of 1812. Uncovered at the beginning of 1822, just as the insurrection was due to begin, the conspiracy resulted only in arrests, death sentences and exile.

Among those condemned to death was Andrea Mangiaruva, grand master of one of the thirty lodges created to organise the revolution, called the 'Imitators of Cato'. Mangiaruva had been a member of the delegation sent to Naples to negotiate a settlement with the constitutional government in 1820, and during the revolution had been appointed an officer of the national guard.[46] Forced to flee Sicily by boat, he did not return to the island until 1836. Although in 1823 a military commission had acquitted him of all responsibility for the conspiracy, there being

45. Valentino Labate, *Un decennio di Carboneria in Sicilia (1821–1831)* (Rome: Società Editrice Dante Alighieri, 1904), pp. 161–209; Amelia Crisantino, *Introduzione agli 'Studi su la storia di Sicilia dalla metà del XVIII secolo al 1820' di Michele Amari* (Palermo: Mediterranea, 2010), pp. 21–29. On Mangiaruva's role, see Labate, *Un decennio*, p. 166.

46. Michele Palmieri, *Le duc d'Orléans et les émigrés français en Sicile, ou Les italiens justifiés* (Paris: Delaunay et Dentu, 1831), p. 20.

insufficient evidence, he nonetheless spent the following years as an economic migrant and freedom fighter between North Africa and the Iberian peninsula, via the British imperial outposts of Malta and Gibraltar, describing his adventurous life in a highly fictionalised autobiography published in 1849.[47] Having arrived in Malta at the end of 1822 under an assumed identity, he was forced to leave after a few days, and with a Spanish passport he reached the Spanish coast after a short period spent in Gibraltar. His arrival in Spain coincided with the French military expedition that had been agreed upon during the Congress of Verona, to crush the constitutional regime and reinstate Fernando VII as absolute monarch. As a consequence Mangiaruva, having lived in Algeciras with other Italian migrants for only four months, was drafted into Sir Robert Wilson's foreign legion, which had been entrusted with the task of defending Seville, the city to which the constitutional government and the Cortes had retreated in the face of the French invasion. The constitutional government had decided to recognise the ranks that the foreigners had previously held while in their national armies, and therefore Mangiaruva regained the title of major in the foreign legion.[48] His activity as a 'volunteer' was short-lived: the capitulation of General Ballesteros in Granada, where he had been ordered to join the general's constitutional forces, and an attack by royalist guerrillas, during which he was wounded, forced him to go back to Cádiz just before the surrender of the city to the French army.[49]

Mangiaruva's forced departure from Spain marked a new phase of his exile, turning him from a military volunteer and freedom fighter into an economic migrant. Crossing the sea once more via Gibraltar and quitting the Mediterranean, he spent almost three years in the city of Tangiers in Morocco, where he traded in perfumes and powders and served at the emperor's court. In Tangiers he found himself in the company of many other Spanish and Italian migrants. Yet a plague and the death of the Italian woman whose support had enabled him to settle on the Atlantic coast of North Africa led to his decision to abandon Morocco and move to Portugal, once more by way of Gibraltar. His arrival in Lisbon in 1826 coincided with the popular celebrations for the introduction of the new constitution granted by Dom Pedro, the emperor of Brazil, who had decided that his under-aged daughter Dona Maria would be the future

47. Andrea Mangeruva [Mangiaruva], *Avventure di un esule* (Palermo: Stamperia Console, 1849). On his acquittal, see Valentino Labate, *Un decennio di Carboneria in Sicilia (1821–1831): Documenti* (Rome: Società Editrice Dante Alighieri, 1909), pp. 173–75.

48. Mangeruva, *Avventure*, p. 160.

49. Ibid., pp. 164–77.

queen of an independent and constitutional Portugal, and had appointed his sister Dona Isabel Maria as temporary regent.[50] Here Mangiaruva established his professional credentials as a portraitist and miniaturist on tortoiseshell snuffboxes for the royal court, joining a thriving community of Italian-speaking artisans and merchants, mainly from Genoa and Naples. This time, however, he decided not to engage actively in politics. After 1828, when Dom Miguel returned to Portugal and abolished the constitution, he continued his professional activities without any direct involvement in the military and civilian mobilisation in the defence of the constitutional government, which had produced a number of military revolts across the country and attracted some Italian revolutionaries. Yet in 1830, like many other migrants and Portuguese sympathetic to the constitution, he became a target of the Miguelist repression, and only just escaped capture and imprisonment by hiding for a while in Lisbon, and by fleeing to Paris for the following six years.[51]

Mangiaruva's biography is illuminating at many levels, as it offers insights into a number of patterns characterising migration across and beyond the western Mediterranean in the 1820s. First of all, it shows the importance that the Iberian peninsula had as a revolutionary pole of attraction in the period. Admittedly, former revolutionaries fleeing Sicily, Naples and Piedmont from 1821 onwards did not exclusively go to Spain. Among the five hundred individuals suspected of conspiracy or condemned for revolutionary activities who had left the Kingdom of the Two Sicilies by 1829, either of their own accord or because they had been expelled, many also reached other destinations, from North Africa to the Greek islands and northern Europe.[52] Yet Spain remained a major destination among former revolutionaries, second only to Greece, not only for those whose origins lay on the Italian peninsula, but also for those from other European countries.

The reasons for this choice were manifold, but they were all related to support for the cause of constitutional internationalism. The Cádiz Constitution, adopted in Piedmont and Naples during the revolutions, represented the most powerful symbol of liberalism across the Mediterranean after 1812. Its defence represented at the same time a commitment to the cause of freedom as a universal rallying-cry beyond national boundaries, and an investment in a struggle against the forces of despotism that,

50. Ibid., p. 264.
51. Ibid., pp. 284–306.
52. ASR, Fondo Statella, 248, 24–25: 'Registro degli attuali espatriati ed esiliati Napolitani', September 1829.

supposing it were to triumph abroad, could provide new opportunities to reintroduce a constitutional regime where it had just been repressed. Thus the initial mode of engagement chosen by exiles fleeing into Spain was that of fighting first the counterrevolutionary guerrillas, and then, in 1823, the French invading forces. More than 1,100 exiles had reached Spain after the end of the revolution in Piedmont, arriving mainly from Genoa with Spanish passports in the ports of Catalonia, where the constitutional government offered them temporary subsidies and the recognition of their previous military occupations or ranks. Former soldiers and army officers represented a significant proportion of these exiles: out of 776 emigrants to Spain whose profession is known, there were 438 former combatants (equally divided between soldiers and officers); it is therefore not surprising that many of them ended up joining the ranks of the Spanish constitutional armed forces. The most famous of their number was Giuseppe Pacchiarotti, who had been involved in the Piedmontese revolution. After fighting with honour against the royalist guerrillas, Pacchiarotti obtained permission to found an independent national regiment which included two hundred Italians, and whose units, comprising also Spanish and Swiss soldiers, were invariably led by Italian officers.

The combination of national and international objectives is confirmed by the establishment of this regiment. The priority of its officers was to affirm the constitution in Spain against its enemies, but these Italian officers indubitably nursed a hope that in future, their regiment might also play a part in the emancipation of their own country. The regiment had an Italian tricolour as its flag, a distinctive uniform with special colours, and its own hymn, entitled 'Inno all'esule' (Hymn to the exile), the text composed by a Piedmontese exile, Luigi Monteggia.[53]

The ideological foundations of French military volunteerism in Spain were different, as they were primarily geared to the revolutionary plans of the Charbonnerie against the Bourbons; but those involved, like their Italian counterparts, drew inspiration from internationalism. Their leader, the former Napoleonic officer Charles-Nicolas Fabvier, put together a regiment of 110 individuals, including the journalist Armand Carrel and a few Spanish and Italian volunteers, to try and stem the French invasion of Spain. Fabvier had already tried to convert the French army approaching the Spanish border to his plans, which envisaged the re-establishment of a Napoleonic regime and the declaration of the young Napoleon II as

53. Carlo Beolchi, *Reminiscenze dell'esilio* (Turin: Tipografia Nazionale, 1852), pp. 109, 116–17.

emperor under the temporary regency of Maria Luisa. Waiting for the arrival of the French invading army on the shores of the Bidasoa river between Spain and France, Fabvier's force issued one manifesto in the name of the 'majestic cause of the people's freedom' and of 'Napoleon II'. A second broadsheet, addressed to 'the headquarters of the army of free men', associated the Napoleonic cause with the introduction in France of a constitution that would abolish all types of aristocracy.[54] The foreign legion organised by Sir Robert Wilson in 1823, meanwhile, which comprised Spanish, French, Swiss, British and Italians (including Andrea Mangiaruva himself) was the one that espoused the most explicitly internationalist language, addressing in its proclamations all the peoples and soldiers of Europe and condemning in no uncertain terms the principles of the Holy Alliance.[55] At the same time, however, like the Italian and French volunteers, Wilson linked the Spanish war to political plans back home: he considered the cause of the Spanish constitution as a crucial step towards reform of the British political system and its constitution.

Military volunteerism, however, was not the only concrete form of revolutionary internationalism that drew exiles to the Iberian peninsula. Another and equally important related phenomenon was the flow of southern European patriots into and from Spain and Portugal to garner support for their own revolutionary cause and to organise transnational revolutionary plots. The activities of these individuals combined conspiracy, the setting-up of international secret societies and informal revolutionary diplomacy with a view to fostering cooperation between constitutional governments and revolutionary groups in Portugal, Spain, Naples and Greece. The former leader of the Neapolitan revolution Guglielmo Pepe was one of those most active in inviting foreign revolutionary governments to support his plans for insurrections in southern Italy after 1821, plans for which he requested the intervention of Spanish and Greek volunteers. He did so first by extending the membership of his secret society, the Fratelli costituzionali europei, and also by meeting politicians and ministers in both Madrid and Lisbon. However, apart from attracting the sympathy of a few deputies of the left in the Spanish Cortes and the Portuguese Congresso, he failed to make much progress with his plans. In

---

54. Antonin Debidour, *Le Général Fabvier, sa vie militaire et politique* (Paris: Plon, 1904), pp. 221ff; proclamations to be found in Jean Baptiste Honoré Raymond Capefigue, *Récit des opérations de l'armée française en Espagne*, [. . .] (Paris: E. Guide, 1823), pp. 68–73.

55. Beolchi, *Reminiscenze*, p. 133; 'Al pueblo y soldados de Europa', 15 May 1823, republished in Brennecke, 'Internacionalismo liberal', p. 472.

Lisbon he managed to obtain the written endorsement of the Portuguese minister of war for his request to the Greek government to provide volunteers for the insurrection in Calabria, although without any practical consequences.[56] Pepe's revolutionary diplomatic efforts were not unique. Others, without the international reputation and the credentials of the Neapolitan general, tried to advance their revolutionary agenda by connecting the cause of the revolutions in Greece, Portugal and Spain. In the summer of 1822, for instance, a Captain Nikolas Chiefala (Kefalas), the self-appointed representative of the Greek government, travelled to Portugal and met up with the Portuguese minister of foreign affairs and other Portuguese politicians, communicating summaries of these meetings to the Portuguese press, with a view to securing diplomatic recognition for Greece and to request that the Portuguese government rally to the cause of Greek national liberation. In his enthusiastic response to Mavrokordatos, entrusted to Chiefala, minister Silvestre Pinheiro Silveira went so far as to imagine the creation of a federation of all southern European countries against despotism and dictatorship, although he did not append any offer of concrete aid to his declaration of moral support.[57] Moving in the opposite direction, that is to say, to Greece, at the end of 1821, three Italian exiles declared themselves to be delegates of Spain, a dubious claim since it was probably made on their own initiative and in order to advance their own interests, when they addressed the national assembly of Epidavros. In their petition to the members of the legislature of Greece, described as 'liberators of a great people', Palma, Morales and Vourinos asked them 'to accept at the same time our offer to establish relationships and unity with the Spanish patriots, with that heroic and free nation which, had it not had to consolidate its own freedom, would have come in its entirety to fight in Greece'. The document included a request for Greek citizenship to be granted to all those Italian 'friends of freedom' who had come from Naples and Piedmont to shed their blood for Greece—in recognition of their signal contribution to the cause.[58]

56. Pepe, *Memoirs*, 3, pp. 251–52.

57. ANTT, Ministério dos Negócios Estrangeiros, Arquivo Central, Correspondência Ministro Pinheiro Silveira, Grécia, livro 175. On Portuguese foreign policy in the period, see Grégoire Bron, 'Il Mediterraneo dei portoghesi all'inizio del secolo XIX: Diplomazia e internazionalismo liberale, 1808–1835', *Daedalus* 5 (2014): 214–42.

58. Palma, Morales and Vourinos, 18 December 1821, in Αρχεία της Ελληνικής Παλιγγενεσίας (Archives of the Greek Regeneration), 25 vols (Athens: Library of the Hellenic Parliament, 1971–2012 [1st edn 1857]), 1, pp. 235–36 (available at https://paligenesia.parliament.gr/, accessed 15 August 2022).

Mangiaruva's account is instructive, secondly, insofar as his movements into and out of Spain and Portugal via Gibraltar highlight the importance that the maritime and coastal space between these three different states played in establishing transnational connections for revolutionary and counterrevolutionary movements. The borders between Gibraltar, Spain and Portugal not only separated different countries, but provided an interface that proved crucial to both the termination and the reactivation of revolts, providing shelter alternatively to absolutists and revolutionaries from various countries, and for Portuguese and Spanish political migrants even more than for those, such as Mangiaruva, hailing from the central Mediterranean. It is important to take into account the fact that this frontier region was already well connected before the revolutions. The openness of the coast and the presence of a wealthy class of merchants accounts for the pro-liberal nature of the towns and cities of the area, from the Spanish port of Cádiz to those of Faro and Portimão. The only exception to the pro-constitutional attitudes of the coast between Spain and Portugal was perhaps Tavira, a city which, given the presence of a military garrison, an aristocracy and a declining trading role, had much stronger absolutist inclinations. Strong economic links integrated the continental interiors of both the Algarve and Andalusia with each other, and their coasts with Gibraltar and North Africa. The Portuguese ports of the Algarve, and Faro and Portimão in particular, traded intensively with Gibraltar and Spain. They exported to Lisbon, as well as to Spain, Gibraltar, Britain and other countries.[59] These commercial exchanges included also a thriving contraband trade: authorities were well aware of the illegal traffic in *trigo* (wheat) and tobacco from Spain and Gibraltar into Portugal.[60]

Depending on political vicissitudes, migrants flowed in one or the other direction by boat via Gibraltar or, less frequently, moving by land across borders. While it was less important than the maritime region, and much less so than the frontier between Trás-os Montes and Spain further north, nonetheless the internal border between the Algarve and Andalusia represented a 'hotspot'. In 1823, the end of the revolution in Spain and the arrival of the French occupying army in Cádiz and Huelva on the other

59. José Carlos Vilhena Mesquita, 'A instauração do liberalismo em Portugal numa visão global socioeconómica: A participação do Algarve', in *Estudos 1. Faculdade de Economia da Universidade do Algarve* (Faro: Faculdade de Economia da Universidade do Algarve, 2004), pp. 23–48; Mesquita, 'O Algarve no processo histórico do liberalismo Português (A economia e a sociedade 1820–1842)', 2 vols, unpublished doctoral dissertation, Universidade do Algarve, Faro, 1997.

60. ANTT, IGP, Algarve 243, ff. 34–35: February 1826.

side of the border was accompanied not only by a flow of officers, soldiers and civil servants, but also by civilian refugees, including many elderly people and children, moving towards the Portuguese border.[61] During the constitutional biennium of 1826 and 1828 the Andalusian territories bordering on the Algarve guaranteed the survival of a regional Portuguese royalist resistance. In October 1826 the fourteenth infantry regiment and the fourth regiment of Caçadores based in the city of Tavira declared Dom Miguel as absolute monarch and set up a provisional governmental junta of the Algarve. While this insurrection was defeated after a only few days, the troops from absolutist regiments who had mutinied managed to cross the border into Spanish territory where they regrouped, reorganised themselves and created a base from which to recruit new sympathisers. Thanks to the protection guaranteed by the Spanish authorities they managed to launch attacks against the constitutional government in Portuguese territory over the following two years.[62]

Besides being a zone of transit between the British Empire, Spain and Portugal, Gibraltar was also a place where politics were conducted, and new uprisings were planned and initiated. Thanks to its direct links with Britain, where many revolutionaries had settled, it also offered a platform from which to plot insurrections and nurture contacts with local liberals in Andalusia intending to resurrect the practice of the military pronunciamiento, in the hope that the events of 1820 would be replicated.[63] A first major plot was organised by the exiled revolutionaries in the summer of 1824. The proclamation they sent round to the Spanish troops invited them to revolt in the memory of Riego and Padilla against the French occupier, as they had done in 1808.[64] It was from Gibraltar that the last maritime insurrection was attempted against Fernando VII's absolute monarchy in 1831. Plans for this insurrection had started as early as 1829, circulated by a group of exiles led by José María Torrijos in London, with financial aid from Britain and France, the support of tradesmen and liberal activists based in Gibraltar and on the Spanish coast and with the contributions of other exiles conspiring from France and North Africa.

61. Ibid., Algarve 240, f. 119: juíz de fora of Lagos to intendente geral de polícia, 28 June 1823.

62. Ibid., Algarve 243, ff. 225–34: October 1828.

63. Castells, *La utopía insurreccional*; Simal, *Emigrados*; Rafael Sánchez Mantero, 'Gibraltar, refugio de liberales exiliados', *Revista de Historia Contemporánea* 1 (1982): 81–107.

64. ANTT, Ministério dos Negócios Estrangeiros, caixa 283, Consulados, Gibraltar, f. 58: José Agostinho Parral to the Marquis of Palmela, 9 August 1824. This includes a copy of the proclamation to the 'Militares españoles', with no date.

Taking advantage of the favourable context created by the 1830 revolution in France, these exiles were hoping that their intervention from Gibraltar would stir an insurrection across the entire country coordinated by local juntas. The forty-nine insurgents who landed on the mainland in November were arrested one and all on the coast of Málaga, however, and executed in December 1831.[65]

Gibraltar was also a foreign space where national ideological divisions were replicated, and the transition from one regime to the other was felt as intensely, if not more so, than in continental Portugal. Concerned for the survival of his sister's regency and for his daughter's rights, Dom Pedro decided in 1828 to send his daughter Dona Maria from Brazil to Portugal to prevent an absolutist coup. In accordance with an agreement desired and promoted by Dom Pedro, she was pledged to marry Dom Miguel and become queen upon reaching adulthood. However, by the time she was nearing Portugal, having arrived in Gibraltar, Dom Miguel had left Vienna and reinstated an absolute regime by abolishing the constitution. Besides hosting the queen and other exiled Portuguese liberals, Gibraltar had offered temporary shelter to the crew of a warship belonging to the naval squadron of the Algarve, the *Ninfa*, that had remained loyal to Dom Pedro and had left Faro upon the reinstatement of the absolute monarchy. In the British colony, the Portuguese consul had hastened to recognise Dom Miguel, and refused to pay a salary to the crew, though the commander of the warship had asked him to do so. Before leaving for London, the exiled Portuguese liberals based there were received by Dona Maria on her vessel for the ceremony of the *beija-mão*: the constitutionalists thus performed a gesture, the kissing of the hand of the monarch, traditionally employed for absolute sovereigns, to signal instead their loyalty to a constitutional ruler.[66]

Thus Mangiaruva's constant, although temporary, passage via Gibraltar to and from Spain towards other destinations exemplifies a larger and very significant movement of revolutionaries across borders within the Mediterranean and between the Mediterranean and the Atlantic that facilitated the continuation of insurrectionary activities throughout the 1820s, enabling the survival abroad of the defeated party at each regime change.

Finally, Mangiaruva's life as an exile shows the overlap existing between the categories of revolutionary volunteer and economic migrant,

65. Simal, *Emigrados*, pp. 318–26; Castells, *La utopía insurreccional*.
66. ANTT, Ministério dos Negócios Estrangeiros, caixa 283: Consulados, Gibraltar, ff. 12, 32: consul to the Viscount of Santarém, 7 June and 11 September 1828.

and the relationship between new revolutionary mobilities and older migrant communities. On the Iberian peninsula, the wave of political exiles such as Mangiaruva did not mark the very first presence of Italian communities in the country. As he noted in his own biography, the coastal regions of Portugal (Lisbon and the Algarve in particular) had welcomed migrants arriving from other parts of the Mediterranean, from Genoa to Naples, since at least the previous century. The Italian community represented the third largest foreign cohort in Portugal, after the French and the Spanish-Galician. Made up of individuals first and foremost from Genoa and Piedmont, but also from Naples and the southern regions, it included tradesmen, merchants and shopkeepers as well as artisans and artists working in the theatre industry, mostly based in Lisbon. Since 1800 they had been organised in a 'conservatória' with their own magistrate. The community also included itinerant tinsmiths from Basilicata.[67] After 1821, and in particular after 1826, a new wave of exiled Spanish and Italian revolutionaries, such as Mangiaruva, drawn to the new constitutional government, reached Lisbon from Gibraltar, London and other parts of the Mediterranean. While some of them took part in the military operations in defence of the constitutional regime against the absolutists in 1827 and 1828, they also sought employment alongside the Italians already living there. Thus the renewal undertaken by the Greek diaspora during the Greek revolution was not a unique phenomenon, as the Italian diaspora was going through similar transformations.[68]

Like the Greek communities across the Mediterranean, the Portuguese Italian contingent became entangled in the political conflicts unleashed by revolution and counterrevolution. In 1823 first, but increasingly after 1828, they became the target of the violence of the Miguelistas, the supporters of Dom Miguel. On the one hand, the absolutist authorities' repressive measures against their enemies resulted in the imprisonment not only of thousands of Portuguese liberals, but also of Italian émigrés. Dom Miguel imprisoned or expelled from the kingdom both former revolutionaries like Mangiaruva and wealthy tradesmen and merchants, and debarred them from recruiting Portuguese workers. He also expelled the itinerant tinsmiths who had come from Basilicata, as he considered them

67. Carmine Cassino, '"Lisboa dos italianos": Presença italiana e práticas de nacionalidade nos primeiros trinta anos do século XIX', Cadernos do Arquivo Municipal, 2nd series, 3 (2015): 211–37.

68. Grégoire Bron, 'Révolution et nation entre le Portugal et l'Italie: les relations politiques luso-italiennes des Lumières à l'Internationale libérale de 1830', unpublished doctoral dissertation, Paris EPHE and Lisbon ISCTE, 2013.

to be agents of sedition and crime as dangerous as foreign revolutionary volunteers. These legal measures had been preceded by mob attacks: the urban underclasses mobilised by the Miguelistas also targeted foreigners (Galician workers and Italian migrants) in their acts of violence against the constitutionalists. In counterrevolutionary nationalist discourse the notions of liberal and foreigner were conflated, both being described as threats to the national community, to its values and integrity.[69] Therefore ideologically driven volunteerism and economic migration were overlapping categories not only because individuals like Mangiaruva moved from one to the other while living abroad, and because the two communities interacted with each other, but also because foreigners, considered equally as criminals and as potential threats to Dom Miguel's regime regardless of their actual social status and political opinions, were subjected to violence and persecution.

Conclusions

The stories explored in this chapter point to how different the material conditions, circumstances and motivations were that turned individuals into revolutionaries and led them to cross the Mediterranean, as well as illustrating the different meanings that individuals attributed to these experiences. By so doing, they call into question the assumption that all fighters joined revolutions in the name of nationalism and constitutionalism, and put the phenomenon of military volunteerism into a broader context of older and new mobilities. These biographies confirm the important part that the Napoleonic era and the era of the 1820s revolutions played in exacerbating displacement. However, they also show that the Mediterranean crossings of this period need to be understood in continuity with longer-term migratory trends that had connected the coasts of the sea for centuries.

As the case studies discussed here demonstrate, traditional patterns of migration and early modern understandings of migrant communities continued to survive into the 1820s. Support for new principles of nationality, along with a commitment to the constitution, may or may not have played a role in determining revolutionary mobilities. This applies not only to migrants belonging to 'foreign' groups abroad and resident there for centuries, but also to the army officers who had embarked upon a Mediterranean career during the Napoleonic wars. In the southern and eastern

---

69. Carmine Cassino, 'La comunità italiana in Portogallo tra rivoluzione e reazione (1820–1828)', *Memoria e Ricerca* 48 (2015): 121–41.

peripheries of Christian Europe, national values may have been subordinate to a vague defence of the values of civilisation against barbarism, or to the interest that the British Empire had in expanding further in the region. In an age of increased politicisation and multiple wars, the ability to take advantage of new and even competing political causes, and to offer one's services as a fighter, may well have been as important as a commitment to the ideologies of 'modernity'. The stories of Church, Scordili and Mangiaruva blur the boundaries between revolution and counterrevolution, freedom fighter, economic migrant and mercenary, national and imperial aspirations. Thus political, intellectual and cultural affiliations created under circumstances of increased mobility did not necessarily all conform to a linear trajectory moving from the ancien régime into the age of liberalism, or from the age of empires to that of nationalism. The biographies of the individuals discussed here invite us to understand experiences like revolution, but also categories like the nation, liberalism and volunteerism in a far more fluid and nuanced way than we have generally been accustomed to do, and to blend together material circumstances and personal choices relating to the great ideological and political transformations of the period.

The broader context of the lives of Church, Scordili and Mangiaruva also shows that, in an era of increased violence, forced migration, not military volunteerism, represented the most prominent or commonest form of mobility in this decade. While violence against migrants and intolerance towards foreigners was rooted in a range of different contexts and causes, it was to be found everywhere. As in previous centuries, crossing the Mediterranean continued to offer possibilities of renegotiation and the acquisition of new and unexpected cultural and political affiliations. At the same time, the increased movements of people across borders had a substantial impact on the way in which states policed their frontiers and controlled transnational conspiratorial activities. Although in the years to follow revolutions and sundry economic motivations continued to spawn movement across southern Europe, an immediate consequence of the 1820s uprisings was the tightening of borders by the states affected by them. The restored absolute regimes did all they could to expel all undesirable individuals and increase controls at their frontiers. This happened at the borders between Portugal and Spain and between Spain and France. It would happen also in the newly established Greek state from the 1830s onwards. After that, foreign revolutionaries would no longer be welcomed for their ideological sympathy for the cause of Greek nationalism, but feared as a threat to the new absolute state. The Neapolitan government not only increased border controls, but started also to project internationally its police and intelligence activities via its diplomatic and consular services. More than ever before, in the eyes of the governments of the southern European monarchies, economic migrants and revolutionaries came to be conflated as dangerous classes of person, potentially importing subversive ideas and undermining domestic stability.[70]

70. Laura Di Fiore, *Alla frontiera: Confini e documenti di identità nel Mezzogiorno continentale preunitario* (Soveria Mannelli: Rubbettino, 2013); Carmine Cassino, 'Portugal e a Itália: Emigração, nação e memória (1800–1832)', unpublished doctoral dissertation, Universidade de Lisboa, 2015, pp. 145–46; Christos Aliprantis, 'Lives in Exile: Foreign Political Refugees in Early Independent Greece (1830–53)', *Byzantine and Modern Greek Studies* 43, no. 2 (2019): 243–61; Simal, *Emigrados*, p. 119.

PART II

Experiencing the Constitution

CITIZENSHIP, COMMUNITIES AND TERRITORIES

Introduction

In December 1820 the municipal authorities of Novi, a village in the district of Vallo in Lucania, a Neapolitan province south of Salerno, submitted a petition to the parliament calling for the abolition of the law for the privatisation and distribution of state land. This law, they complained, had led to the appropriation of public land by a small number of proprietors to the detriment of the villagers, who had lost their traditional grazing and farming rights as a community. The petition claimed that only its abolition could finally demonstrate the benefits of the new constitutional government. In the days that followed, four hundred peasants took possession of the public lands they claimed had been illicitly sold, starting a peaceful movement of land occupation by peasants across the entire district. Peasants carried out such acts to the cry of 'Long live the constitution!' The authorities representing the central government, the intendente and his deputy, tried unsuccessfully to evict these villagers, but in the end not even the intervention of the local militia could persuade the peasants to withdraw. Such resistance by the villagers was not only a vindication of their communal rights against wealthy landowners, but also a defence of municipal autonomy in the face of state interference and its foremost representative, the intendente.[1] This episode is illustrative of themes central to Part II of this book.

1. Aurelio Lepre, *La rivoluzione napoletana del 1820–21* (Rome: Editori Riuniti, 1967), pp. 107–27.

The chapters that follow look at how political constitutions transformed the relationship between citizens, communities and the state. They discuss what people (both individuals and communities) sought from a constitution, what expectations their constitutions raised once they had been introduced and how they were understood in different regional and national contexts and by different social groups. They do so by exploring both the administrative and the legal arrangements that created new political rights for individuals at local and national level, and reordered the relations between towns, provinces and central governments. More importantly, they look at the new, related practices that constitutions introduced, the expectations they gave rise to, and the various ways in which these legal arrangements were interpreted.

An analysis of these practices sheds light on the appeal of the constitution to ordinary citizens, and on the aspirations they thought a constitution could satisfy. While this analysis shows that most constitutions did cater to widespread aspirations for political participation from below, whether through elections or petitions, it suggests also that such participation might be understood in different ways. As the case of the peasants in the district of Vallo shows, the desire to participate was often geared to demands for autonomy, whether communal, provincial, regional or national, or a combination of all of these. This was particularly true in Naples, Sicily and Greece, where their constitutions appealed to a broad coalition of social constituencies by guaranteeing the self-government of communities or territories whose autonomy had been threatened or eroded in the preceding years. As discussed also in the previous chapters, these aspirations arose from an expectation, especially in Portugal, Spain, Piedmont and Naples, that monarchical power had to be limited, or at least combined with a recognition of popular sovereignty. These various demands were combined in different ways, and different people and communities and social groups gave priority to some of them over others.

Crucially, in the context of the struggles that exploded during the revolutions, political actors interpreted what a constitution might do in novel and unexpected ways, and made new claims about the manner in which its various elected institutions, local, regional and national, should relate to each other. This was the case, for instance, with regard to the role of municipalities in Spain. The administrative organisation envisaged by the constitution guaranteed governmental control over the municipalities, although their governing bodies were elected by the local communities. But the tensions between exaltados and moderados created conflicts within cities and towns, and between these latter and central government, that politicised local administrations in unforeseen ways. New claims emerged about the right of municipalities to act in defence of the constitution, and their duty to do so on behalf of the nation. The birth of the Greek state represents a comparable case, for there a new centralised administration was the unpredictable result of the recognition by all regional groups that central coordination and control was required to win the war.

The next three chapters seek to retrieve the plurality of expectations, reactions and practices related to the political rights and territorial reorganisation granted by the various constitutions. The first explores the revolutions as territorial crises, and looks at the impact that the emerging constitutions had on the reorganisation and governance of territories, and the relationship between local communities, provinces and the state. It shows that while all constitutions reorganised territories and introduced uniform administrative control at national level, requests by local communities and regions that their autonomy—under threat from central government—be safeguarded led to constitutional revisions and compromises. The second chapter goes on to discuss the national elections based on quasi-universal male suffrage introduced by the revolutions. It argues that, given that indirect electoral systems prevailed in the 1820s, voting for a national assembly remained a local experience. At the same time, popular sovereignty reaffirmed the role of communities as constitutive elements of the nation, exacerbating tensions between local identities and national unity. The final chapter explores petitioning as a form of participation and a process of representation by citizens, professional groups and local communities. It demonstrates in each case the existence of widespread support for the constitutions, and of mobilisation in their defence against their enemies. But it also shows that there existed conflicting interpretations of what the constitution stood for, reflecting the social and economic tensions in play during the period. As the behaviour of the peasants of Novi and the surrounding villages vividly demonstrates, local communities argued for the preservation of common land against privatisation as a constitutional right, much as professional groups argued against liberalisation on similar grounds, while conversely, others attacked these traditional prerogatives in the name of the individual rights guaranteed by the constitution.

Thus in the 1820s the nation was understood at one and the same time both as the sum of individuals delegating power to national parliaments, and a single territory subject to uniform laws, and as a collective entity made up of social groups with their own privileges as corporate entities, and of communities and regions defending their own autonomy. The nation of the 1820s was therefore a blend of new ideas of citizenship endowed with individual rights with older communitarian concepts of rights as privileges.

CHAPTER SIX

Re-conceiving Territories

THE REVOLUTIONS AS TERRITORIAL CRISES

Introduction

What do Navarre, the Basque country, the city of Genoa, Sicily, the Peloponnese and the island of Samos tell us about the revolutions of the 1820s? This chapter will seek to respond to this question by exploring the impact that the introduction of constitutions had on the territorial organisation of states in this period. It does so by looking both at the concrete impact of the reforms introduced by the revolutionaries and at debates about territorial reorganisation before and after those reforms. What was at stake in the revolutionary debates across southern Europe about administrative reorganisation was therefore whether decisions were to be taken at the central or at the regional level, whether local communities could govern themselves independently, who should elect local governments and how local interests should be represented or defended at the centre.

In the decades before the revolutions, central authorities in Portugal, Spain, Piedmont, Naples and the Ottoman Empire had increasingly reasserted their control over the peripheries, either permanently or temporarily. The Napoleonic expansion across southern Europe had dramatically increased state intervention and territorial centralisation in the territories controlled by France, enhancing existing trends in administrative reform evident within ancien-régime states. Fiscal and military pressures had similarly forced the Ottoman administration to exert more direct control over its territories, and had upset the balance between imperial centre and regional elites. Between 1799 and 1815 the Napoleonic wars, the expansion of French institutional structures and experimentation with new constitutional systems in southern Europe, whether inside or outside the orbit of imperial France, brought with them the idea of the nation as sovereign. In the name of the nation, France exported an idea of the state whose territories were ruled uniformly from the centre. In southern Europe this idea fostered a debate about how national sovereignty was to be distributed inside the nation's boundaries. What were its constitutive elements, from an institutional and territorial point of view, how did they relate to each other, and in which of them did sovereignty actually lie? Was sovereignty confined to the actions of the central administration, or was it shared with peripheral institutions and territories?

The 1820s revolutions in Spain, Piedmont, Naples, Sicily and Greece (but less so in Portugal) represented in their turn junctures when, at least temporarily, central control was challenged and localities tried to reassert their rights. While they varied in intensity, decentralising tendencies can be detected almost everywhere during the revolutions, and constitute a distinctive feature of these events. Throughout southern Europe, the outbreak of the revolutions was marked by displays of initiative on the part of local authorities. But while this initial federal moment would soon come to an end in some areas, in others it became a permanent feature of the revolutionary experience. These tendencies were very pronounced in the Kingdom of the Two Sicilies and in Greece, and very modest in Portugal. One of the most important consequences of the introduction of constitutional government was the recasting of the administrative and institutional relationship between centre and peripheries. The revolutions in turn provided opportunities for local communities, regions and provinces to voice their own requests, and formulate and present new or traditional claims about their autonomy and their privileges. The administrative reorganisation of territories introduced by the constitutions revived existing and long-standing conflicts and rivalries between different cities and different provinces and regions, and precipitated others that were in essence new. Arguments in favour of constitutional liberties, and claims about the nature of constitutional government, were by turns employed to defend local autonomy and to justify central control against particularism. In other words, the revolutions revived or exacerbated conflicts that were both vertical (between centre and periphery) and horizontal (between different and competing territories).

As a matter of fact, the introduction of constitutions and constitutional debate provided a space for a very broad range of different visions of territoriality. These visions were associated with a remarkable variety of arguments, and a plurality of social as well as political interests and stances. Disagreements were often articulated in terms of clashes between federal and centralised notions of the constitutional order. There were also clashes between those who called for the abolition of local and corporate privileges and those who fought in their defence, or advocated their reintroduction. However, as I shall demonstrate, for a number of reasons it is not possible to draw a clear-cut distinction between those in favour of, and those opposed to, the administrative ancien régime, or between those in favour of, or against modernisation—between those defending a new order and those rallying to the one recently overthrown. In fact, the revolutions opened up new possibilities for rethinking the territorial structure of the state that were often hybrid in nature, from both an intellectual and an institutional point of view. This was the case for a number of reasons. First of all, the new administrative and territorial dispensation was at times built up not in opposition to the old institutions, but rather using them as a starting point. The administrative reforms of the Greek revolution, for instance, built on existing Ottoman practices of territorial representation, but a blend of new and old institutional solutions can also be found elsewhere. Second, there existed genuine supporters of the constitution and representative government who nevertheless detested centralisation. These latter were happy to retain some features of ancien-régime communal freedoms or local privileges, but were equally keen to combine these with representative government and universal suffrage. Those critical of centralisation in Naples, Sicily or Greece, and to a lesser extent in Spain, did not simply yearn for a return to a past order. As a result, it is not always easy to divide 'progressives' from conservatives in this debate.

These different reactions to the introduction of a constitution depended on a variety of factors. Sometimes they were related to the fact that the fracturing or dismantling of earlier forms of control or privilege created new opportunities. Sometimes they were the result of expectations and resistance from below prompted by the imposition of a new territorial order from above. Sometimes they were simply responses to the nature of the constitution itself, or were a combination of all of these factors. Nonetheless, a set of converging features can be detected in all these revolutions. First of all, the outbreak of the revolutions was marked by centrifugal tendencies and the proliferation of local committees that in Spain, Portugal, Piedmont and Naples harked back to the experience of juntas created on the Iberian peninsula during the war against Napoleon. Second, the efforts by revolutionary authorities to extend and reinforce administrative uniformity against legal pluralism and local privileges were met with resistance on the part of those regions that had enjoyed a marked degree of self-government. During the revolutions, areas traditionally marked by high levels of autonomy resisted resolutely attempts at enforced centralisation, or rebelled against them. This was the case, in particular, with Navarre and the Basque country in Spain, with Liguria in the Kingdom of Sardinia, with Sicily in the Kingdom of the Two Sicilies, with certain Aegean islands such as Samos, or with the Peloponnese in Greece. These regions invariably reacted against state interference. In some cases, such resistance coincided with an outright rejection of the constitutional system; in others regional leaders proposed compromise solutions that combined the defence of administrative particularism with recognition of the constitution. In yet others, British imperial protection was sought in order to defend autonomy. Resistance led to civil wars between territories in the Kingdom of the Two Sicilies, Spain and Greece.

A third converging feature of these revolutions is that they brought with them municipal elections, and turned local authorities into agents of revolutionary politics. And finally, towards the end of the revolutionary experience, in an effort to find a compromise between conflicting interpretations of the constitutions, the revolutionary elites put forward reforms that extended and reinforced controls from the centre, but recognised at the same time a degree of local self-government as a pillar of the constitutional system. The capacity of revolutionary governments to manage, undermine or defeat this resistance was a decisive factor in determining the eventual success, or otherwise, of the revolutions and in guaranteeing popular support for them.

Constitutional devolution and federal royalism in Spain

The territorial reorganisation adumbrated by the Cádiz Constitution was central to these debates. In Spain, Piedmont and Naples and Sicily, where the revolution was implemented in its name, the 1812 charter was interpreted in different and even contrasting ways. Divergent reactions coexisted both within each national context and from region to region, and depended on prior administrative structures and territorial organisation. To make sense of the reception granted to the Cádiz Constitution, however, it is necessary to go back to the context that led to its formulation, and to the intentions of those who drafted it, not least because the revolutionaries of the 1820s made constant reference to them. Those who drafted the 1812 constitution had produced a document that abolished all forms of territorial privilege, increased the control of the centre over the peripheries and was based on the principle of the legal and institutional uniformity of the nation. This did not mean the total rejection of the importance of local territories and the endorsement of a Jacobin notion of the nation: the existence of provinces was acknowledged in the constitution, and their participation in government was guaranteed through its new institutions. The 1812 constitution had nonetheless rejected the principle of federalism and the sovereignty of each territory.

In 1808, in the context of the revolt against Napoleon, city or provincial juntas had been set up. The absence of royal authority had justified the exercise of sovereignty by these assemblies, which had sent their representatives to a central junta. Although some provincial juntas, like that of Valencia, had claimed that national sovereignty was made up of the individual sovereignty of each of them, in general juntas had acted in the name of the entire Spanish nation and on behalf of monarchical authority. However, the establishment of local and provincial juntas and their appointment of representatives to a 'Junta Suprema Central' represented only a temporary federalising moment in the reorganisation of power in those parts of the kingdom not occupied by the French—one that was soon to be superseded by the convocation of the Cortes in 1810, and the drafting of the new constitution of the Spanish nation approved in 1812.[1]

In its final version, the Cádiz Constitution that was approved in 1812 had introduced a uniform administrative system anchored to the figure of the jefe político who, like the French prefect, was appointed by the central government to administer provinces on its behalf and guaranteed the application of central decisions throughout the territory.[2] In recognition of the importance of provinces as administrative units, the constitution had also stipulated the creation of *diputaciones provinciales*, provincial committees chaired by the jefe político, which included the jefe político himself and the intendente (the representative of the Hacienda, or Ministry of Finance) along with some elected members from the ayuntamientos. The *diputación* had both political (the execution of governmental decisions) and administrative/economic responsibilities, these latter ranging from discussion relating to the promotion of agriculture, industry and commerce to the financing of public works and the approval and supervision of the budgets of individual ayuntamientos. These tasks rendered

1. Portillo Valdés, *Revolución de nación*, pp. 462–91; Moliner Prada, *Revolución burguesa*, pp. 35–89.

2. Francisco Carantoña Álvarez, 'Liberalismo y administración territorial: Los poderes local y provincial en el sistema constitucional de Cádiz', in *La revolución liberal*, ed. Alberto Gil Novales (Madrid: Ediciones del Orto, 2001), pp. 135–57.

these institutions important for the everyday life of provinces. They also allowed local concerns and demands to be raised by individuals elected locally—during the general elections by the very same representatives who elected the deputies to the Cortes. However, in the minds of the liberals who had drafted the constitution, the diputaciones were not representative bodies at the provincial level, but intermediary administrative bodies. In their view, in fact, the will of the people could be expressed only in the national Cortes. The very idea of provincial representation was considered to be dangerous, as it would lead to the disintegration of the nation. The diputaciones presided over by the jefe político also supervised local administrations. While the constitution introduced new elective municipal governments that granted towns a high degree of administrative autonomy, it also extended central controls over them through the supervision of the diputaciones. Finally, the constitution stipulated the introduction of uniform and universally valid commercial, criminal and civil codes cross the country. It also entailed the application of a taxation system throughout the country, with no regional exemptions.[3]

The principles underpinning this new administrative system stood in sharp contrast to the institutional and legal pluralism of the Kingdom of Spain as it had been organised up until the eve of the French invasion of 1808. While in the eighteenth century the monarchs had done much to strengthen their authority over the peripheries of their realm, what had remained in place until the Napoleonic wars were in particular the privileges enjoyed by the Kingdom of Navarre and the provinces of the Basque country, otherwise known as *fueros*. This term indicated either the ancient charters that defined the existence of the three provinces of the Basque country and the Kingdom of Navarre, or statutes and laws passed by the assemblies of these provinces as part of the right to self-government enjoyed by them, or laws passed by the king but approved also by the assembly and therefore integrated into their fueros.[4] Unlike other provinces of Spain such as Catalonia, Aragon and Valencia, which had lost their distinct privileges in the early eighteenth century, Navarre

3. José Antonio González Casanovas, *Las diputaciones provinciales en España: Historia política de las diputaciones desde 1812 hasta 1985* (Madrid: Mancomunidad General de Diputaciones de Régimen Común, 1986), pp. 24–30. On this peculiarity of Spanish early federalism, see also Florencia Peyrou, 'Los orígines del federalismo en Espãna: Del liberalismo al republicanismo 1808–1868', *Espacio, tiempo y forma, Serie V, Historia Contemporánea* 22 (2010) (*República y monarquía en la fundación de las naciones contemporáneas: América Latina, España y Portugal*, ed. Àngeles Lario): 257–78.

4. John Coverdale, *The Basque Phase of Spain's First Carlist War* (Princeton, NJ: Princeton University Press, 1984), p. 22.

and the Basque provinces had retained them until the beginning of the nineteenth. The Kingdom of Navarre had Cortes formed of three estates which by the end of the eighteenth century were no longer summoned by the monarch, whereas the Basque provinces had juntas composed of representatives from local communities and civil servants which wielded considerable powers. Under the rubric of the fueros persisted an array of specific legal and institutional privileges that enabled these provinces to retain a high degree of autonomy. In particular, and most importantly, there existed fiscal privileges. The Basque country was exempt from customs duties, so that trade flowed freely between it and France, and goods were taxed only when crossing the river Ebro on its southern border. In addition, while not exempt from taxes, the people of the Basque country were not subject to the same range of fiscal impositions as inhabitants of other provinces, and managed some of their own taxation for internal purposes. Secondly, the populations of these provinces were exempt from the so-called *quintas*, the military conscription that all others were subjected to in times of military emergency. Finally, municipal government enjoyed a high degree of autonomy if compared to the rest of Spain, where local officials were crown appointments.[5] These privileges were entirely abolished for the first time in 1810, when Napoleon created separate governments, dividing off these provinces from the Spanish territories controlled by his brother. Guerrilla warfare developed in Navarre and the Basque country as much as anywhere else in Spain, but here the rebellion was justified not only in the name of the rights of the king and religion, but also in defence of the ancient constitution of the kingdom and of the fueros, and these latter were to be fully reinstated with the revocation of the constitution by King Fernando in 1814.[6] The Cádiz Constitution also completed the demise of ancién-regime administrative pluralism with a new and uniform system of local administration. This new municipal government abolished the various pre-existing types of local administration, whether they had been under royal authority (through royal civil servants, the *corregidor* or *alcalde mayor*), or under seigneurial jurisdiction. It replaced the previously existing municipal authorities controlled by local aristocratic oligarchies with elective governments, the ayuntamientos, selected through an indirect system that granted voting rights to all resident heads of family.[7]

5. Ibid., pp. 23–27.

6. Ibid., p. 28.

7. Concepción de Castro, *La revolución liberal y los municipios españoles* (Madrid: Alianza Editorial, 1979), pp. 34–56.

The 1820 revolution unleashed a series of reactions across the territories of Spain inspired by the events between 1808 and 1812 that had led to the approval of the new constitution. In 1808, faced with the Napoleonic invasion and in the absence of the monarch, local committees, the juntas, were set up throughout the country, acting in the name of Fernando VII. Soon afterwards representatives from all these local bodies were appointed to the Junta Suprema Central in Seville, which in 1810 agreed to organise elections to create the Cortes. Likewise, Riego's later pronunciamiento resulted in the organisation of local juntas throughout the country, a phenomenon shared in differing degrees of intensity by all the other revolutions across southern Europe. However, the aims and composition of these bodies were very different from previously. While in 1808 juntas had been created in the name of the absent monarch, and were made up of representatives of the traditional local elites, in 1820 such temporary institutions acted in the name of the sovereign nation and the constitution. In addition, demands to follow scrupulously the script of 1808 and appoint a central junta with representatives from all the local juntas came only from La Coruña in Galicia, and from individual revolutionaries such as Juan Romero Alpuente in Murcia. For the junta of Galicia, the only guarantee that the constitution would be properly implemented and therefore secured against its enemies would be the creation of a central junta.[8] In the other cases, the committees set up in the individual cities took on the powers of the government and acted on behalf of the nation only temporarily, in expectation of the recognition of the constitution by the monarch and the convocation of the Cortes. This 'temporary' federalism, marked by local initiatives in the name of the defence of the constitution re-emerged once more, although not in a generalised fashion, between the end of 1821 and 1822, when the exaltados controlling most local administrations accused the moderate Bardají-Feliú government of facilitating counter-revolution in the wake of Riego's removal from the captaincy-general of Zaragoza and stirred up popular protests in the name of the defence of the revolution. In Valencia, for instance, the local radical leadership that controlled the militias and the tertulia patriótica, and was represented on the ayuntamiento, called for the creation of a local independent junta, thus following the script of the events of 1808 and 1820. According to the signatories of a manifesto to the diputación of the Cortes, it was the duty of the city of Valencia, along the lines of what the cities of Cádiz, Seville, La Coruña, Cartagena and Murcia had done, to re-establish their rights and

8. See Moliner Prada, *Revolución burguesa*, pp. 101–2.

their sovereignty and, by ceasing to recognise the authority of the government, to prevent the nation from succumbing to slavery.[9]

Besides these temporary resurgences of local committees, after 1820 the implementation of the centralised system of control over the territories of Spain delineated in the 1812 constitution produced new tensions and conflicts between centre and peripheries, and gave rise to a novel set of debates about the need to rethink its principles and rules. A first set of tensions preceded and accompanied the revision of the political and administrative map of the country introduced in January 1822. This revision increased the number of provinces from thirty-two to fifty-two, and led to the abolition of territorial enclaves, the reorganisation of administrative units on the basis of contiguity, the transfer of a number of territories from certain historical provinces to others and the creation of various new provincial capitals at the expense of others.[10] The contest between certain cities in Galicia at the time of its reorganisation as a province provides an example of such disputes: in a controversy originally ignited years before through public debates, petitions and, more recently, discussions in the Cortes, the ancient seat of the archbishop, Santiago, proclaimed its right to replace La Coruña as the provincial capital. When it became clear that La Coruña would nonetheless be preferred on account of its liberal credentials, Santiago tried unsuccessfully to win the right to host the Real Audiencia (royal tribunal) of the province.[11]

Another source of tension between centre and periphery stemmed from the revival of local politics occasioned by the reintroduction of the elective municipal system of the Cádiz Constitution. One of the first acts of the provisional government was to reintroduce temporarily the constitutional ayuntamientos that had existed in 1814, in anticipation of the organisation of local elections.[12] Competition between moderados and exaltados encouraged participation, intensified pre-existing conflicts and turned

9. María Cruz Romeo Mateo, *Entre el orden y la revolución: La formación de la burguesía liberal en la crisis de la monarquía absoluta (1814–1833)* (Alicante: Instituto de Cultura Juan Gil-Albert, 1993), pp. 162–68. See also CD, serie general, legajo 5, exp. 101: representation by the *alcalde constitucional* and the members of the local militia to the Diputación Permanente de las Cortes, 21 December 1821.

10. Aurelio Guaita, *División territorial y descentralización* (Madrid: Instituto de Estudios de Administración Local, 1975), pp. 45–62.

11. Eduardo Cebreiros Álvarez, 'Conflictos entre municipios gallegos durante el Trienio Liberal: La lucha por la capitalidad', *Revista de Dret Històric Català* 14 (2015): 149–81.

12. Ricardo Gómez Rivero, *Las elecciones municipales en el Trienio Liberal* (Madrid: Boletín Oficial del Estado, 2015). On the contested nature of local elections, see also Arnabat Mata, *Visca el rei*, pp. 83–86.

these elections into fertile ground for contestation, in particular when new social groups aspired to power. Attempts by anti-revolutionary candidates to win the elections were another source of local turbulence. Local factions would therefore often appeal to the central authorities to resolve their own political dissensions, and to challenge electoral results. In the town of Luque in the province of Córdoba, as a consequence of irregularities—'tumults' and 'a spirit of party'—the local elections were annulled by two consecutive jefes políticos. However, since the new alcalde refused to comply, a group of one hundred enraged inhabitants wrote directly to the Cortes to demand that the decree of annulment be enforced.[13]

Representatives of the central government in turn intervened to favour one group over another, depending on their own political affiliations. While the Cortes was often called upon to adjudicate in controversial local elections, sometimes the jefes políticos meddled in, and challenged, the results. In some cases, procedural irregularities were the pretext, but interventions were often highly political in nature, as they occurred in particular when royalist ayuntamientos were elected.[14] A particularly spectacular case of interference from above took place in Murcia, where the jefe político Tomás O'Donojú was also the commander of the army. In 1820 he intervened militarily to invalidate the elections in the town of Hellín, re-establish the council that had been in power in 1814 and call for new elections. This case, discussed in the Cortes, demonstrated that deputies were divided between those who believed O'Donojú's intervention, like any other carried out in similar circumstances by other jefes políticos, to be legitimate, on the grounds that it represented a defence of the national interest, and those who argued against it in the name of the autonomy of the independently elected communal government.[15] In 1821 Antonio Alcalá Galiano, then intendente at Córdoba, intervened to annul the elections in Lucena, the second largest city of the province, where the electorate was divided into two warring parties. Although justified in terms of procedural irregularities, it is clear that Galiano's decision was in fact highly political. An exaltado himself, Galiano acted in defence of his own political group, whose local members had called upon him to intervene.[16]

Such conflicts and constant meddling by the authorities did not prevent, but on the contrary may in some cases have encouraged, the

13. CD, legajo 41, no. 12: a group of citizens of Luque to the Cortes, 17 March 1821.
14. AHN, Estado, legajo 133-I, f. 25.
15. Ibid., f. 16; entry for 8 March 1821 in *Diario de las actas y discusiones de las Córtes: Legislatura de 1820 y 1821*, 13 vols (Madrid: Imprenta de las Cortes, 1820–21), 12, pp. 1–26.
16. CD, legajo 35, no. 80. Details also in Gómez Rivero, *Las elecciones*, pp. 109–21.

participation of electors. The highest percentages of participation in local elections, when often only 10 per cent of those entitled ended up voting, can be detected in those cities where clashes between absolutists and supporters of the constitution were harshest. It was thus in Lleida, a city deeply divided between royalists and liberals, that the highest percentage of voters in all of Catalonia took part in the electoral process: 48 per cent. These conflicts and divisions between moderados and exaltados, meanwhile, in turn did not prevent the emergence of a new local political class, to be distinguished from that in charge of the ayuntamientos earlier, under absolutism. In urban centres such as Barcelona and Reus, where noblemen had represented respectively 30 per cent and 8 per cent of local officials, they disappeared entirely from the list of *regidores* (members of the municipal government), and were replaced by higher numbers of lawyers, tradesmen, artisans and manufacturers (these latter rose from zero to 10 per cent in Barcelona). The proportion of noblemen also went down from 7 to 3 per cent in the city of Girona. In Valencia, the proportion of lawyers and tradesmen increased substantially at the expense of that of the landowners, which fell from 40 to 4 per cent. In Zaragoza, the numbers of both noblemen and landowners were reduced, to be replaced by tradesmen and artisans. In both the smaller towns and the rural villages controlled by liberals or by royalists during the three years of constitutional government there was a considerable turnover within the groups controlling local administrations.[17]

The greatest threat to the administrative and territorial reorganisation of the kingdom envisaged by the constitution came however from the Basque country and the Kingdom of Navarre. In these provinces counterrevolutionary insurrections had much to do with frustrations among the elites and the local populations at the loss of the special privileges guaranteed by the fueros, privileges incompatible with the administrative unity and centralised supervision adumbrated by the constitution. The abolition of some of the privileges associated with the fueros had a considerable impact on the popularity of the counterrevolutionary cause. In particular, the introduction in 1820 of military conscription, a measure that ran counter to local traditions, was bitterly resented. In 1818 the king had already demanded that conscription be introduced in Navarre, but he had then accepted financial compensation in lieu.[18] The abolition of customs

17. Ramon Arnabat Mata, 'Cambios y continuidades en los ayuntamientos constitucionales del Trienio Liberal (1820–1823)', *Bulletin d'Histoire Contemporaine de l'Espagne* 54 (2020): 1–18.

18. María Cruz Mina Apat, *Fueros y revolución liberal en Navarra* (Madrid: Alianza Editorial, 1981), p. 89.

exemptions created additional resentment, as it deprived the region of an income deriving from trade with France, along with imposing increases in taxation and new institutions.

As a consequence, in Navarre as well as in the Basque provinces, the question of the defence of the fueros came to inform the ideological and political clashes between liberals and counterrevolutionaries. Entertaining a historicist notion of freedoms, and embracing *pactismo*, that is to say, the notion that the mutual areas of authority of the monarch and the province were the result of a jointly agreed pact that limited royal authority, anti-constitutional proclamations asserted the ancient liberties of the Basque country, and their right of secession, deprived arbitrarily as they had been of their legitimate rights. In the words of a manifesto issued in 1821, 'If the current ministers dare to suppress [the fueros] by force, anybody could argue that it is your right to separate from the rest of your nation, be independent or put yourself under the protection of the august sovereign of France.'[19] In Navarre, *fuerismo* was supported by those aristocrats who were not wealthy enough to benefit from the sale of church land and the enclosure of common land, and who had suffered from the abolition of primogeniture.

The counterrevolutionary regencia established in La Seu d'Urgell in August 1822 took on the defence of provincial identities and privileges as a key element of its political propaganda against the constitution. Because of these peculiar cultural and institutional features, one historian has defined it as a 'federal counterrevolution', one based not on legal and administrative uniformity, but rather on respect for legal particularism. Admittedly, political differences existed between the various members of the regencia, as some of them were hostile to regional particularism. Yet what would seem to have prevailed were the views of the Marquis of Mataflorida, who was convinced of Spain's plural nature and of the need to take these features into account when fighting to re-establish the absolute monarchy. He insisted on the need to create local and provincial juntas coordinating military and civil matters and reporting back to the regencia itself, similar to those established during the Napoleonic war. This strategy would be supported by propaganda addressing individual provinces and highlighting their peculiarities.[20] The defence of the fueros was an important aspect of this programme from the very beginning. In the first address to the Spaniards written to justify its establishment, the members

19. Llanos Aramburu, *El Trienio Liberal*, pp. 274–76.
20. Arnabat Mata, *Visca el rei*, pp. 36–37.

of the regencia reaffirmed the king's commitment to re-establishing the 'fueros and privileges that some peoples [enjoyed]' before the revolution, and to summon representatives of all peoples and provinces according to ancient fueros, to address all the grievances arising out of the revolution.[21] The importance of defending provincial diversity was also declared in documents sent by the regencia to the sovereigns gathering at the Congress of Verona, at which plans for the future reorganisation of the kingdom were discussed. According to one of these, drafted by the Baron de Eroles, Spaniards, on account of their valiant and proud character, were used to 'the true independence of vassals', and were passionately attached to their fueros and customs. It was not through the Cortes introduced by the revolution, argued the document, but through the voice of the ancient cortes already in existence for centuries that Spaniards should regain the freedom of their ancient constitution.[22] In addition, in accordance with Mataflorida's earlier plans, the regencia targeted all provinces of the kingdom with specific proclamations celebrating their diversity and contribution to the struggle against the revolutionaries.[23] The manifesto addressing the Catalans, for instance, insisted on the preservation of their own 'peaceful and timeless customs and very ancient privileges', and praised their contribution to the fight against Napoleon.[24] Ultimately, royalist culture was not intrinsically in favour of the fueros or of provincial autonomies. In fact, the absolute monarchy had been hostile to them and had tried to erode their scope and applicability since the eighteenth century. However, given the circumstances of the civil war and the need to guarantee a social basis for its struggle against the revolution, emphasis on provincial autonomy and ancient freedoms stood alongside defence of royal prerogatives and religion. At the end of the Trienio the king reinstated the fueros; but in 1829 he undermined them once again.

Faced with the threat of the counterrevolution, both wings of the revolutionary movement were united in support of a uniform administrative system against provincial particularism. Moderados and exaltados alike viewed such particularities as a threat to the unity of the state not simply

21. APR, Papeles Reservados de Fernando VII, 21, ff. 5–6: the Marquis of Mataflorida, the archbishop of Zaragoza and the Baron de Eroles, 'Proclamation entitled "Español!"', Urgell, 15 August 1822.

22. Ibid., 22, ff. 184–90: the Baron de Eroles, 'Exposición de la regencia a los soberanos al congreso de Verona', 12 September 1822.

23. On the competing position of the regencia on the fueros, see Arnabat Mata, *Visca el rei*, pp. 251–57.

24. APR, Papeles Reservados de Fernando VII, 21, ff. 160–64: manifesto addressed to the Catalans, 22 October 1822.

in peninsular terms, but above all in its imperial dimension. In 1821 the moderado Count Toreno dismissed the notion that there was an innate federal tendency in Spain. On the contrary, he said in the Cortes, making reference to the anti-Napoleonic insurrection, 'whatever the difference[s] between Catalans and Gallegos, Andalusians and Castellanos, the idea of making a single nation is widespread among all Spaniards'. The civil war that erupted in 1822 reinforced these concerns among other supporters of the constitution, demonstrating the threat that local oligarchies mobilising large sectors of the populations could pose to the unity of the nation. An exaltado such as José Moreno Guerra, for instance, would denounce the risks of 'a partial and provincial dissolution, which will result in a federal union, more or less good, according to circumstances, but always preceded by the most appalling [*espantosa*] anarchy'.[25]

During the Trienio, meanwhile, a significant proportion of supporters of the constitution based in the provinces in fact came to believe that a higher degree of autonomy should be granted to the provinces, and that the diputaciones provinciales should be granted more powers. From 1820 onwards a number of diputaciones started to complain about the constant need for approval from above for their decisions regarding provincial administration and about its impact on the promptness of the decision-making process, and demanded that their own representative and popular nature be granted official recognition. By so doing, they were calling also for a revision of the regulations that limited their powers and made the jefe político the arbiter of any decision at the provincial level.[26] As a Basque liberal journalist representative of this tendency argued, the diputaciones 'constitute a veritable bulwark against the usurpations of the executive, next to whose principal agent and under whose immediate presidency they have to act as a constant barrier in favour of popular interests'.[27] It is important to note that although the supporters of the constitution frequently recognised the historical and cultural legacies of the provinces of Spain, their demands for a modicum of devolution were neither accompanied by requests for the reintroduction of legal particularism, nor did

25. Conde de Toreno, Cortes, 22 March 1821, in Conde de Toreno, *Discursos parlamentarios*, ed. Joaquín Varela Suanzes-Carpegna (Oviedo: Junta General del Principado de Asturias, 2003), p. 55; José Moreno Guerra, 'Manifiesto a la nación española', 16 February 1822, in Iris M. Zavala, *Masones, comuneros y carbonarios* (Madrid: Siglo XXI de España, 1971), p. 253, both quoted by Claude Morange: Morange, *Una conspiración fallida*, pp. 280, 283.

26. Castro, *La revolución liberal*, pp. 95–98.

27. *El Liberal Guipuzcoano*, no. 147, 26 November 1821, quoted in Llanos Aramburu, *El Trienio Liberal*, p. 336.

they question the idea of the administrative unity of the Spanish nation. In Catalonia and in the Basque country, the constitutionalists may often have celebrated the ancient liberties of their provinces, but were never nostalgic for their revival.[28] It was only the invasion by the French army and the war against it in the spring and summer of 1823 that provided an opportunity for a de facto devolution of powers. These circumstances greatly enhanced the political and military powers of the diputación of Barcelona, which became an executive body controlled by the radicals of the province acting almost independently from the Cortes, assuming the powers that the juntas had exercised in similar circumstances in 1808, and controlling tightly the city's ayuntamiento.[29]

At the end of the Trienio, a revolutionary compromise between those advocating strict governmental controls over provinces and councils and the supporters of a degree of autonomy from the centre was reflected in a revision of the regulations concerning the diputaciones provinciales that was approved in February 1823. While this regulation was never in fact implemented, it did take into account some of the demands emanating from the provinces and amounted to a genuine attempt to delegate power and decentralise the decision-making process. It did so by making a clearer distinction between political and administrative/economic functions, leaving the former firmly in the hands of the executive, but allowing for autonomous decision-making powers regarding expenditure on public works benefiting the province. In addition, it made the diputaciones, rather than the Cortes, responsible for any appeal related to elections.[30] This reform, which was voted through thanks to the support of the exaltados' majority in the Cortes, did not in any way undermine the uniformity of the state that liberals upheld against Navarre and the Basque country. In spite of the multiple critiques of excessive centralisation voiced during the Spanish Trienio as a result of the implementation of the Cádiz

28. Ramon Arnabat Mata, 'Província, pàtria, nació i estat a l'inici de la revolució liberal (1820–1823)', in *Identitats nacionals i nacionalismes a l'estat espanyol a l'època contemporània*, ed. Sebastià Serra Busquets and Elisabeth Ripoll Gil (Palma de Mallorca, Institut d'Estudis Baleàrics, 2019), pp. 31–48; Arnabat Mata, 'Los catalanes y la nación española durante el Trienio Liberal (1820–1823)', in *VII Simposio Internacional: Ciudadanía y nación en el mundo hispano contemporáneo*, ed. José M. Portillo Valdés and Javier Ugarte (Vitoria, Instituto de Historia Social Valentín de Foronda, 2001), pp. 63–78; Javier Fernández Sebastián, *La génesis del fuerismo: Prensa e ideas políticas en la crisis del Antiguo Régimen (País Vasco, 1750–1840)* (Madrid: Siglo XXI de España, 1991), pp. 249–51, 264–66.

29. Vernet, *La Barcelona revolucionària*, pp. 290–96. On the role of the diputación, see also Ramon Arnabat Mata, *La revolució de 1820 i el Trienni Liberal a Catalunya* (Vic: Eumo, 2001), pp. 91–98.

30. Castro, *La revolución liberal*, pp. 98–102.

Constitution, in the rest of Spain, radicals and moderates alike saw in provincial royalism and *fuerismo* the gravest threat to the unity of the nation.

Resisting centralisation: Genoa, Sicily and provincial freedoms

The initial steps of the revolution in Piedmont replicated the provisional federal moment that had been precipitated by Riego's pronunciamiento in 1820. The juntas that were created in Piedmont in 1821, in Alessandria, Asti and in other smaller cities such as Ivrea, followed the Spanish model, acting as they did in the name of the entire nation and justifying their own authority on that very same basis. They therefore saw their authority as temporary and geared to the introduction and defence of the constitution. As the insurgents of Alessandria declared on 10 March 1821, they were setting up a 'Giunta provinciale provvisoria di governo', which was independent of any other authority. They also stated that it would consider the existence of a 'Giunta nazionale' legitimate only when the king would commit himself to a war against Austria in favour of an Italian federation.[31] In accordance with the principle on the basis of which it had been created, the giunta of Alessandria dissolved itself in favour of the central one in Turin in anticipation of the war against Austria, in order to strengthen its military and civil organisation. Piedmontese revolutionaries took pride in the peripheral origin of their revolution, but did not consider it as an affirmation of peripheries against the centre. Writing in the *Sentinella Subalpina*, a journalist praised 'the energy of the provinces' which, in Piedmont as much as in Spain, were putting pressure on the capital city to revitalise the revolution by appointing new *capi politici* (the local representatives of the central government—the equivalent of the jefes políticos of the Spanish constitution) and new municipal authorities.[32] Therefore we cannot detect in Piedmont a radical federalism similar to that entertained by the exaltados in Spain.

In the Kingdom of Sardinia centripetal, albeit not profoundly disruptive, tendencies came from Genoa, the capital of Liguria, rather than from the provisional juntas set up in provincial cities. Such tendencies owed their origin to the city's recent loss of its status as the capital of an independent republic, being now part of the Kingdom of Sardinia. In 1797

---

31. MRM, Bertarelli, Proclami di Alessandria, 05946: broadsheet, 'In nome della federazione italiana', 10 March 1821.

32. *La Sentinella Subalpina*, 27 March 1821, p. 26.

Genoa had been taken over by the French army and turned into one of its 'sister republics', or satellite states on the Italian peninsula, and was directly annexed to the French Empire in 1805. Its ruling class, an aristocratic oligarchy that owed its wealth to centuries of international trade and banking, begrudged Napoleonic rule, and with the collapse of the empire was keen to reassert its political leadership over the city and its territories. Hopes that this could happen had been reinforced by Lord Bentinck's proclamation of the independence of the city on his arrival in Genoa with the British army in April 1814. Over two months, from April to May 1814, a provisional government led by the aristocrat Girolamo Serra re-established the old financial, administrative and judicial structures of the republic, reaffirming the aristocratic and elitist nature of the state, while retaining the Napoleonic civil and commercial legislation. In the same year, however, a deputation to Paris and Vienna failed to make the case either for the reconstitution of the Republic of Genoa as an independent state, or for the creation of a separate constitutional monarchy united to Piedmont only by the monarch.[33] Instead, the former republic was absorbed into the Kingdom of Sardinia as the Duchy of Genoa. Its aristocracy was not minded to tolerate the loss of political autonomy, and the Piedmontese military presence, along with what was perceived to be the diminished economic role of the city, was widely resented. The revolution therefore opened up a space in which both aristocratic nostalgia for the past and desires for greater autonomy under the auspices of the Cádiz Constitution could emerge. The nature of this federal tendency issuing from Genoa was therefore ambiguous, wavering between aristocratic municipalism and an updated, more democratic version of it that was compatible with support for the Cádiz Constitution.

Some Genoese supporters of the revolution sought both more autonomy for Liguria and a constitution. The students' demonstrations that had erupted in Genoa at the end of March 1821, when news of the repeal of the constitution by King Carlo Felice reached the city, combined cries of 'Viva la costituzione!' with 'Viva la repubblica di Genova!' At the same time, reports sent from Genoa to the revolutionary government in Turin mentioned Girolamo Serra as the leader of a counterrevolutionary 'republican-aristocratic' faction of the city. According to rumours circulating in the city, Serra, who had been appointed to the provisional giunta

33. Giovanni Assereto, 'Dall'antico regime all'unità', in *Storia d'Italia: Le regioni dall'Unità a oggi; La Liguria*, ed. Antonio Gibelli and Paride Rugafiori (Turin: Einaudi, 1994), pp. 161–98.

in Turin on 14 March 1821, was also trying to take advantage of the revolution to reconstitute the ancient republic, and had offered the governor of Genoa substantial sums of money if he would try to convince the British government to support such designs.[34]

In Naples and Sicily, far more than in Spain or Piedmont, the Cádiz Constitution was interpreted by a large majority of the supporters of the revolution as a federal, decentralising document that was incompatible with the existing institutional and territorial set-up of the Bourbon administration. It was precisely the widespread hostility to the radical transformation of the administrative structure of the kingdom that had taken place since 1806 under Napoleon that provided fertile ground for support for the revolution in 1820. The Napoleonic centralised administrative system had been introduced in Naples by Joseph Bonaparte between 1806 and 1808, when the kingdom had been divided into fourteen provinces run by the intendenti. These representatives of the central administration were vested with the powers of a French prefect, and they presided over provincial councils appointed by the government. Crucially, this centralised administrative system took control of the communes, the former *parlamenti*, whose officials, traditionally elected independently, were now chosen from local landowners, and whose mayors were now appointed by the intendente. This reorganisation was accompanied by a reform of the judicial system which abolished all the judicial authorities at the local level, and created a new intermediate layer of tribunals in the provinces. A major consequence of these reforms was therefore a loss of autonomy suffered by local communities, and the creation of intermediate administrative units. While the existence of the councils and the new tribunal lent new importance to provincial capitals and provided opportunities for local concerns to be heard at the centre, these intermediate institutions were designed to guarantee the uniform application of law and order across the country, rather than to provide opportunities for provincial self-government. The provincial councils had no consultative powers, and their members were appointed by the government.[35] Significantly, this system was retained, albeit with minor modifications, under the restored Bourbon

34. AST, Segreteria di Stato Affari Interni, Alta Polizia, Sconvolgimenti politici, Impiegati, 27: 'Memorie relative allo stato politico di Genova', signed by the 'Amici della Costituzione e dell'Indipendenza italiana', n.d. [third week of March 1821]. On these events, see also Bornate, 'L'insurrezione di Genova'.

35. Davis, *Naples and Napoleon*, pp. 182–84, 163–64, 188–92, 276–77. On earlier institutions and municipal organisation, see also Aurelio Musi, 'L'amministrazione locale del regno di Napoli: Dall' "università" d'antico regime alla "comune" del decennio murattiano', *Clio: Rivista Trimestale di Studi Storici*, 27 no. 3 (1991): 501–13; Stefano Vinci, 'Dal

regime after 1815, when it was confirmed and extended to Sicily. Here the application of this administrative system to the island in 1817 represented a novelty, and its consequences were more radical than anywhere else in the kingdom. With the extension of the system of the *intendenze* (provinces under an intendente) to the island, Sicily lost its status as an independent kingdom with separate institutions and jurisdiction. Palermo became just one of the centres of the seven new intendenze set up in Sicily and answerable to Naples, and therefore relinquished its status as the administrative and political capital. No other city on the Italian peninsula had been subjected to such a humiliating loss of power, apart from Genoa. During the Napoleonic period this sense of separateness and the strong institutional identity of the island had been bolstered by two factors. First, the island had served as an asylum for the royal family, which withdrew from Naples and settled in Sicily under British protection. Although the experience did not help to overcome a degree of mistrust existing between the monarchy and the Sicilian feudal aristocracy, at the end of the Napoleonic wars the latter expected to be rewarded for their loyalty and support during the war. More importantly, in 1812 the British had introduced into the island a constitution which inaugurated parliamentary government in the form of a bicameral system inspired by British institutions. This constitution provided the Sicilian elites with a new set of institutions that confirmed their separate political identity, and could be interpreted as the modernised version of their traditional parliaments.[36]

As a consequence, both on the mainland and in Sicily resentment at the creation of the intendenze was already simmering before 1820, and the outbreak of the revolution was marked by an immediate rejection of the authority of the intendenti. Supporters of the revolutions in the kingdom interpreted the constitution as a document that would first and foremost guarantee the freedom of the communes, according to an interpretation that could be found in other states of the Italian peninsula during the restoration.[37] In some provinces the initial steps of the Neapolitan revolution in fact bore some resemblance to the federal moment marking the beginning of the Spanish revolutions, but had an even stronger decentralising bias. Thanks to the initiative of groups of carbonari, local lodges

Parlamento al decurionato: L'amministrazione dei comuni del regno di Napoli nel decennio francese', *Archivio Storico del Sannio* 13 (2008): 189–218.

    36. Enrico Iachello, 'Centralisation étatique et pouvoir local en Sicile au XIX siècle', *Annales* 49, no. 1 (1994): 241–66.

    37. On this aspect of Restoration constitutionalism, see Marco Meriggi, *Gli Stati italiani prima dell'unità: Una storia istituzionale* (Bologna: Il Mulino, 2011).

set up autonomous institutions which, in the name of provincial freedom, took over the authority previously held by the intendenti. In Foggia, for instance, the Carboneria literally replaced the intendenza and declared the 'Supreme Magistracy of the United Provinces of Daunia', a giunta made up of civilians and army officers that claimed the right to exercise full legislative and executive powers and issued executive decrees on its behalf. Similarly, in the city of Potenza, the *senato* of the Carboneria seized control of the institutions of the state.[38]

While these were temporary initiatives, and as such swiftly suppressed, the revolution provided the opportunity for demands to revise the centralised administrative structure of the state in favour of self-government and decentralisation. These demands came directly to the parliament from the peripheries and individual municipal governments, keen to recover some of the autonomy lost in the past. Since the administrative reorganisation of the kingdom introduced after 1817 envisaged the presence of judges in the capital of each *circondario*—an intermediary territorial unit between commune and district—this administrative privilege fuelled rivalries between towns. Many communes petitioned the parliament requesting that they become the capitals of their *circondari*, while others simply called for the abolition of these administrative units and the reintroduction of a judge in each commune.[39] Some municipal authorities merely called for the outright abolition of the intendenti and sottintendenti, dismissing the current administrative system as one based on 'tyrannical and despotic principles'.[40]

While many petitions would seem to have displayed a nostalgia for pre-Napoleonic autonomy, supporters of the revolution reframed municipal freedoms in the light of a federalist reading of the Cádiz Constitution more radical than that entertained by many supporters of the constitution in the provinces of Spain, and based on the idea that the *deputazioni provinciali* (equivalent to the Spanish diputaciones provinciales) were representative bodies. Commenting on Benjamin Constant's views regarding municipal

38. Davis, *Naples and Napoleon*, p. 303; Pietro Colletta, *Storia del reame di Napoli*, ed. Nino Cortese, 3 vols (Naples: Libreria Scientifica Editrice, 1953–57), 3, p. 161.

39. On the role of the *circondari*, see Achille Moltedo, *Dizionario geografico–storico–statistico de' comuni del regno delle Due Sicilie* (Naples: Gaetano Nobile, 1858), p. xi; petitions are in ASN, Polizia Generale II, 40, f. 3; 42, f. 333; and 34, passim.

40. ASN, Polizia Generale II, f. 34: petition from the town of Carbonara (Bari), 27 November 1820. See Angelantonio Spagnoletti, 'Centri e periferie nello stato napoletano nel primo Ottocento'; Paola Verrengia, 'Le istituzioni a Napoli e la rivoluzione del 1820–21', both in *Il Mezzogiorno preunitario: Economia, societá, istituzioni*, ed. Angelo Massafra (Bari: Edizioni Dedalo, 1988), pp. 379–92; 549–64.

power to be found in an Italian translation of his *Principes*, an anonymous Neapolitan publicist wrote that the Cádiz Constitution came very close to guaranteeing full autonomy to freely elected councils. He further insisted, however, on the importance of preventing the executive power from interfering in municipal affairs by rendering the diputaciones provinciales free of any intervention from the jefes políticos.[41] According to this vision, what the Cádiz Constitution therefore offered was an idea of the sovereignty of the people as something that was shared throughout the territory and across the institutions, and not simply delegated to the representatives in the national parliament. A constitutional catechism claimed that thanks to the Spanish constitution 'our communes, our *circondarii*, our provinces must be considered as equal in their political rights, and having an equal share in sovereignty'.[42]

When the parliament started debating the administrative reorganisation envisaged by the Cádiz Constitution, these ideas were embraced by a majority of its members. The parliamentary debate dividing those in favour of central control over the territories from those in favour of local autonomy mirrored that taking place in Spain, although supporters of decentralisation were more numerous here on the Italian than on the Iberian peninsula. Those revolutionaries who had served under Joachim Murat, and supported the centralising institutional reforms carried out under Napoleonic rule, were on the other hand sceptical of these tendencies. Giuseppe Zurlo, who in 1820 was the minister of interior, is representative of this attitude. A man educated in the principles of the Enlightenment, Zurlo had been a royal magistrate at the forefront of the anti-feudal movement in the 1790s: after the revolution of 1799, as director of finances first and between 1809 and 1815 as justice and interior minister, he had pioneered the administrative reorganisation of the kingdom and the dismantling of the feudal order. For him, by abolishing privileges and transforming society from above, the state administration was accomplishing a civilising mission and providing the preconditions for economic development. Zurlo and the other former Muratist civil servants involved in the revolution in 1820 therefore held that the discarded Napoleonic administrative system should have been preserved and maintained while introducing the institutions envisaged by the Spanish constitution, since the benefits of the *decennio francese* were worth cherishing.

41. *Saggio di costituzione di Benjamin Constant* (Naples[?]: 1820[?]), pp. 22–23.
42. 'Appendice: Frammenti di un catechismo costituzionale', annexed to *Saggio di costituzione di Benjamin Constant*, p. 6.

Not surprisingly, Zurlo's initial proposal for a revision of the administrative organisation of the kingdom integrated the Spanish system of elected deputazioni provinciali and municipalities into the existing system of central control implemented by the intendenti and their *consigli* (councils).[43]

But this was precisely what the majority of members of parliament sought to avoid, and the proposal was subjected to a barrage of criticism. As the Pugliese revolutionary Vincenzo Balsamo argued when putting forward a proposal for administrative reform in line with the dominant views of the parliament, in order to guarantee the independence of the communes, that is to say 'the first of all freedoms', it was imperative to abolish the despotic system of the intendenze. The addition of the Spanish-style deputazioni provinciali to the existing administrative structure, would have been tantamount to 'adding to a Gothic building an elegant and noble Greek structure'.[44]

In the end, these demands for a full implementation of the Spanish model within the Neapolitan administrative system resulted in a reform of the state administration that was approved by the parliament only on the eve of the Austrian invasion of the kingdom. This circumstance, along with the veto of the vicar of the kingdom and heir to the throne, who refused to jettison the system of intendenze, prevented this reform from being carried out. However, the law, without dismantling entirely central controls over the peripheries, did abolish the *consigli di intendenza* and replicated the Spanish model of the deputazioni provinciali with scant modification of the Spanish legislation. By so doing, the Neapolitan parliament took on board what most of its members considered a fully decentralising reform, one that would give due recognition to the demands of towns and provinces.[45] In harmony with this polycentric idea of the state, and inspired at the same time by the requests of local groups of the Carboneria, the parliament reintroduced the ancient, pre-Italic names of each region, whose new denominations were added to the Neapolitan version of the Spanish constitution. These denominations, that confirmed the aspirations to federalise the kingdom, owed their existence to a tradition of the Neapolitan Enlightenment, revived during the French period, which had celebrated the ancient pre-Roman tribes in order to champion the local and federal

43. On Zurlo's activities, see Davis, *Naples and Napoleon*, passim; Alfonso Scirocco, 'Il problema dell'autonomia locale nel Mezzogiorno durante la rivoluzione del 1820–21', in *Studi in Memoria di Nino Cortese* (Rome: Istituto per la storia del Risorgimento italiano, 1976), pp. 485–528 at 516–28.

44. Vincenzo Balsamo, *Sulla amministrazione civile* (Lecce: Vincenzo Marino, 1820).

45. Scirocco, 'Il problema'.

origins of freedom against imperial despotism. As a consequence, the former province of Principato Citeriore, whose capital was Salerno, was renamed the 'Repubblica Lucana Occidentale'; and Basilicata (whose capital was Potenza) was reborn as the 'Repubblica Lucana Orientale'; while the provinces of Avellino, the so-called Principato Ulteriore, and the Terra d'Otranto took on the new names of 'Repubblica Irpina' and 'Salento'. Similarly ancient names were attributed to other provinces, among them 'Sannio' (for the province of Campobasso) and 'Marsia' (for L'Aquila).[46]

The most violent reactions against centralisation and the most radical reading of constitutional government, not surprisingly, came from Sicily, where a separate revolution momentarily threatened the very survival of the kingdom. The aristocracy of the capital demanded nothing less than independence, supported in this regard by two hundred communes in western Sicily, while the eastern part of the island sided with Naples against Palermo. In Sicily too, the intendente was considered the symbol of a despotism that had deprived the island of its traditional freedoms. As a journalist writing in the official journal of the Sicilian revolution, the *Giornale la Fenice*, had claimed, the intendenti were simply 'petty tyrants, unworthy children of the fatherland', and 'the men most hated by the population, incapable of being the organ of the general will'. Since, the anonymous journalist continued, they were 'always ready to become slaves of those who pay them, or who shower them with gifts, [. . .] they fan the flames of civil war, and seek disorder, anarchy, and the destruction of the entire nation'.[47] For the supporters of the insurrection led by Palermo, it was first and foremost its free communes that made the Kingdom of Sicily what it was. The request for independence submitted by the giunta of Palermo to the king, calling upon him to reinstate Sicily as a separate kingdom, was indeed signed by the communes, divided into districts.[48]

The conflicts dividing Sicily in 1820 show that the introduction of the constitution had the capacity to split the island into opposing camps, and fuel existing rivalries between different cities and different territories. It also showed that not all Sicilian towns supported independence for the island led by Palermo. The city of Catania on the east coast sided with

46. See 'Del territorio delle Due Sicilie', art. 10, 'Costituzione del Regno delle Due Sicilie' (30 January 1821), in Alberto Aquarone, Mario D'Addio and Guglielmo Negri, eds, *Le costituzioni italiane* (Milano: Edizioni di Comunità, 1958), p. 466. On this tradition, see Melissa Calaresu, 'Images of Ancient Rome in Late Eighteenth-Century Neapolitan Historiography', *Journal of the History of Ideas* 58, no. 4 (1997): 641–61.

47. *Giornale la Fenice*, Palermo, 15 August 1820, pp. 1–2.

48. Alfonso Sansone, *La rivoluzione del 1820 in Sicilia* (Palermo: Tipografia Fratelli Vena, 1888), pp. 54–55, 310–15.

Naples, for fear of being subordinated once again to the elites of the former capital. The supporters of the constitution in the cities of Catania and Messina dismissed Palermo's proclamation of independence as a bid by the feudal barons to reintroduce their aristocratic privileges, and to exert again their exploitative control over the rest of Sicily. For these cities, the constitution was the best guarantee against the nobles of Palermo. It was precisely the lack of an aristocratic upper chamber, and the fact that a parliament would be set up in Naples and not in Palermo, that led the provincial elites of the cities of eastern Sicily to rally to the Spanish constitution.[49]

Further conflicts divided not only the island as whole between east and west, but also single provinces and districts, in which tensions escalated into violent confrontations that split villages or pitted town against town. The breakdown of law and order within the intendenza of Catania is a case in point. During the civil war the town of Caltagirone, capital of one of three subunits (*distretti*), of this intendenza, decided to side with Palermo—along with many smaller communes that resented the administrative hegemony of Catania. But such divisions were replicated within individual communes: in the town of Mineo, one faction competing for the control of the municipal institutions sided with Palermo against its enemies backing Catania and Naples.[50] In general, the civil war across the island put an end to the administrative structure imposed in 1817 also in eastern Sicily, where both the important cities of Catania and Messina and most small villages had sided with Naples against Palermo, being opposed to the independence of the island. Under the pressures occasioned by the emergency of the civil war, the intendente of Catania, the Duke of Sanmartino, was obliged to co-opt the local elites and share powers with them by creating so-called 'deputazioni di pubblica sicurezza'.[51] Centralised government was everywhere put to the test.

Besides leading to an island-wide civil conflict, the war against Naples at first, and the negotiations between Palermo and Naples shortly afterwards, opened up a debate about the relationship between Sicily and the mainland. The institutional dimension of this debate, related to the renegotiation of the relationship between Palermo and Naples, was closely connected to the question of whether or not Sicily ought to be considered a separate nation. For supporters of constitutional government in Messina,

49. *Nuova parlata de' catanesi contro i palermitani* (Naples, 1820), pp. 9–11; *Un siciliano alla nazione napoletana* (Naples: Agnello Nobile, 1820), p. 4.
50. De Francesco, *La guerra di Sicilia*, esp. pp. 168–70.
51. De Francesco, *La guerra di Sicilia*, pp. 17–73.

the island was lucky enough to be united to 'a great national body' and for geographical reasons could not enjoy full independence.[52] Conversely, for Count Aceto, whose opinions as a journalist in Palermo only partly coincided with the views of the revolutionary and independentist giunta di governo, Sicily was undoubtedly a fully-fledged nation. The optimal solution of the conflict between island and mainland would in his view be the creation of a federation between the two brother nations, Sicily and Naples; one that would recognise their mutual autonomy while maintaining the integrity of the state. For Aceto, the revolution against Naples was justified by the arbitrariness and despotism of the institutions imposed upon Sicily, but was not a cause rooted an aristocratic oligarchy nostalgic for the past: the cause it represented was rather that of freedom, and as such supported by society at large. Aa a former member of the parliament elected under the Sicilian constitution of 1812, and a pupil of Sicilian Enlightenment philosophers who had supported the reforms of the island's institutions in the eighteenth century, Aceto had welcomed the abolition of feudalism and the introduction of the anti-aristocratic Spanish constitution.[53] Like the Genoese noblemen the following year, some Sicilian aristocrats looked to the British imperial presence in the Mediterranean to legitimise their desire for self-governance. In reconceiving the sovereignty of their 'nation', an imperial umbrella seemed to be more desirable than an overly intrusive Neapolitan state. The fact that Britain, when ruling over the island, had also introduced an aristocratic constitution that many of them preferred to the unduly democratic Spanish variant, and that certain British politicians and imperial agents favoured a consolidation of the imperial presence in the central Mediterranean, made this option both plausible and welcome to some aristocratic circles in Palermo. For members of the provisional government such as Baron Francesco Ventura, Sicily's commercial and geopolitical interests drew it towards the great maritime powers of the Mediterranean like Britain, and were thus incompatible with those of a continental power like Naples. As a consequence, contact was made with the British navy, and a plea was made for protection.[54]

52. See for instance, Antonio Sarao, *Dialoghi sul governo democratico e costituzionale in rapporto al siculo* (Messina: Michalangelo Nobolo, 1821), p. 61.

53. Giovanni Aceto, in *Giornale Patriottico di Sicilia*, nos 205 and 206, 28 and 31 August 1820; 'Allocuzione ai napoletani', *Giornale la Fenice*, 5 August 1820. On Aceto's ideas, see also Renda, *Risorgimento*, pp. 130–38.

54. On these debates, see Giuseppe Grieco, 'British Imperialism and Southern Liberalism: Re-shaping the Mediterranean Space: 1817–1823', *Global Intellectual History* 3,

While such overtures to the British Mediterranean fleet with a view to obtaining a protectorate and thereby guaranteeing independence from Naples were not successful—the British navy rejected these requests in a public document—negotiations with the Neapolitan army in Sicily led to the recognition of a range of demands for greater autonomy.[55] The agreement reached on 22 September 1820 between the commander of the Neapolitan army, General Florestano Pepe, and the representative of the Palermitan giunta, the Prince of Villafranca, reflected the ideas put forward by Count Aceto: it envisaged the election of a separate parliament in Palermo within the framework of the Spanish constitution, the recognition of Sicily as a separate kingdom and the abolition of the intendenze.[56] But this deal was resented by other cities, Messina or Catania among them, which saw this as a dangerous bid on the part of Palermo to regain its former preeminence; by the populace of Palermo, who considered it to be a betrayal of the declaration of independence; and by most of the members of the Neapolitan parliament, who thought this arrangement threatened the cohesion of the kingdom.[57] As a Neapolitan pamphlet argued, it was through the contribution of Sicilian deputies sitting in the parliament in Naples that the Two Sicilies would become 'a single family'. Another commentator noted that the existence of a separate parliament had wisely been avoided both in Great Britain, where there was no separate Scottish parliament, and in the Spanish Empire, where the differences between the colonies and the metropolis were much more pronounced than in the case of the Two Sicilies.[58]

In the end, the idea of a separate parliamentary representation was discarded and Pepe's agreement was itself rejected by the parliament and the government. However, demands to treat Sicily as a separate territorial entity re-emerged in the context of the parliamentary debate regarding the creation and composition of a Council of State, a debate opposing federalists and centralists (the former Muratists). A majority of deputies

---

no. 2 (2018): 202–30. See in particular Francesco Ventura, *De' diritti della Sicilia per la sua nazionale indipendenza* (Palermo: Reale Stamperia, 1821), pp. 79–82; Leonardo Vigo, *Problema di politica sulla indipendenza della Sicilia* (Palermo, 1821).

55. BCUC, Raccolta di Fogli Sciolti: broadsheet, Camillo de Clario, 'Risposta data per mezzo dei maltesi dall'ammiraglio inglese a' palermitani', Malta, 19 August 1820.

56. Cortese, *La prima rivoluzione*, pp. 152–54.

57. See, for instance, *Pensieri politici di tre filantropi messinesi P. S. R., O. S. N., ed A. S. sul trattato conchiuso tra il comandante generale Florestano Pepe e lo ex-principe Paternò* (Naples: Presso Giovanni de Bonis, 1820).

58. *Idee sulla Sicilia* (Naples: Reale Tipografia della Guerra, 1821), p. 15; Raffaele Lucarelli, *Pretensioni de' siciliani confutate da un napolitano* (Naples, 1821), p. 3.

wished the composition of the Council of State to be based on equal representation from each province, in order to create an institution in which the provinces would serve as a check upon the power of the executive. Among them, some Sicilian deputies expected a specific quota of the council to be assigned to their island, in recognition of its traditional separateness. Conversely, the former Muratists, inspired by the model of the Napoleonic Council of State, rejected the idea of any form of territorial representation, and sought an institution that would defend the independence of the administration and its uniform application across the state.[59] While the notion of separate Sicilian representation was rejected, the parliament did approve a law that envisaged a membership based on provincial origin, and therefore Sicily itself also obtained seven members along with the other provinces.[60]

So it was in Naples, much as in Spain during the Trienio, that some of the aspirations for decentralisation were taken on board by the parliament in formulating its administrative reforms; but the majority of the revolutionaries remained by and large hostile to the idea of recognising Sicily as a separate administrative, let alone political, unit. Provincial and local autonomy were principles supported by the majority of Neapolitan revolutionaries, but within an administratively uniform and unitary constitutional kingdom.

Emancipating local councils; creating a new state: Portugal and Greece

The introduction of the constitution in Portugal did not lead to a radical recasting of the relationship between centre and periphery, as was the case in Naples, Sicily and Spain. The civil war that divided the country throughout the 1820s had a territorial dimension, in that the northern province of Trás-os-Montes was resolutely absolutist, and the centre of liberalism, the city of Porto, was also in the north. However, this division was not accompanied by sharply different ideas as to the administrative organisation of the country. This is because, unlike the Kingdom of the Two Sicilies and Spain, there were no territorial privileges to be abolished, or to be defended against centralising tendencies. The most dramatic territorial crisis with which Portugal had to deal was the revolution in Brazil, but no province inside its own territories had ever enjoyed autonomous

59. Alberti, *Atti del parlamento*, 1, pp. 270–75.
60. Verrengia, *Le istituzioni*.

government comparable to that of the Kingdom of Navarre, the Basque country or Sicily.[61] At the same time, Portugal had not experienced anything like the radical territorial reorganisation of Spain in 1812, or of Naples from 1807 onwards, and ancien-régime territorial structures had therefore not been shaken to their foundations. Admittedly, the Napoleonic invasion of the country in 1808 had temporarily introduced the French centralising administrative model to the territories controlled by General Junot's administration, which appointed so-called *corregedores-mores*, the equivalent of French prefects.[62] Yet these reforms were not maintained after the French occupation. The proliferation of local and provincial patriotic juntas, meanwhile, that acted in the name of the monarchy in the centre and the north of the country during the military conflict against the French, did not represent the starting point, as in Spain, for a novel and alternative constitutional experience. The central junta of Porto, which in 1808 took on the leadership in a national war against the French, and the others which proliferated in the same period, were noteworthy for their political conservatism. Their members were local representatives of the traditional orders of society: clergy, aristocracy and people, who spoke in the name of monarchical patriotism, as vassals who wished to restore the king's rights and authority.[63] This temporary administrative 'federalism' was not replicated in 1820. While the junta of Porto may have drawn inspiration from its predecessor, it remained the only temporary junta to intervene on this occasion in the name of the nation and to introduce a constitution, until such time as the revolutionary government should be transferred to the capital.

The territorial structure inherited by the revolutionaries in 1820 was that which resulted from the partially successful attempts made in the previous century by the monarchy to tighten its hold over the state. This was a system that, compared to the other southern European states, had no provincial intermediate bodies, and left at the same time a great deal of leeway to councils: the câmaras. A degree of central control over local communities was possible through the corregedores, royal officials at the head of the *comarcas*—the districts into which each province was

61. Nuno Gonçalo Monteiro, *Elites e poder entre o Antigo Regime e o Liberalismo*, 3rd edn (Lisbon: ICS, 2012), pp. 37–60.

62. António Pedro Manique, *Mouzinho da Silveira: Liberalismo e administração pública* (Lisbon: Livros Horizonte, 1989), pp. 37–38.

63. Capela, Matos and Borralheiro, *O heróico patriotismo*; José Tengarrinha, 'La batalla de las ideas: Conservadores y reformistas en Portugal (1808–1810)', in *Guerra de ideas: Política y cultura en la España de la guerra de la independencia*, ed. Pedro Rújula and Jordi Canal (Madrid: Marcial Pons Historia, 2011), pp. 57–72 at 64–66.

divided—who drew up lists from which members of the municipalities, the câmaras, would be elected. Yet these central controls were not uniformly exerted across the territory of the kingdom. Not all corregedores were appointed by the monarch, as in a few comarcas this right was exercised by great aristocratic families endowed with seigneurial rights (such as the dukes of Cadaval) or by houses that belonged to the royal family (Bragança, Rainhas and Infantado). While in 1790 the *ouvidorias*, the districts in which holders of seigneurial rights—the donatários—were entitled instead of the king to appoint the magistrates, were abolished, in partial contradiction to these same measures, the rights of these great families to appoint the corregedores had been maintained, thus, in theory at least, limiting central controls. Another form of control from above was exercised by the *juízes de fora*—officials either appointed by the crown or by the above-mentioned aristocrats endowed with seigneurial rights who presided over the câmaras. However, before 1820, the juízes de fora held sway over only one fifth of the câmaras: the rest were free to appoint the judges who presided over them. Consequently the câmaras (local councils) of each *concelho* (subdivision of the district), often but not always dominated by noblemen, enjoyed a high degree of autonomy in presiding over local affairs. In the small pre-revolutionary câmaras, voters could include workers and artisans, while in the larger and more important ones they were confined to local propertied elites.[64]

After 1820, although no radical rethinking of the territorial organisation of the state had been implemented, Portuguese administrative and legal reforms converged with those of the other southern European revolutions, and this at two different levels. First of all, the autonomy of municipalities was reinforced and the administrative system of the country rendered uniform through the abolition of any remaining privileges. With the introduction of a new constitution in 1822, the Portuguese revolutionaries approved an electoral law that rendered all municipal posts elective. By this law any male citizen of at least twenty-five years of age and of independent means could be elected, while anyone with electoral rights pertaining to the national Cortes would have equivalent rights regarding local bodies. The *vereador* (councillor) who had obtained the highest number of votes, would be president of the câmara and the câmaras were granted substantial administrative powers. At the same time, the constitution anticipated an administrative reorganisation of the territories into districts, and then the districts into concelhos. In each district

64. See Monteiro, *Elites e poder*, pp. 19–50.

an *administrador geral* appointed by the king would be supported by a *junta administrativa*, composed of representatives from the concelhos. The remaining rights of the great aristocratic families to appoint other local officials were thus abolished.[65] Second, the abolition of feudalism and all its seigneurial rights, including rights to appoint other local officials, extended the administrative and legal scope of the state over all of its lands. While the local elites controlling the câmaras before the revolution were often confirmed by these local elections, sometimes the reform enabled individuals from a more modest social background, even shopkeepers and tradesmen, to accede to power.[66] These reforms were abandoned with the end of the revolution, in 1823, but the question of the administrative reorganisation of the state and the strengthening of its controls re-emerged during the *cartismo* of 1826–28. Although, for lack of time, no overall administrative reform of the country was implemented, between 1826 and 1827 debates in the parliament demonstrate the extent to which a number of deputies supported further centralisation in accordance with the Napoleonic model. A proposal for administrative reform put forward in 1827 by a committee of the Cortes (but not approved, as a result of the political impasse generated by the imminent return of Dom Miguel, who would dissolve them in 1828) envisaged the implementation of a centrally controlled administration that would introduce for the first time authorities at the provincial level, as well as in the comarcas. Significantly, such a proposal included provisions for the appointment of the presidents of the câmaras by the central Ministério do Reino, in contrast to the reform during the Triénio that had allowed for their election by the members of the câmaras themselves. As in Spain, Naples, Sicily and Greece, so too in Portugal liberal opinion was split, and some *vintistas* (1820s liberals) remained critical of what they saw as an attempt to extend to Portugal Napoleonic centralism, dismissing it as an inherently despotic model.[67]

Of all the uprisings of southern Europe, the Greek revolution represented the most radical attempt to put forward a novel territorial order. In comparison to other revolts, the Greek case stands out as the only one

65. On this territorial reorganisation and the eligibility of the *vereadores* in the câmaras, see *Diário das cortes geraes* 7, 1 October 1822, pp. 644–45.

66. Cardoso, *A revolução liberal*, pp. 126–27; Paulo Jorge da Silva Fernandes, 'Elites locais e poder municipal: Do antigo regime ao liberalismo', *Análise Social* 41, no. 178 (2006): 55–73 at p. 62.

67. Manique, *Mouzinho de Silveira*, pp. 39–42. The text and debates on the proposal are in Marcelo Caetano, *Os antecedentes da reforma administrativa de 1832 (Mouzinho de Silveira)* (Lisbon: Universidade de Lisboa, 1967), pp. 11–17, 40–104.

to produce an entirely new state. The revolution represented in itself a dramatic territorial crisis, as it constituted a rebellion against a central authority, that of the Ottoman Empire, at a time when this, it seemed, was ready to reaffirm its control over regions that had traditionally enjoyed a large degree of autonomy and self-government. Since the middle of the eighteenth century, the elites of the Peloponnese had consolidated their local power and substantial independence from Ottoman interference. For them, therefore, joining the Philiki Etaireia and the revolution represented first and foremost an attempt to protect such autonomy.[68] In 1820 the Ottoman decision to crush the semi-autonomous rule of Ali Pasha, whose influence extended beyond Yannina in Epirus to Roumeli, and the intervention of the Ottoman army led by Hursid Pasha, the newly appointed governor of the Morea, alerted the Peloponnesian primates to the risk that their own status might also soon come under threat. As discussed earlier, in Roumeli the early stages of the rebellion enabled the armatoloi to protect their territorial power by disregarding Ottoman rule entirely. As a consequence, they consolidated the autonomy they had enjoyed in the pre-revolutionary past. The power vacuum created by the rebellion reaffirmed the self-governing nature of the islands of the Aegean, which had been nominally subject to the kapudan pasha, the commander of the Ottoman fleet. Therefore, once Ottoman rule had been shaken off, it was unclear whether these individual regional and local territorial units would be able to replace it with something new, or simply retain their full independence.

Yet beyond this glaring peculiarity, the Greek revolution shared many features with the others of the period.[69] First of all, the early phase of the uprising converged with the federal moment of the Spanish and Neapolitan revolutions, and it was likewise marked by the proliferation of local authorities. The outbreak of the uprising in the Peloponnese coincided with an efflorescence of local committees that acted in the name of localities as well as on behalf of the Greek nation. Between the spring and summer of 1821 local assemblies were spontaneously set up in order to cope with the needs of the war, under a variety of different names. We thus encounter either *vouli* (in the case of Messinia, the assembly under the leadership of Petrobey) or *ephories*, *kagellaries* and *koinotites*, instituted across the Peloponnese (in Karytaina), in Athens and at Mount Athos, as well as on very many islands. In other cases, Ottoman local municipal

68. Anscombe, *State, Faith, and Nation*, pp. 64–68; Fleming, *Muslim Bonaparte*; Kostantaras, 'Christian Elites'.

69. John Anthony Petropulos, *Politics and Statecraft in the Kingdom of Greece, 1833–1843* (Princeton, NJ: Princeton University Press, 1968), pp. 27–37.

authorities were turned into revolutionary bodies.[70] Thus in its initial stages the revolt was nothing more than the reaffirmation of the autonomy of local and provincial bodies, although these often embraced the language of the nation.

Second, although the Cádiz Constitution played no role in Greece as an administrative model, the debate about the territorial organisation of the new community was, as everywhere else, marked by divisions between those in favour of federal solutions and local autonomy and those who preferred a stronger, centralised administration. In different phases of the revolution one or the other option prevailed: temporary compromises were achieved, followed by territorial conflicts that resulted in short-lived civil wars. If we take 1827 and the third constitutional agreement as the end of our story, we can discern another important feature that represented a point of convergence with the other revolutions: in Greece too, a revolutionary compromise combined recognition of the importance of central controls over peripheries, in the person of the eparch, with a degree of provincial and local autonomy through the election of local and provincial councils. What was peculiar about Greece was perhaps the fact that support for the creation of a central administration and central government was very much due to the pressure arising out of the war against the Ottomans, and the negotiations between regional factions.

The tensions between those in favour of central control and the advocates of autonomy emerged soon after the beginning of the revolution, when attempts were made first at coordination among the local revolutionary committees, and then at creating rudimentary regional bodies. From the very beginning of the revolution, it was the leaders of the Philiki Etaireia who advocated the need for stronger coordination, and took the initiative to set up state administrations and assemblies, first at a regional and then at a national level. These leaders were all from Greek Phanariot families, and therefore belonged to the Ottoman Greek elites that had actually been employed in the service of the sultans either at Constantinople, where they acted as interpreters, or in the principalities of Moldavia and Wallachia, where they governed in the sultan's name. By the beginning of the nineteenth century this elite had consolidated its power to such an extent that, although positions within the imperial administration were always subject to individual appointment, in practice specific families had become princely dynasties retaining sole control over specific

70. Dakin, *Greek Struggle*, pp. 79–80.

posts.[71] Paradoxically, therefore, the Phanariots' determination to impose central control over the Greek territories rebelling against the Ottomans, and to avoid territorial particularism, owed much to their own experience as imperial servants. At the same time, their political instincts and ideas about state administration and territorial control, which they developed also in relation to other European models, had striking similarities to those of the Neapolitan Muratists or many Spanish supporters of the constitution, and were moulded by direct experience of Europe.

The most prominent diasporic leaders of the revolution, Alexandros Mavrokordatos, Theodoros Negris and Dimitrios Ypsilantis, shared a Phanariot background. In 1812, when his uncle Ioannis Karatzas was appointed hospodar of Wallachia, Mavrokordatos became his secretary, and was soon promoted to the position of 'grand *postelnikos*' (secretary for foreign affairs). Negris had been secretary to the hospodar of Moldavia and on the eve of the revolution was appointed secretary of the Ottoman diplomatic representation in Paris. Dimitrios Ypsilantis had been educated in France and, like his brother Alexandros, had served the czar in the Russian army. Their father was Konstantinos, grand dragoman and prince of Moldavia and Wallachia.[72] These three leaders were at the forefront of the earliest efforts to create central organs of government. On arriving in Greece, Mavrokordatos, after failing to organise a national assembly in Zarakova on the Peloponnese, set up an assembly of western Greece based in Messolonghi; in November that same year Negris and Karatzas summoned an assembly in the town of Salona in central Greece, and in December at Argos an assembly of Peloponnesian primates was set up under the presidency of Dimitrios Ypsilantis. These assemblies earned their legitimacy by gathering representatives from across the localities of each region. Attempts were made in each of the three regions to exert a degree of control over their territories, but these attempts relied on officials elected locally, since regional administrations required the support of localities for their very survival. The administrative systems put in place in western Greece and the Peloponnese were based on provincial representatives known as ephors, who, while responding to their regional assemblies and taking orders from them, were appointed by villages. The system envisaged by Negris for eastern Greece was even more decentralised, since

71. Christine M. Philliou, *Biography of an Empire: Governing Ottomans in an Age of Revolution* (Berkeley, CA: University of California Press, 2010), pp. 27–28. See also Loukos, Αλέξανδρος Μαυροκορδάτος (Alexandros Mavrokordatos).

72. Philliou, *Biography*, pp. 85–86.

it allowed for local administrative autonomy based on the power of local primates.[73]

More than in any other southern European revolution, the Greek experience was marked by repeated attempts on the part of local and national Greek leaders to negotiate the relationship between territories and a central administration. They were choosing constitutional arrangements in the midst of a war, and so experienced something close to 'constructing a ship at sea'. This process had moments of temporary crisis, leading to deadlock, to civil wars and to compromises. As in Spain, in the Neapolitan provinces and in Sicily, interference from representatives of the central administration was often resented and rejected. The first national constitution, agreed at Epidavros in January 1822, represented a major step towards the integration of these regional entities into a larger framework. This document introduced an executive of five members elected by an assembly and a national parliament, or legislature, that would bring together representatives from the whole of Greece. Both of these bodies were elected annually. However, the constitution left the existing regional assemblies in place without specifying in detail how regions and central administration would relate to each other. Although it is a term used neither by those who drafted it nor by Greek contemporaries, foreign commentators defined it as a 'confederal constitution'. This finally introduced a uniform system of fully elective municipal authorities—an important change from existing practices, at least in principle. Up to the revolution, in fact, the selection system for the local administrators, called *demogerontes*, varied hugely from place to place.[74] Differing electoral procedures (rarely formalised) were employed also in provinces with large Orthodox communities to appoint district governors, known as *ayan*, either through petitions, acclamation, voting in assemblies, public protests or a combination of all of these practices. In the Peloponnese, villages and towns voted by majority for their demogerontes, who in turn would appoint a Greek *kotzabasi* and a Turkish *ayn* to sit in the council at provincial level. On most islands, the demogerontes were selected exclusively by the primates, the local elites. However, on the island of Psara, off the coast of Chios,

---

73. Georgios Dimakopoulos, *Η διοικητική οργάνωσις κατά την Ελληνικήν Επανάστασιν, 1821–1827* (Administrative organisation during the Greek revolution, 1821–1827) (Athens: Klisiouni Brothers, 1966), pp. 63–85.

74. *Constitution, loix, ordonnances*, p. 40. On Ottoman local government in these areas, see Henry Headley Parish, *The Diplomatic History of the Monarchy of Greece* (London: J. Hatchard & Son, 1838), pp. 37–44; Yaycioglu, *Partners of the Empire*, pp. 139–49, 154–56.

every year the population chose forty electors who would in turn appoint the three demogerontes to govern the island.[75]

The constitution made it clear, meanwhile, that municipal autonomy was to be limited. It stated that 'every local government body, organised before the sitting of the national assembly, is uniformly and entirely subject to the decisions of the central government'; in practice, however, attempts at exerting control over the individual regions of Greece proved challenging, to say the least.[76] Thus just after the Epidavros assembly, in the spring of 1822, efforts were made to create a national and centralised administration, and, crucially, one that was controlled from above. For the first time since the outbreak of the revolution, the state would be divided into administrative units and subunits, the so-called eparchies and anteparchies, controlled by civil servants appointed by the central government, and not elected locally, as before.[77] Unsurprisingly, all efforts at reinforcing control from the centre would from now on be met with intermittent resistance, disaffection and rebellion, and eparchs were often viewed by local communities with the same hostility as that encountered by the jefes políticos in Spain or the intendenti in the Kingdom of the Two Sicily. Nevertheless, these centralising efforts continued throughout the course of the revolution and could only be halted temporarily.

The reception accorded these new administrative structures was, at the local level, very mixed. In early 1822 Count Constantin Metaxas was charged with extending the system of eparchies to the Aegean islands, in order to facilitate the execution of governmental orders and the levying of the taxes needed to fund the war. The islands of Naxos, Sifnos, Serifos, Paros, Kimolos, Tinos and Mykonos welcomed him, agreed on the appointment of eparchs and anteparchs and declared their willingness to pay taxes.[78] However, attempts at central control did meet with some resistance in the Aegean. Thus, the four villages on the island of Amorgos accepted in principle that they should pay certain taxes, but refused to submit to an anteparch appointed by the central government, preferring to defer decisions to locally elected primates. Payment of taxation took place only after meetings and negotiations with the assembled population.[79] But

---

75. Trikoupis, Ιστορία (History), 1, p. 145.

76. *The Provisional Constitution of Greece*, p. 91.

77. BMA, F1, doc. 51: law on the organisation of the Greek eparchies of 20 April 1822.

78. BMA, F3, docs 1–63: letters to the central administration or to the commissioners (*armostes*) of the islands, sent between April and July 1822.

79. BMA, F4, doc. 47: village of Aigiali (Island of Amorgos), 22 June 1822; BMA, F5, doc. 3: letter of the *armostes* of the islands to the villages of Amorgos, 2 July 1822; ibid.,

the maritime war with the Ottomans rendered any further steps towards integration challenging at best. No sooner had Metaxas disembarked on the island of Santorini than he was placed under arrest. Since the Ottoman fleet was just then approaching the island, its inhabitants and the primates, fearful of imminent retaliation, decided to reject Metaxas's authority. In August 1822 riots against the revolutionary administration broke out on Mykonos. On Santorini, as on other islands, a reluctance to recognise the central administration also stemmed from hostility on the part of the Catholic communities, whose members suspected that their religious rights might well be afforded more protection under Ottoman rule.[80] Circumstances were yet more fraught in the Peloponnese, where Kolokotronis and the chieftains held the local communities on a tight rein. Here no eparchies were set up, with the exception of one in Corinth.[81] In addition, it was unclear how the surviving regional assemblies would interact with these administrative structures.

With the Constitution of Astros of 1823, some of these institutional inconsistencies were resolved, and further centralisation, at least on paper, was achieved: the regional assemblies were in fact abolished, and on the islands eparchies were reorganised and reallocated. Islands such as Santorini that had previously challenged the central administration were now willing to recognise the authority of the eparchs and confine the authority of the municipalities to dealing with strictly local matters.[82] This system was also extended to the Peloponnese, and there territorial structure now mirrored the pre-revolutionary administrative divisions of the Ottoman districts or *kazas*. The only other major novelty introduced by this constitution was that ephors would now be appointed by the legislative assembly, and not by the executive. In 1823, when specifying exactly what an eparch's duties were, the provisional administration stated that he was expected 'to make the people of the province respect the administration and the nation; to do your utmost to make our national political system and its constitution known throughout the province, in order for the nation to understand that it needs an administration; and that without it, it can neither be called a nation, nor claim that it is actually a nation'. The

doc. 10: eparchs Charalampos Stekoulis and Savvas Odysseas to the *armostes* of the islands, 5 July 1822.

80. Constantin Metaxas, *Souvenirs de la Guerre de l'indépendance de la Grèce* (Paris: Ernest Leroux, 1887), pp. 88–94; BMA, F5, doc. 40: the anteparchos of Mykonos to the provisional government, 20 July 1822.

81. Dakin, *Greek Struggle*, p. 89.

82. Eparch of Santorini to the primates of Hydra, 7 June 1823, in Lignos, Αρχείον (Archive), 9, pp. 218–21.

eparch was invited to serve the administration in the name of the common interest and in the spirit of its 'liberal constitution' without ever succumbing to the 'spirit of tyranny'. The administration also requested eparchs to conduct a census of the people living in the province, and to provide information about the state of the national land it contained.[83] At the same time, the constitution confirmed the elective principle for municipal authorities, stating explicitly that the demogerontes should be elected by all male members of the local community.[84]

Where centralisation and cooperation were achieved—in the core areas of the revolution—they were the result of constant negotiation. As decisions taken at Epidavros and at subsequent constitutional assemblies demonstrated, the existence of central administrative, executive and legislative institutions depended on the readiness or otherwise of the various regional leaders to cooperate, on the recognition of their respective interests and on the equal representation of regional groups at the centre, both in the executive and in the assembly. Whenever regional groups felt they were not equitably represented, institutions lost legitimacy. What further complicated these regional divisions were the tensions discussed in chapter three above between the military classes and the propertied elites of the primates in the Peloponnese, as well as between the former and those in favour of civilian controls over the army: that is, the Phanariot Greeks of the diaspora. In 1824, across most of the Peloponnese, the military class of the kapetanaioi (kapoi) managed to exert its authority at the local level at the expense of that of the centrally appointed eparchs. The eparch of Venetico, for instance, was forced to flee his eparchy because of the hostility of the local kapos. In other cases, eparchs simply acted independently of governmental control, and used their position to pursue their own interests by abusing their powers and displacing local power groups.[85] These rivalries among different factions and individuals within the same region were transferred to the national institutions, as were those between the islands, the Peloponnese and other parts of continental Greece. Finally, the pressures of war determined at different stages the conduct of the various parties and affected negotiations between regional groups.

83. Ministry of the Interior to Ioannis Kolettis, eparch of Evripos, 23 May 1823, in Vasiliki Plagianakou Bekiari and Aristotelis Stergellis, eds, Αρχείο Ιωάννη Κωλέττη (Archive of Ioannis Kolettis), 2 vols (Athens: Academy of Athens, 2002), 1, doc. 284.

84. Kallinikos Kritovoulides, *Narrative of the Cretan War of Independence, Vol. 1*, ed. A. Ioannides (London: n.pub., 1864), pp. 101, 205–7.

85. Julius Millingen, *Memoirs of the Affairs of Greece, Containing an Account of the Military and Political Events which Occurred in 1823 and Following Years; With Various Anecdotes relating to Lord Byron* (London: John Rodwell, 1831), p. 182.

The constitutional history of Greece between 1821 and 1827 reflects the unstable nature of the agreements between these groups, and demonstrates at the same time that the end of the revolution was marked by a compromise among them. The first national constitution of January 1822 had been agreed by committees that included individuals from all regions. The executive, presided over by Mavrokordatos, as well as the assembly, were dominated by primates from the Peloponnese and leaders from the islands, along with the Greeks of the diaspora. But the hostility of the military class and military defeat discredited this constitutional arrangement. In 1823, at Astros, an agreement among regional groups led to the approval of a new constitution which abolished regional assemblies and bolstered the powers of the senate at the expense of the executive. The executive elected by the senate included the leader of the military faction, General Kolokotronis, a seat being offered to him at the last minute after threats by him to create a separate assembly, along with representatives of the Peloponnesian primates and the islands.

The language used by the revolutionaries in their public documents mirrored this tension between the local, the regional and the national, and the relationship between these concepts evolved along with the consolidation of the new state and the legitimation of a central administration. In 1821 the first public manifestos of the local revolutionary assemblies employed the language of the traditional *patridai*: regions, that is, already recognised under the Ottomans as territorial entities, such as the Peloponnese, Roumeli and the islands, but also spoke of the Greeks as an *ethnos*, or nation. In the succeeding years, references to individual regions did sometimes remain, although subsumed under the broader umbrella of Greece and the Greek nation. In an unusually lengthy proclamation, published on the eve of the first civil war, in December 1823, the then president of the executive Petros (Petrobey) Mavromichalis condemned the individual lust for power that undermined the quest for national independence, but recognised at the same time the contribution of each region to the struggle for emancipation, as the Peloponnesians, the men of Sterea Ellada and the islanders had fought both for their own fatherland (their region) and for the entire nation.[86]

Yet the truce between these factions reached in 1823 proved to be only temporary, as the drive towards centralisation produced a backlash. The

---

86. Proclamation of the president of the executive, December 1823, in Lignos, Ἀρχεῖον (Archive), 9, pp. 591–95. On these tensions in the public document of the period, see Sotiropoulos and Hadjikyriacou, '*Patris, Ethnos,* and *Demos*'.

appointment of a new president of the executive, an islander, Koundourio-tis, at the expense of an ally of Kolokotronis, Anagnostis Deliyannis—after Mavrokordatos's refusal to accept this post—created a rift that resulted in a brief civil war in spring 1824, and in the emergence of two competing governments, one in Argos and one in Tripolitsa. This war opposed the primates of the Peloponnese (in particular their powerful leaders Zaimis and Lontos), allied with the islanders, to the military class of the same region led by Kolokotronis. This was therefore both a conflict within the Peloponnese, and, in the main, between the Peloponnese and the islands. But in November 1824 a second civil war ensued, this time with far more sharply defined regional connotations: by now the primates and the military classes of the Peloponnese had formed an alliance with a view to opposing the preponderance of the islanders in government. The hegemony of the lat-ter over the executive had become a much more threatening factor for the primates than competition with the kapetanaioi. Significantly, the conflict started with the Peloponnesian primates' refusal to allow a government official to enter their provinces, and resulted in the invasion of the Pelo-ponnese by the detested Roumeliot troops, which led to the destruction and pillaging of the entire region.[87] In spite of the peculiarity of the fac-tionalism of the Greek context, these two civil wars were similar in many ways to the territorial crisis of Sicily: one that combined hostility to central government, conflicts between different provinces and tensions between different social groups within the same territories.

This second Greek civil war was the most serious regional crisis since the beginning of the revolution. Yet it also represented a turning point in the construction of the Greek state. Ibrahim Pasha's invasion, followed by the seizure of Messolonghi and Athens, threatened the very survival of the revolution, and greatly reduced the territories held by the insurgents, who were now left with only the islands and some parts of the Pelopon-nese. A consequence of these events was to force all regional factions to cooperate and to recognise the importance of a central administration. As Mavrokordatos himself had declared in a speech delivered in Decem-ber 1823, on the eve of the first civil war, integration and cooperation were a necessity: 'Although it will be difficult to combine the different interests and opinions that the members of the congress hold, notwithstanding these different interests, the goal is to contemplate the common interest.' Rejecting the allegation that he aimed to unify all continental Greece to

87. Dakin, *Greek Struggle*, p. 130; Brewer, *Greek War*, pp. 232–33.

the detriment of the Peloponnese, he stated that 'we all know the need for unity and for centralisation [*sygkentrismos*] at the expense of division'.[88]

Ibrahim's invasion meanwhile forced the revolutionary elites to come up with a new solution to defend their recently acquired autonomy, and to seek the support of foreign powers. In much the same fashion as the Genoese or Sicilian ruling classes had resisted Piedmontese and Neapolitan interference, so too the Greeks looked to Britain as a possible source of protection against the Ottomans. The document in question, drafted on the island of Zante, endorsed by all the leading figures of the revolution, and approved by the senate in July 1825 after being circulated widely through all territories so as to receive written support from local leaders, stated that the Greek nation 'places the sacred deposit of its liberty, independence and political existence, under the absolute protection of Great Britain'.[89] This attempt, immediately rejected by the British foreign secretary Canning, was one of a broad range of possible solutions entertained by the Greek revolutionaries, sometimes as a united front and at others on the initiative of regional groups, to renegotiate the protection of their sovereignty either under the aegis of a foreign imperial power, or with the Ottoman authorities themselves. When the British option faded, supporters of Russia in consultation with Count Ioannis Kapodistrias drew up a similar request to be submitted to the great Orthodox empire, which was sent to St. Petersburg in December 1825.[90] But in previous years the leaders either of the Peloponnese or of the islands had also contemplated the possibility of acquiring the same status as Serbia had negotiated in 1817, involving formal recognition only of Ottoman authority, and thereby paying annual taxation as a tributary state while otherwise enjoying full self-government.

Besides forcing all factions and regional groups to cooperate and to sue for foreign protection, Ibrahim's invasion had a dramatic impact on the very nature of government, resulting as it did in a radical simplification and centralisation. In the circumstances created by the gravest military threat so far offered to the actual survival of Greece, the assemblies were no longer summoned and Greece was governed by a directory headed by representatives from the regions. In addition, the eparchies

88. Ελληνικά Χρονικά [*Ellinika Chronika*], nos 4–5, 12 and 16 January 1824, in Koumarianou, *Ο Τύπος στον Αγώνα* (The press in the 'Struggle'), 2, pp. 30–34.

89. Dakin, *Greek Struggle*, pp. 161–66. The text of the act can be found in Gordon, *History*, 2, p. 283.

90. Dakin, *Greek Struggle*, p. 166.

were temporarily abolished and, in order to guarantee the support of local elites, Ottoman administrative structures were revived.

What continued to undermine centralising efforts was the fact that some territories tried to retain their full autonomy by either serially—and temporarily—recognising the Ottoman or the Greek administrations, or simply by refusing to submit to any other authority or superior institution whatsoever. The rebellion of the armatoloi that marked the origins of the revolution in continental Greece, and their ability to carve out independent fiefdoms encompassing their former military administrative units, were noted above in Part I. Other regions simply remained resolute in their determination to protect their full autonomy. The commitment of the island of Samos to retaining its full independence during the revolution is a case in point. The island had had a special status within the empire, as it was subject to a religious institution—a mosque in Constantinople to which the island's taxes were sent—and not to the central administration. The revolution of the island was not only a rebellion against the Ottomans, but also the victory of one of the two existing political factions dividing the island, the 'Karmanioloi' (Carmagnolists: those who represented the newly rising social and economic forces), led by Lykourgos Logothetis, opposed to the so-called 'Kalikantzaroi' (Goblins: representing the old order), whose irreconcilable hostility had already resulted in many years of civil war even before the revolution.[91] Logothetis ruled over an independent island through institutions based on pre-existing Ottoman practice: villages sent their representatives (ephors) to an assembly that elected three political judges who governed the island alongside the Logothetis as governor-general. Attempts by the Greek governments to subject Samos to their authority failed notwithstanding Logothetis's temporary imprisonment in 1822. The islanders refused to accept the authority of an eparch appointed by the central administration that same year, and in 1823 the island's assembly once more refused to recognise the Greek state, stating that it rejected any form of tyranny. A state of war between the

91. Michael B. Sakellariou, Ένας συνταγματικός δημοκράτης ηγέτης κατά την Επανάσταση του 21: ο Γ. Λυκούργος Λογοθέτης της Σάμου (1722–1850) (A constitutional democrat leader during the revolution of 1821: G. Lykourgos Logothetis of Samos (1772–1850)) (Irakleion: Crete University Press, 2014), pp. 40–62; Sophia Laiou, 'Political Processes on the Island of Samos Prior to the Greek War of Independence and the Reaction of the Sublime Porte: The Karmanioloi–Kallikantzaroi Conflict', in Political Initiatives 'From the Bottom Up' in the Ottoman Empire, ed. Antonis Anastasopoulos (Rethymno: Crete University Press, 2012), pp. 91–105.

island and the Greek administration persisted until 1826, when the latter recognised Logothetis as legitimate ruler.[92]

In the heartlands of the revolution, however, free from permanent Ottoman military interference, but in response to the persistent threat it posed, central institutions continued to be consolidated. In 1827 the summoning of a third assembly led to further disagreements and the emergence of competing factions. Nonetheless, on this occasion the tension was short-lived and an agreement was immediately reached. There was no going back from the recognition of a central authority and some degree of centralisation. The constitution agreed at Troezena confirmed the role of eparchies in guaranteeing a measure of control over the territories of the state by catering for the military and fiscal needs of the government. At the same time the new dispensation took into account the demands for local autonomy emanating from the provinces: while the respective powers of the locally elected and centrally controlled representatives were not clearly defined, the new constitution confirmed the elective principle for municipal administrations, through the appointment of demogerontes in numbers proportionate to the populations of the various towns, and introduced also committees of general demogerontes (from five to ten, according to the extent of the eparchy) elected at provincial level.[93] By the end of 1827, therefore, the need to recognise a central authority by co-opting all the regional leaders had come to seem uncontroversial, and while some local administrative autonomy had been recognised, a degree of central control had been established. By this year, in fact, in Greece as in the other countries whose revolutionary upheavals are here discussed, a compromise had been reached between the demands of local and regional elites and the priorities of state control. The creation of the administrative structure of the Greek state thus converged with the compromise attained between the different revolutionary groups during the other southern European revolutions.

---

92. Sakellariou, Ένας συνταγματικός δημοκράτης ηγέτης (A constitutional democrat leader), pp. 88–92, 200–3, 227–33, 242, 353–57.

93. See 'Constitution politique de la Grèce (1827)', in Pierre-Armand Dufau, *Collection des constitutions, chartes et lois fondamentales des peuples de l'Europe e des deux Amérique*, 7 vols (Paris: Picon et Didier, 1823–30), 7, p. 84. See discussion also in Kaltchas, *Introduction*, p. 53. For the political context, see Petropulos, *Politics and Statecraft*, pp. 105–6.

CHAPTER SEVEN

Electing Parliamentary Assemblies

NATIONAL ELECTIONS REPRESENTED the most important collective experience introduced by the constitutions, and voting for national representatives the most important new political right acquired by male citizens in the 1820s, across all southern European states experiencing revolution. No other practice could more vividly demonstrate to citizens the implications of constitutional government. Although electoral practices had existed in southern Europe well before that decade, especially at the local level, the extent of voting rights and participation varied enormously, and tended to be limited to a small proportion of the population, based on a certain income threshold.

The novelty of the 1820s was that for the first time, national assemblies were elected throughout southern Europe by male quasi-universal suffrage, whether direct or indirect. This had happened before the 1820s only in Spain, where national elections had been held to appoint the Cortes extraordinarias in Cádiz in 1810 and in 1813 on the basis of the new electoral system introduced by the constitution.[1] A Sicilian parliament was elected in Palermo during the British occupation in 1813, following the introduction of a new constitution inspired by Britain's. However, an

---

1. The elections of 1810 to create a constituent assembly, summoned by the Junta Central, introduced male universal suffrage, but established three different types of electoral procedures, one to elect a deputy for each administrative division, a second to appoint representatives from each military junta that had composed the Junta Central, and a third to appoint representatives from each city. See Quintí Casals Bergés, *La representación parlamentaria en España durante el primer liberalismo (1810–1836)* (Lleida: Edicions de la Universitat de Lleida, 2014), pp. 55–78.

income threshold for both active and passive voting rights applied.[2] The
only other forms of universal suffrage experienced before the 1820s were the
Napoleonic plebiscites organised in Spain, in Piedmont and on the Italian
peninsula.

In the 1820s an unprecedented number of male citizens acquired new
political rights in the region, and they were called upon to elect representative assemblies in Portugal, Spain, the Kingdom of the Two Sicilies and
Greece. In 1820 and in 1822, out of a population of respectively 10,541,221
and 11,661.865, 3,216,460 citizens (30.51 per cent in 1820; 27.58 per cent
in 1822) obtained the right to vote in Spain, while in Portugal 752,710
fogos (hearths)—a term referring to heads of households—were accorded
this right (thus around 25 per cent of a population of 3,026,450).[3] In
the Kingdom of the Two Sicilies, whose total population amounted to
6,734,234, a roughly similar percentage was called upon to vote.[4] Universal male suffrage was also extended to communal elections in all of
these countries.

Indirect elections remained the principal form of electoral participation, thereby ensuring that people's participation as voters was experienced
first and foremost as members of a local community, whether a village
or a parish. The most important example was set by the Cádiz Constitution, whose electoral procedures, followed in Spain in 1820 and 1821, were
replicated almost to the letter in Naples in 1820 and in the elections for
the Portuguese constituent assembly of the same year. This system was
based on four successive electoral phases in three different territorial units
progressing from the smaller to the larger: the first two in parishes, the
third at a level known as *cabeza de partido*, and the final one at provincial

2. Alfio Signorelli, 'Partecipazione e generazioni in Sicilia dalla costituzione del 1812
all'unità', in *Rileggere l'Ottocento: Risorgimento e nazione*, ed. Maria Luisa Betri (Turin:
Carocci, 2011), pp. 203–23.

3. These dates are found in Juan Linz, José Ramón Montero and Antonia Ruiz, 'Elecciones y política', in *Estadísticas históricas de España: Siglo XIX-XX*, ed. Albert Carreras
and Xavier Tafunell, 2nd edn, 3 vols (Bilbao: Fundación BBVA, 2005) 1, pp. 1025–1154 at
1089, and Pedro Tavares de Almeida, ed., *Legislação eleitoral portuguesa, 1820–1926* (Lisbon: Imprensa Nacional-Casa da Moeda, 1998), p. 38. In Portugal, voting rights applied to
male citizens above the age of twenty-five, or twenty if married. Children living with their
father, even when above the age of twenty-five, were excluded. See the electoral regulations of 1822 as published in July 1821, available in Maria Namorado and Alexandre Sousa
Pinheiro, eds, *Legislação eleitoral portuguesa: Textos históricos (1820–1974)*, 2 vols (Lisbon:
CNE, 1998), 1, p. 39.

4. These data were published in the instructions for the elections issued on 20
July 1820 by the minister for home affairs, Giuseppe Zurlo. See *La Voce del Secolo*, no. 3,
1 August 1820, p. 10.

level of the. In the first, members of a parish (of at least two hundred) elected the so-called *compromissorios*, who would in turn immediately elect a single *elector de parroquia* (parish elector). All the parish electors gathered in a *cabeza de partido* appointed the *electores de partido*. It was only these latter who, meeting in the capital of each province, voted for the representatives to be sent to the Cortes. The Cádiz Constitution gave voting rights to men above the age of twenty-one. Among those excluded were women, individuals in domestic service, those with no permanent abode and people condemned for debt or criminal acts. To be eligible for election themselves, citizens had to be above the age of twenty-five and resident in the territorial unit where they were elected. The constitution also made reference to property requirements to be defined in future. It thereby combined extensive popular participation with a system that selected economically independent individuals.[5]

In Greece too, the revolution introduced indirect elections to the national assemblies after 1822. According to the regulations, 'people of every class and condition' had a right to vote. Each village, depending on the number of families, would appoint a number of electors, who would in turn assemble in the capital of the eparchy to elect a deputy by majority vote. This system, in contrast to that envisaged by the Cádiz Constitution, therefore had only two, rather than four phases (degrees) in the electoral process for the appointment of representatives. The Greek preference for indirect elections had nothing to do with the influence of the Cádiz Constitution: in fact these procedures owed much to earlier Ottoman practices. Before the revolution, in provinces with predominantly Greek populations, communes elected the administrators called demogerontes who gathered at district level as an assembly and elected representatives for the council advising the Ottoman voivode, an agent appointed by the pasha, to discuss budgetary and taxation issues.[6] Besides the influence of this legacy from the past, during the revolution public authorities—as stated in the official guidelines on electoral procedures—came to believe that indirect elections were the only viable choice, given the impossibility, during the war, of organising simultaneous voting procedures at the national level.[7]

5. An analysis of its procedures is provided by Blanca Esther Buldain Jaca, *Las elecciones de 1820: La época y su publicística* (Madrid: Ministerio del Interior, Secretaría General Técnica, 1993), pp. 49–62.

6. Petropulos, *Politics and Statecraft*, pp. 27–28.

7. 'Proclamation of the Executive', 9 November 1822, in Lignos, Αρχείον (Archive), 8, pp. 613–17.

A noteworthy exception to these indirect systems was the Portuguese elections for the Congresso of 1822. While in 1820 the electoral procedures of the Cádiz Constitution had provided a template to elect and appoint a constituent assembly, when discussing and approving a new constitution the majority of the deputies (sixty-six in favour and twenty-six against) opted for direct elections based on universal male suffrage, albeit with some restrictions. The lively debate that preceded this decision high-lighted what the Portuguese deputies considered to be the advantages offered by a direct electoral system. Portuguese partisans of indirect elections held them to be more compatible with Portuguese traditions (as the *vereadores*—local councillors—and the câmaras were sometimes elected indirectly), and believed they would avoid disturbances and riots known to affect elections in Britain and preclude the election of individuals unknown to citizens. But the majority of the deputies reckoned on the contrary that the general will of the nation would be more directly and fairly represented through direct selection of the candidates to be sent to the Congresso. They were convinced that the representative institutions introduced by the constitution would grow in legitimacy, as the delegates were a direct emanation of the electors' choice. In addition, they hoped that this system would encourage popular participation. Deputies attributed the indifference displayed by the populations of many villages in 1820 in the election of the *compromissórios* to the fact that voters could not see the direct effect of their vote. Partisans of direct elections also believed that this system would make it more difficult for the executive or for individuals to corrupt the process and influence voters. References were made to elections in Britain and America both to criticise and to support direct electoral processes.[8] As in Spain and Greece, this direct system was likewise experienced by local communities gathering in parish churches. Portugal reverted to an indirect electoral system only in 1826, under a different constitution, the Carta, which substantially reduced suffrage by granting voting rights only to those male citizens with an annual income of 100,000 *réis*.[9]

The Sicilian elections for a pro-independence assembly in the capital city of Palermo were also based on an indirect system, although they did not involve a uniform set of procedures. The provisional and pro-independence government set up in Palermo invited the towns of Sicily to send representatives to the capital from each district, chosen with

8. *Diário das cortes geraes*, 3, no. 161, 27 August 1821, pp. 2030–31, 2034–36.
9. Almeida, *Legislação eleitoral portuguesa*, p. 44.

the agreement of all the municipalities within it.[10] It was the provisional government's intention that this assembly should meet temporarily, as its exclusive task would be to oversee the preparations for the election of a parliament according to the Spanish constitution as the charter of an independent island, presumably in line with that constitution's electoral procedures. However, the invitation to the towns of Sicily to send delegates did not include specific instructions about elections. Therefore communities improvised. In some cases, deputies were acclaimed at public meetings gathering entire communities; in others it was the provisional giunta elected during the revolution that nominated the representatives to be sent to Palermo.[11]

Participation in parliamentary elections as a duty to the nation was a central theme of electoral literature. The public instructions delivered by both central and local authorities to guide voters conceived the vote not simply as an individual right, or the act whereby 'each individual concurs in the exercise of sovereignty', but above all as a patriotic duty towards the nation, one understood in political as well as territorial and religious terms.[12] This idea recurred in the addresses to voters or electors, geared to instructing and educating them about procedures. Underpinned by pedagogical intent, as well as by concerns to avoid disorder, these documents demonstrate how voting was understood by authorities and citizens alike, and more generally casts an important light on how the constitution and representative government were interpreted in this decade. Instructions on how to vote were accompanied by speeches and sermons. Given that in Spain, Portugal and Naples parishes represented the primary electoral unit, and that churches or other religious buildings were employed everywhere to organise the vote, it is not surprising that priests and bishops featured prominently as the authors of such speeches. Along with them, jefes políticos in Spain and corregedores in Portugal also read out addresses to electors. These speeches, sometimes conserved today as manuscripts only, were often printed as broadsheets or as publications consisting of just a few pages. They could also be found in newspapers, or as manifestos containing public declarations or instructions produced by the authorities to be read out in public and displayed in squares in anticipation of the electoral process.

10. BCP, Manoscritti, Qq H 138, ff. 240–41: broadsheet, Gaetano Bonanno Cancelliere, 'Alle municipalità del Regno', 26 July 1820.

11. See the documents in ASP, Real Segreteria, Incartamenti, Giunta provvisoria, 5035.

12. See, for instance, AAM, Secretaría, Acontecimientos Políticos, 2–230, no. 30: 'Manifiesto a los vecinos de Madrid', 22 September 1821.

In similar fashion a Spanish parish sermon stated that the object of the electoral meeting in the parish was the glory and interest of the nation, whose definition in the constitution the author painstakingly explained in its territorial, political and religious dimensions. In short, he concluded, elections aimed at guaranteeing the 'felicidad de la patria' (happiness of the fatherland).[13] A parish priest, speaking before the election in a church in Naples, similarly claimed that the election of good candidates was an act of duty towards the nation as well as the monarch.[14] The president of an electoral assembly in Portugal associated the regeneration of nation, its emancipation from monarchical despotism, economic decline and subjection to its former colonies, in short its independence, to the introduction of the constitution and the election of new legislators. It warned voters against the enemies of the constitution.[15]

What was notably absent from all of this abundant printed material (which in the case of the Greek revolution was limited to official manifestos alone) was the voice of the candidates themselves. In this respect the southern European elections of the 1820s reflected a longer tradition, revived during the French revolution, that condemned self-promotion and canvassing. This tradition was in sharp contrast with the nature of elections in Britain, where popular participation—even by those without voting rights—revolved around the performances of candidates who interacted with the public and defended their programmes speaking from the hustings. A member of a collegiate church overseeing the elections of the partida in the Spanish city of Jerez de la Frontera in fact echoed Plato's view, that office should be held by those who least aspired to it: 'the high posts the fatherland makes available must be denied to those who aspire to them, and awarded to those who flee them or refuse them'.[16] In southern Europe public advocacy was seen as an unacceptable form of interference with the free choice of the voters, equated with intrigues, corruption and manipulation. Those who tried to advance their own candidature were

13. Baldomero de Frías, 'Discurso pronunciado en la iglesia parroquial de San Sebastian de Madrid en el dia 30 de abril de 1820', in Buldain Jaca, *Las elecciones*, pp. 162–63.

14. Electoral sermon summarised in *L'Amico della Costituzione*, no. 32, 22 August 1820, pp. 2–3.

15. AHP, secções I/II, caixa 131, maço 90, no. 59: 'Discurso pronunciado na Assamblea eleitoral da cabeça do concelho da Montaelegre pelo seu Presidente Vereador segundo bacharel José dos Santos Dias', Montalegre, 17 August 1822.

16. Francisco de Paula, *Discurso que se pronunció en la insigne iglesia colegial de Xerez de la Frontera el domingo 7 de mayo de 1820, con motivo de las elecciones del partido de la misma ciudad* (Cádiz, 1820), p. 11.

considered to be acting immorally and against the public good. In short, as another Spanish parish priest stated, the righteous man is 'happy to deserve to be elected, but without soliciting it'.[17] Or, as another Spanish electoral pamphlet concluded, 'any citizens who intrigue to be a deputy, [are] not worthy of being elected'.[18] In its instructions prior to the elections in 1822, the Portuguese *Correio do Porto* warned citizens against all parties (*partidos*) that would spontaneously emerge in constitutional regimes to try and influence voters and ensure the appointment of candidates representing special interests. Such attempts to interfere in the process had to be resisted, and public acclamations at the beginning of the voting procedures avoided as illegal.[19]

The absence of direct canvassing and the lack of any reference to specific candidates show that what mattered in electoral processes were not specific party programmes, but rather the selection of the individuals with the best possible virtues and professional skills. Much was in fact written about the qualities needed for an ideal representative. Whether in Portugal, Spain or Naples, this literature adopted the language of republicanism and civic virtues when discussing both the qualities required of deputies and the nature of voting as the public duty of each and every citizen. Ideal candidates were described as those politicians with the loftiest attributes of wisdom, honesty, control of passions and patriotism. The public instructions published by the national administration of Greece at the end of 1822 in anticipation of the elections explicitly pointed to the need to appoint men who 'had given unequivocal proof of patriotism and public virtue'.[20] In an address to Portuguese voters published by the Minerva patriotic society based in Lisbon, electing the deputies to the Congresso was described as the utmost act of popular sovereignty. In order to create an enlightened and incorruptible body, it was argued, the deputies required the qualities of moral virtue: that is to say, 'humanity, religion, love for the other and generosity'; and of social virtue: that is to say, 'patriotism, love for the cause, a noble heart and an eternal hatred

17. D. Tomás Martínez del Hortal, *Discurso pronunciado en Villanueva de la Serena el dia 8 de mayo de 1820 al congreso de electores parroquiales en la eleccion de electores de partido* (Madrid, 1820), p. 10.

18. *Mis apuntes sobre elecciones de diputados* (Valencia, 1820), p. 4.

19. 'Novas eleiçoes', *Correio do Porto*, 15 August 1822.

20. Comstock, *History*, p. 265; 'Proclamation of the Executive', November 1822, in Lignos, Αρχείον (Archive), 8, p. 615.

of despotism'. A love for the constitution, along with these qualities, was deemed to be essential over and above any consideration regarding a candidate's social status and wealth.[21] As a priest stated on the day of the elections in his parish in the Portuguese city of Coimbra, deputies must be 'above passions, in order to listen more clearly and distinctively to the impartial voice of truth'.[22] Electoral sermons included narratives of historical events used as morality tales. Examples of the rise and collapse of ancient empires and republics were deployed to demonstrate the need to elect politicians endowed with civic virtues and avoid those corrupted by money, ambition and selfishness.[23]

In pure republican fashion, these virtues were in fact deemed to be incompatible with any partisan belief: therefore parties or factions (translating terms often used interchangeably) were universally condemned as threats to the body politic and incompatible with patriotism and a healthy political life. Party politics and the dominance of specific interests would result, it was believed, in the collapse of the constitutional regime. As a Neapolitan publicist wrote, a plurality of different interests could result in harmony in an assembly of individuals forced to find a compromise. However, if individual interests and passions prevailed, as had happened in the assemblies of the French revolution, instability, constant constitutional revisions and anarchy would ensue.[24] Besides choosing the right candidate, on the grounds that 'a good candidate would make good laws', it was important to avoid the enemies of the constitution. A Spanish priest argued in his church before the parish election that those citizens 'who criticise the constitution, or are opposed to complying with it, have to be seen as enemies of God, of the nation, of the King and of yourselves'.[25] An electoral sermon by the prior of a church in Lisbon divided society into two parties: the party of despotism and selfishness, and the party of the law of nature, reason and true religion, otherwise called 'the party of the

21. *Illustração aos povos para fazerem com acerto as elleições dos deputados para a proxima legislatura, feita pela sociedade patriotica denominata Gabinete de Minerva* (Lisbon, 6 August 1822), pp. 2–3. Similar themes can be found in *Discurso de D. Manuel Maía de Acevedo, gefe político interino de Asturias, leido el dia 22 de Mayo en la Junta Electoral de Provincia* (Oviedo: Oficina de Francisco Pérez Prieto, 1820).

22. *O reitor da freguezia da Sé de Coimbra, aos cidadãos seus parochianos*, broadsheet available online at http://purl.pt/1357 (accessed 14 August 2022).

23. Anonymous untitled broadsheet (n.p., n.d. [Naples 1820]), in SNSP, Opuscoli 1820–21, 13, f. 113713.

24. Antonio Giordano, *Idee generali sulla scelta de' deputati e pensieri di costituzione per un governo rappresentativo* (Naples: Tipografia di Porcelli, 1820), pp. 15–17.

25. De Frías, 'Discurso', in Buldain Jaca, *Las elecciones*, p. 166.

Liberals'. It was this latter, he argued, representing the majority of the population, that must prevail in the elections.[26]

Rooted in hostility to factions, parties and the enemies of the fatherland—the regeneration of which was to be guaranteed by the appointment of a representative assembly—the idea of the fatherland emerging from the electoral discourse was therefore holistic, homogeneous and incompatible with pluralism, universally considered a lethal threat rather than a resource and a precondition for parliamentary life. It seemed to confirm the preeminence of the nation as an entity over and above the individual; and in this sense voting represented the fulfilment of an individual's duty towards this supreme, superior community, endowed with shared moral and civil attributes.

In practice, however, through voting people became aware of belonging to a broader national community in an indirect and mediated way, assembling as heads of families at the parish level or at the level of the village, in local public and religious buildings. This communitarian understanding of voting was reinforced by the fact that electors gathered in parish churches, cathedrals or monasteries, listened to an electoral sermon by a priest and attended mass before fulfilling their voting duties. Electoral practices thus confirmed the religious demarcation of the nation as a sum of local religious congregations, highlighting the religious content of the newly acquired political right and its consensual and harmonious nature.[27] The religious setting was meant to provide these events with a composed and inspired atmosphere, one that the contemporary literature considered to be a vital precondition for the successful performance of this civic duty and for the dignity of the occasion. A dialogue in a Neapolitan constitutional catechism ran as follows:

Q: Do elections have to be carried out with solemnity?

A: With as much as possible of it. This is the most important and august act a people can carry out. Religion must contribute to it with its prayers.[28]

The exiled Lombard revolutionary Giuseppe Pecchio noted 'the order, dignity and general decorum' of elections in Spain during the Trienio, a

26. *Astro da Lusitania*, no. 15, 15 December 1820, p. 2.

27. On this aspect, see Gian Luca Fruci, 'Democracy in Italy: From Egalitarian Republicanism to Plebiscitarian Monarchy', in Innes and Philp, *Re-imagining Democracy*, pp. 25–50 at 39–40.

28. Luigi Galanti, *Catechismo costituzionale per uso del regno unito delle Sicilie* (Naples: Domenico Sangiacomo, 1820), pp. 66–7.

feature of Spanish elections that was in stark contrast with the disorder and noise of those taking place in Britain at the time.[29] Sometimes elections would indeed seem to have measured up to expectation. Reports confirmed that parish elections in Naples had gathered people together in an orderly fashion, patiently waiting to fulfil their duties for three continuous days and with no interruption. The general elections on the mainland appear to have taken place without any disturbance.[30] In the province of Bari, the authorities triumphantly stated that 'it is a consolation to see that in these assemblies the best possible order reigned'.[31] Whenever circumstances allowed it, the solemnity and dignity of the procedures was followed by public celebrations and displays of joy. In the city of Oviedo in the Spanish province of Asturias, for instance, where the electoral process had unfolded without any disturbance or controversy, its termination was marked by a public ceremony in which a military band and members of the local patriotic society led a procession into the hall where the elections had taken place and sang patriotic songs. They were followed by three children representing peace, concord and abundance, and by two *literati* (academics) holding flags and strewing flowers at the feet of the members of the electoral junta.[32]

Very often, however, the peace, concord and unanimity advocated in addresses to voters and described by some contemporary observers was a far cry from the actual experience of voting in parishes, villages and cities, where conflicts and disorders frequently arose. If parishes and villages were the primary unit of the sovereign nation, local politics and their relationship with national ones led to disagreements and even violence. In the city of Campobasso in the Abruzzo, for instance, the electors could not vote for the deputy, as the assembly, disrupted by armed men, was disbanded.[33] In 1820 in the town of Acireale in eastern Sicily, a disagreement degenerated into a dispute that resulted in the interruption of the electoral procedures. In the village of Trecastagne in the province of Catania, elections were interrupted by the threats of an individual, supported by part of the population, who demanded to be appointed a secretary of the *giunta elettorale*.[34] In the Portuguese city of Aveiro some citizens denounced the

29. Giuseppe Pecchio, *Anecdotes of the Spanish and Portuguese Revolutions* (London: G. & W. B. Whittaker, 1823), p. 114.

30. *La Minerva Napolitana*, no. 1, 1820, pp. 59–60.

31. ASN, Polizia Generale II, 41, ff. 123–25.

32. María Jesús Aguilar, *La imagen del Trienio Liberal en Asturias* (Oviedo: Universidad de Oviedo, 1999), p. 54.

33. Letter dated 30 August 1820, in Alberti, *Atti del parlamento*, 4, p. 207.

34. ASN, Ministero degli Affari Interni, App. II, 2014, ff. 96, 124–26.

fact that, thanks to the interference of 'military factions' led by a lieutenant colonel, 336 votes were declared void.[35]

Although officially condemned, attempts at influencing voters were
common at all stages of the electoral process, and may have reinforced the
general understanding of national elections as local affairs. Considering
themselves guarantors of the sovereignty of the people, Spanish patriotic
societies intervened to praise the conduct of authorities and welcome the
election of constitutional candidates with public addresses. But they
often went beyond this simple role as watchdogs to play an important
role in determining electoral choices. The selection of candidates, especially
in the last round to determine the choice of deputies, was often discussed
and agreed among their members.[36] Besides patriotic societies, the networks of sociability offered by secret societies such as the Carboneria in
southern Italy and the Comunería in Spain were also employed for similar
purposes. In the Spanish elections at the end of 1821, for instance, the
society of the Comunería openly supported individual candidates and did
not hide its satisfaction when voters had followed its recommendations.[37]
Efforts by priests to control voters were reported very frequently, and
vehemently denounced. If priests had a key role in organising and preaching on the eve of elections, they were also often the object of complaints
for interfering unduly in electoral choices in Portugal, Spain and Naples
alike. In the town of Bisceglie in Puglia, the priests had distributed lists of
names to citizens participating in the appointment of the *compromissori*,
along with sums of money and warnings that if they dared to vote for
carbonari they would go to hell.[38] In the town of Albufeira in the Portuguese Algarve, a prior was denounced for circulating lists of candidates
in advance of the elections;[39] while in the absolutist northern region of
Trás-os-Montes priests were allegedly supporting the election of royalist
candidates: in Bragança two abbots had tried to influence the outcome
of elections by bribery, and in Algoso a parish priest intervened in the
electoral assembly to suggest candidates, claiming that the fatherland was
in peril. Similar reports of clerical interference, bribery and advocacy of

35. AHP, secções I/II, caixa 131, maço 90, no. 70: electoral report of 26 October 1822.

36. Miraflores, *Apuntes histórico-críticos*, p. 54.

37. APR, Papeles Reservados de Fernando VII, 67, exp. 20, f. 277: letter of the merindad of Zamora, 4 December 1821. On the political context, see Matilde Codesal Pérez,
La ciudad de Zamora en el Trienio Liberal (1820–23) (Zamora: Ayuntamiento de Zamora,
2008), pp. 201–2.

38. *Le trame de' preti di Bisceglie contra la libertá* (Naples, 1820).

39. ANTT, IGP, Algarve 239, f. 352.

anti-constitutional candidates also came from other regions.⁴⁰ On the eve of the Spanish elections of 1821 a Basque constitutional newspaper warned the voters against listening to the advice of priests, since 'clerics are in general those who believe that more than anybody else they have something to lose from the reforms introduced by the constitution'.⁴¹

Another factor that rendered elections and the contribution of each family, parish or local community to the construction of a sovereign nation less than harmonious was interference by government officials or local administrators, who intervened directly in conflicts pitting candidates and local or regional factions against one another, often manipulating the outcomes of the elections at local and provincial level. In Spain the contested nature of the elections at the end of 1821 owed much to the fact that the tone of the political debate had become more tense and acrimonious in the last few months of the year, and the political situation across the country had become unstable and polarised. On the one hand, fears of counterrevolution resulted in the murder of the Cura Vinuesa, accused of involvement in a plot against the constitution, while the organisation of a growing number of royalist partidas was threatening the constitutional order. Perhaps more importantly, the moderado government led by Eusebio Bardají was in open conflict with the exaltados: the elections had been called just after the public protests against the dismissal of Riego from the captaincy-general of Zaragoza, and the demonstrations against the government that had erupted across the country. As a consequence, the government did not hesitate to use its powers to try to guarantee a victory for its own moderado candidates. A confidential note sent out by the Ministry of Interior to the jefes políticos invited them to ensure that the deputies elected would meet the following requirements:

1. Adherence to the constitution and the constitutional king.
2. Not having belonged to the *afrancesados* [supporters of past Napoleonic rule in France].
3. Not belonging to the party which public opinion rightly defines as advocates of exaggerated principles and doctrines.
4. [...] if possible, to be a property owner or among those who by their position or social relations resist any dangerous innovation.⁴²

40. Benedicta Maria Duque Vieira, *O problema político português no tempo das primeiras Cortes liberais*, vol. 1 of Miriam Halpern Pereira, ed. *A crise do Antigo Regime e as Cortes constituintes*, 5 vols (Lisbon: João Sá da Costa, 1992), pp. 303–5, 312.

41. *El Liberal Guipuzcoano*, no. 132, 5 October 1821.

42. Quoted in Miguel Artola Gallego, *La España de Fernando VII*, 2nd edn (Madrid: Espasa Calpe, 1999), pp. 559–60; for the context, see also Gil Novales, *El Trienio Liberal*, pp. 43ff.

In this context, denunciations of irregularities were employed to challenge electoral results that had favoured opposing parties.[43] The enemies of the exaltados often accused them of having employed soldiers and the local militias to circulate their list of candidates, and of imposing their choices on voters in parishes with threats and violence.[44] In the city of Salamanca, the mayor of which was known to have anti-constitutional leanings, a group of citizens featuring both moderados and absolutists refused to accept the outcome of an election that had given the victory to three exaltado deputies. This interclass group of citizens, which included army officers, civil servants, lawyers and even a day-labourer, submitted a request via the ayuntamiento to the Cortes that the results be invalidated, on the grounds that before the elections a group of exaltados, including some of the *electores de partido*, had tried to put pressure on all voters to influence the outcome.[45] In other towns, it was the exaltados who challenged electoral results. In the city of Baza in Andalusia, the *elecciones de partido* ended in uproar, with the local population divided between those supporting a representative of the Comunería, who had obtained eighty votes, and a canon from the local minster (*collegiata*) who had gained eighty-seven votes and was the apparent winner. It was only the intervention of the national militia from a neighbouring town that put an end to the disorders and violence.[46]

This combination of interference by the executive and local factionalism also accounts for the contested nature of electoral results in Greece. The controversy dividing the citizens and villages of the eparchy of Leontari (in the region of Arcadia, in the Peloponnese) regarding who had been legitimately elected in their eparchy as representative in the summer of 1824 is a case in point. Some citizens backed one Nikolaos Milianis, while another group argued that it was Petros Salamonos who had been lawfully elected. Supporters of Salamonos complained about the interference of the executive, and in particular of the minister of interior Papaflessas, who had intervened to support the election of Milianis, and had gathered signatures in his favour. As a consequence, the electors' own choice had

43. Gil Novales, *Las sociedades patrióticas*, 1, p. 555.

44. Sebastián Miñano y Bedoya, *Histoire de la révolution d'Espagne de 1820 à 1823: Par un espagnol témoin oculaire*, trans. Ernest Poret, vicomte de Blosseville, Meissonier de Valcroissant and Andrés Muriel, 2 vols (Paris: J. G. Dentu, 1824), 1, pp. 56, 270–71.

45. Claudio Calles Hernández, 'La lucha política durante el Trienio Liberal: El enfrentamiento electoral de diciembre de 1821 en Salamanca', *Salamanca: Revista de Estudios* 53 (2006): 71–134.

46. Antonio Guillén Gómez, *Una aproximación al Trienio Liberal en Almería: La milicia nacional voluntaria (1820–1823)* (Almería: Instituto de Estudios Almerienses, 2000), pp. 105–7. Details can also be found in CD, legajo 8, no. 14.

simply been ignored, and their votes had allegedly disappeared. While it is impossible to know where the truth lay in this conflict, it highlights a genuine desire for participation felt by ordinary citizens. Five hundred citizens had signed the letters to the administration in support of the election of Milianis, while around two hundred different villages from the eparchy had done the same to defend the election of his competitor. Two hundred citizens complained in writing about the interference from the minister of interior, stating that they had revolted precisely so that they could take decisions freely.[47]

Participation and turnout at the voting assemblies would seem to have varied hugely. The only data available for a national election are for Portugal and refer exclusively to second ballots, required when candidates had not reached an absolute majority of votes.[48] Individual case studies therefore offer a more complex picture and suggest the uneven nature of participation. In large cities it was often very substantial. In December 1820 in Lisbon, the parish elections for the constituent assembly were marked by a high turnout, to the extent that in some parishes additional secretarial support was needed to count all the lists in time.[49] Reports from Naples and the neighbouring towns also suggest a very high turnout. Although during the first day of the elections only a fourth of the voters had turned up in Naples, queues to vote continued for several nights and days. In addition, evidence suggests that the *compromissori*, those elected at the parish level, were not only professionals or property owners, but also individuals of more humble origins. Those appointed in the parishes of the province of Naples included *proprietari* (property owners), priests, notaries and surgeons, but also shopkeepers such as greengrocers, artisans such as tailors, dyers and shoemakers, and tenant farmers and carters.[50] Many of these *compromissori* would have been illiterate and, not surprisingly, signed the electoral documents with a simple cross.[51]

47. BMA, F8, docs 59–66: letters signed by the inhabitants and the electors of Leontari for two different plenipotentiaries to the legislature, and the letter to the legislature by inhabitants of various villages, between July and September 1824.

48. AHP, secções I/II.

49. *Menmosine Constitucional*, no. 73, 18 December 1820, pp. 2–3.

50. ASN, Polizia Generale II, f. 112: Tommaso de Liso, 'Giunta preparatoria della Provincia di Napoli: Rapporto del delegato speciale presidente al segretario di stato ministro degli affari interni', Naples, 16 October 1820.

51. As demonstrated by the documents of the parish elections in the town of Castellammare di Stabia. See Angelo Acampora, *I moti del 1820–21 a Castellammare* (Castellammare di Stabia: Pianeta Giovani, 1985), p. 16.

In other cities or regions participation was more limited. Many reasons account for this. Although electoral sermons used the language of duty and civic virtue to encourage people to vote, there did not seem to be a widespread concern among revolutionaries to ensure a high turnout. Organisers occasionally lamented the lack of participation, and a variety of strategies were employed to call citizens to elections: the tolling of church bells or fireworks were commonly used devices. However, they appeared to be more concerned with the orderly execution of the voting than with guaranteeing a maximum turnout. In general, these attitudes seem to confirm what Pierre Rosanvallon has observed about indirect elections during the French revolution, especially at their first stage: namely, that this participation had a primarily symbolic meaning, serving as it did to legitimise the process by confirming the will of the nation and its sovereignty.[52] In some instances local elites explicitly discouraged participation, or simply ignored electoral procedures. In 1824 ordinary citizens from many different districts of Greece voiced their frustration about their right to vote being completely disregarded. In their petitions to the central administration they stated that village elders selected delegates to be sent to the assembly, keeping ordinary citizens out of the process.[53] Sometimes candidates were acclaimed rather than chosen by secret ballot, and either because of circumstances or because of deliberate choice, delegates were chosen exclusively by members of the army or by the primates. Sometimes individuals appointed themselves to represent districts.[54]

In some cases, lack of interest and apathy were the principal cause, but in others external circumstances played a larger role. The war in Greece and the civil war in Sicily, for instance, greatly affected participation and the smooth organisation of voting. In the province of Catania, which had sided with Naples against Palermo, voting was a sign of allegiance to the integrity of the kingdom and the constitution, but threats issued by supporters of independence and fears of retaliation played a role in limiting the turnout of electors. In the town of Randazzo, nobody turned up to vote, as citizens knew that the surrounding towns supported independence. In Militello only a hundred out of and electorate of 1,900 took advantage of their right to vote. Supporters of Palermo had spread rumours that the pro-independence army was approaching and that it

52. Pierre Rosanvallon, *La rivoluzione dell'uguaglianza: Storia del suffagio universale in Francia* (Milan: Anabasi, 1994), pp. 201–2.

53. *Φίλος του Νόμου* [*Filos tou Nomou*], no. 85, 9 January 1825, in Koumarianou, *Ο Τύπος στον Αγώνα* (The press in the 'Struggle'), 3, pp. 66–68.

54. Brewer, *Greek War*, pp. 181–82.

would abolish all duties, while by voting citizens would confirm their willingness to pay them. Because of the civil war elections were completely suspended in Biancavilla and Gagliano. Yet in some smaller villages like Accibonaccorsi, all heads of family dutifully voted.[55] In Greece the war often prevented or delayed compliance with voting procedures by ballot. In 1823 more than fifty delegates at the assembly of Astros, where a new constitution for Greece was to be discussed and approved, had not been appointed through the formal electoral process, but had joined the gathering with petitions from their villages, anxious to be represented and to participate in the activities of the national assembly.[56] In early 1826 the harshness of the winter and the proximity of the enemy delayed the election of delegates to the third national assembly from the town of Ipatis, in western Roumeli, whose population was either hiding in caves or migrating to safer areas. When the election became possible, it was carried out by the demogerontes alone.[57]

Sometimes, however, it was regulatory constraints, not disregard for rules or conflicts, that excluded citizens otherwise keen to be engaged in the process. In Portugal the most vocal group to complain about its exclusion from elections was that of university students. In 1820 the 1,500 students of the University of Coimbra complained about the decision of the câmara to exclude them from voting for the election of the constituent assembly on the basis of an interpretation of the Cádiz Constitution that they rejected. To challenge the câmara, they sent petitions to the government with the support of the academic body of the university—one of the petitions was signed by the poet and writer Almeida Garrett—and organised demonstrations reading out their proclamations in public. Some of them went so far as to take an oath that they would rather die than give up the sacred right of voting: 'Votar, ou morrer!'[58]

The elections in Spain, Portugal and Naples produced national political classes with strikingly similar social and professional profiles: parliamentary assemblies in these countries were dominated by clerics, army officers, lawyers and civil servants. The dominant group among the

55. ASN, Ministero degli Affari Interni, App. II, 2014, ff. 168–72, 315, 327–28, 363; De Francesco, *La guerra di Sicilia*, pp. 238–41.

56. Blaquiere, *Greek Revolution*, p. 256.

57. Andreas Z. Mamoukas, ed., *Τα κατά την αναγέννησιν της Ελλάδος, ήτοι συλλογή των περί την αναγεννώμενην Ελλάδα συνταχθέντων πολιτευμάτων, νόμων και άλλων επίσημων πράξεων από του 1821 μέχρι τέλους του 1832* (On the regeneration of Greece: Collection of constitutions, laws and other formal acts of the regenerated Greece from 1821 to 1832), 11 vols (Athens: Vasiliko Typografeio, 1839–52), 5, p. 78.

58. *O Liberal*, no. 14, 3 January 1821 p. 5.

hundred delegates elected for the Portuguese constituent assembly in 1820 was that of lawyers (39) and professionals (21), with army officers and civil servants representing the second largest groups (16 and 10 respectively), and the final group including medical doctors (6), landowners (5) and tradesmen (3).[59] In the Spanish Cortes of 1820, the first professional group among the elected was that of the ecclesiastics, who represented 27.6 per cent of the total. They were followed by army officers (17 per cent), and immediately afterwards by lawyers (15 per cent) and civil servants (12 per cent). As in Portugal, so too in Spain, landowners and estate managers (9.82 per cent), and then tradesmen and industrialists (4.2 per cent) constituted clear minorities.[60] As in Spain, in Naples the breakdown of the ninety-one deputies elected in 1820 confirms a predominance of clerics (17), followed by lawyers and judges (10 and 11 respectively), and then by military officers and civil servants (8 and 7).[61] In general, therefore, the educated and professional middle classes prevailed, while aristocrats represented a marginal presence in the assemblies of Spain, Portugal and Naples. Compared to the membership of these parliaments, the first Greek national assembly of 1821, made up of fifty-nine individuals, had a much larger share of landowners (20), followed by entrepreneurs—there were sixteen merchants, thirteen of them shipowners—and intellectuals (14). In 1821 only three members of the assembly were military men, yet their share increased significantly in the following two assemblies.[62] In general, therefore, the election of representative assemblies weakened the power of

59. Fernando Piteira Santos, *Geografia e economia da revolução de 1820* (Lisbon: Edições Europa-América, 1962), p. 91.

60. This distribution of professions did not vary enormously after the elections of 1822, which replaced the moderado majority of the previous Cortes with an exaltado one. The percentage of ecclesiastics decreased noticeably, to 17.79 per cent, along with the share of military officers (15.34 per cent), and the percentage of landowners remained stable, while lawyers' share grew to 16.56 per cent of the elected, along that of civil servants (13.5 per cent) and industrialists and tradesmen (9.2 per cent). This substantial homogeneity between the two Cortes of the Trienio shows that the exaltado and moderado political elites came from similar social backgrounds. Their biographies meanwhile show that this was by and large a new political class, as Only thirty-three deputies out of 160 appointed in 1820 (13.6 per cent) had sat in the Cortes elected in 1813 in Cádiz: Casals Bergés, *La representación parlamentaria*, pp. 135–37,150–51; Juan Francisco Fuentes, 'La formación de la clase política del liberalismo español: Análisis de los cargos públicos del Trienio Liberal', *Historia Constitucional* 3 (2002): 1–37.

61. Daum, *Oscillazioni*, p. 163. No record of professional background is available for twenty-six deputies.

62. Nikos Alivizatos, *Το Σύνταγμα και οι εχθροί του στη νεοελληνική ιστορία, 1800–2010* (The constitution and its enemies in modern Greek history, 1800–2010) (Athens: Polis, 2011), pp. 42–48.

the aristocrats. It was only the Portuguese constitution of 1826 that gave them an institutional role as members of the Câmara dos Pares, to which seventy-two aristocrats had been appointed.[63]

Even after the elections, however, the relationship between these national delegates and citizens, or between the local and provincial communities and the parliament could prove controversial. This was firstly because no agreement existed about the degree of autonomy of the delegates. The Cádiz Constitution recognised the full independence and inviolability of people's representatives, whose freedom in deliberating and expressing opinion was guaranteed by Article 128.[64] While many in Naples, and in Portugal likewise, accepted and endorsed this principle, republican concerns regarding the accountability of deliberations led some contemporary observers to question what they considered to be an unchecked delegation of power, and an unqualified autonomy of judgement. Indirect elections did not prevent some observers from demanding close scrutiny of the activities of members of the parliament. Referring to the ideas of Mably and Rousseau, a Neapolitan publicist argued that in order to defend the sovereignty of the nation, prevent any abuse of their role as delegates and sustain civic virtues, it was necessary to establish a tribunal of censorship that would enable ordinary citizens to denounce deputies in breach of their mandate. This project echoed those put forward in 1793 during the French revolution by Condorcet and Hérault de Séchelles, who had endeavoured to provide the people with additional means to censor and monitor the acts of the representative assembly acting on its behalf.[65] Likewise in Spain, the Rousseauian emphasis on the centrality of popular sovereignty entertained by the exaltados led some of them to emphasise the responsibility and accountability of the elected deputies towards the nation, and to stress the fact that they were dependent on it.[66]

63. Lousada and Ferreira, *D. Miguel*, p. 189.

64. See for instance, support for this principle in the Portuguese periodical *Genio Constitucional*, as quoted in Telmo dos Santos Verdelho, *As palavras e as ideias na revolução liberal de 1820* (Coimbra: Instituto Nacional de Investigação Científica, 1981), p. 214, where it is stated that freedom of discussion cannot exist without the perfect inviolability of deputies. For Naples, see Vincenzo Balsamo, *Addizioni del traduttore: Sui deputati*, in Benjamin Constant, *Ragionamento di un elettore con se stesso* (Lecce, 1820), pp. 41–44.

65. Michele Farina Crotoniate, *Della responsabilità de' deputati, ossia Breve osservazione sull'articolo 128 della costituzione delle Spagne* (Naples: Giovanni de Bonis, 1820), pp. 2–3. On these projects, see Pierre Rosanvallon, *La Démocratie inachevée: Histoire de la souveraineté du peuple en France* (Paris: Gallimard, 2000), pp. 61–64, 66–81.

66. Ramón de los Santos García Auñón, *Teoria de una constitución politica para España* (Valencia, 1822), now republished in Ignacio Fernández Sarasola, ed.,

Secondly, there was no agreement as to whether delegates represented first and foremost the nation in its entirety, or the province that had sent them to the parliament, or both at the same time. Although the electoral literature had defined the vote as a patriotic act, the sovereign nation could conversely be seen as the sum of provincial entities or a unit that could not be broken down. In Spain, Naples and Portugal, the interpreters of the constitution tended to be in agreement that members of the Congreso, the Cortes and the Parlamento represented the people's sovereignty in its unitary and indivisible nature.[67] A cornerstone of the theory of representation enshrined in the Spanish and Portuguese constitutions was the notion that deputies were representatives of the entire nation. Acknowledging that individual representatives might act on behalf of a specific province or district would have implied the federalisation of their countries. This interpretation of representation had been advanced at Cádiz in 1812 by some royalist deputies, who considered the nation as an aggregate of kingdoms and provinces, and deputies as their delegates; but this option was then dismissed by the vast majority of the liberals, and the constitution confirmed the idea of a national representation. In Portugal the adoption of this notion entailed the rejection of the proposal to reconstitute the ancient Cortes of the kingdom, a body composed of the three separate estates nobility, clergy and people. This idea had first been proposed by the governadores do reino when confronted by the revolution on 1 September 1820. However, while this idea continued to have some supporters, the majority of members of the revolutionary Junta das Cortes, set up to decide the rules for the election of a constituent assembly, favoured the creation of a national representation based on the idea of the sovereignty of the nation as a sum of all its individuals, and not of separate groups, a principle that would also be recognised by the 1822 constitution.[68] In Spain, the idea of deputies being representative of the provinces sometimes emerged only in the penultimate stage of the electoral process. When addressing the *electores de partido*, local priests occasionally claimed that it was imperative to appoint appropriate deputies

Constituciones en la sombra: Proyectos constitucionales españoles (1809–1823) (Oviedo: Universidad de Oviedo, 2014), pp. 267–451; see esp. p. 291.

67. On Spain and Naples, see Jens Späth, 'Promotori del liberalismo: I parlamenti del regno di Spagna e del Regno delle Due Sicilie, 1820–1823', *Rivista Storica Italiana* 130, no. 2 (2018): 615–38.

68. Joaquín Varela Suanzes-Carpegna, 'Nació, representació i articulació territorial de l'Estat a les Corts de Cadis', *Afers* 68 (2011): 47–70. On the Portuguese debates, see Isabel Nobre Vargues, *A aprendizagem da cidadania em Portugal (1820–1823)* (Coimbra: Livraria Minerva Editora, 1997), pp. 116–28.

to represent the interests of both the fatherland and the province.[69] But once elected, they were first and foremost described as national figures. The Sociedad Patriótica Mallorquina extolled the wisdom of the *electores de partido* in choosing representatives of the province noteworthy for their patriotic virtues.[70]

This notion that delegates were national figures was one replicated by the revolutionary presses. National elections produced a pantheon of exceptional individuals who represented the best talents of their countries, and reconciled public with private virtues. In the words of a Neapolitan journalist, deputies like Cardinal Firpo showed that a priest could also be a good citizen; the young Tito Berni was equipped with a patriotic soul and a morality 'worthy of the times of the patriarchs'; and Francesco Lauria was a sincere friend, outstanding patriarch and brilliant lawyer who would undoubtedly defend the rights of citizens in the parliament.[71] In Spain, for instance, the Sociedad Patriótica Mallorquina published a eulogy of the three deputies elected in 1820 in its periodical, praising their impeccable political trajectory as army officers, former members of the Cortes of 1813 and former member of the Holy Inquisition converted early on to the principles of the constitution.[72] For a Portuguese journalist, the newly elected deputies of the constituent Cortes, comprising the best individuals from all classes chosen from each province, stood in stark contrast to those 'lying favourites (*validos*), insatiable parasites, courtly sycophants and adulatory ministers full of ignorance' that had surrounded the king and prevented him from listening to his people.[73] Such patriotic credentials were reaffirmed even when these pantheons were the target of irony and criticism.[74]

Nonetheless, in the 1820s the idea persisted among voters and local elites that representation in national assemblies was the representation of

69. Hortal, *Discurso*, pp. 21, 22.

70. *Sociedad Patriótica Mallorquina*, no. 1, 25 May 1820, p. 1.

71. *La Voce del Popolo*, Naples, September 1820, pp. 85–90, 111–15, quotations at 88, 114.

72. 'Un ciudadano de la Sociedad con motivo dela acertàda eleccion de diputados en Córtes, pronunció el siguiente discurso', *Sociedad Patriótica Mallorquina*, no. 2, 28 May 1820, pp. 5–6.

73. *O Liberal*, 3 January 1821, no. 14, p. 1.

74. Sebastián Miñano y Bedoya, *Condiciones y semblanzas de los diputados a Cortes para los años de 1822 y 1823* (Madrid: D. Juan Ramos y Compañía, 1821); Miñano y Bedoya, *Condiciones y semblanzas de los Sres. diputados a Cortes para los años de 1822 y 1823* (Madrid: Imprenta del Zurriago de don M. R. y Cerro, 1822); see the response to the former by Bartolomé José Gallardo in his *Impugnacion joco-seria al folleto titulado Condiciones y semblanzas de los Diputados a Cortes para la legislatura de 1820 y 1821* (Madrid: Librería de Paz, 1821).

a sum of local interests, or that delegates represented at one and the same time the province and the nation. In Greece in particular, the notion of national representation was ambiguously conflated with the idea that deputies were elected to represent their territories. The survival of this interpretation reflects well the nature of the nation building process, which relied on the coming together of localities and regions that had enjoyed extensive autonomy under the umbrella of Ottoman administration. The first national assembly gathering at Epidavros in December 1821 was made up of—mostly unelected—delegates from western Greece, eastern Greece, the Peloponnese and the islands, selected according to very varying procedures to represent these different regions. The delegates from eastern Greece were partly sent by its individual eparchies, and partly directly appointed by its assembly, the Areios Pagos.[75] But a territorial understanding of representation persisted at a later stage of the revolution, once electoral procedures had been put in place. In 1823, soon after the elections, the administration of the island of Hydra, for instance, authorised the deputies taking up their seats in the national assembly 'to represent our island in the second term of the high administration of Greece', expecting at the same time that they would sacrifice their own private interests for those of Greece.[76] In announcing the results of the election by the population of their island, the authorities on Santorini declared that their 'plenipotentiaries' had full authorisation 'to speak and act according to what they think is in the interest of our *patrida*'. What they meant by *patrida*, or fatherland, was made clear when they invited the high administration 'to listen to our plenipotentiaries, because they are the face of our community, the voice of all the residents'.[77] Four years later, most of the deputies elected at the assembly of Aegina, as contemporaries observed, still considered themselves representatives exclusively of their *patrida* of origin, rather than of the whole of Greece.[78]

An even more overtly fragmented notion of sovereignty and representation underpinned the election of representatives in revolutionary Sicily. The decision to create an assembly of delegates representing districts in the capital city of Palermo reflected an understanding of freedom in local

75. Among the Aegean islands, only Spetses, Hydra, Psara, Kassos and Skopelos elected delegates. The other territories selected delegates without resorting to elections: Trikoupis, Ιστορία (History), 2, pp. 100–19. See also Sotiropoulos, '"United we stand"'.

76. The primates of Hydra to the provisional government, 5 and 28 May 1823, in Lignos, Αρχείον (Archive), 9, pp. 171, 195–96.

77. The primates and demogerontes of Santorini to the primates of Hydra, 10 July 1823, in Lignos, Αρχείον (Archive), 9, pp. 266–67.

78. Kasomoulis, Ενθυμήματα στρατιωτικά (Military memoirs), 2, p. 673.

terms. But even this federal notion of representation may not have met all the expectations of the towns supporting the anti-Neapolitan stance of Palermo, whose idea of the Sicilian nation seemed to be that of a congeries of smaller territories. In fact, some towns would have preferred direct representation for each individual village in the Sicilian assembly, rather than one mediated through the process of districts selecting a number of deputies chosen from among those sent by all the communes within its jurisdiction. The giunta of the town of Gibellina wrote to the government in Palermo to advocate a system of communal representation that, once the Cádiz Constitution had been introduced, would not exclude any village. Similar concerns were raised by other towns, Poggioreale among them. Palermo did not ignore these views, or the fact that support for it depended on the recognition of local freedoms. It is significant that from August 1820, the decrees of the provisional government of Palermo were signed in the name of the giunta 'together with the representatives of the communes of the kingdom'.[79]

The election of national representatives therefore made a significant contribution towards realisation of the idea that citizens belonged to a broader national community, but it did not weaken the importance of local communities. This was for two reasons. First, the widespread use of indirect electoral systems had turned these communities into the constitutive elements of the nation. Second, the conflicts surrounding electoral procedures in towns and districts, and the interference of government authorities, reinforced an understanding of voting as a practice in defence of local interests. In the end even national delegates could be seen as representatives of provincial interests. As the next chapter will demonstrate, local communities and individuals petitioned revolutionary governments in the name of the constitution both in defence of their own localities and on behalf of the nation. They did so also to defend professional and community privileges, as well as individual rights, combining these in different and even unexpected ways, but always in the name of the constitution.

79. ASP, Real Segreteria, Incartamenti, 5035: decrees published from late August 1820.

CHAPTER EIGHT

Petitioning in the Name
of the Constitution

THE RIGHT TO APPEAL directly to constitutional authorities through petitions was central to the way in which citizenship was understood during the revolutions. Indeed, the practice of petitioning did much to shape the way in which constitutions were understood, and to legitimise revolutionary institutions. Revolutionaries considered petitioning to be an act of popular sovereignty exercised by individuals and communities alike. A Sicilian revolutionary newspaper, for instance, referred to the right to petition, along with that of the vote, as a political right that benefited both the individual and the entire community.[1] As such, it represented one of the ways in which politics was carried out publicly. Contemporaries viewed it as a vehicle for public opinion to express itself, and treated it as integral to the right to freedom of expression. They saw it as an additional way of expressing the will of the people. For a Neapolitan newspaper, the right to petition was to be considered sacred under a representative government, and the ability to influence governmental decisions through this almost unlimited right could be considered 'the popular element of present society', and 'a very powerful means to achieve peace, harmony, and public order'.[2]

Petitioning was not a novel political practice. In fact, it was common in ancien-régime societies, and its use had proliferated and intensified since the latter part of the eighteenth century, throughout southern Europe. Submitting petitions to the monarch represented an important vehicle

1. *Il Corrispondente Costituzionale*, 26 August 1820, p. 3.
2. *La Voce del Popolo*, Naples, December 1820, pp. 305–11, quotations at 308, 311.

of communication for peripheries and localities subjected to increasing interference from the state and central authorities, and provided opportunities for protest and the submitting of complaints. Ancien-régime protests or riots were also understood as forms of petitioning. In Spain, for instance, food riots were accompanied by specific requests for intervention on the part of the city councils. A frequent subject of petitions was taxation, whose existence was accepted but whose fairness was the subject of contention. Petitions might also demand material benefits. Communities used petitions more frequently in exceptional circumstances, when calamities or emergencies required the intervention of governments: in the case of famines or earthquakes, for example. They provided opportunities for marginalised social groups to take centre stage, or to communicate to the central authorities grievances between different communities. Supplicants could call for clemency or the redress of a grievance in the name of mercy or justice.[3] In eighteenth-century Portugal professional corporations, represented by the juíz do povo, as well as rural communities, regularly submitted *representações* to the authorities relating to the protection of their privileges. In the Ottoman Empire, this practice had likewise existed well before the Greek revolution. The practice of petitioning, known as *şikayet*, enabled any subject of the empire, including the Christian populations, women and slaves, to address the sultan, the grand vizier or the kapudan pasha, but also provincial governors and vice-governors, who might be called upon to judge their complaints instead of local tribunals. Governors and their *diwan* (council) issued decrees in response to each of the requests they received.[4] Unlike petitions written during the constitutional period, these ancien-régime documents were private. What the Napoleonic regimes established in the regions of southern Europe did was to turn this into a public practice, but also to manipulate it so as to justify in the name of the people the establishment of its new regimes, and to demand mass displays of loyalty and submission. In January 1809 twenty-five

3. Domenico Cecere, 'Scritture del disastro e istanze di riforma nel regno di Napoli (1783): Alle origini delle politiche dell'emergenza', *Studi Storici* 58 (2017): 187–214; Cercere, 'Suppliche, resistenze, protesta popolare: Le forme della lotta politica nella Calabria del settecento', *Quaderni Storici* NS 46, no. 138 (2011): 765–96; Costanza D'Elia, 'Supplicanti e vandali: Testi scritti, testi non scritti, testi scritti dagli storici', *Quaderni Storici* NS 31, no. 92 (1996): 459–85.

4. Michael Ursinus, *Grievance Administration (şikayet) in an Ottoman Province: The Kaymakam of Roumelia's 'Record Book of Complaints' of 1781–1783* (London: Routledge-Curzon, 2005).

thousand inhabitants of Madrid signed petitions in recognition of Joseph Bonaparte as the new king of Spain.[5]

The petitioning movement of the 1820s marked a new phase in the history of the practice, in terms both of its unprecedented scale, and of a change in its nature. In Naples, Spain and Portugal the right to petition was guaranteed by the constitutions. The Cádiz Constitution of did not explicitly mention the right to petition. Article 373, however, guaranteed the citizens' right to denounce to the king and the Cortes infringements to the constitution by authorities, assigning to the Cortes the duty of intervening to redress the abuse and prosecute culprits. During the Trienio this right was interpreted in the broadest possible way, as legitimising all sorts of complaints and requests in the name of the safeguarding of the constitution.[6] In Greece, likewise, the constitution of Astros in 1823 explicitly required the legislative body to examine all petitions received and to submit them to the relevant institutions. The Constitution of Troezena in 1827 then confirmed that it was the senate's duty to accept and respond to citizens' petitions. Mavrokordatos considered petitions an important tool to connect the territories of the state to the newly established central administration.[7]

This new political and legal context changed the meaning of this practice, even when petitions were sent, as often still happened, to the king or to regional or local leaders, as these documents were now drafted in the name of the new constitutional order. They were addressing individuals whose authority was based on new sources of legitimacy, and these documents reflected those important shifts. The practice of combining messages of congratulation to new monarchs, on special occasions such as weddings and births, with requests from local communities was either retained with a new meaning (as they now addressed constitutional monarchs), or transferred to mark the establishment of the revolutionary assemblies and the introduction of the constitution. The spontaneity of

5. Diego Palacios Cerezales, 'Re-imagining Petitioning in Spain (1808–1823)', *Social Science History* 43, no. 3 (2019): 487–508 at p. 11.

6. Marta Lorente Sariñena, *Las infracciones a la Constitución de 1812* (Madrid: Centro de Estudios Constitucionales, 1988), pp. 29–39. For the case of Naples, see Dario Marino, 'La "nostra politica rigenerazione": Petizioni e rivoluzione nel Regno delle Due Sicilie (1820–21)', unpublished doctoral dissertation, University of Salerno, 2022, p. 44.

7. *Constitution, loix, ordonnances*, pp. 74, 181. In 1824, in an assembly of all the eparchs and kapetanaioi of western Greece, he asked them to submit individual and group petitions regarding the public good from their territories to the assembly: Millingen, *Memoirs*, p. 221.

these developments signalled a growing desire for political participation on the part both of individuals and of communities and patriotic associations, and in turn provided a powerful legitimacy for the constitutional order and its institutions. Petitioning was part and parcel of the political mobilisation and the public demonstrations that exploded during the revolutionary period. In general, during the revolutions, petitions were no longer private documents, but public interventions in the political sphere that could be published in the press, and whose discussion in the parliamentary assemblies was made available in official documents. Petitions could also, as in the past, be used to convey professional and economic grievances, but these too were now formulated in new ways and with reference to the new language of constitutionalism. The following pages will explore both the petitions sent by citizens and communities to support and defend the constitution and those submitted to communicate narrower—and often long-standing—professional and economic grievances in a new institutional framework.

Depending on the circumstances in which they were produced, petitions in favour of the constitution by towns and groups of citizens had different purposes and were the outcomes of different circumstances. At the beginning of the revolution, petitions could be used to put pressure on authorities and convince them to accept the constitution. In 1820 on the island of Madeira, when its governor hesitated to rally to the revolution that had started in Porto and then conquered Lisbon, 120 citizens signed a petition addressed to him and delivered by five individuals accompanied by a large crowd gathering in the square.[8]

Soon after the outbreak of the revolutions, petitions also signalled support for the new political regime. In Naples, a wave of *felicitazioni* (congratulations) from villages and local communities was addressed to the parliament in support of this new institution. These petitions were acts of solidarity with the constitution (whether spontaneous or solicited by the new government) that show how it was understood in the smallest and most remote communities of the kingdom. They often contained references to the fact that Europe would be full of admiration for the regeneration of the kingdom resulting from the revolution, and that a new era

8. Sebastião José Xavier Botelho, *Historia verdadeira dos acontecimentos da ilha da Madeira depois do memoravel dia 28 de Janeiro* (Lisbon: António Rodrigues Galhardo, 1821), pp. 16–17; quoted in Diego Palacios Cerezales, 'Embodying Public Opinion: From Petitions to Mass Meetings in Nineteenth-Century Portugal', *E-Journal of Portuguese History* 9, no. 1 (2011): 1–19, http://www.brown.edu/Departments/Portuguese_Brazilian _Studies/ejph/html/Summer11.html (accessed 14 August 2022) at p. 4.

of happiness was starting with the introduction of the constitution. In their address to the parliament, the authorities of the town of Colosimi in Calabria Citra stated that liberty was now flourishing again as it had done in the ancient republics, and that all countries envied the constitution of Naples. The city of Altamura in the province of Bari welcomed the new constitution as the 'most liberal [ever known with] a democratic-monarchical government'. The town of Molfetta proclaimed that the Neapolitans had been virtuous to ask for a 'liberal government that, by destroying any arbitrary power, and returning its sovereignty to the people, inaugurates an era of happiness for the nation'.[9]

During the revolutions, however, petitions in support of the constitution took on more explicitly defensive and militant overtones: they were associated with public mobilisation against perceived threats to its survival and became expressions of the political conflicts dividing revolutionaries. This is true in particular in the case of Spain, where conflicts between moderados and exaltados, the outbreak of the civil war and the hostility of the monarch raised permanent concerns about the very survival of the constitution. Every time town councils, sociedades patrióticas and militias felt that the constitution was under threat from internal or external enemies, their first act was to submit, either to the monarch or to the Cortes, a petition raising specific complaints, concerns or requests. In these circumstances, therefore, petitions served also the purpose of imposing vetoes or acting as judicial pronouncements. A recurrent request included in petitions was to keep the Cortes in permanent session in order to defend the constitution. For instance, in May 1821 dozens of ayuntamientos wrote petitions to the monarch asking him to use his constitutional right to turn the current Cortes into *cortes extraordinarias*, such that they would function until their next election, thus forestalling any interruption to their activities.

Although these petitions stressed the antiquity of the practice of addressing the monarch in cases of emergency, the alcaldes and regidores of the individual towns who signed them invoked the will of the people to justify their request to keep the Cortes functioning in defence of the fatherland against its internal and external enemies (the recent Austrian invasion of Naples often being cited). While addressing the monarch, the signatories to these documents nevertheless referred explicitly to the new foundations that legitimised his power, adopting a theme that had been

9. ASN, Polizia Generale II, f. 34: addresses dated respectively 15, 20 and 24 November 1820.

used to justify the pronunciamiento by Rafael Riego in his public proclamations in 1820. These petitions reminded Fernando that despotism had
been irremediably defeated, and that the contribution of the people to
the salvation of the monarchy during the Napoleonic invasion needed to be
rewarded now by acknowledging popular sovereignty and respecting the
prerogatives of the parliament.[10]

A new and even more substantial wave of petitions was unleashed in
the wake of public protests that exploded in most Spanish cities at the end
of the same year, when the dismissal of Riego from the captaincy-general
of Zaragoza, the appointment of a number of counterrevolutionary generals and jefes políticos and the removal of exaltados from positions of
power across the country was taken as a sign that the revolution was under
threat. Between October and December 1821 petitions from Cádiz, Seville,
La Coruña, Cartagena and many other cities were sent to the monarch
or the Cortes by the ayuntamientos to challenge such decisions. Listing
all the acts that were undermining the constitutional regime, these documents called for the ousting of the military leaders and the resignation of
the government. Signed by local authorities and local militias, they were
written in conjunction with public protests and meetings organised to put
pressure on local authorities to respond to the population's grievances.
In some cases, such petitions were followed by direct—whether peaceful
or violent—interventions in the public life of the communities involved.
Events in Cádiz are a case in point. The population of this city responded
to the governmental appointment of a new military leader for the city, the
Baron de Andilla, chosen despite widespread opposition there, with mass
mobilisation. In mid-November large crowds gathered in the Plaza de la
Constitución, summoned the local administration, read out a petition that
confirmed the signatories' refusal to accept Andilla's appointment, and to
recognise the authority of the current ministry until a new government
might be appointed. The local regiments passed on the request to the
Andilla, who as a consequence did not enter the city.[11] These local conflicts
over appointments could sometimes mobilise large numbers of citizens.
In February 1822 the removal of the leader of the national militia in Barcelona resulted in a petition submitted to the Cortes in his defence that

10. Forty-five petitions from towns to the monarch are held in AAM, Secretaría, Acontecimientos Políticos, 2–230, no. 7.

11. Guillaume de Vaudoncourt, *Letters on the Internal Political State of Spain during
the Years 1821, 22 and 23* (London: Lupton Relfe, 1824), pp. 76–78, 85–87; *Examen critique
des révolutions d'Espagne, de 1820 à 1823 et de 1836*, 2 vols (Paris, 1837), 1, pp. 98–101,
104–6.

was signed by three thousand citizens.[12] After the failed anti-revolutionary military coup of July 1822, suspicions that the king had colluded with the insurgents were made public and resulted in yet more petitions and public demonstrations. In these circumstances petitioning became a tool directly and explicitly to rebuke the monarch. The national militia of Irún in the Basque country wrote to King Fernando warning him that resisting change was dangerous, as people would resort to excessive measures, and reminding him that princes without the support of the people were intrinsically weak. The militia asked the monarch publicly to declare his allegiance to the constitution, and to summon the Cortes immediately.[13]

While women presumably also took part in these public demonstrations, the documents discussed thus far were signed exclusively by male citizens, or generically by communities whose leaders were men. However, there is some evidence that petitions could be a tool for women to express citizenship rights and participate in the new political space provided by the constitution. Although they represent a tiny minority compared to the mass of documents signed by men, these documents evince a desire by women to lend their support to the revolution in their own right.[14] In Spain the political activism of liberal women coincided with the public defence of the constitution and the wave of petitions submitted in its defence after the failed counterrevolutionary coup of 7 July 1822.[15] In its aftermath eighty 'women citizens' from the city of Logroño addressed the monarch, calling upon him to protect the constitutional government against its enemies. Likewise the defence of the constitution was taken on by the Junta Patriótica de Señoras, a patriotic society set up in the spring of 1821. Its members, launching a public subscription publicised also by the *Diario de Madrid*, decided to collect money in support of the national militia that had defended the constitution against the attempted coup of 7 July 1822. The 101 signatories included the president of the junta, Vicenta Oliete, who was the housekeeper of the exaltado politician Juan Romero Alpuente, its secretary, and Isidra Minutria, the widow of Manuel Losada y Quiroga, an important protagonist in the intellectual life of the Madrid. The petition was addressed, significantly enough, to

12. CD, legajo 44, no. 200. On these events, see Vernet, *La Barcelona revolucionària*, pp. 123–38.

13. Reproduced in Llanos Aramburu, *El Trienio Liberal*, pp. 390–91.

14. On Portugal, see Diego Palacios Cerezales, '"Assinem assinem, que a alma não tem sexo!": Petição coletiva e cidadania feminina no Portugal constitucional (1820–1910)', *Análise Social* 205, no. 4 (2012), pp. 740–65.

15. Juan Francisco Fuentes and Pilar Garí, *Amazonas de la libertad: Mujeres liberales contra Fernando VII* (Madrid: Marcial Pons, 2014), pp. 82–87.

the queen, an explicitly gender-specific gesture, although the signatories praised the king's own alleged devotion to the constitution. The king's spouse responded by endorsing the subscription and by adding her own contribution.[16]

In Portugal too, one of the first public acts by the câmaras after the revolution was to submit to the monarch acclamations in its support. This often happened in association with public ceremonies organised to swear an oath to the constitution.[17] As in Spain, attempts to overthrow constitutional government account for an even larger and more spontaneous mobilisation by communities and citizens. A wave of public demonstrations that produced petitions in support of the constitution followed the defeat of Count of Amarante's royalist insurrection in the province of Trás-os-Montes in March 1823. More than a hundred câmaras, along with a number of military regiments and patriotic societies, reacted to this pronunciamiento by voting and submitting documents of condemnation of the revolt to the king. What is remarkable about these displays of loyalty to the constitution is precisely the fact that they took place just two months before the end of the Triénio, demonstrating that in spite of the erosion of its popularity, the regime still enjoyed considerable support. All these *autos de aclamação* shared a similar language. They were always addressed to, and took the form of expressions of loyalty to Dom João VI, who was, however, almost always explicitly defined as constitutional king. They also stressed the binding nature of the oath sworn to the constitution, or 'the constitutional system', or 'the sacred constitutional code', which had been broken by Amarante. Their approval was accompanied by hurrahs for religion, the constitution, the Cortes and the constitutional king.[18] The *auto* approved by the câmara of Figueira da Foz contained an explicit reference to the fact that Amarante had wanted to reintroduce slavery to Portugal by withdrawing the rights and freedoms guaranteed by the constitution.[19] The approval of such petitions was often accompanied by their public reading and official celebrations. In Figueira da Foz, for instance, the petition in support of the constitution was read out in all parish churches. In the town of Moura this act of support was first approved and read out in the câmara in the presence of all the civil, military and religious authorities, and then read out again in the public arena following a parade through the mains streets of the town, whose

16. APR, Papeles Reservados de Fernando VII, 23, ff. 130ff.

17. ANTT, Ministério do Reino, Autos de Aclamação, maço 7.

18. Ibid., maço 33, nos 5940, 5945 and 5950.

19. Ibid., no. 5967.

houses had been decorated. Abundant rain and hail did not discourage the crowds from attending the reading of the petition.[20] Although much more rarely than in Spain, in Portugal too petitions could be used as direct acts of political intervention to censor governmental decisions deemed a threat to the constitution. Evidence of this is only available, however, for the second constitutional period, from 1826 to 1828. Thus in 1826 protests in Lisbon and Porto over the resignation of the liberal General Saldanha resulted in a public demonstration in which petitions in his favour and more broadly in defence of the constitution were addressed to the regent Dona Isabel Maria by the crowds and by the juíz do povo.[21]

It was precisely the popular mobilisation and even violent protests associated with this practice that led most revolutionary authorities to place restrictions upon its use. Petitions were a resource for the constitutional governments, but could also be seen as a threat, the fear being that they could undermine the formal decision-making process and enable local communities or opposition groups to question governmental authority. In Portugal the petitions against the resignation of General Saldanha from the Ministry of War led to claims that this constituted an illegal interference in governmental decisions.[22] The 1826 constitution guaranteed the right of any citizen to submit petitions to the legislative or executive and recognised as legitimate their use to denounce infringements to the constitution. However, the more restrictive interpretation of popular sovereignty underpinning this second constitution encouraged its supporters to view popular mobilisation with more suspicion than ever.[23] In Spain, the right to petition became one of the bones of contention between moderados and exaltados. For the latter, petitions were part and parcel of the exercise of popular sovereignty. They represented an important instrument to denounce threats to the constitution and to put pressure on the Cortes in the name of public opinion. But the moderados considered a constant and systematic use of these public representations to be an abuse of power, a threat to the institutions and the state, rather than a legitimate vector for the exercise of popular sovereignty. As a consequence, in February 1822 restrictions were introduced to make collective petitions from

20. Ibid., no. 5948.

21. Santos, *Documentos*, 3, pp. 817, 824, 829.

22. Ibid., pp. 817, 824, 829; Palacios Cerezales, 'Embodying Public Opinion', p. 5.

23. *Carta constitucional da monarchia portugueza* (Lisbon: Impressão Regia: 1826), p. 62; for a version in French, *Charte constitutionnelle pour le royaume de Portugal: Algarves et leurs dépendances*, Titre VIII, Artt. 145–28, in Édouard La Ferrière, *Les Constitutions d'Europe et d'Amérique* (Paris: Cotillon, 1869), p. 509.

specific bodies or associations illegal, as well as petitions in the name of the people. This decision was designed to thwart undue interference from the sociedades patrióticas and the militias, and to curb the influence and the subversive potential of the exaltados and their social base.[24] Similar concerns led the Neapolitan Giunta Provvisoria di Governo, appointed after the revolution and dominated by the Muratists—civil servants who had served and supported the Napoleonic regime in Naples—to allow only petitions signed by no more than three people, and make public gatherings to influence public authorities illegal.[25]

The practice of petitioning and reactions to it are therefore revealing of the way in which relations between centre and periphery, between the state, localities and citizens, were being renegotiated and reshaped in this period. The petitions analysed so far confirm the extent to which local communities on the Iberian peninsula gave explicit support to the constitution and saw themselves as the temporary repository of a national sovereignty threatened by governments or by external enemies. As discussed in chapter six above, while Spanish and Portuguese cities, villages or revolutionary organisations considered themselves as the foremost defenders of the general interest, in Naples towns and villages used petitions also to lay claim to a central role in the architecture of the new constitutional state. A substantial percentage of the petitions addressed to the Neapolitan parliament came from villages lamenting the loss of autonomy resulting from the introduction of the French system of the intendenze that enabled decisions to be taken by centrally appointed officials akin to the French prefects, and the reorganisation of the judicial system that had deprived villages of their traditional tribunals. In Greece too, local communities occasionally adopted petitions as a means of defending their autonomy from central authorities. Often governmental representatives themselves were the object of complaints by villages. In September 1823 the national authorities decided to remove the eparch of the island of Santorini from his post following petitions from three plenipotentiaries appointed for this specific purpose, who denounced to the legislative assembly the eparch's abuse of his powers as borne out by his 'collecting more taxes, imprisoning

24. See 'Decreto LXVIII' of 12 February 1822, law prescribing the just limits of the right of petition; original available at http://legishca.edu.umh.es/1822/02/12/ (accessed 14 August 2022).

25. Alberti, *Atti del parlamento*, 1, p. lii; Nino Cortese in Colletta, *Storia del reame*, 3, p. 186.

innocent men, forcing people to purchase bonds and indulging at the same time in excessive personal expenditure'.[26]

However, in most cases Greek local communities did not see their own interest as being incompatible with the recognition of the national administration. As a result, petitions represented an important tool of communication between centre and periphery. They provided opportunities for local communities to ask for the protection of the central administration in the face of the proliferation of violence, lawlessness and civil strife occasioned by the war against the Ottomans, and for local authorities to obtain legitimation from the centre. They demonstrate the recognition and legitimacy that communities accorded the new state, owing to the impact of these events at the local level, and they highlight the extent to which complaints from the peripheries were being taken seriously by the national governments. They also reflect tensions unleashed by the revolution between different social groups. In the Peloponnese, it was the rebellion of the military class against the *kotzabasides*, the local notables who had traditionally held administrative power under the Ottomans. Given the state of lawlessness in the Peloponnese resulting from the rebellion of the kapetanaioi against the representatives appointed by the central government, villages addressed the central authorities to request protection. The inhabitants of the eparchy of Vlacho complained to Governor-General Mavrokordatos, asking him to intervene to re-establish order in the face of the looting and depredations carried out by a local kapos.[27] While mainland communities complained about the impact of independent warlords, the islands lamented the predatoriness of piracy, a phenomenon on the increase in some areas of the Aegean due to the lawlessness produced by the war at sea. The inhabitants of the island of Karpathos, for instance, petitioned the legislative assembly to ask for protection against pirates from the Sporades who had settled on their territory and imposed their authority over them. By so doing, the pirates were taking control of the local administrative structures and challenging the authority of the central state on the island.[28] The displacement of populations into the territories

26. Plenipotentiaries of the Three Islands to the Legislature, 12 September 1823, in Lignos, Αρχείον (Archive), 9, pp. 432–34.

27. Letter signed by 'the inhabitants of the prefecture of Vlachó', with no date, in Millingen, *Memoirs*, p. 181.

28. The petition, dated 10 December 1827, is addressed to the legislative body. It is quoted in Dimitris Dimitropoulos, 'Πειρατές στη στεριά; Πρόσφυγες, καταδρομείς και καθημερινότητα των παράκτιων οικισμών στα χρόνια του Αγώνα' (Pirates ashore? Refugees, irregulars and everyday life in coastal areas during the War of independence), in Όψεις της

controlled by the revolutionaries fuelled demands for protection by the central administration. Refugees fleeing from their provinces of origin to safer places addressed the government to complain about the treatment meted out to them by the communities that had received them. They petitioned the government at the same time to obtain military support and to be exempted from paying taxes, given the dramatic circumstances of the war, but asked for this as a temporary measure only.[29]

Since the territorial organisation of a state bureaucracy was also serving military purposes, and the war had a considerable impact on local life, it is hardly surprising that petitions were sent to military authorities as well. What is perhaps more striking and worth noting is the fact that, as the petitions demonstrate, local communities were willing to recognise national military authorities in order not to have to take orders from, and give exclusive allegiance to, regional chieftains. In 1827 several villages petitioned the head of the national army, General Church (see chapter five above), to complain about unreasonable demands placed upon them to provide the army with foodstuffs, ammunition and livestock, at the expense of the wellbeing of their own communities.[30] They also reported the tyrannical behaviour of local military leaders who had unfairly imposed taxation, looted towns and burned down properties. Petitions, signed by both village leaders (demogerontes) and ordinary citizens, revealed clashes between military leaders as well as between local civil and religious authorities.[31]

Besides conflicts between military and civil authorities, or between different political groups competing to be recognised by the centre, petitions reveal also the existence of incompatible economic and professional interests within local communities. By petitioning parliaments, different social and professional groups articulated their own peculiar interpretations of what the constitution stood for in relation to their own grievances. In Naples, Spain and Portugal, a high proportion of petitions emanating

---

Ελληνικῆς Ἐπανάστασης του 1821: Πρακτικά συνεδρίου, Αθήνα 12 και 13 Ιουνίου 2015 (Aspects of the Greek Revolution of 1821: Proceedings of a conference, Athens, 12 and 13 June 2015), ed. Dimitris Dimitropoulos, Christos Loukos and Panagiotis Michailaris (Athens: EMNE, 2018), pp. 87–105.

29. GSA, Administrative Committee, file 174, no. 73: refugees from Thiva in Salamina, n.d.; ibid., file 183, nos 1 and 24: Salonite refugees in Loutraki, 28 May and 4 July 1826.

30. BL, Church Papers, respectively in Add MS 35545, f. 138, demogerontes of Vostitsa to Church, 1827; ibid., f. 152, inhabitants of the eparchies of Salona and Arahova to Church, 4 May 1827; Add MS 35546, f. 175, inhabitants of Divri to Church.

31. BL, Church Papers, 35546, f. 46, commission of province of Mistra to General Church, 24 August 1827.

from villages addressed conflicts existing between local communities and feudal landowners, whether aristocratic families or clerical institutions such as monasteries, about whether lands belonged to the community or to the lord. In Spain and Naples these conflicts had been exacerbated by anti-feudal legislation introduced in the first decade of the nineteenth century, which abolished seigneurial privileges and recognised private property only, forcing landowners and communities to prove their entitlement to lands they claimed to own.[32]

Thus while some of these conflicts were not new, the constitution provided opportunities to frame them in a new language. Petitioners wanted to be heard, either to veto the dismantling of certain privileges, or to support it. For local communities, the constitution represented a tool to protect communal rights against aristocratic abuses. A minority of petitions favoured also the privatisation of common lands, and therefore appealed to the principle of private property as a constitutional right. In Spain, petitions denouncing the outcome of elections at the municipal level were often expressive of a conflict between the supporters of the local holder of seigneurial rights, who before the electoral reform had been able to control councils, and their middle-class enemies. While denouncing electoral fraud, petitions denounced also usurpations of communal lands by feudal lords, or included complaints by leaseholders.[33] Likewise, villages in the Kingdom of the Two Sicilies petitioned the parliament and denounced the illegitimate appropriation of common land by local aristocrats, and often referred back to the anti-feudal decrees of 1808, which had ordered the division of property between villagers and their former lords, in support of their demands.[34] The citizens of di Corleto in Basilicata, for instance, denounced the usurpation of their grazing rights by Duke Riaro.[35] The village of Castelpagano near Benevento asked the parliament to reinstate them in the *diritti civici* (communal rights) usurped by the 'feudal aristocracy' that was illegally treating communal lands as its own. Municipalities meanwhile demanded that church properties be sold and divided into small allotments for the sake of the benefits that the distribution of private property would bring to the community.[36] Property rights were

32. Hamnett, *La politica española*, pp. 151–59; Davis, *Naples and Napoleon*, pp. 234–40.

33. Castro, *La revolución liberal*, pp. 104–13.

34. Davis, *Naples and Napoleon*, pp. 236–37. On these types of petitions see Marino, 'La "nostra politica rigenerazione"', pp. 280–299.

35. ASN, Polizia Generale II, f. 40: Nicola Lapenta to the members of parliament, 3 January 1821.

36. Ibid., 43, letter signed by 11 villagers of Castelpagano, 19 December 1820.

therefore interpreted and understood in different ways in these petitions: sometimes as an individual right, sometimes as a collective right and a community privilege. As a consequence, petitioners referred to the constitution for conflicting purposes and with reference to diametrically opposed principles.

Unlike Spain and Naples, Portugal before 1820 had not reformed its feudal legislation. In 1820 some individual privileges and dues known as *direitos banais* (related to the milling of grain, and production of bread and wine) and various forms of taxation guaranteed by charters and known collectively as *forais* were still in existence. These were partly abolished during the revolution in 1821 and in 1822. Similarly to their Neapolitan and Spanish counterparts, however, petitions emanating from the Portuguese countryside appealed to the constitution both in the name of the private property of individuals and to defend communal rights, or simply to lament the excessive weight of the *forais*. Out of the 213 surviving petitions sent to the Congresso's commission for agriculture by câmaras, groups of villagers or single individuals, thirty concerned village common lands (*baldios*), and most of them denounced abuses by local landholders with seigneurial rights.[37] In 1821 the *câmara constitucional* of Bemposta, in the province of Beira Baixa, expressed its hostility to the complete abolition of common lands or *pastos comuns*, arguing that the *Bases da constituição* did not sanction the right of property in an absolute fashion.[38] In other cases, however, individuals wrote in favour of their privatisation, also invoking the constitution. For instance, two relatives from the villages of Meimoa and Benquerença, in the same province of Beira Baixa, submitted a petition attacking the system of *pastos comuns* and asking for the recognition of their individual rights of property over the land cultivated by them, given that the 'bases of the constitution guarantee full property and its effects'.[39]

Conflicting interpretations of the rights protected by the constitution did not exclusively pertain to the world of landed property in feudal and post-feudal societies. Tensions in relation to commercial interests also gave rise to competing understandings of what principles the constitution stood for. The petitions sent to the Portuguese Cortes by artisans

37. Albert Silbert, *Le Problème agraire portugais au temps des premières cortes libérales (1821–1823)* (Paris: Fondation Calouste Gulbenkian, 1985).

38. Ibid., pp. 235–37. On the importance of common lands in the region, see Silbert, *Le Portugal méditerranéen à la fin de l'ancien régime: XVIIIe siècle–début du XIXe siècle; Contribution à l'histoire agraire comparée*, 2 vols (Lisbon: SEVPEN, 1966), 1, pp. 296–321.

39. Silbert, *Le Problème agraire*, p. 141.

organised in corporations and by independent manufacturers reflect the growing competition between these, and point to the antithetical ways in which the constitution could be interpreted with regard to the production and sale of industrial goods and crafts. The corporations were professional bodies that regulated access to a profession, their membership giving individuals a permanent status and rights to practise what was considered an art, and therefore different from manual work. They had also a political role, especially in Lisbon, where their association, the Casa dos Vinte e Quatro, took part in the running of the government of the city. Yet by 1820 their role had been undermined by the state. Since 1809 the monarchy, through the Junta de Comércio, had encouraged manufacturing outside the corporative system, by granting privileges to individual producers who were in competition with the corporations. The corporations' very existence was now being questioned by many leaders of the revolution, in the name of the principles of free trade.[40] But artisans struck back through petitions. The corporation of comb-makers (*penteeiros*), for instance, denounced to the Congresso the fact that ivory comb makers, who did not belong to their corporation but were protected by the Junta de Comércio, had obtained the right to produce also tortoiseshell combs: for them, this encroachment on their privileges was nothing less than a usurpation of the rights of the individuals protected by the 'wise constitution'.[41] For the corporation of the 'Estreito', a liberal constitution stipulated that all citizens could 'produce and sell all the goods related to their trade'; the fact that the privilege of producing 'galoes, e franjas de ouro e prate fina' (strips and fringes of fine gold and silver) had been given to individuals outside their corporation was the result of 'despotism and absolute power'.[42] Besides attacking those producers working outside their ranks and protected by the Junta, corporations complained about competition from foreign producers.[43] Needless to say, meanwhile, producers working *outside* the corporations made appeals to the constitution against the latters' privileges.

40. Miriam Halpern Pereira, *Sob o signo da Revolução de 1820: Economia e sociedade* (Lisbon: Assembleia da República, 2020); Pereira, 'Artesãos, operários e o liberalismo: Dos privilégios corporativos para o direito ao trabalho', in Pereira, *Do Estado liberal ao Estado-providência: Um século em Portugal* (Bauru: EDUSC, 2012), pp. 105–80; Pereira, *Negociantes, fabricantes e artesãos entre velhas e novas instituições: Estudo e documentos*, vol. 2 of Pereira, ed., *A crise do Antigo Regime e as Cortes constituintes*, 5 vols (Lisbon: João Sá da Costa, 1992).

41. Pereira, *Negociantes*, p. 431.

42. Ibid., p. 427.

43. Ibid., pp. 432–33.

Admittedly, petitions could be submitted to authorities by individuals to address personal grievances that did not entail a specific understanding or rethinking of the political order, or were without any pretensions to a more collective or national benefit. The provisional government set up in Palermo in 1820, for instance, was inundated with petitions from individuals simply seeking employment.[44] In 1825 citizens from the island of Hydra whose relatives had been captured and imprisoned by the Turks asked the Greek authorities (either the primates of the island or Koundouriotis, an islander who was then president of the national executive committee) to exchange Turkish prisoners for their relatives, usually making the case for a close relative.[45] However, what is undeniable is that the petitionary movement of the 1820s in Greece, as well as in Portugal, Naples and Spain, demonstrates the legitimacy that the constitution had acquired across different social groups at the local level. It also shows the ambiguous and hybrid nature of the political culture produced by the revolutionary experience, and the unresolved tensions it unleashed. Petitions reveal the extent to which the principles of representation, popular sovereignty and the rule of law were endorsed, but also betray the existence of conflicting interpretations of their nature: first, because for some, petitioning could be used to veto governmental decisions or as a parallel form of representation—an interpretation of the practice considered dangerous by others; and second, because broad swathes of society associated support for representative government with the defence of corporate privileges, the protection of local communities from state interference, hostility to competition and an ambiguous understanding of what individual rights meant, while others, but by no means representing the opinion of the majority, were more concerned to dismantle any form of protection for corporate economic life. In the end, a communitarian understanding of political participation often went hand in hand with requests for new individual rights, and defence of the rule of law and the state (as Greek petitions show). In short, petitions show how new political rights were supported alongside the defence of older forms of freedom and privileges. As a consequence, however, revolutionary governments could neither satisfy equally all of these competing interests, nor respond to all the demands, vetoes and expectations of the motley coalition of constituencies that had decided, at least temporarily, to support the constitutional regimes.

44. ASP, Real Segreteria, Incartamenti, Giunta provvisoria, 5032.
45. The petitions all date from May 1825. See Lignos, Αρχείον (Archive), 11, pp. 324–26.

Conclusions: political participation and
local autonomies after the 1820s

The 1820s revolutions provided new opportunities for the populations of southern Europe to participate in the decision-making process, both at a local and at a national level, thanks to a new set of rights (direct and indirect, electoral as well as petitionary). These new rights enabled them to renegotiate the relationship between citizens and local as well as provincial and national institutions in new and unprecedented ways. They led to the emergence of a new political class at the local level (in Spain and Portugal), and at the national level with the election to the parliaments of the educated classes, including professionals, civil servants, army officers and clerics. They could also offer an opportunity for recently dispossessed social groups, such as the artisans and aristocrats in Palermo, to reclaim their political role. They led furthermore to the reaffirmation of the social standing and political leadership of existing privileged classes in a new institutional context. This was the case with the Greek Phanariots, who forfeited their role as a ruling and administrative elite in the service of the Ottoman Empire, but many of whose members regained preeminence as holders of the highest institutional positions in the new Greek state.

At the same time, as I have sought to demonstrate, the populations of southern Europe understood the relationship between these institutions in different ways. The explosion of political conflicts between opposing parties, the impact of civil and national wars and the enduring legacies of pre-existing territorial privileges led to a proliferation of conflicting interpretations of their mutual relations. Local communities could understand local government either as subject to the central government, or as a form of self-rule that was not only autonomous but also independent from state interference. Different social groups often supported at the same time new individual political rights and territorial, professional or communal privileges, instead of viewing them as incompatible. As the petitionary movement in Spain, Portugal, Naples and Sicily suggests, rural communities and peasants were not necessarily hostile to the new constitutional regime, but demanded at the same time the distribution among themselves of public lands, or their protection against privatisation. Furthermore, in most cases voters considered local and national politics to be complementary and mutually reinforcing, and believed participation in each to be of equal importance.

The post-revolutionary restorations then proved unable to resolve in a satisfactory way the tensions between central administrations, government at provincial level and local councils unleashed during the revolution. While the restored governments withdrew voting rights at local and national level, they never fully reverted to the pre-revolutionary administrative pluralism. As a consequence, the intolerance of some territories for administrative interference that had emerged during the revolutions did not subside with their end, and frustration at the loss of political rights at local and national level exacerbated hostility towards the state. An oscillation between impulses from the centre towards further centralisation and reactions in defence of local patriotisms and autonomy therefore continued in the following decades. During the revolutions and counterrevolutions that erupted in the decades after the 1820s, popular mobilisation re-emerged both to resist administrative centralisation and to reclaim those political rights (to vote in municipal and national elections) temporarily acquired during the 1820s and repealed at their end, and simply to reclaim ancient territorial privileges After the 1820s, popular support for constitutional government and representation was often associated with hostility to excessive governmental interference (whether fiscal or administrative or both). Thus the uprisings that took place between the 1830s and 1850s cannot be understood without taking into account the demands and expectations first raised during the 1820s.

With the end of the revolutions, the Bourbon dynasties in Spain and in the Kingdom of the Two Sicilies tried to appease their provinces in order to retain their loyalty, but the desire already shown before the revolutions to secure a firmer grip on their territories was not abandoned. As a consequence, tensions were not slow to re-emerge. In 1823 Fernando VII of Spain abolished the territorial reorganisation envisioned by the constitution, and reinstated the traditional fueros. However, the tendency previously demonstrated by the absolute monarchy before 1820s to erode these was soon confirmed. As early as 1829, a royal order decreed that Navarre would be ruled like any other province, while a ministerial junta would examine the origin and legitimacy of each fuero. The death of Fernando VII and the decision of the regent to reintroduce constitutional government led to a dynastic crisis and to a civil war during which alternative reactions to centralisation emerged. On the one hand, it contributed to the popularity of the Carlist movement in those provinces where the counter-revolution had thrived during the 1820–23 revolution: it is no surprise that this de facto abolition of provincial privileges prompted Navarre to rally to Don Carlos during the first Carlist war that raged between 1833 and

1840.[46] On the other hand, it fostered demands for popular participation in local and national politics alike that the royal statute of 1834, with its merely consultative assembly, failed to satisfy. The radical wing of the constitutional front was calling for the reintroduction of municipal autonomy and universal male suffrage for national elections, against the wishes of the moderates. As in 1820, during the provincial insurrections that broke out in 1836, revolutionaries created local municipal committees, or juntas, that acted in the name of the sovereignty of the nation, and demanded the reintroduction of the Cádiz Constitution. As in the years from 1821 to 1823, what revitalised the power of local administrations between 1835 and 1836 was both their fight against the Carlist movement and their protest against the moderate government in Madrid. This activism continued under the new constitution introduced in 1837; firstly, because radicals demanded the reintroduction of universal suffrage for national elections, while the new constitution granted electoral rights only to a small percentage of the population; and secondly because, while this constitution reintroduced the local government legislation of Cádiz based on male suffrage, the moderates were keen to repeal it and did all they could to this end. Since municipal councils were in the hands of the radicals and the *progresistas*, moderates wanted to replace the existing municipal legislation with a system that both reduced electoral rights for local elections and imposed governmental controls over them. It was widespread urban mobilisation against this proposed moderate curtailment of municipal freedom that enabled the rise to power of General Espartero in 1840, against the moderados. Espartero's regime between 1840 and 1843 represented the (temporary) victory of this municipal constitutional movement.

In the Kingdom of the Two Sicilies after 1821, King Ferdinando retained the much-hated administrative structures he had inherited from Murat and reinforced in 1817, but made a number of concessions to Sicily to appease its aristocratic elites. In 1821 he had agreed to create a separate Sicilian administration and a 'Consulta' in Palermo—a consultative body composed of local aristocrats entitled to offer their opinions on draft legislation. However, the reintroduction of a Ministry for Sicily in Naples and a secretariat of state attached to the *luogotenente* (royal representative) in Palermo in 1832 did much to reignite the hostility of the Sicilian aristocracy, exacerbated further by the governing style of the luogotenente himself. The purge of those individuals who had compromised themselves with the revolution from the lists of *eleggibili* used by government officials

46. Mina Apat, *Fueros*, pp. 110ff.

when selecting local administrators, and the government's failure to update these same lists, created a further breach between the island and the monarchy, and alienated support for Naples also in those Sicilian cities traditionally hostile to Palermo. In 1837, when a popular revolt against Naples broke out in Sicily at the time of the cholera epidemic, the crowds blamed the king for having spread the disease, and called for the independence of the island. The elites of Catania and eastern Sicily, who in 1820 had supported Naples against Palermo, now sided with their capital city and demanded, in concert with the Palermitan aristocracy and populace, independence from the mainland.[47] The 1848 revolution on the island led once more to a declaration of independence from Naples, although this time under the 1812 Sicilian constitution. On the mainland too, during the 1848 revolution, as in 1820, supporters of constitutional government, mostly concentrated in the provinces of the kingdom, demanded administrative decentralisation along with universal suffrage.[48] In Genoa, the insurrection of 1848 reaffirmed, as it had done in 1821, the distinctive municipal identity of this ancient republican capital against Turin. By then Genoese revolutionaries were no longer calling for the introduction of the Cádiz Constitution as they had in 1821. By 1848 they had embraced the new republican and democratic ideals of Mazzini and the introduction of universal suffrage, and favoured the creation of an Italian federation. However, as in 1821, their political agenda aimed at challenging the bitterly resented rule over them of the Piedmontese.[49]

In Portugal and Greece, governments pressed on more steadily with centralising reforms—as the lesson learnt from the revolutionary years was that only stronger central controls could prevent further civil disturbances. Working between the Azores and the city of Porto before the end of the civil war for and against Dom Miguel, Minister Mouzinho da Silveira produced in 1832 a radical reform of the state administration that he considered to be a necessary complement to the 1826 constitution. Drawing

47. Giuseppe Giarrizzo, 'La Sicilia dal Cinquecento all'unità d'Italia', in Vincenzo D'Alessandro and Giarrizzo, *La Sicilia dal Vespro all'unita'd'Italia* (Turin: UTET, 1989), pp. 692–730; Antonino De Francesco, 'Vulcano di patriottismo: Catania nella politica rivoluzionaria dell'ottocento', in *Catania: La grande Catania; La nobiltà virtuosa, la borghesia operosa*, ed. Enrico Iachello (Catania: Sanfilippo editore, 2010), pp. 323–31; Alfio Signorelli, *Catania borghese nell'età del Risorgimento* (Milan: FrancoAngeli, 2015), pp. 225–39, 236–37.

48. Viviana Mellone, *Napoli 1848: Il movimento radicale e la rivoluzione* (Milan: FrancoAngeli, 2017)

49. Antonella Grimaldi, 'L'insurrezione genovese del 1849', *Rassegna Storica del Risorgimento* 95 (2008): 323–78.

inspiration from the French Napoleonic model, his reform reorganised the territories of Portugal into *províncias, comarcas* and *concelhos*, and introduced as representatives of the state in each of these units a *prefeito*, a *subprefeito* and a *provedor*, appointed by the government, and assisted by elected councils. Besides reinforcing state controls at provincial level, this reform abolished completely any form of autonomy of the câmaras, since the government-elected *provedor* held sway over their activities. Not surprisingly, the cities protested against this loss of autonomy. Shortly afterwards the number of concelhos, the municipal units of the country, was also radically reduced. The local elites forced a revision of these measures, but their success was only temporary, as they were finally reconfirmed in 1842.[50] This administrative centralisation was accompanied by a drive to complete the abolition of seigneurial privileges started in the 1820s, and by increased fiscal pressure upon localities. It was this seemingly unstoppable drive towards the strengthening of the state that led to the revolts in the provinces of the 1840s. These revolts supported conflicting political agendas. In 1846, during the so-called Maria da Fonte revolt in Minho, Trás-os-Montes and the Douro valley, rebels protested against taxation and a law prohibiting burials around churches, and all in the name of Dom Miguel. During the civil war of 1847, the so-called Guerra da Patuleia, in the northern province of Trás-os-Montes rebels supported the Miguelist absolutist pretender, while the towns allied to a revolutionary junta set up in Porto demanded the repeal of the 1826 Carta (restored in 1842), and the reintroduction of the more progressive constitution of 1838. The 1847 war was marked, in fact, by the multiplication of local juntas and the assertion of the rights of local councils against the central state. Thus in 1847 Portuguese towns reacted against their governments exactly as Neapolitan cities had done in 1820, and the Spanish municipal authorities in 1837.[51]

In Greece, centralisation continued first under the administration of Kapodistrias, between 1828 and 1831, and subsequently, under the Othonian regency, from 1833. Under Kapodistrias local autonomy was abolished, as heads of the municipalities came to be directly appointed by the

50. Manique, *Mouzinho da Silveira*, pp. 74–91; Rui Ramos, 'A Tale of One City? Local Civic Traditions under Liberal and Republican Rule in Portugal', *Citizenship Studies* 11 (2007): 173–86.

51. On popular revolts, see Maria de Fátima Sá e Melo Ferreira, *Rebeldes e insubmissos: Resistências populares ao liberalismo (1834–1844)* (Porto: Edições Afrontamento, 2000). On these reforms, see Rui Ramos, 'A revolução liberal (1834–1851)', in *História de Portugal*, ed. Rui Ramos, Bernardo Vasconcelos e Sousa and Nuno Gonçalo Monteiro (Lisbon: A Esfera dos Livros, 2017), pp. 491–519, esp. 507–14. On the 1837 civil war, see Maria de Fátima Bonifácio, *D. Maria II* (Lisbon: Círculo de Leitores, 2014), pp. 224–26.

government, and in practice representative government came to an end. In the following year a territorial reorganisation of the state divided Greece into nomarchies (provinces), eparchies (counties or sub-prefectures) and *demoi* (demes, or municipalities). Municipalities were now granted a larger degree of autonomy than they had enjoyed under Kapodistrias, and their mayors were appointed by the government from a list of three names chosen by the local councils; but as in Portugal, municipalities were dramatically reduced in number, the new deme consisting of a number of formerly independent villages. In addition, the nomarchies and eparchies were run by governmental officials, and central governments did all they could to undermine the influence of the elected councils at nomarchy and eparchy level.[52] As a consequence, local rebellions against state authorities proliferated in this period: in 1830 they broke out on the peninsula of Mani and the island of Hydra. In 1832, after the assassination of Kapodistrias, a civil war seemed to replicate the regional conflicts that had occurred in 1825, as once more Roumeliot troops loyal to the governing commission invaded the Peloponnese, and civil strife divided islands and individual provinces like Messinia, in the Peloponnese. In 1834 another rebellion against taxation broke out, in Arcadia and Messinia. During these episodes protest against excessive taxation and administrative interference was often accompanied by demands for representative government and universal suffrage.[53] But perhaps it is the curious history of the island of Samos that serves as the most eloquent testimony to the complex nature of the territorial crisis triggered by the revolution in the 1820s in the Aegean. Having been excluded from the new Greek state, a settlement for Samos became, in 1832, the object of negotiations between its fiercely independent elites, the European powers and the Ottoman administration. A range of possible solutions was discussed, from full independence to the sort of tributary relationship towards the Ottomans that the Greeks in the Peloponnese had seen as a viable solution up until 1825 and beyond. In the end, it was decided that Samos would revert to being under the full sovereignty of the Ottoman state, but recognised as a separate principality under a Christian prince representing the

52. Anne Couderc, 'Nation et circonscription: Construire et nommer le territoire grec, 1832–1837', in *Nommer et classer dans les Balkans*, ed. Gilles de Rapper and Pierre Sintès (Athens: École française d'Athène, 2008), pp. 217–35; Couderc, 'Structuration du territoire et formation des élites municipales en Grèce (1833–1843)', in *Construire des mondes: Élites et espaces en Méditerranée XVI–XX siècle*, ed. Paul Aubert, Gérard Chastagnaret and Olivier Raveux (Aix-en-Provence: Presses Universitaires de Provence, 2005), pp. 163–84; Petropulos, *Politics and Statecraft*, pp. 172–75.

53. Petropulos, *Politics and Statecraft*, pp. 120–22, 131–34, 218–25.

sultan. A member of the same Phanariot elite that had served the empire for centuries but had also assumed the leadership of the Greek revolution was appointed in 1832 as its prince: Vogoridis. Although the island took two years to accept the representative of the new prince, this settlement may not have been any worse than submitting to the authority of a Greek eparch. The conflicts between opposing parties that had divided the island during the Greek revolution indeed persisted in this new context, as sections of the island's elites continued to bridle at any form of external control; the unruliness of the island did not subside, and rebellion broke out again in 1849 and 1850.[54] Thus the reimposition of Ottoman imperial rule over Samos as an autonomous principality, a seemingly traditional administrative set-up, turned out to be one of the possible outcomes of the territorial crises and demands for local autonomy that had emerged during the revolutions of the 1820s.

54. Philliou, *Biography*, pp. 114–16, 136–38.

PART III

Building Consensus, Practising Protest

THE REVOLUTIONARY PUBLIC
SPHERE AND ITS ENEMIES

Introduction

This section explores the new public space that the revolutions opened up for the discussion of politics. It looks at the impact that this had in shaping a new public opinion, and at the opportunities it offered for popular mobilisation, be it for or against those revolutions. The chapters that follow are devoted to an analysis of the ways in which political information and political culture circulated, to the social actors and social spaces that contributed to these processes and to the networks of communication that were associated with them. It also scrutinises the rituals, related symbols and cultural practices that revolutionaries adopted to regain control over public space, and to demonstrate their allegiance to the revolution. The study of these phenomena reveals a tension between two coexisting and potentially conflicting processes. On the one hand, revolutionaries strove to educate citizens in the values of their constitution (and their state, in the case of Greece), so as to inculcate loyalty to these. Such aspirations required efforts to build consensus, and to guarantee that a set of shared beliefs would be agreed upon. To this end, revolutionary governments and publicists endeavoured to control the public sphere, employing the new circuits of communication and public rituals to reshape the public sphere in an orderly fashion. On the other hand, the new public space conceded to politics facilitated the eruption of a new set of violent conflicts or disagreements, both among revolutionaries and between them and their enemies. Such conflicts, resulting both from wars and from civil conflicts, were reflected also in a new culture of protest and dissent. As the chapters below will show, war both interfered with, or limited, the public sphere and, conversely, contributed to its expansion, in the process fuelling public opinion.

Historians have highlighted the existence as early as the eighteenth century of information societies with plural channels of communication, in which orality was as important as printed media, and popular opinion was created in specific social and spatial contexts. They have also increasingly questioned the separation between these two worlds of oral and print culture.[1] The study of these revolutions likewise demonstrates the extent to which their public sphere resulted from the interaction between different media and different social spaces. The revolutionary culture that emerged from it was arguably politically fragmented in nature, but at the same time a plurality of social groups, both educated and uneducated, and a plurality of media participated in its creation.

Chapter nine below construes the birth of a revolutionary public opinion in terms of the interaction between print culture and orality. This resulted from the sudden growth in the production and circulation of printed material, and its discussion in patriotic societies, cafés, streets and squares. It is shown that the revolutionaries' attempts to control the public sphere and to educate the general population were at least partly successful, as support for the constitution percolated down among the uneducated classes. Public opinion, however, was also influenced by rumours and unverified information. The interaction between printed news and orality in a context of wars and conflicts led to an unprecedented production of misinformation. Its proliferation was not simply the result of popular fears, but also the product of campaigns organised by revolutionary and counterrevolutionary elites.

Chapter ten considers the various ways in which governments and society regained ownership of public space during the revolutions. Attempts to control public space led revolutionary authorities and associations to organise and perform a set of public rituals to foster consensus and demonstrate the unity of the nation. The first section looks at revolutionary festivities, quintessentially urban practices which included religious and civil ceremonies organised to erect monuments, and celebrate martyrs

1. See for instance Robert Darnton, 'An Early Information Society: News and the Media in Eighteenth-Century Paris', *The American Historical Review* 105, no. 1 (2000): 1–35. On the post-Habermasian debate on the public sphere, see Massimo Rospocher, *Oltre la sfera pubblica: Lo spazio della politica nell'Europa moderna* (Bologna: Il Mulino, 2013).

and heroes. At the same time, key elements of these public rituals (music, banquets and processions) were adopted independently and autonomously by organisations and individuals, forging in their turn a culture of protest and contestation. The second section explores this culture by focusing in particular on the ubiquitous practice of singing. More than any other practice, singing was adopted in public to define political identities and challenge political enemies. The third section then turns to secret societies as key agents of public mobilisation. It shows the extent to which, in Naples and Spain in particular, the Carboneria and the Comunería respectively combined secrecy with an active role in the public sphere in their defence of the constitution, alternatively supporting or contesting governments. A striking feature of revolutionary mobilisation was the great debt it owed to older and independent traditions of popular protest. The fourth section considers how much the political activism of artisans in Madrid and Palermo, and of sailors on Hydra, owed to the defence and decline of corporate professional structures. In the 1820s these workers and artisans were not simply manipulated by the revolutionary elites, but themselves took the revolutionary initiative in ways highly reminiscent of the protagonists of early modern urban revolts.

Chapter eleven, finally, focuses on the counterrevolutionary public sphere. It discusses the emergence in Portugal and Spain, and to a lesser extent in Naples, of a popular culture supportive of absolutism and with its own peculiar practices, rituals and media that all targeted the revolution. While these practices can only be understood in relation to the constitution, the chapter shows that popular support for absolutism also gave rise to a range of public opinion and to forms of protest independent of the existing absolute monarchies, and capable of challenging them. In the 1820s, public opinion and popular protest could thus operate independently of both the constitutional and the absolute regimes, and by the same token be equally critical of both.

CHAPTER NINE

Shaping Public Opinion

*Communicating the revolution, educating
citizens: information and sociability*

One of the most striking effects of the revolutions was a dramatic expansion in the quantity and circulation of printed media both across society and across space. The press played an important role in facilitating the circulation of political information. Among the many types of printed material produced during the revolutions, newspapers and periodicals played a central role in the creation of the complex circuits of communication that facilitated a dialogue between society and revolutionary institutions, and shaped a new revolutionary public opinion. By so doing, newspapers helped to define the new political affiliations and allegiances that emerged at national and local level, and produced new understandings of the constitution. They also enabled new forms of protest, participation and contestation. At the same time, the press shared with other revolutionary media, such as political catechisms, the aim of educating citizens and encouraging consensus as regards the new regimes. The pages that follow address the various ways in which political information circulated and was consumed in a variety of public spaces.

Newspapers and periodicals were not previously unknown to southern European societies. The Napoleonic invasion of the Iberian peninsula had created the space for the birth of political journalism and the temporary enjoyment of freedom of the press, particularly in Spain under the constitution, and to a lesser extent also in Portugal. In Naples a genuinely free press thrived only very briefly, during the republican experiment of 1799. In the Ottoman Empire a Greek public sphere had existed before the revolution, thanks to the circulation of literary periodicals among the

Greek educated elites. Printed in the communities of the Greek diaspora in Vienna and in Paris, these circulated throughout the empire. While they were not explicitly political, these periodicals played a role in fostering new ideas of the literary, linguistic and historical dimension of the Greek national community.[1] There is no doubt, however, that the explosion of political journalism that took place during the 1820s revolutions represented an entirely new phenomenon. Although the number of political periodicals published in this period varied from country to country, their sheer quantity was unprecedented. At one extreme there were the 345 newspapers published in Spain, at the other, the much smaller Greek political press which boasted no more than five different titles printed between 1824 and 1827. This latter number is nonetheless significant, as the printed press had been introduced into the territories concerned for the first time only at the end of 1823, thanks to the initiative of a number of philhellenes. To these newspapers must be added a small number of manuscript magazines produced in the early years of the revolution.[2] In Portugal between 1820 and 1823, 112 newspapers appeared, and between 1826 and 1828 another thirty-eight (and an additional twelve hostile to the constitution); in Naples during the nine months of the revolution there were no fewer than thirty-five different titles, supplemented by eight and six respectively in the Sicilian cities of Palermo and Messina.[3]

Distribution across each state was—not surprisingly—uneven, and concentrated mainly in and around major cities. In Spain, the publication and circulation of the periodical press was not confined only to the capital city of Madrid, but was strong also in the coastal regions of the south, and in Galicia in the north, with Murcia and Granada being the only major provincial capitals of journalism not on the coast. The geographical distribution of the moderado and the exaltado press differed: the latter was mainly concentrated in the capital, where it accounted for the lion's share

1. Catherine Koumarianou, 'The Contribution of the Intelligentsia to the Greek Independence Movement, 1798–1821', in Clogg, *Movement for Greek Independence*, pp. 67–86; Nassia Yakovaki, 'Ο *Λόγιος Ερμής* ως τόπος διαμόρφωσης του ελληνικού κοινού' (The *Logios Ermis* as a *topos* for the shaping of the Greek public), in *Λόγος και χρόνος στη νεοελληνική γραμματεία (18ος–19ος αιώνας): Πρακτικά συνεδρίου προς τιμήν του Αλέξη Πολίτη, Ρέθυμνο, 12–14 Απριλίου 2013* (Discourse and time in modern Greek letters (18th–19th centuries): Proceedings of a conference in honour of Alexis Politis, Rethymno, 12–14 April 2013), ed. Stefanos Kaklamanis, Alexis Kalokairinos and Dimitris Polychronakis (Irakleion: Crete University Press, 2015), pp. 207–38.

2. Aikaterini Koumarianou, 'Εισαγωγή' (Introduction), in Koumarianou, *Ο Τύπος στον Αγώνα* (The press in the 'Struggle'), 1, pp. 12–30.

3. Tengarrinha, *Nova história*, pp. 320, 415.

of the newspapers, while the former's imprints were more evenly distributed across the provinces. According to a conservative estimate, at least 345 different periodicals were printed during the Trienio in Spain.[4] In Greece, meanwhile, because of the lack of postal services and the disruption occasioned by the war, the very small number of copies printed had little circulation beyond the cities where they were produced. For instance, the Hydriot newspaper *Filos tou Nomou* was circulated more widely in the British Ionian Islands and in Europe more generally than in the rest of revolutionary Greece. No newspapers there had more than two hundred subscribers, who were confined to the educated classes.[5]

While the constitutions invariably guaranteed freedom of the press, revolutionary regimes for their part considered the public sphere as a space to be regulated and controlled. Some form of censorship was therefore introduced everywhere. Although it proved impossible to monitor and regulate the unprecedented production of printed material, revolutionary administrations justified interference in journalistic activities by the need to prevent disturbances and avoid attacks on government and representative institutions. In Spain and Naples the revolution reintroduced the article of the Cádiz Constitution that guaranteed freedom of the press and abolished any form of prior censorship. In Naples, however, the existing penal provisions for punishing those writing, producing or selling publications against religion, the government and *buoni costumi* (respectable behaviour) were not only maintained, but rendered even harsher, as were checks on public displays of printed material, which were vetted by the *banditore pubblico* (town crier). In practice, such restrictions were employed during the revolution to limit the circulation of foreign news and foreign publications.[6]

4. On the Spanish press, see Juan Francisco Fuentes, 'Estructura de la prensa española en el Trienio Liberal: Difusión y tendencias', *Trienio* 24 (1994): 165–96 (these data at p. 167). See also Fuentes and Javier Fernández Sebastián, *Historia del periodismo español: Prensa, política y opinión pública en la España contemporánea* (Madrid: Síntesis, 1997). On Naples, see Daum, *Oscillazioni*, pp. 70–71.

5. Emerson, Pecchio and Humphreys, *Picture of Greece*, 1, p. 340; Giuseppe Pecchio, *Relazione degli avvenimenti della Grecia nella primavera del 1825* (Lugano: Vannelli, 1826), p. 61.

6. See 'Decreto per la libertà di stampa', 26 July 1820, in Alberti, *Atti del parlamento*, 3, p. 90, and on the debates around it, as well as on governmental interference, see Daum, *Oscillazioni*, pp. 117–34, 264–68. On Spain, see Alicia Fiestas Loza, 'La libertad de imprenta en las dos primeras etapas del liberalismo español', *Anuario de Historia del Derecho Español* 59 (1989): 351–491; Beatriz Sánchez Hita, 'Libertad de prensa y lucha de partidos en el Trienio Constitucional: Los procesos contra el *Diario Gaditano* de José Joaquín de Clararrosa', *El Argonauta Español* 2 (2005), DOI: https://doi.org/10.4000/argonauta.1194.

In Portugal and Greece governmental controls were even tighter. In the former, unlike Naples and Spain, prior censorship, the key feature of pre-revolutionary printing regimes, remained in place during the revolution, and interference in political journalism would seem to have been more intense. While the constitution of 1822 and the Carta of 1826 both defended freedom of the press (as a natural right) and freedom of thought, Portuguese liberals put equal emphasis on the need to prevent attacks on their governments and on the pivotal figures of the regime. They also sought to avoid the dissemination of destabilising foreign news. In practice, however, it was difficult to exert control over all printed material, and censorship was applied particularly to the radical press, since it was considered to be a threat to the stability of the regime. Popular ultra-liberal periodicals such as the *Astro da Lusitania* were frequently targeted, so much so, indeed, that this latter was forced to close down in the face of systematic persecution. A degree of governmental control was likewise exerted over the much smaller sphere of Greek revolutionary journalism. The second national constitution, or law of Epidavros of 1823, was the first document explicitly to recognise freedom of the press in one of its articles, but in accordance with the wishes of Mavrokordatos in particular, or so it is supposed, it also set certain limits on the exercise of this freedom, by requiring respect for Christianity and for public morality as well as for individuals. In practice, from then on the Greek revolutionary press remained under the influence of powerful political interests. The content of *Filos tou Nomou* for instance, published on Hydra, was subject to systematic prior censorship by the senate of the island, and the government interfered also with the content of the Athenian *Efimeris ton Athinon*.[7] Mavrokordatos controlled closely the content of the *Ellinika Chronika* in Messolonghi.[8]

Bitter political disagreements and conflicts divided the revolutionary press in the post-revolutionary period, opposing radical to more moderate newspapers (for instance, in Spain *El Censor*, a moderado paper, was pitted against *El Zurriago*, an exaltado publication), or pro-government periodicals to independent ones (in Naples the official *Giornale Costituzionale del Regno delle Due Sicilie* against *L'Amico della Costituzione*, and in Greece *Geniki Efimeris* against the Hydriot *Filos tou Nomou*). However, in spite of these divisions, all journalists saw themselves as having two

7. See Emerson, Pecchio and Humphreys, *Picture of Greece*, 1, pp. 340–41; Comstock, *History*, p. 365.
8. Beaton, *Byron's War*, p. 223.

roles to play: they considered themselves as supporters of the revolutionary governments and of the constitution, and at the same time as guarantors of an independent space of critique and debate. This commitment
to defend the constitutional regimes can be detected in the most widely
circulating official-governmental gazette newspapers that displayed official declarations, published decrees, reported parliamentary debates and
disseminated important information regarding public life, from elections
to public ceremonies.[9] Furthermore, the journalists writing for the independent press considered themselves to be first and foremost educators
and instructors of the public, a public that had to be broadened to include
as many citizens as possible: to this end the free press saw itself as the best
tool in the search for truth, to defeat errors and undermine those factions that might threaten the very survival of the constitution. Thus they
aimed at forging a rational public opinion that was united by a number of
beliefs and was supportive of the new regime.[10] In Greece, in particular, the
press emphasised the need to defend the unity of the nation. The manifesto
announcing the publication of the *Ellinika Chronika* stated that through
newspapers the Greeks would seek 'to learn about the progress which good
laws foster, about the sense of autonomy that the rule of law creates, about
the heroic deeds and the acts for the common good of the military and
political leaders of the nation, about the sacred duties of the citizen and about
the discipline that is needed before the laws and the administration'.[11] In
the Greek context in particular, the defence of the integrity of the nation
and of the rule of law entailed a condemnation of those leaders who had
divided it by waging civil war. *Filos tou Nomou* declared itself to be hostile
to factions, understood as those who challenged the 'contract [*synthiki*]
by which the Greeks from the very beginning of their glorious struggles
sought to act politically together', and stated respect for the law to be its
primary objective.[12]

At the same time, journalists viewed the press as the most powerful anti-
dote to despotism, by virtue of the channel of communication it created between society and government. For one Neapolitan writer, under
the constitution newspapers helped politicians to learn about innovations

9. Fuentes 'Estructura de al prensa'; Tengarrinha, *Nova história*, pp. 336–38; Daum,
Oscillazioni, pp. 248–54; Koumarianou, Ἐισαγωγή' (Introduction), p. 9.

10. *L'Imparziale*, no. 1, 28 July 1820, p. 2.

11. This was published on 18 December 1823. Quoted in Koumarianou, *Ο Τύπος στον
Αγώνα* (The press in the 'Struggle'), 2, p. 9.

12. Φίλος του Νόμου [*Filos tou Nomou*]. no. 1, 10 March 1824, in Koumarianou, *Ο Τύπος
στον Αγώνα* (The press in the 'Struggle'), 3, pp. 11–12.

and the needs of the people, and served to inform public opinion about governmental decisions.[13] For the Portuguese *Mnemosine Constitucional*, the prosperity of nations derived from the existence of the freedom of the press, their decadence from the lack of it.[14] Revolutionaries in their turn assented to the notion that the independent opinions conveyed by the press and constitutional institutions were mutually reinforcing. Since they were in either case an expression of the people's will, they contributed together to the defence of freedom. For the Greek *Ellinika Chronika*, publicity was 'the heart of justice'.[15] *Filos tou Nomou* too argued that it was desirable to criticise laws, as this would ultimately lead to their improvement. As a consequence, when the government fired Theoklitos Pharmakidis, the editor of the *Geniki Efimeris*, *Filos tou Nomou* decided to intervene in his favour. Although critical of Pharmakidis for having been, in his role as editor-in-chief, insufficiently independent of the provisional government, it condemned his removal as undue interference in the autonomy of the press, and as a backwards step as far as the publicity of governmental affairs was concerned.[16]

Publicists produced material even more specific than newspapers to educate the popular classes in particular, and turn them into citizens. Revolutionaries employed short dialogues, dictionaries and political catechisms, often limited to just a few pages, to close the gap between the educated and uneducated classes, and win the latter over to the revolutionary project. They did so by explaining in simple words the meanings of the new concepts introduced by the revolution, to demonstrate the advantages brought by a constitution. Dialogues typically involved an educated member of society and supporter of the constitution, whether a priest or a teacher, and an illiterate person, or an enemy of the new regime (often a priest), and were often satirical in tone. Political catechisms adopted the format of pre-existing educational printed material produced

13. 'Dell'utilità dei giornali in uno stato costituzionale', *L'Imparziale*, no. 3, 9 August 1820, pp. 3–4.

14. Compare the article 'Libertà di stampa', in the Neapolitan *La Voce del Popolo*, September 1820, pp. 97–105, with the Portuguese 'Discurso sobre a liberdade de escrever', *Mnemosine Constitucional*, no. 9, 4 October 1820, pp. 1–2, and the Greek articles in the Ελληνικά Χρονικά [*Ellinika Chronika*], no. 61, 26 July 1824, this last in Koumarianou, *O Τύπος στον Αγώνα* (The press in the 'Struggle'), 2, pp. 121–23. On the limits of censorship, see also *Astro da Lusitania*, no. 20, 9 December 1820, pp. 1–2.

15. Ελληνικά Χρονικά [*Ellinika Chronika*], no. 6, 19 January 1824, in Koumarianou, *O Τύπος στον Αγώνα* (The press in the 'Struggle'), 2, p. 36.

16. Φίλος του Νόμου [*Filos tou Nomou*], no. 156, 2 November 1825, and no. 193, 12 March 1826, in Koumarianou, *O Τύπος στον Αγώνα* (The press in the 'Struggle'), 3, pp. 132–34, 152.

for the religious and moral education of the faithful. In particular, a number of earlier French or Spanish models were taken as sources of inspiration by contemporary imitators. Sometimes revolutionaries would replace their entire content, but more often they just added to pre-existing sections devoted to religion and private and public morals notions related to the constitutional system and its relationship with the moral and religious spheres.[17] An early example of these new revolutionary versions, the French revolutionary *Catéchisme patriotique* written by Jacques Vincent Delacroix in 1789, for instance, was translated and adjusted to the constitutions in Portugal and Naples.[18] The most widely circulated Spanish catechism, entitled *Catecismo político arreglado á la constitución de la monarquía española*, first appeared in 1812, and was then republished in 1820 in Spain in various cities, and translated or adapted with some minor modifications into Italian and Portuguese.[19] This literary genre was introduced into Greece by a Piedmontese volunteer, Alerino Palma, who published a *Political Catechism* on Hydra in 1826, addressed especially to Greek youth, and adjusting these literary models to the Greek context.[20]

To maximise the impact and circulation of their ideas, revolutionaries often published this popular literature in vernacular languages and dialects, to reach out to the uneducated and adjust their messages to local or regional contexts. In Naples, for instance, a series of dialogues in the Neapolitan language between the inhabitants of one of the neighborhoods of the city were printed in 1820. One of these, specifically addressed

17. On the Italian case, see Luciano Guerci, *Istruire nelle verità repubblicane: La letteratura politica per il popolo nell'Italia in rivoluzione, 1796–1799* (Bologna: Il Mulino, 1999); on Spain, see Jean-René Aymes, 'Du catéchisme religieux au catéchisme politique (fin du XVIII siècle–début du XIX)', in *École et Église en Espagne et en Amérique latine. Aspects idéologiques et institutionnels*, ed. Jean-René Aymes, Eve-Marie Fell and Jean-Louis Guerena (Tours: Presses Universitaires François-Rabelais, 1988), pp. 17–32.

18. Jacques Vincent Delacroix, *Catéchisme patriotique à l'usage de tous les citoyens françois, dédié aux états-généraux* (Paris: Guffier, 1789), translated into Italian as *Catechismo patriottico estratto di La Croix ed adattato al Regno delle Due Sicilie tradotto dal francese da Giovanni Taddej* (Naples: Luca Marotta, 1820); and into Portuguese as *Catecismo patriotico para uso de todos cidadãos portugueses, de M de la Croix*, trans. Manuel Ferreira de Seabra, published in *O Patriota*, 22 and 29 October 1820.

19. The full title was *Catecismo político arreglado a la constitución de la monarquía española para illustracion del pueblo, instruccion de la juventud y uso de las escuelas de primeras letras* (Barcelona: Piferrer, 1820 [1812]); also republished in Valencia and Madrid.

20. Alerino Palma, Κατήχησις πολιτική εις χρήσιν των Ελλήνων συνταχθείσα μεν ιταλιστί υπό του φιλέλληνος Κ. Α. Π. Μεταφρασθείσα δε παρά Νικολάου Γ. Παγκαλάκη (Political catechism for the use of the Greeks written in Italian by the philhellene K. A. P., translated by Nikolaos G. Pagkalakis) (Hydra, 1826).

to children, optimistically claimed that one of the consequences of the promulgation of the constitution would be the complete eradication of illiteracy in the kingdom, and all in the space of ten years.[21] In the Basque country and in Catalonia, versions of catechisms in Euskera and in Catalan instructed citizens about the articles of the constitution, but took also into account the implications that the text had for the life of these specific provinces.

These publications provided a variety of definitions of what a constitution was, explaining in particular how it would serve to renegotiate the relationship between the nation and the monarchy. For the Spanish *Catecismo político* the constitution was 'an orderly collection of the fundamental and political laws of the nation'. Under the constitution, it was the nation, through its representatives, that legislated. The *Catecismo* defined Spain as a constitutional monarchy, or 'monarquía justa', since the authority of the monarch was defined by the constitution itself.[22] For Manuel López Cepero in his *Catecismo religioso, moral y político*, what defined the Spanish constitutional government and made it different from absolute government was the rule of law (the fact that those who governed could not separate themselves from a set of established rules and laws), and the laws regarding the three separate powers.[23] Such publications often highlighted the moderate nature of the new constitutions. According to Galanti's *Catechismo* published in Naples, the virtue of constitutional government (otherwise defined by him as mixed government) lay precisely in its equidistance from the extremes of despotism and anarchy. Galanti rejected the notion that it brought with it revolution; in fact, he argued, it prevented it.[24]

Along with definitions of the constitution, all these publications set out to explain what it meant to be a citizen. The sections regarding the requisite qualifications to be a Spanish citizen constituted the largest section of the *Diccionario provisional de la constitucion política de la monarquía española* (1820), for example. Most publications, however, elaborated primarily on the rights attached to citizenship and their consequences for individuals. The Neapolitan dialogues in dialect stated that the purpose

21. Salvatore Grasso, *La scola custetuzionale pe li piccirilli: Primma lezione cuntenuvazione de li penzieri de chillo che scrivette la primma chiacchiariata tra lu Sebeto e lu cuorpo de Napole* (Naples: Antonio Garruccio, 1820).

22. *Catecismo político arreglado*, pp. 3, 27.

23. Manuel López Cepero, *Catecismo religioso, moral y político* (Madrid: Imprenta de García, 1821), pp. 76–77.

24. Galanti, *Catechismo*, pp. 10, 12.

of a constitution boiled down to two objectives: first, to protect the rights nature had given to each and everyone, and second, to make individuals aware of the means necessary to enjoy them. These publications were generally addressed either to all citizens, or to children and youth. Although they often discussed private morality and family life, they rarely addressed women alone. A rare example of a catechism expressing a specific concern for the education of women was Joaquina Cândida de Sousa Calheiros Lobo's *Cathecismo religioso, moral e politico para instrucção do cidadão portuguez* (1822). This Portuguese writer in fact aimed at educating both male and female citizens. In her catechism she argued that while women were physically weaker, they suffered from no inferiority as regards their mental faculties and talents. Without suggesting that they should acquire political rights like men, Joaquina nonetheless lamented men's determination to keep women ignorant, and advocated education for them, and the granting to them of a more prominent place in society.[25]

Public readings were necessary prerequisites to the communication strategies of revolutionaries, and access to these educational texts thus required the support of intermediaries. Indeed, it was for cultural mediators, who could read out and explain them to larger audiences in public spaces, that catechisms were printed. The clergy was absolutely crucial to the pedagogic strategies of the revolutionaries, but intermediaries included also teachers, civil servants and local administrators: in other words, individuals belonging to the educated middle classes. Not surprisingly, these were the audiences listed in the introduction of the above-mentioned *Diccionario provisional* as those deemed to be the appropriate users of this text.[26]

While the catechisms tended to be printed in the larger cities, the presence of local supporters of the revolution across the territories of Portugal, Spain and Naples made it possible for them to be employed for educational purposes even in remote localities. Some evidence in fact suggests that they were read also in smaller towns or villages, at any rate in some regions. In the Kingdom of Piedmont-Sardinia this was happening both in the small coastal towns of Liguria and in villages in the provinces of Asti and Cuneo, where mayors, deputy mayors and provincial and municipal administrators instructed villagers in public squares about the benefits of

25. Joaquina Cândida de Sousa Calheiros Lobo, *Cathecismo religioso, moral e político para instrucção do cidadão portuguez* (Coimbra: Imprensa da Universidade, 1822), pp. 46–47.

26. *Diccionario provisional de la constitucion política de la monarquía española* (Madrid, 1820), p. 1.

the Spanish constitution.[27] In Cherasco, in the province of Cuneo, it was the *riformatore delle regie scuole*, the provincial magistrate supervising schools, who read out and explained a political catechism on the Spanish constitution to the local civic militias, and told them how to interpret the colours of the constitutional cockades he was wearing.[28] In Portugal too, catechisms were read and commented upon in smaller towns far from the capital city. For instance, teachers used a catechism as an educational tool in the city of Castelo Branco, a district capital in the centre of the country. Copies of a catechism written in Lisbon by a shopkeeper circulated as early as 1822 in even smaller villages in this district, and continued to be illegally distributed among young people also after the end of the Triénio in 1823.[29] Catechisms were also read out to the illiterate across Catalonia.[30]

Oral communication contributed also to the maximisation of the impact of the revolutionary press. High rates of illiteracy characterised southern European societies in this period, which along with the price of periodicals was a serious limitation upon their circulation and reception, but these limitations could, at least in part, be overcome. The circulation of such publications was undoubtedly multiplied by their availability in public spaces and by the widespread practice of public reading. Historians suggest that during the Spanish Trienio each copy could have had a readership of ten to fifteen individuals.[31]

This public consumption of political information took place in a variety of spaces, from cafés to reading societies, from public streets and squares to private houses. On the Iberian peninsula in particular, patriotic societies played a key role in providing spaces for the public reading and discussion of political periodicals. Although they existed in greater numbers in the capital cities, these clubs could be found everywhere, in both countries. During the Trienio, no less than 250 were launched in Spain, in 164 different localities, sometimes as entirely new institutions, and in Portugal they appeared in all the district capitals of the kingdom.[32] In both countries

27. See the cases of the towns of Primeglio and Baldichieri near Asti, where mayors and municipal secretaries explained the constitution in public: AST, Segreteria di Stato Affari Interni, Alta Polizia, Processi politici del 1821: Deliberazioni della Commissione superiore di scrutinio, 59, Operazione Giunta scrutinio, no. 3, Torino (Turin), nos 6–8.

28. Ibid., Operazione Giunta scrutinio no. 4, Cuneo, no. 11.

29. ANTT, IGP, Castelo Branco 276, f. 206: juíz de fora to intendente geral de polícia, 18 June 1822; ibid., ff. 333–34: juíz de fora to intendente geral de polícia, 19 July 1823.

30. Ramon Arnabat Mata, 'La divulgación popular de la cultura liberal durante el Trienio (Cataluña, 1820–1823)', *Trienio* 41 (2003): 55–83 at p. 82.

31. Fuentes, 'Estructura de la prensa', p. 184.

32. Gil Novales, *Las sociedades patrióticas*, 1, pp. 25–36.

they were sometimes established on the matrix of pre-existing economic or literary societies: in Portugal in particular, after 1820 a number of literary and economic societies were set up along much the same lines as the late eighteenth-century institutions, in parallel with the more explicitly political patriotic clubs.[33] These organisations were hosted in cafés, private houses, reading societies, former convents or even in town halls, and therefore their activities overlapped with those offered by these spaces. They almost always published their own political periodicals, but during their sessions these 'home-produced' political newspapers were read out and discussed along with other newspapers and a variety of different types of publications. In turn they often had the speeches delivered during their sessions published as leaflets or in their newspapers. The public reading and discussion of newspapers was associated with the reading of other types of texts. The meetings of the newly formed patriotic society of the Portuguese town of Setúbal, for example, focused on reading out and commenting on the *Diário das Cortes*, the proceedings of the national assembly, a routine that was common also among some societies in Spain.[34]

Membership of patriotic societies varied in size, and ranged from a few dozen to two hundred or so individuals. Subscription costs may have limited access, as a flat rate or different fees according to membership types existed for all of them. Membership was in fact mostly, if not exclusively, middle-class in nature. The presidents were almost invariably army officers, lawyers, government officials (such as the jefes políticos in Spain) or local politicians, but ordinary subscribers included also members of the secular and regular clergy, and also shopkeepers. The seventy-six members of the Sociedade Patriótica de Juventude Portuense included twenty-four students, nine shopkeepers, seven clerks, five property owners, four members of the army, three professors, three members of the clergy and three writers; among the 269 who had joined the Sociedade Literária Patriótica of Lisbon there were seventy-eight shopkeepers, thirty-one military men, twenty-seven members of the Cortes, fifteen physicians, ten judges, eight property owners and eight members of the clergy.[35] These institutions did nonetheless attempt to make contact with all sectors of the population. To encourage the participation of the poorer urban classes, some societies

33. Vargues, *A aprendizagem*, pp. 171–200.
34. ANTT, IGP, livro 20, 1820–22, ff. 8–9.
35. Maria Carlos Radich, 'Formas de organização política: Sociedades patrióticas e clubes políticos, 1820–1836', in *O liberalismo na Península Ibérica na primeira metade do século XIX*, ed. Miriam Halpern Pereira, Maria de Fátima Sá e Melo Ferreira and João B. Serra, 2 vols (Lisbon: Sá da Costa Editora, 1982), 1, pp. 117–41 at 125.

made provision for a category of non-paying members. A number of the most radical patriotic societies in Spain, and in Madrid in particular, reached out to the artisans, who sometimes spoke at their meetings and were invited to their banquets. What broadened the audiences of patriotic societies even further was the fact that the gatherings of most of them were open to the public.[36] The statutes of the Portuguese Sociedade Literária Patriótica explicitly stated in fact that 'for no reason whatsoever can there be secret sessions: spectators are admitted to all of them'.[37] Thus it is safe to say that, by creating new, open and inclusive forms of sociability, patriotic societies had the potential to amplify dramatically the impact of their discussion of political information. Reports suggest that audiences could be very large, amounting to several hundreds. They also refer to the routine presence of women at the public gatherings,[38] who sometimes they acted as a separate group of supporters of a given society: for instance, in March 1822, on the return of Rafael Riego to Madrid, the ladies of the capital's Fontana de Oro café dedicated and offered him a wreath of laurel and roses.[39]

Like journalists, most members of patriotic societies considered the shaping of public opinion and the education of citizens as the primary task of their institutions. In this respect, the role they sought to play in the public sphere was similar to that envisaged by the members of the economic and literary societies of the late Enlightenment, who endeavoured to enlighten the public, so that it might lend its support to the state and its government. Patriotic societies replaced this explicit support for monarchies with a commitment to the defence of their constitutional version. As the periodical of the patriotic society of the Andalusian city of Córdoba, the Asociación del Bien Público, stated, its aim was 'to instruct your fellow men [. . .] explaining the constitution [. . .] instilling one thousand times the advantages produced by complying with it [. . . and] recommending the respect due to the law'.[40] It was by educating citizens, the founders believed, that sedition and insubordination would be avoided. Thus they openly declared their submission to the law and the constitution, and often viewed themselves as supporters of the Cortes and the constitution at the local level. In similar terms, the statutes of the Portuguese constitutional patriotic society Gabinete de Minerva claimed to 'lead public opinion according to the

36. Gil Novales, *Las sociedades patrióticas*, 1, p. 11.
37. Radich, 'Formas de organização', p. 123.
38. Gil Novales, *Las sociedades patrióticas*, 1, pp. 119, 597–98.
39. Ibid., p. 660.
40. *El Amigo de los Pobres*, Córdoba, 4 June 1820, pp. 6–7.

spirit of the constitution [and] prove the necessity and advantages of the constitutional system'.[41] Some Spanish societies regarded their function in the public sphere in far more autonomous terms, however. Educating citizens did not necessarily mean turning them into passive and uncritical supporters of the authorities' decisions. Patriotic societies controlled by the exaltados in particular became also agents of contestation of governmental acts, instigating forms of public participation that were antagonistic in nature. This is a role that patriotic societies in Portugal, by contrast, never claimed for themselves. There, patriotic societies never set out to criticise constitutional governments, but intervened of their own accord to condemn the enemies of the constitutions. For instance, when Count of Amarante's royalist insurrection broke out in the province of Trás-os-Montes in March 1823, the patriotic society of Porto wrote both to the monarch, to declare its members' allegiance to him as a constitutional monarch, and to the inhabitants of that province, to invite them to reject the insurrection.[42] Conversely, the Spanish societies felt entitled to intervene legitimately in the public sphere not simply to support the Cortes or the government, but as independent agents entitled to challenge their acts. They did so by virtue of representing directly popular sovereignty, or so they claimed, no less than the Cortes did themselves.[43] (Some of these protests will be further explored below.) In the name of the sovereign people, therefore, patriotic societies also justified violent forms of protest to denounce wrongdoings, to submit demands and even to challenge the lawfulness of governmental decisions.

It was this mobilisation of crowds against the government by the exaltados that led the moderate liberals, the moderados, to be critical of an unchecked production of political journalism. The moderate *El Censor* argued for a distinction between a 'natural majority' and a 'legal majority'. The former could never replace the latter, represented in the parliament, as otherwise the nation would fall prey to the 'spirit of factions' and to 'the spirit of party', and one single faction might impose its views.[44] For *El Censor*, only a press controlled by the educated classes could advance the

41. Vargues, *A aprendizagem*, p. 177.

42. See, for instance ANTT, Ministério do Reino, Autos de Aclamação, maço 33, no. 5977: proclamation signed by the Sociedade Patriótica.

43. Jordi Roca Vernet, 'From the *Cortes* to the Cities, Exercising and Representing Popular Sovereignty: Barcelona during the *Trienio Liberal* (1820–23)', in *1812 Echoes: The Cadiz Constitution in Hispanic History, Culture and Politics*, ed. Stephen G. H. Roberts and Adam Sharman (Newcastle upon Tyne: Cambridge Scholars, 2013), pp. 130–49.

44. 'Sobre la mayoría de la opinion, y modo con que se forma', *El Censor*, no. 91, 27 April 1822, pp. 69–75.

truth, the lower classes being capable only of emotions, passions or senti-ments, not opinions. Public opinion forged in the sociedades patrióticas, dominated by the radicals and directly associated with the mobilisation of urban mobs, could only lead to 'demagogic anarchy'.[45]

Patriotic societies were not the only spaces where political news was dis-cussed. Cafés were quintessentially urban and middle-class spaces of socia-bility in which the consumption of refreshments (tea, liqueurs, punch) went hand in hand with the discussion of political information. It is not by chance that the main patriotic societies of Madrid had their headquar-ters in cafés such as the Lorencini, Cruz de Malta or Fontana de Oro, as did those in other Spanish cities, Cádiz among them. Since cafés started to appear only in the period between the late eighteenth century and the war of independence, and tended to exclude the poorest strata, they did not have a monopoly as public spaces where information was commented on, however.[46] News was commented on also in *tabernas*—older and more popular spaces of sociability where wine was the drink of choice—along with shops, squares and streets.

The expansion of the public sphere across a variety of spaces was not of course a uniquely Spanish phenomenon. It was taking place in most southern European cities. In Lisbon too, during the revolution, discussions about politics took place both in traditional and popular spaces of socia-bility such as *tabernas*, *tendas* and *casas do pasto* (where the public could drink wine, eat food and buy groceries), and in the more recently estab-lished cafés (or *lojas de bebidas*). Cafés appealed to a more middle-class public, were rarer than *tabernas*, and offered a more sophisticated choice of spirits, coffee, tea and chocolate, and cakes.[47] By 1825 there were no less than 1,600 of these older and more recent establishments in Lisbon,

45. Claude Morange, 'Opinión pública: Cara y cruz del concepto en el primer iberal-ismo español', in *Sociabilidad y liberalismo en la España del siglo XIX*, ed. Juan Francisco Fuentes and Lluís Roura (Lérida: Milenio, 2001), pp. 117–46; Morange, 'Teoría y prác-tica de la libertad de la prensa durante el Trienio Constitucional: El caso de "El Censor" (1820–1823)', in *La prensa en la revolución liberal: España, Portugal y America Latina*, ed. Alberto Gil Novales (Madrid: Universidad Complutense de Madrid, 1983), pp. 203–32; Ignacio Fernández Sarasola, 'Opinión pública y libertades de expresión en el constitucio-nalismo español (1726–1845)', *Historia Constitucional* 7 (2006): 160–86.

46. Juan Francisco Fuentes, 'De la sociabilidad censitaria a la sociabilidad popular en la España liberal' in *Sociabilidad y liberalismo en la España del siglo XIX*, ed. Juan Francisco Fuentes and Lluís Roura (Lérida: Milenio, 2001), pp. 207–24.

47. Maria Alexandre Lousada, 'Public Space and Popular Sociability in Lisbon in the Early 19th Century', *Santa Barbara Portuguese Studies*, 4 (1997): 220–32; Lousada, 'Sobre a alimentação popular urbana no início do século XIX: Tabernas e casas de pasto lisboe-tas', in *Desenvolvimento económico e mudança social: Portugal nos últimos dois séculos;*

a city of two hundred thousand inhabitants. It is in the area of Lisbon near the quayside (Cais) of the river Tagus and its side streets that the highest density of *tabernas* and *lojas de bebidas* could be found, and that a decidedly interclass pro-constitutional public opinion emerged in these years. The police reported conversations critical of Dom Miguel and supportive of Dom Pedro taking place in this area in *lojas de bebidas* and in barber shops at the beginning of the absolutist restoration of 1828. In the arsenal of the same neighbourhood, head carpenters, caulkers and sailors could also be heard voicing their support for the constitution.[48] A similar expansion of the public sphere was evident in the capital of the Kingdom of the Two Sicilies. According to a contemporary pamphlet with a fictional description of life in Naples after the pronunciamiento, conversations about politics were not confined to educated men and members of the clergy debating constitutional tracts, or to poets writing verses in honour of the revolution. During festive days women could now be found commenting on the patriotism of Sicilian ladies while on a promenade; army and militia members discussed the public addresses of General Pepe in a tavern; a gentleman explained constitutional dialogues in dialect to a group of sailors playing *morra* outside an inn; and students argued about the benefits of freedom of the press in the street.[49] Although such accounts reflected the aspirations of the Neapolitan revolutionaries in particular, they nonetheless suggest that all sectors of society were now contributing to the creation of 'public opinion' as a novel phenomenon.

In Greece the press, because of its limited size and circulation, played a more restricted role than in Portugal, Spain and Naples in informing citizens. Messengers delivering governmental decrees and manifestos to localities had a more important part to play. Other informal channels of communication were opened up by sailors conveying the latest news to the islands, and by soldiers returning from war zones. Although military events dominated the press, verbal reports were much more important than newspapers as sources of detail regarding the conduct of the war and international events. In addition, information travelled via private correspondences. Chieftains and notables, often illiterate, used personal scribe-secretaries to draft their letters.[50] Verbal reports were likewise important also for political

Homenagem a Miriam Halpern Pereira ed. José Vicente Serrão, Magda A. Pinheiro and Maria de Fátima Sá e Melo Ferreira (Lisbon: ICS, 2009), pp. 227–48.

48. ANTT, IGP, Romulares 228, 1828, ff. 425–26, 445–45.

49. Pasquale Tisi, *Il quattro agosto a Posillipo* (Naples, 1820).

50. Emerson, Pecchio and Humphreys, *Picture of Greece*, 1, p. 340; Kasomoulis, Ενθυμήματα στρατιωτικά (Military memoirs), 1, p. 421. See also Mazower, *The Greek Revolution*, pp. 191–94.

communication. It was often local civilian or military leaders who brought back to their provinces or villages fresh political information after attending regional or national assemblies. Military leaders often had their own troops stationed close by, and constantly interacted with them at the margins of the key assemblies taking decisions about war and peace, or making new political and institutional arrangements among various regional groupings. We are aware of the creation of only one Greek society whose structure is comparable to those established in Portugal and Spain, a 'Philanthropic Society' established in 1824 in Nafplion. Its aim was not explicitly political, as it focused on maintaining poor children and contributing to their education. Still, it allowed its members to publish their debates, and declared its support for the government. As its statutes read, 'Every member of the society has the right to publish his speeches or opinions, through the medium of the press.'[51] In Greece, however, the proliferation of para-Masonic lodges played a role comparable to that of patriotic societies in Spain or Portugal, providing as it did a space for debate between politicians, their supporters, their clienteles and foreign Philhellenes. Their meetings took place close to the sites of the national assemblies that met year after year.

The emergence of revolutionary public opinion across southern Europe thus resulted from a combination of public reading practices, verbal reports and conversations both within organised spaces that were revolutionary in nature and outside of them. Admittedly, some spaces of sociability catered for specific social groups, and public opinion was therefore partly fragmented and divided according to class distinctions. At the same time, as I discuss below, some revolutionary organisations, such as patriotic societies, the army and the lodges of secret societies, along with workplaces, shops and the streets, did offer spaces for class interaction. And, as the next section will show, the interaction between written and verbal communication lead also to an unprecedented generation of rumours and misinformation.

Invasions and conspiracies: rumours and the international imagination

In February 1821 the Spanish newspaper *El Universal* condemned the malignity and ignorance that produced 'false news to seduce the simple-minded inhabitants of villages who fear the eruption of Vandals, Goths, Alans and Moors, but also of all the nations that are known in the world' as an increasingly widespread and worrying phenomenon that created

51. Comstock, *History*, p. 496.

public disturbances.[52] Concern about the increasingly uncontrolled dissemination of false news came to be a common theme of the revolutionary press in the period. The Portuguese newspaper *O Liberal* denounced the practice as an attempt to spread anarchy among the free citizens of the country.[53] While the growth of political journalism gave rise to a dramatic increase in the production and circulation of news, the fast and effective communication of information, in particular in the international arena, still remained extremely difficult, at a time when extraordinary changes were taking place at an unprecedented pace. The press had to cater to an anxious public constantly looking for confirmation of claims whose reliability was hard to test. Thus while in the nineteenth century rumours were no longer dominated by fantastical 'facts', as they had been in previous centuries, they continued to be part of everyday life, and their production intensified in an almost uncontrolled way.[54] Rumours were a key feature of the public sphere during the revolution, and constantly interacted with information to shape public opinion.

As the above-mentioned Spanish article suggested, the interaction between official news, real events, and rumours concerned primarily international affairs and foreign invasions, as well as revolutions and conspiracies abroad. This is hardly surprising. Their production can be understood in the context of the decisions leading to the suppression of the revolutions taken by the Holy Alliance during the congresses held from 1820 onwards, whose debates and consequences were covered by the press in the countries concerned. The invasion and occupation of the Kingdom of the Two Sicilies debated and decided by the European powers at Troppau and Laibach, and the French military expedition into Spain approved at Verona at the end of 1822, turned the possibility of international military interference into a favourite topic of speculation, and furthermore gave rise to rumours and reports of invasion, war and international plots. The interaction between official national or international news and less reliable information facilitated the circulation of misinformation. By their nature, rumours were in fact rarely entirely false, and almost always had some relation to current events or ongoing political and diplomatic discussions. They often anticipated the desired outcome of future political decisions or events, or twisted existing political facts in a specific way.

52. *El Universal*, 9 February 1821, p. 147.

53. *O Liberal*, no. 15, 10 January 1821, p. 1.

54. On this, see François Ploux, *De bouche à oreille: Naissance et propagation des rumeurs dans la France du XIXe siècle* (Paris: Aubier, 2003).

This interaction between reliable news and informal sources of information did not come to an end with the suppression of the revolutions in Naples, Portugal and Spain. On the contrary, with the abolition of a free press, some political information continued to travel across borders, although in a more limited way. First of all, some printed material circulated illegally, following transnational commercial routes: for instance, periodicals and other forbidden printed material continued to be smuggled from Spain and Britain into the coastal cities of the Portuguese Algarve after the end of the constitutional period in the summer of 1823.[55] Second, thanks to conversations in foreign ports, seamen and traders brought with them information about international events across the sea from country to country. Between 1822 and 1823 the crews of Sardinian and American commercial ships en route from both the western and the eastern Mediterranean brought to the Sicilian port of Messina news about the most recent events. In Messina these seamen were the first to speak about the French invasion of Spain, the withdrawal of the constitutional troops to Cádiz, the fall of the constitutional regime in Portugal and the naval battles between Greek insurgents and the Ottoman fleet.[56] Once a free press was no longer available, the oral transmission of information, combined with the circulation of limited numbers of illegally imported foreign newspapers, increased the uncontrolled dissemination of false news and rumours.

What the above-mentioned article from *El Universal* suggests is that the constitutional press considered rumour to be the opposite of public opinion, the latter being understood by the educated classes to comprise a space for rational judgement. Liberals associated rumours either with the gullibility of the uneducated, or with vicious attempts by the revolution's enemies to undermine it. As it was put in the Portuguese *Astro da Lusitania* in 1823, 'rumores' and 'falsos boatos', unlike public opinion, would lead to the destruction of social bonds and to anarchy.[57] The reality, however was much more complex than the revolutionaries wished their readers to believe. In practice, the dichotomy between a rational public sphere, in which political journalism acted as a channel of communication between an educated public and revolutionary institutions, and a popular space dominated by rumour was a false one. Exploring the production,

55. ANTT, IGP, Algarve 240, ff. 128 and 134: July 1823.

56. ASP, Real Segreteria di Stato presso il Luogotenente di Sicilia, Polizia, 20, 1220: 22 December 1822; ibid., Direzione Generale di Polizia, 3 (1823), fascicolo 37, incartamento 1, 7 August 1823.

57. *Astro da Lusitania*, no. 48, 1 March 1823, p. 1.

circulation and impact of rumours invites us to break down the boundaries between elite printed information on one side and a popular public sphere dominated by orality on the other, as well as the notion of the separate existence of a rational public sphere as opposed to the uncontrolled spread of irrational news triggered by fear, panic or hope. Printed information may appear more authoritative and reliable to the public, but official journalism was not impervious to the influence of rumours, and often contributed to their dissemination. Thanks to the press, unverified information reached foreign countries. Well after Ypsilantis's military defeats in the Danubian Principalities in 1821, the French and British press continued to report his imagined victories, along with news of non-existent Greek naval successes and the liberation of the Morea.[58]

In addition, an analysis of the revolutionary public sphere shows that rumours were not only the product of unverified information travelling from a distance, but were also intentionally made up and intentionally spread by the educated and the elites. Specific groups fabricated information to serve their interests and undermine their political enemies. At the same time, the constant fear of foreign invasion and war rendered the impact of such false information unpredictable, distorted further and exaggerated the false news created for political purposes, or simply made it impossible to distinguish between news created by expectations and anxiety in a context of impending crisis and information fabricated for specific political objectives.

Whether the product of key political actors, national or local revolutionaries, diplomats or local populations, such rumours and misinformation remained a key feature of all the political conflicts and civil wars that marked this revolutionary wave. Sometimes they were produced by political groups temporarily out of power who were striving to reacquire it. Occasionally they could be employed by those in power to undermine their enemies, win greater popular support, or build a consensus for political decisions that required justification. The contested nature of revolutionary politics in Spain provided ideal opportunities for the production and dissemination (both intentional and unintentional) of false news to discredit political enemies. During the Trienio, one carefully orchestrated counterrevolutionary campaign based on the dissemination of rumours and false news stands out in particular: in January 1821 a plot was organised, probably with the support of the king, to stir up public demonstrations

58. Hervé Mazurel, *Vertiges de la guerre: Byron, les philhellènes et le mirage grec* (Paris: Les Belles Lettres, 2013), pp. 281–83.

against the constitution, imprison the leading authorities of the revolutionary regime and, with the backing of the army, reintroduce absolutism. It was probably to support this specific conspiracy that a disinformation campaign aiming to foment popular opposition to the constitution was organised. To this end, false manifestos in which a Russian general, allegedly quartered in Munich, addressed his soldiers were sent by military officers from Madrid to Cádiz, where they circulated before being confiscated by the jefe político. In these manifestos the general encouraged Russian soldiers to take up arms and march to Madrid to liberate the country from that 'terrifying black cloud that has discharged and continues to discharge over this kingdom thunder and lightning, hail, death, desolation and extermination'. He compared the political principles by which Spain was being ruled to Napoleon's 'philosophism'. The messages of this manifesto were aimed more at a Spanish audience than at any imaginary Russian soldier: the general ordered his troops to maintain the most rigorous discipline and to respect religion, properties and people when marching towards the capital of Spain—an order meant to reassure Spanish readers of the honourable intentions of the Russian expedition.[59]

Rumours were also an important ingredient of the political campaign to limit the political visibility, undermine the moral authority and weaken the immense popularity, acquired nationally soon after his pronunciamiento, of the hero of the revolution, Rafael Riego, on the grounds that he was conspiring against the monarchy. Judgements about his career were in fact made in a context dominated not only by political disagreements about whether he and the constitutional army represented a threat to civilian government and the monarchy, but also in the midst of rumours about attempts made by him to establish a military dictatorship. Moderates and absolutists alike were behind the circulation of insinuations against Riego. These groups were equally hostile to granting any prominent role to an army officer, on the grounds that popular government supported by a group of officers amounted to nothing less than government by an armed faction. Rumours about Riego's determination to establish a military power in competition with the Cortes and the government started to circulate in Madrid during the summer of 1820, when the government decided to dissolve the army of the Isla de León. Other rumours suggested that Riego wanted to murder the king and establish a republican

59. On the context, see Miraflores, *Apuntes histórico-críticos*, pp. 84–87; La Parra López, *Los Cien Mil Hijos*, pp. 89–91. See AHN, Consejos Suprimidos, legajo 11296, f. 143: 20 February 1821.

government, or at least force the resignation of the existing provisional government. The power and influence of such rumours was so substantial that in early September 1820 many deputies denounced them in the public debates of the Cortes, highlighting the need to defend Riego's reputation in the face of the government's move to dismantle his army, and to explain the reasons for such a decision to the public in order to safeguard his reputation as a patriot.[60]

What dealt a final blow to Riego's credibility, however, and justified the government's decision to remove him from any public responsibility were rumours concerning his association with international conspiracies and foreign invasions. At the end of 1820 his appointment to the captaincy-general of Aragon had laid the ground for a compromise between all forces supporting the constitution. Yet by September 1821 the political context was no longer favourable to him. The government's decision to remove him from the captaincy-general in Zaragoza had created an uproar and led to public demonstrations in defence of the constitution across the country; but his local enemies still had no difficulty in manipulating ongoing investigations about alleged international plots to undermine his reputation. The arrival of foreign refugees following the end of the revolutions in Naples and Piedmont, the organisation by Bonapartist refugees of a military expedition from Spain into France to reintroduce the 1791 constitution (as reported by the French to the Spanish authorities) and the arrest of some exaltados allegedly plotting to establish a republic in Zaragoza were all circumstances Riego's enemies used against him. Allegations of his involvement in such conspiracies would seem to have been groundless, but he nevertheless stood accused of being a criminal and a republican. False news circulated about his efforts to organise the military intervention of Russia. In other words, his demotion was accompanied by a serious attempt at character assassination.[61]

In Portugal too, what fuelled the dissemination of rumours was the clash between constitutionalists and absolutists. Here the emergence of different waves of spurious information went hand in hand with the rise and fall of constitutional governments, and with the organisation of military coups. Such rumours aimed either to undermine the existing regime

60. See for instance *El Universal*, 25 August 1820, pp. 390–92.

61. On the plot, see Gil Novales, *Las sociedades patrióticas*, 1, p. 228; Vaudoncourt, *Letters*, pp. 36–37; on the rumours, see Gil Novales, *El Trienio Liberal*, p. 41; Pedro Rújula, *Constitución o muerte: El Trienio Liberal y los levantamientos realistas en Aragón (1820–1823)* (Zaragoza: Edizions de l'Astral, 2000), pp. 66–68; *Diario de las actas y discusiones de las Córtes*, 4, pp. 401, 403–4.

or to lay the ground for the consolidation of a new one, but were also the by-product of the fears, expectations and hopes on both sides of the conflict. Rumours of a Russian invasion of the Iberian peninsula circulated in Lisbon roughly at the same time as the disinformation campaign orchestrated in Cádiz involving the publication of fake manifestos by a Russian general. This was probably the product of an independent initiative, but was similarly aimed at destabilising the constitutional regime. The circulation in the streets of the capital of the news that two hundred thousand Russian soldiers were crossing from France into Spain to reach Portugal was denounced in the Cortes in February 1821, and the absolutist *prior mor* of the Ordem de Cristo was accused of disseminating such information.[62]

The Spanish border played an important role in facilitating the transmission of these stories. It was often itinerant workers, artisans, muleteers and carters, or shepherds practising transhumance, moving from one village to the other, and between Spain and Portugal, who performed the role of collectors and communicators of rumours. In peripheral regions close to the border such as Trás-os-Montes, information arrived first from the border and then from the capital city, and communication between local authorities and Lisbon was slow. In 1822 rumours brought by people coming from Spain replicated those circulating the year before in the capital about an imminent Russian invasion to rescue absolutism. Not surprisingly, the French expedition into Spain in early 1823 increased fears and magnified the rumours about foreign invasions, but in subsequent years France and Spain replaced Russia as the invading country in Portugal's and Spain's popular imagination.[63] In spring 1827 Spanish emissaries who had crossed the border into the province of Castelo Branco were spreading the rumour that Dom Miguel was on his way to Madrid where he would join Don Carlos, and soon afterwards, protected by the French, would arrive in Lisbon to re-establish absolutism.[64]

The transition from constitutional government to absolutism in 1828 was in turn marked by the fabrication of rumours by liberals against Dom Miguel. In the province of the Algarve, local supporters of the constitution

62. António Monteiro Cardoso, 'Notícias "aterradoras" e pasquins "incendiários": A circulação de rumores em Trás-os-Montes no tempo das lutas liberais', in *Contra-revolução, espírito público e opinião no sul da Europa: Séculos XVIII e XIX*, ed. Maria de Fátima Sá e Melo Ferreira (Lisbon: Centro de Estudos de História Contemporânea Portuguesa, 2009), pp. 109–16 at 111–12.

63. Cardoso, 'Notícias "aterradoras"'.

64. ANTT, IGP, Castelo Branco 277, f. 478: juíz de fora of Idanha-a-Nova to intendente geral, 25 April 1827.

tried to undermine Dom Miguel's restoration of absolute government with the circulation of false news about his ill-health. In the city of Faro, which in the civil war and military clashes of May 1828 had sided with Dom Miguel, local authorities denounced the existence of 'notícias atterradoras' (terrifying news) promulgated by the constitutionalists, who had spread the story that Dom Miguel, apparently unwell, had actually died. The lack of any details about the medical condition of the monarch for a few days left both the authorities and the general population in turmoil, until news of the improvement to his health was published by the corregedor.[65]

The success of rumours, whether they are fabricated on purpose for political purposes, or the product of imprecision, confusion or misunderstanding, is directly related to their ability to express existing anxieties, hopes and prejudices. This is because they can reflect certain features of a 'collective conscience' or a collective emotional state, and tend to respond to the existing expectations of ordinary individuals.[66] In other words, their impact and credibility are more effective when they amplify and multiply existing hopes. This is why not all rumours are equally effective and credible, and therefore in revolutionary contexts some of them had more direct consequences than others. While in some circumstances they might lead to nothing more than public gatherings and discussions, in others they had very significant consequences in terms of events: rumours could actually affect and shape reality.

During the insurrection of the city of Genoa, triggered by the publication by the governor Giorgio de Geneys of the Piedmontese king's condemnation of the constitution, a rumour circulated that the former had received money from the Austrians to hand the city over to them, although their troops had finally been defeated and the constitution was in fact safe. As a consequence, not only was the governor's palace attacked, but a ship in port in which the money paid to him was allegedly stored was assaulted.[67] The Greek insurrection, however, is the most obvious case in which rumours served to encourage the uprising and escalate the conflict. Rumours on both sides exaggerated the size of the insurrection, although for different reasons: the Greeks to stir up additional support, and the Ottomans out of sheer fear and panic. As a result, rumours and false news

65. Ibid., Algarve 244, ff. 550, 551, juíz de fora of Faro to intendente geral, 23 October 1828.

66. Marc Bloch, 'Reflexions d'un historien sur les fausses nouvelles de la guerre', *Revue de Synthèse Historique* 33 (1921): 13–35.

67. Bornate, 'L'insurrezione di Genova', p. 357.

helped to turn localised violence and limited conspiratorial networks into a widespread and generalised conflict.

Rumours prompted by fear made a substantial contribution to the escalation of the Greek–Ottoman confrontation in 1821. The overreaction of the Ottoman authorities in Constantinople to news about the military expedition by Ypsilantis and the revolt in the Morea was based on unfounded reports of an extensive conspiracy involving the Greeks living in the capital of the empire, along with its entire Greek population. This fear resulted in consecutive waves of executions of prominent members of the Phanariot elite ordered by the authorities in the capital, but also in murders carried out spontaneously by the populace, targeting both Greeks and other Europeans.[68] These unchecked rumours were soon circulating throughout the empire. As soon as tales of a generalised Greek conspiracy against the Muslims reached the city of Smyrna and its environs in Asia Minor, where nobody had risen up in imitation of the insurgent population of the Peloponnese, the local Greek inhabitants became the target of unbridled violence. At first the Janissaries managed to stem the violence inside the city, restricting it to a small number of isolated murders, while armed squads attacked and murdered Greek peasants in its rural hinterland; but when news of a military defeat suffered by the imperial fleet at Lesvos reached the city, the violence escalated again and the local population plundered Greek properties and murdered those who had not yet fled.[69]

Rumours had a powerful effect also in encouraging the insurrection among the Greeks. In this case in particular, what increased the impact and credibility of rumours in Greece was that while they were disseminated by the leaders of the revolution for political purposes, they also reflected pre-existing expectations and beliefs. The rumour of a generalised revolt was spread on purpose by the revolutionary leaders in the Peloponnese, Papaflessas and Kolokotronis among them, to foment further violence against the Turks and to convince people to join the revolution. What played an even more important role in the ensuing mobilisation was the belief that the uprising had the support of the Russians, and the notion that the Russian army was going to intervene soon in their defence did much to push those who had at first been hesitant to side with the revolution.[70] The story of Russia's support for the conspiracy against the

68. See Philliou, *Biography*, pp. 65–72; on these massacres, see also Ilikak, 'Radical Rethinking', pp. 130–33.

69. Gordon, *History*, 1, pp. 189–91.

70. Apostolos Vakalopoulos, *Φήμες και διαδόσεις κατά την Ελληνική Επανάσταση του 1821: Συμβολή στην ψυχολογία των ελληνικών επαναστατικών όχλων* (Rumours and news

Ottomans had circulated well before the actual outbreak of the revolution, in the context of the recruitment of members of the Philiki Etaireia, and was based on the aspirations of its leaders. The fact that the name of the leader of the secret society was for long not known, and that the highest echelons of the organisation were themselves hoping for the support of the czar, served to foster the misplaced conviction that Russia was behind the whole revolutionary project. Count Ioannis Kapodistrias, then foreign minister of Russia, had turned down a request to become the leader of Philiki, but some of its members spread the rumour that he was in actual fact its leader. This misconception was disseminated among its members in the Peloponnese.

Before 1821 the coffee houses, churches, markets and workshops where the members of the Philiki gathered, whether in Odessa or in Constantinople, were also sites where such rumours were exchanged and communicated. Admittedly the networks of the Philiki may indeed have informed individual Russian military officers such as Count Pavel Kiselev and Mikhail Orlov, who were stationed in southern Russia, of Ypsilantis's plans. Orlov in particular, as a leader of the secret society Union of Welfare, was sympathetic to the idea of coordinating an insurrection in Greece and Russia. In addition, the governor of New Russia, the Count of Langeron, was also aware, it would seem, of Ypsilantis's plans. Langeron did not see fit to denounce these, as he probably assumed, or had been told, that Czar Alexander I was prepared to back them. These isolated cases do not at all mean that any substantial portion of the Russian civilian and military authorities were involved in Ypsilantis's plans or had been compromised by dealings with him. Nonetheless, when launching his military expedition, Ypsilantis himself referred in his proclamation to the Moldavians to a certain 'power', thus reinforcing the expectation of Russian backing for his venture. As a matter of fact, the czar was not only apparently unaware of Ypsilantis's plans, but no sooner had he got wind of the expedition, while attending the Congress of Laibach, than he vehemently condemned it. Ypsilantis himself wrote to the czar to seek his support in liberating Greece, but Alexander dismissed his act as shameful and criminal.[71]

As soon as the revolution broke out, the emissaries of the Philiki who arrived in the Aegean islands brought with them assurances of direct

during the Greek Revolution of 1821: A contribution to the psychology of the revolutionary masses) (Thessaloniki: Triantafyllou, 1947).

71. On Russian attitudes towards the revolt, see Frary, *Russia*, pp. 27–31; Bitis, *Russia*, pp. 101–5; Stites, *Four Horsemen*, p. 202.

Russian involvement in the expedition. The emissary who arrived on the island of Naxos, for instance, reported that Ypsilantis, with no less than 150,000 troops, was fast approaching Constantinople. Following his victory, this same emissary went on, an agreement with the Ottomans had given the Russian imperial fleet permission to cross the Dardanelles, to liberate the Aegean islands from Ottoman rule, and to reach the Kingdom of the Two Sicilies to lend support to the king there against the carbonari.[72] This information was also replicated in public proclamations reported by the manuscript revolutionary press: in August 1821 the ephors of Messolonghi communicated to the population of the city 'the decision of the emperor of Russia to become an ally of our *genos* [race] and to defend our national rights'.[73] News of the success of Ypsilantis's expedition, along with reports of a Russian invasion of the Ottoman Empire and the conquest by Greek insurgents of Constantinople, was widespread in the first months of the revolution, and was exploited by prominent leaders such as Papaflessas and Kolokotronis when negotiating with their enemies.

The pervasiveness of such rumours, and their capacity to mobilise, requires further elaboration. Indeed, such misplaced expectation was both credible and rich in consequences, because it built on historical antecedents and popular religious tradition. Admiral Orlov's revolt of 1770, when the Russian imperial fleet had supported an anti-Ottoman rebellion, and the subsequent role accorded to Russia as the protector of the Orthodox community in the Ottoman Empire by virtue of the rights granted to it by the Treaty of Küçük Kaynarca (1774), had entitled Russia to intervene in the domestic affairs of the Danubian Principalities in defence of their Christian populations, a right that was interpreted as extending to all the Christians of the empire. These rights were reinforced by the Treaty of Jassy in 1791.[74] The rumours owed some of their power also to the revival of an Orthodox oracular tradition that had prophesised liberation from Turkish servitude through the intervention of a saviour. In other words, they found a receptive population, because Russian intervention tallied with millenarian expectations based in religious culture. Notions that Russia was indeed the saviour had already been revived in the previous two decades, and revitalised by the revolutionary language of Rigas Velestinlis.[75]

72. Walsh, *Residence at Constantinople*, 1, pp. 186–87, 308–20.

73. Εφημερίς Αιτωλική [*Efimeris Aitoliki*], no. 1, 10 August 1821, in Koumarianou, *Ο Τύπος στον Αγώνα* (The press in the 'Struggle'), 1, pp. 6–7.

74. On these treaties, see Bitis, *Russia*, pp. 20–21.

75. For more details on this oracular tradition, see chapter thirteen below.

During the revolution false information about victories continued to circulate in the context of the war, often reported by manuscript gazettes, at times emerging spontaneously out of fear and hope, and at times devised, like many other rumours, by military leaders anxious to sustain morale in moments of difficulty. It also triggered specific episodes of anti-Ottoman violence that were thus justified as forms of retaliation or revenge in the face of perceived, albeit unsubstantiated, impending threats. In May 1822 the siege of Athens by the Greek insurgents resulted in the capitulation of the Ottoman garrison on the basis of an agreement, guaranteed by the consuls of France, Austria and the Netherlands, that the Turks would be spared their lives and, having made over their possessions and properties to the Greeks, could decide either to remain in the city or leave unharmed. However, the rumour that a large Ottoman army was approaching, only later confirmed, led the Greek population to murder four hundred men, women and children, regardless the terms of the capitulation and the efforts made by the ephors, the government and the French consul to protect the prisoners and allow them to embark on ships.[76] In 1824 on the island of Hydra, the rumour that a Muslim slave had set fire to a Greek ship where he was being held captive resulted in the execution by the local population of no less than two hundred Muslim prisoners in the public square.[77]

With the end of the revolutions, foreign occupation, the re-establishment of absolutism and the disappearance of a free press, rumours became instead a by-product of the suppression of public debate. Their production and circulation itself became evidence of the moods of the population and a test of public attitudes towards the restored monarchies. In other words, their proliferation helps us to appreciate the extent to which the restored regimes enjoyed popular support. In both Naples and Madrid the police became obsessed with monitoring the public spirit, and with reporting regularly and intensively the mood of the urban population; exploring public attitudes in both cities helps us to understand how far the regime, and with it its institutions, had lost legitimacy in the two Bourbon monarchies. In both cities, hostility to government went hand in hand with mistrust of official sources of information and a search for alternative ones. However, in each case this hostility and the rumours it produced had different and antithetical political overtones. In Naples the members

76. Gordon, *History*, 2, pp. 410–12.
77. Finlay, *History*, 2, p. 58.

of the Carboneria, whose networks were reorganised and reactivated soon after the end of the revolution, remained confident that the restoration of absolutism would be but temporary. Rumours were circulated to facilitate their new revolutionary plans. After 1821 in the Terra di Lavoro (Caserta), on the coast of Puglia, and in other provinces, a rumour circulated, presumably spread by the Carboneria, that the Greeks and Russians were soon to come by sea in support of a revolution in favour of a constitution.[78] In 1823, meanwhile, liberal public opinion in Naples refused to accept that the constitutional regime in Spain had come to an end. There was much talk about the resilience of the Spanish constitutional army, and of an imminent British military intervention in its support.[79] A further set of rumours demonstrates the extent to which the Bourbon dynasty had lost credibility and prestige after 1821: what discussions in the cafés and streets of Naples demonstrate is how the Austrian invasion had undermined the king's authority by highlighting the weakness of the kingdom in the face of foreign powers. Many took it for granted that the king would soon be murdered and a republic would be established in Naples. It was also believed that the French army, on its way to join the conflict between Russia and the Ottomans, would invade the kingdom and appoint the king's brother Leopoldo as regent, while the British would annex Sicily once more.[80]

In Madrid, conversely, the most troubling rumours demonstrated the existence among the popular classes in the barrios of a widespread hostility towards the liberals, both at home and abroad. Here rumours about international and domestic affairs were fuelled by the arrival of the mail at the Puerta del Sol, a public space where stories were created and disseminated. The liberals, the so-called *negros*, were blamed for the rise in the price of bread.[81] But the popular classes of the capital, aware of the relationship between domestic and international politics, also had a keen interest in international affairs. In 1825 the death of Czar Alexander I produced a flurry of different hypotheses about the death itself and speculations about its impact on European politics. While the French who lived in the city welcomed the czar's demise as an opportunity to liberalise the continent, many *madrileños* claimed either that the news was false,

78. See ASN, Borbone, 726, f. 117: 'Rapporto dello spirito pubblico', 1821; ibid., 278, part 2, ff. 174–78.

79. ASN, Borbone, 278, ff. 328, 357: 'Rapporto dello spirito pubblico', 28 Sept. 1822, June 1823; ibid., f. 423: 'Spirito pubblico della capitale', 28 June 1823.

80. Ibid., ff. 219, 238, 273: 'Bollettino segreto', 7 August. 1821, 'Bollettino segreto', 11 August 1821, 'Rapporto segreto', 30 September 1821.

81. AHN, Consejos Suprimidos, legajo 12334-5, ff. 10, 15: reports of 12 and 13 December 1825.

manufactured by the *negros* to subvert the European order, or that the czar had been murdered by the French or the British.[82] Thus comparing the rumours reported in Madrid and in Naples and its provinces helps us understand the different directions opinion was taking after the revolutionary period in the two countries, and the impact the constitutional experience had had on society at large. While the constant production of rumours in the Kingdom of the Two Sicilies confirmed that the revolution had consolidated a constitutional opposition—although not one that developed, at least for time being, into new uprisings—in Madrid rumours bear witness to the emergence of a new absolutist public opinion determined to persecute any former revolutionary. As will be shown in chapter eleven below, this opinion would soon become an insidious threat to the monarchy, as it was at the same time both hostile to the constitutionalists and increasingly critical of Fernando's brand of absolutism, deeming it too lenient towards his enemies.

82. Ibid., ff. 28ff; f. 27: reports of 28 and 29 December 1825.

CHAPTER TEN

Taking Control of Public Space

Revolutionary ceremonies as rituals of concord

On 9 March 1820 in the city of Segovia, the proclamation of the constitution turned out to be a grand public event attended by most of the population: a public banquet was organised for the troops, and drinks were offered to the officers, while bands played patriotic tunes all night. The celebrations continued in the following days, and included the installation of a constitutional plaque and a ceremony during which the local militia garrison took a public oath of allegiance to the constitution. On 19 March, the anniversary of the ratification of the Cádiz Constitution, a solemn Te Deum was celebrated in the cathedral, and followed by fireworks, music, banquets and dances across the city.[1] In the succeeding months the focus of the public ceremonies shifted from celebration of the constitution to celebration of the heroes of the revolution, Quiroga and Riego. The entry of Quiroga into the city of Madrid on 23 June 1820 and that of Riego on 3 September were both carefully planned public events, and followed similar patterns. The patriotic societies got involved in their planning alongside the ayuntamiento: while the government was not itself officially represented, it nonetheless gave its approval. Each of the two heroes made a triumphant entry into the city standing on an open carriage flanked by members of the patriotic societies, and was cheered and acclaimed by

1. On this ceremony, see Francisco Juan Fuentes, 'La fiesta revolucionaria en el Trienio Liberal español (1820–1823)', *Historia Social* 78 (2014): 43–59 at pp. 46–47. On Spanish festivals, see also Gonzalo Butrón Prida, 'Fiesta y revolución: Las celebraciones políticas en el Cádiz liberal', in *La revolución liberal*, ed. Alberto Gil Novales (Madrid: Ediciones del Orto, 2001), pp. 159–77; Jordi Roca Vernet, 'Fiestas cívicas en la revolución liberal: Entusiasmo y popularidad del régimen', *Historia Social* 86 (2016): 71–90, esp. pp. 71–78. For Portugal, see Vargues, *A aprendizagem*, pp. 340–50.

FIGURE 15. The taking of an oath to the Constitution of 1812 by the garrison of Madrid, 9 March 1820 (aquatint by Johann Lorenz Rugendas II, c. 1826; Museo de Historia de Madrid, Madrid). The scene is depicted as taking place in front of the old Royal Alcázar, which was in fact destroyed by fire in 1734. Image: Biblioteca Digital memoriademadrid

the crowds of the capital on both sides of the streets that connected the Puerta de Atocha through the Calle de Alcalá to the Casas Consistoriales. Here Quiroga was welcomed by the alcalde, who delivered a speech in his honour (while Riego himself spoke from the balcony of the town hall). Immediately afterwards they attended a banquet at the patriotic society Los Amigos del Orden, together with public authorities, members of the society, artisans, workers and soldiers, in an atmosphere that the sources describe as marked by fraternal equality. In the evening the theatre organised performances in the heroes' honour, and in both cases the 'Himno de Riego' was sung along with other patriotic songs. The next day, more public events were organised at the premises of the patriotic societies.[2]

2. Gil Novales, *Las sociedades patrióticas*, 1, 107–11, 124–27. On Riego's celebrations, see also *Miscelánea de Comercio, Política y Literatura*, no. 188, 4 September 1820, p. 2. On

As had happened in Madrid for the reception of Quiroga and Riego, the triumphal entry into Lisbon of the officers making up the provisional junta of Porto with their troops, on 1 October 1820, was accompanied by banquets, public dances and the singing and playing of the 'Hymno nacional' and 'Hymno constitucional'. Welcomed first outside Lisbon by the juíz do povo and another four delegates from the Casa dos Vinte e Quatro (the union of artisans' guilds) and then by the members of the senate, the officers paraded through streets adorned for the occasion. After entering the main square of the city, Rossio, already filled with military regiments, they appeared to the crowds from the balcony of the Palácio do Governo. A key difference between these ceremonies and those taking place in Spain, however, was that here the symbolic celebration of the (absent) monarch provided a counterpoint to those dedicated to the heroes of the revolution. Public festivities therefore emphasised the transformation of the monarchy into a constitutional one. A number of boxwood arches decorated with bay leaves were set up along the road that connected the town of Sacavém to Lisbon, and no fewer than six of these were erected inside the city. The most imposing of them all, located on a street that led directly into the Rossio square, crammed with allegorical figures and verses, devoted the central space of the arch to the figure of Dom João VI, portrayed in the act of graciously receiving the constitution from the *Génio lusitano* (Spirit of Portugal). On the pinnacle of the arch, above the portrait of the monarch, stood a statue displaying the distich of the 'Constituição'. The two columns raised on either side of the arch featured tablets that represented Religion and Hope. Above and below these, inscriptions elaborated on these same themes. The combined message of these tablets and inscriptions was that God, listening to the voice of the Portuguese nation, had drafted and sent down the constitution, and that the Portuguese should be grateful to the 'gods of their country'; the inscription dedicated to Hope addressed the Cortes, auguring the latter's promotion of the wellbeing of the state. Under the inscriptions, surmounted by the figures of Religion and Hope, lay symbolic representations of defeated fanaticism, hypocrisy, despotism and tyranny.[3]

The centrality of the monarchy was confirmed also during the celebrations that took place at the beginning of the second constitutional period, in 1826, when Dom Pedro IV conceded the Carta to Portugal,

---

the preparation for Quiroga's and Riego's arrival in Madrid, see AAM, Secretaría, Acontecimientos Políticos, 2–229, no. 30.

3. Details can be found in the *Mnemosine Constitucional*, no. 7, 2 October 1820, pp. 2–4.

FIGURE 16. Portuguese allegory of the Constitution: *O Triumpho maior da Luzitania* (engraving by Constantino de Fontes, after Luís António, Lisbon, 1821; Biblioteca Nacional de Portugal, Lisbon). Image: BNP Biblioteca Nacional Digital

abdicated in favour of his daughter Dona Maria, then still a minor, on the understanding that she would marry her own uncle Dom Miguel, and confirmed his sister Dona Isabel Maria as regent of Portugal. The entire city of Lisbon was decorated with arches adorned by laurel leaves; temporary monuments were set up in most public spaces in the capital and remained in place for several days. Representations of Dom Pedro and

Dona Maria dominated the decorations erected for the public ceremonies that followed the granting of the constitution at the end of July, of which the swearing of an oath of allegiance to the Carta by the regent was the central event. In the square of Romurales, for instance, on the four sides of the monument on which an obelisk was raised were featured the portraits of the emperor Dom Pedro, Dona Maria, Dona Isabel Maria and Lysia, the mythical founder of Lusitania; in the Rua de São Roque a half-bust portrait of the emperor in the act of granting the constitution was hung at the centre of an arch erected across the street. Similar installations could be found across the city.[4]

Revolutionary ceremonies were public rituals whereby society was refounded by the turning of individuals into a community of citizens who shared the same values and beliefs. These rituals were thus designed to foster a new political militancy that would sustain the revolutionary regimes, and stir up civic enthusiasm. Such festivities signalled the extent to which the revolution had broken away from the past, had marked the beginning of a new era and had created a new order expressed in the adoption of new symbols.[5] The official celebrations described above had marked the victory of the revolutions in Spain and Portugal. Public festivals were not confined to the beginnings of the revolutions, however. The authorities continued to employ public ceremonies to forge consensus and reinforce the legitimacy of the new order by turning them, in intention at least, into permanent practices that would mark each important moment in the public life of the constitutional regimes, from elections to the opening of parliaments. They also turned the anniversaries of the revolutions and of the introduction of the new institutions into national festivals, to highlight the extent to which such events marked the beginning of a new era in the history of their countries. In January 1821, for instance, the Neapolitan parliament voted to mark 7 July, the day upon which the monarch had accepted the constitution, and 30 January, when it had been published, as national festivals. In Portugal the revolution led to a multiplication of national commemorations: in 1821 the Cortes declared the days of the revolutions in Porto and Lisbon (24 August and 15 September), of the anniversary of the union between the two provisional governments (1 October) and of the opening of the Cortes and the oath taken by the

4. See *Relação dos festejos que tiverão lugar em Lisboa nos memoraveis dias 31 de julho, 1, 2 etc. de agosto de 1826* (Lisbon: J.F.M. de Campos, 1826), pp. 28–31 and passim.
5. On revolutionary ceremonies, see Mona Ozouf, *La fête révolutionnaire, 1789–1799* (Paris: Gallimard, 1976); Michel Vovelle, *Les métamorphoses de la fête en Provence de 1750 à 1820* (Paris: Aubier/Flammarion, 1976).

king to the constitution (26 January and 26 February) all to be national days. In 1822 a new wave of national celebrations that put the monarch at the centre of the revolution was approved: the day of his return to Portugal was added to the already long list of revolutionary landmarks to be commemorated on a regular basis.[6]

As the ceremonies of Madrid, Segovia and Lisbon suggest, these revolutions shared a number of symbolic practices, although local peculiarities and national differences persisted. The pages that follow will explore further the practices adopted during festivities to foster concord and create consensus. The staging of public banquets, processions and religious ceremonies which included public blessings and masses, and the unveiling of temporary or permanent monuments and renaming of public spaces, almost invariably accompanied by music and official songs, all aimed at creating unanimous support for the nation or the constitution (often represented by ancient or recent heroes) and emphasised the principles of concord and brotherhood. While the success of these efforts by authorities to create greater enthusiasm for the revolution is often hard to assess, their adoption in various contexts and by various political and social actors undoubtedly multiplied their impact and contributed to the civic education of the populations.

No other practice shows more strikingly the variety of meanings that concord and brotherhood could assume, and the broad range of contexts in which these could be evoked and celebrated, than the public banquet.[7] Unlike the principle of equality, that of brotherhood did not refer to specific rights, and did not necessarily entail a revision of the economic foundations of society on a more egalitarian basis. Rather, it pointed to the need for an ethical refounding of society, based on the rejection of divisions and factions, that recognised the unity of all its members against its enemies. The underlying assumption of these celebrations was that concord was in itself a vital precondition for the preservation of the social fabric, whose integrity was necessary for the survival of the constitution. While emphasis on inclusivity did not necessarily entail a desire to overcome social inequalities or a critique of the unequal enjoyment of rights, sometimes public displays of brotherhood had explicit social connotations,

6. For Naples, see Alberti, *Atti del parlamento*, 3, p. 303; for Portugal, see Vargues, *A aprendizagem*, pp. 272–76.

7. On fraternity, see Mona Ozouf, 'Fraternité', in *Dictionnaire critique de la révolution française*, ed. François Furet and Mona Ozouf (Paris: Flammarion, 1988), pp. 731–40; specifically for the Italian case, see Catherine Brice, ed., *Frères de sang, frères d'armes, frères ennemis: La fraternité en Italie (1824–1914)* (Rome: École française de Rome, 2017).

aiming as they did to integrate the lower classes into the new political communities.

Public events often conveyed concord and brotherhood in military terms, a principle most vividly illustrated by the participation of soldiers and officers sitting next to each other. In such circumstances what was highlighted were the new egalitarian, anti-despotic foundations of revolutionary armies. One of the first banquets organised after the revolution in Naples was attended by no less than ten thousand troops, who at the end of the meal, holding hands with each other, swore to defend the constitution, the *patria* and the king. A central pavilion was erected to accommodate the heir to the throne and his wife, the Duke and Duchess of Calabria, and various courtiers. Emphasising the extent to which the event showed the new principles underpinning the monarchy, General Pepe, who attended it, wrote that 'a universal sympathy seemed to bind us together', and 'the expression of patriotic enthusiasm was such that even the courtiers might have been taken for Jacobins'.[8] Similar events took place across the kingdom. In other circumstances, it was the alliance between civilians and the army that served to symbolise the foundation of the constitutional order to be celebrated. In the city of Lisbon, for instance, on the first anniversary of the revolution in September 1821 the patriotic society of the capital offered a banquet to the cavalry regiment stationed in Belém, as a sign of gratitude for the support offered by them to the revolution and a symbol of unity, regaling them with abundant 'rice, bread and wine'.[9] In Greece, military victories, and the missions of revolutionary emissaries travelling far and wide to meet with local military leaders, were often marked by banquets, or *trapezia*. When travelling to the islands in 1821, Grigorios Salas, who had been appointed commissioner of Macedonia by Ypsilantis, and Nikolaos Kasomoulis, plenipotentiary of Olympos, were welcomed by the local notables and leaders with lavish feasts. These were traditional events, often accompanied by singing and dancing, but in revolutionary circumstances they took on new meanings. Banquets were now fostering for the first time a sense of shared belonging to the Greek nation among fighters and politicians from far-flung regions, whose affiliations were primarily with other provinces and localities.[10] Given their strong symbolic association with ideas of brotherhood, when disagreements or even hostility had previously existed, banquets could be

---

8. *L'Amico della Costituzione*, 24 July 1821, p. 1. See also Pepe, *Memoirs*, 2, p. 270.

9. *Astro da Lusitania*, no. 248, 22 September 1821, p. 4.

10. Kasomoulis, Ενθυμήματα στρατιωτικά (Military memoirs), 1, pp. 164–71.

employed to mark a renewed or much desired harmony and reconciliation between enemies. The banquet organised by the Alta Vendita of the Carboneria in Naples in honour of all the generals, on the eve of the defensive war against the Austrian invasion, served to show that the Carboneria, in spite of its doubts about the revolutionary credentials of some of the armed forces (such as, in particular, Carrascosa, whom they saw as their political enemy), was determined to show its support for the army, and did not wish to quarrel with the parliament and the regent.[11]

Admittedly, participation in some banquets was confined to military and civil authorities, and many of these events, while aspiring to represent the support for the constitution in society at large, in practice involved mainly commercial and professional elites, besides army officers and prominent civilians. A *jantar constitucional* (constitutional dinner) organised in the arsenal of Lisbon under the presidency of José Xavier Mouzinho da Silveira, then in charge of the customs as *administrador geral*, and under the vice-presidency of a member of the Cortes, and claimed to be the first of its kind ever organised in Portugal, was attended by no fewer than 160 people, who toasted the Cortes, the Portuguese nation, the Portuguese who had initiated the revolution, the constitutional king Dom João, the army and all 'constitutional peoples'. Yet the fact that each subscriber agreed to raise money and make a donation in aid of the prisoners at the arsenal suggests that its participants did not belong to the popular classes.[12] Sometimes the middle-class nature of such events could be discerned also in the banquets organised by secret societies according to the model of Masonic sociability. Following the declaration of the constitution in the town of Voghera in Piedmont in March 1821, members of the society of the Federati organised a banquet at the premises of the Albergo del Moro. Its fifty-two participants were either lawyers, military officers, shopkeepers or landed proprietors.[13]

Banquets might more explicitly assume socially inclusive connotations, however, when their organisers took care to ensure that the participants belonged to all classes. Patriotic societies in particular made a point of involving the lower strata of society in these events, and the offering of food could therefore serve to convey a social message. In so doing they built on pre-existing religious practices: in pre-revolutionary societies it had been religious institutions that had attended to the organisation of

11. Pepe, *Memoirs*, 3, pp. 118–19.

12. *Astro da Lusitania*, no. 225, 27 August 1821, p. 2.

13. AST, Segreteria di Stato Affari Interni, Alta Polizia, Processi politici del 1821, fascio 53, f. 49.

feasts for the indigent. Inspired by such practices, patriots in revolutionary France and in Italy during the revolutionary triennium of 1796–99 provided banquets for the poor to prove that misery could be relieved through brotherhood, and that those at the margins of society could be won over to the cause of democracy and republicanism.[14] In the 1820s this practice was revived to win over the indigent and the popular classes to the constitutional monarchy in Spain, Portugal and Naples alike. The patriotic societies of Madrid insisted on having some artisans and workers attend the banquets in honour of Quiroga and Riego, pointing to their desire to demonstrate the popular foundations of the constitution. In the Kingdom of the Two Sicilies a memorable banquet was organised by the local patriotic society in the main square of the town of Pizzo in Calabria on 1 January 1820 as a means of showing the benefits of the constitution to the poor. The event was covered by the revolutionary press. The patriotic society proudly wrote to the parliament that two thousand paupers, who had been offered a copious lunch served by its young members, confirmed their attachment to the new regime with cries of 'Viva il Re! Viva la nazione! Viva il parlamento nazionale!'[15]

Regardless of their social composition, it should not be forgotten that in the 1820s the organisation of public banquets as markers of political belonging represented a Europe-wide phenomenon whose intensification went hand in hand with the expansion of a liberal public sphere across the entire European continent and beyond. In France, banquets became the hallmark of a new middle-class sociability that favoured liberalism both at home and abroad. Funds for the Greek armed struggle were raised during such public events, at times in the presence of foreign exiled revolutionaries.[16] Public dinners became rituals of solidarity and support for the revolutions abroad among European internationalists, although with potentially different underlying ideological premises. In London, support for the Greek cause was given official status by the invitation of the Greek deputies Anastasios Orlandos and Ioannis Louriottis, sent by the Greek government in 1823 to negotiate a loan, to a dinner in their honour at the Guildhall in the city. This event was attended by the lord mayor and by

14. Glauco Schettini, 'Un rito rivoluzionario: I banchetti per i poveri in Emilia Romagna, 1797–1798', *Contemporanea* 18 (2015): 197–220.

15. ASN, Polizia Generale II, ff. 34, 12: patriotic society to the parliament, 4 January 1821.

16. Vincent Robert, *Le Temps des banquets: Politique et symbolique d'une génération (1818/1848)* (Paris: Publications de la Sorbonne, 2010). For an example of a banquet organised to raise funds for the Greek war, see in *Le Mercure du Dix-Neuvième Siècle*, vol. 13 (1826), pp. 329–30.

George Canning, the secretary for foreign affairs. In Britain sympathy for all revolutionary struggles in southern Europe had nonetheless a quintessentially radical overtone. In October 1820 Major Cartwright, supporter of all international causes for freedom, and convinced of the direct relationship between constitutional reform at home and revolution in continental Europe, publicly embraced the cause of revolution in Portugal, Spain and Naples by organising a dinner with other radical politicians, Sir Robert Wilson among them, Spanish exiles and some Whig grandees. A singer entertained the assembled company with Spanish music, and busts of Riego and Quiroga were mounted on a pedestal for display during the event. This type of sociability supportive of international brotherhood had in turn an impact on the revolutionary public sphere in the south. First of all, events organised in France and Britain resonated in southern Europe too, as wider European backing for southern constitutionalism was reported at great length by the revolutionary press in the countries concerned.[17] Second, the practice of using banquets to celebrate international fraternity travelled along with volunteers to the Mediterranean, who introduced it in Greece. As in France or Britain, depending on the political beliefs and background of their advocates, such rituals could interpret and represent internationalism in differing ways. One particular brand of philhellenism, for instance, was that celebrated by the French naval officer Olivier Voutier, a philhellene who had joined the war under the command of Dimitrios Ypsilantis in 1821. Committed to the cause of independence as an intrinsically Christian one, Voutier recognised the crucial role that France and its king had traditionally played in protecting the Catholic minorities of the islands. In November 1826, having recruited and trained a new regiment, he organised a banquet on Syros on the birthday of the king of France, an event attended by the island's Greek Catholic bishop, its civil authorities and the commander of the French ship docked there, who all toasted the health of the Catholic monarch. The feast took place after the blessing of the regiment's flag by the bishop and a mass for the king.[18]

At these celebrations of the national community regenerated by the revolution, its heroes past and present, including its ancient and its more

17. *Life and Correspondence of Major Cartwright*, ed. F. D. Cartwright, 2 vols (London: Henry Colburn,1826), 2, pp. 201–2; William St. Clair, *That Greece Might Still Be Free: The Philhellenes in the War of Independence* (Cambridge: Open Book Publishers, 2008), p. 209.

18. Jean-Philippe-Paul Jourdain, *Mémoires historiques et militaires sur les événements de la Grèce depuis 1822, jusqu'au combat de Navarin*, 2 vols (Paris: Brissot-Thivars, 1828), 2, p. 274. On his activities in Greece, see also Olivier Voutier, *Mémoires du Colonel Voutier sur la guerre actuelle des grecs* (Paris: Bossange Frères, 1823).

recent martyrs, were given centre stage. As discussed above, the pronunciamientos provided opportunities for the military officers who proclaimed the revolutions to carve out a space for themselves in the public sphere: declaring the revolution was in itself a public event that put them at the heart of rituals deemed to be necessary to legitimise their acts. This in turn fostered a cult of personality for these military heroes. While the nature and intensity of this varied from country to country, it was generally associated with the production of poems and songs, as well as the immediate historical reconstruction of their deeds in the revolutionary press. This cult also had a transnational dimension, encouraged by the press.[19] Spain was the country where the cult of personality and the personification of the revolution was most fully developed. The great public ceremonies organised in honour of Riego and Quiroga's entry into Madrid were only two examples of the series of mass demonstrations, promoted across Spain, that focused on the heroes of the revolution. Riego's presence in the public sphere gradually but steadily gained preeminence at the expense of Quiroga's, the former continuing to be celebrated as a symbol of the constitution in most cities of Spain, either during his visits or through the use of his portrait in public demonstrations.

A second feature of the revolutionary culture of this decade in Spain was the celebration of past heroes and martyrs of the national cause. Their commemoration entailed the reinvention of history through the creation of new revolutionary genealogies and myths of origin for the new political order. What took centre stage as a national official festivity during the Trienio in Spain was the commemoration of the victims of Dos de Mayo (2 May) 1808, the day of the popular insurrection in Madrid, supported in part by Spanish troops, and brutally repressed by the French army. This cult confirmed the argument advanced in Riego's revolutionary manifestos, that the sacrifice of the people in defence of the monarchy against Napoleon deserved to be rewarded by the constitution in 1820. The celebration of these martyrs for the freedom of the nation dated back to 1809, when the Junta Suprema invited all ayuntamientos to commemorate the anniversary of the insurrection, but was organised in a detailed and elaborate way by the Cortes in 1814, once such commemorations could again be staged in the capital city. It was in 1814 that the ashes of the civilian victims of the insurrection were buried in the Campo de la Lealtad, and those of

19. Pierre-Marie Delpu, 'Eroi e martiri: La circolazione delle figure celebri della rivoluzione napoletana nell'Europa liberale, 1820–1825', *Rivista Storica Italiana* 130, no. 2 (2018): 587–614.

the soldiers in a separate memorial in the Parque de Artillería. The burial represented the culmination of an imposing civic procession which included deputies, children and survivors of the insurrection, and which made its way from the Ayuntamiento to the Cortes and took part in a solemn religious commemoration in the church of San Isidro. Maintained by King Fernando during the restoration but celebrated then with exclusively religious ceremonies, the celebration in Madrid was reactivated during the Trienio along the lines first experimented with in 1814. Between 1820 and 1823 the commemoration of the victims of 2 May 1808 became more explicitly a celebration of popular sovereignty, and an endorsement of the liberties enshrined in the constitution. In 1822 detailed plans to raise a monument in Madrid to the victims were ratified, although the ending of the revolution put a stop to its construction. The association between Riego's pronunciamiento and the anti-Napoleonic insurrection in Madrid became common currency also in the speeches during the reunions of the patriotic societies within and beyond Madrid.[20]

The commemoration of martyrs was extended to include those who had died during the revolutions themselves, when fighting in their defence: their funerals became public ceremonies employed for political and patriotic purposes. A collective funeral was organised in Madrid for those members of the civic militia who had died in July 1822 suppressing the attempted counterrevolutionary military coup, and their death was commemorated in a public ceremony also in Barcelona.[21] In Greece, the war provided opportunities to establish a link between the heroes of ancient Greece and the fighters involved in the war against the Ottomans, and turn the death of prominent warriors into tools of patriotic propaganda to encourage resistance against the Ottomans and reactivate the struggle for emancipation. The war produced a pantheon of heroes and martyrs to be employed both for domestic purposes and to stir up international support for the Greek cause. One of these was Markos Botsaris, a Suliot leader who had participated in the insurrection from its earliest stages and had joined the defence of Messolonghi between 1822 and 1823. In August 1823 he died during the battle of Karpenisi in central Greece, while leading 350 Souliots against the vastly superior Albanian army of the pasha of Shkodra. Before he was killed by a bullet his unit had managed to massacre a great number (allegedly eight hundred) of enemy soldiers

20. See Christian Demange, *El Dos de Mayo: Mito y fiesta nacional (1808–1958)* (Madrid: Madrid: Centro de Estudios Políticos y Constitucionales, 2004), pp. 135–47; Gil Novales, *Las sociedades patrióticas*, 1, pp. 70–71, 89–91.

21. Vernet, *La Barcelona revolucionària*, p. 239.

taken by surprise in their camp at night. As soon as this military chieftain died, the provisional government issued a decree signed by the president of the executive Mavromichalis, announcing the heroic death of 'another Greek Leonidas', and inviting all Greeks to imitate Botsaris, 'shake off the lethargy' and 'hasten to the field of Mars to gather crowns of laurel'.[22] The much less heroic death of Lord Byron in Messolonghi in April the following year—the English philhellene died after a short illness—turned out to be a very powerful tool of international propaganda for the Greek cause of independence, providing the war with its most effective symbol. Commemoration was carefully organised as a public event to reconfigure the poet as one of the great martyrs of the war. After being embalmed, his mortal remains were drawn through the streets of Messolonghi, lined with a thousand soldiers, in a procession led by the bishop of Arta, followed by priests and all the civil authorities including Mavrokordatos, and his coffin was laid next to the tombs of the German philhellene Karl von Normann-Ehrenfels and Markos Botsaris. Similar public ceremonies to commemorate Byron were held across the country.[23]

In Naples and Portugal, no individual came to symbolise the constitutional order in quite the same way as Riego did in Spain, nor did new martyrs acquire the same degree of fame as those who died during the Greek war of independence. However, historical events were chosen as precedents for the new constitutional regime, with a view to crafting national revolutionary traditions. In Naples, Masaniello, hero of the 1647 uprising against the Spanish government, was turned into an anti-despotic symbol and a forerunner of the current revolution. A broadsheet published in 1820 entitled 'La Rivoluzione di Masaniello' referred to the symbolic date of disturbances in the market against taxation that had led to Masaniello's revolt, 7 July—the same date as the promulgation of the constitution in that year—praising the reforms that the Neapolitan tribune of the people had implemented but also warning against the excesses of his despotic power. For the anonymous writer, Masaniello's authority was 'admirable and singular' and yet, unfortunately, he became 'intolerable to his own supporters, and cruel to everybody', which led to his fall.[24] In Portugal it was the much more recent memory of General Gomes Freire de Andrade, who was executed in 1817 for his participation in a conspiracy against William Beresford's regency, that would be commemorated as the main

22. Gordon, *History*, 2, pp. 32–34, 42–43.
23. Ibid., pp. 116–18.
24. SNSP, Miscellanea 1820, f. 242: broadsheet, 'La rivoluzione di Masaniello', n.d.

precedent for the 1820 revolution in Porto. For the newspaper *Genio Constitucional*, it was by no means by chance, but rather a sign of providence, that Beresford should have quit Portugal on 18 October 1820, exactly three years after the execution of Freire de Andrade. A public speech delivered on the anniversary of his death declared that Freire finally deserved to be remembered and to be mourned as belonging to the company of martyrs for the fatherland who had died in the struggle against tyranny and despotism, and called for the erection of a marble statue in his memory. A biographical sketch published in 1822 in the *Astro da Lusitania* denied that the general had played any part in the conspiracy, and recalled in detail his final hours, when Freire listened to the tribunal's death sentence and awaited his execution in tranquillity and dignity. For the journalist of the *Astro* these events demonstrated the perversity and despotism of the governadores of Portugal, a despotism that had led directly to the events of 24 August 1820.[25]

In these countries the proliferation of public events in support of the revolution did not simply result in the marginalisation of the church and its ministers with regard to the public sphere, let alone in a dechristianisation. Unlike the public rituals created by the French revolution, in southern Europe (as in restoration France) public ceremonies were not simply aimed at replacing religion, but rather reappropriated it.[26] Revolutionaries were indeed at pains to illustrate in their public rituals the compatibility between their beliefs and religion: a common feature of public celebrations of the revolutions was the presence of religious symbols, and the systematic integration of religious services into these. This transfer of sacrality was designed to confer legitimacy upon the new political order, rooting its origins in the divine order, and grounding it in the moral principles of religion. By so doing, revolutionaries were at times changing the meaning of religion itself, but not thereby denying it.[27] The representation of God bestowing the constitution upon Portugal in the temporary arch raised in Lisbon in 1820 is a case in point. In addition, the Te Deum and religious ceremonies were almost invariably an element in revolutionary celebrations, from the commemoration of the martyrs

25. *Mnemosine Constitucional*, no. 48, 18 November 1820, pp. 2–4; *Astro da Lusitania*, no. 222, 12 November 1822, pp. 1–5. See also *Genio Constitucional*, no. 21, 25 October 1820, p. 4.

26. This observation made by Fuentes for the Spanish case is valid for all the southern European revolutions. See Fuentes, 'La fiesta revolucionaria', p. 58.

27. On the sermons and speeches delivered during these services, see further the section on preaching in chapter thirteen below.

of the Dos de Mayo to the erection of monuments to commemorate the constitution. Sermons had to confirm that a justification for constitutional government or for the national struggle for liberation could be found in the Gospels.

Admittedly, the importance of the religious element varied from ceremony to ceremony, and from context to context. It was in Greece that the blurring of the distinction between the religious and the political in public events was perhaps more pervasive than anywhere else. This was due to the fact that the struggle against the Ottomans and war itself were sacralised. Ceremonies were held both before battles and after them on the actual battlefields. It was on the battlefield at Kalamata that a sequence of rites famously was held after the victory of the two thousand troops led by the Maniot leaders Petrobey Mavromichalis and Dionysis Mourtzinos, who had managed to capture the city in March 1821, enslaving its surviving Muslim inhabitants, in only two days. The following day a thanksgiving ceremony was held on the banks of the river that flowed alongside the city, in which twenty-four priests celebrated a Te Deum in front of five thousand soldiers.[28] What the revolution brought was also an explicit sacralisation of the sacrifice of those fighting for the liberation of the fatherland. But this was not confined to those who had died already, as in the case of the grand funerals for military leaders or volunteers like Byron. The soldiers themselves understood their participation in the war as a sacred mission for the fatherland which required their personal sacrifice. In March 1822, reassured by the arrival of Ypsilantis's 1,200 Peloponnesian troops, Colonel Voutier decided to launch an assault against the citadel of Athens, which had been under protracted siege from his 2,500 Athenian, Boeotian and Aeginian forces. On the day of the attack, during a religious ceremony held in the military camp and attended by the bishop of Athens, soldiers swore on the Gospels, in front of temporary altars consisting of heaped-up stones, to face death. Having adorned their heads with laurel branches blessed by the prelate, they all retired to their tents to perform their funerary rituals.[29] In summer 1823 Botsaris offered a banquet to 240 of his soldiers in honour of the Holy Virgin, protector of Souli, in advance of a major battle in the region of Agrafa in Roumeli. The banquet was followed by a ritual bath in the river, after which the soldiers, washed, dressed and adorned with flowers, awaited their leader's orders

28. Finlay, *History*, 1, pp. 184–85.

29. Alexandre Soutzo, *Histoire de la révolution grecque* (Paris: Didot, 1829), pp. 187–88.

and were encouraged by him to be ready to sacrifice themselves in order to exterminate the encamped enemy troops where they slept at night.[30]

These celebrations of the national community, its martyrs and the constitution were not realised only through the constant enactment of new spatial practices and rituals. Revolutionaries also tried to assert their control over public space in a more permanent way, rearranging it by means of the inauguration of new monuments and the appropriation of existing buildings used now for new purposes and given new meanings. It was also through the monumental reorganisation of cities that the relationship between the sacred and the civil was renegotiated. What drove the revolutionaries' intervention in urban spaces was their determination to destroy the symbols of past regimes, to commemorate the events marking the revolution and to celebrate its own most important symbols. The most systematic attempts to mark public space occurred in Spain. Across the country, plaques were raised to commemorate the promulgation of the constitution, and squares were renamed after it. As some of the events mentioned above suggest, the inaugurations of such squares were among the most important public ceremonies of the Trienio. They were celebrated by civil and military authorities alike.[31] In the town of Dolores, near Alicante, the unveiling of the constitutional plaque on the facade of the town hall was accompanied by speeches, children's dances and a parade of eight individuals on horseback dressed like ancient Spaniards and native Americans to represent the harmony of the empire under the constitution. A triumphal carriage with a throne and a portrait of the king, accompanied by five nymphs, dispensing poems to those in attendance and holding up the text of the constitution, closed the procession.[32] While local councils often footed the bill, sometimes public subscriptions were launched to raise money in support of such patriotic endeavours.[33] In Naples, a financial shortfall and lack of time meant that such plans were not carried out; here too, however, projects for the erection of columns to celebrate the constitution in each town of the kingdom had been discussed in the parliament.[34] The transformation of the monumental space of towns and villages in Greece, started by acts of vandalism carried out during wartime operations, was completed by the conversion of Ottoman buildings.

30. François Pouqueville, *Histoire de la régénération de la Grèce*, 4 vols (Paris: Firmin Didot, 1825), 4, p. 408.

31. AAM, Secretaría, Acontecimientos Políticos, 2–230, no. 2.

32. *Diario de la Ciudad de Valencia*, no. 46, 15 November 1821, pp. 206–8.

33. AHM, Assuntos Militares Gerais, 14/1/11.

34. Daum, *Oscillazioni*, pp. 345–46.

Those mosques which had not been destroyed were used for new purposes. Some of them were turned into Orthodox churches, sometimes thus reconverting them to their original use. This is what happened, for instance, in Argos. In other cases mosques were turned into public buildings and used by the revolutionary authorities. In the city of Tripolitsa, conquered by the Greek insurgents in 1821, for example, the palace of the pasha and its mosque were completely destroyed, but by 1825 one mosque had been used to host the eighty representatives of the Greek legislative assembly, and another had been turned into a school. In Athens too, the assembly of notables met to discuss the administration of the town in a former mosque.[35] Whereas in Portugal, Spain and Naples the defeat of the revolution precluded a permanent reconversion of public space, it was in Greece that the most radical attempts to obliterate the religious past of the region were made, with the reconversion of public and religious buildings proving there to be the most enduring.

Rituals of contestation: singing the revolution

As some of the circumstances discussed so far already suggest, while official celebrations were carried out at the initiative of local or national military and civil leaders, public demonstrations of support for the revolution were not always official events sponsored by state apparatuses. It is important to note that the process of reappropriation of public space discussed above had begun in the form of spontaneous actions carried out by individuals or groups in the earliest stages of the revolution. Violence against public symbols of authority and destruction of monuments had been one of the earliest forms of political participation in these revolutions. These early episodes of iconoclasm were both acts of revenge against the existing regime and affirmations of the popular will.[36] In Palermo in July 1820, for instance, the crowds toppled the statues of the Spanish Bourbons, Philip V and Charles III, going on to first abuse and then pull down the statue of the existing king Ferdinando I.[37] In the city of Pizzo Calabro in Calabria, only the intervention of the local judge prevented a group of

---

35. Pecchio, *Relazione*, pp. 16, 24–25, 28, 48, 95.

36. Emmanuel Fureix, 'L'Iconoclasme: Une pratique politique (1814–1848)?', in *La Politique sans en avoir l'air: Aspects de la politique informelle, XIXᵉ-XXIᵉ siècles*, ed. Laurent Le Gall, François Ploux and Michel Offerlé (Rennes: Presses Universitaires de Rennes, 2012), pp. 117–32; Fureix, *L'Œil blessé: Politiques de l'iconoclasme après la Révolution française* (Ceyzérieu: Éditions Champ Vallon, 2019).

37. Daum, *Oscillazioni*, p. 471.

carbonari from tearing down the statue of the monarch. Parading across the city, they gathered around the statue singing satirical verses suggesting that the king was afraid of being torn down by the miller.[38] In Spain too, the first steps of the revolution were accompanied by acts of iconoclasm. In March 1820 in the city of Valencia, crowds tore down the monument erected in 1814 to commemorate the return of the monarch from his exile, and replaced it with one commemorating the constitution.[39] Again, the most systematic destruction of the symbols of the past regime was carried out in Greece. Here iconoclasm targeted first and foremost mosques and the buildings that represented the authority of the Ottomans. Vandalism towards these buildings took various forms. The first was symbolic: as ultimate acts of humiliation and defiance horsemen and troops entered and fouled these religious buildings, gestures that vividly demonstrate an identification in the minds of those rebelling between religion and the enemy, the Ottoman Empire. Often the armies simply set fire to the premises: this is what Samian fighters did to two mosques during their expedition to the island of Chios when they entered the town there.[40]

Although revolutionary authorities hastened to introduce and organise new public rituals, they never managed to acquire a complete monopoly of the public space: spatial practices in fact continued to enjoy a degree of autonomy. They could even be used to challenge the newly constituted authorities, thus competing with governments or revolutionary leaders. Moving as they did across society, public practices were adopted in a range of different circumstances and for varying purposes. The highly conflictual nature of revolutionary politics, marked as they were by civil strife and deep social and political contrasts, facilitated their use in a variety of circumstances. The circulation and adoption of existing practices, and the spontaneous creation of new ones, help us understand the role played by ordinary citizens in the creation of a popular revolutionary culture, one at least to some degree independent of those devised or sponsored by elites or, indeed, by revolutionary institutions themselves. It also shows that revolutionary culture not only aimed at encouraging unity and reconciliation, but also provided tools for protest, contestation and the redefinition of specific political groups when pitted against their enemies. Divisions within the revolutionary front, tensions between local authorities and national government and the social conflicts precipitated

38. ASN, Borbone, 726, f. 239.
39. Romeo Mateo, *Entre el orden*, p. 88.
40. St. Clair, *That Greece*, p. 39; Gordon, *History*, 1, pp. 298, 355.

by civil wars all encouraged new cultural practices, or lent new meanings to existing ones.

A number of revolutionary organisations played a key role in adopting these practices, not only in support of local and national governments, but also when challenging them. As will be discussed below, the lodges of the Carboneria in Naples and the Comunería in Spain in a similar fashion took on this twofold role of providing public support but also challenging national governments. Spanish patriotic societies likewise not only joined official ceremonies (as described previously) in order to give their backing to revolutionary governments but, in the case of those controlled by the exaltados, felt entitled to challenge governments.

The transformation of Riego from a symbol of national consensus and unity behind the constitution into the most powerful instrument of exaltado contestation against the moderados exemplifies the transformation that public cults could undergo. Patriotic societies controlled by the supporters of the exaltados played a key role in this shift. Riego's immediate popularity throughout Spain stemmed from his being regarded as the saviour incarnate of the fatherland and of freedom, and his figure came to be closely identified with the defence of the constitution. Evoking his name in public demonstrations with cries of 'iViva Riego!' equated to cheering the constitution. As a matter of fact, the consensus regarding his public role had been unstable from the very outset. When he was welcomed in Madrid in early September 1820, the public authorities banned a banquet in the Plaza de Toros, fearing popular excesses, and the disturbances that erupted in the theatre, where he was accused of having sung the 'Trágala' in a less than wholly veiled attack upon the government, led to his dismissal from the captaincy-general of Galicia and his expulsion from the capital.[41] Yet it was his dismissal from the captaincy-general of Aragon in September 1821 that put him at the centre of a wave of popular protests against the government and the moderados, often organised or at least supported by the patriotic societies. In these public demonstrations Riego's portrait would be carried in procession. The religiosity of this practice, derived from the tradition of displaying images or statues of saints in a solemn fashion during the annual festivities for local saints

41. Víctor Sánchez Martín, '"Que nada importa que yo sufra", o La servidumbre de Riego: Mito y lucha política entre moderados y exaltados durante el Trienio Constitucional', *Ayer*, forthcoming (2022), DOI: https://doi.org/10.55509/ayer/900. On the key features of his myth, see also La Parra López, *Los Cien Mil Hijos*, pp. 244–47. Jodi Roca Vernet, 'Las imágenes de la cultura política liberal durante el Trienio (1820–1823): El caso de Barcelona', *Cuadernos de Ilustración y Romanticismo* 10 (2002): 185–220.

and patrons, was now turned into an expression of political protest, to the extent that in some cities such displays were prohibited by the authorities. In Madrid the jefe político banned the procession organised by the Fontana de Oro, but the public demonstration nonetheless went ahead on 18 September and paraded Riego's portrait through the city, along the Prado towards Puerta del Sol and Calle Mayor. Before it could reach the Ayuntamiento, however, the demonstrators were dispersed by the armed forces. In the city of Seville, processions displaying Riego's portrait took place over two consecutive days (13–14 September). Organised in the local *café constitucional*, the demonstrators mounted the portrait on a cart adorned with flags and military trophies, and flowers, and a combination of clerics, civilians, and soldiers from the local garrisons, all holding candles, paraded through the city singing patriotic songs. The procession was occasionally interrupted to allow a cleric to give speeches in honour of Riego.[42] Admittedly, Riego was not only well aware of his own fame, but presented himself as a *super partes* defender of the constitutional order appealing to the entire nation, disapproving of party politics and public disorder and submitting himself not only to the authority of the Cortes, but also to that of the government and the monarch. Yet his appeals for peace and unanimity, which he made repeatedly in public speeches across the country, often went unheeded, and between 1821 and 1822 he became a tool of protest and contestation.[43]

In these circumstances, therefore, the public display of political objects by men and women alike constantly changed meaning. From the outset of the revolution, individuals demonstrated their support for the constitution by wearing green ribbons attached to cockades or hats. Some of this material culture was gender-specific: women used fans decorated with images of Riego and Quiroga, or allegorical images of the constitution. They also wore *mantillas* (shawls) with green ribbons or inscriptions referring to the constitution. Soon after the revolution, however, these symbols became explicitly associated with exaltado politics, with ribbons and hats bearing the motto 'Constitución o muerte' (constitution or death), or 'Constitución o venganza' (constitution or revenge).[44]

42. Gil Novales, *Las sociedades patrióticas*, 1, pp. 457–60, 655–58.

43. Sánchez Martín, '"Que nada importa"'.

44. Álvaro París Martín and Jordi Roca Vernet, 'Green Ribbons and Red Berets: Political Objects and Clothing in Spain (1808–1843)', in *Political Objects in the Age of Revolution: Material Culture, National Identities, Political Practices*, ed. Carlotta Sorba and Enrico Francia (Rome: Viella, 2021), pp. 61–96. On the uses of these mottos on clothing, see AHN, Consejos Suprimidos, legajo 12271: comandante geral of Jean (Catalonia) to the secretario de estado, 24 August 1823.

Singing, music and dancing were undoubtedly the most popular elements of revolutionary culture in the 1820s. They became a pervasive feature of the public sphere precisely because individuals or groups adopted
them in a variety of circumstances beyond the public celebrations organised by the revolutionary authorities. A study of the prevalence of singing
in fact tells us more about public backing for the revolutions than does
examination of any other practice. It provides evidence in particular of
women's participation in the public sphere: by singing, women demonstrated their support for the revolutionary cause in a wide range of contexts. Singing turned their role at public events from that of being passive
spectators into that of protagonists and active participants; for by their
very nature songs were 'uniquely accessible means of communication'.[45]
Singing was a communal practice that long pre-dated the revolutions, representing an important feature of the popular culture of ancien-régime
societies, and one that often provided the raw material—the tunes and the
rhymes—that would be adapted to fit new political circumstances. What
enhanced the circulation and adoption of songs was the fact that they
occupied a position between oral and print cultures. During the revolutions they became available in very cheap and easily reproducible song-
sheets, often reprinted in newspapers, but circulated also in manuscript
form. In addition, songs were amenable to being learnt by heart; their
oral communication facilitated their adoption, as well as their adaptation
to different contexts, and their reappropriation and new interpretation. In
addition, singing (along with dancing) created a actual bodily sense of unity,
arousing and expressing emotions as no other political practice could. As
one scholar has recently observed, it was precisely the deeply physical and
emotional nature of singing and dancing that 'helped to weave people's daily
lives into the political and military conflicts of the period'.[46]

For these reasons, in this same period the introduction of national
anthems was accompanied by a proliferation of patriotic songs. In Spain
the 'Himno de Riego', commissioned by Riego himself on the eve of the
pronunciamiento as a song to be sung by his own soldiers and composed by his comrade Evaristo San Miguel, almost immediately acquired

45. On this feature of music as a revolutionary medium, see Laura Mason, *Singing the
French Revolution: Popular Culture and Politics 1787–1799* (Ithaca, NY: Cornell Univer-
sity Press, 1996), p. 3. See also Oskar Cox Jensen, *Napoleon and British Song, 1797–1822*
(London: Palgrave Macmillan, 2015). On its centrality in popular culture, see David Hop-
kin, *Voices of the People in Nineteenth-Century France* (Cambridge: Cambridge University
Press, 2012).

46. Mark Philp, *Radical Conduct: Politics, Sociability and Equality in London,
1789–1815* (Cambridge: Cambridge University Press, 2020), p. 210.

universal fame across Spain. With its refrain that exhorted soldiers to defend the fatherland or die ('Soldiers, the fatherland calls us to the fight. / Let us swear for her to vanquish or to die') and its reference to Riego's love for the fatherland, the 'Himno' became the most popular tune of the revolution. It also acquired official status, as in 1822 the Cortes declared it to be the army's official march. Yet it was not the only patriotic *himno* composed in the period: at least two more were dedicated to the citizen Riego, and others still to the re-establishment of the constitution.[47] An equally popular patriotic song was the 'Trágala'. Composed in the city of Cádiz in March 1820, this rapidly acquired national fame but, unlike the 'Himno de Riego', it almost immediately took on far more radical and popular overtones, and became associated with the liberalism of the exaltados and their supporters. At least three different versions circulated, but in each case the text defended the constitution and defied its enemies: the absolutists, and the moderates who advocated the creation of a second chamber, as well as friars and all those parasitical groups who lived at the expense of the popular classes, and who were told in forthright terms, 'Trágala, perro', or 'Swallow it, dog'.[48]

Similarly in Portugal, a 'Hymno constitucional' gained official status in 1820 as the national anthem, replacing a 'Hymno patriotico da nação portugueza' composed in 1808 in honour of the monarch; but plenty of other constitutional and patriotic songs were composed for specific occasions, such as the union of the provisional governments of Porto and Lisbon, the gathering of the Cortes in January 1821 and the first anniversary of the revolution in Porto in August 1821. Their production was not confined to the capital, moreover, since a spontaneous multiplication of works belonging to this musical genre can be detected also in many provincial towns: in provinces such as Beira, for example.[49] In 1826 the introduction of a new

47. A collection of Spanish revolutionary songs is in Mariano de Cabrerizo, *Coleccion de canciones patrióticas que dedica al ciudadano Rafael del Riego y a los valientes que han seguido sus huellas* (Valencia: Venancio Olivares, 1822), which includes the 'Himno a Riego' and other songs dedicated to him. On the origins of Riego's 'Himno', see Antonio Alcalá Galiano, *Memorias de Antonio Alcalá Galiano, publicadas por su hijo*, 2 vols (Madrid: E. Rubiños, 1886), 2, pp. 16–18. See also La Parra López, *Los Cien Mil Hijos*, pp. 233–40.

48. Versions of the 'Trágala' are included in Cabrerizo, *Coleccion de canciones*, pp. 45–47, 52–54. On this song, see also Emilio La Parra López, La canción del *Trágala*: Cultura y política popular en el inicio de la revolución liberal en España', *Les Travaux du CERC en Ligne*, no. 6 (2009), in *La Réception des cultures de masse et des cultures populaires en Espagne (XVII–XX siècles)*, ed. S. Salaün and F. Etienvre, available at https://crec-paris3.fr/wp-content/uploads/2011/07/actes-03-La-Parra.pdf (accessed 14 August 2022).

49. On Portuguese music, see Vargues, *A aprendizagem*, pp. 276–83.

FIGURE 17. Front cover, *Coleccion de canciones patrióticas, 1823* (book of 'Patriotic songs . . . dedicated by Citizen Mariano de Cabrerizo to Citizen Rafael de Riego and the brave men and women who followed in his footsteps'; Valencia, printed for Venancio Oliveres, 1822). Image: Biblioteca Valenciana Digital/ Creative Commons

constitution was marked by a new wave of publication of patriotic songs that might be sung alongside the new official anthem of the kingdom, the 'Hymno constitucional' dedicated to Dom Pedro. Various anthems were composed specifically to be sung and played at the beginning of theatre performances.[50] This proliferation of songs to celebrate the revolution was undoubtedly facilitated by the widespread practice of improvisation, not only by professional musicians but also by ordinary citizens. At the beginning of the revolution in Piedmont, and in particular in the town of Porto San Maurizio in the coastal region of Liguria, a teacher was reported to have recited poetry and written patriotic songs with his students. In another coastal town, Ventimiglia, on the day of the official celebrations of the constitution a notary had composed and sung a 'canzone patriottica' during a public banquet.[51] In the Kingdom of the Two Sicilies constitutional balls were organised, with music and songs commissioned to welcome the revolu-

tion. In the town of Melfi in Basilicata, for instance, at a ball attended by the members of the local vendite of the Carboneria, an anthem composed for the occasion was sung by all the participants. Its verses were dedicated to King Ferdinando, as prince and father of the (Carboneria's) squads and the fatherland.[52]

50. *Hymno constitucional: Cantado no Real Theatro do Porto em Julho de 1826* (Porto: A. L. de Oliveira, 1826).

51. AST, Segreteria di Stato Affari Interni, Alta Polizia, Processi politici del 1821, 59, no. 4: notes on Bonfante, Contado di Nizza; ibid., Moti del 1821, Sconvolgimenti politici, 29, 4: notes on Domenico Laura, Contado di Nizza (Nice).

52. ASN, Borbone, 726, f. 221: 'Memoria su Giovan Battista Rega'.

Like other practices, however, after the initial phase of the revolutions singing became a key element of partisan politics. No longer expressing unity in support of the revolution, it came to signify political affiliations in a context of contestation and even violent confrontation. The political battles of the period greatly contributed to the autonomous use of songs, changing the value of singing itself. In Spain, the meaning of patriotic singing altered along with that of the cult of Riego discussed above, taking on the same politically divisive and subversive meaning as Riego himself did. The notorious incident that led to the expulsion of Riego from Madrid and his banishment to the Asturias—the allegation that he had sang the 'Trágala' during the theatre performance organised in honour of his visit on 3 September 1820—is a case in point. While the 'Himno de Riego' was sung without disorder or opposition in the interval after the second act of the performance, the public then decided to sing the much more contro-versial 'Trágala', against the orders of the jefe político of Madrid, who was attending the event. The government considered this to be a subversive act, directed as much against it as against the monarch.[53] From then on singing not only the 'Trágala', but also the 'Himno de Riego' became an act of protest by the exaltados and their supporters in the patriotic societies against the moderate governments of Spain. The public disorder following the decision of the government to expel Riego from Madrid for singing was accompanied by more public singing by protesters in the streets and in the square in front of the theatre. The public demonstrations against the government that took place from the end of 1821 onwards after the dismissal of Riego not only had their most prominent symbolic element in the display of Riego's portrait, but were almost invariably accompanied by the singing of his 'Himno'. This 'Himno' and the 'Trágala' became tools to exert pressure on local authorities and the government. Singing them became also acts of defiance against absolutists. The tertulia patriótica of the town of El Carpio in Andalusia concluded each of its public sessions, attended by crowds that included women, with the singing of the 'Trágala' and the symbolic burial of the *serviles* (absolutists).[54] Besides adopting the 'Trágala' and the 'Himno de Riego', the culture of protest and opposition of the exaltados made use of other songs that explicitly celebrated their own values and condemned their enemies as enemies of the revolution. One song dedicated to the exaltados in fact defined them, for their patriotic

53. Gil Novales, *Las sociedades patrióticas*, 1, pp. 126–28; Description of the protests on 5 September in AAM, Secretaría, Acontecimientos Políticos, 2–230, no. 26.
54. Gil Novales, *Las sociedades patrióticas*, 1, p. 483.

qualities, as 'the most valued class of the nation', and 'Law or Death' as the motto that best defined *exaltación*.[55]

Given how easily they could be reproduced and communicated, songs travelled far and wide, even across state borders. Their transnational circulation contributed to the multiplication of their uses and meanings. Once they started to be adopted, their uses and dissemination were no longer under the control of those who had first produced them. There is some evidence, for instance, that the Spanish revolutionary tunes were adopted in Portugal in particular, as a mark of support for the constitution both during the Triénio and the 'Biénio Cartista' (1826–28), at a time when the civil war and anti-constitutional insurrections made the survival of the constitution seem precarious. For example, in the pro-constitutional coastal city of Figueira da Foz in September 1827, the public attending a performance at a theatre spontaneously stood up and sang not only the more predictable Portuguese 'Constitutional', but also the Spanish 'Himno de Riego' and the 'Trágala'.[56] However, the revolutionary space across which singing culture travelled furthest was the Greek. During the Greek revolution it was Rigas Velestinlis's famous 'Thourios hymnos' that acquired the status of a semi-official national anthem, but its circulation had started well before, crossing the boundaries of empires and seas from Vienna, where it had first been printed in 1797, along with the author's revolutionary proclamation and a republican constitution for Greece. It was through this republican text and his early but failed revolutionary attempt that ended with his arrest in Trieste and his execution by the Austrians, that Rigas became transformed into a protomartyr of the Greek national cause. Since most of the original printed copies had been confiscated, in the years that followed the hymn circulated mostly in manuscript form, independently from the constitution, as its four pages of text were much more easily transcribed than the other texts originally attached to it. On the eve of the revolution the members of the Philiki Etaireia adopted the 'Thourios' as their own song: their networks further facilitated its adoption in the Danubian Principalities, in the Greek community of Constantinople, in the Peloponnese and on the islands.[57] The religious ceremonies marking the arrival of Ypsilantis in Bucharest in March 1821 were accompanied by the singing of the 'Thourios'. But this practice marked the beginning of the revolution everywhere. In the village of Therisos on

55. Cabrerizo, *Coleccion de canciones*, pp. 64–66.

56. ANTT, IGP, Coimbra 286, f. 236: juíz de fora to intendente geral, September 1827.

57. Apostolos Daskalakis, '"Thourios Hymnos", le chant de la liberté de Rhigas Velestinlis', *Balkan Studies* 4 (1963): 315–46.

Crete, for instance, a musician noted for his playing the lyre had been singing the 'Thourios' long before the revolution on the island, and continued
to do so after its outbreak.[58] In the city of Salonica it was reported that in
the early days of the revolution a man had been arrested by the Ottoman
authorities for teaching this same song to children.[59]

The 'Thourios' was not, however, the only hymn sung during the Greek
revolution to reach new audiences and circulate for the first time in new
territories. What the revolution did was to intensify the adoption and circulation of pre-existing folk music. Popular songs often belonged to the
culture of local communities, and ballads performed on some islands were
not known on others, but during the revolution some traditional music
acquired a more general 'national' appeal. The fortune of klephtic ballads
is a case in point.[60] These were popular songs dedicated to the Christian
brigands of continental Greece who were often repressed, but sometimes
also employed, by the Ottoman authorities, and their verses turned those
who had lost their lives in conflicts with leaders like Ali Pasha into heroes,
and their deeds into patriotic endeavours. Some of these ballads also told
stories of other exceptional individuals, and of Greek women. Belonging to
a tradition of the mainland, and unknown on the islands, during the revolution these ballads were adopted everywhere and became vastly popular
as national songs.[61] What additionally enhanced their fame is the fact that,
more than any other corpus of revolutionary songs of the period, those of
Greece acquired too an international appeal. For the philhellenes, their
texts bore evidence of the existence of an ancient national popular culture that was proof of the resistance of the Greeks against the Ottomans.
It was in particular Claude Fauriel's best-selling collection of verses that
stressed the continuity between modern and ancient Greek culture, and
their translation contributed to the popularity of the Greek cause and the
literary appeal of the philhellenic movement.[62]

The practice of singing became a pervasive feature of the Greek revolutionary experience above all because it was not restricted to peacetime, but

58. Kritovoulides, *Narrative*, p. 13.

59. Mark Mazower, *Salonica: City of Ghosts; Christians, Muslims and Jews, 1430–1950*
(London: Harper Collins, 2004), pp. 133–34.

60. Finlay, *History*, 1, pp. 27–29, 77.

61. Kasomoulis, Ενθυμήματα στρατιωτικά (Military memoirs), 1, pp. 164–72.

62. Claude Fauriel, *Chants populaires de la Grèce moderne*, 2 vols (Paris: Dondey-
Dupré, 1824–25); English translation as *The Songs of Greece* (London: Longman, Hurst,
Rees, Orme, Brown & Green, 1825). Another example of European translation of Greek
songs is represented by Panagiotis Soutsos, *Odes d'un jeune grec, suivies de six chants de
guerre* (Paris: Emler Frères, 1828).

also featured during military activities by soldiers and civilians, men and women, on the mainland and the islands alike. When Nikolaos Kasomoulis, an affiliate of the Philiki acquainted with many revolutionary leaders, travelled from the Peloponnese to the islands in autumn 1821, he noted that the sailors and captains of vessels from Psara were all committed to the liberation of the nation, and among them 'you could not hear anything else but songs for freedom'.[63] The newly appointed leader of the insurgent army on Crete was reputed to have sung patriotic tunes all night to embolden his troops prior to their assault upon the fortress of Rethymno.[64] In general, singing was very closely associated with military pursuits.

Although women might not be directly involved in the fighting, singing enabled them to show their support for the war in a variety of circumstances. In the Adriatic city of Trieste the women of the local Greek community sang the 'Thourios' while sewing flags with the symbols of the Philiki for the army of Dimitrios Ypsilantis, about to embark for Greece and fight.[65] On the eve of the patriotic war against the Austrians, it was through music that Neapolitan women contributed to public displays of solidarity for rearmament and military mobilisation. Women sang on the nights preceding the expedition, and thus made manifest their support for the members of the legions and the provincial militias, singing verses in favour of national independence in the streets of the towns around Avellino.[66]

In Spain too, the intensification of the civil war and the invasion by the French army in 1823 changed once again the context in which constitutional songs were used, and their purpose. Taking on the role that anthems had recently acquired in Greece and in Naples on the eve of the Austrian invasion, the 'Himno de Riego' regained its quintessentially military quality and was adopted in the armed struggle against the enemies of the constitution, whether foreigners or not. This was the spirit in which it was revived by the troops of General Mina in Catalonia, the last bastion of constitutional resistance in an occupied country. In an environment increasingly hostile to the constitution, singing came more generally to be employed as a signal of defiance, and became a part of rituals that involved direct confrontations, sometimes violent, with political enemies. A few

63. Kasomoulis, Ενθυμήματα στρατιωτικά (Military memoirs), 1, p. 147.

64. Kritovoulides, *Narrative*, pp. 74–75.

65. Ioannis K. Mazarakis-Ainian, Η ιστορία της ελληνικής σημαίας (The history of the Greek flag) (Athens: National Historical Museum, 2007), p. 17.

66. 'Relazione dal Principato Ultra', 9 March 1821, in Alberti, *Atti del parlamento*, 3, p. 610.

weeks before the end of the war, when the French army had advanced into the territory of Spain and was already besieging the Cortes in Cádiz, the refusal of certain regiments and their supporters to accept the terms of the capitulation agreed by most constitutional generals did not remain unnoticed by the French occupying authorities. In the town of Úbeda in the province of Jaén, the fortieth regiment of Navarre thus not only refused to follow the example of General Ballesteros and of José María Torrijos, who had by then given up fighting, but rather continued to declare their public support for the constitution in front of the local realistas. The open confrontation between the two parties, which resulted in the temporary victory of the constitutional forces, was carried out through singing: the regiment sang the 'Himno de Riego' and other constitutional songs, while the realistas sang their own anthems before retreating. The presence of these troops had also in fact encouraged a final act of allegiance to the revolution by a number of local civilians, who decided to erect a constitutional plaque.[67]

Civil war and military confrontation were equally important in redefining the meaning of singing patriotic tunes in Portugal. The oscillation between singing as an act of celebration of the revolution and singing as an act of contestation and defiance is best demonstrated by its public use in the years from 1826 to 1828. The introduction of the Carta by Dom Pedro in 1826 took place in a highly divided society, and repeated military insurrections and constant civil strife put it under a constant threat of being revoked (until its final abolition by Dom Miguel in March 1828). Even when the civil war formally came to an end in early 1827, the political divisions within individual communities persisted. In this context of divisions and permanent tensions between rival groups, singing became an explicit act of allegiance and a means of reaffirming a specific set of political values. It was employed by individuals or groups to challenge their political enemies in public and remind them that, although under threat, certain political beliefs were still alive and widely shared in the community. The public practice of singing in the town of Sabugal, in the comarca of Castelo Branco on the border with Spain, is a case in point. Here popular support for the constitution was also matched by an equally strong hostility towards it: the town had in fact been the scene of a royalist insurrection in December 1826, and in the months to follow it hosted absolutist armed groups that until then had been hiding in Spanish territories. In

June 1826 the introduction of the Carta was welcomed by its supporters in Sabugal with the public singing of the 'Hymno constitucional', but this was also a self-conscious act of defiance against its enemies in a divided community: its opponents were in fact equally outspoken in venting their public hostility to such acts of loyalty to the constitution, and demonstrated in their turn against its supporters.[68]

Once Dom Miguel had returned to Portugal from his exile, seized power and, in 1828, abolished the constitution, singing the 'Hymno constitucional' became an act of resistance in a politically hostile environment. The announcement of Dom Miguel's landing in Lisbon in 1828 provoked public demonstrations of joy, but also clashes between his supporters and the advocates of the constitution, and in these violent confrontations music and singing were employed to mark affiliation to distinct political 'parties'. In the university city of Coimbra the arrival of Dom Miguel was celebrated with public ceremonies that included a Te Deum, and for three consecutive nights the town was lit up as a sign of rejoicing. During these nights, however, the supporters of the constitution did not fail to make their dissatisfaction public, and on the evening of 28 February two groups confronted each other, one playing the 'Hymno' of Dom Pedro and the other the 'Hymno real' (probably the one composed for Dom João VI as absolute monarch in 1809), until midnight. The public authorities had no doubts that such determination to sing and play the constitutional hymn in the midst of the festivities was an act of defiance against the new regime.[69]

In the same month Dom Miguel made the 'Hymno constitucional' illegal. Establishing absolutism required censorship and control over musical and singing activities as much as over information and printed material. Putting an end to the revolution meant also silencing it. From the perspective of his supporters and the police forces of the new absolute monarchy, singing was no longer a sign of political enthusiasm but a source of disorder, a dangerous indication of insurrection and dissent that had perforce to be repressed. From then on, therefore, singing became not only an act of defiance, but also an activity that could lead to imprisonment, as an explicit and undeniable sign of insubordination. Opposition to Dom Miguel continued to be marked by musical and singing activities, nevertheless. During the constitutional pronunciamientos and insurrections that took place in May 1828 in Porto, Coimbra and the Algarve, both civilian and military

68. ANTT, IGP, Castelo Branco 277, f. 297: 22 June 1826.
69. Ibid., Coimbra 286, f. 289: juíz de fora to intendente geral, 2 March 1828.

officers sang the 'Hymno'—as did some Franciscan friars in their monastery in Tavira, to demonstrate their own support for the constitution during the military uprising against Dom Miguel.[70] This practice continued in public also in the months following the suppression of these constitutional uprisings, signalling the permanence of a liberal public opinion that, even if by increasingly isolated acts, was not shy of demonstrating its existence and asserting its beliefs in the face of political defeat. Singing may thus have become a way of continuing political activism and engagement, and the only one possible at the time. By the end of 1828, when Lisbon was under the control of Dom Miguel, groups of individuals were still reported to be acclaiming Dom Pedro with hurrahs and the singing of his 'Hymno' in Lisbon while crossing the river Tagus from the Cais do Sodré.[71] With the consolidation of Dom Miguel's power, such isolated acts of resistance ceased to feature in public spaces, but far from disappearing entirely, the practice of singing constitutional hymns came to be confined to the (not entirely) safer sheltered interiors of people's houses. In the liberal city of Lagos in the Algarve, women were denounced for singing the 'Hymno' in their own homes after the suppression of the military pronunciamiento in favour of the constitution in the city just a few weeks before.[72] The disappearance of singing from the public sphere followed a similar trajectory in Spain. In October 1823 the death penalty was introduced for those who dared to shout 'Viva Riego, viva la constitución, viva la libertad!', along with any other form of public support for the previous regime, as demonstrations of insubordination against the monarch.[73] The practice of singing was still occasionally reported by informers even after 1823, however—as a dangerous sign of insubordination and evidence of the threats posed by liberal conspiracies in provincial cities.[74] The end of the revolution and the re-establishment of absolutism in Portugal and Spain were thus marked by the disappearance from the public arena of all revolutionary practices, and by the repression of all public acts of protest. It was in the confinement of the private sphere that the singing of constitutional anthems, the last and only possible remaining form of political dissent available to those who could not resign themselves to absolutism, survived and continued to be practised. This, the most common of

70. Ibid., Algarve 244, f. 540, juíz de fora to intendente geral, Tavira, 19 December 1828.

71. Ibid., Romulares 228, f. 464: 13 November 1828.

72. Ibid., Algarve 244, f. 405: 2 October 1828.

73. La Parra López, *Fernando VII*, p. 503.

74. APR, Papeles Reservados de Fernando VII, 71, f. 313: report on the public mood, March 1827.

public revolutionary practices, was also the hardest to eliminate once it had retreated from the streets, squares and public buildings; but even if exercised in private, it could often still be detected by its enemies.

Secret societies: from clandestine opposition to public advocacy

The outbreak of the revolutions marked a new phase in the life of secret societies. Rather than simply losing their raison d'être and disappearing, secret societies gained new influence and radically changed in nature, taking on new roles and broadening the scope of their activities. Although some simply disintegrated soon after the initial stages of the revolution, other, new ones emerged. Those that survived the transition underwent a profound transformation and increased their membership. Admittedly, these old and new societies never abandoned the principle of secrecy that had defined their clandestine nature, nor the rituals of initiation necessary to join them. With the revolutions, however, most secret societies gained a key role in the public sphere. Their members came to believe that the duty to defend the revolutionary order could only be honoured through a range of new public activities. Along with patriotic societies and civil militias, 'secret' societies used their organisational structures to intervene in the political life of their countries, to influence the new revolutionary public opinion and to mobilise people in public protests. In his memoirs, a prominent member of the Carboneria, Orazio De Attellis, wrote that as soon as the revolutionary army with the flags of the Carboneria entered Naples in July 1820, 'the words carbonaro, liberal and patriot became synonyms. The Kingdom of the Two Sicilies became one great lodge [*vendita*], and as a consequence the sect was no longer a sect.'[75] It is to this new role of secret societies—acquired in Naples, Greece and Spain during the revolutions—that this section is devoted.

Given the crucial role the secret societies played in planning and carrying out the pronunciamientos, the first context in which they went public was a military one. Having planned and lead the military insurrections in the Ottoman Empire and in Naples respectively, the Philiki and the Carboneria employed their symbols and banners publicly from the earliest stages of the uprisings. Armed insurrections, whether peaceful or not, were thus explicitly carried out as secret society initiatives, and

75. De Attellis, *L'ottimestre costituzionale*, p. 131.

revolutionary armies continued to display the societies' symbols during the military activities that were conducted beyond the initial stages of the revolution.

Ypsilantis's army had owed its organisation to the efforts of the Philiki, and his military expedition was therefore publicly advertised as their own. The flag featuring the symbols of the Philiki had first been adopted by Ypsilantis's Sacred Band at the end of February 1821 in Jassy, where it had been blessed in a public ceremony after a solemn procession in a church. Ypsilantis was presented with the flag in front of soldiers and civilians who all swore an oath to liberate the fatherland. According to the military laws of the Philiki, drafted at the end of the previous year by Alexandros Ypsilantis's brother Nicolaos, who led the Sacred Band, the Greek flag should have three colours: namely, white, black and red; and should also include the symbols of the cross on one side and a phoenix on the other. White symbolised the innocence and the justice of the enterprise against tyranny; black referred to death for freedom and the fatherland; and red to the self-determination of the Greek people and the resurrection of its fatherland.[76]

These symbols and colours, with allowance made for a degree of freedom and adaptation, were employed both by the military units and the revolutionary navy during the first year of the revolution. They thus represented the struggle for national liberation and the anti-Ottoman war, in a blend of religious and national references that combined the notions of regeneration, struggle in the name of Christianity and martyrdom for freedom.[77] Likewise, the first revolutionary fleet organised on the islands of Hydra, Spetses and Psara adopted the symbols of the Philiki on the flags of its warships: a vigilant eye, along with a cross on a crescent, an anchor, a serpent and a bird, which referred to the struggle against the Ottoman Empire.[78]

However, this systematic military use of the symbols of the Philiki did not last long, coming to an end with the disintegration of the organisation. Two factors determined its disappearance. First, Dimitrios Ypsilantis's attempt to apply the centralised and quasi-military model of the Philiki to the structures of the Greek administration proved intolerable to the Greek

76. Ypsilantis to the Ephors of Patras, 23 February 1821, in Alexandre Ypsilanti [Alexandros Ypsilantis], *Correspondance inédite*, ed. Gregori Arš and Constantin Svolopoulos (Thessaloniki: Institute for Balkan Studies, 1999), pp. 73–74.

77. Mazarakis-Ainian, Η ιστορία (The history), pp. 15–17; Comstock, *History*, p. 182.

78. John Meletopoulos, *The Greek Navy in 1821* (Athens: Commercial Credit Bank, 1971).

primates. The decision officially to abolish the symbols of the Philiki was taken during the first national assembly in 1822, thanks to the vote of the primates, who lent their support to Mavrokordatos, by then a rival to Ypsilantis and deeply hostile to his personal power.[79] Besides its association with centralised controls, what determined the organisation's disappearance from the public sphere was the awareness of the Greek leaders that in order to render their cause respectable in the eyes of European public opinion and the relevant governments, their revolution had to be disassociated from conspiracy and secret societies. As a result of the abolition of the organisation and its symbols in 1822, public use of the latter decreased dramatically, and they were gradually replaced by others on the flags of each military unit.

The end of the Philiki did not signal the disappearance of secret societies from Greece during the revolution, however, but opened up a new phase of their life that coincided with the arrival of European philhellenes and foreign emissaries. In these new Masonic or para-Masonic organisations Greek revolutionaries interacted with foreign representatives and foreign volunteers. A vendita of the Carboneria, for instance, was established in Nafplion, along with other lodges, by European philhellenes between 1821 and 1828. In 1824 another secret society, called the 'Sacred Body' was founded in Russia to promote that country's political and diplomatic interests in Greece, with the aim of putting Grand Duke Constantine on the throne of independent Greece. By the following year it had sent emissaries, established contacts and acquired members on the Ionian islands and the islands of the Aegean and in continental Greece, who vouchsafed their support for the czar himself and Count Kapodistrias.[80] Kapodistrias, concerned with the damage secret societies might do to the reputation of the newly formed state in the eyes of the foreign powers, but also with the threat they posed to him personally, resolved when he took power in 1828 to crack down on their activities and therefore declared them illegal. Nonetheless, their presence continued to be felt, and transnational networks remained in association the presence of European philhellenes. As in the previous years, their activities oscillated

79. Loukos, *Αλέξανδρος Μαυροκορδάτος* (Alexandros Mavrokordatos), pp. 22–23.

80. Douglas Dakin, *British Intelligence of Events in Greece, 1824–1827: A Documentary Collection* (Athens, 1959), pp. 129–31; Christos Rizopoulos and Andreas Rizopoulos, *Φιλέλληνες και Έλληνες τέκτονες το 1821* (Philhellenes and Greek freemasons in 1821), 2nd edn (Athens: Tetraktys, 2008), pp. 144–51; Walter Bruyère-Ostells, 'Réseaux maçonniques et para-maçonniques des officiers de la Grande Armée engagés dans les mouvements nationaux et libéraux', *Cahiers de la Méditerranée* 72 (2006): 153–69.

between secret and public ones, and between national and international objectives. A 'Società Rigeneratrice', for instance, combined the hierarchical structure of the Freemasonry and its cult of secrecy with the establishment of a network of clubs not only in the various cities of Greece, but also in other countries across the Mediterranean and in France. Its ranks included mostly Italian, French and Greek members, along with Russians, Britons, Irish and Americans who had settled in Greece as freedom fighters and had joined the Greek army or government. Its clubs, assembled in anticipation of the meeting of the national assembly in Argos in 1829, mirrored the divisions in the parliament and among Greek revolutionaries into parties supporting different European powers and different candidates for the throne of Greece. Besides discussing domestic politics, and taking sides on whether to support Kapodistrias, the Società Rigeneratrice was a space where the regeneration of Europe through the relaunch of revolutionary activities could be discussed and planned. In particular, it was at its secret meetings (when not all members could be recognised, as they disclosed neither their names nor their identities) that the possibility of organising insurrectionary expeditions from Greece to southern Italy (whether to Calabria or other regions) were explored. Both the membership of the organisation and its projects confirm the extent to which secret societies could promote initiatives that oscillated between revolution, diplomacy and conventional politics. Their meetings provided a site of interaction between diplomats, foreign envoys, army officers, international volunteers and adventurers. Notwithstanding the formal illegality of such organisations, even high-ranking officials and other individuals employed by the Greek government could not afford to ignore them.[81]

In Naples, soon after the entry of the constitutional army into the capital—marked by a display of carbonaro colours and cockades—the Carboneria turned to public advocacy and took on many of the functions performed by patriotic societies in Spain and Portugal. In these new circumstances, indeed, their lodges came to be dubbed 'società patriottiche'. This emergence into the public sphere was dictated by a commitment to bolster the constitutional order. To this end, members attended official events with their cockades and banners, sometimes taking a leading role in organising them. They also made their presence felt during the religious festivities of towns and cities, contributing thus to the politicisation of religious ceremonies and to the sacralisation of politics during the revolution. A key feature of the statutes of the Carboneria had been the adoption of

81. Korinthios, *I liberali napoletani*, pp. 35–42, 55, 59–69, 80–88.

the language of Christianity and a readiness to lend its support to religion. This association with religion was therefore replicated also in the public sphere. In the Neapolitan provinces and in Sicily, the Carboneria turned annual festivities devoted to patron saints into demonstrations of loyalty to the constitution. By so doing, revolutionaries sought to demonstrate the bond between local cults, the village and national politics. In Mormanno in Calabria, on 15 August 1820, the day of the town's patron saint, don Martino, the founder of the local Carboneria, accompanied by a large group of carbonari along with priests, entered the main church holding the tricolour flag of the secret society and its ceremonial daggers, declared the statue of the Holy Virgin a 'giardiniera' (the name applied to women belonging to the Carboneria), and adorned her with a carbonaro cockade and sash. The statue was then taken in procession around the town crowded with bystanders and devout citizens, as tradition prescribed.[82] In the Sicilian city of Messina in 1821, the local carbonari decorated one of the carts set up for the celebration of the saint of the city with a statue representing freedom dressed in white, wearing a Phrygian cap and holding the tricolour flag of the Carboneria.[83] In this specific context the adoption of the colours of the Carboneria represented a plighting of allegiance to constitutional Naples against the claims for autonomy of the island made by Palermo and its allied cities.

In Spain, the role played by the Carboneria in Italy was taken on by an entirely new society that similarly combined clandestine activities with public mobilisation: the Comunería. Established at the end of 1820, it was set up by twenty-eight freemasons, who included the famous general Francisco López Ballesteros, its first leader or *comendador*, Francisco Serrano, the exaltado politician José María Torrijos and a member of the Cortes, Juan Romero Alpuente. These revolutionaries had decided to abandon Freemasonry and create a new society in order to defend the constitution against its enemies, at a time when the appointment of well-known anti-constitutional officers was creating great apprehension. The name they chose for their organisation had patently anti-despotic overtones, as it made an explicit reference to the sixteenth-century revolt of Castile against Charles V.[84] Like the carbonari in Naples, its members—*comuneros*—could be found attending religious and civic ceremonies

82. ASN, Borbone, 726, ff. 233–35: 'Memoria sulle scelleraggini [. . .] dell'accanito settario sacerdote Don Nicola Martino [. . .]'.

83. D'Alessandro and Giarrizzo, *La Sicilia*, p. 683.

84. Marta Ruiz Jiménez, *El liberalismo exaltado: La confederación de comuneros españoles durante el Trienio Liberal* (Madrid: Editorial Fundamentos, 2007), pp. 20–29;

alongside those of other revolutionary organisations and constitutional authorities, thus giving their association an almost official and institutional role. In the city of Cuevas de Vera, for instance, the mass for the oath to the constitution to be taken by the newly formed national militia of infantry and cavalry was held on 23 April 1823, the anniversary of the decapitation of Juan López de Padilla, the leader of the original comuneros, who had been executed for his part the rebellion against the monarch in 1520. The ceremony was attended by the municipal constitutional administration along with the members of the local comunero lodge, or *merindad*, and the symbols and ceremonial paraphernalia of the organisation were given centre stage in the church. A pedestal placed in the middle of the church held a catafalque surrounded by four towers; a motto inscribed on one of its sides referred to the 'comuneros of Castile, noble victims of an insane monarch'. The priest himself recalled during his sermon the first comuneros and their leader Padilla, inviting the modern Comunería to imitate its historical predecessor in the virtues of its members.[85] What contributed to the public visibility of the Comunería was the overlap between its membership and that of patriotic societies and national militias, organisations that were often direct emanations of the secret society, or were supported by its local leaders. Even the ceremony of swearing an oath to the society, generally considered to be a crucial step in a member's initiation, could now be public. In the city of Lorca for instance, the local merindad of the comuneros staged the taking of an oath to the organisation in the public square, where the flag of the Comunería was displayed. The infantry and cavalry members of the national militia took an oath to the comuneros too, and a priest closed the ceremony with a speech.[86]

The introduction of freedom of the press made it easier to publicise the activities of the Carboneria and the Comunería. It enabled them to engage in public advocacy by advertising themselves, and by defending their contribution to public life against their detractors. They did so in a variety of ways. To begin with, they published the sort of literature addressed to the people that had been produced to instruct the uneducated in the principles of the constitution. This practice of circulating catechisms was a legacy of Freemasonry, an organisation that had already publicised its principles in a similar manner in the eighteenth century. In addition to

Ruiz Jiménez, 'La confederación de comuneros españoles en el Trienio Liberal (1821–23)', *Trienio* 35 (2000): 155–86.

85. Quoted in Ruiz Jiménez, *El liberalismo exaltado*, pp. 89–90.

86. AHN, Consejos Suprimidos, legajo 3635–54, ff. 69–71: minutes of meeting of the comuneros of Lorca, 22 February 1822.

the catechism dialogues, broadsheets directed at the popular classes and other such material produced in defence of the constitution were printed, to instruct the uneducated in the principles of the Carboneria. In a dialogue printed in Naples in 1820, in which a peasant posed his questions in Neapolitan dialect to a carbonaro, the principles of the Carboneria were explained with a view to denying their incompatibility with religion, and with Catholicism in particular. The carbonaro explained that he was called 'carbonaro'—a term referring literally to a charcoal-burner—as he was 'the son of a virtuous society' and that, burned like a piece of wood, he had been purified and turned into 'the friend of God'. He thus reassured the peasant that the Carboneria was in line with their sacred 'Christian, Catholic, Roman religion', and that it was based on 'divine, human and natural right, and on the Holy Gospels'. The dialogue became explicitly political when it stated that the aim of the organisation was to defend the rights of men 'by breaking down, and trampling oppressions, and despotism'.[87] The Carboneria and Comunería also publicised their principles and their role in defending the constitution in a number of poems, anthems and songs. An 'Inno carbonaro', addressed to the 'popolo carbonaro' but written for the army, celebrated freedom and the constitution, the defeat of aristocracy and tyranny and the religious values of faith, virtue, probity and hope that the Carboneria had embraced in its secret rituals. Its verses were regularly interspersed by a choir singing the praises of the patron saint of the organisation, Saint Theobald. Another poem, 'Il trionfo della virtù' (The triumph of righteousness), celebrated as the 'legge carbonara' (law of the Carboneria) the prowess needed for the survival of the constitution. This ephemeral literature included also *canzoni* (songs) written in Neapolitan dialect, and poems or musical odes containing direct attacks on the arch-enemies of the Carboneria, the absolutist secret society of the Calderari.[88]

In addition, the carbonari circulated summaries of some of their debates, going so far as to issue public appeals that were displayed in public and made easily available in the market and at booksellers. Both the Comunería and the Carboneria published manifestos and addresses to parliament, and publicised the decisions of their assemblies.[89] As was

87. *L'ignoranza illuminata: Dialogo tra un carbonaro ed un contadino* (Naples: Francesco del Vecchio, 1820), pp. 10, 12.

88. Michele Natale, 'Inno carbonaro ed analogo' (Naples, n.d.); 'Canzone nna accaseione da venuta de li cravonare a Nnapole' (Naples, n.d.); 'Il Caldararo vinto dal Carbonaro' (n.d.); Giosuè Alfieri, 'Il trionfo della virtù' (broadsheet, n.d.); available, like the other broadsheets mentioned here, in SNSP, Miscellanea 1820.

89. Daum, *Oscillazioni*, p. 107. An example of such publications is *Manifiesto y otros documentos de la Sociedad de Comuneros* (Cádiz: Esteban Picardo, 1823).

recognised by the Neapolitan minister of justice, in a circular to the clergy of the kingdom issued in December 1820, the Carboneria was no longer a secret organisation: the danger posed by a foreign invasion and the dramatic growth in its membership had made its discussions and deliberations public and turned it into an association devoted to the defence of the nation's institutions, as 'no class of citizens can now be ignorant of the purposes of their meetings'.[90]

In Spain, meanwhile, the comuneros, to intervene directly in public debates, employed sympathetic periodicals to voice their views about contemporary policy issues, criticise governmental decisions and attack their enemies. The Comunería enjoyed the support of *El Zurriago* and *El Eco de Padilla*, periodicals which more or less became its official mouthpieces. *El Zurriago* went so far as to publish the Comunería's statutes in its pages, and attacked the competing secret society of the Anilleros. For *El Zurriago*, the comuneros were 'the firmest support of the fatherland'.[91] The association between the historical memory of the 1520 comuneros and contemporary quests for a constitution, promoted by revolutionary literature, journalism and theatre performances, did much to advertise the Comunería. As recalled by a foreign visitor in Madrid at the time, a drama focusing on Juan de Padilla's attempt to re-establish the rights of the people against Charles V was very popular as, 'although the piece is not considered as possessing much merit, it excites applause for the analogy between the former and present epoch'.[92] References to the historical experience of the comuneros were adopted also into the statutes of patriotic societies, whose membership did not necessarily always overlap with that of the secret society. Songs and odes written in their honour circulated throughout Spain. The song dedicated 'a los ilustres comuneros', and the 'Himno a los comuneros' invited Spaniards to visit the tombs of Bravo and Padilla, to adorn them with laurels and swear by their memory to defend freedom.[93]

What accounts for their public visibility is the fact that both the Comunería and the radical wing of the Carboneria embraced a 'populist' ideology based on the belief that politics should not be confined simply to parliament, but should spill over into society at large, and that it was their duty to defend the rights of the people, and in particular liberty of public opinion and freedom of the press and of association. This is why they

90. Bartholdy, *Memoirs*, p. 167.
91. *El Zurriago*, nos. 67–69 (n.d. [1822]), p. 7.
92. Pecchio, *Anecdotes*, p. 85.
93. Cabrerizo, *Coleccion de canciones*, pp. 28–38, 67–69.

attributed great importance to the patriotic societies, whose activities they saw as being in harmony with their own, and did not refrain from mobilising crowds and instigating public demonstrations to protect the constitution. Both organisations were capable of activating sectors of the popular classes, directly or indirectly, in order to put pressure on the government and the legislative assemblies. Although only a minority of the members of the representative assemblies belonged to these secret societies, their ability to influence public opinion through their social base had a major impact on parliamentary politics and governmental decisions.

In Naples, two major public protests organised by the Carboneria stand out for their size, impact and legacy. The first is associated with an attempt at a coup d'état, in order to withdraw the Spanish constitution, planned by the monarch with the support of his ministers of the interior and foreign affairs, Giuseppe Zurlo and the Duke of Campochiaro, in early December 1820. Summoned by the European powers meeting at Laibach, the monarch responded with a public declaration in which he accepted the invitation and, implicitly rejecting the current constitution, promised that at Laibach a new charter, allowing for a narrower set of liberties than those guaranteed by the constitution (the proclamation including a generic reference to the protection of individual rights and national representation), would be discussed. The king's attempt to withdraw the constitution was supported by some regiments of the army that favoured the return of the absolute monarchy, and by his ministers Zurlo and Campochiaro, whose preference was for a constitution more moderate than the Spanish one. A few days before, a diplomatic dispatch from Paris, read out during a secret session of the parliament, had confirmed the determination of the European powers to put an end to the constitution in Naples. No sooner was the monarch's declaration made public, on the evening of 6 December, when it was displayed in the streets of Naples, than the Carboneria activated its networks.[94] On the same night it summoned an assembly to discuss the threats posed to the constitution and the measures to be taken in its defence, but the discussion did not remain secret. Significantly, the discussion spilled out of the assembly to involve people gathering in the square outside the Carboneria's headquarters, and armed demonstrators instigated by the organisation roamed the streets of the city of Naples shouting 'Costituzione o morte!' The following day, members of the Carboneria and their supporters not only filled the streets around the

94. On these events, see Daum, *Oscillazioni*, pp. 377–81, 395–402. The king's declaration is available in Alberti, *Atti del parlamento*, 2, pp. 361ff.

parliament, but went on to occupy the courtyard of the national assembly, enter the building and throng its corridors and public galleries prior to the parliamentary discussion of the implications of the edict. According to a contemporary observer, the carbonari cried from the gallleries 'Costi- tuzione o morte!' and brandished the ceremonial dagger of the organisa- tion at the assembled deputies. Making reference to the murder of the dictator Julius Caesar—carried out by a group of senators—one of the demonstrators warned the deputies that there were now 'one hundred Brutuses' in the chamber ready to defend freedom: here the dagger of the Carboneria had become a symbol of resistance against despotism. Dem- onstrations continued across the city thanks also to the arrival of members of the Carboneria from the powerful provincial lodges of Avellino and Salerno, who assembled around the gates of the city, Porta Capuana and Porta Nolana: young affiliates were seen tearing down and ripping up the edicts displayed in the streets, and students gathered around the castles of the capital to prevent the king from fleeing. A few days after these demon- strations and clashes between armed groups, the former head of the Bour- bon police Francesco Giampietro was kidnapped and murdered.[95] After heated parliamentary debates between government and opposition, the latter supported by the Carboneria and the moderates, the constitutional crisis was resolved by the resignation of the government and a demand put to the king, who accepted it, for a public declaration of allegiance to the Spanish constitution, in exchange for the parliament's approval of his trip to Laibach. Zurlo and Campochiaro, compromised by their drafting of the manifesto, were impeached, and a new government which included Muratists loyal to the constitution such as the Duke of Gallo and Pietro Colletta, along with Giuseppe De Thomasis, was appointed.[96]

Although the joint intervention of the parliament and the Carboneria had neutralised the monarch's attempt to withdraw the constitution, the Carboneria continued to be vigilant in its defence. This pattern of public mobilisation was in fact replicated in January 1821, when the Carboneria intervened in defence of freedom of religion. The parliament had proposed a minor modification to the constitution to allow forms of worship other than Catholicism to be practised in private, but the heir to the throne, under pressure from the archbishop of Naples, had vetoed it. Hundreds of carbonari and the members of the legions controlled by them invaded

95. The activities of the Carboneria are described by Ulloa: *Sulle rivoluzioni*, ff. 249–54.

96. On this institutional crisis, see also Emilio Gin, *L'aquila, il giglio e il compasso: Profili di lotta politica ed associazionismo settario nelle Due Sicilie (1806–1821)* (Mercato San Severino: Edizioni del Paguro, 2007), pp. 149–52.

the parliament building, filled the galleries and, directly addressing the deputies, demanded that they punish the archbishop, reject the veto and abolish the committee of public safety chaired by Pasquale Borrelli, the head of the police. That evening clashes between the national guards and the legions mobilised by the Carboneria broke out in various parts of the city.[97]

The Carboneria associated itself with the defence of the integrity of the constitutional state in all military contexts during the revolution. Luigi Minichini's tour of Sicily, from Messina to Catania, during the war against Palermo, was marked by crowds using the secret society's ribbons and banners to welcome the hero of the revolution and show their support for defend the constitutional unity of the kingdom.[98] The radical wing of the Carboneria, meanwhile, in order to increase its capacity to mobilise the population in defence of the constitution, did its utmost to control the militias and legions—military units made up of ordinary citizens—in Naples. Through these forces the Carboneria was able to mobilise for military purpose also the labouring classes who were affiliated to, and had close ties with, their vendite, and were organised as turbe. When the time arrived to mount a defence against the Austrian military threat, the secret society marshalled its own guerrilla units sporting its colours. In Nola, on the eve of the clash with the Austrian army, military uniforms in the colours of the Carboneria were hastily sown for the regiments assembled by the association for the occasion. In this context these became symbols of resistance against the foreign invasion.[99]

In Spain, the comuneros too turned to public demonstrations when they felt that the constitution was under threat, although without going so far as to occupy the Cortes. The role played by the comuneros at the local level to influence parliamentary elections has already been noted above. As early as the end of 1821, when the dismissal of Riego was taken as evidence of attempts to undermine the revolution, local *torres* (lodges) of the Comunería took the initiative also by collecting signatures for petitions to the Cortes in defence of the constitution.[100] But the public activities of the comuneros would seem to have escalated by the following year, as they backed and became involved in extensive public demonstrations. The

97. Bartholdy, *Memoirs*, pp. 164–66.

98. See Minichini, *Luglio 1820*, pp. 317–18.

99. Stassano, *Cronaca*, p. 415. On these legions and militias, see the section 'The Failure of the revolutionary script in Naples, Piedmont and Spain' in chapter four above.

100. APR, Papeles Reservados de Fernando VII, 67, exp. 20, f. 277: letter of the merindad of Zamora, 4 December 1821.

widespread popular reaction across the country to the attempted military coup on 7 July 1822 owed much to the initiative of the merindades of the Comunería throughout Spain. The public protests that exploded in Cádiz, Valencia, Cartagena, Alicante and La Coruña had been encouraged by the organisation and by the patriotic societies that enjoyed close ties with it.[101] The commitment of the Comunería to defending the constitution was confirmed in times of danger during the civil war. Faced with the threat of the counterrevolution and an attack on the capital city, the merindades of the city of Toledo set up a subscription and mustered a group of armed volunteers, a decision that was publicised throughout the organisation and praised in its published minutes.[102] Close ties would seem to have existed between members of the Comunería and the voluntary national militias established in 1822 to fight the royalist guerrilla bands: even in a small towns such as Yébenes, in the province of Toledo, the officer in charge of a voluntary cavalry unit comprising sixty members had access to lists of names of prominent comuneros at local and national level, including members of the Cortes.[103]

The public visibility of secret societies and the shift of their activities towards political mobilisation was not without problems and tensions, creating as it did a debate both within the societies themselves and outside. When *El Zurriago* published the minutes of meetings and the substance of the agreements to forge an alliance between the Comunería and the freemasons, a decision that had been contested and that had caused controversy among the members of the former organisation, some comuneros denounced this as being in breach of the secrecy of its proceedings and an infringement of its regulations that must be discussed during their meetings and avoided in future. In the town of Lorca similar concerns were raised regarding the fact that lodges of the Carboneria had been invited to use the same premises as the Comunería and its members had attended meetings of the latter.[104]

But the most vehement attacks against the comuneros came from their political enemies and from governmental authorities. In particular the 'populist' language and appeal of both the Carboneria and the Comunería

101. Michel Mondejar, 'Alliances et conflits au sein des sociétés secrètes libérales: La Confédération des chevaliers comuneros, ou les limites de l'illusion démocratique durant le triennat constitutionnel 1820–1823', unpublished doctoral thesis, Université de Provence, 2007, pp. 383ff; Zavala, *Masones*, pp. 82–83.

102. Ruiz Jiménez, *El liberalismo exaltado*, p. 111.

103. AHN, Consejos Suprimidos, legajo 12269, f. 180.

104. Ibid., legajo 3635-54, ff. 34–35: minutes of meeting of the comuneros of Lorca, 22 February 1822.

became the target of criticism by their political antagonists, who viewed them as organisations filled with 'fanatics' set upon subverting the constitutional system, creating anarchy by disregarding the laws, or conspiring to abolish the monarchy and establish a republican regime. This was the language used by the Spanish moderate press and by moderado politicians to undermine the legitimacy of the comuneros' political activities. The moderate liberal periodical *El Látigo Liberal contra el Zurriago Indiscreto*, for instance, defended the principle of political moderation and accused the comuneros of trying to create a state within the state.[105]

Against these attacks the comuneros responded by pointing to the public nature of their statutes, whose principles transparently defended the constitution against its enemies, and unmasked the hypocrisy of their critics, the moderates of the Anilleros, who pretended to defend the constitutional regime in public and at the same time undermined the free press, weakened the authority of the diputaciones provinciales, and denied to one and all the right to cry 'Viva Riego!'[106] They also continued to defend the secrecy of some of their activities as necessary to the survival of an independent public sphere, rather than being a threat to it. In a revealing passage from a pamphlet in defence of the role of the comuneros, the anonymous writer argued for a direct relationship between secret activity, secret discussion and public freedom. The arbitrary decisions of moderate governments could only be countered by secret societies, which guaranteed 'the sacred right to meet and talk about what matters to citizens'.[107]

In Naples the Muratists, once they had seized power, continued to be suspicious of the capacity the carbonari demonstrated before and during the pronunciamiento to mobilise the local populations, treating them as a potential threat to public order. As early as 3 August 1820, the Giunta di Governo issued a decree that restricted the right of assembly, and empowered the intendenti to prohibit public gatherings aimed at influencing governmental decisions. But the decree would seem not to have been successful in containing or repressing either the Carboneria's constant public engagement with politics or its ability to muster armed groups. In a report read out during a secret parliamentary session in November 1820, the

105. *El Látigo Liberal contra el Zurriago Indiscreto*, no. 22 (1822), p. 3. More generally on allegations of conspiring against the monarchy, see Juan Luis Simal, 'Conspiración, revolución, y contrarrevolución en España, 1814–1824', *Rivista Storica Italiana* 130, no. 2 (2018): 526–56, esp. pp. 550–51.

106. *El observador de las sociedades secretas* (Madrid, n.d. [1822]), pp. 21–23; *La voz de la patria: Observaciones que hace un español á los que hayan leido el papel titulado cosa sobre Comuneros* (Málaga: Luis de Carreras, 1823).

107. *El observador*, pp. 17–18.

minister of justice denounced the ongoing influence that patriotic societies exerted on 'the exercise of the executive and legislative power', which
'disturbed the public mood', and he invited the parliament to discuss those
patriotic societies that acted 'as legislative bodies', the military Carboneria,
and 'the suppression of military organisations', as well as 'the suspension
of the organisation of legionaries in the capital'.[108]

Publicity did much to increase the appeal of both Carboneria and
Comunería, and by the same token to boost their memberships. Their
social composition, however, requires some elaboration. The constitution of the Repubblica Lucana Orientale stipulated that membership as
open to any free man who 'has the wherewithal to provide for himself an
employment, a trade, from which he can support himself and his family',
thus including the smallest landowners and artisans, but leaving out
domestic servants, the unemployed and the poorest sections of the population.[109] Of the 1,441 carbonari recorded by the police in the province
of Bari in Puglia, to take one example, some 28 per cent were property
owners, 15 per cent members of the clergy, 8 per cent lawyers, notaries and
judges, 8 per cent artisans, including shoemakers and tailors, 7 per cent
pharmacists, doctors and surgeons, 6 per cent civil servants, 6 per cent
peasants, 2.5 per cent tradesmen and entrepreneurs and 1 per cent innkeepers and food sellers.[110] However, the data available, and the regulations of the organisations, while confirming their overall middle-class or
lower middle-class character, nonetheless do not take into account the
ability of the lodges, well illustrated by events during the revolution, to
connect with and involve in their activities the lowest strata of the population. Contemporary accounts confirm the extent to which, at least in the
capital city of Naples, the Carboneria made efforts to recruit and mobilise also servants, fishermen and the *lazzaroni* (beggars and street folk).[111]
But evidence for the penetration of the organisation among the classes
of shopkeepers, small artisans and both skilled and unskilled workers
can be found for other cities. In Tropea in Calabria, for instance, members of the two local vendite, called La Pace Costante and I Seguaci della
Virtù included not only, predictably, priests and property owners, but also

108. Nino Cortese in Pietro Colletta, *Storia del reame*, 3, p. 186; Lepre, *La rivoluzione napoletana*, pp. 60, 62–64.

109. *Giornale Patriottico della Lucania Orientale*, no. 1 (1820), p. 58.

110. ASN, Borbone, 726, ff. 106–7; Aurelio Lepre, 'Classi, movimenti politici e lotta di classe nel Mezzogiorno dalla fine del Settecento al 1860', *Studi Storici* 16, no. 2 (1975): 340–77.

111. Bartholdy, *Memoirs*, pp. 84, 93.

artisans and goldsmiths, carters (*vaticali*), carpenters, barbers, dyers, builders, shoemakers, innkeepers and porters.[112]

The membership profile of the Comunería is more difficult to establish. One of its founding members, Juan Romero Alpuente, went so far as to claim that it had no less than a hundred thousand members by the end of the Trienio. More conservative estimates suggest that its membership amounted to something between forty thousand and sixty thousand.[113] The social background of Spanish Freemasonry seems to have been more select than that of the Comunería, although during the Trienio its membership grew steadily. In Madrid Masonic lodges included large numbers of members drawn from the army and the civil service, but also tradesmen and lawyers, many students, and only a few workers, farmers, shopkeepers and chemists.[114] The police gathered evidence of the penetration of both Freemasonry and the Comunería into the ranks of two categories: the clergy, and the educated and professional classes—the so-called *letrados*—which included lawyers, judges, notaries and court clerks; a choice that reflects the authorities' anxieties regarding these social groups in particular. In the case of both categories, membership of the Comunería was higher than for Freemasonry.[115] Evidence at local level too suggests that there was a broader social and professional representation, and a larger membership, in the Comunería than in Freemasonry. While local comunero leaders tended to belong to the political and military elite of the cities and towns where the the provincial branches of the society—the merindades—were based, local membership undoubtedly went beyond these groups. Among the comuneros of the Andalusian city of Almería, the police recorded mainly individuals belonging to the national guard, civil servants, tradesmen and small landowners. Yet the presence there of six *torres* surely indicates a much wider social base among members.[116]

Neither Carbonería nor Comunería was confined to the larger cities, but developed a capillary presence throughout the territories of their states, traceable even in the smallest villages and in all the provinces of both kingdoms. In the case of the Carbonería, this was due to the fact that from its very origin it had served the purpose of mobilising

112. ASN, Polizia Generale II, fascio 4603: 'Quadro delle vendite carbonare', 1821.

113. Zavala, *Masones*, pp. 74–75; Juan Romero Alpuente, *Historia de la revolución española y otros escritos*, ed. Alberto Gil Novales (Madrid: Centro de Estudios Constitucionales, 1989), p. 316.

114. APR, Papeles Reservados de Fernando VII, 67: the list of civil-servant freemasons is in exp. 5, ff. 89–120; another list of freemasons in Madrid is in exp. 8, ff. 159–207.

115. Ibid., exp. 3, ff. 71–80 (eclesiásticos); exp. 4, ff. 81–88 (letrados).

116. Guillén Gómez, *Una aproximación*, pp. 82–84.

provincial political interests against the capital. At the end of the revolutionary period, the police noted the existence of *vendite carbonare* in virtually every town of Calabria, down to the tiniest hamlet. In the town of Pizzo Calabro, for example, where the Carboneria does not appear to have existed before 1820, the vendita called Perfetta Unione had acquired by the end of the revolution a membership of four hundred individuals, out of 6,300 inhabitants. In the urban centres of Calabria, from the smallest to the largest, the proportion of the population who were carbonari varied, for those towns where specific numbers are known, between 2 and 6 per cent.[117]

An equally capillary presence of the Comunería can be detected throughout the territory of Spain by the end of the Trienio. Merindades could be found in all provincial capitals, including Almería, Badajoz, Cuenca, Jaén, Murcia, Oviedo, Soria, Valencia, Zamora and Barcelona.[118] In the city of Almería itself, as noted above, there were no fewer than six *torres*, but lodges were set up also in the villages of its province.[119] In Catalonia, there were at least five hundred members of the Comunería, and the organisation also controlled two periodicals, the *Diario Constitucional de Barcelona* and *La Voz del Pueblo*. Its presence was felt not only in Barcelona, but also in Manresa, Mataró, Reus, Tarragona, Lleida, Vic, Girona and Figueres. At times the comuneros were at odds with the freemasons, and there were clashes between the two organisations in Barcelona and in Tarragona, but otherwise they were prepared to cooperate between 1822 and 1823 to fight the absolutists, when they engaged jointly in activities of public mobilisation.[120]

Their presence in the public sphere, their public advocacy and their coordination of activities between the local and the national did not turn secret societies into modern political parties. Although they debated and voted on programmes and objectives, coordinating their responses to governmental decisions at the national level, the engagement of both the Comunería and the Carboneria with the politics of the revolutions lacked cohesion. In fact, their ranks included individuals with a variety of political orientations, as they had done in previous years when their activities had been entirely clandestine. They also modified their political strategies during the revolutions, and the shifts in attitudes, objectives and strategies led to disagreements and conflicts between different

117. ASN, Borbone, 726, f. 329.
118. Ruiz Jiménez, *El liberalismo exaltado*, pp. 34–37.
119. Guillén Gómez, *Una aproximación*, pp. 82–84.
120. Arnabat Mata, *La revolució*, pp. 139–44.

groups within the same organisations. Thus it would make better sense to refer to the existence of several 'Carbonerie', and several 'Comunerías'. The Carboneria comprised both a radical and a more moderate component. Divisions and distinctions could oppose also the vendite of specific provinces to certain others. For instance, in 1820 the carbonari of Cosenza in Calabria were approached by the those of the *repubbliche* of Lucania Orientale, the Principato Ultra and the Principato Citra and asked to join them and build a confederacy of all the provinces. The former declined the offer, however, and remained independent, concerned as they were that this initiative was the product of 'democratic ideas', that would make the revolution appear as 'licentious and demagogic' in the eyes of Europe.[121] In addition, the nature of the organisation itself changed during the revolution. As government officials observed, the Carboneria now began to attract an increasing number of moderate supporters of the revolution, both landowners and civil servants, who were content with the status quo and not in favour of permanent mobilisation. This modified the internal political balance of the lodges at the local level in the provinces.[122] It also led to conflicts between more moderate and more radical vendite. For instance, in August 1820 three members of the Neapolitan vendite, Paladini, Vecchierelli and Maenza, obtained the endorsement of some provincial groups of the Carboneria when mustering an army to prevent a foreign invasion and organise a coup in defence of the revolution. What came to be remembered as the 'Paladini Conspiracy' was however reported by the more moderate elements of the Carboneria to the head of the police, Pasquale Borrelli. As a consequence, Paladini and another radical, Giuseppe Lattanzi, were arrested.[123] In Sicily, meanwhile, an obvious political bone of contention was the question of the independence of the island from Naples. Mirroring the division of the island's elites, the Carboneria in Palermo and the cities allied with the island capital were committed to some form of autonomy, if not full emancipation, from Naples, while the members of the vendite of eastern Sicily converged with those of the mainland on this issue. But such divisions could be replicated at the local level, too, where different lodges advanced different political agendas mirroring conflicts between factions competing for the control of municipal institutions.[124]

121. Davide Andreotti, *Storia dei cosentini*, 3 vols (Naples: Salvatore Marchese, 1869–74), 3, pp. 211–12.

122. Lepre, *La rivoluzione napoletana*, pp. 57–60.

123. Ibid., pp. 60–62; Gin, *L'aquila*, p. 162.

124. Giuseppe Barone, *L'oro di Busacca: Potere, ricchezza e povertà a Scicli (sec. XVI–XIX)* (Palermo: Sellerio, 1998), p. 213.

In Spain, similarly, the Comunería not only modified its 'official' political line during its existence, but its membership likewise became divided over the strategies to pursue and the stance it should adopt in relation to the other secret societies and, indeed, the governments. It became a more politically radical organisation only after the failed military coup of 7 July 1822, when it came to be more closely associated with the exaltados, and in particular with the political agenda set by the patriotic society Sociedad Landaburiana. Nonetheless, not all of its members were satisfied with this militant new style and explicit hostility against the moderados, nor with its displaying such a confrontational attitude towards government and Freemasonry. They also resented the political line of *El Zurriago*, blaming the periodical for undermining and slandering members of the Cortes and the government. By the end of the year, a number of comuneros had become convinced that a united front among all supporters of the revolution was needed against the threat posed both by the counterrevolutionary movement and a putative foreign invasion. To this end they advocated an alliance with the *masones*. By the beginning of 1823, these disagreements divided the organisation. In February, in fact, the Junta de Gobierno of the comuneros based in Madrid issued a statement in which, citing as its justification the urgent need to defend the constitution and the sovereignty of the nation, it decreed a union between Comunería and Masonería, and its commitment to support or criticise constitutional authorities jointly. As a result, those comuneros who were hostile to any political compromise, and wished to remain loyal to the earlier radical stance of the society, voted against the proposal, created a separate assembly and abandoned the organisation. On 24 February they set up a new organisation called Comuneros Españoles Constitucionales. According to its statutes all members were explicitly forbidden to belong to other secret societies, although it declared its commitment to cooperate with the freemasons.[125] These divisions and disagreements were replicated on the local level, where the assemblies discussed and voted whether or not to support decisions taken in Madrid.[126] Spanish Freemasonry was similarly divided within its ranks. At a time when a pact was forged between a wing of the Comunería and the Masonería, some members of this latter

125. Ruiz Jiménez, *El liberalismo exaltado*, pp. 20–29; Ruiz Jiménez, 'La confederación'. Both the decision taken by the Junta Preparatoria in Madrid and the founding document of the new Comunería established in February 1823 can be found in *Manifiesto y otros documentos*, at pp. 1–7 and 8–10 respectively.

126. AHN, Consejos Suprimidos, legajo 3635–54, ff. 19–35: minutes of meeting of the comuneros of Lorca, 22 February 1822.

organisation, defining themselves as representative of pure Freemasonry, came to the conclusion that it was time to move beyond the revolution, which had been hijacked by the comuneros and the exaltados, to defend the authority of the king and safeguard religion. They claimed that the majority of the Spanish people were devoted to the monarch, and were ready to support a new type of government which, while not reverting to the absolutist practices of 1814–20, would safeguard both the throne and citizens, and guarantee equal justice to one and all.[127]

Thus the political influence and visibility that secret organisations continued to enjoy during the revolutions was due precisely to their flexibility and to their capacity to take on a variety of different roles and tasks. Above all, it was their ability to combine secrecy and publicity in different ways according to circumstances that enabled them to remain at the centre of revolutionary politics. Secret societies had provided spaces of sociability and discussion at a time when no public debate was tolerated. They continued to play this role during the revolutions, when they took full advantage of the existence of a new public space granted to politics, contributing thereby to the shaping of it.

Protest and corporate interests in Madrid, Palermo and Hydra: artisans and sailors

The instances of popular protest discussed above, whether spontaneous or resulting from the intervention of radical political leaders, point to the existence of a variety of forms of participation from below in defence of the constitution, and to the adoption and dissemination of revolutionary practices among the popular classes. However, the transfer or reappropriation of revolutionary practices will not in themselves serve as an exhaustive explanation of the processes of politicisation and the mobilisation of the popular classes in the 1820s. For this, we also need to take into account specific and autonomous forms of popular 'agency'. What facilitated popular participation was also the existence of older traditions of popular protest, characterised by the performance of a set of repertoires and rituals, by specific understandings of justice and morality and by the defence of corporate-professional interests. In early modern revolts, specific notions of equity and moral economy had shaped people's expectations and justified their demands with regard to the local or national governments, as well as the monarch. The personal attacks, temporary imprisonments and

127. APR, Papeles Reservados de Fernando VII, 67, exp. 27, ff. 288–97.

looting of properties that took place during them amounted to retribution for misdeeds perceived as violations of trust perpetrated by specific individuals against the population at large. Whether fully independent forms of popular intervention, or determined also by competition for leadership at the local level, urban riots were not simply eruptions of incoherent violence, but reflected the ability of urban populations to obtain satisfaction of specific demands, and to pursue clear political objectives. They represented forms of negotiation, with a view to reinstating the principles of justice and honour expected of the authorities.[128] These early modern patterns of popular protest not only persisted, but were revitalised during the 1820s, when popular groups combined traditional professional and political demands with support for the constitution.

This section analyses popular protest in Madrid and Palermo, and on the island of Hydra in the Aegean, all noteworthy as centres of sustained popular revolutionary initiative in the 1820s. At a time of economic crisis, unemployment and legislative reforms together were serving to erode the bargaining power of workers across the southern peripheries of the European continent, and thereby creating the preconditions for a mobilisation of skilled labour, and for its support for the revolution. As noted above, in Lisbon the artisans' corporations had intervened early on to support the immediate introduction of the Spanish constitution and of universal male suffrage. Thus in November 1820 they backed a second military pronunciamiento, following on from the first in Porto. In Barcelona artisans were at the forefront of demonstrations in favour of the constitution, held shortly after Riego's pronunciamiento. Yet in the 1820s it was in Madrid, Palermo and Hydra in particular that urban popular groups gained an unprecedented degree of political influence, took the revolutionary initiative and influenced the overall course of events. In these centres, revolts presented striking similarities to patterns of popular protest that had taken place in European cities in previous centuries. In this period the behaviour of the popular classes of Palermo, Madrid and Hydra does not necessarily demonstrate new forms of class consciousness, as artisans and sailors often continued to defend their professional privileges against competition, and did not therefore question existing social hierarchies. Yet the popular groups protesting in Madrid, Palermo and Hydra were powerful enough to force existing institutions and governments, both at a local and at the

128. William Beik, *Urban Protest in Seventeenth-Century France: The Culture of Retribution* (Cambridge: Cambridge University Press, 1997); Francesco Benigno, 'Rivolte in città', *Storica* 10 (1998): 164–70.

national level, to negotiate with them, to forge alliances with individual revolutionary leaders in defence of their interests, and also to shape constitutional politics.

By the 1820s in Madrid, a city with a population of around two hundred thousand, there were around twenty thousand artisans, working mainly in the construction, textile and food industries, along with ten thousand day-labourers. These were in turn divided between those working in small factories with an average of nine workers, especially in the construction, textile, food and printing businesses, and those working in smaller workshops, which included shoemakers, carpenters, tailors, tinsmiths, locksmiths and gilders. Only one segment of the artisan class, the most professionalised and skilled, belonged to the *gremios* (corporations), organisations that provided official recognition for the skills necessary to become a qualified artisan (by granting *cartas de examen*), and managed competition by controlling access to their ranks. Since the end of the previous century the proportion of this class working outside corporative structures had grown dramatically, and the greater part of industrial production was no longer controlled by them. Yet they did still play a role, and trained new apprentices to join their ranks. The economic crisis of the post-Napoleonic period resulted in high unemployment, especially among unskilled workers, and increased the gap too between the few rich artisans and the majority of impoverished ones.[129] The support of these groups for the constitution dates back to the first constitutional period, when a number of public demonstrations in solidarity with the constitution were organised according to patterns revived during the Trienio: meetings in cafés such as the Fontana de Oro, parades with music, cheering the constitution and condemning its enemies, and gatherings at the Puerta del Sol. This does not mean that all artisans were necessarily in favour of the constitution. In fact many of them sided with the absolutists, and must surely have participated in the riots against the constitutionalists that marked the return of the monarch in 1814 and in 1823. However, their presence among the members of the sociedades patrióticas, as well as in the ranks of the Guardia Nacional testify to the existence among them of many supporters of the constitution.

During the Trienio artisans spoke during the meetings of the patriotic society Los Amigos de la Libertad (at the Café Lorencini) and of the

---

129. París Martín, 'Artesanos y política'; José A. Nieto Sánchez and Álvaro París Martín, 'Transformaciones laborales y tensión social en Madrid: 1750–1836', *Revista Encuentros Latinoamericanos* 6, no. 1 (2012): 210–74.

society called San Sebastián de la Corte, denouncing counterrevolutionary gatherings and lamenting the impact that unemployment and the rising prices of staple foodstuffs (flour, bread and wheat) were having on them, and their concerns were taken seriously by the members. For these, the constitution represented a guarantee against those speculating and profiteering at the expense of the population of the city. Some members of the sociedades became sympathetic regarding the conditions of the workers: drawing a distinction between the poverty and destitution associated with immoral conduct and that of the 'virtuous' poor, deserving of support and solidarity, they advocated the collection of funds to relieve the misery and wretchedness of the latter.[130] While the precise social composition of the protesters gathering regularly in the public spaces of the city is not easy to determine, artisans, along with day-labourers, were present at all the public demonstrations organised with the support of the exaltados and the patriotic societies. Artisans and journeymen added to the crowds that moved between the venues of the societies themselves, in the large open space surrounding the Puerta del Sol, the Plazuela de la Villa. This is the square where they addressed their demands directly to the city authorities in front of the the the Casas Consistoriales (city hall).

In Madrid artisans had been key protagonists of ancient régime riots, or *motines*, at least since 1766. Elements of continuity between eighteenth-century *motines* in the capital and popular mobilisation during the Trienio included not only the participation of artisans as their key protagonists, but also their belief, and that more broadly of the general population, that the king himself was the ultimate guarantor of the people's demands. Since the previous century, the population of Madrid had enjoyed a special relationship with the monarch, one that was not questioned even at times of discontent. Urban protests were in fact also a direct dialogue between the population and the king, and the people of the capital considered his very presence in the Madrid as evidence of his commitment to redress the wrongdoings that were at the origins of their unrest. Between March and April 1766, during the so-called Esquilache riots, the population of Madrid managed to obtain the resignation of the highly unpopular minister the Marquis of Squillace, at a time of grave economic crisis, high prices of staple foodstuffs and unemployment. The uprising was suspended when the monarch accepted the popular demands by addressing the crowds from the balcony, as they had asked him to do. Yet the following day his departure for the royal palace of Aranjuez triggered a second revolt, as

130. Gil Novales, *Las sociedades patrióticas*, 1, pp. 65–66, 83, 87–90.

the population considered this act a disavowal of his earlier promises. The protests came to an end only when the monarch gave additional guarantees of his commitment to his promises. Although he refused to return to the capital before the re-establishment of law and order, he eventually did so, accompanied by troops.[131] In the new circumstances created by the occupation of the country by the French army in 1808, popular insurrections broke out in both Aranjuez and Madrid when the populace got wind of the flight of members of the royal family. 'Running like a mobilizing thread through all of these risings', one historian has observed, 'was the fear, solidly embedded in popular consciousness, of living in a world without their king.'[132]

Not dissimilarly during the Trienio, protesters considered the presence of the monarch in the capital as evidence of his support for the constitution, and of his commitment to defend it against its enemies. In November 1820 the appointment by the king of a new captain-general of Castile, the reactionary José de Carvajal, provoked fears of a potential move to revoke the constitution. The king's decision had not been approved by the government, however, and was therefore soon withdrawn; but the fact that it coincided with the temporary closure of the session of the Cortes raised concerns about the monarch's loyalty to the new regime. Unlike earlier urban protests, when the crowds had been addressing the monarch directly, demonstrators were now calling upon the constitutional council of Madrid to intervene on their behalf to present their demands to the monarch. Large crowds of demonstrators gathered day after day in the Puerta del Sol, outside the Fontana de Oro and in front of the Casas Consistoriales, where they asked for the Cortes to be reopened, and demanded that the jefe político, the city administration, and the *diputación permanente* of the Cortes recall the king to Madrid. As a consequence, the municipal authorities officially asked the king, 'worthy father of his people', to return to the city. The king complied, and his decision was communicated to the population from the balcony of the Casas.[133] The monarch in fact responded to the request with a public letter in which he accepted to return to the capital provided the protests would come to an end. His entry into

131. José Miguel López García, *El motín contra Esquilache* (Madrid: Alianza Editorial, 2006), passim, and esp. pp. 116–29.

132. Fraser, *Napoleon's Cursed War*, p. 57. See also José A. Nieto Sánchez and Álvaro París Martín, 'La participación popular en la crisis política de la monarquía: Del motín contra Godoy al 2 de mayo de 1808 en Madrid', *Investigaciones Históricas: Época Moderna y Contemporánea* 37 (2017): 109–48.

133. AAM, Secretaría, Acontecimientos Políticos, 2–229, no. 28.

the city attracted large crowds shouting 'Long live the constitution!' and, according to some sources, also addressing him with insults.[134]

This pattern of behaviour was replicated in September 1821, after the demotion of Riego from the captaincy-general of Aragon, an event that had huge repercussions. The crowds demanded that the city administration appoint a delegation of its choice to ask the monarch to return to the capital, and to submit on its behalf a petition to the Cortes. The ayuntamiento agreed to put pressure on the king to come back to Madrid, although it refused to let the protesters decide the composition of the delegation charged to see the monarch. This dialogue between the crowds filling the Plazuela de la Villa and the city authorities was carried out again from the balcony of the Casas Consistoriales, where the intendente spoke to the demonstrators who had been denied entry. Although on 5 September it was publicly announced that the king would come back to Madrid, this time demonstrations in support of Riego continued for some time longer.[135]

In Palermo, the revolutionary mobilisation of the artisans was far more closely associated than in Madrid with the defence of the professional and political privileges traditionally granted to their trade associations. It resulted in the artisan corporations' direct participation in the revolutionary provisional government of the city and of the whole island, along with representatives of the city aristocracy. In 1820 these two groups shared a political programme based on the defence of the autonomy of the city from Naples, and a desire to regain the privileges lost in the previous years. It was to defend the island's autonomy that they introduced the Cádiz Constitution.

Since well before the eighteenth century, the seventy-two corporations representing the different trades and the aristocratic leadership of Palermo had been traditionally bound together by relationships of patronage and by their participation in the governance of Palermo. While the *pretore* (city mayor) and the members of the *senato* of the city were aristocrats, the corporations were entitled to the membership of the *consiglio civico* (city council). The *pretore* had the right to appoint the *consoli*, the leaders of each corporation, as well as the members of their councils, who in turn were called upon to confirm the election of the members of the senate as city representatives in the parliament of the island. The members of the

---

134. Letter contained in Miraflores, *Documentos*, pp. 206–7; on the king's return, see *Miscelánea de Comercio, Política y Literatura*, no. 267, 22 November 1820, p. 2.

135. AMM, 2–230.26; also Gil Novales, *Las sociedades patrióticas*, 1, pp. 653–56.

corporations traditionally played an important role in the defence of the city, as they filled the ranks of the *guardia civica*. In addition, the corporations had been involved in the management of grain provisions for the city, the *annona*: their representatives on the city council voted the price of bread, while some corporations were entrusted with the task of enforcing the regulations and the decisions taken by the city magistrates with regard to grain provisions.[136]

By 1820 the economic might and political role of the corporations had been weakened. In the 1780s a comprehensive reform had reduced their numbers by abolishing seventeen of them, deprived them of the *privativa* (the exclusive practice of its trade by each *corporazione*), and put most of them under the direct control of the royal magistrates, leaving only the so-called *arti annonarie* (food-related guilds) under the control of the city senate. The reforms also liberalised the production and sale of bread, and forbade members of the corporations from bearing arms.[137] In 1812 the king partly reinstated the corporations' ancient privileges, by recognising their right to the *privativa* and by putting them back under the control of the city authorities. He did so in an attempt to gain the support of the population of the city for absolutism during the Napoleonic occupation of the mainland and the British protectorate over the island. In reality, however, this partial reintegration of past privileges did not redress the economic grievances of the corporations: even after 1812 the senate could not reinstate the corporations abolished in 1784 without royal assent, and all the workshops not belonging to the corporations were allowed to continue producing or trading outside their structures.[138] The economic crisis that affected the island after 1815 further exacerbated the difficulties experienced both by the members of the corporations and by artisans working outside their ranks. By 1820 the economic crisis and the severe unemployment fuelled by the high costs of primary materials and the scarcity of commissions made taxation and the Bourbon administration more unpopular than ever.

As in Madrid, so in Palermo, the fundamental role played by the artisans in the 1820 revolution derived from a longer tradition of protest and

136. Simona Laudani, *'Quegli strani accadimenti': La rivolta di Palermo del 1773* (Rome: Viella, 2005), pp. 17–20, 41.

137. On the reforms, see Francesco Luigi Oddo, *Le maestranze di Palermo: Aspetti e momenti di vita politico/sociale (sec. XII–XIX)* (Palermo: Accademia nazionale di scienze, lettere e arti, 1991); Laudani, *'Quegli strani accadimenti'*, pp. 196–202.

138. ASP, Real Segreteria, Incartamenti, 5476: 'Ripristino maestranze', and in particular the text of the decree of 1812.

mobilisation that dated back at least to the previous century. In 1773 in particular, the population of the city had risen up against the viceroy, accused of speculating on the sale of bread and more generally criticised for his maladministration. The insurrection led to the departure of the viceroy, who after moving to the city of Messina was finally dismissed by the king. It also resulted in the ritual punishment and humiliation of members of the aristocracy and merchants accused of collusion with the viceroy: while they were not physically harmed, their palaces were looted and their furniture burned in acts of ritual justice.[139]

In 1820 the patterns of behaviour of the population, and the artisans in particular, manifested striking similarities to those displayed in 1773. As in 1773, so too in 1820 what triggered the revolution was the trans- formation of a public act of popular devotion into a protest against the authorities representing the monarchy, who became the primary target of popular anger. The outbreak of the revolt in fact coincided with the festivities in honour of the patron saint of the city, Santa Rosalia, which took place twice a year for several days, and were marked by religious cer- emonies in all the city churches, culminating in the procession of the statue of the saint along the main street, the Cassaro. It was during this procession that the crowds attacked General Richard Church, the military officer in charge of the defence of the city and seen as representing Bourbon despo- tism, with the streets echoing to cries of 'Hurrah for independence!' and 'Down with the tyrants!' They looted the hotel where the general was stay- ing, burning its furniture in the middle of the aristocratic Piazza Marina, the main square of the city, throughout the night. They then moved on to attack all the buildings considered to be symbols of monarchical oppression, from the revenue office to the land registry and those of city and provincial jus- tice, burning their archives The royal palace was also looted and its furnish- ings burnt, and the representative of the king, the Luogotenente Naselli, was forced to leave the city. As in 1773, so too in 1820 the prisoners held in custody at the city harbour were set free and even armed, while the general population seized control of the castle (Castellammare), and took the arms stored in it. The contribution of the corporations and their members to the insurrection was crucial, and that of the corporation of the *conciapelli* (tan- ners) in organising the armed groups was particularly noteworthy.[140]

As in 1773, this hostility against royal authority was accompanied by acts targeting specific members of the aristocratic leadership of the city

139. Laudani, *'Quegli strani accadimenti'*, pp. 66–71.
140. Palmieri, *Saggio storico*, pp. 321–41.

deemed responsible for misdeeds old and new against the population. What explained and justified this behaviour was therefore a traditional 'culture of retribution', but one which was designed at the same time to achieve specific political aims. The first victim of popular revenge was the Prince of Aci, who had been *pretore* of the city twice, and who had acted as one of the leaders of the revolution in its early stages, inciting the population to rise up and goading on the crowds to seize the castle. However, the excessive controls exerted over grain sellers, and alleged acts of extortion, were deeply resented by the population and some corporations, and led to the prince's murder.[141] The second victim was the Prince of Cattolica, who was accused of being an ally of Bourbon despotism and, according to some, wanted the reintroduce the English aristocratic constitution of 1812, disliked by the majority of the population, who favoured the Spanish constitution.

While the inclusion of the artisans' corporations in the new provisional government temporarily appeased the population, the *maestranze* (lower ranks of artisans and corporations) were not yet ready to give it carte blanche, and continued to watch over its decisions. When in September 1820 the provisional government of Palermo and the Neapolitan army agreed on a deal that envisaged the creation of a separate Sicilian parliament, the population, unhappy with its terms, rose up once again. Since they interpreted this deal as a partial repudiation of the earlier declaration of independence, they refused to let the Neapolitan army led by General Florestano Pepe into the city, as the terms of the truce had stipulated. The insurrection resulted in the condemnation of those individuals perceived to have acted against popular interests. Once more, the principles of retribution determined the behaviour of the population: those deemed to have betrayed the population were punished by the crowds with acts of retributive justice. On 25 September, when the Neapolitan army was supposed to enter Palermo, the population took control of the city and attacked the palace of Prince Villafranca, who had led the negotiations with Florestano Pepe on behalf of the provisional government. It also imprisoned a number of other negotiators, occupied the fortresses of the city and managed to fend off an attack by the Neapolitan troops.

Nor did this second insurrection entail an outright dismissal of aristocratic leadership, however. The population instead selected another

141. See Michele Amari's reconstruction of the events, written and left unpublished in 1842, and now published as Amari, *Studii su la storia di Sicilia dalla metà del XVIII secolo al 1820*, ed. Amelia Crisantino (Quaderni Mediterranea—ricerche storiche 15) (Palermo: Accademia nazionale di scienze, lettere e arti, 2010), p. 425; and Palmieri, *Saggio storico*, p. 323.

FIGURE 18. Popular action in Palermo: *Ostinata zuffa tra la Civica e la bassa Plebe* ('Violent clash between civic guards and the common people', 25 September 1820; etching by Calogero De Bernardis, in *Raccolta di 20 stampe, che rappresentano al naturale li fatti più rimarchevoli successi in Palermo dal giorno 15 luglio sino li 5 ottobre 1820*, Palermo[?], 1820). Image: Museo centrale del Risorgimento, Rome, www.risorgimento.it, with permission

aristocrat, Prince Paternò, whom they trusted more than Prince Villafranca, as chief negotiator. Paternò's intervention was in fact much more effective than that of the artisans' own leaders, the *consoli*, in putting an end to the insurrection. His ability to involve the artisans in his negotiations was crucial to their success. He kept in constant communication with the population by addressing the crowds street by street, explaining in detail the terms of the armistice, and promising tax relief. His parade across the city with the white cockade of Sicily's independence, along with promises of money and bribes to some *capipopolo* (leaders of the popular insurrection), made his offers more compelling and convincing. At the end of the negotiations Paternò re-entered the city triumphally, was treated as a liberator by the population, which offered the fortresses to him, and could finally welcome in the Neapolitan troops, this time more prudently arrayed in the dress uniform.[142] General Pepe, meanwhile, when justifying

142. Cortese, *La prima rivoluzione*, pp. 154–56; *Del modo che tenne il principe di Paternò D. Giovanni Luigi Moncada per indurre il popolo di Palermo alla capitolazione*

his controversial deal, much criticised by the Neapolitan government and the parliament, argued that he had had only two options: either to take advantage of Prince Paternò as a mediator to reach an agreement, or simply to level the entire city and its population with it, thus permanently alienating Sicily from Naples.[143]

Corporate structures and relationships of patronage were at the basis of the maritime business and of the administration of the common good also on the Aegean island of Hydra. On this island, sailors constituted the professional category most active in taking the revolutionary initiative. As in the case of the artisans of Palermo, the mob and sailors of Hydra did not fundamentally question existing social hierarchies, but were capable of organising protests to challenge the decisions of the island's elite when they considered that the principles of equity and justice underpinning the shipping business and the governance of their own community had been undermined.

Unsurprisingly, there was a confluence between the economic and political hierarchies of the island. The merchant shipping business was dominated by wealthy investors whose profits were regulated by the existence of two different partnerships, one related to the ownership of the ship, the other to the ownership of the cargo bought for each commercial venture. Along with a small number of wealthy investors, the captain of the ship and the entire crew likewise participated in such partnerships. Sailors could in fact invest their small pots of money in each individual venture instead of being paid a wage, and in any case the crew shared both profits and losses equally. The very nature of commercial shipping therefore made this business a 'communal' activity whose success would benefit the entire island.[144] The wealthy shipowners dominating the business were also the primates or aristocrats of the islands, the so-called *noikokyraioi*, who ruled over the island through a supreme council, where common affairs were discussed often in the presence of their own ships' captains, and who appointed paid adminstrators, the demogerontes. Thus the existing political factions overlapped with business interests and relations of patronage.[145]

---

col comandante delle armi del Re il ten. Col. D. Florestano Pepe segnata a 5 ottobre 1820 (n.p., n.d. [1821]).

143. Cortese, *La prima rivoluzione*, p. 176.

144. On the organisation of labour and profit sharing, see Pissis, 'Investments', esp. pp. 154–57.

145. Trikoupis, Ιστορία (History), 1, pp. 143–44.

The revolts on the island of Hydra in 1821 and 1826 took place in the context of the disruption of commercial ties between the islands and continental Europe triggered by the revolution. They also took place at a time of acute economic depression. As mentioned in chapter two above, during the Napoleonic wars the Greek merchant fleet had benefited from the exclusion of British trading interests from the Mediterranean, and the opportunities offered by the continental blockade imposed by the French after 1807; the ensuing post-war reduction in trade had a marked impact on profits and wages. There is evidence that under the pressure of this crisis some merchants were now offering fixed wages to the sailors, abandoning the traditional profit-sharing system. The revolution further contributed to this transformation of the modus operandi of the Greek merchant fleet.[146]

In 1821, at a time of grave economic crisis precipitated by the insurrection on the mainland and the interruption of trade, it was the mob that intervened to push the island's shipowning notables to support the revolution. One of the island captains, Antonis Oikonomou by name, had joined the revolt with some of the notables, members of the Philiki, and was ready to support the political change advocated by the networks of the secret society. Since the majority of the notables hesitated and seemed to be reluctant to lend their support to the revolution, Oikonomou took the initiative and recruited an army composed of unemployed seamen— described by a philhellene witness as a 'nautical mob'—to join the siege of the fort of Akrokorinthos, which was held by the Ottomans. Oikonomou's army ended up by seizing control of the island, however, displacing the authority of the *noikokyraioi*, with the support of its entire population. The populist regime of Oikonomou lasted only forty days, during which the island officially joined the revolution, but he made himself very unpopular by appointing the captains of his own faction to all the islands' ships. In the end he was deposed and arrested thanks to another popular insurrection, supported by some notables and led in particular by Emmanouil Tombazis, brother to Admiral Iakovos 'Yakoumakis' Tombazis and a member of a prominent shipowning family.[147]

In the years that followed ships from the islands played a crucial role in supporting the war effort at sea. The contribution of the navy to the revolution continued to be made possible by the financial support of its shipowners, who became also prominent leaders of the revolution and

146. Vasilis Kremmydas, Προεπαναστατικές πραγματικότητες: Η οικονομική κρίση και η πορεία προς το 21' (Pre-revolutionary realities: The economic crisis and the path to 1821), Μνήμων [Mnimon] 24, no. 2 (2002): 71–84.

147. Trikoupis, Ιστορία (History), 1, pp. 233–47; Gordon, *History*,1, pp. 165ff.

famous admirals. In 1826 the *Filos tou Nomou*, a newspaper aligned with the Hydriot shipowner Koundouriotis, defended his reputation against those who doubted his sacrifices, sang his praises and by the same token lauded the seamen for their selfless generosity, noting that they 'take ten times less than the privates of the army'.[148] The reality may have been more complex and less heroic. Since neither the revolutionary administration nor the shipowners could afford to pay for the services of all seamen, many of them took to piracy as an alternative, or supplementary, source of income.[149] In addition, the seamen expected the system of profit-sharing employed in commercial shipping to be transferred to the new wartime circumstances, and to be applied to the distribution of the booty. It is hardly surprising that as soon as the islands of Hydra, Spetses and Psara joined the revolution, the organisation of a military fleet led to agreements between them about how to manage each ship as well as about how the booty should be shared.[150]

It was against this background of financial hardship, maritime war and unemployment that in 1826 a second popular insurrection broke out on the island, challenging once more, at least temporarily, the authority of the shipowning oligarchy, and determining a shift in the power balance between two opposing factions, one led by the Koundouriotis brothers and the other by Tombazis, Miaoulis and Boudouris. At the end of the previous naval campaign, the admirals and shipowners of the islands had withdrawn their ships to the island of Poros, a decision that was seen by the population as an attempt to avoid sharing the booty with them, and as a refusal to provide much-needed financial support to the community in times of hardship. This perceived violation of trust triggered a revolt, that followed the perennial rationale of a culture of retribution. The population attacked the houses of the admirals Miaoulis and Emmanouil Tombazis (temporarily absent), arrested their magistrates and established two committees made up of captains and simple seamen to maintain order and voice their demands. Meanwhile, those other members of the shipping oligarchy who were still on the island managed to escape to Poros—with the exception of the Koundouriotis brothers, who were thrown into prison.

148. Φίλος του Νόμου [*Filos tou Nomou*], no. 181, 29 January 1826, in Koumarianou, *Ο Τύπος στον Αγώνα* (The press in the 'Struggle'), 3, pp. 147–48.

149. Dimitris Dimitropoulos, 'Pirates during a Revolution: The Many Faces of Piracy and the Reaction of Local Communities', in *Corsairs and Pirates in the Eastern Mediterranean. Fifteenth-Nineteenth Centuries*, ed. Gelina Harlaftis, Dimitris Dimitropoulos and David J. Starkey (Athens: AdVenture SA, 2016), pp. 29–40.

150. Trikoupis, *Ιστορία* (History), 1, pp. 154–55.

In this situation a captain supported by 150 seamen with one of Koundouriotis's ships went on to engage in acts of piracy and to loot two Ionian vessels. The situation returned to normality only with the intervention of the British philhellene Captain Hamilton, who guaranteed the protection of the admirals and their ships anchored off Poros. More importantly, the local authorities promised to cater to the material needs of the population over the winter by raising money to feed them.[151]

FIGURE 19. Sailor from Hydra (lithograph by Louis Dupré, Paris, 1827). Image: Wikimedia Commons

The insurgency thus reaffirmed the right of the community to be supported, and displayed the features characteristic of early modern factional strife over local leadership. It also had important consequences in determining the solution of yet another crisis that was dividing the revolutionary front, and marked the consolidation of the authority of Koundouriotis over the other notables. Indeed, while in 1821 the popular insurrection had remained a localised event, the outcome of the protest affected political alignments at the national level. At the time, the factions leading the revolution were divided between those meeting in Aegina and those in Ermioni. The victory of Koundouriotis led to the withdrawal of the representatives of Hydra, along with those of Spetses and Psara, from the meeting in Aegina, and the recognition of the assembly sitting in Ermioni.[152]

The ability of sailors and artisans to influence and shape revolutionary politics failed to stem the erosion of their corporate privileges, however, which was already well under way before 1820. In Sicily, soon after the revolution, the trade *corporazioni* were abolished for good. By 1822 they were no longer considered to be a tool of support for the restored regime, but rather as a permanent threat to law and order: their crucial role in the events of 1820 had to be punished.[153] After 1823 in Madrid, the *gremios* for their part continued to exist and function, but in the succeeding years

151. Gordon, *History*, 2, p. 356, Trikoupis, Ιστορία (History), 4, pp. 105–13.

152. Gordon, *History*, 2, pp. 358–60.

153. ASP, Real Segreteria di Stato presso il Luogotenente di Sicilia, Polizia, 7, 1822, f. 22.

their representativeness decreased, as most of the workers in the industrial sectors of the city acted outside their organisations. On the Aegean islands too, the end of the revolution marked a break from the existing practices of the shipping industry and a radical change in its structure. Whereas up until the revolution the great merchants and investors had also been the owners of both ships and cargos, after it trading and shipping became separate activities, and ownership of the vessels was confined to their masters alone. After the revolution increasing numbers of ships were built, but profits in general decreased under the pressure of foreign competition. Crucially, the profit-sharing system that the sailors had fought to maintain during the war steadily declined and remained confined to coastal shipping: most sailors became earners of greatly reduced wages.[154]

Nonetheless, the revolutionary potential of these professional groups was not lost. The ancient corporate structure that had shaped their professional identity left an enduring legacy of political awareness that did not disappear after their dissolution. Another revolt broke out on Hydra in 1838, apparently also as a response to the predicament of the shipping industry: during these events shipmasters committed barratry, sinking some of their ships to pay off their debts. The population of Palermo, meanwhile, intermittently recovered its revolutionary potential in the succeeding decades, although outside the purview of the corporations and without their backing; indeed, it was destined to play a crucial role in the revolutions of 1837 and 1848. The political activism of skilled and unskilled workers in Madrid did not disappear either, but found new outlets after the Trienio. As I shall discuss in the next chapter, some of them, especially those from the lower ranks of each trade, in fact joined the organisations representing the realistas. Others continued to support constitutional government, and in the decades to follow joined republican and democratic organisations. The protests of the 1820s marked the transition from the culture and expectations of early modern protests to the political culture of the new nineteenth-century political movements.

154. Christos Hatziiossif, 'Conjunctural Crisis and Structural Problems in the Greek Merchant Marine in the 19th Century: Reaction of the State and Private Interests', *Journal of the Greek Diaspora* 12 (1985): 5–20 at pp. 14–16.

CHAPTER ELEVEN

A Counterrevolutionary Public Sphere? The Popular Culture of Absolutism

WITH THE END of the constitutional regimes in Naples, Spain and Portugal, the monarchs regained control of the public spaces of their capitals, and obtained popular recognition for their fully restored powers through a sequence of public ceremonies. In May 1821, the return of Ferdinando to Naples from Florence and Rome was carefully planned and organised by the city authorities. For his arrival a number of temporary pavilions and arches had been set up along the designated route from the city outskirts all the way to the royal palace. The first, a pavilion erected at Santa Maria degli Angeli just outside the city, contained four statues representing the virtues of the sovereign, and was held up by poles featuring the emblems of each province of the kingdom. The second, set up within the city itself, a triumphal arch dedicated to the clemency of the monarch, was decorated with the lilies of the Bourbon dynasty. To welcome their king, the Neapolitans displayed tapestries on their balconies and windows, and erected busts of him outside their houses. His public entry into his capital aimed also at effacing the memory of events that had taken place only ten months or so before. In its final stretch, the king's procession in fact followed the route taken by the constitutional army led by Guglielmo Pepe in July the previous year. Indeed, Pepe's military parade along Via Toledo down to the royal palace had marked the victory of the revolution and the submission of the monarch to the constitution. This time, however, the troops were stationed at intervals along the street, leaving its space unencumbered for the king alone to be cheered by the jubilant crowds. The following day, after receiving court dignitaries and aristocrats, and attending a Te Deum, the king appeared on the balcony of the royal palace with his son, the Duke of Calabria, who embraced him publicly. On this occasion he was acclaimed again by the population of the capital as absolute monarch.[1]

In October 1823 it was the turn of King Fernando VII to reclaim Madrid as absolute monarch. He did so after a triumphal journey from Cádiz, where he had spent the previous two months as a hostage of the besieged constitutional regime before its defeat by the French army. Now reinstated in his power, Fernando entered each city neither accompanied nor welcomed by any public authority. The king was in fact determined to stand alone, when acclaimed by his people. Each of these events followed a similar pattern. The royal family entered each city in an open carriage. Groups of 'Voluntarios Realistas', the absolutist equivalent of the constitutional national guard, then took the place of the horses and pulled the carriage themselves. Ceremonies were organised for the monarch to receive the *besamanos* (kissing of the hand); the city was lit up at night and firework displays invariably followed. Unlike the celebrations organised for his return at the end of the Napoleonic wars, those organised in 1823 did not have a markedly religious connotation. Religious rites and visits to churches and monasteries had been kept to a minimum. Fernando's new public cult of personality did not require a constant reminder of the sacrality of his authority, or his homage to the Catholic church.

In Madrid, the reassertion of his authority entailed also domination or the regaining of control of the urban space previously marked by the celebrations of Rafael Riego: like Ferdinando in Naples, Fernando sought to erase the memory of the hero of the revolution. Just as Riego had done in 1820, the king likewise entered Madrid on open conveyance. His procession into the capital culminated with his entrance into the Plaza Major (renamed Plaza Real), through the Arco de Platerías, where in 1821 protesters had held up the portrait of Riego as a symbol of revolutionary resistance. But the arch now featured his own portrait, and portraits of the monarch were at the same time displayed on the facades of most buildings between the Paseo del Prado, the Calle Alcalá and the Puerta del Sol, the itinerary Fernando followed once inside the capital.[2] Thus the king was

---

1. Francesco de Angelis, *Storia del regno di Napoli sotto la dinastia Borbonica*, 7 vols (Naples: G. Mosino, 1817–33), 6, pp. 47–52; *Giornale del Regno delle Due Sicilie*, no. 48, 18 May 1821, p. 188.

2. Emilio Soler, Francisco Sevillano and Emilio La Parra López, eds, *Diarios de viaje de Fernando VII (1823 y 1827–1828)* (Alicante: Universidad de Alicante, 2013), p. 241. On the nature of these ceremonies, see David San Narciso Martín, 'La monarquía ante la nación:

FIGURE 20. The entry of King Fernando VII into Madrid, 13 November 1823: *Entrada triunfal en Madrid, 1823* (oil painting, artist and date unknown, Museo de historia de Madrid, Madrid. Image: Biblioteca Virtual del Patrimonio Bibliográfico, https://bvpb.mcu.es/es/

embracing the self-same personalisation of politics as had first emerged during the constitutional period.

In Portugal, a celebration of the authority of Dom Miguel and the constant presence of his vassals would likewise mark his return to Lisbon from his exile, in February 1828. Unlike Fernando VII of Spain and Ferdinando of Naples, Dom Miguel was, at least in theory, not regaining power as an absolute monarch. On the basis of an agreement with his brother Dom Pedro, Emperor of Brazil, and of a protocol signed in Vienna by himself, Austria and Britain, Dom Miguel was in fact set to become regent of the kingdom only after swearing an oath to the 1826 constitution, and on condition that he marry his niece Dona Maria, still then a minor, but the legitimate heir. However, his public conduct upon his arrival anticipated his determination to reinstate absolutism. Behaving in a fashion similar

---

Representaciones ceremoniales del poder en España (1814–1868)', unpublished doctoral dissertation, Universidad Complutense de Madrid, 2020, pp. 95–98; Pedro Rújula, 'Una monarchia populista? Potere assoluto e ricorso al popolo nella restaurazione spagnola di Fernando VII', *Memoria e Ricerca: Rivista di Storia Contemporanea* 27, no. 62 (2019): 421–35.

to the heads of the Neapolitan and Spanish dynasties upon their return to their capital cities as absolute monarchs, his first acts made it clear that his power was not to be shared with any other institutions. Significantly, he made a conscious effort not to imitate the rituals that had marked the return of his own father Dom João VI from Brazil to Portugal in 1821 as a constitutional king. On that occasion, Dom João in fact had landed at the Terreiro do Paço, the large square by the river Tagus in the centre of the city, known also as Praça do Comércio, only after receiving a delegation from the Cortes on his ship. Having disembarked in the square, Dom João had remained constantly surrounded by the army, the members of the senate of the city council and the parliamentary delegation, who escorted him to the Cortes to swear an oath to the constitution. The presence of these institutions was a reminder of the limitations that the constitution imposed upon monarchical power.

Dom Miguel, on the contrary, took the decision in February 1828 to disembark at Belém, far outside the city, whence he went straight to visit his mother, Dona Carlota Joaquina, in the Ajuda Palace. In Belém he refused to receive a delegation from the Chamber of Deputies, or indeed the keys of the city from the senate of Lisbon, though they had been offered to him. He did the same when he arrived at the Ajuda Palace, where he otherwise received the *beija-mão* (kissing of the hand) from a public, but not from the parliamentary, delegation. It was only the following day that he took an oath to the Carta in front of the members of the lower and upper chambers inside the palace. Yet, as eyewitnesses reported, he did so begrudgingly, in the most muted tone. Popular displays of support would seem to have been what mattered to him most. Unencumbered by the presence of any institutional delegation, while travelling from Belém to the Ajuda Palace just outside Lisbon he had been welcomed by large crowds and by acclamations as 'King Miguel'. Popular support for his reinstatement of absolutism was made more explicit less than two months after his arrival in Belém, on 25 April, the birthday of the queen-mother Dona Carlota Joaquina, when he was acclaimed as Dom Miguel *rei absoluto* by large crowds gathering at the senate of the city council of Lisbon.[3] Just a few days later, he put an end to the constitutional regime, summoned the traditional Cortes made up of the three estates, and declared himself absolute monarch.

3. Maria Alexandre Lousada, 'A contra-revolução e os lugares da luta política: Lisboa em 1828', in *Contra-revolução, espírito público e opinião no sul da Europa: Séculos XVIII e XIX*, ed. Maria de Fátima Sá e Melo Ferreira (Lisbon: Centro de Estudos de História Contemporânea Portuguesa, 2009), pp. 83–108; Lousada and Ferreira, *D. Miguel*, pp. 136–41.

As these public ceremonies demonstrate, the monarchs eagerly sought displays of popular loyalty: popular consensus, albeit granted by subjects and not by citizens, had to be publicly demonstrated to legitimise their return. No other authorities or institutions participated in these festivities, so as not to interfere in the direct relationship between sovereign and people. Crucially, these events suggest also that there already existed genuine popular support for the return to absolutism. The enthusiasm expressed by the populations for the return of their monarchs to their capitals therefore invite us too to think of absolutism in the age of revolutions as a popular movement. Although the presence of the population at these ceremonies certainly owed much to the organisational efforts of local authorities, and was partly regimented, popular enthusiasm was not exclusively the result of a mobilisation from above. As we have seen earlier, genuine popular enthusiasm for the end of the liberal experiment had in fact already expressed itself independently in Spain and Portugal. It is to the culture and spatial practices of popular royalism, to the complex relationship it had with monarchical power and to the ways in which kings themselves responded to it that the pages below are devoted.

A few preliminary remarks are required to make sense of royalist popular culture and its supporters, known at the time as *realisti* (in Naples), or *realistas* (in Spain, and in Portugal, where they were also defined as 'Miguelistas'). First of all, to understand the emergence of a royalist public opinion and of something that could be defined as a 'counterrevolutionary public sphere', we need to acknowledge the interdependence of revolution and counterrevolution. The emergence of such separate, autonomous and antithetical political identities, each with its own original features, owed much to this interaction. Counterrevolutionaries (or royalists) and revolutionaries (known then as liberals or constitutionalists) defined themselves against their enemies and their enemies' symbols through a cycle of group and personal acts of revenge and of punitive justice. While alternative and incompatible, at the same time the revolution and the counterrevolution constantly influenced each other. The public rituals organised to celebrate restored absolutism described above represented a rejection of revolutionary rituals, but they had also adopted some of their features. This interdependence is true also for the counterrevolution as a grass-roots movement. Such a movement in fact developed a set of political behaviours and practices comparable to those of the revolution. It employed secret societies and other forms of sociability already adopted by the constitutionalists. Although the critics of the revolution attacked freedom of the press and journalism as vehicles for atheism and anarchical principles, they for their part claimed to be the representatives of the 'true public opinion', of a majority that was hostile to the new ideas.[4] The apologists of absolutism were therefore forced by circumstances to seek publicity, to engage in propaganda and to produce a sizeable journalistic output, in a variety of media, that attacked constitutionalism and revolution and subjected the political ideas, the arguments and the practices of constitutionalism to systematic scrutiny.

Like the supporters of the revolutions, counterrevolutionary publicists in Spain, Portugal and Naples (and in the Ottoman Empire) related events in their own country to those taking place across southern Europe. For them, events at home belonged to a Europe-wide crisis that was leading to national humiliations and imperial disintegration.[5] Although these events demonstrated that anarchy was spreading across the continent's outlying southern European territories, they were convinced that, for geopolitical as well as moral reasons, these revolutions were doomed to fail. Supporting the cause of Dom Miguel, argued a proclamation published during the civil war of 1826, would in fact save Portugal from being subjected to a shameful invasion and occupation, similar to that carried out in 1808, by the French—and such as Naples, Piedmont and Spain had experienced more recently at the hands of foreign powers—and would help to restore its national honour.[6]

Second, like popular liberalism, popular royalism developed also as a phenomenon independent of the institutions it sought to defend. Although hostile to the notion of popular participation in politics, absolute monarchs needed popular mobilisation and participation to win their war against the revolution. The harmonious relationship between absolute monarchs and their peoples displayed during the public ceremonies organised for the return of the kings was, however, only a temporary phenomenon. For, once reinstated in their absolute power, monarchs no longer wanted a public that could question their authority, but only subservient subjects that acknowledged it. This is why they closed down all periodicals, including those that had supported the restoration of their

4. See for instance *O Braz Corcunda e o Verdadeiro Constitucional*, no. 2, 1823, pp, 38–39. For one counterrevolutionary periodical, freedom of the press would lead to the abolition of Christianity: see *O Punhal dos Corcundas*, no. 12, 1823, p. 125.

5. For the eastern Mediterranean, see *Le Spectateur Oriental: Feuille Littéraire, Critique et Commerciale*, no. 13, 21 July 1821, p. 1, and no. 15, August 1821, pp. 2 and 3. For Naples, see for example the *Enciclopedia Ecclesiastica, e Morale: Opera Periodica, Compilata da G.V.T*, vol. 1 (June–August 1821; 21 June), pp. 55–62; vol. 2 (September–November 1821; 30 October), pp. 275–93.

6. ANTT, IGP, Coimbra 286, f. 151: proclamation published in 1826.

absolute authority: in order to tighten their grip over the public sphere. Moreover, the tensions between the expectations of absolute kings and the aspirations of their supporters could not always be resolved. In the new circumstances of the restoration of absolutism, the dynamic of contestation shifted from being against the constitutionalists to being against the so-called moderate royalists (at least in Naples, where they were labelled *realisti moderati*, and in Spain, where they were dubbed *realistas moderados*). This was the label attached to those ministers and administrators in the service of the absolute monarchs whom the royalists deemed to have betrayed their cause by protecting the liberals. In Spain and Portugal (but not in Naples), popular royalism managed to challenge the monarchy by stirring up insurrection and by supporting alternative royal pretenders. A new royalist opinion critical of the terms of the restoration first emerged in Naples, where absolutism was reinstated after the revolution earlier than in any other southern European monarchy.

In the Kingdom of the Two Sicilies, the first government of the restoration had been dominated initially by the figure of the minister of police, the Prince of Canosa, the leading champion of ultra-royalism. Canosa was determined to root out any revolutionary threat by purging the justice system, the army and the civil service, along with the clergy and the educational system, of all those who had been compromised by the constitutional regime. This agenda led to an indiscriminate witch-hunt, the establishment of military tribunals and arbitrary incarcerations and death penalties for former revolutionaries. This approach to restoration clashed with the wishes of the Austrian foreign minister Prince Metternich, and his representative in Naples, Count Ficquelmont, who wanted justice to be enforced by scrupulously following the law, in a spirit of reconciliation. Austrian pressures led to the appointment of Luigi de' Medici as president of the council and the dismissal of the ultra-royalists in government, Canosa in particular.[7]

Medici had been in power already between 1816, when he replaced his arch enemy Canosa as president of the council, and the revolution of 1820. Suspicious of any form of consultation, he was a committed supporter of the prerogatives of the absolute monarch, and an advocate of reformism from above. For this reason, after coming to power in 1816 he had retained the administrative and legal reforms of the French period. In a spirit of reconciliation, between 1816 and 1820 he had tried to create a new social consensus around the restored monarchy by merging the

7. Walter Maturi, *Il Principe di Canosa* (Florence: Le Monnier, 1944), pp. 150–84.

recently established Napoleonic civil service with the previous service loyal to the Bourbons. These policies had laid the foundations for the new post-Napoleonic administrative monarchy. After 1821 Medici was resolved to govern by the same principles as had guided him before the revolution. Determined, in the name of law and order, to punish any form of private revenge and violence, he sought to pursue a policy of pacification in the wake of the revolution. Given the polarisation of opinion produced by the constitutional period, and its end by foreign military means, this would prove more difficult than in 1816.[8] Medici's approach in fact disappointed many supporters of absolutism. In this context, an ultra-royalist opposition to restored absolute monarchy emerged out of the sense of betrayal felt by all those who had welcomed the withdrawal of the constitution and the return of the king from Laibach in 1821.

A number of recurring complaints were voiced by the realisti in Naples after the revolution. Even when Prince Canosa still held power, the ultra-royalists lamented the fact that their foremost champion was not in control of the government. They noted his isolation in the council of ministers, which undermined his ability to pursue his objectives, and were convinced that most of its members were protecting the Carboneria.[9] They criticised the head of the Austrian occupying army, General Frimont, and the minister the Duke of Ascoli for failing to persecute the political enemies of absolutism, and for colluding with the Carboneria.[10] They went so far as to accuse the heir to the throne himself, the Duke of Calabria, of being in charge of some lodges of the Carboneria and of protecting their networks. They regretted the fact that too many liberals were still enjoying privileges, and that military and civil authorities in the provinces were granting them favours.[11] They resented too the slow and irregular pace of the purges of the army and the ministries, and denounced the extent to which both the directors of several ministries and local civil servants protected or favoured former members of the Carboneria. The replacement of Canosa by Medici only exacerbated this disappointment of the realisti, who considered the latter to be the candidate of the liberals and the so-called 'pseudo-royalists', a group that included those who had accepted Medici's compromise with the French regime after 1816. In this new context, many of these realisti became very critical of the monarch himself: as

8. Gaetano Cingari, *Mezzogiorno e Risorgimento: La restaurazione a Napoli dal 1821 al 1830* (Rome: Laterza, 1976).

9. ASN, Borbone, 726, f. 6: 'Spirito pubblico dei realisti', 9 April 1822.

10. Ibid., 278, f. 277: 'Bollettino segreto', 9 October 1821.

11. ASN, Borbone, 726, f. 8, 'Spirito pubblico dei realisti' 12 April 1822.

one of their number noted, the fact that they called him father, and loved him unconditionally, while he was in reality favouring the liberals, only showed how mad the realisti themselves were.[12]

The carbonari were the *bêtes noirs* of the Neapolitan royalists. As an anonymous counterrevolutionary writer argued, Cromwell and the French Jacobins had been the ideological heroes of the 'sect', as he defined the carbonari, who had planned and organised the revolution. Their aim was not to 'restore humanity to the happiness of the golden age', but rather to put an end to monarchical power. Fortunately, if attacked with sufficient rigour, *liberalismo* would disappear 'like a phantom'.[13] As other royalist writers confirmed, the carbonari were targeting, besides the monarchy, revealed religion, which they wanted to replace with a form of indifferentism, and with the rituals and cult of their own 'religione carbonaria'. Defence of church and state thus went hand in hand.[14]

The Neapolitan realisti tended to meet and debate in sites different from those occupied by supporters of the constitution or the Carboneria, their ideological divisions thus being reflected in their control of different urban spaces. They often gathered around the royal palace or in specific coffee houses and shops. Many of the most virulent enemies of the Carboneria belonged to the secret society of the Calderari, first set up in 1816 by the Prince of Canosa in defence of the Bourbon dynasty, and whose reorganisation in 1821 was attributed again to him. While the Calderari rarely exchanged views or debated with the constitutionalists in shared spaces, they often clashed with them when they abandoned their 'strongholds' and roamed through the streets of Naples, where the police reported acts of violence between members of these rival groups, including the murders of both realisti and carbonari. After 1821 the government did all it could to suppress not only the Carboneria but also this royalist secret society, whose networks were present both in the capital and the provinces of the kingdom, and whose members were accused of 'fomenting anarchy' with their acts of personal revenge against members of the Carboneria.[15]

12. Ibid., f. 3, 'Spirito pubblico dei realisti', 22 March 1822.

13. Ibid., f. 47, 'Considerazioni sui settarj, e di loro condotta'.

14. ASN, Borbone, 269, ff. 417–22, 'Memoria anti-carbonaria'. See also ASN, Borbone, Carte Canosa, 724, f. 171, 'Carteggio filosofico-politico della rivoluzione accaduta in Napoli il luglio 1820 [. . .] di un cittadino calabrese, che scriveva ad un suo amico in Napoli'.

15. ASN, Borbone, 278, f. 267: Intonti to the king, 15 September 1821; ibid., f. 208: 'Bollettino segreto', 5 August 1821; ibid., ff. 227 and 233: 'Bollettino segreto', 8 August 1821. On the spatial politics of the carbonari and the realisti in Naples, see also Castellano, *Spazi pubblici*, pp. 86–91.

FIGURE 21. *Funeral of the Constitution* (drawing by unknown artist, Naples, 1821; Archivio di Stato, Naples: Archivio Borbone, carte Fardella di Torrearsa. Image: ASN, with permission

However, in Naples in the 1820s there emerged no popular royalist movement determined to attack the constitutional regime or willing to challenge the Bourbon absolute monarchy after its restoration, as did occur in Spain during these same years. In 1799 a royalist popular movement led by Cardinal Ruffo, the Armata della Santa Fede (army of the holy faith), had attacked the French army, and rioters rose up against the republican authorities in Naples. More royalist uprisings had challenged the French occupation in Calabria in 1806, the so-called *insorgenze*. But the events of 1799 or 1806 were not replicated in 1820, as many landowners supportive of the revolution had feared would happen. For Guglielmo Pepe, the fact that the popular classes in Naples and in the provinces did not rise up against the revolution in 1820 as they had done in 1799 owed much to the progress education and enlightenment had made throughout the society of the kingdom during the previous twenty years.[16] Likewise,

16. Pepe, *Memoirs*, 2, p. 250. On 1799, see John A. Davis, 'Rivolte popolari e contro-rivoluzioni nel Mezzogiorno continentale', in *Folle controrivoluzionarie: Le insorgenze populari nell'Italia giacobina e napoleonica*, ed. Anna Maria Rao (Rome: Carocci, 1999),

although ultra-royalist public opinion remained a source of concern for public authorities after the restoration of absolutism in 1821, it did not produce a mass movement capable of destabilising the monarchy. This was for a variety of reasons. First, since the final years of the French period the Carboneria, by presenting itself as a patriotic and anti-French organisation had become a hegemonic force in terms of its capacity to control, rouse and influence popular opinion, as well as to mobilise the lower classes in urban and rural areas. It remained such also at the end of the revolution in 1821, as the police in Naples and from the provinces consistently reported.[17] This is why, in spite of the economic crises, felt in particular in the countryside, no royalist insurgencies broke out in Naples. Ultra-royalism appealed only to limited sectors of Neapolitan society: those defeated and sidelined already during the decade of French rule, the legal and land ownership reforms of which would remain in place after 1815. Second, in Naples there was no alternative dynastic candidate willing to challenge the authority of the ruling monarch to lead or stir up opposition. Admittedly, the revolution produced tensions between the occupant of the throne and his heir, who in practice acted as regent (appointed lieutenant of the kingdom by the king) during the revolution, when his father was abroad, and appeared to be more sympathetic to the cause of the constitution than his father would have wished. But these tensions were overcome with the return of the king to Naples. In spite of rumours, and in the face of the hopes of some carbonari, the Duke of Calabria had no interest in acting as the leader of an internal opposition (possibly constitutional) to the existing king.[18] The Duke's public homage to his father on the balcony of the royal palace the day after the king's return to Naples was intended to demonstrate his loyalty and the renewed harmony between the monarch and his son.

Although both constitutionalists and ultra-royalists were very critical of King Ferdinando after 1821, albeit for different reasons, the sudden death of this elderly monarch in 1825 did not undermine the popularity of the monarchy. On the contrary, it turned out to be an important moment to reaffirm the authority, unity and sacrality of the Bourbon dynasty against its enemies. A set of funerary ceremonies replicated across the kingdom

---

pp. 349–68; Davis, '1799: The Santafede and the Crisis of the *ancien régime* in Southern Italy', in *Society and Politics in the Age of the Risorgimento: Essays in Honour of Denis Mack Smith*, ed. John A. Davis and Paul Ginsborg (Cambridge: Cambridge University Press, 1991), pp. 1–25.

17. ASN, Borbone, 278, f. 269: Intonti to the king, 22 September 1822.

18. On the tensions between father and son, see Galasso, *Storia*, 5, pp. 222–24.

the official funeral that had taken place in the capital, which had been officiated at by Cardinal Ruffo. These ceremonies transformed the Church into the guarantor of dynastic legitimacy. A catafalque was erected in every church of the kingdom to hold an urn, and the effigy of the king had to be displayed during the services. Funerary sermons were delivered in all churches, and many of them were published. While the literary genre of funerary sermons belonged to an older royal tradition, in 1825 the public reading of these texts provided an opportunity specifically to defend the restoration after the revolution, and to celebrate the history of the dynasty and the virtues of a monarch whose throne had been attacked during successive political upheavals. They described Ferdinando as a benign father devoted to his family and his people, a pious man who had endured with great virtue and 'equally heroic fortitude' all sorts of 'misfortunes', including the recent 'political upheaval'. Thanks to another of his virtues, firmness, he had 'rescued his kingdom from the immense horrors of anarchy'.[19]

To observe much larger and more turbulent popular royalist movements than in the Kingdom of the Two Sicilies, it is to the Iberian peninsula that we should turn. There, counterrevolutionary public opinion with specific cultural and ideological features had already emerged during the revolutions themselves, when it provided support for armed insurrection against the constitutional governments. In both Spain and in Portugal, efforts to undermine the political and intellectual credibility of revolutionary ideas, to advance an alternative set of values and to reclaim urban spaces controlled by the constitutionalists had started well before the restoration of absolutism. The civil wars in Spain and Portugal were marked by the proliferation of broadsheets, proclamations, short dialogues, songs and poetry that vehemently attacked the ideas of the revolutionaries, highlighting their inconsistency and absurdity, while advancing their own alternative values. These ephemeral publications were often transcribed or circulated along with manuscript texts in a clandestine fashion.[20] In Spain in particular, many of these texts attacked the main heroes of the revolution. In a dialogue entitled 'Doctrina de los serviles' (the derogatory

19. Quotations from Michele Basilio Clari [Clary], *Orazione funebre in morte di Sua Maestà Ferdinando I* (Naples: Angelo Trani, 1825), pp. 20–22, 41, 54. On this literary genre, see Giovanni Montroni, 'Linguaggi di regalità: L'uso pubblico della retorica a Napoli nel primo Ottocento', *Contemporanea* 1 (1998): 703–30. For other examples of this genre, see Giuseppe Plumari, *Orazione funebre per il piissimo, clementissimo, invittissimo Ferdinando I* (Messina: Giuseppe Fiumara, 1825), and Francesco Silvestre, *Per la morte di S.M. Ferdinando I* (Naples: Saverio Giordano, 1825).

20. Ramon Arnabat Mata, 'Propaganda antiliberal i lluita ideologica durant el Trienni Liberal a Catalunya (1820–1823)', *Recerques: Història, Economia i Cultura* 34 (1996): 7–28.

term employed by the revolutionaries to define their enemies, and evidently embraced also by the latter themselves), Riego was dismissed as 'a freemason libertine, drunkard, *pícaro* [rogue] and coward who led the army against his king in order to avoid going to America'. The same dialogue described the Cortes as a hell full of demons who worked to demolish the throne and the altar: its members were the most depraved individuals of each province, who did not follow God's commandments, lived as libertines, and 'have ruined the nation'. It also attacked the appropriation of the public sphere by the revolutionaries, claiming that while the liberals sought glory in the cafés and theatres, the *serviles* did so through 'beatitude'.[21] These themes were further elaborated in a range of other satirical compositions. For instance, the description of Riego as a traitor recurred in political poetry; in a poem devoted to the heroes of the revolutions, he was similarly described as a deserter and (not without reason) a plotter who had never actually fought in a war. In sum, 'he gained his fame as a traitor and directed the farce of the insurgency'.[22]

Besides lampooning the leaders of the revolution, much of this Spanish *realista* literature specifically attacked the constitution. According to one poem, the constitution subverted not only religion but also the very foundations of society. Indeed, it sought to 'modify God's plans, make Christ sin and change the Ten Commandments'. It also aspired to 'equate all classes, rob all property, turn authority into a deck of cards, protect the wildest and authorise treason, conspire against the throne and make the soldier rebel'. Finally, it turned the king into a citizen, and introduced republicanism into Spain. To ridicule it, gendered metaphors were often used to personify the constitution as a young and amoral girl. One poem described the history of constitutionalism as the biography of an illegitimate girl, never christened in a Catholic church, who had grown into an adulterous young woman, and had made herself easily available to other men not only at home but also abroad. This metaphor thus served the purpose of condemning the constitutional internationalism of the 1820s, representing international admiration for Spanish constitution and its adoption in other countries as an act of national betrayal. It also pointed to the idea that the Spanish nation was incompatible with cosmopolitan beliefs.[23]

21. APR, Papeles Reservados de Fernando VII, 21, ff. 189–90: 'Doctrina de los serviles'.

22. Ibid., f. 180: broadsheet, 'A los heroes de farsa del ano 20. Versos'.

23. Ibid., 21, ff. 219–26: 'Poema historico que contiene la vida y muerte de una niña adulterina de infame nacimiento, salida à luz en Cádiz ano de 1812: no bautizada por la iglesia, y no obstante confirmada militarmente en la isla de Leon; hija de los padres mas viles y execrables de todo el mundo'.

But critiques of constitutionalism were not confined to pasquinades, satirical squibs or anti-revolutionary pamphlets. The enemies of the revolution also challenged the constitutional regime by threatening its symbolic control of public space. They did so by individual acts of iconoclasm, sporadically at first, in 1820, and then intensifying during 1822 with the outbreak of the civil war. These targeted the numerous plaques and monuments in honour of the constitution that had been erected across the country, and were often responses to the public destruction of monuments or symbols carried out by the constitutionalists in 1820. Within months of Riego's pronunciamiento and the reintroduction of the constitution, local authorities were to be found denouncing the desecration or vandalism of these monuments. Such events often prompted official responses on the part of the local constitutional forces, who organised ceremonies to honour the constitution in the face of what for them amounted to sacrilege.[24]

During the summer of 1823, when the French army invaded and occupied Spain, paving the way for the end of the constitutional regime and the reintroduction of absolutism, these iconoclastic acts both increased in number and changed in nature. They became public rituals organised and attended by large groups of people. In Madrid soon after the arrival of the French army, constitutional plaques were removed from their sites and burned in public spaces. In the Plazuela de la Cebada, for instance, a group of people burned an inscription removed from the building of the Real Junta de Farmacia and dedicated to the constitution by the students of a religious college.[25] In other towns acts of destruction of constitutional plaques were turned into fully-fledged ceremonies during which these were replaced with portraits of the monarch or by crosses. The organisers of such events were trying to eradicate all visible references to the revolution, and to complete the reclamation of public space by substituting the symbols of the past regime with their own. By these acts they sought to reaffirm the values of Catholicism in the face of revolutionary impiety and the sacrality of the monarchy violated by the constitution, and made reference at the same time to the martyrdom of the king during the constitutional period.

24. See for instance, Florencio Idoate, 'La merindad de Tudela durante la guerra realista', *Príncipe de Viana* 27, nos 104–5 (1966): 277–300; Gregorio Sánchez Romero, *Revolución y reacción en el nordeste de la región de Murcia* (Murcia: Real Academia Alfonso X El Sabio, 2001), p. 207; Francisco Javier Díez Morrás, '*La Antorcha de la libertad resplandece': La Sociedad Patriótica de Logroño y los inicios del liberalismo* (Logroño: Ayuntamiento de Logroño, 2016), pp. 146–56.

25. AHN, Consejos Suprimidos, legajo 12270, f. 187: 25 September 1823.

The spontaneous nature of these initiatives is clear from the fact that the public authorities did not encourage them when the regime changed: on the contrary, they sought to suppress them, so as to prevent disturbances or disorders. In the small town of Mentrida in the province of Toledo, the local authorities could not prevent the burning of a plaque and its replacement by the emblem of the monarch, an act carried out in the presence of a large crowd. Yet they managed to forestall the burning of the statue of Riego, against the wishes of the same people. In these moments of regime transition, the competition for the symbolic reappropriation of the public space resulted in 'agonistic rituals':[26] revolutionaries wanted to declare that the revolution was not over yet, while counterrevolutionaries aimed at putting an end to it permanently. The meaning of symbols was constantly questioned in these circumstances.[27] In the village of San Lorenzo de la Parrilla, in the province of Cuenca in Castile, ritual destruction was preceded by the appointment of a leader by the crowd, which then marched to the public square, where they smashed to pieces the constitutional plaque. They then entered the town hall, crying 'Long live the king! Long live religion!' and 'Death to the constitucion!' The following morning, they returned to the square to replace the plaque with an image of the crucifixion. Yet the supporters of the constitution did not resign themselves to the destruction of the plaque; the following night they tore the image from the crucifix and replaced it with a sheet with the seal of the year 1820 and the inscription '¡Viva la constitución!' This act prompted much public outrage, and the crucifix was restored amid hurrahs for the king.[28]

Once the king had been fully reinstated, and public symbols of the constitutional regime had been erased, the authorities completed their reclamation of urban spaces with a new set of rituals and commemorations in honour of those who had fought and died to defeat the revolution. Like the revolutionaries, absolutists created their own official cult of martyrs and heroes. Most of these martyrs turned out to be clerics. The most famous and most important of them, without any doubt, was the *cura* (parson) Vinuesa, who had been arrested and murdered in the prisons of Madrid in 1821 for organising an anti-revolutionary plot with the acquiescence of the monarch. Counterrevolutionary propaganda employed his murder as evidence of the brutality of the constitutionalists, and of their disregard

26. I borrow the expression from Fureix, *L'Oeil blessé*, p. 53.

27. AHN, Consejos Suprimidos, legajo 12271: report on events in Mentrida, 4 June 1823.

28. Ibid., f. 246: report from Cuenca de Castilla, 10 June 1823.

for religion and the clergy.[29] His martyrdom was celebrated not only in Spain, but also in Portugal, Naples and Piedmont. For the *Giornale del Regno delle Due Sicilie*, his murder amounted to 'the historical summary (*compendio*) of the Spanish revolution'. In March 1824 his funeral and the procession for the translation of his body to the royal church of San Isidro in Madrid was turned into a grand and solemn affair attended by large crowds. A group of Voluntarios Realistas on horseback led the procession, followed by all the religious communities and all the parish priests of the capital. The coffin was borne by priests and was followed by Vinuesa's family, His Majesty's preachers, and by more Voluntarios. The king with his family witnessed to the event from the balcony of the royal palace, while the chaplains to the king awaited the arrival of the martyr's mortal remains at the entrance to the church. The following day all the military, civil and religious authorities of the capital, including the commander of the French troops, were present at a pontifical mass in Vinuesa's honour. This was a wholly religious event dominated by religious authorities but, as the epitaph upon the urn where Vinuesa's bones would be deposed made plain, his sacrifice symbolised the cause of absolutism, as he had been murdered by the enemies of both throne and altar.[30]

Other cities commemorated their own local martyrs for the monarchy and religion. In Toledo, for instance, the memory of Don Atanasio García Juzdado was celebrated by a much-delayed funeral in June 1823. This priest had been garrotted by the constitutional authorities in November 1822 for his anti-revolutionary activities. As a guerrilla leader, he had led a group of seventy infantry fighters and twenty horsemen in the mountains outside Toledo, hosted meetings to organise resistance and written and disseminated proclamations inciting insurrection against the constitutional government. His remains were now exhumed—the press reporting that his body was found to be miraculously still intact a full seven months after his execution—and put on public display in a church. A procession accompanied his coffin back to the square where he had been executed, and where a temple had been erected to host it. That same day

29. *Giornale del Regno delle Due Sicilie*, no. 67, 9 June 1821, p. 269; Eduardo José Rodriguez de Carassa, *Oración fúnebre que en las solemnes exequias celebradas en el convento de religiosas de la encarnación (vulgo San Plácido). Por el alma de don Matías Vinuesa, capellán de honor de S.M., arcediano de Tarazona, y cura antes de Tamajon, asesinado en la cárcel en la tarde de 4 de mayo de 1821* (Madrid: Imprenta de Nuñez, 1823).

30. *Gazeta de Madrid*, 30 March 1824, p. 174. The *Gazzetta Piemontese* noticed that the king of Spain had wanted his funeral to be as solemn as for those of the heroes of 2 May 1808, thus connecting the memory of these two episodes as both being acts in defence of the rights of the monarchy: *Gazzetta Piemontese*, no. 44, 13 April 1824, p. 244.

he was finally buried in the cathedral of the city in the presence of the clergy, the city authorities and the Voluntarios Realistas.[31] Ceremonies for lay victims of the revolutions were less frequent; but in 1823 in Valencia it was the memory of a prominent military officer, General Francisco Javier de Elío, a former captain-general of the city, that would be revived in the name of absolutism. On the anniversary of his execution, which had taken place a year before to punish him for organising a military coup against the constitution, a memorial service and funeral was held in the metropolitan church of the city. But the status of martyr was awarded by the counterrevolutionary press mainly to those clerics who by their sacrifice had borne witness to the cause of religion and the king, rather than to laymen: while Vinuesa and many other priests and monks who had lost their lives were classified as martyrs, General Elío remained first and foremost a 'hero'.[32] The reclamation of the public space of Spanish cities, meanwhile, was completed by the erection of new monuments and symbols that celebrated the monarch.[33]

However, these attempts to create a new cult of absolutism supported by a loyal public were not wholly successful. The transition from revolution to restoration raised expectations and hopes that were not to be satisfied. Disappointment with the reality of the restoration in Spain led to the emergence of a royalist opposition much larger in size, and more violent in nature, than that in Naples. The first source of dissatisfaction stemmed from the king's attitude towards the Church and from the style of his reorganisation of state administration. As Ferdinando had tried to do in Naples after 1821 with the appointment of Medici, Fernando VII in Spain sought after 1823 to reinforce his power by appointing governments made up by a majority of so-called moderate royalists: individuals whose principles were in line with eighteenth-century regalism. Their aim was not to turn the clock back to the pre-revolutionary era, but on the contrary to reinforce monarchical absolutism, when necessary even with some administrative reforms, so as to undermine or eliminate any competing authority. For these reasons, although they saw the Church as an ideological ally in the fight against the revolution, they did not want it to hold any power that could otherwise be exercised by state authorities. Thus while

31. *El Restaurador*, no. 8, 8 July 1823, pp. 58–59; no. 10, 10 July 1823, pp. 84–86. Julio Porres Martín-Cleto, 'Curiosidades Toledanas', *Toletum: Boletín de la Real Academia de Bellas Artes y Ciencias Históricas de Toledo* 42 (2000): 9–42.

32. *El Restaurador*, no. 69, 14 September 1823, pp. 633–42.

33. Emilio La Parra López, 'El rey ante sus súbditos: Presencia de Fernando VII en el espacio público', *Historia Constitucional* 20 (2019): 3–23.

Fernando had repealed at one stroke all the legal reforms of the revolutionary period, he never fully reinstated the Holy Inquisition, which was indeed effectively abolished. He only temporarily allowed some of its local tribunals, controlled by the dioceses, to function for a brief period, and he entrusted a newly created police department under governmental supervision with the task of controlling and suppressing any form of opposition.[34] To regain control of the state, the king also carried out a radical purge of the bureaucracy, removing all those who might be deemed his enemies. This meant the dismissal or enforced retirement not only of liberals, but also of ultra-royalists, supporters of a more radical political agenda aimed at a return to the (pre-revolutionary) status quo ante. More than ideological reliability, it was civil servants' personal loyalty to the king that would serve as the main criterion for selection of the new administrative class; and even some former collaborators with the French regime could thus be confirmed in their posts.[35] Ultra-royalists considered these purges a betrayal of their cause, however, and the reintroduction of the Holy Inquisition to be a necessary prerequisite for the consolidation of absolutism and persecution of the *liberales*.

Dissatisfaction stemmed secondly from the king's attitude towards the Voluntarios Realistas, the royalist version of the revolutionary national guard. This organisation had grown out of the guerrilla groups of the civil war of 1822 and 1823 that evolved into militias of volunteers. It was formally recognised in 1823, first by the regency that was in control of the realista army, and then by the king, to defend the restoration against its enemies.[36] Yet, while ultra-royalists were keen to turn the Voluntarios into a militia for persecuting the liberals, the king saw the suppression of any form of violence as a priority for the stabilisation of his regime, and regarded the organisation as a popular armed force in defiance of his authority.

The king's stance was thus at odds with an important sector of monarchical public opinion, made up of various social groups, including not only many bishops, members of the clergy, civil servants and former guerrilla fighters, but also urban and rural populations and the foremost royalist

---

34. Emilio La Parra López, 'Ni restaurada, ni abolida: Los últimos años de la Inquisición española (1823–1834)', *Ayer* 108 (2017): 153–75; La Parra López, *Fernando VII*.

35. Jean-Philippe Luis, *L'Utopie réactionnaire: Épuration et modernisation de l'état dans l'Espagne de la fin de l'ancien régime (1823/1834)* (Madrid: Casa de Velázquez, 2002), pp. 83–135.

36. Gonzalo Butrón Prida, 'Pueblo y élites en la crisis del absolutismo: Los Voluntarios Realistas', *Spagna Contemporanea* 25 (2004): 1–20.

organisation, the Voluntarios Realistas themselves. They all reproached the moderate monarchical governments in power after 1823 for being unduly lenient with the former revolutionaries, or for colluding with them and with the freemasons. These groups converged around a set of shared political demands. Their main preoccupation was the reintroduction of the Holy Inquisition with its full former powers. The Holy Inquisition, claimed *El Restaurador*, mouthpiece of the realistas, represented the only effective means to defend the monarchy and religion from their enemies, and from the descent of Spanish society into anarchy. Furthermore, they asked for reinforcement of the Voluntarios Realistas, to defend absolutism. Requests to reintroduce the Inquisition were submitted to the king not only by bishops and civil servants, but also by the Voluntarios Realistas and members of the army. Neither the king nor his governments were amenable to these demands, however. In September 1825 the king forbade members of both the Voluntarios and the army from submitting petitions to him except in relation to wholly personal matters.[37]

These frustrated aspirations fuelled royalist conspiracies or rebellions, and led to the emergence of popular protests against both the liberals and the existing government. In Madrid and other Spanish cities, towns and villages it was the foremost popular royalist association, the Voluntarios Realistas, that in fact became the agent of popular mobilisation against the king's governments. In Madrid, as in most Spanish cities, their ranks were filled primarily by artisans (shoemakers, carpenters, masons) and by day-labourers (*asalariados*).[38] Their social composition overlapped with that of the constitutional Guardia Nacional, and the workers in the sociedades patrióticas during the revolution, but also differed substantially from them. Unlike the Guardia Nacional, the Voluntarios Realistas were mainly made up of the rank and file of artisanal guilds, and not by their *maestri*. In addition, the professional classes were absent from them. Therefore their social composition was more 'plebeian' in character. Another mark of distinction between them and the artisans supporting the constitution was that, as in Naples, so too in Madrid, ultra-royalist public opinion was cultivated in specific public spaces sharply distinguished from those controlled by the liberals. It was in the squares or *tabernas* of the popular barrios of

37. La Parra López, 'Ni restaurada, ni abolida'.
38. Álvaro París Martín, 'Los Voluntarios Realistas de Madrid: Politización popular y violencia contrarrevolucionaria (1823–1833)', in Rújula and Ramón Solans, *El desafío*, pp. 89–123; Juan Sisinio Pérez Garzón, 'Absolutismo y clases sociales: Los Voluntarios Realistas de Madrid (1823–1833)', *Anales del Instituto de Estudios Madrileños* 15 (1978): 295–310.

Madrid that the Voluntarios Realistas met, discussed and protested, in a defensive space they considered their own. As in Naples, however, to fight with their political enemies they would also move outside it and invade the space controlled by the liberals, to defeat them and claim a wider spatial dominance. The realistas moved to areas of the city dominated by the bourgeois sociability of cafés to threaten, attack and provoke that public, which they knew to be in favour of the constitution. Demonstrations in defence of the constitution during the Trienio had taken place at Puerta del Sol. In contrast, it was in the popular barrios of the city that royalist protests erupted in 1825; but they spilled out into the city centre, where protesters attacked coffee houses and middle-class individuals. Triggered by the rise in bread and grain prices, these disturbances targeted in particular merchants and shopkeepers selling staples, whom the Voluntarios denounced as *negros*, supporters of the past regime, accusing the government of protecting them. In the popular barrios of Madrid, women, and in particular market women such as fruit and vegetable sellers, represented a key component of this royalist public opinion. They denounced merchants as liberals, and berated the king for betraying his most loyal supporters and favouring to the revolutionaries instead.[39]

The royalist conspiracies that proliferated in this period manifest a continuity with the counterrevolutionary mobilisation during the civil war between 1822 and 1823, and with the counterrevolutionary sociability that emerged from it. Those who had fought against the constitutional regime between 1820 and 1823 redirected their protest, soon after its end, against the absolutist order. Jorge Bessières, who led a failed ultra-royalist conspiracy in the summer of 1825, had in 1822 been in charge of a successful *partida realista* on behalf of the regency, and the following year his troops entered the capital city. With the collapse of the constitutional regime they were disbanded, but in 1825 he made himself available to organise a column of 270 individuals, including many Voluntarios Realistas, in the village of Brihuega, and lead it towards the capital to murder those *negros* who threatened the monarchy. The expedition was almost immediately defeated by regular troops. However, Bessières along with two other military leaders had not acted in isolation and had been supported by a network of sympathisers scattered across many provinces

---

39. París Martín, 'Los Voluntarios Realistas', p. 105; Álvaro París Martín, 'Royalist Women in the Marketplace: Work, Gender and Popular Counter-Revolution in Southern Europe (1814–1830)', in *Popular Agency and Politicisation in Nineteenth-Century Europe: Beyond the Vote*, ed. Oriol Luján and Diego Palacios Cerezales (London: Palgrave Macmillan, 2023), pp. 55–77.

as well as in Madrid. These groups acted within realista secret societies, such as El ángel exterminador or La purísima, that had proliferated at the beginning of the restoration. These events show that royalist conspiracies enjoyed support in both cities and rural areas. They also confirm that the groups of Voluntarios Realistas created in smaller centres were plebeian in composition. Local authorities reporting about these events described the members of these militias as 'miserable workers, some thieves, other tramps'.[40]

As the outbreak in 1827 of the revolt of the *agraviados* (or *agraviats*) demonstrates, such conspiracies could also enjoy large popular followings. This uprising, centred in Catalonia, but affecting also the neighbouring provinces of Aragon, Valencia, the Basque country and Navarre, mobilised around thirty thousand individuals. Their social composition was interclass in nature, ranging from peasants to artisans. While the motivations of the day-labourers, artisans, clerics, guerrilla fighters and Voluntarios Realistas who joined this movement no doubt differed, the members of the armed partidas that rose up were agreed in demanding the reintroduction of the Inquisition and the ousting of the much-hated moderate members of the government. After 1824 anti-governmental protests against the had occasionally resulted in public demonstrations of support for the king's brother, Don Carlos, as an alternative monarch. His sympathies with the demands of the ultra-royalists were well known, although the precise extent of his own active involvement in fomenting the royalist conspiracies of this period is difficult to establish. Public displays of support for Carlos remained isolated, however, and popular royalism (at least during this decade) never questioned the legitimacy of the existing king. What is striking about the revolt of the *agraviados* was that its participants claimed to have intervened to defend the royal prerogatives, considering the monarch to be a prisoner of freemasons and liberals.[41] As the participants of the eighteenth-century *motines* had done, its leaders demanded that the king act as a guarantor for their demands, a request that could only be satisfied in his physical presence. To reaffirm his authority and pacify the country, military intervention led by the Count of España was not sufficient: the king was once again required to travel across the country to re-establish a public bond with his subjects. This was clearly an effective

40. Fontana, *De en medio del tiempo*, pp. 186–94, quotation at 188.

41. On this rebellion, see Jordi Canal, *El Carlismo*, 2nd edn (Barcelona: RBA, 2006), pp. 44–50; Núria Sauch Cruz, *Guerrillers i bàndols civils entre l'Ebre i el maestrat: La formació d'un país carlista (1808–1844)* (Barcelona: Publicacions de l'Abadia de Montserrat, 2004), pp. 215–42; Fontana, *De en medio del tiempo*, pp. 217–30.

strategy, since soon after the beginning of his tour the country was fully pacified. The revolt forced him to continue the public campaign of promoting his own authority, which had started with his return to Madrid in 1823. With his consort, Queen Amalia Josefa, he travelled from Valencia to Tarragona and Barcelona, and from there to the Basque country and Navarre. In some respects the ceremonies to celebrate the king's presence followed a pattern already established in 1814 and 1823, involving visits to religious institutions, public *besamanos* (hand-kissings) and attendance at religious ceremonies or at the parades of the Voluntarios Realistas. Even more than before, the emphasis was put on the close relationship between the king and his people, and on the support of all ranks of society for the monarchy: the parades organised in Pamplona and Bilbao included representatives of all professional corporations, and in the Basque country the royal couple attended events celebrating local folklore.[42]

The counterrevolutionary public sphere in Portugal bore some striking similarities to that in Spain, but also had some distinctive features. As in Spain, in Portugal royalist public opinion first emerged in opposition to the constitutional regime between 1820 and 1823. Anti-revolutionaries made their dissent known first by individual clandestine acts of defiance such as the production and circulation of *pasquins* (singular *pasquim*). These were short anonymous manuscript texts, often satirical in content, written on scraps of paper and displayed in public spaces, whose production belonged to an early modern popular tradition of lampooning authorities and denouncing political enemies. In this new controversy between revolution and counterrevolution, such texts took on new meanings, and had the constitution as the main, if not exclusive, object of their attacks. Anti-revolutionary pasquins were first reported and collected by the police in 1821. They included satirical texts attacking 'people attached to the liberal system' (as in the case of a large number of those appearing in the city of Elvas, not far from Lisbon) or targeting the Cortes and their members. A pasquim found in a university college in Coimbra ridiculed the Cortes by comparing it to Gulliver's island, expressing the wish that it would soon be blown up.[43] The number of such pasquins increased between 1823 and 1824, and in 1826 again. After 1823 they explicitly signalled support for Dom Miguel and started to circulate along with handwritten

42. On the king's tour, see La Parra López, *Fernando VII*, pp. 562–68; San Narciso Martin, 'La monarquía', pp. 104–13.

43. For the pasquim in Coimbra, see ATT, IGP, Coimbra 284, ff. 40–41; on Elvas, see ATT, IGP, livro 20, 1820–22, f. 93: July 1821. For other examples of pasquims, see Vargues, *A aprendizagem*, pp. 258–65.

proclamations, becoming an important tool of propaganda in his favour. They often included simple messages (written in large capital letters) such as 'Death to the constitution', 'Death to the freemasons', and 'Long live Dom Miguel and religion'.[44]

The authors of the pasquins and their channels of circulation remain in most cases unknown. Yet the available evidence suggests that although they were the product of the initiatives of individuals or small groups, their consumption was not exclusively local. They could travel wide and far across the country and could be easily replicated in manuscript form. The pasquim against the Cortes found in 1821 in a college in Coimbra had been sent by mail to a student from Lisbon, and was allegedly a copy of a text already displayed at many crossroads throughout the capital. Informal networks of individuals belonging to different social groups were involved in their production and dissemination. The sudden reappearance and proliferation of pasquins attacking the constitution in public in Coimbra in October 1826, while the uprising against the Carta was raging across the country, was due to the activities of a capitão mor visiting the city just for a few months and for business purposes. Convinced that the constitutional regime was doomed, he distributed pasquins and handwritten proclamations through his contacts with a friar, a tailor and several shopkeepers. He does not appear to have acted on behalf of other parties, whether provincial or local military leaders of the insurrection.[45]

Also as in Spain, popular royalism celebrated the end of Portugal's constitutional period with the annihilation of its physical signs, and in particular with the destruction of the monuments celebrating the constitutional regime.[46] A common popular practice, adopted by the supporters of absolutism to mark the end of the revolution, was the symbolic burial of the constitution. These rituals took place at the end of the Triénio, between 1823 and 1824, intensified again with Dom João's death in 1826, and reappeared in 1828. Such events often entailed the personification of the constitution as a *menina* (little girl) who was to be interred. In other circumstances a puppet made of straw symbolising the constitution or the 1826 Carta was burned to demonstrate hostility to the revolution. This

44. ANTT, IGP, Castelo Branco 276, ff. 488–89: 1823; Castelo Branco 277, ff. 307–8, 315–16: August 1826; Coimbra 286, f. 165: November 1826.

45. Ibid., Coimbra 286, f. 270: October 1826.

46. Maria de Fátima Sá e Melo Ferreira, 'A política na rua: Festa liberal e festa contrarevolucionária no Portugal do século XIX', in *A Rua: Espaço, tempo, sociabilidade*, ed. Graça Índias Cordeiro and Frédéric Vidal (Lisbon: Livros Horizonte, 2008), pp. 155–64; Ferreira, '"Vencidos pero no convencidos": Movilización, acción colectiva y identidad en el Miguelismo', *Historia Social* 49 (2004): 73–95.

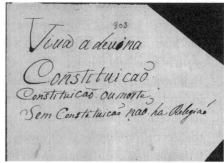

FIGURES 22A AND 22B. *Pasquins* against (22a; Coimbra, 1826) and in favour of (22b; Castelo Branco, 1826) the constitution, produced during the civil war in Portugal (Arquivo Nacional Torre do Tombo, Lisbon: IGP.286, f. 170; IGP.277, ff. 307–8). ATT, with permission

practice was not entirely original: it derived from early modern popular traditions and carnivalesque rituals during which villagers burned or buried representations of their enemies. While the evidence to hand refers to these as mainly rural rituals, such symbolic practices were given wider currency in printed material published in cities. In printed satires too, the end of the constitution was described as the death of a young woman. In one, she appears as the daughter of Manuel Fernandes (one of the leaders of the revolution) and Freemasonry, and the granddaughter of the Spanish constitution. In her will she left her heirs, the Portuguese people, a legacy of poverty and destitution, involving commercial crisis and financial disarray.[47]

Like its Spanish counterpart, the Portuguese royalist press responded to the cult of the heroes of the constitutional period with the fabrication of its own heroes of the royalist cause. Thanks to her uncompromising conduct and demeanour, Queen Carlota Joaquina became the symbol of resistance to the revolution. The mother of Dom Miguel and spouse of Dom João VI, who was also the eldest sister of King Fernando VII of Spain, had in fact refused to swear an oath to the constitution approved by the Cortes Constituintes in 1822. She did so by retiring to the residence of Ramalhão, and by claiming that since she was ill she could not move from there. The government decided to revoke her political and civil rights and asked her

47. José Daniel Rodrigues da Costa, *Novidades de Lisboa dadas por Bento Aniceto, lavrador ao seu compadre: Cura da sua freguezia na provincia da Beira* (Lisbon: João Nunes Esteves, 1823); *Testamento que fez à hora da morte a illustrissima e excellentissima senhora Dona Constituição à hora da sua morte* (Lisbon: Impressão de A. L. da Oliveira, 1828).

to leave the country as soon she recovered from her alleged infirmity.[48] Her acts of courage earned her great popularity among absolutists: unsurprisingly, she featured prominently in the counterrevolutionary press. An article in *O Punhal dos Corcundas* praised her as a 'true Christian heroine' and 'the most illustrious victim of Lusitanian Freemasonry' in the name of an imaginary national sovereignty. Her reputation for standing up for the rights of the monarchy crossed national borders. A Spanish pamphlet argued that the queen provided an example for all monarchs in the world of how to defend their rights; for this reason a bust of her should be erected in all their residences.[49]

Yet the greatest hero of the counterrevolutionary cause was indubitably Dom Miguel. What made Portuguese popular royalism distinctive—more extensive and different in character from its counterparts elsewhere—was its identification with this alternative pretender to the throne. The fact that, since at least 1823, Dom Miguel had sought to gain power and repeal the constitution made him a consistent point of reference and a symbol of the counterrevolution. Counterrevolutionary journalism did much to create a public sentiment in his favour. No fewer than seventy-seven of the 316 periodicals published between 1820 and 1834 (mostly in Lisbon) supported Dom Miguel, who became the unmistakeable figurehead of counterrevolution from 1823. In spite of its fragmentary nature (some titles were only published in a handful of issues), and despite the fact that some periodicals changed their political line to adjust to new political circumstances, the Portuguese royalist press was far more extensive that elsewhere in southern Europe.[50] Dom Miguel was its hero, and represented an idea of the Portuguese nation to rival that upheld by the constitutionalists. In short, he was the *restaurador da Lusitânia* (restorer of Portugal).[51]

But it was not such a copious royalist press alone that fuelled Dom Miguel's popularity. Enthusiasm for him accounts for another striking Portuguese peculiarity: namely, a proliferation of public demonstrations of popular support in cities and towns, which had no equivalent in terms of number and size anywhere else in southern Europe. The end of the

48. Lousada and Ferreira, *D. Miguel*, pp. 43–45.

49. *O Punhal dos Corcundas*, no. 28, 1823, pp. 400–401; APR, Papeles Reservados de Fernando VII, 21, ff. 707–71: Félix Ramón de Alvarado y Velaustegui, 'Reflexiones imparciales de un español acerca del estranamiento de S. M. F. la Reyna dona Carlota del territorio portugues', Madrid, 1823.

50. Maria Alexandre Lousada, 'Imprensa e política: Alguns dados sobre a imprensa periódica portuguesa durante as lutas liberais (1820–1834)', *Finisterra* 24, no. 47 (1989): 88–104.

51. *O Braz Corcunda e o Verdadeiro Constitucional*, no. 8, 1823, p. 78.

constitutional regime, triggered by Dom Miguel's failed military coup against his own father Dom João VI, the 'Abrilada' of April 1824, was marked by an unprecedented wave of public demonstrations across the entire country. Spontaneous displays of devotion in streets and squares interacted with the decisions of câmaras, along with those of religious corporations and military garrisons, to submit declarations of support for him. Local authorities read these out to the crowds during public events and ceremonies which culminated in his acclamation or that of his father as absolute monarchs.[52] It was in these circumstances that a counterrevolutionary public attained its fullest potential in Portugal. These written addresses contained a number of recurring themes, adopted time and time again by different signatories (including, although not exclusively, the members of each local council) across Portugal, that echoed those featuring in the counterrevolutionary press. They show the extent to which such language was circulating throughout the kingdom, both in major urban centres and in rural towns and villages. First, they praised Dom Miguel, a heroic and providential figure sent by God to save the monarchy, often referring to the key role he had played in 1823 in putting an end to the revolutionary period with the Vilafrancada.[53] They described his adversaries as enemies of religion and of the legitimate sovereign; indeed, as traitors to the national community: the Miguelistas made a distinction between the true Portuguese, loyal to their country, to religion and to Dom Miguel, and their enemies, often dismissed as a faction, freemasons who had betrayed all of these things in the name of false principles of foreign origin.[54]

The authorities writing to Dom Miguel referred to the local populations no longer as citizens, but by the traditional term of faithful and loyal *vassalos*. As this word suggests, these documents were meant to be acts of submission. They were written on behalf of the 'true' or 'good' (*verdadeiros, bons*) Portuguese who supported the absolute monarchy, as opposed to the revolutionaries, who were dismissed as a faction. As the document submitted by the câmara of Santarém stated, the constitutionalists upheld 'anarchical opinions' and wanted to amalgamate the monarchy with a 'revolutionary democracy'. Second, they complemented Dom

52. ANTT, Ministério do Reino, Autos de Aclamação, maço 27.

53. Maria Alexandre Lousada, 'O Miguelismo (1828–1834): O discurso político e o apoio da nobreza titulada', unpublished Master's thesis, Faculdade de Letras, Lisbon, 1987, p. 66. Armando Barreiros Malheiro da Silva, *Miguelismo: Ideologia e mito* (Coimbra: Edições Minerva, 1993).

54. ANTT, Ministério do Reino, Autos de Aclamação, maço 27, nos 5002; 5003: Vila Real to Dom Miguel, 13 May 1824; Faro to Dom Miguel, 8 May 1824.

Miguel upon intervening to reinstate the monarchy with its full sovereign rights. At the same time, they referred to the reintroduction of the ancient liberties of the Portuguese nation, although these were rarely spelled out, and the constitution was conceived in purely historicist terms, on the basis that the 'best constitution of a people has always been that to which they are accustomed, based on its old customs; any reform that has departed from these foundations always proved fatal to the nations'.[55]

Although a few weeks later the king decided to relieve Dom Miguel of his command of the army, a decision leading to his departure in exile for France, this coup in 1824 marked the end of any constitutional government for the following two years.[56] In this new context, those who supported the repeal of the constitution temporarily redirected their public enthusiasm for absolutism towards Dom João VI. A second wave of public ceremonies and popular displays of loyalty took place in the weeks that followed, in celebration of Dom João's birthday on 13 May. These events were intended to mark the restoration of the rights of the monarchy: in the words of a local administrator reporting on these demonstrations, people were celebrating 'the destruction of the impious, partisan and usurping Masonic government'.[57] In the city of Coimbra, for instance, a pontifical mass was organised in the royal chapel of the university to celebrate the king's birthday in the presence of the military, religious and civil authorities, university students and ordinary citizens. At night both the public and private buildings of the city were lit up and the population of the city thronged the streets and the public squares along with army regiments.[58] On the same evening in the town of Oliveira de Azeméis, a public concert was staged, during which a choir supported by an orchestra sang the 'Hymno real' and a number of odes composed in honour of the monarch were recited in front of the population, who interrupted with hurrahs for Dom João VI.[59]

What fuelled yet more popular demonstrations in favour of Dom Miguel was the civil war that broke out after the death of Dom João in April 1826, when Dom Pedro introduced a new constitution and temporarily appointed the Infanta Dona Isabel Maria as regent. The royalist insurgency that erupted between April 1826 and February 1827 led to

55. Ibid., maço 27, no. 5010: acclamation from the city of Santarém, 17 July 1824.

56. On these events, see Lousada and Ferreira, *D. Miguel*, pp. 75–84.

57. ANTT, IGP, Castelo Branco 276, f. 477: juíz de fora of Idanha-a-Nova to intendente geral de polícia, 11 May 1824.

58. ANTT, Ministério do Reino, Autos de Aclamação, maço 27, no. 5026.

59. Ibid., maço 27, no. 5063.

mobilisation of civilians in support for absolutism, and to many clashes between opposing factions in the villages and cities. As described in the previous chapter, during such clashes the singing of the 'Hymno real' became an act symbolic of support for Dom Miguel. In December 1826, in the town of Penamacor in the province of Castelo Branco, the determination of both supporters of the constitution and their enemies to defend their respective causes resulted in large public gatherings.[60] In the same month in Sabugal, crowds took advantage of the market day to demonstrate against the constitution, and to hang up manifestos in favour of Dom Miguel throughout the town.[61] Some acts of defiance continued until February, when individuals were reported to be breaking into the town halls of the province of Castelo Branco crying 'Death to the constitution!' while the national guards were meanwhile singing the 'Hymno constitutional'.[62]

The largest wave of public acclamations in favour of Dom Miguel took place in 1828, with his physical return to the country. Some public displays of enthusiasm exploded before his landing at Belém outside Lisbon. When news of his imminent return arrived in the village of São Vicente da Beira, people descended into the streets, illuminations were organised and church bells were rung in jubilation.[63] But most such celebrations took place after his arrival, and were organised with the support of local authorities. Admittedly, the question as to whether popular mobilisation was necessary to legitimise the restoration of absolutism was controversial. In 1828, when Dom Miguel seized power and repealed the second constitution, popular mobilisation and the role of the câmaras in confirming his ascent to the throne became a bone of contention among counterrevolutionary publicists as well as among his ministers. Absolutist writers were divided between those who favoured public displays of loyalty, and agreed that the câmaras had a role in confirming the monarch's ascent to the throne, and those who rejected such acts of municipal acclamation as implicitly undermining the legitimacy of his absolute power, which did not require any popular recognition.[64] Nonetheless, in 1828, as in 1824, local supporters of Dom Miguel and at least one minister (secretly) did all they could to mobilise the crowds and create a palpable atmosphere of popular enthusiasm. As a result, his return from exile coincided with a

60. ANTT, IGP, Castelo Branco 277, f. 421.
61. Ibid., f. 426.
62. Ibid., f. 459.
63. Ibid., f. 554: November 1827.
64. On this debate, see Lousada and Ferreira, *D. Miguel*, pp. 146–48, 156–58.

further wave, larger than ever, of public events, acclamations and declarations of loyalty.[65]

This popular mobilisation continued also after 1828, when yet another civil war broke out between the constitutional army and Dom Miguel's forces. The involvement and the organisational efforts of local authorities are however not sufficient to account for the existence of his large popular following. The peculiarity of the Portuguese royalist popular movement is that an abiding conflict between constitutionalists and absolutists served to transform Dom Miguel into a figurehead for counterrevolutionary public opinion. This was not a privilege that Ferdinando had in Naples after 1821, or that Fernando VII enjoyed in Spain after 1823. Moreover, this support was not simply the product of manipulation from above. In Portugal, as in Naples and Spain, the impact of revolution and counterrevolution transformed the monarchy, with kings coming to recognise the need for public legitimation of their power, and thereby acknowledging 'the people' as a new political actor. At the same time, however, the nature of the royalist public opinion that emerged demonstrates the impossibility for absolute monarchies of acquiring an unqualified consensus even among those opposing the constitutional option. Royal authority, first questioned by revolutionary constitutionalism, came also to be questioned by those who were, in principle, the kings' most loyal supporters.

Conclusions: from revolutionary practices to public memory

The pages above have sought to reconstruct the efforts made by a variety of competing social, political and institutional actors to reclaim public space during and after the revolutions. This is a history of opposed attempts to control the public sphere by eliminating permanently any visible symbolic presence of political enemies. However, neither the constitutional regimes nor the absolutist dispensations managed to reclaim fully all public spaces and to obtain universal consensus. In addition, during the period discussed here civil wars and the enduring presence of groups hostile to the existing regimes meant that political enemies operated in discrete areas of the same cities. Political divisions thus often created physical divisions within the same urban space. In Naples and Madrid supporters of the constitution and their enemies gathered in different neighbourhoods, and used squares they each particularly favoured to engage in public protests.

65. ANTT, Ministério do Reino, Autos de Aclamação, maço 21 and maço 33.

A remarkable consequence of these events was moreover the unprecedented broadening of the public space devoted to the discussion of politics, which was itself associated with a proliferation of different types of sociability, both formal and informal. Although it remained fragmented and contested, in the 1820s the public sphere therefore grew in size across in southern Europe, and this to a marked degree. It did so not only in urban centres, but also in rural communities and peripheral areas. As the capillary dissemination of the Carboneria in southern Italy suggests, sociability grew also in the provinces. The circulation of rumours across territorial and maritime borders in turn demonstrates that a mobilisation of political information had the potential to affect even the most remote areas and regions, far from capital cities and provincial centres.

At the same time, the revolutions and counterrevolutions of the 1820s inaugurated an entirely new cycle of conflicting claims over urban spaces: in the succeeding decades civil wars, revolutions and dynastic crises reopened conflicts over the symbolic reappropriation of cities and rural communities throughout southern Europe.[66] The restoration of absolutism only temporarily put an end to the practices of the revolutionary public sphere and the symbolic reconfigurations of the public spaces discussed in the pages above. The impact of the rituals, practices and forms of mobilisation of this decade was in fact deep and lasting. One of its enduring legacies was to give specific political connotations to certain urban spaces. Just to give one example: the Rossio square in Lisbon remained indelibly associated with constitutional and radical mobilisation, even after its monument to Dom João VI as constitutional king had been dismantled. Another important legacy of these revolutions had to do with the peculiar forms of sociability engendered by them. The Iberian revolutionaries of the 1830s and 1850s inherited from the popular constitutionalism of the 1820s the use of revolutionary clubs and patriotic societies as organisations to mobilise support and educate ordinary citizens in their values. While many of the republicans and democrats of these decades belonged to the younger generation, some had already been active during the 1820s. The patriotic societies and political clubs set up in the 1830s in Portugal, and in the 1840s and 50s in Spain, in particular retained

66. On attempts by counterrevolutionary movements to reclaim the public space after the 1820s, see, for Naples, Marco Meriggi, *La nazione populista: Il mezzogiorno e i Borboni dal 1848 all'Unità* (Bologna: Il Mulino, 2021); for Portugal, Tengarrinha, *Nova história*, and Lousada and Ferreira, *D. Miguel*, pp. 335–78; for Spain, Pedro Rújula and Javier Ramón Solans, eds, *El desafío de la revolución: Reaccionarios, antiliberales y contrarrevolucionarios (siglos XVIII y XIX)* (Granada: Editorial Comares, 2017).

striking elements of continuity with those established during the Trienio. The interclass nature of the forms of sociability established in the 1820s was reiterated in the following decades; the political mobilisation of artisans of that decade continued and even intensified, in forms both old and new. In Portugal, the role of political organisations was revived at the end of the civil war, when they played a crucial role in mustering support for either the 1826 Carta or the constitution of 1822. Indeed, in 1836 mobilisation of the artisans and workers of the arsenal of Lisbon was instrumental in guaranteeing the victory of the revolution that reintroduced the 1822 constitution: it was by taking part in the meetings of the Clube do Arsenal, and as members of the Guarda Nacional, that they made a decisive contribution to its victory. As in the previous decade, artisans combined support for universal suffrage with defence of their rights, income and commercial interests.[67] The presence of artisans and workers in the republican and democratic societies of Spain was equally important. Admittedly, the patriotic societies—tertulias—established at the beginning of the 'Trienio Esparterista' between 1840 and 1841, or those created during the 'Bienio Progresista' (1854–56), were speaking new political languages and employing a vocabulary different from that of the 1820s. As in the 1820s, however, these patriotic societies represented spaces devoted to the exercise of the sovereignty of the people, their purpose being to influence governmental decisions, educate citizens and democratise the revolution.[68] In Naples, the resilience of absolutism prevented any resurgence of the public sphere until 1848, when full-scale revolution finally broke out. In the Kingdom of the Two Sicilies, therefore, secret societies represented the only form of sociability hostile to absolutism that endured between 1821 and that year. After 1821 the Carboneria survived at the local level, but never reconstituted a strong enough national network to lead a revolution covering the whole territory of the kingdom. By the early 1830s it had disintegrated. Yet the new secret societies set up in the 1830s and 40s, such as Benedetto Musolino's Figlioli della Giovine Italia (1832) took inspiration from the organisational structure of the Carboneria. While they embraced a novel language based on the notions of democracy and equality, between the

67. Radich, 'Formas de organização, pp. 133–38; Maria de Fátima Bonifácio, 'Os arsenalistas da Marinha na Revolução de Setembro, 1836', *Análise Social* 17, no. 65 (1981): 39–65.

68. Florencia Peyrou, *El republicanismo popular en España, 1840–1843* (Cádiz: Universidad de Cádiz, 2002); Peyrou, *Tribunos del pueblo: Demócratas y republicanos durante el reinado de Isabel II* (Madrid: Centro de Estudios Políticos y Constitucionales, 2008), pp. 268–69.

1830s and 40s the Figlioli retained the Carboneria's ability to integrate into its ranks both the local elites and members of the popular classes (shopkeepers and artisans) of the provinces of the kingdom, and in particular in Calabria. Both the old Carboneria (in 1828 in Cilento, for instance) and the new clandestine organisations (in 1844 and 1847 in Calabria) continued to conspire and foment uprisings, albeit without success.[69]

Perhaps what best demonstrates the lasting impact of these experiences is the role that memory of them would play across a wide variety of political movements. The celebration of the nation (in Italy and Greece) and the return of constitutional government (in Spain and Portugal) provided opportunities to integrate the events and the protagonists of the 1820s into the political cultures of these countries, and to celebrate them in public ceremonies and spaces. Unsurprisingly, such public memories remained contested, as both opposition movements and constitutional governments attributed different and selective meanings to them, or challenged their use. What gave a broader currency to the memory of 1820–21 in Naples was the integration of its protagonists into martyrologies celebrating Italian nationalism. Even in the course of that same decade, and all over Europe, exiled patriots were publishing historical narratives of these events and commemorations of their heroes. But it was the 1848 revolutions that provided the most favourable context for their dissemination and reception. The creation of a new Italian national platform supported by Piedmont encouraged a bipartisan reading of the martyrdom of the Neapolitan, and more broadly Italian, patriots who had fought, had been executed or had lived in exile abroad. Piedmont's endorsement of the ideology of Italian nationalism after 1848, and the existence of a substantial exile community from the other Italian states in its capital, Turin, facilitated a close association between its constitutional governments and such commemorative agendas. In 1851 the exiled Neapolitan lawyer Gabriele D'Amato founded a society to edit a collection of biographies of Italian martyrs, the *Panteon dei martiri della libertà italiana*, with the financial backing of the Piedmontese government. The book, published that same year, included also the biographies of the Neapolitan patriots executed after the revolution of 1799, and those of Michele Morelli and Giuseppe Silvati, who had organised the pronunciamiento in Nola in 1820,

---

69. On secret societies in this period, see Pierre-Marie Delpu, *Un autre Risorgimento: La Formation du monde libéral dans le royaume des Deux-Sicilies (1815–1856)* (Rome: Collection de l'École française de Rome, 2019), pp. 214–22, Mellone, *Napoli 1848*, pp. 36–46, Berti, *I democratici*, p. 196.

and likewise suffered martyrdom after the reintroduction of absolutism in 1822.[70] Such cooperation between exiled revolutionaries and government was not without its tensions, however. The Piedmontese authorities, concerned about the potential democratic and republican appeal of this enterprise, finally dissolved the association in 1853.[71] In addition, alternative martyrologies whose ideological connotations were more obviously at odds with Piedmontese monarchical constitutionalism were published in the course of these same years. Atto Vannucci's *I martiri della libertà italiana*, for instance, gave as much space to the memory of the Neapolitan martyrs as had D'Amato's *Panteon*, but was a resolutely Mazzinian and democratic enterprise.[72]

In Greece, what was central to the commemoration of the revolution for decades was not the celebration of its key protagonists and martyrs, but rather the notion of a continuity between the nation emancipated in 1821 and ancient Greece. The celebration of the anniversary of the outbreak of the Greek revolution on 25 March was officially introduced as early as 1838, under King Otto. In 1835 Ioannis Kolettis, minister of home affairs of the same king (and a key political figure during the revolution) issued a detailed proposal for athletic games to commemorate the most important battles of the revolution. In Kolettis's view these festivals, modelled on the athletic games and religious festivals of Greek antiquity, would benefit the new nation and the monarchy alike, and reinforce international support for the Greek state. It took time, however, for such patriotic celebrations to be turned into a regular practice: the first to be staged were the Zappas Olympics in 1859. Another link between the new Greek state and classical antiquity was reflected, however, in the architecture and toponomy of the new capital, Athens, soon after independence. The Bavarian regency approved plans for the spatial reorganisation of the city as early as 1833. In the subsequent decades a number of streets were dedicated to notable figures from antiquity. Between the 1830s and 1840s the construction of a number of imposing new buildings inspired by classical architecture was started: the royal palace (1836–1843), the city hospital (1836–1858), the Gennadios house (1846–1856) and the university

70. Gabriele D'Amato, *Panteon dei martiri della libertà italiana* (Turin: Gabriele D'Amato Editore, 1851), pp. 23–116; 203–16.

71. On the circulation of historical accounts of the Neapolitan revolution, see the 'Epilogue', below. On the cult of Neapolitan martyrs, see Delpu, *Un autre Risorgimento*, pp. 359–62. On the memory of exiles, see also Isabella, *Risorgimento in Exile*, pp. 213–21.

72. Atto Vannucci, *I martiri della libertà italiana nel secolo decimo nono* (Florence: Società Editrice Fiorentina, 1848).

(1839–1864). It was, finally, in anticipation of the fiftieth anniversary celebrations of the revolution that in 1869 three statues of more recent historical figures were commissioned and erected in front of the university. Nonetheless, the key protagonists of the revolution remained strikingly absent from this triad and from public space in general. These monuments celebrated the protomartyr of Greek patriotism, Rigas Velestinlis (1757–98), and stressed the religious dimension of the nation by honouring the memory of another martyr, Patriarch Grigorios V, who had been executed by the Ottoman authorities in 1821 in retaliation for the outbreak of the revolution. In 1875 the statue of the humanist and philosopher Adamantios Korais was added to those of Rigas and Korais. An integration of the protagonists of the revolution into the public space of the capital took place only later on, during the 1880s. New street names were used to honour politicians who had served both during the revolution and in the new Greek state (Metaxas, Zaimis, Mavromichalis, Deliyannis), and also a handful of fighters, Karaiskakis and Miaoulis among them. A possible explanation for the belated nature of this homage to the heroes of the revolutions is that its former fighters in particular had been among the most vocal opponents of the Bavarian dynasty that ruled Greece from 1835 to 1862. In their own memoirs and historical accounts many of them produced interpretations of the revolution implicitly or explicitly critical of the authoritarian nature of the Bavarian regime. With the demise of this regime in 1862 and the introduction of a new and popular constitution, their memory had become less threatening and controversial; but until the fiftieth anniversary of the revolution a pressing concern to commemorate the historical and cultural lineage of the Greek nation had prevailed over any wish to remember those who had fought against the Ottomans in the 1820s.[73]

One type of recognition of their services to the nation was however accorded to those revolutionary leaders who died in the aftermath of the

73. Gonda Van Steen, 'Anniversaries', in *The Greek Revolution: A Critical Dictionary*, ed. Paschalis M. Kitromilides and Constantinos Tsoukalas (Cambridge, MA: Harvard University Press, 2021), pp. 694–707; Ellie Skopetea, *Το 'Πρότυπο Βασίλειο' και η 'Μεγάλη Ιδέα': Όψεις του εθνικού προβλήματος στην Ελλάδα, 1830–1880* (The 'Model Kingdom' and the 'Great Idea': Aspects of the national problem in Greece, 1830–1880) (Athens: Polytypo, 1988); Leonidas Kallivretakis, 'Athens in the 19th Century: From Regional Town of the Ottoman Empire to Capital of the Kingdom of Greece' (17 June 2017), available at https://brewminate.com/athens-in-the-19th-century-from-regional-town-of-the-ottoman-empire-to-capital-of-the-kingdom-of-greece/ (accessed 14 August 2022); Vangelis Karamanolakis, 'The University of Athens and Greek Antiquity (1837–1937)', in *Re-imagining the Past: Antiquity and Modern Greek Culture*, ed. Dimitris Tziovas (Oxford: Oxford University Press, 2014), pp. 112–27.

war of independence, in the form of state funerals. Those of them who had served the Bavarian monarchy rather than opposing it were deemed to merit burial with full honours. This applied even to a former fighter like Theodoros Kolokotronis. Although he had been imprisoned, tried and condemned for treason with a capital sentence in 1834, in 1835 he was released by King Otto, with whom he then formed a close friendship. On his death in 1843, Kolokotronis was honoured with a grand state funeral attended by all military, civil and ecclesiastical authorities in Athens, including many veterans from the revolution. He was buried as an *archistratigos*, or commander-in-chief, a Turkish flag laid symbolically at his feet in homage to his military victories. More than ten thousand people accompanied the three-hour-long procession and attended the burial in Athens, while funerary ceremonies were organised too across the whole country.[74]

In Portugal and Spain, meanwhile, the memory of the 1820s was reintegrated into public space much earlier than in Greece. In these two countries the return to constitutional government in the mid-1830s smoothed the path to public recognition of the revolutionaries of the previous decade. In contrast to the case of the Greek uprising, the key protagonists of the Spanish and Portuguese revolutions did not have to wait until the 1880s to be celebrated. However, in these countries too, the meaning of the revolutions of the 1820s remained open to alternative readings. What caused that memory to be contested in the case of Portugal was the existence of two alternative constitutional periods, 1820–23 and 1826–28, whose different constitutions divided the supporters of representative government into two hostile camps until 1852. The defeat of Dom Miguel's troops and the end of the civil war in 1834 were immediately reflected in the urban spaces, and paved the way to public celebration of the victory of liberalism. The capital of Portuguese liberalism, Porto, celebrated the end of the siege by Dom Miguel's troops in 1833 by revising the city's toponomy: the square called Praça Nova das Hortas, which in 1820 had been called Praça da Constituição, in 1833 was dedicated to Dom Pedro; in 1835 a street was dedicated to Manuel Tomás, a member of the secret society the Sinédrio, key organiser of the 1820 pronunciamiento in Porto and member of the provisional government of that year; and five years later

74. 'Πρόγραμμα περί της εκφοράς του νεκρού, του αοιδίμου Θ. Κολοκοτρώνη, αντιστράτηγου, συμβούλου της επικρατείας εις τακτικήν υπηρεσίαν αναπαυθέντος εν Κυρίω τη 4 Φεβρουαρίου 1843' (Programme for the funeral procession of Th. Kolokotronis, commander-in-chief, councillor of state who rested in the Lord on 4 February 1843), broadsheet held at BMA. An account of the funeral is in Dimitropoulos, *Θεόδωρος Κολοκοτρώνης* (Theodoros Kolokotronis), pp. 96–97.

another street was dedicated to yet another member of the Sinédrio, Francisco Barros de Lima. In 1837, the year after the revolution that had reintroduced the constitution of 1822, the name of Bernardo de Sá Nogueira, since 1834 Viscount of Sá da Bandeira, was added to the toponomy of the city to remember his heroic role in the civil war, during which he had lost an arm.[75] The 1840s put a temporary halt to the public retrieval of the memory of 1820. The victory of moderate liberalism under António Bernardo da Costa Cabral, who reintroduced the 1826 Carta in 1842, made possible the recognition of this constitution alone in urban toponymy. Only in the 1850s was the process of the integration of 1820 into the public space restarted. In 1858 in Porto a street dedicated fifteen years before to Cabral's restoration of the Carta, was significantly renamed '24 August 1820', the actual date of the 1820 pronunciamiento. After years of turbulence and civil strife, it was only in the context of the 1850s *Regeneração*, a time of mutual recognition for the various brands of Portuguese liberalism under a new constitutional compromise, that 1820 no longer seemed a subversive date.

In Spain, what made it possible to rescue the memory of the 1820s was the decision by the regent María Cristina, after King Fernando VII's death in 1833, to abandon absolutism and promote reconciliation between the monarchy and the liberals by granting a moderate constitution, the 'Estatuto'. In 1835 Riego's memory was officially rehabilitated by his former companion in the pronunciamiento of 1820, then prime minister, Juan Álvarez Mendizábal, with a decree that not only reinstated the general in his military rank and honour, but gave his family a pension and put them under the direct protection of the queen and the regent. In 1836 a revolution carried out in the name of the Cádiz Constitution, led to a new constitutional compromise between the various political groups favourable to representative government the following year. The fact that by 1837 the Cádiz Constitution was no longer seen as relevant to the solution of the problems of Spain does not mean that the Trienio was forgotten. On the contrary, the progresistas—the left-wing supporters of the new constitutional compromise who celebrated popular sovereignty, defended the role of the national guard and advanced municipal liberty and a modicum of decentralisation—did much to retrieve it. To legitimise themselves they strove to build a consensual national memory that would satisfy liberals

75. Paulo Alexandre Vasconcelos, 'A memória do liberalismo no espaço público do Porto (Santo Ildefonso, Bonfim e Campanhã)', in *Omni Tempore: Atas dos encontros da primavera 2017* (Porto: Universidade do Porto, Faculdade de Letras, 2018), pp. 447–72; Magda Pinheiro, *O liberalismo nos espaços públicos: A memória das revoluções liberais através dos monumentos que a celebram* (Oeiras: Celta, 2000).

of every stripe by integrating into a new historical narrative all examples of martyrdom and sacrifice for the winning of freedom against despotism. This narrative included those who had fought against Napoleon and the revolutionaries of the Trienio, as well as those who fought against Carlismo. To this end inscriptions of the names of the martyrs for the fatherland would be added to the halls of the Congreso, including those of 'El Empecinado' (Juan Martín Díez), the famous guerrilla fighter against the French invader after 1808, Rafael Riego himself (significantly not for his role in the pronunciamiento, but as a member of the Cortes), the liberal heroine Mariana Pineda, executed in 1831 for conspiracy and José María Torrijos, who had died in his failed constitutional pronunciamiento near Málaga the same year. Another example of this ambition to build a national memory was the decision to erect the Panteón de Hombres Ilustres de Madrid, a monument approved first in 1837 and completed only after 1868, to honour the victims of despotism after 1823.[76]

The Spanish progresistas, however, were not the only ones to adopt the memory of the 1820s for their own political purposes. In the same period a new and more radical democratic and republican popular opposition took over the memory of those who had challenged despotism. It integrated this memory into an insurrectional culture to criticise from the left the existing constitutional order and 'official' progressive liberalism. Under the regency of Baldomero Espartero in particular (1840–43), republicans and democrats celebrated the people's ability to defend themselves from oppression through insurrections, revolts and pronunciamientos as instances of popular sovereignty in a new wave of civic festivities, monuments and ceremonies that sprang up across the country. In 1841 a square was dedicated to the memory of Mariana Pineda in Granada, and the following year a monument in honour of Torrijos and his companions was inaugurated there. In that same period in Cádiz, festivities were organised to commemorate the suppression of the popular demonstrations in favour of the constitution that had erupted in March 1820, while in Madrid, public homage was paid to the memory of Riego on the anniversary of his death on 28 November in the very square where he had been executed, the Plaza de la Cebada. The memory of the Trienio and its protagonists was also integrated into the democratic culture of workers' organisations. In

76. María Cruz Romeo Mateo, 'Memoria y política en el liberalismo progresista', *Historia y Política* 17 (2007): 69–88; Carolyn P. Boyd, 'Un lugar de memoria olvidado: El Panteón de Hombres Ilustres en Madrid', *Historia y Política* 12 (2004): 15–39; Javier Pérez Núñez, 'Conmemorar la nación desde abajo: Las celebraciones patrióticas del Madrid progresista, 1836–1840', *Historia y Política* 35 (2016): 177–202.

Barcelona the Associations of Mutual Aid of the *tejedores* (weavers) organised public events to celebrate the anniversary of their foundation and the rights of their members by singing the 'Himno de Riego'.[77] At the same time the members of the Partido progresista continued also in the following two decades to view themselves as belonging to an anti-despotic tradition in Spanish history that connected 1812 to 1820 and 1837, and associated Riego with their founder Juan Álvarez Mendizábal. By so doing, they asserted their own contribution to the establishment of liberalism in Spain against the more conservative moderados.

Although in Spain such commemorations remained primarily the agenda of the left, between the 1860s and the 1870s in Italy, Greece and Portugal the public memory of these revolutions even came to be a preoccupation of officialdom, by the same token becoming less associated than before with partisan politics. In Italy, the republication of Vannucci's *Martiri della libertà* and of Giuseppe Ricciardi's *Martirologio italiano* in 1860, when the new Kingdom of Italy came into existence, reminded the public of the sacrifices that had paved the way to the final emancipation of the nation in that year.[78] In 1871 Greece celebrated in grandiose fashion its own fiftieth anniversary of the revolution. On that occasion the bones of Patriarch Grigorios V were translated from the Russian-imperial city of Odessa where they had been kept since his execution. In a solemn ceremony attended by the King George I and Queen Olga they were buried in the cathedral of Athens. In Portugal in 1878, on the fiftieth anniversary of the 1828 constitutional insurrection of Porto, a ceremony was organised to bury the bones of the martyrs for freedom, the constitutionalists executed by Dom Miguel in 1829, in a mausoleum in the city's cemetery. Thus, although they had been subjected to diverse, even competing readings, by the 1870s the memory of the revolutions of the 1820s had become less controversial than in the previous decades. It had been accorded public recognition and had acquired an important place in the national history of each of the countries concerned.

77. Jordi Roca Vernet, 'Las fiestas cívicas del Trienio Progresista (1840–1843): Progresistas enfrentados y desafío a la Regencia', *Historia Contemporánea* 56 (2018): 7–45.

78. Giuseppe Ricciardi, *Martirologio italiano dal 1792 al 1847; libri dieci* (Florence: Le Monnier, 1860).

PART IV

Citizens or the Faithful? Religion and the Foundation of a New Political Order

Introduction

Between February and March 1821, the otherwise quiet life of Nicosia, a hillside town in inland Sicily and the seat of a bishopric, was disturbed by some extraordinary events. The vicar-general of the cathedral, Don Francesco la Motta, had sent out a letter to all his parish priests, warning them against 'the poison [. . .] being spread' and exhorting them to 'muster all their zeal to check its progress'. What he was referring to in this note was the worrying fact that some members of the clergy in his diocese were filling the ranks of the Carboneria. In the case of at least two priests from his own town, Don Sebastiano D'Amico, and Don Bartolomeo Pidone, his warning was to no avail. To deal with these unrepentant carbonari, in fact, the vicar-general had to resort to extreme measures. As a punishment for their insubordination he decided to suspend them *a diviniis*, forbidding them to hear confession and to celebrate the mass. Yet the two priests not only ignored their superior's order, but engaged in open acts of rebellion with the complicity of the revolutionary leadership of the town, who belonged to the local vendita of the Carboneria. Don D'Amico, accompanied by the mayor of Nicosia, the *vice-intendente* (the equivalent of a vice-prefect), and the head of the police force (the *capitan d'armi*), on different occasions verbally and physically threatened the vicar-general, and followed him to the door of his place of residence demanding, although without success, the withdrawal of the suspension. In a flagrant challenge to their superior's authority, the two priests decided to celebrate the mass together in the cathedral before the civil authorities, whose very presence betokened their support of this act of defiance, the city population and the entire cathedral chapter, one and all astonished by the audacity of these two individuals.[1]

The conflicts that exploded in Nicosia in 1821 were by no means unique. Indeed, analogous episodes could be identified in many localities in all southern European countries during the revolutions. What these events indicate is a constant upsurge in violent disagreements regarding the relationship between secular and religious institutions and, more importantly, regarding the relationship between religion and the political order. These disagreements erupted both within the ranks of the church and between clerics and local authorities. Such conflicts remind us that revolutionaries were then having to combat a counterrevolutionary ideology whose principles were incompatible with freedom of expression and, indeed, with any form of popular government. In the minds of counterrevolutionary thinkers and church authorities, 'the secular order required a sacred foundation', one based on a divine authority and absolute religious truth that could neither be questioned nor undermined without the destruction of society, and that could only be guaranteed by the existing monarchical and absolutist political order.[2] This was not only true for Catholicism, but also for Orthodoxy: the Orthodox church did indeed condemn revolutionary principles and any form of political critique or rebellion against Ottoman rule, on the grounds that submission to the Porte was consistent with the divine plan, and would serve to ensure the ultimate survival of the Orthodox faith.[3] However, the revolutionaries—along with their supporters within the ranks of the clergy—themselves in fact considered religion and religious morality to be prerequisites for the success of their political projects. As historians of the Ibero-American World and the Balkans have shown, the values of the Enlightenment and those of liberalism emerged

1. ASC, Miscellanea Risorgimentale, 251–52, ff. 288ff: sottointendenza di Nicosia to intendenza di Catania, 13 June 1821.

2. Emile Perreau-Saussine, *Catholicism and Democracy: An Essay in the History of Political Thought* (Princeton, NJ: Princeton University Press, 2011), pp. 32–33.

3. Richard Clogg, 'The "Dhidhaskalia Patriki" (1798): An Orthodox Reaction to French Revolutionary Propaganda', and 'Anti-Clericalism in Pre-Independence Greece, c. 1750–1821', in Clogg, *Anatolica: Studies in the Greek East in the 18th and 19th Centuries* (Aldershot: Routledge, 1996), chs 5 and 8 respectively.

within these religious cultures, at times challenging them, at times arriving at more or less awkward accommodations with them.[4]

As Part IV here will go on to demonstrate, rather than rejecting religion, revolutionaries strove to find an accommodation between their own values and revealed truth. They did so at a time, after the collapse of the Napoleonic order, when church and religion had re-emerged with a renewed prestige and enhanced popular support. Thus, rather than being defined as simply a step towards the secularisation of the political sphere, the revolutions of the 1820s need to be understood as junctures at which the relationship between religion and politics, faith and freedom, church and state were renegotiated, and new political tenets and sources of legitimacy were combined with older ones, and with religious justifications and principles in particular. This process involved the participation of civilians and members of the churches alike, at both national and local level. Although religion in some respects constrained, or limited, the ways in which freedom of expression and toleration were conceived and put into practice, it also provided tools and opened up possibilities to rethink the political order. This, however, was not a peculiarity of southern Europe. Reconciling religious values with the novel political framework of the post-revolutionary world, rethinking religion itself so that it might mount a challenge to the status quo, and establishing an accommodation between the sacred and revolution, constituted central problems for early nineteenth-century supporters of constitutional government.[5] Revolutionaries in southern Europe at this time were engaging with problems similar, in fact, to those facing their counterparts in other parts of Europe and the wider world. While the revolutions were unfolding in southern Europe, an intense debate about the relationship between religion,

4. See Javier Fernández Sebastián, 'Toleration and Freedom of Expression in the Hispanic World between Enlightenment and Liberalism', *Past and Present* 211 (2011): 159–97; Stuart B. Schwartz, *All Can Be Saved: Religious Tolerance and Salvation in the Iberian Atlantic World* (New Haven, CT: Yale University Press, 2008). On the relationship between Orthodoxy and enlightenment, see Larry Woolf, *Enlightenment and the Orthodox World: Western Perspectives on the Orthodox Church in Eastern Europe* (Athens: Centre for Neohellenic Research, 2000); Paschalis Kitromilides, 'Orthodoxy and the West: Reformation to Enlightenment', in *The Cambridge History of Christianity*, vol. 5: *Eastern Christianity*, ed. Michael Angold (Cambridge: Cambridge University Press), pp. 187–208.

5. Gareth Stedman Jones and Ira Katznelson, eds, *Religion and the Political Imagination* (Cambridge: Cambridge University Press, 2010). More specifically for the French revolution, see at least Dale K. Van Kley, *The Religious Origins of the French Revolution: From Calvin to the Civil Constitution, 1570–1791* (Basingstoke: Palgrave, 2000).

freedom and toleration was taking place among both Catholics and Protestants in France, where a Catholic revival was met with a renewed anticlerical movement.[6] In Britain too, in the 1820s, the relationship between politics, national education and religion was fiercely contested, not least because of the debate leading ultimately to the emancipation of Catholics.[7]

A striking consequence of the religious understanding of the political order entertained by the 1820s revolutionaries was their propensity to defend a notion of the sovereign nation as, in religious terms, essentially homogeneous. The homogeneity of their societies would in this way, or so they reckoned, be protected. Setting aside the Waldensians in the Alpine valleys of Piedmont, and the Greek Orthodox minorities in the Kingdom of the Two Sicilies, the populations of Catholic countries were exceptionally homogeneous from a religious point of view. In Greece too, the association between religion and nationality was very intimate, although the relevant affiliation was sometimes Orthodoxy, sometimes Christianity more broadly. But this was the outcome of the revolution itself, an event that had put an end to the multiethnic and multireligious nature of the part of the Ottoman Empire that acquired independence. As chapter twelve below will show, this religious notion of the nation, protected by all the constitutions introduced during these revolutions, resulted in limitations to freedom of thought and toleration. Given the importance they attributed to religion as a foundation of their new political order, revolutionaries considered the clergy to be a key ally in their project of social and political regeneration. The chapter explores the policies that constitutional governments imposed upon their national churches, showing that, while constitutional authorities saw the regular clergy as an unproductive burden upon society, they saw parish priests in particular as fulfilling the vitally necessary role of educating citizens, and asked all members of church hierarchies to rally around the constitution. Reactions among the ranks of the churches were, however, mixed, and clerics divided in their attitudes. Chapter thirteen discusses the responses of both bishops and ordinary clerics to the revolution. It demonstrates that popular mobilisation both for and against the new order, especially during civil wars, owed much to clerical activism, and that in Catholic countries monks and friars tended to be more hostile to the revolution than were priests. These responses often reflected political divisions that had first emerged after the

6. Helena Rosenblatt, *Liberal Values: Benjamin Constant and the Politics of Religion* (Cambridge: Cambridge University Press, 2008).

7. Joanna Innes, 'L'"éducation nationale" dans les îles Britanniques, 1765–1815: Variations britanniques et irlandaises sur un thème européen', *Annales* 5 (2010): 1087–116.

French revolution and during the Napoleonic wars. They also had much to do with pre-existing tensions between low and high clergy, and with the material circumstances of the lower clergy. In Catholic countries clergies were thus divided; in Greece, however, the overwhelming majority of priests, monks and bishops embraced the revolution from the very outset, regarding it as morally legitimate inasmuch as it represented a struggle in the name of Christian civilisation against Ottoman barbarity.

It was through preaching in churches that priests either publicly condemned or supported the revolution and the constitution. The chapter goes on to explore the nature of the sermons delivered during religious ceremonies, whose content was at once political and religious. It highlights the extent to which both counterrevolutionary and constitutionalist priests would justify their views by adopting and providing alternative understandings of a shared set of concepts. Yet neither clerics nor revolutionaries were in full control of the uses of religious culture. A study of the numerous miracles and prophetic apparitions reported as taking place in the period demonstrates the importance that popular understanding of the divine played in the period. Attempts made by political and religious authorities to control and manipulate such phenomena were not always successful. All types of religious expression were therefore central to the culture wars that divided societies during the revolutions.

CHAPTER TWELVE

Christianity against Despotism

Religious nations, intolerant nations?

A remarkable feature of the constitutionalism in southern Europe in the 1820s was the centrality it accorded to a religious definition of the nation. The relationship between nationality, religion and citizenship was shaped across the region by the reception and discussion of the Cádiz Constitution of 1812, which the Spanish revolutionaries reintroduced in 1820 without any major modifications. Article 12 stated that the religion of the nation was Catholic, a religion that the nation had a duty to protect by prohibiting the exercise of any other. This centrality of a religious idea of nationality had a number of implications. As has already been observed, given the subordination of individual rights to the supreme community of the nation, citizenship itself acquired a religious connotation. Admittedly, religious faith was not one of the requirements listed explicitly in the Cádiz Constitution to define citizenship; but specific legislation implemented in 1822 in the Spanish penal code nevertheless stipulated that those guilty of apostasy risked forfeiting their rights as Spanish citizens.[1] The link between state and religion proposed (or implied) by the constitution was in part a legacy of the pre-revolutionary era. The association between religion and monarchy had represented one of the central features of the ideology of the Ibero-American world, as well as of the Bourbon dynasties. This same association was in fact reaffirmed by the revolutionaries, who did not question monarchical rule in Spain, Portugal or the Italian states. On the contrary, they acted in the name of the king, the constitution and

---

1. See Article 233 in the *Código Penal Español* (Madrid: Imprenta Nacional, 1822), p. 46. On this new crime of apostasy, see Fernández Sarasola, *La Constitución de Cádiz*, pp. 112–14.

religion alike. The military pronunciamientos were started in the name of God, king and constitution, thus signalling both an ideological and an institutional continuity with existing institutions. However, legal recognition of the hegemony of a religious faith in society was not simply a sign of political and cultural continuity with the past. Religion was now also associated with the rights of the nation. Through invoking the principle of nationality, the Cádiz Constitution had put sovereignty at the heart of the political system it was founding. It had likewise affirmed the supremacy of this same principle over any individual rights, of which indeed no detailed catalogue was attached; the constitution stated that 'sovereignty lies essentially in the nation', and that 'the nation is obliged to preserve and protect by wise and just laws the civil rights, property and other legitimate rights of all the individuals who compose it'.[2]

In Greece, for its part, the break with the past was far more radical than it had been in the cases of Portugal, Spain, Piedmont and Naples. Unlike these other revolutionary contexts, marked by a high degree of religious homogeneity, the Greek revolt resulted in multiple interfaith conflicts that opposed the majority Orthodox rebels to Jews, Catholics and, above all, Muslim minorities (commonly, and tellingly, referred to as 'Turks', whatever their ethnic origin).[3] The birth of a new, religiously homogeneous state was a product of the revolution itself. As it unfolded, Muslims and Jews were either massacred or expelled from the territories controlled by the revolutionaries. Tensions emerged also with the Catholic minorities, as their community was accused, like the Jewish one, of siding with the Ottomans.[4] There was no previous relationship between state and religion to provide an element of continuity between the pre-revolutionary and the revolutionary polities. On the contrary, the Orthodox community in the Ottoman Empire was organised according to the *millet* system. This guaranteed, through the Greek Orthodox patriarchate, a degree of autonomy to the Orthodox population, an ethnically diverse community bound together both by their religion and its universal principles, and by an allegiance to the empire—with its own rules and legal system, but politically subordinate to a Muslim-defined imperial governance.[5] It was

2. Articles 3 and 4 in the *Constitución política de la monarquía española*, p. 2.

3. Anscombe, *State, Faith, and Nation*, pp. 68–69.

4. For the specific case of the Jews living in Greece, see Katherine Fleming, *Greece: A Jewish History* (Princeton, NJ: Princeton University Press, 2008), pp. 15–17.

5. On the *millet* system and religious diversity in the Ottoman Empire, see Karen Barkey, 'In the Lands of the Ottomans: Religion and Politics', in Stedman Jones and Katznelson, *Religion and the Political Imagination*, pp. 90–111; Benjamin Braude and Bernard

the emergence of the notion of a separate ethnic and cultural community in the late eighteenth century that introduced a powerful element of diversity within those groups that had otherwise until then been united under the umbrella of a universal Orthodox Christianity. Thus nationalism put an end to the post–imperial Byzantine legacy of religious unity. Rather than rejecting religion or the legacy of Orthodoxy, however, the revolution represented a step towards its nationalisation, and this at a number of different levels.[6] First of all, some revolutionaries advocated the creation of an autocephalous church. During the first year of the revolution, while closely following Greek events from Paris, Adamantios Korais called for the establishment of a national Greek church.[7] Second, they soon adopted religion as one of the key cultural traits that defined the Greek nation, along with ethnicity and, above all, language. The existing interconnection between religion and language within the framework of the Ottoman Empire as guaranteed by the *millet* system, with the supremacy it granted to the Greek Phanariot families and the Greek-speaking clergy, therefore provided the background for the rise of Greek nationalism and its manipulation and adaptation of religion.

A political language combining demands for emancipation with assertions of religious identity can be detected in the earliest documents of the revolution. Admittedly, in some public manifestos the revolutionaries claimed that 'we don't fight Muslims but we fight injustice and tyranny' as 'the Turks themselves have taken up arms many times against the unjust and tyrannical'.[8] However, it was primarily in the name of the defence of religion that the Greeks fought their long war against their Ottoman rulers, and that popular participation was advocated and fomented. In 1821 a handwritten revolutionary gazette argued that the rebellion was that of

Lewis, eds, *Christians and Jews in the Ottoman Empire: The Functioning of a Plural Society* (New York: Holmes and Meier, 1982).

6. Paschalis Kitromilides, 'From Orthodox Commonwealth to National Communities: Greek–Russian Intellectual and Ecclesiastical Ties in the Ottoman Era', in Kitromilides, *An Orthodox Commonwealth. Symbolic Legacies and Cultural Encounters in Southeastern Europe* (Aldershot: Routledge, 2007), pp. 1–18; Kitromilides, *Enlightenment, Nationalism, Orthodoxy: Studies in the Culture and Political Thought of South-Eastern Europe* (Aldershot: Routledge, 1994), pp. 149–92.

7. Paschalis Kitromilides, 'Itineraries in the World of the Enlightenment: Adamantios Korais from Smyrna via Montpellier to Paris', in *Adamantios Korais and the European Enlightenment*, ed. Paschalis Kitromilides (Oxford: Voltaire Foundation, 2010), p. 26.

8. Dimitrios Ypsilantis to Serif Mehmed Pasha, 25 July 1821, in Κρητικά ιστορικά έγγραφα, 1821–1830 (Historical documents from Crete, 1821–1830), vol. 1 (one vol. published) ed. Nikolaos V. Tomadakis and Anthoula A. Papadaki (Athens: Ministry of Culture and the Sciences, 1974), pp. 25–27.

the Greek *genos*, that is to say a community 'united by our eternal faith', whose religion had been insulted by the Turks.[9]

The very first attempts to assert the existence of Greece as an autonomous political entity therefore made reference to its religious nature. Only a few months after the outbreak of the revolution Theodoros Negris, gathering together the leaders of eastern Roumeli in what came to be known as the Areios Pagos, drafted a first political document about the organisation of the state, which stated that while all religions were tolerated, 'the Eastern Church of Christ and the current language only are recognised as the authorised religion and speech of Greece'.[10] In the same year, 1822, the first formally recognised charter of the state, the Constitution of Epidavros, linked Christianity, rather than Orthodoxy specifically, to Greek citizenship. The document stated that 'every individual of the Christian faith, whether a native or definitively settled in Greece, is a Greek, and entitled to an equal enjoyment of every right'. While this, as was made clear by the English translators of the document, countered any allegation of Orthodox intolerance against the existing Catholic communities in the Greek islands, the definition of citizenship along religious lines had an explicitly anti-Muslim flavour (although Muslims who converted to Christianity could become Greek!)[11] The revised constitution approved in Troezena in 1827 confirmed Orthodoxy as the state religion, but with citizenship granted to all Greeks of the Christian religion, it being declared more emphatically than before that 'everyone professes his own religion freely, and obtains freedom for his worship (or sect)', and that citizenship was also extended to those living abroad but with a Greek father, and to foreigners who were living on Greek soil and wished to be naturalised.[12] The explicit acknowledgement in the Greek constitution of the rights of other Christian denominations was forced upon the revolutionaries by foreign powers and by the revolutionaries' awareness that this would encourage

9. *Σάλπιγξ Ελληνική* [*Salpix Elliniki*], August 1821, in Koumarianou, *Ο Τύπος στον Αγώνα* (The press in the 'Struggle'), 1, pp. 43–44, 46, 47.

10. Charles A. Frazee, *The Orthodox Church and Independent Greece, 1821–1852* (Cambridge: Cambridge University Press, 1969), pp. 45–46.

11. See the English version of the constitution, *The Provisional Constitution of Greece*, p. 39.

12. On these aspects of the constitutions, see Iakovos D. Michailidis, 'The Formation of Greek Citizenship (19th Century)', in *Citizenship in Historical Perspective*, ed. Steven G. Ellis, Gudmundur Halfdanarson and Ann Katherine Isaacs (Pisa: Edizioni Plus, 2006), pp. 155–62; Anne Couderc, 'Religion et identité nationale en Grèce pendant la révolution d'indépendance (1821–1832): Le creuset ottoman et l'influence occidentale', in *La Perception de l'héritage ottoman dans les Balkans*, ed. Sylvie Gangloff (Paris: L'Harmattan, 2005), pp. 21–41.

support for the Greek cause in other European and in extra-European countries. It should not be forgotten, however, that the Greek revolution not only opposed Orthodox to Muslim, but was also riven by tensions between the Orthodox majority and the Catholic minority, which was concentrated on four Cycladic islands: namely, Syros (where they were in the majority), Tinos, Hydra and Santorini. When the insurrection started to spread, this latter community decided to remain neutral and loyal to the Turks, convinced that its interests were better preserved by the Ottoman authorities, and claiming to be under the protection of France. The Orthodox bishop in Naxos reacted with violence to this decision, conflating the Catholic minority with the Turkish enemy.[13] The revolutionaries did try to enlist the support of the Catholic communities, however, especially at times when the war was not proceeding successfully. In 1823 the minister of the interior Grigorios Dikaios (best known as Papaflessas), who was himself a priest, wrote to the Catholic community—the so-called Latins—inviting them to join the struggle for liberation, and arguing that 'only barbarous nations put religion together with nationality, such that a small religious dispute serves to divide them', and that since by the constitution all Christians were Greek, the 'old Christians of the Western Church' were an integral part of the nation.[14] However, this reassurance did not entirely persuade the Catholic communities to embrace the revolutionary cause, and Catholics continued until 1829 to question the authority of the new administration.[15]

Generally in revolutionary societies, the recognition of a state religion raised a number of questions regarding its compatibility with other principles enshrined in their constitutions, and in particular with freedom of conscience and freedom of expression, and its relationship to citizenship. Although a compromise between competing principles clearly needed to be found, southern European revolutionaries were determined to devise legal solutions that protected the religious homogeneity of their societies and recognised individual rights only within this religious cultural space. As a consequence, toleration and freedom of expression came to be substantially limited by this pre-existing cultural characteristic of the nations concerned. The assumption everywhere was that toleration for other

13. See Frazee, *Orthodox Church*, pp. 42–43.

14. As quoted in Frazee, *Orthodox Church*, p. 61. See Konstantinos I. Manikas, 'The Relations between Orthodoxy and Roman Catholicism in Greece during the Revolution (1821–1827): Contribution to the History of the Church in Greece', unpublished doctoral dissertation, University of Athens, 2001, pp. 179–202.

15. Frazee, *Orthodox Church*, pp. 82–84.

faiths was an issue that regarded foreigners and foreigners alone, since southern European liberals held themselves to be ruling over religiously homogeneous societies.[16]

In Naples, members of the Neapolitan parliament agreed at first to confirm Article 12 of the Spanish constitution, but appended the word 'public' to the stipulation regarding forms of worship that were banned, implying that the private exercise of other faiths was acceptable if foreigners were prepared to pray in the privacy of their own households. This limited form of toleration seemed to win universal agreement in the parliament. Yet this same word was dropped in the final version of the constitution, in the face of bitter hostility from the leaders of the Catholic church, and from the clergy in general.

Most prominent among the senior clerics hostile to the constitution was the archbishop of Conza, Arcangelo Lupoli, a highly educated and energetic prelate, committed to the reform of his bishopric, to which he had been appointed in 1818, and the renovation of its churches. For Lupoli, any attempt to undermine the role of Catholicism as state religion by permitting even the mildest form of toleration represented first and foremost an attack on the freedom of the Church and an assault upon religion, since it would limit the scope of God's own reign, which represented in turn the foundation of any state and community: 'the Church is the kingdom of God on earth, a sign as free in majesty as the King of Kings, through whom it has been communicated, is free,' he asserted. A state religion, he concluded, was a vital support to government, since without religion the social order would disintegrate: 'far from finding ourselves in society, we would find ourselves in a wood or in a forest'.[17] Hostile though the Catholic hierarchy may have been to the constitution, it was precisely by appealing to its wisdom that they condemned the parliament's proposals to modify it. The archbishop of Naples, Cardinal Ruffo, who led the opposition to the wording of the article, claimed that any deviation from the original text of the constitution would betray its nature, and repudiate its rightly acknowledged Catholic foundation. For a priest by the name of Felice Racioppi, writing to the parliament to oppose the toleration accorded to foreigners in their worship, the inclusion of the word 'public'

16. On foreigners in Naples, see Luigia Caglioti, *Vite parallele: Una minoranza protestante nell'Italia dell'Ottocento* (Bologna: Il Mulino, 2006).

17. *Rimostranza dell'arcivescovo di Conza per la libertà della chiesa* (Conza: Giuseppe De Bonis, 1821), quotations at pp. 5, 14–15. On Lupoli, see Antonio Cestaro, *Le diocesi di Conza e di Campagna nell'età della Restaurazione* (Rome: Storia e Letteratura, 1971), esp. pp. 47–100.

in the text might well lead to a plurality of creeds entering the kingdom and destroying its unity:

> Soon in the Kingdom of the Two Sicilies we would see as many religions as there are individuals composing it. We would see private oratories, and we would see even in our own times one great fanatic practise the Lutheran cult here, and another the cult of Calvin there, and since man is proud and tends by virtue of mingling to become individualised, we would once again see mosques rise up in private gardens, and finally the introduction of monstrous idolatries, the offshoots of pagan theogonies.[18]

Society would dissolve, families be divided, and in the end, Racioppi concluded, civil war would break out. Heeding this opposition, the king used his right of veto to modify the final text and leave the wording of the Cádiz Constitution intact.[19] This decision provoked a reaction from the Carboneria of the capital, whose members invaded the parliament to protest against it.[20] In spite of this bitter conflict, which resulted in victory for the Church, the views of the Neapolitan hierarchy and those of the majority of the deputies were in fact closer than they might seem at first sight. What brought together both supporters of the constitution and its critics was the conviction that the religious uniformity of the nation had to be protected, and that religious pluralism was a threat to society. In his *Catechismo costituzionale per uso del regno unito delle Sicilie*, the Benedictine monk Luigi Galanti, an unflinching supporter of the new order elected to the Neapolitan parliament in 1820, confirmed that the religious homogeneity of the Neapolitan nation was a source of strength, unity and cohesion, a characteristic of its culture in which the country could and should take pride. In order to avoid potential religious conflicts, the kingdom therefore did not need toleration, but rather the protection of the religious status quo. The introduction of other cults was seen as a threat to national unity and to the social fabric, while the public practice of other faiths could easily give rise to anarchy:

> Having just the one religion, we do not need to proclaim freedom of worship, as other countries, where there are followers of different religions, have been obliged to do. Happy as we are to have this powerful

18. *Al parlamento nazionale, petizione del canonico Felice Racioppi di Apice in P.U.* (Avellino, n.d.).

19. Lepre, *La rivoluzione napoletana*, pp. 247–53.

20. On this episode, see the account in the section on secret societies in chapter ten above.

bond, we will not live in fear of those bloody scenes between Catholics and Protestants witnessed even in recent years in France.[21]

Admittedly, certain revolutionaries were keener to defend toleration for foreigners. In Spain some of them, especially among the exaltados, would ideally have supported this measure, and put forward constitutional projects that supported it.[22] In practice, however, they preferred to defend the constitutional text in its entirety from any external attacks. Prudence moreover dictated that all direct confrontation with the Church over such matters be avoided. Since religious tolerance was not a cause that would win the Spanish exaltados or, for that matter, the Neapolitan, Portuguese and Greek patriots any additional support from their social base, but might in fact alienate popular opinion, they opted not to embrace it.[23]

The principle did become law in Portugal. In the 1822 Portuguese constitution, the affirmation of the existence of, and the need to protect, a state religion was associated with explicit toleration of the public practice of other religions for non-nationals. But here too, the basic assumption that the nation was, and should remain homogeneous from a religious point of view was not questioned. Article 25 of the *Bases da constituição* discussed in 1821 stated that 'the religion of the Portuguese nation must be Catholic, Apostolic, Roman. All foreigners are permitted the private exercise of their respective cults.' Many deputies associated religious toleration with economic progress, and observed that the great prosperity of countries such as the United States of America, Great Britain and the Netherlands was evidence for the link between the peaceful coexistence of different religious beliefs and economic success. Likewise, it was argued, the Portuguese Empire could only thrive if foreigners were allowed to flock into its territories and practise their faiths.[24] Toleration, after all, some went

21. Galanti, *Catechismo*, p. 16. On Galanti, see Enrico Narciso, 'Illuminismo e cultura sannita nel secolo XVIII', in *Illuminismo meridionale e comunità locali*, ed. Enrico Narciso (Naples: Guida, 1988), pp. 25–62 at 49–50.

22. See for instance the constitutional proposal by Ramón de los Santos García Auñon (Santos García Auñón, *Teoría de una constitución*), who supported toleration of any cult in private for foreigners. On this radical priest, see Cayetano Mas Galvañ, 'La democracia templada según un "clérigo del lugar": Perfiles biográficos e ideológicos de D. Ramón de los Santos García', in Fernández Sarasola, *Constituciones en la sombra*, pp. 211–66. (The text itself is republished in the same volume at pp. 267–51. Article 9 on toleration is at pp. 411–13.)

23. Juan Francisco Fuentes, 'El liberalismo radical ante la unidad religiosa', in *Libéralisme chrétien et catholicisme libéral en Espagne, France et Italie dans la première moitié du XIXᵉ siècle: Colloque internationale 12/13/14 novembre 1987* (Aix-en-Provence: Université de Provence, 1989), pp. 127–41.

24. *Diário das cortes geraes*, 3, no. 143, 3 August 1821, pp. 1771–73.

so far as to claim, was first and foremost a Christian virtue, one praised in the New Testament and advocated by Jesus Christ and the Apostles, a Catholic duty towards foreigners compatible with historical praxis across the world. Intolerance was coterminous with fanaticism, violence and civil strife. Although there was a duty to defend Catholic truth, Christianity also taught its followers to tolerate those who erred.[25] However, while deputies in principle acknowledged the importance of respecting the religious beliefs of foreigners, they took seriously the notion that the Catholic nature of the monarchy and the nation must be defended. In their view the text of the *Bases* seemed to reconcile these two seemingly antithetical principles. As Francisco Manuel Trigoso, a member of the constitutional assembly suggested, individual freedom of conscience should be protected to the same extent as the religious integrity of the Portuguese nation: the unchecked proliferation of religious sects was as dangerous to society as complete intolerance of individual religious opinions.[26] Some went so far as to suggest, just as most Neapolitan members of parliament had done, that only the private, not the public, practice of other faiths should be tolerated.[27] Thus the text of the Portuguese constitution did not challenge the assumption that the religious unity of the nation had to be safeguarded, while making allowances for aliens in a far more generous and explicit manner than the Neapolitan and Spanish revolutionaries had permitted. No one in these countries argued publicly for the complete neutrality of the state towards religion.[28] The only state where religious toleration for nationals was protected was Piedmont, where in 1821 the revolutionaries decided to amend the Spanish constitution to allow 'the practice of other confessions'. This revision was introduced in order to take into account the existence of the small Protestant communities of Waldensians, who lived in certain secluded Alpine valleys, and whose faith had been tolerated since the 1690s (although they had otherwise still been discriminated against, in terms of their rights as citizens).[29]

Rather than embracing religious toleration, revolutionaries chose to fight other battles against the clerical opposition, in particular in favour of freedom of the press. This freedom was bitterly opposed by many senior

25. Ibid., no. 145, 6 August 1821, pp. 1799–1802.

26. Ibid., p. 1802.

27. Bispo de Beja, in *Diário das cortes geraes*, 3, no. 143, 3 August 1821, p. 1772.

28. For the text of the *Bases*, see Vieira, *O problema político português*.

29. See Aquarone, D'Addio and Negri, *Le costituzioni italiane*, p. 513. On the Waldensians, see Augusto Armand-Hugon, *Storia dei valdesi*, 2 vols (Turin: Claudiana, 1989), 2, pp. 197–204.

members of the clergy, who saw it as a direct attack on divine right as the origin of monarchical authority. In this sphere too, however, most supporters of constitutional government agreed that the protection of religion had to be taken into account, with this requiring the imposition of some limitations upon freedom of expression. The debates on the adoption of Article 372 of the Cádiz Constitution, which concerned freedom of the press, and the scope or limits of censorship, as well as the controversy that they unleashed, are indicative of the prevailing views among members of the parliaments and of the issues that were considered to be at stake.[30] Controversy was exacerbated by the opposition of many, if not quite all, bishops and leaders of the national churches, who loudly voiced their hostility to press freedom and raised concerns about the threats it posed to public order and religion. In Spain, the revolution brought back a revised version of the regulation originally introduced by the Cortes of Cádiz in 1813. While the Inquisition was once again abolished and freedom of the press guaranteed, ecclesiastical preventive censorship was introduced, although strictly limited to religious dogma and to the publication of the Holy Scriptures (thus restricting the scope of the 1813 regulation, which had endorsed the application of ecclesiastical censorship to any publication addressing religious matters). Although at the outset of the revolution most Spanish bishops were hoping to maintain their control over the press, and in fact condemned freedom of the press outright, the archbishop of Toledo, Cardinal Borbón, the leader of the Spanish church and a supporter of the constitutional regime, did not see any incompatibility between religion and press freedom. Since in his view freedom and religion went hand in hand, a free press would ultimately contribute to, rather than undermining, the spreading of religious truth. This argument, whilst replacing reason with Catholicism, in fact mirrored that of Enlightenment philosophers, who were less committed to a pluralism of ideas than to the ultimate victory of reason over superstition and error.[31]

In Naples too, revolutionaries argued that the broadest possible freedom of the press was a vital pillar not only of the constitutional system and of a flourishing society but also of religion itself. For an anonymous journalist writing for *L'Imparziale*, 'the tribunal of public opinion [. . .]

30. Part of the debate is summarised in Lepre, *La rivoluzione napoletana*, pp. 209–11, 233. For the parliamentary speeches, see Alberti, *Atti del parlamento*, 2, pp. 170–77.

31. On the legislation, see Fernández Sarasola, *La Constitución de Cádiz*, p. 263; on the views of Cardinal Borbón, see Rodríguez López-Brea, *Don Luis de Borbón: El cardenal de los liberales, 1777–1823* (Toledo: Junta de Comunidades de Castilla-La Mancha, 2002), pp. 302–4.

knows that in all the triumphs of religion there was no more effective tool than the pen of the impious'.[32] And as another journalist argued, a free press was first and foremost a threat to vice, not to religion, and the Church should be entitled to intervene and condemn only in the case of the handful of works that took advantage of freedom to spread erroneous beliefs. Against the attacks of the archbishop of Naples, who had argued that freedom of the press would bring about the final destruction of religion and undermine revelation, one deputy retorted that by virtue of a free press both reason and the purest principles of the Holy Scriptures would thrive, and the Church itself would be more easily cleansed of any form of corruption affecting its members.[33] These Neapolitan liberals seemed to share an enlightened faith in the emergence of a public opinion founded upon wisdom and rationality, deeming it altogether compatible with the principles of revelation.

As in Spain, so too in Portugal the majority of members of the Cortes agreed that freedom of expression could not question religious dogma. During the discussions in the Cortes a number of positions on the issue emerged. The most liberal was predicated on the notion that freedom of the press was associated with the natural right of freedom of expression, and as such it should have precedence over any religious consideration and should not be limited. Even this stance, however, was not intrinsically anti-religious. On the contrary, while it acknowledged as a fact that religion was beneficial to society and would contribute to its cohesion, it was based on the conviction that religious belief could not be founded upon constraint, but only upon free will and inner conviction. Thus preventive censorship on religious matters could not help but prove harmful and counterproductive as far as religion itself was concerned, since it would foster superstition and, through secrecy, encourage erroneous beliefs. Genuine religious principles could only thrive with free discussion, the sole means by which truth might prevail and errors be challenged. These views were advanced by a member of the Cortes who was also a cleric, the Canon João Maria Soares Castelo Branco, who believed passionately in the full compatibility of religion with individual freedom. The risk, as others observed, was that once the idea of preventive censorship was admitted, it was difficult to

32. 'Dell'utilità dei giornali in uno stato costituzionale', second part, *L'Imparziale*, 14 August 1820, p. 4. Similar arguments can also be found in 'Atti de' varii poteri. Potere legislative. Affari ecclesiastici', *Il Censore*, 16 January 1821, pp. 61–62.

33. See Galanti's 'Rapporto della commissione di esame a tutela della costituzione sulla mozione del signor deputato Catalano', in *Lettera dell'arcivescovo di Napoli al parlamento nazionale e risposta del parlamento* (Naples, 1821), p. 14.

draw a clear distinction between religious and non-religious writings, and the enemies of freedom would easily find reasons to object to the beliefs of most philosophers and to extend the reach of censorship, thereby trampling upon constitutional rights.[34] It was through preaching and pastoral activities, not through laws, that religion would flourish.[35]

But for most deputies, a state religion like Catholicism nevertheless required some sort of protection. The absence of any form of preventive censorship regarding religious publications would encourage the spread of heresies, and therefore pose a direct threat to the integrity of the national community whose shared religious values were those of the Catholic church. For Anes de Carvalho, the backwardness and ignorance of Portuguese society, subjected as it had been to three centuries of despotism by the Holy Inquisition, did not permit an untrammelled freedom of the press on religious matters. Moreover, Portugal had embraced Catholicism, a religion based on a set of unquestionable truths that only the Church itself could shield from error.[36] Only the wisdom of bishops on questions relating to salvation, it was added, could determine what was acceptable or not on matters concerning dogma.[37] This latter position was the one that prevailed. Consequently, following the Spanish example, the Portuguese liberals arrived at a compromise solution that accurately reflected the nature of the parliamentary debate, since it drew on the distinction between civil concerns and matters relating to religious doctrine, allowing ecclesiastical censorship for these latter, while granting the *jurados* responsible for civil censorship the additional right to pronounce as to whether publications censored by the bishops would represent an offence to Christian morality.[38]

Revolutionaries also took pains to communicate these views about the mutually constitutive relationship between freedom and religion in the popular literature directed at the uneducated. In political catechisms, dialogues addressing the illiterate and in journalism, three key messages in

34. The debates are published in full in Augusto da Costa Dias, ed., *Discursos sobre a liberdade de imprensa no primeiro parlamento português (1821)* (Lisbon: Editorial Estampa, 1978). For Castelo Branco's interventions, see pp. 64–68, 122–23.

35. Deputy Fernandes Tomás, in ibid., p. 42.

36. *Discursos sobre a liberdade*, pp. 76–77.

37. Ibid., p. 101.

38. See Ana Mouta Faria, 'A condição do clero português durante a primeira experiência de implantação do liberalismo: As influências do processo revolucionário francês e seus limites', *Revista Portuguesa de História* 23 (1987): 301–31. On censorship, see also José Tengarrinha, *Da liberdade mitificada à liberdade subvertida: Uma exploração no interior da repressão à imprensa periódica de 1820 a 1828* (Lisbon: Edições Colibri, 1993).

particular emerged. First of all, patriots strove to demonstrate the compatibility of the revolutionary experiment with the principles of religion, not least in order to convince the audience most receptive to the Church, namely, the illiterate masses, of the extent to which a constitution had, among other things, become the protector and the defender of religion. Second, patriots and even clerics themselves argued that religion itself represented the foundation of the constitution, this amounting to nothing other than the practical implementation of religious principles in the realm of politics. It should not be forgotten that the preamble to the Cádiz Constitution referred to 'Almighty God' as the author and supreme legislator of society. Finally, political reform, church reform and religious reform would have to go hand in hand, inasmuch as the revolution promised a regeneration that was ethical and moral, and therefore political and religious at one and the same time.

When discussing the content of the constitution with a view to rendering its content intelligible to the public, commentators agreed that one and only one national religion, as confirmed by the constitution, was necessary to the political life of a country, given that it furnished whatever moral principles were needed to defend society and to guarantee compliance with the laws. But this could only work if one religion prevailed over the others: 'tolerance can exist in the individual, not in society'.[39] Popular texts strove to reassure their readerships or audiences that patriotism, secret societies and constitutional principles were a far cry from atheism or heresy. Even children might become the target of a popular literature that proclaimed the compatibility of constitutional principles with religion. In a dialogue published in Seville with the aim of teaching the children of the parish to read through being exposed to the ideals enshrined in the constitution, and to the institutions introduced through it, a priest made it clear that 'he who would be a good Christian must be a good Constitutional', the constitution being founded upon the 'character of the nation, natural law and the religion of the one true Jesus Christ'.[40] The constitution must be respected, among other reasons, precisely because it protected and

39. Nicola Salerno, *Compendio della terapeutica costituzionale, ossia Ristretto ragionamento su la cura de' mali politici e legali nel nuovo governo costituzionale del regno di Napoli* (Naples: Giovanni de Bonis, 1820), p. 13. Similar ideas can also be found in D. De Vecchi, *La voce del cittadino* (Capua, 1821), pp. 38–40.

40. (Don) Apolinar Contoni, 'Cartilla de explicación de la constitución política de la monarquía española, para la instrucción de los niños de la parroquia de Santiago de la ciudad de Baza' [Seville, 1821], in *Catecismos políticos españoles arreglados a las constituciones del siglo XIX* (Madrid: Comunidad de Madrid, Consejería de Cultura, Secretaría General Técnica, 1989), pp. 203–11 at 205.

defended the Catholic nature of Spain. The dialogue explained that the constitution preferred Catholicism to any other faith because the Spanish nation was 'intimately convinced of the truth of the Catholic, Apostolic and Roman religion', and the unity of the religious sentiments of the nation must be safeguarded, it being a precious resource for the political community.[41] This was affirmed also in a Portuguese political catechism which, in spite of the explicit toleration of other faiths enshrined in the constitution of 1822, emphasised that 'following the Roman Catholic religion is the first duty of Lusitanian citizens', the constitution having ruled that this should be the religion of the Portuguese.[42]

These assertions as to the religious foundations of the various constitutions might lead ultimately to the further claim that 'true' Christianity, or 'true Catholicism', as opposed to superstition, was the foundation of the new political system. While tradition and revolution were not deemed to be incompatible, patriots did however make it very clear that what they supported was an evangelical, progressive form of religion at odds with oppression or despotism. In the words of a Sicilian liberal, 'the friends of liberty want a religion as pure as God himself, as simple as the Gospels [. . . and] they impute the same value to social duties and to religious duties, because to their way of thinking social duties are still religious duties'.[43] Thus religious reform and political reform went hand in hand. These ideas also percolated down as far as the revolutionary popular press. For some revolutionaries, the civil rights guaranteed by the revolutions would remain a dead letter without the moralisation of religious practices, the abandonment of merely external forms of worship and conversion to the true spiritual principles of Christianity, of which the nation stood in such need. Political catechisms might therefore sometimes contain critiques of popular forms of religion vitiated by the needless proliferation of devotional chapels and churches that were the object of pilgrimages, often too lavishly endowed, to the detriment of parish churches and the education of the masses.[44] Religious worship had to be reformed to reflect the evangelical principles of the original religion, which, it was argued, 'is

41. Ibid., p. 206.

42. Inocêncio António de Miranda, *O cidadão lusitano: Breve compendio, em que se demonstrão os fructos da constituição, e os deveres do cidadão constitucional, para com deos, para com o rei, para com a patria, e para com todos os seus concidadãos; Dialogo entre hum liberal, e hum servile—o Abbade Roberto e D. Julio* (Lisbon: Neves e filhos, 1822), pp. 48–50.

43. Notizie estere, 'Francia, Parigi, 19 Agosto 1820,' *Giornale Patriottico di Sicilia*, no. 213, 25 September 1820, p. 4.

44. Miranda, *O cidadão lusitano*, pp. 55–56.

FIGURE 23. Portuguese allegory of the Constitution: *A Constituição defendida, o Despotismo aterrado* ('The constitution defended, despotism overawed'; engraving by Constantino de Fontes, after Luís António, Lisbon, 1822[?]; Biblioteca Nacional de Portugal, Lisbon). Image: BNP Biblioteca Nacional Digital

entirely analogous to human rights'. This could only be achieved through the combating of bigotry and of those superstitious practices that sustained the enemies of the revolution, and through the conversion of souls.[45] Constitutions, it was argued, would in turn defeat fanaticism and intolerance and help religion regain its association with enlightenment.[46] This belief in the need to reform religion was associated with the equally heartfelt conviction that religion was the pillar of any and every form of civil life. For the Portuguese liberal João Baptista de Almeida Garrett, the current moral decadence of Portugal was due to the decadence of the clergy, who had transformed religion into an instrument of intolerance. Yet no society could survive, and no public life thrive, without the aid of religion. In the wake of Gaetano Filangieri, Almeida Garrett thus defined religion as 'the supplement to the criminal code of a nation; it is the most sacred bond that brings together men in a society'.[47]

Admittedly, some of this pedagogical literature could go so far as to advance notions of natural religion, identifying the rights of citizens with natural rights, defending forms of deism that were common among freemasons and some members of secret societies, and challenging traditional religiosity. In a Portuguese catechism written in the classic dialogic style, the anonymous writer argued that natural laws, which ruled the universe as well as human existence, coincided with God's order and served as proof of its existence. When the Gospels and the prophets defended social virtues such as justice, charity, humanity, probity and patriotism, they were 'doing nothing less than announcing the precepts of natural law'. Thus the 'partisans of natural law were not godless, but had nobler ideas than most regarding the divine'.[48] But in the majority of cases we are concerned rather with a reformed, anti-despotic brand of religion. In a dialogue published in Naples in 1820, a patriot strove to convince a priest that his own beliefs were by no means contrary to the revealed truths of Catholicism. Quite the contrary: this patriot, Lorenzo by name, argued that patriots were loyal to the king and to religion, as they were 'true followers of Jesus

45. A.C.B.D., *Parlata dell'uomo sincero: Avviso alla più parte della nazione* (n.p., n.d. [1820]).

46. Cândido de Almeida y Sandoval, *O fanatismo e a intolerancia combatidos por hum filosofo Christão* (Lisbon: Imprensa Nacional, 1821), pp. 3–4.

47. João Baptista da Silva Leitão de Almeida Garrett, *O dia vinte e quatro de Agosto* (Lisbon: Typ. Rollandiana, 1821), p. 44. Similar ideas are to be found in *O parocho constitucional: Dialogo entre hum parocho de Riba-Tejo e hum cidadão liberal de Lisboa seu amigo* (Lisbon: Imprensa Nacional, 1821).

48. *Exposição da lei natural; ou Catecismo do cidadão* (Lisbon: Typografia Rollandiana, 1820), pp. 9, 55, 60.

Christ'.[49] As the dialogue made clear, it was God's own plan to combat injustice, 'so that henceforth the will of the nation, expressed through its representatives, not the will of one only, [shall] be the law'.[50] At the end of the dialogue the priest agreed to preach in such a way as to convince his parishioners of the patriots' good intentions and sound principles. Similar dialogues between clergy and ordinary people could be found elsewhere.[51]

Reforming churches: priests as educators

During the revolutions a number of church privileges, both jurisdictional and financial, were repealed or limited. The aims were twofold: namely, to assert the legal authority of the state, and to boost government finances in times of financial hardship. Revolutionary policies towards the Church were very much in line with the regalist, anticurialist attitudes that monarchical governments had entertained towards national churches in the previous century, all aimed at reinforcing state controls over the Church. These attitudes had been given a radical new twist during the Napoleonic period in the territories controlled by France, where authorities seized church properties and tried to put the clergy at the service of the state. They also built on a reformist agenda that in the past had been supported by some sections of the Church itself. It was in Naples and Spain that this same agenda had been most effectively enacted prior to 1820. Between 1806 and 1811 in Naples, the French authorities closed down and sold the properties of 1,300 monasteries, and drew up plans (never in fact implemented) to reduce and reorganise the number of dioceses and parishes of the kingdom. In Spain, in the territories ruled by Napoleon's brother in 1809, all monastic communities and friaries were suppressed. Without going that far, the Cortes of Cádiz likewise pushed the agenda of Spanish regalism further than ever before. In 1810, to finance the war, they seized the revenues of all vacant benefices and half of the tithes collected by a variety of religious institutions, from bishoprics to monasteries. In 1813 they decreed the abolition of the Tribunal of the Holy Inquisition, drafted proposals for a limitation of the number of monasteries and ordered monastic properties ruined by the war to be sold. In Portugal, attempts to undermine the power of religious institutions were more limited in

---

49. *Dialogo tenuto verso la fine di giugno del corrente anno 1820 tra il patriota Lorenzo e l'arciprete D. Fabrizio* (Naples, n.d.), p. 6.

50. *Dialogo tenuto verso la fine di giugno*, p. 10.

51. 'Dialogos de un aldeano con el domine del lugar', *Diario de Barcelona*, 28 March 1820, pp. 57–58.

scope. After the expulsion of the Jesuits and the seizure of their properties decided by the Marquis of Pombal in 1759, and his move to transform
the Inquisition into an arm of the state, Portuguese governments did not
endeavour to reduce the wealth and authority of the Church in any substantial way.[52]

For the leaders of the 1820s revolutions these policies represented an
obligatory point of reference. In Spain, revolutionaries reintroduced the
reforms that had been approved between 1812 and 1814 and withdrawn
by King Fernando at the restoration. The abolition of the Tribunal of the
Holy Inquisition, the suppression of the Jesuits, who had been reintroduced by Fernando in 1814, and the sale of their properties, were among
the first acts of the constitutional government in 1820. Both the Holy
Inquisition and the Jesuits, renowned for their attachment to the crown,
were perceived as symbols of royal absolutism.[53] In Portugal likewise, the
revolution coincided with the substantial erosion of church privileges,
in some cases for the very first time. In March 1821 the Holy Inquisition
was abolished here too; in the same month the suppression of seigneurial privileges such as the *direitos banais* affected the many monastic and
clerical institutions that were their beneficiaries. More specific measures
targeting the Church included the abolition of privileges granting pensions (*aposentadorias*), and of those granting clerics a separate juridical
system (*privilégios pessoais de foro*). The revolution also sought to benefit
from the income of church institutions that were not considered of any
utility. The state thus decreed its acquisition of the income deriving from
vacant clerical benefits, and introduced additional taxation on the income
of clerical and secular institutions above 600,000 *réis*.[54] In Naples, the
parliament decided to abolish ecclesiastical tribunals.[55] In Greece, meanwhile, the revolutionary governments embarked upon a process of partial
imitation of these regalist policies, in order to replace the legal framework

52. See Derek Beales, *European Catholic Monasteries in the Age of Revolution, 1640–
1815* (Cambridge: Cambridge University Press, 2003); Brian Hamnett, *The Enlightenment
in Iberia and IberoAmerica* (Cardiff, University of Wales Press, 2017), pp. 72–77; William J.
Callahan, *Church, Politics, and Society in Spain, 1750–1874* (Cambridge, MA: Harvard University Press, 1984); Davis, *Naples and Napoleon*, pp. 177–78, 249–51.

53. Callahan, *Church, Politics, and Society*, p. 122.

54. Faria, 'A condição', pp. 310–12; ANTT, Leis e Ordenações, Leis, maço 10, no. 16:
'Decreto de extinção do Conselho Geral do Santo Ofício, inquisições, juízes do fisco e todas
as suas dependências no reino de Portugal', 31 March 1821; ANTT, Ministério dos Negócios
Eclesiásticos e da Justiça, maço 112, no. 1 (19): 'Decreto das Cortes Gerais abolindo os privilégios de aposentadoria activa e passiva', 25 May 1821.

55. Lepre, *La rivoluzione napoletana*, p. 211.

provided by the *millet* system. During the revolution there one of the outcomes of the introduction of the new constitution was a substantial transfer of authority from church to state. The first national constitution, approved on 1 January 1822, in fact not only created a Ministry of Religion to supervise the Orthodox church, but implicitly also abolished the judicial authority that the it had exercised over the faithful on a broad range of 'religious matters', loosely understood, by establishing a new independent judiciary.[56]

In Catholic countries, the main target of revolutionary policies besides ecclesiastical privileges was the regular clergy. Similarly to the 'enlightened' reformers of the previous century and to Napoleonic administrators, revolutionaries in the 1820s attacked monks and nuns on the grounds that their activities lacked all public utility. They were, it was argued, an economic burden on society—individuals living a parasitical existence whose resources could be used otherwise for the general good. In Portugal and Spain legislation was therefore introduced to limit the number of monasteries or to arrange for their gradual extinction. Consequently in Portugal the admission of novices was prohibited (21 March 1821) and a threshold was set on the number of monasteries that might exist (18 October 1822). In Spain, attacks on monastic establishments were more radical than in Portugal, and took seriously the proposals discussed but never implemented after 1812. A set of laws known as the *ley de monacales* decreed the abolition of all monastic orders; non-monastic orders such as the mendicant ones were treated more leniently, as friaries containing more than twenty-four ordained priests were not closed down, although for these too a ban was introduced on the initiation of novices. These measures resulted in the suppression of a considerable number of monasteries—over eight hundred by 1822, although something over this number remained in existence.[57] These Spanish policies in turn inspired the Neapolitan revolutionaries who, following the example of the Spanish Junta's first acts, suspended the admission of novices, with the exclusion of nuns, notwithstanding the letter of the concordat signed in 1818 between the Church and the kingdom, until 'further notice'. A number of much more radical measures, mirroring the ecclesiastical policies of the Napoleonic era, were discussed in the parliament and taken into serious consideration, but were not followed up. Echoing earlier debates, deputies in fact proposed the abolition of all religious orders, with the distribution

56. Frazee, *Orthodox Church*, p. 47. See *The Provisional Constitution of Greece*, pp. 87ff.
57. Callahan, *Church, Politics, and Society*, pp. 122–23. Faria, 'A condição', pp. 312–13.

of their property in emphyteusis to peasants and the selling of the properties associated with the *mense arcivescovili* (archepiscopal dues), and went so far as to recommend that all church properties be declared *beni nazionali* (national assets).[58]

The attitude of the government towards the lower clergy was entirely different. Revolutionaries across southern Europe saw priests, unlike monks, nuns and friars, as necessary allies in the regeneration of the nation and the education of the masses. They were thus regarded, in their role as educators, not simply as the long arm of an authority to which the people should submit, but also as allies of the constitutional government in the emancipation and liberation from ignorance and despotism. An anonymous writer setting his own agenda for the new Spanish regime in 1820 argued that instruction was needed to make sure that the people would understand and respect the law, as well as to appreciate and defend their interests, but these objectives could not be achieved without the cooperation of priests, who as the most persuasive 'guardians of public morality' were best placed to reach out to the population.[59] Greek patriots likewise associated the regeneration of their country with a renewed role for the clergy in the instruction of the people, and viewed religion as a vital element in rebuilding public morality, without which no new political community could be constructed. Count Ioannis Kapodistrias argued, for example, that instruction was the key to the national renewal, and this was not simply a question of teaching young Greeks their own literature and language, but rather of providing them also with moral education, which, he wrote, 'ought on the one hand to have for its object to bring to prominent notice men worthy of the respect and the confidence of the nation; and on the other to accustom the nation gradually to respect, to listen to, and to believe in such men'. This task, he concluded, would be accomplished only with the support of the priesthood. Admittedly Kapodistrias was highly critical of the Orthodox church, and of its hierarchy in particular: not only had it failed until then to provide moral leadership, but it had also been responsible for the moral degradation of the Greeks. But though the Church was thus the problem, it was also an important part of the solution to Greece's decadence. He believed that the 'immense authority of the Church' could be mobilised to its proper end by contributing to public education in its own dioceses, as well as to the administration of justice.

58. Gennaro Maria Monti, *Stato e Chiesa durante la rivoluzione napoletana del 1820-21* (Milan: Vita e Pensiero, 1939).

59. *Lo que espera la España de sus representantes en el próximo congreso nacional* (Madrid: Imprenta de Núñez, 1820), pp. 33–34.

This would require, however, more careful selection of the senior clergy, and in particular of bishops and metropolitans, who ought to be selected on the basis of their own educational and moral standing.[60]

The crucial role of the clergy in contributing to public morality, and the importance of a regenerated or 'true', rather than corrupt or superstitious, religion as the foundation of social progress was emphasised also by Neapolitan liberals. 'Monks are incompatible with the social order as much as priests are necessary to sustain it,' wrote one Nicola Salerno in his commentary on the constitution, likening clerics to magistrates in an empire, and arguing that they should not be distracted by the ownership and management of land from the only responsibilities properly associated with their duties, namely 'education, instruction, preaching'. To this end it was important that their own education be improved, since many members of the clergy were mired in ignorance and moral decay.[61] For a university professor at Coimbra writing to the *Gazeta de Lisboa*, meanwhile, it was the cleric's duty to 'instruct the people in their legitimate rights, and in their rigorous obligations'.[62]

Given the conviction that priests did indeed have a useful role to perform, governments made some genuine attempts to ameliorate their circumstances, by ensuring, for example, that they had sufficient financial means to carry out their duties. In 1820 the Spanish Cortes set up a committee for the reform of the Church dominated by priests already committed to this agenda. The result was a set of legislative proposals to rationalise the payment of salaries, reducing those granted to bishops and suggesting specific rates for parish priests, and to reorganise the size and number of parishes according to the actual needs of the population. The plans to reorganise parishes were turned into law, although they were carried out unevenly across the territories of the monarchy. Towards the end of the Trienio, in 1823, when the influence of the exaltados grew in the Cortes, more sweeping reform proposals were put forward. Although never approved, these envisaged a radical territorial reorganisation of dioceses, the strengthening of the role of the state in the appointment of bishops, and the abolition of tithes and their replacement with a tax to

60. Ioannis Kapodistrias's 'Address of Count Ioannis Kapodistrias to the Greeks' [1819], in Clogg, *Movement for Greek Independence*, pp. 131–36, quotation at 133. On Korais's ideas about religion see also Richard Clogg, 'The Correspondence of Adhamantios Korais with the British and Foreign Bible Society (1808)', in Clogg, *Anatolica: Studies in the Greek East in the 18th and 19th Centuries* (Aldershot; Routledge, 1996), ch. 16.

61. Salerno, *Compendio*, pp. 14–15.

62. 'Papel de hum academico, impresso de ordem do Governo. Conimbricenses', *Gazeta de Lisboa*, 3 October 1820.

cover the financial needs of parish priests.[63] In Portugal too, a parliamentary committee proposed the diversion of all ecclesiastical revenues above a certain threshold to the fund used to support parish priests.[64] To relieve priests from excessive fiscal burdens, the Neapolitan parliament abolished a set of financial contributions paid by parish priests and other ecclesiastics to the *mense vescovili* (episcopal dues) which, though repealed in 1813, had been reintroduced in 1819.[65]

In Greece, from the earliest stages of the revolution, its leadership had grasped the importance of utilising the clergy to lend legitimacy to the struggle and to educate the citizens of the new national community in the virtues of patriotism. One of the main aims of the newly established Ministry of Religion was precisely to employ the Orthodox clergy for civic purposes. The duties of a clergyman, in the words of the president of the executive, entailed leading the flock and teaching it 'its duties towards religion and towards the fatherland'.[66] According to the provisions for the new government of Greece established in 1822, such a minister of religion must 'use all his power to ensure that the holy clergy teaches the people of Greece to respect, subject itself to and love the lawful administration of Greece, upon which their wellbeing depends'.[67] In practical terms this meant that tangible efforts were made to guarantee the presence of preachers in all the provinces of liberated Greece—the eparchies—and by the same token to appoint bishops in charge of the preachers and educators, in order to teach 'the fear of God, the love of one's neighbour, concord, true patriotism and everything that contributes to man's psychological and physical salvation'.[68]

Monastic communities, for their part, had been criticised by protagonists of the Orthodox Enlightenment for their moral turpitude. However, the Greek revolutionaries, by contrast with their Neapolitan, Portuguese

63. Callahan, *Church, Politics, and Society*, pp. 120–21, 124–25; Manuel Revuelta Gonzalez, *Política religiosa de los liberales en el siglo XIX: Trienio Liberal* (Madrid: CSIC—Escuela de Historia Moderna, 1973).

64. Faria, 'A condição', p. 317.

65. See Angelantonio Spagnoletti, *Storia del Regno delle Due Sicilie* (Bologna: Il Mulino, 2008), p. 180; Monti, *Stato e Chiesa*, p. 384.

66. GSA, Ministry of Religion, February–May 1822, first part, A-II-2, doc. 23: the president of the executive to the minister of religion (February 1822 [no exact date])

67. On the duties of the minister of religion, Corinth, 27 February 1822, in *Η εκπαίδευση κατά την Ελληνική Επανάσταση, 1821–27: Τεκμηριωτικά κείμενα* (Education during the Greek Revolution, 1821–27: Sources), ed. David Antoniou, 2 vols (Athens: Hellenic Parliament, 2002), 1, pp. 42–43.

68. The Ministry of Religion to the reverend teacher of Dimitsana Mr. Kallinikon, 22 March 1822, in Antoniou, *Η εκπαίδευση* (Education), 1, pp. 58–59.

and Spanish counterparts, did not seek to undermine the regular clergy financially or legally. Indeed, they sought to gain their support, reckoning that they could serve the same educational purposes as the secular clergy. In the earliest years of the revolution, priests and monks alike were asked to act as teachers or turn their monasteries into schools for children. This happened, for instance, in the eparchy of Athens, where in 1824 the monasteries of Penteli, Petraki, Kaisariani and Vrana were asked to set up two schools.[69] A governmentally imposed commitment on the part of the clergy to educate the faithful in the principles of patriotism was not confined to Greece; but for the revolutionaries it was not sufficient for the clergy to prove their social utility. To achieve this goal they also had to declare their allegiance to the constitution, and give explicit and public support to the government. This could only happen if the church hierarchies declared their loyalty to the new regimes. For this reason, in Portugal, Spain and Naples governments were determined to ensure the Catholic hierarchy's commitment to the constitutional cause, first by requiring all its members to swear an oath of allegiance to the constitution, and second by demanding that they deliver episcopal pastoral addresses and sermons in support of it. Yet while soon after the outbreak of the Greek revolution Orthodox bishops became the foremost champions of the rebellion, in Catholic countries the bishops' attitudes towards the constitution were more complex, and not all of them turned out to be willing to lend their unreserved support.

69. Provisional Administration to the eparchos of Athens, 5 September 1824, in Antoniou, ed., *Η εκπαίδευση* (Education), 1, pp. 265–66.

CHAPTER THIRTEEN

A Revolution within the Church

Begrudging endorsement?
Church hierarchies and the revolutions

The experience of the revolution represented a peculiarly traumatic moment for the Orthodox church, marking a turning point in its history, producing as it did a permanent fracture between the patriarchate and the territories of the newly established Greek state. Although the patriarchate shared with the Holy See hostility towards revolutionary principles, and although both churches condemned in an equally uncompromising way the secret societies, the peculiarity of the Greek insurrection—accounting for the reaction of the patriarchate—is that such a rebellion put a de facto end to the integrity of the Orthodox community as such. Admittedly the patriarch had met up with some members of the Philiki, although the nature of their exchanges and the degree of support offered are unknown. However, he was also quick to condemn unreservedly the insurrection in a number of public documents that circulated across the Otttoman Empire. Soon after Ypsilantis's pronunciamiento, the patriarch issued six encyclicals, reprinted in Greek newspapers, and sent to bishops, which contained a forceful denunciation of the 'apostasy', and an order to all Christians to submit themselves to the 'kingdom that comes from God'.[1] Every one of these documents argued that anybody going against the sultan's rule

---

1. Dimitrios Sofianos, Ἐγκύκλιοι (Αὐγουστος 1821–Ἰανουάριος 1822) του Οἰκουμενικοῦ Πατριάρχη Εὐγενίου ᾿Β περί δουλικὴ υποταγῆς των Ἑλλήνων στον οθωμανό κατακτητή' (Encyclicals [August 1821–January 1822] of the ecumenical patriarch Evgenios II recommending to the Greeks submission to Ottoman rule), Δελτίο του Κέντρου Ερεύνης της Ιστορίας του

was contravening God's rule too. The outbreak of the insurrection had still other consequences for the life of the Church: namely, the condemnation and marginalisation of those sectors within it that had opened up to Enlightenment culture and had entertained contacts with Korais and his circle. As a consequence the Holy Synod that was summoned on 27 March 1821 provided an opportunity for a showdown between the conservative and the more progressive sectors of the Church, and resulted in the condemnation of the teaching of philosophy, and the closing down of all Greek schools in the eastern Aegean (Smyrna, Kydonies, Chios), and also the schools of Constantinople and Patmos, and the departure of their teachers.[2] These acts, however, were not sufficient to secure the patriarch's protection and demonstrate his innocence. The sultan decided that, since the ultimate responsibility for the loyalty of his Christian subjects and for their submission to his authority lay with the patriarch, this latter deserved to be punished. Although the initial acts of retaliation against the Greek elites in Constantinople targeted Phanariot notables and merchants, the escalation of violence affected also a number of bishops first, seven of whom were imprisoned, and culminated in the execution of the patriarch at the end of the Holy Week, on 10 April 1821, when Grigorios V was hanged outside the patriarchate compound. Soon after, a number of other clerics were executed, including high-ranking individuals such as the bishop of Ephesus, and several religious houses and churches in the capital of the empire were attacked and looted by Muslim students.[3]

While the patriarch and the bishops based in Constantinople may not have been responsible for the uprising in the Peloponnese, it is true that the revolutionary leadership of the Peloponnese included a number of prominent bishops, and that most of them had been involved in the early stages of the planning of the uprising. Prominent among them was Germanos, bishop of Patras since 1806 and a leading Etairist (member of the revolutionary secret society). In March 1821 the decision of the Turkish governor of Tripolitsa to summon the bishops and the primates of the Peloponnese to discuss Ali Pasha's revolt precipitated events, and encouraged the insurgents to declare the revolution. While the eight bishops who

---

Νεότερου Ελληνισμού [Deltio tou Kentrou Erevnis tis Istorias tou Neoterou Ellinismou] 2 (2000): 19–43.

2. Kostas Lappas, 'Πατριαρχική σύνοδος περί "Καθαιρέσεως των φιλοσοφικών μαθημάτων" το Μάρτιο του 1821: Μια μαρτυρία του Κωνσταντίνου Οικονόμου' (Patriarchal synod on 'The deposition of the philosophical courses' in March 1821: A testimony by Konstantinos Oikonomou), Μνήμων [Mnimon] 11 (1987): 123–53.

3. For the unfolding of events, see Philliou, Biography, pp. 71–74.

FIGURE 24. *The Bishop of Old Patras Germanos Blesses the Flag of Revolution* at the monastery of Agia Lavra, near Kalvryta in the Peloponnese, March 1821 (oil painting by Theodoros Vryzakis, 1865, The National Gallery of Greece, Athens). Image: Wikimedia Commons

had agreed to go to Tripolitsa were arrested, and five of them lost their lives during their imprisonment, the others assumed the leadership of the insurrection. According to later recollections, in an episode now questioned by historians as a fabrication, Germanos inaugurated the revolt by raising the banner with a cross above the monastery of Agia Lavra.[4]

In the following months and years, bishops took on both military and civil responsibilities, leading troops on the battlefield, joining legislative assemblies and assuming various responsibilities as government ministers. Outside the Peloponnese, however, at least at first, some bishops remained resolutely hostile to the rebellion, and dutifully published and

4. Frazee, *Orthodox Church*, pp. 18–21; on the mythical nature of this event see Mazower, *The Greek Revolution*, pp. 64–65.

disseminated the patriarch's official denunciation of the insurgency. In July 1821 in Cyprus, Archbishop Kyprianos had thus publicly endorsed the imperial decree ordering the disarming of his own religious community, which had been peaceful until then. His compliance with imperial orders did not however prevent him and the three other bishops on the island from being executed by the Ottoman authorities.[5] This indiscriminate killing of so many high-ranking clerics, and that of the patriarch above all, rather than persuading the rebels to submit themselves to the Ottoman authorities, and the clergy to abide by the patriarchate's instructions, pushed them further towards revolt. Among the rumours that soon spread across the Peloponnese and the islands about the events in Constantinople, it was precisely the news that the Ottomans were indiscriminately persecuting the Orthodox priesthood by imprisoning its members that loomed largest in the popular imagination.[6] In the years that followed, public condemnations of the insurrections continued, with patriarchal letters being read in all churches, without however achieving any results. They were reiterated by the successor of Grigorios V, Evgenios, in 1821 and 1822, and after him by Patriarch Agathangelos I in 1828, deploying a similar language, and with threats of excommunication for those rebels in the Aegean and the Peloponnese who would not resubmit themselves to the Ottoman authorities.[7] In response to Evgenios's letter to the revolutionaries, in 1821 a written response was signed and submitted by twenty-eight bishops and more than a thousand priests refusing to comply, and declaring their support for the independence of their country.[8]

Unlike the Orthodox patriarchate, the Holy See decided to adopt a more cautious stance towards the events happening in the Catholic countries. While the papal government offered its protection to those Greek refugees who had crossed the Adriatic, it refused to speak out in favour of the revolutionaries. When in 1822 the Greek revolutionaries sent the bishop of Patras, Germanos, as special envoy to the Holy See, to ask for the pope's support for their cause, and to call for a possible reunion of the Greek and Catholic churches, the papacy declared that it would remain strictly neutral. This was due to pressure from the European powers gathering at the Congress of Verona, and from fear of possible acts of retaliation affecting

5. Michalis N. Michael, 'The Loss of an Ottoman Traditional Order and the Reactions to a Changing Ottoman World: A New Interpretation of the 1821 Events in Cyprus', *International Review of Turkish Studies* 3 (2013): 8–36.

6. Kasomoulis, *Ενθυμήματα στρατιωτικά* (Military memoirs), 1, p. 134.

7. Lappas, 'Πατριαρχική σύνοδος' (Patriarchal synod), pp. 27–38.

8. Frazee, *Orthodox Church*, p. 35.

the Catholic minorities living in the Ottoman Empire.[9] The papal government's attitude towards Portuguese, Spanish and Neapolitan events was somewhat different, however. It did not criticise the revolutions as such, nor the newly established governments, but confined its political intervention to a public reiteration of the older, earlier condemnations of secret societies. As a consequence, in Spain the papal nuncio Giacomo Giustiniani convinced reluctant bishops to adhere to the new government and not give voice to unnecessary opposition and thereby threaten in other respects the interests of the Church. This policy was consistent with the broader stance adopted by the Holy See at the time, of remaining independent with regard to the Holy Alliance in all matters of foreign policy.[10] The Holy See's position, however, did not prevent individual bishops from reacting according to their own judgement or instinct, especially in the early stages of the revolution. In Cádiz, for instance, the bishop was quick to address his flock, warning them against the rule of the military rebellion, which he likened to an act of sacrilege overturning the oath of loyalty to the monarch, whose authority derived directly from God. His public denunciations led to many angry responses from the liberals, and even had an international echo.[11]

In Catholic countries, the importance that the revolutionaries attached to the bishops` attitudes towards the new governments and the constitution owed much to the impact that their public endorsement or condemnation had on the attitudes of both the lower clergy and the faithful towards the new governments. Indeed, they expected bishops to issue pastoral letters in support of the constitution that would be read out by priests in all the churches. Such requests to bishops were by no means a new practice, but belonged to an ancien-régime tradition, renewed in revolutionary times, that employed church hierarchies to instruct subjects regarding the political behaviour they were expected to adopt. This was the most effective tool of propaganda available to ensure that the entire population would rally to the new political order. Therefore the fact that the primate of the Spanish Catholic church, Cardinal Luis de Borbón,

9. Ibid., pp. 52–58.

10. Carlos María Rodríguez López-Brea, 'La Santa Sede y los movimientos revolucionarios europeos de 1820: Los casos napolitano y español', *Ayer* 45 (2002): 251–74.

11. See Francisco Xavier Cienfuegos y Jovellanos, 'Exhortacion del Señor Obispo de Cádiz al estallar la rebellion en la isla', 9 January 1820, in *Colección eclesiástica española*, 14 vols (Madrid: Imprenta de E. Aguado, 1823–24), 3, pp. 30–41. Among the responses, see Antonio Quiroga, *Ejército nacional: Al ilustrísimo señor Obispo de Cádiz* (México: Oficina de D. Alejandro Valdés, 1820). The bishop's condemnation was reported and criticised by the Neapolitan newspaper *La Voce del Secolo*, 15 August 1820, pp. 29–30.

archbishop of Toledo, was prepared to endorse the new regime, and even became a leading proponent of a moderate interpretation of constitutional liberalism, did much to bolster the revolution. His adherence to the newly established political order was in line with his earlier endorsement of the constitutional government during the French invasion that had led to the proclamation of the 1812 constitution. Notwithstanding the resistance of other prominent members of the Church to the request that they swear a compulsory oath of loyalty, in 1810 Borbón had recognised the authority of the Cortes elected in Cádiz in a public ceremony, thus implicitly recognising the sovereignty of the nation. He was therefore appointed a member of the Council of State. His willingness to agree to the clerical reforms of the Cortes, including the abolition of the Holy Inquisition, and to enforce discipline among those clerics who refused to comply with the orders of the government, earned him the trust of the revolutionaries and his appointment to the regency, representing the vacant monarchical authority, in 1813. In 1820 the cardinal, who was also an uncle of the king, once again found himself the head of the provisional junta (Junta Provisional Consultiva) set up with a view to the implementation of the Cádiz Constitution. His prominent role in the Church and his family connections made him the ideal figure to guarantee the transition from autocracy to constitutional government.[12] The cardinal's pastoral in support of the constitution circulated widely beyond his own diocese of Toledo: it was adopted also by other Spanish bishops and reprinted in Naples. Here the revolutionary provisional government that was following closely the activities of its Spanish counterpart recommended that the Neapolitan bishops take it as a model for their own pastorals to the clergy and congregations in support of the new regime. The Neapolitan liberal press paid a great deal of attention to it, and it was published in several newspapers.[13] In this document, Luis de Borbón highlighted the importance of the king's oath to the constitution, emphasised that respecting the new laws was in compliance with an evangelical principle, and that by recognising the Catholic faith as its foundation, the constitution gained legitimacy. For the cardinal, therefore, religion and patriotism bound the Spanish people to the constitution. Although he stressed how, by the constitution, citizens were now called to contribute, albeit indirectly, to the legislative process through elections, for the cardinal respect for the law represented the

12. On this figure, see Rodríguez López-Brea, *Don Luis de Borbón*.

13. For its circulation, see ibid., p. 286. For the echoes of the document in Naples, see Alberti, *Atti del parlamento*, 4, pp. 5–6. The Pastoral appeared also in the Neapolitan *L'Amico della Costituzione*, 31 July 1820, pp. 2–3.

essence of liberty.[14] He was sincerely convinced that the interests of the Church and of religion could be guaranteed under the constitution, and that bishops were obliged to obey the civil power. As chair of the Junta, the cardinal supported the abolition of the Holy Inquisition, and did not oppose the decrees for the secularisation of the regular clergy. It was only after July 1822, when radicalisation of the conflict between exaltados and moderados led to popular protests and to increased political interference in the life of the Church that the cardinal became critical of the regime, and started defending the autonomy of the Church from the government.[15] Besides the initial resistance of the bishop of Cádiz, moreover, in Spain overt critiques of the constitution came from only two of his peers, namely Veremundo Arias Teixeiro, bishop of Valencia, and Simón López y Cañedo, bishop of Orihuela. They for their part refused publicly to endorse the new regime, or to instruct all priests under their authority to teach citizens the key aspects of the constitution. For their refusal to abide by the government's requests, these two bishops were eventually expelled from the country.[16] Teixeiro's pastoral reaffirmed the traditional theological beliefs of the Church. As far as he was concerned, parish priests' commitment to explaining in detail the contents of the constitution could only be at the expense of their primary duty, that of instructing believers in the principles of the Holy Scriptures. Thus he asked his priests to confine their discussion of the constitution to those aspects that were in line with Catholic doctrine and the Gospels. For him, the new constitution was a valid document only insofar as it confirmed Catholic morality. Therefore in the constitution, as in the Gospels, the notions of freedom and equality did not entail 'libertinage, licence, insubordination, and disorder', but rather required 'subordination to authorities'. In the bishop's view the most striking abuse of freedom was perhaps the exploitation of freedom of the press to threaten and subvert the laws of God. Priests were obligedto remind their flocks, he said, that the constitution's main goal was that of protecting and defending religion.[17] Bishop López of Orihuela argued likewise, that entrusting priests with the task of explaining the constitution would pose a fundamental threat to their primary duties, and

---

14. 'Luis de Borbon por la Divina Misericordia Presbítero Cardenal de la santa Iglesia Romana, del Título de Santa María de Scapa, Arzobispo de Toledo [. . .]', pastoral letter, 15 March 1820 (Madrid: Imprenta de la Compañía, 1820), pp. 4–5.

15. Rodríguez López-Brea, *Don Luis de Borbón*, pp. 354–66.

16. Ibid., p. 295.

17. 'Pastoral del Señor Arzobispo de Valencia sobre el único y major modo de explicar los párrocos la constitución', in *Colección eclesiástica española*, 3, pp. 126–33, quotations at 133, 135.

constitute an abuse of the division between religious and political spheres. He exhorted the priests in his charge to warn against 'false promises of happiness, liberty and equality', as 'true liberty is to live free of sins, and not be a slave to passions'.[18]

Unlike the archbishop of Toledo, the leader of the Portuguese church, along with another two bishops, decided not to adhere to the governmental request to endorse the constitution publicly by means of a formal oath of allegiance to *Bases da constituição*. The patriarch (that is, the archbishop of Lisbon) accepted only two articles of the document: that regarding the introduction of ecclesiastical censorship for religious matters, and that proposing to grant Catholicism the status of state religion without toleration for any other cult. Given the importance attached by the provisional governments to official endorsement by the Church hierarchy, it is not surprising that this attitude was punished by the expulsion of the patriarch, who eventually left Portugal, in May 1821. As noted above, only two other bishops refused to accept the constitution in full: Dom Vasco José Lobo, bishop of Olba, who raised objections to many of its articles, and Manuel Nicolau de Almeida, bishop of Angra, who supported the resistance to, and reaction against, the recognition of the liberal regime on the island of Terceira in the Azores, and refused to comply with the requests of the new administration reinstalled there in May 1821.[19] The most enthusiastic endorsement of the new constitution in Portugal came from the bishop of Porto, Dom João de Magalhães, who stressed the need for a Christian to be a good citizen and respect civil authority, and therefore instructed parish priests to call for subordination to the new Cortes, and from Dom José Valério da Cruz, bishop of Portalegre, who declared that the constitution would bring signal benefits to the country, including material improvements.

Notwithstanding the striking divergence between the views held and the decisions taken by the leaders of the Spanish and Portuguese churches, and between the patriarch of Lisbon and the bishops of Porto and Portalegre, the most common attitude among Catholic bishops, from Portugal to Naples, was that of a reluctant acquiescence. This stance was dictated by prudence, and by the need to avoid hostility towards the Church, whose best interests thus lay in lending its support, albeit in a muted fashion, to

18. 'Carta de despedida del Obispo de Orihuela a los curas, clerio y demas diocesanos suyos', Santa Pola, 12 August 1820, in ibid., pp. 153–62, quotation at 61.

19. Ana Mouta Faria, *Os liberais na estrada de Damasco: Clero, igreja e religião numa conjuntura revolucionária (1820–1823)* (Lisbon: Fundação Calouste Gulbenkian, 2006), pp. 96–104.

the authorities. After all, the constitutions gave guarantees with regard to the recognition of of state religions, although at the same time advancing a number of other, more disquieting, principles or policies.[20] In Portugal, the firm reaction by the revolutionaries to the patriarch of Lisbon's open refusal to acknowledge the new regime surely persuaded even those bishops most hostile to the constitution to adopt a prudent approach and comply with governmental guidelines. Yet alignment need not entail full or enthusiastic endorsement; indeed, quite the contrary. While the tone of many of the bishops' pastorals may demonstrate their commitment to supporting established authority, this did not necessarily involve explicit acceptance or approval of the constitution and the new principles it enshrined. Rather than celebrating the constitution, some simply stressed the need to accept the changes brought about by history. This general alignment with the regime, would seem however to have been eroded by the end of the Triénio. When the government asked bishops to issue pastorals condemning the Count of Amarante's rebellion in 1823, fewer of them than in 1820 complied with the official request.[21]

The ambiguity of the Neapolitan hierarchy towards the constitutional order is clearly reflected in the words chosen by the bishops in their pastorals. Only a small minority (the bishop of Pozzuoli and the archbishop of Salerno) explicitly and unreservedly lent their support to the constitution.[22] Otherwise loyalty to the monarch, and relief that the constitution was first and foremost a Catholic document, are what emerge primarily in the stance taken by the majority. Michele Spinelli, archbishop of Sorrento, described the revolution in anodyne language, presenting the recent political changes as the inscrutable result of divine providence. While the archbishop noted the lack of violence or war in the transition to the new order, he emphasised the need for all to follow the principles of Catholicism on the one hand, and on the other a bounden duty to comply with the law and to be subject to authority as the key to 'temporal political happiness'. Finally, he asked his flock to support the throne against anarchy and libertinism, and to manifest their attachment to the constitutional government, to the nation, to the king and to all the royal family.[23]

20. Manuel Teruel Gregorio de Tejada, *Obispos liberales: La utopía de un proyecto, 1820–1823* (Lleida: Milenio, 1996).

21. Ana Mouta Faria, 'A hierarquia episcopal e o vintismo', *Análise Social* 27, nos 116–17 (1992): 285–328.

22. Daum, *Oscillazioni*, pp. 443–44.

23. SNSP, Miscellanea 1820: 'Michele Spinelli arcivescovo di Sorrento al clero e al popolo della diocesi di Sorrento', Sorrento, 15 August 1820.

What enabled most Catholic bishops to lend their support to the new order, in spite of their ideological hostility to many aspects of constitutional government, was therefore their loyalty to the crown and to monarchical rule more generally. As most pastorals demonstrated, support for the constitutions often boiled down to an exhortation to all believers to renew their loyalty to the monarch under the new dispensation. In Piedmont likewise, a majority of bishops unenthusiastically lent their support to the revolutionary order for the sake of their loyalty to the monarch. Strikingly, the pastoral of the bishop of Mondoví, Giovanni Battista Pio Vitale, for instance, only recommended obedience to the king, asking parish priests to pray for the sovereign and preach concord and unity among the faithful, while publishing in small print, at the end of the document, the letter from the government requesting support for the constitution, which was otherwise not even mentioned.[24] In Piedmont too, however, there were exceptions to this cautious attitude. The bishop of Aosta openly refused to comply with the request to explain the constitution, arguing that he could not possibly give instructions regarding a document whose content he did not know himself.[25] At the other end of the spectrum stood the bishop of Asti, Antonio Faá, Count of Carentino, whose pastoral letter enthusiastically endorsed the constitution—so much so that after the revolution he was harshly reprimanded by the authorities for this unequivocal offer of support. Inviting all priests to instruct their parishioners about the new order, the bishop claimed in his pastoral that the Spanish constitution should be welcomed because, rather than having been imposed by a foreign army, it corresponded to the wishes and expectations of the entire country. He likened the establishment of a new government in Piedmont to the seizure of the city of Jericho by the Israelites, ignored for six days as they marched around the city, but whose 'acclamation' succeeded on the seventh in bringing down its walls. The comparison with this biblical example seemed to suggest that the triumphant march of the people that had led to the introduction of the constitution could itself no longer be ignored.[26]

24. AST, Segreteria di Stato Affari Interni, Alta Polizia, 26: pastoral letter, 6 March 1821. The government's request to the bishops to support the constitution in their pastoral letters, dated 16 March 1821 is in AST, Materie Politiche per Rapporto all'Interno, 10, f. 27.

25. AST, Segreteria di Stato Affari Interni, Alta Polizia, 26: Jean-Baptiste-Marie Aubriot de la Palme, bishop of Aosta, to the Ministry of Interior, 19 March 1821.

26. The pastoral, dated 19 March 1821, was published in *La Sentinella Subalpina*, no. 10, 6 April 1821, p. 50. See also Niccola Gabiani, *Il vescovo d'Asti ed i moti del 1821* (Asti: Paglieri e Raspi, 1921).

In Sicily, the peculiar nature of the Church as an institution dependent on royal patronage accounts for the conduct of most of its bishops, who in fact supported Palermo's quest for independence. According to the institutional framework provided by the 'Apostolica legazia', the king of Sicily replaced the pope in the management of the island's church affairs. This set-up created a direct and strong link between the Sicilian monarchy and the island's dioceses, whose bishops were jealous of their prerogatives. Thus during the revolution most of them sided with the rest of the elites of the island they belonged to.[27] During the first phase in Palermo, the provisional government was chaired by the archbishop, Cardinal Gravina. This example was replicated elsewhere across the island: in Piazza Armerina the bishop presided over the provisional council; in Mazzara del Vallo and in Monreale the archbishops Monsignors Emmanuele Custo and Domenico Balsamo were elected to the same role by their respective cities. The archbishop of Lipari, capital of the Aeolian islands, Monsignor Carlo Maria Lenzi, left his bishopric and moved to Palermo to give his full support to the new government, and was later temporarily arrested on that account by the Neapolitan authorities.[28] In western Sicily, it was only Monsignor Giovanni Sergio, bishop of Cefalù, who rejected the island's declaration of independence. In retaliation for his public plea to the faithful to remain loyal to the king, a small army organised in Palermo marched towards Cefalù, occupied the town, and escorted the bishop back to the capital where he was temporarily held in captivity.[29] Thus out of all the Catholic countries undergoing a revolution, in Sicily alone did a majority of the ecclesiastical hierarchy support a move for political autonomy in the same way as the Orthodox bishops did in the territories of the Greek rebellion. Unlike their Orthodox counterparts across the sea, however, Sicilian bishops were equally happy for the revolution to come to an end, as long as an accommodation between the government in Naples and the island's elites could be arrived at that would acknowledge the traditional privileges of the latter.

In some cases, admittedly, the public attitudes of individual bishops directly affected clerical and popular responses towards the revolution and

27. Angelo Gambasin, *Religiosa magnificenza e plebe in Sicilia nel XIX secolo* (Rome: Edizioni di Storia e Letteratura, 1979), pp. 43–69.

28. See ASP, Real Segreteria, Incartamenti, 5034: letters from Monreale, 2 August 1820, from Mazzara del Vallo, 16 August 1820 and from Piazza Armerina, 17 August 1820, all three to the provisional government. On Monsignor Lenzi, see *Giornale Costituzionale del Regno delle Due Sicilie*, no. 59, 14 September 1820, p. 242.

29. Sansone, *La rivoluzione*, pp. 99–100. See also Monsignor Sergio's defence, dated 25 August 1820, in ASP, Real Segreteria, Incartamenti, 5033, no. 129.

the constitution, either stirring up resistance, or encouraging obedience. However, a remarkable feature of these revolutions was that the attitudes of the lower clergy to the new political context was often independent from that of their hierarchy. As the next section goes on to demonstrate, in Greece the war pushed all members of the Orthodox church, from bishops to priests, towards insurrection; but elsewhere the revolution created new fractures and revived old divisions between those priests and monks who enthusiastically supported the new regime, and those who remained resolutely hostile to it.

A divided clergy

Between 1820 and 1822 the cathedral of Málaga, a coastal city in Spanish Andalusia, was the scene of a number of acts of violence and intimidation. Here the chapter of the cathedral and its bishop, Alonso Cañedo, were openly hostile to the constitution. Tensions between the city administration, supported by the constitutional minority of the local clergy, and the bishop and the cathedral's canons first emerged with regard to the reinstatement in the chapter of Canon Francisco Xavier Asenjo. Asenjo was a man of the Enlightenment and an old supporter of French rule in Spain, a so-called *afrancesado*. Appointed in 1810 as temporary administrator (governor) of the diocese of Málaga by the French army, he left with it and lived in exile in France until 1820, when he asked to be reinstalled in his post. The hostility of the chapter's members to his request was overcome only thanks to the pressure of a judge, and as a result of a number of popular demonstrations around the cathedral in support of Asenjo. A more dramatic confrontation, however, took place in 1822. In that year the absolutist bishop, accused of plotting against the revolution, was expelled from the city, and a conflict broke out over the election of a temporary governor to administer the diocese until a new bishop could be selected. The city council, the civil militia and part of the urban population favoured the appointment of Don Pedro Muñoz Arroyo, author of sermons in support of the constitution, vice-president of the local patriotic society, the Confederación Patriótica, and elected to the national Cortes as a deputy in 1820. On the day of the election of the new governor, a crowd invaded the cathedral demanding that the chapter appoint Arroyo. When the canons tried to postpone their decision and leave the building, they were forced back in by a group of people brandishing bayonets, until the protestors' favoured candidate was finally elected. This was only one of the many acts of violence involving crowds, often mobilised by local radical exaltado politicians and by the patriotic societies, against the majority of the canons of the cathedral chapter notorious for being enemies of the revolution.[30]

These events were not unique to the city of Málaga. During the revolutions, members of city councils, governmental representatives and local populations all became involved in clerical appointments. The decisions of church chapters thus became increasingly politicised, and divisions between their members mirrored the political factions that existed in most cities.[31] The ideological fissures caused by the revolution affected the clergy at a local level, and led to conflicts between clerics themselves. Such conflicts varied from village to village, from region to region and from country to country, but occurred more or less throughout southern Europe. Churches were complex organisations whose institutions and members belonged to all social backgrounds. They included members of the aristocracy, learned men and also poor and semi-literate rural priests and members of mendicant orders living off alms. The differing political views of clerics sometimes mirrored social differences outside the Church. Sometimes they simply divided members of the same communities 'horizontally', producing disagreements between peers within individual parishes, bishoprics or cities. The following pages will be devoted to exploring the role played by the secular and the regular clergy in the revolutions, whether in favour of or against. As I hope to demonstrate, important minorities within each clerical category supported the revolution. Many of their members played a key role in political and military mobilisation either for or against the constitution, conferring moral authority upon both revolution and counterrevolution.

The case of Málaga also suggests that the origins of these ideological divisions often pre-dated the revolution, although the revolution may well have revived or exacerbated them. They went back to the late eighteenth century, when supporters of the Enlightenment or of French ideas were pitted against the absolutist clergy, and were further heightened by the impact of the Napoleonic military expansion across southern Europe. In the territories it occupied, the French army and administration waged a

30. On these events, see Luisa Conejero López, 'El clero de Málaga en el Trienio Liberal', *Baetica: Estudios de Arte, Geografía e Historia* 2, no. 2 (1979): 277–93.

31. On similar conflicts arising from the appointment of members of cathedral chapters, see Jesús Millán y García-Varela, 'Autoritat, opinió i mobilització a l'Oriola del Trienni: Una aproximació als significats del liberalisme', *Pasado y Memoria: Revista de Historia Contemporanea* 10 (2011): 219–41. On similar events in Bragança, a city in northern Portugal in the region of Trás-os-Montes, see Cardoso, *A revolução liberal*, p. 91.

war against the Church, requisitioning its lands and closing down monasteries, condemning the perceivedly superstitious nature of Catholicism
and its practices. As a result, the French occupation consolidated a vis-
cerally anti-revolutionary front among priests, who actively contributed
to the *insorgenze*, the popular uprisings of 1799 against the Neapolitan
republic, and that of 1809 against the French regime in Calabria. When
the Prince of Canosa set up the anti-revolutionary secret society of the
Calderari in defence of the restoration of 1816, its ranks were filled with
priests.[32] At the same time many of the Neapolitan priests singled out by
the police after 1821 as liberals had started their political apprenticeship in
1799 as supporters of the Neapolitan revolution, and had viewed the events
of 1820–21 as a vindication of their earlier support for the French revolution and the republican experiment.[33] During the Napoleonic occupation
of the Italian peninsula, some clerics had joined the freemasons first, and
many more joined the Carboneria likewise soon after its establishment,
consolidating the presence of a national and constitutional opposition
across the territory of the Napoleonic Kingdom of Naples. Although we do
not know when the two carbonaro priests of Nicosia engaged in the conflicts discussed in the introduction to Part IV above had joined the ranks
of the secret society, many of their peers had already lent their support to
conspiracies in favour of a constitution before 1820 in various provinces
of the kingdom.[34]

The Napoleonic invasion was similarly divisive among priests in Portugal and Spain. After 1808 many of them had preached in churches
against the invading army, and helped turn the anti-French insurrection
into a religious crusade. While members of the lower clergy participated
in the guerrilla war fighting in the partidas and even leading them, bishops and priors joined the juntas along with members of the army to give
political direction to the insurrection.[35] Although the majority of those
involved in the war against Napoleon did so in the name of religion and

32. Davis, '1799: The Santafede'; Michael Broers, *The Politics of Religion in Napoleonic
Italy: The War against God, 1801–1814* (London: Routledge, 2002). On the priest in the
society of the Calderari, see Di Mauro, 'Le Secret et Polichinelle', p. 366.

33. ASN, Borbone, 726, f. 14; Pierroberto Scaramella, *Il cittadino ecclesiastico: Il clero
nella repubblica napoletana del 1799* (Naples: Vivarium, 2000).

34. Pierre-Marie Delpu, 'Patriotisme libéral et nation catholique: Les Prêtres libéraux
dans la révolution napolitaine de 1820–1821', *Studi Storici* 58 (2017): 545–71; Di Mauro,
'Le Secret et Polichinelle'.

35. On Portugal, see Ana Cristina Araújo, 'Revoltas e ideologias em conflito durante
as invasões francesas', *Revista de História das Ideias* 7 (1985): 7–75; Marques, 'O clero
nortenho'.

the absolute monarchy, in Spain in particular a minority of priests, canons and even bishops genuinely supported the constitutional experiment which emerged out of the defence of the monarchy in the absence of the monarch. The committee for ecclesiastical affairs of the Junta Central, established after 1808 in absence of the king, was filled with clerics who favoured the abolition of monastic communities, the sale of church land and a more austere religiosity.[36] In the Spanish territories under French jurisdiction, the clergy was forced to cooperate with the new regime, and most did so grudgingly. However a minority, larger especially among the members of cathedral chapters, supported it enthusiastically, recognising in the French administration those Enlightenment principles they had already embraced before the invasion. Canon Asenjo, whose return to Málaga in 1820 met with so much resistance, was one of 252 clerics who had gone into exile to France at the time of the French occupation of Spain.[37]

This convergence between sectors of the Church and the constitutional regimes in 1820–21 was in fact facilitated by movements for reform within national churches that had been under way since the eighteenth century. These movements all aimed to reconcile faith with reason and progress, and to purify religious worship.[38] The convergence identified here also owed much to the fact that, in both the Catholic and Orthodox worlds, leading intellectuals of the Enlightenment belonged to the Church, and considered their intellectual agenda to be compatible with their religious beliefs and their vision of a reformed church. The impact of these ideas could be felt both at the local and at the national level. In the city of Catania and in Sicily in general, for instance, an inclination to welcome new

36. Carlos María Rodríguez López-Brea, 'La Iglesia española y la Guerra de la Independencia: Desmontando algunos tópicos', *Historia Contemporánea* 35 (2007): 743–63; Emilio La Parra López, *El primer liberalismo español y la Iglesia:. Las Cortes de Cádiz* (Alicante: Instituto de Cultura Juan Gil-Albert, 1985), pp. 69–72.

37. Maximiliano Barrio Gozalo, 'Los eclesiásticos afrancesados durante la Guerra de la Independencia', in *Las élites y la revolución de España (1808-1814): Estudios en homenaje al profesor Gérard Dufour*, ed. Armando Alberola and Isabel Larriba (Alicante: Publicaciones de la Universidad de Alicante, 2010), pp. 227–56; Gérard Dufour, 'La emigración a Francia del clero afrancesado', in Dufour, José A. Ferrer Benimeli, Leandro Higueruela del Pino and Emilio La Parra López, *El clero afrancesado: Actas de la Mesa Redonda, Aix-en-Provence, 25 de enero de 1985* (Aix-en-Provence: Université de Provence, 1986), pp. 163–206.

38. On these reform movements and their legacies, see Helena Rosenblatt, 'The Christian Enlightenment', in *The Cambridge History of Christianity*, vol. 7: *Enlightenment, Reawakening and Revolution, 1660-1815*, ed. Stewart J. Brown and Timothy Tacket (Cambridge: Cambridge University Press, 2006), pp. 283–301; Mario Rosa, ed., *Cattolicesimo e lumi nel Settecento italiano* (Rome: Herder, 1981); Callahan, *Church, Politics, and Society*.

political ideas in the ranks of both the regular and secular clergy may have owed something to the reformist agenda imposed by the powerful figure of the archbishop of Catania, Salvatore Ventimiglia, chancellor of the local university in the 1760s, and by his circle. His reformist policies shaped the local seminary and revived the university library, opening it up to scientific knowledge and the brilliant culture of the Neapolitan Enlightenment. While Ventimiglia lost his battle against the elites who controlled the local religious institutions, and had to leave the city in 1773, his cultural legacy endured.[39] Twelve members of the chapter of the cathedral, rumoured to have been members of secret societies, were condemned for having spoken in favour of the constitution during mass in 1820.[40] Some priests justified their support first for the 1799 republican experiment in Naples and subsequently for the constitution of 1820 in terms of the ideas of the Neapolitan Enlightenment. Other, more moderate, Neapolitan clerics who had rejected the 1799 republic as a radical French import, however, favoured the 1820 constitutional regime precisely because they considered it to be in tune with the reformist values of their own intellectual tradition. Prominent among these was Luigi Galanti, the Benedictine monk who authored the widely circulated *Catechismo costituzionale per uso del regno unito delle Sicilie*, and was a member of the parliament in 1820. Galanti had been a pupil of the philosopher Antonio Genovesi. He had dismissed the republican values of the French revolution for mistakenly entrusting the people with full powers, and had been hostile to the Neapolitan revolution of 1799. In 1820, however, he welcomed the Cádiz Constitution as a monarchical and moderate document. For him, the institutions introduced by the new constitution owed much also to philosophers such as 'Giannone, who first attacked priestly despotism, Genovesi, who instructed the nation in the true philosophy and in political economy, Filangieri, who spread the good principles on legislation [and] Giuseppe M. Galanti, who [...] unmasked the vices of our government'.[41]

The movement within the Catholic church that most often offered resources to support political reform, in conjunction with ecclesiastical reform, was Jansenism, whose influence across Catholic countries was widespread in the last decades of the eighteenth century (thanks to the circulation of Jansenist catechisms, and the influence of the

39. Lina Scalisi and Arianna Rotondo, 'La città del buongoverno', in *Catania: La grande Catania; La nobiltà virtuosa, la borghesia operosa*, ed. Enrico Iachello (Catania: Sanfilippo Editore, 2010), pp. 13–30.

40. ASC, Intendenza Borbonica, XVII, 3454.

41. Narciso, 'Illuminismo', pp. 49–50. See Galanti's *Catechismo*, p. 15.

Jansenist-leaning Synod of Pistoia's declarations among higher and lower clergy). Admittedly, a transition from Jansenist ideals to support for revolution and constitutions was not a foregone conclusion. Individual members of the movement reacted in different ways in the face of the political upheavals of the end of the eighteenth century and events in France.[42] However, what created potential links between this movement and revolutionary events was not so much its theology, as Jansenist nostalgia for the primitive Church as a poor community whose spirit was closer to the actual teaching of the Gospels. In Spain, this reformist movement flourished at the intersection between the aspirations of the monarchy to strengthen its power at the expense of the Church, and the agenda set by the Jansenist movement, in particular after the influential Synod of Pistoia of 1786. Priests who had been influenced by Jansenism as theology students at the University of Salamanca in the 1790s supported the Cádiz Constitution in 1812, and also promoted an agenda of church reform based on the proposals approved at Pistoia. In 1820 these legacies were still alive. Between 1820 and 1823 several such priests served as deputies in the liberal Cortes, where fifty-four of their number were elected and voted in favour of the suppression of monastic communities and the abolition of church privileges.[43]

An outstanding example of such intellectual trajectories bridging Catholic Enlightenment, reformism and the liberalism of the Trienio is represented by the figure of Joaquín Lorenzo Villanueva (1757–1837). Villanueva was one of the reformist clergy belonging to the circle of the philo-Jansenist Felipe Bertrán of Salamanca. He had joined the Holy Inquisition in 1783, along with those clerics who supported the regalist policies of the Spanish monarchy, argued in favour of more sober forms of worship, was open to cultural innovation and the reading of the Bible in vernacular and was sincerely hopeful that the absolute monarchy would drive political reforms. But elected to the Cortes of Cádiz in 1810, he moved from his earlier reformist and enlightened positions to moderate liberalism. He considered the new constitution discussed and approved there as representing the restoration of Spain's ancient laws rather than being a

42. Dale K. Van Kley, 'From the Catholic Enlightenment to the Risorgimento: The Exchange between Nicola Spedalieri and Pietro Tamburini, 1791–1797', *Past and Present* 222 (2014): 109–62. On the influence of Jansenism across southern Europe, see Ulrich L. Lehner and Michael Printy, eds, *A Companion to the Catholic Enlightenment in Europe* (Leiden: Brill, 2010); Cândido dos Santos, *Jansenismo e antijansenismo nos finais do Antigo Regime* (Porto: CITCEM, 2011).

43. Juan Marichal, 'From Pistoia to Cádiz: A Generation's Itinerary, 1786–1812', in *The Ibero-American Enlightenment*, ed. Alfred Owen Aldridge (Urbana, IL: University of Illinois Press, 1971), pp. 97–110; Callahan, *Church, Politics, and Society*, p. 120.

radical break from the past, and viewed it as a document fully compatible with Catholic principles, in line with the principles of Thomist doctrine. Among his other concerns stood the reform of the Church itself, according to the agenda set decades earlier by the Synod of Pistoia and discussed also in Spain since the 1790s. It was on this subject that he made his greatest contribution to the reform agenda of the Trienio, when he returned to Spain after an exile imposed on him by the monarchy. After his election to the Cortes in 1820, Villanueva was among the priests appointed to a special committee who drafted a series of proposals aimed at giving dignity to the pastoral care of the Church, which included the improvement of the living conditions of parish priests, the reorganisation of parishes according to population size and a reduction in benefices not associated with pastoral work.[44]

Enlightenment ideals, as well as the impact of the French revolution, had an equally important role in creating faultlines within the Orthodox church in the decades preceding the revolution. At one level, it is safe to say that a smaller percentage of the Orthodox than of the Catholic clergy had unequivocally embraced Enlightenment ideals before 1820, especially if we consider ordinary priests. At the same time, however, what makes the case of the relationship between the Orthodox church and the Enlightenment remarkable is precisely the fact that most figures of Enlightenment in the Ottoman Empire were clerics. Thinkers such as Evgenios Voulgaris (1716–1806) did not see any incompatibility between their own faith and philosophical enquiry, although they considered the latter as independent from the divine order. His friend Nikiforos Theotokis (1731–1800), who like Voulgaris also became a bishop, was drawn to scientific knowledge and the natural sciences without explicitly questioning revealed truth. These two very influential figures died before the revolutions, but others demonstrate in their own biographies a direct link between the Orthodox Enlightenment and the Greek uprising. Among these the figure of Theoklitos Pharmakidis (1784–1860) stands out. After serving the Church as a priest in Vienna for eight years, until 1819, Pharmakidis spent time in Göttingen to study Western, and in particular Protestant, theology

44. Brian R. Hamnett, 'Joaquín Lorenzo Villanueva, de católico ilustrado a católico liberal: El dilema de la transición', in *Visiones del liberalismo: Política, identidad y cultura en la España del siglo XIX*, ed. Alda Blanco and Guy Thompson (Valencia: Universitat de València, 2008), pp. 19–42. See the 'Proyecto de decreto acerca de nueva demarcación de parroquías y dotación de párrocos', attached to the *Dictámen de la Comisión eclesiástica sobre el nuevo plan de iglesias metropolitanas y catedrales de la monarquía española, presentado á las Córtes el día 13 de mayo de 1821* (Madrid: Don Mateo Repullés, 1821).

until the outbreak of the revolution, when he moved back to Greece. He worked in the service of Dimitrios Ypsilantis, set up a short-lived newspaper, sat in the Epidavros assembly and played a part in the organisation of a new Greek school system. After a spell in the Ionian Islands, where between 1823 and 1825 he occupied the chair of theology, he returned to Greece to set up the governmental newspaper in Nafplion, and to participate in the 1827 Troezena assembly. The influence of the writings of Korais and of Protestant theology made him one of the foremost advocates of the creation of an autonomous-autocephalous church that would break away from the patriarchate of Constantinople.[45]

The language of the Orthodox Enlightenment was embraced and employed during the revolution also by other prominent members of the clergy, coming increasingly to be associated with the regeneration of the *patrida* (nation). Palaion Patron Germanos (metropolitan of Patras), one of the key leaders of the insurrection, and a member of the first national assembly, along with many other bishops, believed that only the Orthodox faith, embodying the principles of progress and morality, could advance the cause of the nation.[46] Given that its members had failed to fulfil their duties and had been corrupt for centuries, for Germanos the revolution in fact represented an opportunity to reinstate the Church in its ancient glory, and also to defeat the atheism and immorality that had distanced the people from it. He considered moral reform of the clergy so essential for the success of the revolution that he devised a secret society for these purposes not long after the revolution. He conceived the aims of this 'Holy Association' to be 'to consolidate the Eastern Orthodox church and the interests of the nation' (or to 'reform the moral fabric of the nation').[47] The existence of support for these ideas among learned clerics should not however obscure the fact that Enlightenment ideals, as well as notions of national regeneration, created much hostility in the ranks of the Church among the hierarchy and among conservative circles in monastic communities, often isolating the most progressive of its members.[48]

45. Vasilios N. Makrides, 'The Enlightenment in the Greek Orthodox East: Appropriation, Dilemmas, Ambiguities', in *Enlightenment and Religion in the Orthodox World*, ed. Paschalis Kitromilides (Oxford: Voltaire Foundation, 2016), pp. 17–44; Paschalis Kitromilides, *Enlightenment and Revolution: The Making of Modern Greece* (Cambridge, MA: Harvard University Press, 2013), passim. On the career of Pharmakidis during the revolution, see Frazee, *Orthodox Church*, pp. 103–4.

46. Germanos ('Palaion Patron Germanos'), Ἀπομνημονεύματα (Memoirs) (Athens: Spyros Tsaggaris, 1900), pp. 176–77.

47. Ibid., pp. 181, 185.

48. Makrides, 'Enlightenment', pp. 22–23.

Besides pre-existing intellectual traditions and reform movements, what shaped the attitudes of the clergy throughout southern Europe towards the revolution was their own material condition. Unequal access to resources often created tensions within the churches themselves, and especially between the impoverished lower clergy and the hierarchies, and more generally between poor parish priests and the wealthiest and best-endowed of church institutions. A general problem affecting members of the lower clergy across the region was indeed their chronic poverty, and the lack of resources for parishes. These circumstances had been rendered yet more acute by the economic crisis affecting their countries at the end of the Napoleonic wars. In the years before the revolution, the Orthodox clergy had often been at odds with its hierarchy and, above all, with the patriarchate itself. The klephts—bandits hiding in the mountains and living off raids on Muslim landowners and tradesmen—could often count on the connivance and support of local communities, including priests and monks, who would frequently protect them. When at the beginning of the nineteenth century the Ottoman authorities decided to take severe measures to repress the phenomenon, the patriarchate was asked to endorse their request and excommunicate those members of the Church who colluded with banditry. The bishops of the Peloponnese officially endorsed and circulated this decree, but the clergy for their part did not comply.[49] In Naples in 1818, meanwhile, a new concordat between the Church and the Kingdom of the Two Sicilies had tried to deal with the economic conditions of parish priests by guaranteeing higher salaries, or *congrue*. However, these welcome reforms did not have any immediate effect, and were accompanied by new unpopular measures that further eroded the sources of income of the clergy. First, a set of financial contributions paid by parish priests and other ecclesiastics to the *mense vescovili*, abolished in 1813, was reintroduced in 1819.[50] Along with increased financial pressures in 1819 the pope, in agreement with the king, strengthened episcopal controls over the selection, appointment and supervision of the activities of priests attached to churches enjoying until then special privileges, the so- called *chiese ricettizie*. In many areas of the Kingdom of the Two Sicilies, both on the continent and in Sicily, these churches enjoyed a particular legal status. They were independent of the power of the bishops, and were the beneficiaries of a number of sources of revenue that

49. Steven Runciman, *The Great Church in Captivity: A Study of the Patriarchate of Constantinople from the Eve of the Turkish Conquest to the Greek War of Independence*, 2nd edn (Cambridge: Cambridge University Press, 1985 [1968]), p. 398.

50. See Spagnoletti, *Storia del Regno*, p. 180; Monti, *Stato e Chiesa*, p. 384.

traditionally made them appealing to members of the provincial middle classes. Each of these churches provided employment for several priests who formally shared in their duties, but in practice were hardly involved in any pastoral or useful activity and were under no obligation to reside in the parish. As lay institutions they were not accountable to any ecclesiastical authority. The reforms introduced in 1819 were resented by priests, who occasionally refused to collaborate with the authorities to provide information about the nature and wealth of their communities. Acts of rebellion against episcopal authority regarding the management of such communities soared immediately prior to and during the revolution.[51] It is hardly surprising that in the areas where the majority of churches enjoyed this status (and this was the case in many dioceses), priests were inclined to begrudge the erosion of their traditional privileges. Many of them joined the Carboneria and were sympathetic to the revolution.[52] The perennial competition for appointments to such religious institutions, chronic in societies where resources were scarce, led to harsher conflicts during the revolution, as tensions between priests and civil authorities, and also between priests belonging to one and the same parish, began to acquire new, ideological, overtones. Material interests and factional strife were now conflated with clashes between secret societies and their enemies, between supporters of the constitution and absolutists. During the revolution, priests would write petitions to complain about their financial circumstances and about their personal disputes with their own bishops. One Dionisio Petitti, *arciprete* in Curato di Motta, in the Neapolitan diocese of Lucera, for instance, petitioned the parliament complaining about his bishop's attempt to expel him from his own parish. He argued that by asking for the parliament's intervention, he was protecting his civil freedom, a principle enshrined in the new constitution.[53]

In Portugal likewise, hopes for material improvement and for a solution to their financial difficulties led many priests to look favourably upon

51. See, for instance, the case of the arciprete of Bronte, the head of a *comunia* endowed with considerable properties, which refused to collaborate with the bishop of Nicosia, and appointed *procuratori* without seeking his approval: ASP, Real Segreteria, Incartamenti, 5641. For a complaint about the examiner sent by the bishops, see ibid., 5587, ff. 947–48.

52. On the condition of the Church after 1815, see Cestaro, *Le diocesi di Conza*, pp. 66–71. On the 1818 concordat, see the classic work by Walter Maturi, *Il concordato del 1818 tra Santa Sede e le Due Sicilie* (Florence: Le Monnier, 1929); Rosario Romeo, 'Momenti e problemi della Restaurazione nel Regno delle Due Sicilie (1815–1820)', *Rivista Storica Italiana* 57 (1955): 366–417; Gambasin, *Religiosa magnificenza*, pp. 132–35.

53. ASN, Polizia Generale II, Carte del parlamento nazionale, fascio 35: Dionisio Petitti, arciprete at Curato di Motta in the diocese of Lucera, to the parliament, 1820.

the constitutional regime. Petitions to the newly elected parliament are revealing of the financial problems that priests were hoping the constitutional government would resolve. Addressing both the government and the Cortes, these priests urged them to intervene to deal with the unequal distribution of resources, the unsatisfactory allocation of tithes and unfair access to privileges and additional sources of income. They wrote to the Cortes with regard to two main issues: either asking for a higher *côngrua*, or complaining about the fact that tithes were not used for their original pastoral purposes. Priests lamented the fact that the *dizimeiros*—the ecclesiastical institutions that collected tithes—retained the majority of these sources of income, and left insufficient resources for pastoral purposes, for the maintenance of the church buildings and for the relief of poverty.[54]

Thus a combination of factors, which included aspirations for material improvement and belief in Enlightenment notions of religious regeneration, as well as support for church and political reform, led substantial minorities of the clergy to support the revolution or, at least, to be open-minded about it. Among the Catholic countries, the most impressive clerical mobilisation in favour of the revolution was to be found in the Kingdom of the Two Sicilies. It was here that demands for church reform and adherence to the Carboneria created the preconditions for widespread support. In the provinces outside Naples, where there was a high concentration of secret society activities, the presence of an explicitly pro-constitutional clergy was equally substantial. In the district of Castel Sant'Angelo de' Lombardi near the city of Avellino, for instance, out of 742 priests, eighty had joined the Carboneria before the revolution, and an additional 114 did so after it had broken out.[55] In Capua, twenty-five kilometres north of Naples, the ranks of the Carboneria included more than 220 priests. In the province of Bari, in what is today the region of Puglia in the heel of Italy, ecclesiastics represented more than 10 per cent of those condemned by the police as carbonari: out of 1,441 members of the Carboneria, 117 were priests and an additional thirty-two were members of cathedral chapters and collegiate churches.[56] No religious institutions would seem to have been immune from some involvement in the revolution. Ecclesiastics whose primary occupation was education were

54. Faria, *Os liberais*, pp. 245–80. The dispersal of tithes and their use for purposes different from those to which they were originally assigned was another recurrent source of complaint among lay petitioners to the Portuguese Cortes.

55. Quoted in Delpu, 'Patriotisme libéral', p. 562.

56. ASN, Borbone, 726, ff. 106–7.

particularly likely to show sympathy for the revolutionary cause. In the city of Capua at least three priests and prefects of the local seminary were noted for preaching in favour of the new order to their students. In the city of Lecce, the capital of the province of Terra d'Otranto, almost the entire seminary was likewise alleged to have backed the revolution.[57] In Sicily, the geography of such clerical support mirrored divisions within the island community between those siding with Naples and those aligning themselves with secessionist Palermo, and was thus mainly concentrated in eastern Sicily and in the city of Mazzara on the western coast, areas hostile to Palermo's aspirations towards insular autonomy. It is here that we can find the highest numbers of ecclesiastics involved in conspiratorial activities. In Piazza Armerina, for instance, sixty-three ecclesiastics were accused of being carbonari; in the town of Nicosia they numbered 107, and in Catania there were no fewer than 124.[58] Some of these carbonaro priests acquired local or even national visibility as revolutionary leaders. The most famous of them all, of course, was Abate Luigi Minichini. Entering the city of Naples on horseback at the beginning of the revolution, he brandished his sword and wore the tricolour cockade of the Carboneria while dressed in his clerical frock. In October 1820 Minichini's tour of Sicily, at the end of the campaign to stem the rebellion, fully demonstrated his ability to stir up popular enthusiasm, and showed the extent to which the fame he had acquired as a leader of the insurrection had spread through the island. In each of the villages and cities he visited in Sicily, from Messina to Catania, Siracusa and Caltanissetta, parades, processions and celebrations with music were organised: his presence attracted people of all social backgrounds, and everywhere he was feted as the liberator of the fatherland. In Catania altars with his image were set up and thousands of civilians welcomed him into the city.[59] In his communications, Minichini combined political and religious language, presenting himself as a man entrusted by God with a special mission. He went so far as to compare himself to Jesus Christ, who was destined to sacrifice himself for the greater good, and to many he seemed to be imbued with an exceptional, superhuman spirit.[60]

The presence and the increase in number of clerics in the ranks of the Carboneria during the revolution is even more remarkable considering that, on the basis of a papal edict against secret societies issued in 1814

57. Ibid., f. 271.
58. Labate, *Un decennio*, pp. 134–39.
59. Mario Themelly, 'Introduzione', in Minichini, *Luglio 1820*, pp. i–lxxi at lxii–lxvi, and Minichini's own recollection of the tour at pp. 330–37.
60. Minichini, *Luglio 1820*, p. 338.

that reiterated earlier condemnations of Freemasonry, some bishops in Naples were in fact denying members of the Carboneria the sacrament of penitence. The Ministry of Justice had to intervene in defence of the Carboneria with the Catholic hierarchy of the kingdom, denying its secret and morally subversive nature.[61] It was a priest of the collegiate church of San Giovanni in Naples who responded to such papal condemnation by publishing a public defence of the Carboneria. In his pamphlet he argued that the the society professed 'the teachings of the church of Jesus Christ [. . . and] the Catholic Apostolic Roman religion [. . .] practising a moral discipline entirely modelled on that of the Gospels'.[62]

In Spain and Portugal, the minorities in favour of the constitution were more limited than in Naples and Sicily, but in both countries the revolution consolidated the support of a section of the secular clergy for the constitution. In most provinces of Portugal, at least until 1821, only a few priests refused to take a vow of allegiance to the constitution, or to preach on the basis of what its text contained, and even fewer dared to deliver sermons openly hostile to it. In some areas this acceptance of the new regime was unqualified. The priests of Ourique in the district of Beja, for instance, preached in favour of the constitution in spite of the fact that they had not received any pastoral guidance to this effect from their bishop. Likewise in the town of Vinhais in the district Bragança, all were enthusiastic supporters of the revolution. The same happened in the comarca of Castelo Branco, where the clergy endorsed the bishop's pastoral in favour of the constitution.[63] In other cities, however, hostility emerged almost immediately after the declaration of the revolution. In Santarém and Elvas, where the bishop was fiercely hostile to the constitution, some resistance was reported by the civil authorities as early as 1821.[64] The explicit hostility to the constitution manifested by priests in some cities or provinces was due not only to the example of their bishops, but sometimes owed something to the influence of specific clerical movements for spiritual reform. Since the beginning of the eighteenth century, the so-called 'Jacobeia' movement had aimed at the moralisation of religious practices, advocating a more mystical and austere spirituality based on frequent prayer and penitence.

61. ASN, Borbone, 269, f. 232: broadsheet, 'Lettera del ministro di giustizia a vescovi ed arcivescovi', 23 January 1821.

62. Giovanni Arcucci, *Rimostranza della società dei Carbonari al sommo pontefice Pio VII* (Naples: Paci, 1820), pp. 6–7.

63. ANTT, IGP, livro 20, 1820–22, f. 19: 14 June 1821; ff. 94: October 1821; IGP, Castelo Branco 276, f. 9: March 1821.

64. Ibid., IGP, livro 20, 1820–22, f. 30, corregedor de comarca de Alenquer; f. 72, Elvas.

One of its main proponents, the bishop of Bragança Dom António Luís da Veiga Cabral da Câmara, otherwise known as 'Bispo Santo', who died in 1819, was convinced that he had been given the task of defending Catholic religion against the ideologies emerging from the French revolution. His austere religiosity, as well as the aura of sanctity and the miraculous events associated with him, made him extremely popular not only during his lifetime but also subsequently. After 1820 his followers, who were to be found throughout Portugal but in particular around Lisbon, where he had lived for a number of years, turned against the constitution. Many of them joined the counterrevolution.[65]

The emergence of a movement against the constitution, leading to civil strife, polarised opinions in favour of or against the constitution among priests and heightened existing divisions between them. While large sections of the clergy may have simply been indifferent to the constitution, or complied grudgingly with governmental directives, the conflict forced even those who had been indifferent until then to take sides, and encouraged those who had been silently hostile to become vocally critical of the new regime, and assume the leadership in the rebellion against it. In Portugal it was first with Count of Amarante's counterrevolutionary rebellion at the beginning of 1823, and soon after with Dom Miguel's failed military coup (the Vilafrancada), that a clerical mobilisation against the constitution emerged. Individuals such as Father João da Nogueirinha became leaders of the royalist partidas that supported the military revolt in the province of Trás-os-Montes. As a consequence, in the course of the suppression of this rebellion, dozens of ecclesiastics were imprisoned, exiled abroad or to other parts of the country, or emigrated of their own accord. Thirty-two clerics were mentioned in the press a few weeks after the failure of the counter-pronunciamiento for the support they had lent to this challenge to the regime. At the same time, a number of priests stood out for their loyalty to the constitutional cause, which was expressed in a variety of ways. Some volunteered to join the Civil Guard, even if the clergy was technically exempted from this patriotic duty. Others were notable for their generosity in giving financial support to the constitutional cause when it was under military threat. José Cordeiro da Cruz, prior at Repreza, offered some of his benefices for the defence of fatherland, including those obtained by him as a consequence of wounds suffered and limbs lost during the Peninsular War.[66] Others were keen to follow governmental

65. Cardoso, *A revolução liberal*, pp. 58–61.

66. Faria, *Os liberais*, pp. 664, 675–77; Cardoso, *A revolução liberal*, pp. 151, 156.

guidelines and publicly condemned these military coups. The prior of the church of Sé in Coimbra, Manuel Nunes da Fonseca, a fervent supporter of the constitution and author of several writings in its defence, addressed his flock, and in the course of his sermon censured Amarante's military revolt, warning that discord and civil war would lead to anarchy and the 'unravelling of civil society', all events opposed to the teachings of Holy Scripture.[67]

Although absolutist uprisings encouraged many clerics to publicly condemn the revolution, it is safe to say that by the end of the two constitutional periods of 1820–23 and 1826–28 a substantial proportion of the clergy had become resolutely favourable to representative government and hostile to absolutism. The data available about political prisoners detained by the authorities after the establishment of Dom Miguel's regime confirm that this was far from being a negligible phenomenon. Among those who rebelled against Dom Miguel in 1828 in Coimbra, priests ranked among the largest groups in the liberal opposition: they represented 13 per cent of those arrested by Dom Miguel after 1828, second only to the military (24 per cent) and equal in numbers to civil servants and tradesmen.[68] Some clerics took part in the revolt against Dom Miguel in the Algarve in 1828. Among the 261 individuals arrested for their participation in this uprising, mostly members of the army, there were also sixteen priests.[69] Among the sixty 'rebels' who left the Algarve via Gibraltar to go into exile after this failed uprising, there were also four priors and priests.[70] In spite of the Holy See's support for the absolutist Miguelistas during the civil war that ravaged Portugal between 1828 and 1834, many parish priests and clerics were among the most intransigent enemies of Dom Miguel's regime.

In Spain too, the introduction of the constitution and the outbreak of civil war between 1821 and 1823 divided the clergy. In 1820 only a minority of clerics were prepared actively to boycott or criticise the revolution. Hundreds of priests dutifully submitted their oath to the constitution, and many wrote to the government to declare their support for the new regime. Isolated acts of resistance were reported in Andalusia and in the province of Soria, where in a few villages priests disobeyed the civil authorities, refused to sing a Te Deum in honour of the constitution or to support the new regime in their church services. These acts of insubordination were

67. ANTT, IGP, Coimbra 284-2, f. 396: broadsheet, Manuel Nunes da Fonseca, 'Exhortação do reitor da Sé aos seus parochianos', Coimbra, 8 March 1823.

68. Ferreira, *Rebeldes*, pp. 75–81.

69. ANTT, IGP, Algarve 244-2, ff. 532–33.

70. Ibid., ff. 325–27: list of rebels who left the country, Lagos, September 1828.

noted more frequently in some cities and provinces than in others. More substantial from the outset was the hostility of the clergy on the Balearic islands, in Burgos and in Navarre, where reluctance to speak in favour of the constitution was widespread. In the case of Navarre, this was due to the influence of the bishop: it was after his visit to their villages that the province's parish priests stopped preaching the constitution.[71] As in Portugal, moreover, so too in Spain the civil wars led to a polarisation of political attitudes among priests. Members of the clergy made a significant contribution to the planning and organisation of counterrevolutionary activities. From Navarre to the Basque country and Catalonia, the royalist offensive was often led by clerics. Clerical support was of crucial ideological importance to a struggle that was carried out in the name of religion and the monarchy, thus turning the civil war into a religious war. A few of these men attained a semi-mythical standing. The most famous among these clerical guerrilla leaders in the Basque country was Don Francisco Gorostidi, a priest of aristocratic origin, who led the counterrevolution in the province of Guipúzcoa. His exploits were extensively covered by the press, and his bravery, resolve and ability to win support for his cause and for his personal following rendered him famous. Like other clerics leading the partidas, or simply joining the guerrillas, he had already been extensively involved in the battles and skirmishes of the war of independence. Gorostidi's proclamation issued to foment the rebellion was designed to 'defend the Catholic religion threatened by imminent destruction, [. . .] obtain the full freedom of the king [. . . and] preserve the fueros and privileges of this province'.[72] In June 1822 he initiated his guerrilla activities with the support of several hundred individuals, setting up, along with two other priests, a junta to coordinate the insurrection with the other provinces of the Basque country, and managing to capture the political chief of the province. During his incursions into villages controlled by the constitutionalists he famously went so far as to set fire to the churches where his enemies were hiding.[73]

The sacralisation of the war against the constitution was encouraged by the royalist provisional government, or regencia, set up in La Seu d'Urgell with the blessing of the monarch, and presided over by Jaime Creus,

71. AHN, Consejos Suprimidos, legajo 11360: letters from the jefes políticos on the behaviour of the clergy.

72. See documents in Pío de Montoya, *La intervención del clero vasco en las contiendas civiles, 1820–1823* (San Sebastián: Editorial Txertoa, 1971), pp. 121–40, quotation at 129.

73. Pío Baroja, *Siluetas románticas y otras historias de pillos y de extravagantes* (Madrid: Espasa Calpe, 1934), pp. 54–63.

FIGURE 25. *El enfermo por la Constitucion* ('Made sick by the Constitution': the priest 'can't swallow it', but the soldier insists that he can have 'no other remedy', while above hangs the emblem of the Holy Inquisition; satirical etching by unknown artist, c. 1820; Museo de Historia de Madrid, Madrid). Image: Biblioteca Digital memoriademadrid

archbishop-elect of Tarragona. While the political leadership was firmly in the hands of the Marquis of Mataflorida, who had been responsible for its setting up, the presence of a prominent member of the church hierarchy gave an additional seal of authority to the institution. The establishment of the regencia was marked by grandiose religious ceremonies reminiscent of the splendour attaching to the sacralised ancien-régime monarchy. In the territories controlled by the regencia, military expeditions and guerrilla actions were often inaugurated by religious ceremonies and by anti-constitutional speeches in churches. Clerics represented 17.5 per cent of the leaders of the royalist partidas, the highest percentage along with that of the professional military. Members of the clergy represented the highest proportion of the members of the juntas set up in the towns that had joined the counterrevolution, together with army officers, lawyers and landowners. Sometimes they were simultaneously leaders of the partidas and members of the juntas.[74] For constitutionalist observers of such

74. Arnabat Mata, *Visca el rei*, pp. 445–50.

phenomena, the role played by village priests in leading the royalist insurgency exemplified the alliance between backwardness and superstition. As a Piedmontese volunteer wrote when commenting on the hostility of the rural population of Catalonia to the constitution and the international volunteers who had come to its rescue,

> The simple and unrefined Catalan, as fanatical about religion as he is incapable of recognising deceit, gives credence to the rumours of those he believes to be incapable of lying, and with the villages thus being roused and the bands of insurgents formed, public order, security, property and the life of every respectable citizen is at risk. [. . .] A man only has to have a reputation of being a liberal [. . .] for the insurgents to burn him alive as a heretic [. . .]. Everywhere there are levies spreading terror, [. . .] and under the guidance of those meek pastors, to whom God entrusted the shepherding of his flock!!!! [sic][75]

Acts of retaliation against counterrevolutionary clerics were not slow in coming. The participation of the clergy in the absolutist insurgency gave rise to a wave of anticlericalism, supported by an intense campaign in the revolutionary press against those monks and parish priests who had dared to rise against the constitution and betray their role in their communities. By 1822 the radical exaltados dominated both national and local politics, with moderado clerics being expelled from Barcelona, while others accused of supporting the insurrection were arrested and held in detention. The intensification of the conflict and the French invasion accounted also for an escalation in acts of violence against both regular and secular clergy. Around eighty clerics died violently during the civil war and the French invasion, either in reprisals or in military actions.[76] The most prominent victim in the Catalan clergy was the bishop of Vic, Ramón Strauch i Vidal, who was in prison in Barcelona awaiting trial for conspiracy when, on the news of the French invasion, a group of exaltados decided that there was no time for formal justice, took him out of the citadel and executed him outside the city.[77] At the same time, some clerics resolutely sided with the revolution. After 1821, when low-intensity conflicts escalated into full-scale civil war in Catalonia, in Barcelona, its capital city, some of the clergy reacted to the new situation by redoubling their

75. Quoted in Isabella, *Risorgimento in Exile*, p. 39.

76. Gaspar Feliu i Montfort, *La clerecia catalana durant el Trienni Liberal* (Barcelona: Institut d'Estudis Catalans, 1972), pp. 171–79.

77. Florent Galli, *Campagne du Général Mina en Catalogne* (Paris: Philippe, 1831), pp. 179–82.

propaganda efforts in defence of the revolutionary order. In July 1822 prayers to the Virgin Mary were organised by some patriots in Barcelona to ask for her support for a victory of the constitutional army against the French invader. When, under the pressure of the French invasion, Barcelona became the capital of a liberalism under siege, a number of clerics fleeing the countryside entered the capital in order to defend the city, and fifteen of these volunteered for the work involved in the construction of a new fortress protecting it. In 1823 a priest published a plan advocating the organisation of a militia of clerics to act as a civil guard in the city's defence.[78] By the end of the revolution, therefore, not only in Portugal but also in Spain, a section of the clergy had participated in the organised forms of sociability that thrived in all of the peninsula's cities, had mobilised to support the constitutional order and had remained loyal to the bitter end. After the withdrawal of the constitution, the police submitted to the monarch a list of constitutionalist clerics that included sixty-four freemasons, twenty-eight members of patriotic societies, and eighty-five comuneros.[79] Although it is difficult to assess how representative such a sample was of a larger national trend, such numbers confirm the existence of a phenomenon that represented a source of concern for the absolute monarchy even after the end of the revolution.

The revolutionary context most marked by clerical involvement in the cause of revolution was Greece. The archbishop of Patras Germanos himself later claimed that all of the clergy in the Peloponnese had joined the ranks of the Philiki by 1821. This is probably a substantial exaggeration, as historians have suggested that around 10 per cent of their number (about eighty-five) might be a more accurate estimate.[80] This was a relatively small contingent, but these clerics did nonetheless constitute a group crucial to the organisation and planning of the revolution, as they ranked among the first and most important contacts of Germanos and the archimandrite Papaflessas in the Peloponnese. Yet in the initial stages of the anti-Ottoman insurrection, fear of reprisals as well as the condemnation of the patriarchate did much to inhibit clerical support. At the beginning of the revolution, the Greek clergy were as divided as their counterparts in Catholic countries. What caused them to go over in their entirety to the side of the revolution, however, was the nature of the conflict itself—for the Ottoman authorities' initial overreaction, along with their propensity

78. Feliu i Montfort, *La clerecia catalana*, pp. 130–31.
79. APR, Papeles Reservados de Fernando VII, 67, exp. 3, ff. 71–80.
80. Frangos, 'Philiki Etaireia 1814–1821', p. 229.

to renege upon their promises, thereby precipitating unexpected acts of violence against the clergy, often based on suspicion, led to ever greater numbers rallying to the revolutionary cause. For this reason the revolution produced a convergence between higher and lower clergy that had no equivalent elsewhere in southern Europe. It was the military escalation of the conflict, however, that finally turned the clergy into a key element of the insurrection. In the light of the religious definition of the conflict offered by its protagonists, the clergy provided a much needed ideological legitimacy for it. Their preaching to bolster the war effort, and their own direct participation in military activities had an immense symbolic value, and made a decisive contribution to the sacralisation of the war. As a British philhellene noted, in Greece priests 'were greatly instrumental in bringing about the glorious revolution. They traversed the country, and enlisted their votaries in the honourable plot; they fought in the ranks of the noble insurgents, and many of them are permanently engaged as soldiers, and some as captains.'[81] The sacralisation of the conflict by the Greeks was in turn mirrored by the responses of the Ottomans who, from the very beginning, viewed the rebellion as a direct attack on them as a religious community. It was also for this reason, and for the prestige they enjoyed in their communities, that clerics were among the most valued prey of the Ottoman army and targets of their acts of retaliation. According to certain estimates, something between six thousand and seven thousand priests died during the insurrection, along with many bishops.[82]

To fully understand clerical attitudes towards the revolutions, however, it is important to draw a distinction between regular and secular clergies. In Catholic countries the regular clergy tended to feel much more hostile towards constitutional regimes than did the secular clergy. This should be no cause for surprise, given how the former were subjected to attacks by revolutionary governments intent on taking over their properties, abolishing their privileges and regulating or even suppressing their existence. In Portugal and Spain in particular, monastic communities often became sites of counterrevolutionary conspiracy and mobilisation. In Portugal what gave rise to the hostility of great monastic establishments against the constitutional regime was the impact that the partial abolition of seigneurial rights, carried out by the revolutionary governments with the *lei dos forais* in June 1822, had on their privileges and sources of income.

81. Leicester Stanhope, *Greece during Lord Byron's Residence in That Country, in 1823 and 1824*, 2 vols (Paris: Galignani, 1825), 2, p. 104.
82. Frazee, *Orthodox Church*, p. 101.

These reforms exacerbated pre-existing social tensions between wealthy monasteries, the local communities subject to their fiscal rights and their parish priests, and created new political divisions between regular and secular clergy. The reaction to revolutionary legislation of the great monastery of Alcobaça, belonging to the Cistercian order, and located in the Leiria district of Estremadura, may be taken to exemplify this pattern. This monastery was the recipient of tithes, rights and various impositions over thirteen different towns and twenty-five parishes. The promulgation of the above-mentioned *lei dos forais* encouraged parishes to withhold payment to the monastery of these tithes and levies, whose excessive nature had already been reported by them to constitutional authorities in the previous year. In their acts of resistance, the parishioners were also supported by their priests, who in turn lamented and deplored the fact that the tithes gathered by the monastery were not employed for pastoral purposes. At the end of the constitutional period, in 1823, these conflicts took on explicitly political overtones. The friars in fact celebrated Dom Miguel's failed military coup, the Vilafrancada, and welcomed the withdrawal of the constitution in religious ceremonies held specifically for this purpose. The repeal of the *lei dos forais* in 1824 triggered new conflicts between the monastery and the local communities.[83] This state of affairs, and the conflict between monasteries and parish priests, was replicated across the whole country. In 1823 the friars of the monastery of Santa Maria de Seiça, in the concelho of Figueira da Foz, were denounced by a parish priest for plotting against the constitution. This priest had refused to pay the tithes due to the monastery, and encouraged his parishioners to do likewise.[84] Hostility to the revolution could be found not only in wealthy monastic communities, moreover, but also among poorer itinerant preachers, who lived off alms or manual labour, and were in close contact with the poorest strata of the population. Itinerant Franciscan friars were reported to officials for preaching against the constitution in different parts of Portugal.[85] Unsurprisingly, several monastic communities welcomed the return of Dom Miguel in 1828 and the re-establishment of absolutism, sending letters and addresses directly to him, among which were the good wishes of the abbess of the convent of Nossa Senhora da Esperança of Vila Viçosa, in the Alentejo region, sent to him via a preacher. The abbess wrote that

83. Nuno Gonçalo Monteiro, 'Lavradores, frades e forais: Revolução liberal e regime senhorial na comarca de Alcobaça (1820–24)', in Monteiro, *Elites*, pp. 221–99, esp. 221–44.

84. ANTT, IGP, Coimbra 284, f. 308: 30 July 1823.

85. *O Indipendente*, 29 November 1821, p. 33; a Franciscan itinerant preacher was denounced in Braga. See ANTT, IGP, livro 20, 1820–22, f. 80.

her community was thanking the Almighty for his providential return to Portugal, and was praying that the Lord might preserve his prosperity and that of the dynasty.[86]

In Catalonia, the dismantling and closure of monastic houses encouraged the mobilisation of those monks who were no longer attached to any institutions, increasing the likelihood of their participation in military conflict and pushing them towards counterrevolution. In this province between October and November 1822, a number of monastic houses were in fact dissolved; some communities, like that of the Franciscans, were expelled from the city of Barcelona, but those who failed to make good their escape made subject to the ruling that all regular clerics be secularised. Monasteries became important centres of counterrevolutionary activity and military action. They gave shelter to guerrillas, provided logistical and practical support, hosted meetings and acted as points of reference for both military and political coordination. In Catalonia, for instance, the monastery of Poblet i Montserrat played a crucial role in leading the counterrevolution in several of the surrounding districts.[87] While most funding for the guerrillas came from other sources, at times clerics or monasteries provided financial support for the organisation and maintenance of partidas.[88] One of the most famous military leaders of the counterrevolutionary movement in Catalonia was a Trappist friar, Antonio Marañón, better known as 'El Trapense'. He had participated in the war against the French and his bravery earned him promotions from soldier to lieutenant; remaining in the army after the end of the Napoleonic conflicts until 1817, when he lost his position through gambling, he once more joined a monastery. In 1821 he started gathering groups of combatants in the village of Poblet; having survived the anti-French struggle, 'El Trapense' claimed to enjoy divine protection and to have been charged with a divine mission that prevented him from being hit by enemy fire. In his friar's garb, holding a large cross at his neck and sustained by his fiery eloquence and personal charisma, he rode through the villages of the region, where he blessed the local populations and invited them to join the struggle in the name of religion. As Marañón passed through, people knelt down and kissed the hem of his cassock. His fame was greatly enhanced by his role in the seizure in June 1822 of La Seu d'Urgell, which was to become the capital of the regency. He led thousands of fighters and, at least according to contemporary sources, managed to scale the walls of the

86. ANTT, Ministério do Reino, Autos de Aclamação, maço 21, no. 4379.
87. Arnabat Mata, *Visca el rei*, pp. 78–79.
88. Sauch Cruz, *Guerrillers i bàndols*, p. 192.

fortress wholly unscathed, holding a cross in his hands.[89] In his addresses to his soldiers, he likened the current conflict to that waged by their Spanish ancestors against the Moors, and presented it as one that demanded the complete extermination of the enemy.[90]

Exceptions to these patterns did however occur both on the Iberian peninsula and elsewhere. Friars supportive of the constitution were occasionally reported in Portugal.[91] The existence of a small but not insignificant pro-constitutional contingent of regular clergy in Portugal is confirmed by a survey carried out on behalf of the government after the fall of Dom Miguel's absolute regime in 1834. Of 238 friars, 7.6 per cent were 'fanatical Miguelistas', 50.6 per cent were moderate realistas, and only 9.2 per cent were supporters of the constitution.[92] A similar pattern emerges with regard to the Spanish regular clergy. Surprising as it may seem, however, in Spain the dissolution of monasteries did not necessarily play into the hands of the armed insurrection against the constitution. Although in Catalonia these closures prompted many friars to join the conterrevolution, the opposite was true in other parts of Spain. In fact many *exclaustrados*, as the former friars, once they had been secularised, were known, became publicists and worked as journalists in the constitutional press, often writing about the Church in highly critical terms.[93] Even in Catalonia, a prominent constitutional cleric was Albert Pujol, a Discalced Augustinian who, besides being rector of his own monastery, was professor of ecclesiastical history at the University of Barcelona. The local liberal leadership entrusted him with the task of drafting a political catechism to instruct the Catalans in the rights they had acquired under the constitution, which was published in 1820, and in 1822 Pujol was among the founders of the Sociedad Económica de Amigos del País.[94]

In Sicily, meanwhile, the existence of monastic communities supportive of the revolution was more pronounced than in either Portugal or Spain. Many of the island's monasteries were involved to a greater or

89. Miraflores, *Apuntes histórico-críticos*, p. 152; Baroja, *Siluetas románticas*, pp. 54–63.

90. *Gazeta del Gobierno Imperial de Mexico*, vol. 2, no. 94, 12 September 1822, p. 726.

91. ANTT, IGP, Algarve 244, f. 540: juíz de fora to intendente geral, Tavira, 19 December 1828.

92. Armando Barreiros Malheiro da Silva, 'O clero regular e a "usurpação": Subsídios para uma história sócio-política do Miguelismo', *Revista de História das Ideias* 9 (1987): 529–630 at p. 553.

93. Celso Almuiña Fernández, 'Clericalismo y anticlericalismo a través de la prensa española decimonónica', in Carlos Seco Serrano et al., *La cuestión social en la Iglesia española contemporánea* (Madrid: El Escorial, 1981), pp. 123–75 at 137.

94. Gil Novales, *Las sociedades patrióticas*, 1, p. 286; Feliu i Montfort, *La clerecia catalana*, pp. 126–27.

lesser degree in conspiratorial activities before, during and even after the revolution, although a variety of different political reasons might account for monks' and friars' presence in the ranks of the Carboneria. In the town of Randazzo, on the slopes of Mount Etna, it was a monk, Andrea Capparelli, who established the first vendita of the Carboneria, called the Figli di Astrea, and held meetings in his monastery, in which, it was rumoured, up to four hundred members of the secret society had on one occasion participated.[95] Not a single religious institution in the city of Catania, the capital of eastern Sicily, would seem to have been entirely immune to conspiratorial activities. The Dominican convent of Santa Caterina, for instance, whose members were allegedly 'ferociously and publicly carbonari', was not an isolated example. Indeed, in the foremost monastic institution of the city, the Benedictine monastery of San Nicola l'Arena, six out of the twenty monks living there were also carbonari. This powerful institution, whose grandiose buildings dominated the city, was not only an important cultural centre, boasting a large library and an art collection, but also a source of its prosperity, with a substantial income deriving from the extensive properties it owned across the island, including ten fiefdoms. The monks here were traditionally members of both the aristocratic and the non-aristocratic elites of the city.[96] Other, smaller monasteries were dissolved at the end of the revolution because of their communities' support for the revolution. The seven members of the monastery of Santa Anna in the city of Messina, for instance, had to leave, and ended up in various institutions. This community had been an important centre for the dissemination of the Carboneria on the island some years before the revolution.[97] Supporters of the revolution could be found among members of the Third Order of Saint Francis. A Franciscan friar from a monastery in Monreale, Gioacchino Vaglica, acquired great visibility and prestige as the leader of a mob during the insurrection that inaugurated the revolution in Palermo in July 1820. As recognition of his role in the uprising he was promoted to the rank of colonel by the Sicilian provisional government.[98]

95. ASC, Intendenza Borbonica, 3147, no. 438: Randazzo, 26 September 1822.

96. ASC, Intendenza Borbonica, XVII, 3454; Gaetano Zito, 'Benedettini a Catania tra conflitti e riforma: La visita abbaziale del 1822 a S. Nicola l'Arena', in *Monastica et Humanistica. Scritti in onore di Gregorio Penco O.S.B.*, ed. Francesco G. B. Trolese (Cesena: Badia di Santa Maria del Monte, 2003), pp. 519–60.

97. ASP, Real Segreteria di Stato presso il Luogotenente di Sicilia, Polizia 12, doc. 538: intendente of Messina, 4 July 1822.

98. BCP, Manoscritti, Qq H 138, f. 227: broadsheet, 'Avviso' signed by Bonanno Cancelliere, 25 July 1820.

More than anywhere else, however, it was in Greece that, during the insurrection, monastic communities were at the forefront of popular mobilisation, both civil and military, in defence of the revolution. Since the struggle for national emancipation was closely identified in this case with the Orthodox faith, their contribution was no less significant than that of the secular clergy. Monasteries as communities and as buildings played a crucial role at all stages of the revolution both in Wallachia, where Prince Ypsilantis and his generals used them during their expedition of 1821, and throughout the Peloponnese and the islands.[99] Monasteries likewise provided shelter to the emissaries of the Philiki crossing the country in the years preceding the revolution and at its inception.[100] It was in the monastery of Agia Lavra in Kalavryta that the most important meeting between the emissaries of the Philiki and the primates of the Peloponnese was held, in March 1821, when the decision to proceed with the rebellion was taken.[101] Monks could moreover be found in the ranks of irregular troops throughout the revolutionary war. The most famous among them, and the most important emissary of the Philiki in that region on the eve of the revolution, was Papaflessas, who sat in the first national assembly as a delegate, was elected to the senate of the Peloponnese and was appointed minister of the interior by the second national assembly. As in the case of Minichini in Naples or Vaglica in Palermo, Papaflessas's fame was due both to the charisma he derived from his clerical status and to his feats of arms. He died in combat, in fact, losing his life in 1825 on the battlefield at Maniaki in the Peloponnese, where he led over a thousand fighters.[102]

The most remarkable mass mobilisation of monastic communities dated back to the early days of the insurrections and was centred around the monasteries of Mount Athos. These institutions had enjoyed a large degree of autonomy from Ottoman rule since 1806 and held sway over the peninsula of Chalkidiki. Under the leadership of the emissary of the Philiki Emmanouil Papas, the monastery of Esphigmenou became the epicentre for the organisation of the insurrection. When rebellions broke

99. Gordon, *History*, 1, pp. 111, 121, 127, 137.

100. Fotakos (Chrysanthopoulos Fotios), *Βίος του Πάπα Φλέσα συγγραφείς μεν υπό Φωτάκου πρώτου υπασπιστού του Γέρω Κολοκοτρών εκδοθείς δε υπό Σ. Καλκάνδη* (Life of Papa Flessa written by Fotakos, first adjutant to Old Man Kolokotronis, published by S. Kalkandi) (Athens: Typois Nomimotitos, 1868), p. 46.

101. Panagiotis Michailaris and Vassilis Panagiotopoulos, *Κληρικοί στον Αγώνα: Παλαιών Πατρών Γερμανός, Ιγνάτιος Ουγγροβλαχίας, Νεόφυτος Βάμβας* (Clerics in the 'Struggle': Palaion Patron Germanos, Ignatios Ouggrovlachias, Neophytus Vamvas) (Athens: Ta Nea, Istoriki Vivliothiki, 2010), pp. 32–33.

102. Fotakos, *Βίος του Πάπα Φλέσα* (Life of Papa Flessa), pp. 40–70.

out in the villages, after some initial hesitation, the monastic communities declared for the revolution, and along with the bishop of Maroneia Konstantios and leading laymen they recognised in Papas as 'chief protector of Macedonia'. Under his leadership a number of archimandrites led an army of more than a thousand monks against the Ottoman troops.[103] By the end of 1821 the rebellion had been suppressed and the Ottomans had reoccupied Mount Athos, granting a pardon and ordering in return that the monasteries support the army financially. By then, however, more than half of the monks who had resided there before the insurrection had left to join the war effort permanently elsewhere.[104] In the years that followed the monastic buildings were besieged, and fierce fighting raged around them. In 1825, during Ibrahim's famous expedition in the Morea, the pasha wrote to the monastery of Mega Spilaion calling upon them to surrender, but the monks, who had with them a community of more than ten thousand refugees, refused, preferring to fight, and mounted a successful defence of their monastery.[105]

During the civil war monasteries sought to avoid being directly involved in military activities, hoping to be spared the most grievous consequences of the conflict. In 1824 some of them petitioned the national government to obtain its protection from any military incursion, in compliance with an act that precluded any armed men entering into monasteries, promising to allow only civilians affected by the war into its buildings, and declaring at the same time their obedience to the national government.[106] Their communities continued to be the target of military attacks, however, and their premises often suffered destruction or very serious damage.

Preaching in favour of or against the new order

Preaching to the faithful was the main and potentially the most effective public activity that the clergy could conduct either in favour of or against the revolutions. In Spain, and in Naples, where Spanish regulations were imitated, the catechisation of those attending mass in the principles of the constitution represented a government policy the clergy was obliged to implement. The Spanish authorities requested that priests endeavour to explain the constitution during mass on Sundays or during various

103. See John Vasdravellis, *The Greek Struggle for Independence: The Macedonians in the Revolution of 1821* (Thessaloniki: Institute of Balkan Studies, 1968), pp. 75–81.

104. Gordon, *History*, 1, pp. 176–78, 287.

105. BL; Church Papers, Add MS 36546, f. 40; Add MS 36547, f. 182.

106. 16 December 1824, in Plagianakou and Stergelles, *Αρχείο* (Archive), 2, p. 559.

festivities, extending the same obligation to priests teaching in seminaries and schools, as well as to convents, and insisted that the bishops instruct their clergy accordingly. Likewise in Naples—although these decisions do not seem to have been followed up by the hierarchy—the Giunta Provvisoria decided to target not only parish priests but also those clerics who were in charge of *cappelle serotine*—street conventicles—and students' chapels, blamed for having been particularly outspoken critics of the latest political developments, and asked the bishops to appoint inspectors to supervise the enforcement of regulations.[107] In Portugal, meanwhile, the authorities asked for the priests' public support at various stages during the revolution. In February 1821 the Cortes ordered parish priests to pray in support of the constitution in all churches. After the failed absolutist military coup by Count of Amarante, priests were invited publicly to condemn his rebellion, and to preach in defence of the constitution.[108] And in Greece, as was mentioned above, the revolutionary government invited the clergy to instruct the faithful in the values of patriotism.

Priests often spoke on a variety of other occasions, too. They delivered sermons in churches specifically to thank the king for having granted the constitution, to mark the inauguration of parliamentary sessions, to commemorate key revolutionary events or to condemn the enemies of the revolution. Such sermons—*sermones, sermões* or *allocuzioni*—were traditional religious practices in ancien-régime societies, combining the communication of sacred content with elements of sheer theatricality in public performance, and could turn successful practitioners into popular figures.[109] These preachers discussed political matters from the pulpit or altar, but also in the public square. As the world of politics underwent a rapid expansion, so too the religious and political spheres were increasingly merging in novel ways. Priests thus became key interpreters of the new revolutionary discourse, while at times they also condemned, attacked and challenged the new political culture.

A common theme of the orations delivered by members of the clergy in Catholic countries was the biblical or evangelical roots of constitutional government. Priests reminded voters on the eve of elections for the new

---

107. For Spain, see Gérard Dufour, 'Estudio preliminar y presentación', in *Sermones revolucionarios del Trienio Liberal (1820–1823)*, ed. Gérard Dufour (Alicante: Instituto de Cultura Juan Gil-Albert, Diputación de Alicante, 1991), pp. 7–57 at 36–7; for Naples, see Alberti, *Atti del parlamento*, 4, p. 79.

108. See Faria, 'A condição', p. 322.

109. On these, see Dufour, 'Estudio preliminar'; Fausto Nicolini, *Aspetti della vita italo-spagnuola nel Cinque e Seicento* (Naples: Guida, 1934), pp. 325ff.

parliamentary assemblies of the divine origin of laws, and of the need for legislators to be inspired by divine wisdom in their legislative activities, which should be based on respect for God, love for the people and prudence.[110] Theology and biblical narratives might thereby be used to buttress the constitutional regimes. In a sermon delivered in Porto in Portugal to celebrate the new provisional government, the Augustinian friar and philosophy professor Francisco de Santa Bárbara highlighted God's endorsement of representative government by referring to the book of Exodus, according to which God had ordered that the Jewish legislator be advised by seventy wise men who would share with him the burden of power. He argued that the Catholic church should also be based on such anti-despotic principles. It was Jesus Christ's wish that 'the sovereign power of the Church reside in the ecumenical councils: and what are these councils, if not Cortes, that represent Christian society?'[111] Indeed, Santa Bárbara told his audience, it was precisely when it had opposed these principles that religion (including the bishop of Porto and the bishop of Cabo Verde, as well as the political leadership of the city) had become no more than 'fanaticism, superstition, simony, intolerance and cruel persecution'.[112]

What contributed to stirring up popular support and to encouraging popular aspirations were also the millenarian expectations used by members of the clergy and laymen alike to justify them. The period between the late eighteenth and the mid-nineteenth centuries can be described as a 'millenarian moment' throughout the Mediterranean area, during which revolutions, anticolonial rebellions and demands for people's rights were often justified in a providential and prophetic language that presented

110. Don Mariano García Zamora, 'Breve discurso o sermon que en la misa de espíritu-santo celebrada en la iglesia catedral de Cartagena sita en Murcia. [. . .] A los electores de partido' [1820], in *Sermones revolucionarios del Trienio Liberal (1820–1823)*, ed. Gérard Dufour (Alicante: Instituto de Cultura Juan Gil-Albert, Diputación de Alicante, 1991), pp. 85–97 at 89, 92–93.

111. António de Santa Bárbara, '*Sermão em acção de graças pela desejada e muito feliz união da Junta Provisoria do Governo Supremo do Reino com o governo interino de Lisboa—verificada no 1.º de outubro de 1820, que na igreja dos monges benedictinos da cidade do Porto, e no dia 22 do mesmo mez, quando o corpo do commercio deu o maior testemunho da sua gratidão ao Deos dos exercitos por tão memorando beneficio*', p. 27. The text is attached to this publication, which includes a description of the event: *Relação da solemne acção de graças que o Corpo do commercio da cidade do Porto ordenou se rendesse ao Altissimo dia 22 de Outubro, pela feliz união do Supremo Governo do Reino com o governo interino de Lisboa* (Coimbra: Real Imprensa da Universidade, 1821).

112. Santa Bárbara, *Sermão*, p. 20.

them as the inevitable outcome of a divine design.[113] In Naples, sermons delivered in churches by priests supportive of the new regime proclaimed the inevitable establishment of constitutional regimes whose principles could be found also in the Bible, and itinerant preachers announced the advent of a new era. Addressing his parishioners in a town not far from Naples, a priest who was presumably himself a member of the Carboneria announced, with the establishment of constitutional government, the advent of 'the reign of freedom, of peace and benevolence'.[114] In Sicily, itinerant priests, who abounded on the island at the time, were reported to have adopted messianic language in order to link the cause of revolution with moral regeneration and the message of the Gospels when addressing their audiences in public spaces.[115]

In some cases, the adoption of providential or millenarian themes derived from the manipulation and readaptation of older local prophetic and messianic traditions. In Portugal, for example, 'Sebastianismo', a venerable prophetic tradition based on the belief that the wise King Sebastião (1554–78) would come out of his concealment to lead the Christians and create a fifth empire, was given a new and final lease of life during the Napoleonic invasions, when it helped in mobilising anti-French opposition among the populace of Lisbon. In Portugal during the Triénio some revolutionaries argued that Dom João VI who after thirteen years in Brazil had made his way back to Portugal in order to accept the constitution, was in truth the legendary monarch at long last returned from his place of hiding.[116] While Sebastianismo was in decline after the 1820s, other millenarian traditions flourished and won a large popular following. Greek revolutionaries for their part adapted the literary genre of the oracle in order to reframe the Greek struggle as the final fulfilment of centuries-old prophecies foretelling the emancipation of the faithful from Ottoman captivity. Oracles took the form of commentaries upon the Apocalypse, in which the Ottomans were cast as the Antichrist, and a future liberation

113. I borrow the expression from Sanjay Subrahmanyam, 'Sixteenth-century Millenarianism from the Tagus to the Ganges', in Subrahmanyam, *Explorations in Connected History: From the Tagus to the Ganges* (New Delhi: Oxford University Press, 2005), p. 107.

114. *Allocuzione del sacerdote Don Luigi Ammendola, recitata nella parrochiale chiesa di S. Giuseppe di Otajano nel di' 16 luglio 1820* (Naples: Marotta, 1820), p. 6.

115. ASC, Intendenza Borbonica, 3146, ff. 191–95.

116. António Pereira de Figueiredo, *Os Sebastianistas combatidos, o egregio encoberto apparecido, o caso raro e maravilhoso acontecido* (Lisbon: J.F.M. de Campos, 1823). On this tradition, see Francisco Bethencourt, 'The Unstable Status of Sebastianism', in *Utopia in Portugal, Brazil, and Lusophone Africa*, ed. Francisco Bethencourt (Oxford: Peter Lang, 2015), pp. 43–69.

from oppression, occasionally associated with a specific date, was fore-seen. The famous revolutionary Rigas Velestinlis had been among the first to adopt this historical, millenarian framework for the call for emancipa-tion, in 1790, when he republished the the scholar-priest Theoklitos Poly-eidis's *Oracles of Agathangelos* in Vienna. But a similar language could also be found in the martyrologies, or the 'sermons of consolation', that constituted the most common forms of religious text, accessible to ordi-nary *reyes* (Christian subjects of the Ottomans) for centuries. It should therefore come as no surprise that a messianic language inscribing the emancipation of the Greeks within a providential design, and a narrative of oppression and resurrection, became common coinage during the revo-lution among all social groups, from monks and priests involved in the insurrection to peasants and military leaders. In this context Russia came to be seen as the saviour that would come to the rescue of the insurgents in the name of their shared Orthodoxy.[117] On the eve of the revolution as he crossed the region to gain support for the uprising, Papaflessas earned his fame through his oratory and the message he spread that Russia, the new Messiah, was ready to support the rebellion.[118] Even when it had become clear that Russia was not interested in sustaining the revolution, cler-ics continued to invoke its duties towards the Orthodox community, in the hope that it would finally intervene. On the inauguration of the first national assembly in Epidavros in December 1821, the Bishop Neophytos of Talantios spoke about the historical link between Russia and the Hel-lenes, concluding his sermon with a prayer to the czar.[119]

A variety of political languages and themes was thus grafted onto these providential frameworks. In Greece, centrality was given to the theme of patriotism, so vital was it to sustaining the war effort. In 1825, for instance, the bishop of Messolonghi called to arms priests, monks and the entire population, asking them to gather after mass and contribute to the

117. Marios Hatzopoulos, 'Oracular Prophecy and the Politics of Toppling Ottoman Rule in South-east Europe', *The Historical Review/La Revue Historique* 8 (2011): 95–116. On Rhigas's interest in this tradition, see Paschalis Kitromilides, 'Athos and the Enlight-enment', in Kitromilides, *An Orthodox Commonwealth: Symbolic Legacies and Cultural Encounters in Southeastern Europe* (Aldershot: Routledge, 2007), pp. 257–72 at 269. On the most important of these commentaries on the Apocalypse, their circulation and their relationship to popular religious culture among the Orthodox living under the Ottomans before the revolution, see Astérios Argyriou, *Les Exéges grecques de l'apocalypse à l'époque turque (1453–1821): Esquisse d'une historie des courants idéologiques au sein du people grec asservi* (Thessaloniki: Society for Macedonian Studies, 1982), pp. 101–2.

118. Millingen, *Memoirs*, p. 270.

119. Pouqueville, *Histoire*, 3, pp. 341–42.

reconstruction of the city walls. He defined this as an act of patriotism, and cursed those who would not give their contribution, dismissing them as 'unworthy of freedom and indifferent to this deleterious situation'.[120] In Naples, Spain and Portugal priests employed biblical episodes to communicate a number of different interpretations of the constitutional regime, often firmly within the liberal camp, but sometimes also bolstering a reductionist or anti-liberal reading of the meaning of recent political events. Santa Bárbara's sermon was primarily a celebration of enlightenment and of constitutional monarchism: he condemned the excesses of the French revolution, and referred to the 1791 monarchical constitution as its wisest institutional result. However, the sermon also mounted an explicit defence of revolutions against those who claimed that they were 'fatal to the happiness of the people', since it was calumny and oppression, not philosophy, that caused political convulsion, 'philosophy, as daughter of reason, [being] the most passionate friend of order'.[121] In words reminiscent of Madame de Staël's famous dictum, Santa Bárbara claimed that despotism was a modern phenomenon, while liberty was ancient. Thus he described the recent events in Portugal as peaceful, based on the concord of all the people and forces, and as a 'restoration' of Portuguese institutions, damaged in recent decades against the monarch's own wishes. This historicist interpretation of the events did not however prevent Santa Bárbara from stressing that the fundamental principle recognised by the revolution was that of popular sovereignty, a principle that justified the establishment of the constituent assembly of the Cortes. Priests might indeed at times go so far as to defend in churches the radical principles of the Carboneria. Don Luigi Amendola, addressing his congregation, phrased the transformations introduced by the constitution in personal terms, by listing what it was doing for each and every one of them:

It restores to you the first right of man, that will henceforth never be alienated[; . . .] it renders the press necessary to you, so that your voice may reach the king [. . .]. *Religion is yours* [emphasis in the original]. And so that you may with inner worship and outer adore the one Creator, it allows you to profess the One, True, Catholic and Roman religion [. . .]. It grants the right of representation.[122]

120. Ελληνικά Χρονικά [*Ellinika Chronika*], nos 102–3, 23 December 1825, in Koumarianou, Ο Τύπος στον Αγώνα (The press in the 'Struggle'), 2, pp. 329–30.

121. Santa Bárbara, *Sermão*, p. 17.

122. Gennaro Campanile, *Allocuzione nel rendimento di grazie all'altissimo per l'ottenuta costituzione* (Naples, 15 July 1820), pp. 27–28.

Thus an analysis of literature for the masses and of sermons and addresses demonstrates that while revolutionaries were borrowing from the Church the language of religion, the Church was itself engaging at the same time with the rights introduced by the constitution in order to find ideological accommodation between its own values and those advanced by the revolutionaries. That said, the Church hierarchies and a part of the clergy also endeavoured to combat liberal manipulations of religion, and the ensuing ideological conflict, during the revolution and in its aftermath, was bitter indeed. Sermons represented one of the key and most effective tools of communication in this culture war against the revolution. Some were delivered during the civil wars, and represented acts of defiance against the constitutional regimes by priests expected by these to preach the constitutions. Others were official acts of support for absolutism, delivered to celebrate its restoration. Whether they belonged to the first or to the second of these categories, counterrevolutionary sermons challenged the constitution at two levels. First, they emphasised and ridiculed the absurdity of revolutionary ideas. A parish priest forced to explain the constitution against his wishes in the province of Gerona in Catalonia observed that there was nothing remarkable about the concept of the nation as enshrined in the constitution. To state that the 'nation is the reunion of all Spaniards of both hemispheres' concealed the fact that it was thanks to the constitutionalists that the American territories had been lost. It was also self-evidently absurd, as all Spaniards could never be reunited in the same space, and therefore this 'nation' was a meaningless concept. A true Catholic could not have any doubts as to choosing between faith or freedom, religion or atheism, the constitution or Christ.[123] Second, these sermons challenged understandings of the constitution purportedly compatible with religion by reclaiming the 'correct' interpretation of the revolutionaries' own favourite vocabulary. In this respect, the anti-revolutionary homilies published by Archbishop Clary of the city of Catanzaro in the Kingdom of the Two Sicilies, just after the end of the revolution in 1821, significantly entitled *Il liberalismo cristiano*, represents an interesting case in point.[124] Clary aimed to provide an anti-revolutionary interpretation of the concepts that constituted the foundations of *liberalismo*: namely, liberty, society, nationality and

123. APR, Papeles Reservados de Fernando VII, 21, ff. 133–35: 'Sermon que el día 25 de agosto del presente año [1822], pronunció en la Yglesia el Párroco del Pueblo de **la Provincia de Gerona'.

124. Michele Basilio Clary, *Il liberalismo cristiano: Omelie sacro-politiche* (Messina: Giuseppe Pappalardo, 1821).

patriotism, so that Christians could be true 'liberals', rather than 'libertines'.[125] For Clary, moral freedom could only exist in association with virtue, and political freedom in compliance with law and with respect for authority. In either case, freedom thus found its rightfulness in obedience to God. Outside these boundaries there existed only slavery and vice. The Christian, as opposed to the revolutionary, nation was an organic and living whole bound together by the principle of fraternity, whose head, represented by the king, could not be separated from the body. This is why the truly liberal nation was the one loyal to the monarch who had put an end to the constitutional experiment.[126] In 1823 in Portugal, meanwhile, José Agostinho de Macedo, a prominent counterrevolutionary intellectual, celebrated the end of the constitutional period with a sermon attacking one of the central principles of the revolution, that of political regeneration. For Macedo this principle was nothing less than a hatchet used to cut the roots of the social tree, such as to destroy everything. What Portugal needed instead was to combine a true political regeneration with a moral regeneration, one that would require a contribution from all classes, from the aristocrats, to the clergy, the army, the civil servants and youth, to re-establish the true and full sovereignty and independence of the Portuguese nation.[127] The explanation to the faithful of the supposedly correct meaning of the concepts needed to rebuild the national community after the revolutionary cataclysm constituted one of the priests' most important contributions to the return of absolutism.

The politics of miracles

As mentioned previously, supporters of the constitutions tended to look down on popular cults and often dismissed popular religiosity as mere superstition to be replaced by a rational, well-ordered form of worship. They often considered such cults to be the expression of a credulity that was itself the product of a lack of enlightenment and could only reinforce despotism. However, against the revolutionaries' expectations, the revolutions were in fact marked by a resurgence of popular forms of religiosity, and, in particular instances, miraculous apparitions and prophecies proliferated. For ordinary men and women, divine intervention seemed to be the only explanation available to account for the exceptional circumstances

125. Ibid., pp. 3–5, 14–17.
126. Ibid., pp. 93–120.
127. José Agostinho de Macedo, *Sermão de acção de graças pelo restabelecimento da monarquia independente* (Lisbon: Impressão da Rua Formoza, 1823), pp. 34–39.

they were experiencing, to render acceptable what seemed to be the break-down of ordinary life, to make sense of the upheavals brought about by these events and to give expression to the fears or anxieties they produced. The divine thus offered explanations for the exceptional.

Although their content was not necessarily new, in such circumstances these phenomena took on new meanings, and their occurrence often had unpredictable and even enduring consequences. In Palermo, for instance, where the insurrection had coincided with the festivities in honour of the city's patron saint Santa Rosalia, insurgents searched for signs that the saint protected their actions and approved of the role they were playing in fomenting the revolution. The urban crowds took the fact that the candles lit during that night continued to burn during the following days without the need for additional oil as a miracle, and evidence of the saint's blessing of their own deeds. In this case, miracles represented also a form of legiti-mation of the island's right to be independent from Naples.[128]

Some of these spontaneous religious phenomena had even broader political and institutional implications. Secular and religious elites in fact tried to manipulate and exploit them to serve their own political pur-poses, or would sometimes attempt to control or suppress them to prevent disturbances. Analysis of the circumstances surrounding their birth and development may therefore also cast some light on the religious, political and social disagreements that exploded as a result of the revolutions. In Naples, the military pronunciamiento coincided with numerous miracu-lous apparitions of the Virgin Mary being recorded on the outskirts of the city, and the mass gatherings that followed made the authorities anxious about the revolutionary potential of such religious events. The response of the populace of Naples to the declaration of the constitution was to associate this regime change with otherworldly signs; and when similar phenomena resurfaced in 1825, four years after the return of absolutism, it was thus natural for the authorities to become concerned that such public displays of piety would lead to demonstrations, disorders or even revolu-tion. In that year in the church of San Nicola in Caserta, just a few kilo-metres from Naples, where the Bourbons had their summer residence, a boy declared that an image of the Virgin had miraculously appeared to him. From this apparition a new cult would seem to have emerged:

128. BCP, Manoscritti, Qq F 162: 'Cronica degli avvenimenti di Palermo in luglio, agosto, settembre ed ottobre del 1820. Scritta da Don Giacomo Dané orologiaio della Corte e della Specola nel momento in cui gli avvenimenti andavano succedendo l'uno all'altro', p. 22.

the church became the object of pilgrimages from the entire province, and crowds started to gather around images of the Virgin that were hung on poles along the roads leading into the capital city. As a consequence, and precisely because of fears of new revolutionary disorders, the government took measures to reduce permits to travel across the province, and the police intervened to disperse the crowds and dismantle the sites of worship.[129]

Not all apparitions seemed to suggest divine support for the constitution, however. During the ten months of constitutional government, miraculous events interpreted by many as signs of God's disapproval represented a serious threat to the revolution. In July 1820, in the city of Cosenza in Calabria, the carbonari had successfully taken control of the city by ousting the intendente and organising the city militia, with the explicit approval of the local population. However, between the summer and the autumn of 1820 a famine affecting the region did much to undermine their popularity. In November 1820 the appearance and subsequent explosion of a meteorite in the sky above the city provided fertile ground for prophetic interpretations: for the enemies of the revolution this event signalled a divine punishment directed against it. The persistence of the famine in the region was blamed upon the constitution. To the revolutionaries' dismay, many were willing to believe these interpretations.[130]

More than anywhere else, it is in Portugal and Greece that miraculous apparitions (in both cases related to the cult of the Virgin Mary) cast light on the political divisions between clerics and civil authorities produced by the revolutions, and highlight the extent to which popular piety could not be easily controlled. In these countries certain local events gave rise to cults with a remarkable popular following. Controversies about miracles in Portugal demonstrate the degree to which the struggle between revolutionaries and counterrevolutionaries was waged also in the domain of the sacred. The discovery in May 1822 of an image of the Virgin Mary on the bank of a river in Carnaxide, on the outskirts of Lisbon, seemed at first to be just one of the very many apparitions and interrelated prophecies pervading Portugal in the aftermath of the revolution; soon after the establishment of the new regime, in fact, angels announcing the end of the constitutions started to appear to nuns in convents, and prophecies describing the revolutionaries as the Antichrist circulated along with rumours that the constitution was to be blamed for crop failures and the

129. ASR, Fondo Statella, 245, 18, ff. 96–99: Della Torre to Statella, Turin, 4 July 1825.
130. Andreotti, *Storia*, 3, pp. 208, 210, 211.

harsh winter weather.[131] However, the apparition of Nossa Senhora da Rocha de Carnaxide soon acquired a fame greater than any other contemporary miracle or prophecy. It at once attracted large numbers of pilgrims from the surrounding villages and from the capital. Its remarkable popular following turned this new cult into a bone of political and religious contention. At first the controversy it produced was primarily religious, opposing as it did clerical members of the Jacobeia movement to the supporters of enlightened religiosity. While the former, who tended to be antirevolutionary, were very supportive of these forms of popular devotion, the latter condemned them as mere signs of superstition. But soon the counterrevolutionaries started to take ownership of this cult, with aristocrats visiting the site and Queen Carlota sending a lamp made of silver. Concerned about the potential threat to order posed by this new cult, and keen to control and institutionalise it, the constitutional authorities decided to transfer the image from Carnaxide to the cathedral of Lisbon only two months after the miracle. This decision was met with stiff resistance from the local population, however, and constitutional troops had to accompany the public procession for its translation to the capital, to prevent further disturbances.[132] In fact the constitutional regime failed in the end to take control of this cult, and royalist propaganda turned it into one of its symbols.

For the counterrevolutionary press, the apparition of the Senhora da Rocha presaged the end of the constitution: it represented a providential intervention. Retrospectively, as absolutist publicists were to note, the very date when the Virgin revealed herself on the shores of the river was also seen to constitute a prophetic message. The Count of Amarante's military pronunciamiento in Vila Franca de Xira that led to a restoration of the absolute monarchy in fact took place on the first anniversary of the apparition, at the end of May 1823.[133] From then on, the royal family, and in particular Dom Miguel and Dona Carlota Joaquina, made regular public homages to this Virgin, turning it into a symbol of the absolutist cause. A visit to the the shrine of Nossa Senhora in the cathedral of Lisbon was one of the first public acts of Dom Miguel when he came back to Portugal to reclaim the throne in February 1828. The re-establishment of the absolute

131. Faria, *Os liberais*, pp. 937–39.

132. Maria de Fátima Sá e Melo Ferreira, 'Nuestra Señora de Rocha de Carnaxide: Una devoción del miguelismo', in *Discursos y devociones religiosas en la península ibérica, 1780–1860: De la crisis del antiguo régimen a la consolidación del liberalismo*, ed. Rafael Serrano García, Ángel de Prado Moura and Elisabel Larriba (Valladolid: Ediciones de la Universidad de Valladolid, 2014), pp. 151–61.

133. *O Punhal dos Corcundas*, no. 3, 1823, pp. 27–28; *Refutação da constituição dos insurgentes* (Lisbon: Simão Thaddeo Ferreira, 1823), pp. 1–18;.

monarchy was in turn celebrated with popular ceremonies in honour of the Senhora da Rocha in many parishes around the capital.[134]

In Greece, meanwhile, and specifically on the island of Tinos, in 1821 apparitions of the Virgin Mary ('Panagia') took place in the context of a breakdown in the pre-existing institutional and power relations, and the intensification of conflicts between the local Catholic and Orthodox communities. The discovery of icons in specific places thanks to dreams and visions pre-dated the events of Tinos of 1821 and belonged to a venerable tradition. But unlike earlier apparitions, always linked to objects found along the coastline, those on Tinos related to icons buried in the ground rather than floating on the sea.[135] Between 1821 and 1822, at the inception of the Greek revolution, the Virgin did in fact appear again and again in dreams to the inhabitants of Tinos. At first the church authorities ignored or even condemned these

FIGURE 26. *Verdadeiro retrato da Milagroza Imagem de N. S. da Conceição da Rocha* . . . ('True depiction of the miraculous image of Nossa Senhora da Rocha [de Carnaxide], discovered 31 May 1822'; engraving from the workshop of António Joaquim Ribeiro, Lisbon, 1822–1830[?]; Biblioteca Nacional de Portugal, Lisbon). Image: Wikimedia Commons

signs. It was not until a nun repeatedly dreamed about the presence of an icon in a field that efforts were made to find it. In the end, in 1823, an ancient icon was indeed discovered in a field, inside a piece of wood. This discovery led to the almost immediate construction of a church. By 1824 a site of worship had been established in the icon's honour, called 'Evangelistria', in the town of Agios Nikolaos. The island was in turmoil at the time: plague was raging, and thousands of refugees would soon disembark, greatly increasing the size of the local population. In addition, the

---

134. Lousada, 'A contra-revolução'; Ferreira, 'Nuestra Señora', p. 157.

135. Charles Stewart, 'Dreaming of Buried Icons in the Kingdom of Greece', in *Networks of Power in Modern Greece: Essays in Honour of John Campbell*, ed. Mark Mazower (London: Hurst Publishers, 2008), pp. 89–108.

reluctance of the local Catholic community and their leader, Bishop Collaro, to join the revolution increased Orthodox hostility against them. By 1824 such hostility had escalated, resulting in unprecedented acts of violence: armed Orthodox villagers launched attacks on Catholic communities. In turn the arrival of representatives of the central government revived old rivalries between local factions, and between the local Orthodox bishop, who was lukewarm towards the revolution, and these factions. Against this background, in 1825 another miracle, involving the restoration of sight to a blind child, the son of a prominent Phanariot associated with Tinos, Georgios Mavroyeni, earned Panagia an even wider, national, reputation: that year the fame of this religious site started to spread beyond the island and to attract a steady flow of pilgrims across the Aegean. This cult represented much more than simply a new religious phenomenon, however: its institutionalisation provided an opportunity to resolve most of the social and political tensions that had exploded in the previous years. It enabled the local Orthodox church to reassert itself after the collapse of Ottoman rule, providing all the local factions with an opportunity to settle their disagreements as members of the board running the site (chaired by the Orthodox bishop). Last but not least, it gave Tinos a new national visibility. The net result of these novel circumstances was to bring about a pacification of the island.[136]

What the cults of Panagia in Tinos and of the Senhora de la Rocha de Carnaxide in Lisbon thus demonstrate is that in this period miracles did not always remain temporary phenomena, but could engender enduring popular cults associated with new and permanent sites of worship. Their gradual—and not always uncontroversial—institutionalisation contributed to the consolidation of some of the legacies of the revolutions: namely, the full integration of local communities into the national project in Greece, and the establishment of a powerful popular counterrevolutionary movement supported by a royal pretender in Portugal.

Conclusions

During the 1820s revolutions, a variety of actors, both within and beyond the churches, competed to advance religious justifications for alternative types of civil authority. These culture wars not only opposed priests to revolutionary elites, but divided the ranks of those within churches too.

136. An account and analysis can be found in Mark Mazower, 'Villagers, Notables and Imperial Collapse: The Virgin Mary on Tinos' in *Networks of Power in Modern Greece: Essays in Honour of John Campbell*, ed. Mark Mazower (London: Hurst Publishers, 2008), pp. 69–87.

As a result, the populations of Spain, Portugal, Naples, Sicily and Greece were constantly exposed to a wide variety of new and conflicting brands of religion. Although the effective impact and influence of clerical preaching is hard to gauge, it is undeniable that priests played a fundamental role as cultural mediators in the education of local communities in the new political vocabulary of nationalism and constitutionalism, mobilising them either in favour of or against the new political order. What made religion a particularly effective and convincing tool of mobilisation were civil wars on the Iberian peninsula, its integration into the language of the Carboneria in Naples, and the confessional nature of the conflict in the case of the Greek revolution. The emphasis on a reconciliation between religious values, nation and constitutional government advocated both by some clerics and by civilians demonstrates the markedly communitarian dimension of the early liberal ideology of the 1820s revolutionaries.

When looking back at the period of the revolutions and reflecting upon the causes of their failure, many of their protagonists, from their places of exile abroad, considered that both the role played by the clergy and religious questions more generally had determined their fate, and more effective solutions were needed if further attempts at introducing representative government were ever to succeed in future. Many of them agreed that although the context had not been favourable to it, failure to defend religious toleration more vocally had been an error. Life in France and Britain, and exposure to the ideas of, and criticism by, some of their supporters in these countries convinced them that in order to obtain the backing of public opinion abroad, support for religious toleration was needed.[137] They often blamed the clergy for the failure of the revolutions, and lamented the extent to which it had supported the counterrevolution. From his London exile Guglielmo Pepe argued that it was the Catholic clergy who had thrown 'back into slavery the people of the peninsula'. To interest the Spanish clergy in the cause of freedom, he believed that the constitutional government should have sent its most conservative element to the Americas, and let younger clerics get married.[138]

However, both the exiled revolutionaries of the 1820s and later generations remained convinced that the solution to the problem of freedom and the defeat of fanaticism still lay in religion and in the reform of the clergy. On the Iberian peninsula religion was lauded as a salve to heal

137. See Fernández Sebastián, 'Toleration'.
138. Guglielmo Pepe, 'The Non-Establishment of Liberty in Spain, Naples, Portugal and Piedmont Explained', *The Pamphleteer* (London: A. J. Valpy, 1824), pp. 223–86, quotations at 230, 268.

the wounds of societies affected by civil conflicts, to replace the materialism and the fanaticism that had caused previous revolutions to fail in the 1820s. In Portugal, once the civil war had ended in 1834 and the revolution of September 1836 had abolished the moderate 1826 constitution, emphasis on the beneficial effects of religion reflected the debate staged by the elites regarding the desirability or otherwise of popular participation in the constitutional order. In his *A voz do profeta* (1837), the liberal Alexandre Herculano defended constitutional government and, in language reminiscent of the French liberal philosopher-priest Félicité de Lamennais's *Paroles*, identified in the Gospels a message in favour of human liberation and against despotism. Mindful, however, of the popular support that the absolutist Dom Miguel had enjoyed, he also argued that the rule of the *plebs*, which he described as democracy, would lead to a despotism of the masses, thereby associating popular sovereignty with the *gentalha* (rabble). Only the educated belonged to the 'people'.[139] Looking back at the failures of the earlier liberal experiments of the 1820s, the Portuguese poet João Baptista de Almeida Garrett for his part concluded that, after the traumatic experience of the civil war, only Christianity could reinvigorate liberalism, by washing away the materialism and irreligiosity of *vintismo*—the radicalism of the early 1820s.[140] The perceived need in the late 1830s to refound liberalism on the basis of a reformed Christianity in order to defeat Carlism also affected the adoption of a religious message in Spanish literary circles, and among the political elites. In his introduction to the translation of Lamennais's *Paroles*, which appeared as *El dogma de los hombres libres* (1836), the Spanish *progresista* Mariano José de Larra thus argued that Spain required a revolution based on a pure and tolerant religion allied with freedom and with liberty of conscience (an alliance that liberals had failed to forge in the past), in order to defeat the fanaticism recently displayed during the civil wars. That alliance could not be re-established on the basis of the Cádiz Constitution of 1812, given the excessively prominent role that this had assigned to Catholicism. Such views became increasingly common from the 1830s onwards among Spanish republicans and democrats.[141]

139. Alexandre Herculano, *A voz do Profeta* [1837], now in *Opúsculos*, ed. Jorge Custódio and José Manuel Garcia, 5 vols (Lisbon: Presença, 1982–85), 1, pp. 43–77.

140. João Baptista da Silva Leitão de Almeida Garrett, *Viagens na minha terra*, with an introduction by João Gaspar Simões, vol. 1 of Almeida Garrett, *Obras completas de Almeida Garrett*, 10 vols (Lisbon, Círculo de Leitores, 1984 [1846]), pp. 329–30.

141. Félicité de Lamennais, *El dogma de los hombres libres: Palabras de un creyente* (Madrid: José Maria Repulles, 1836); Emilio La Parra López, 'El eco de Lamennais en el progresismo español: Larra y Joaquín María López', in *Libéralisme chrétien et catholicisme*

The end of the revolutions was marked by a renewed alliance between church and state in the name of the principles of absolutism. The pope went on to condemn secret societies, first in September 1821, when he issued a bull explicitly targeting the Carboneria, and then again in 1830 when he renewed his condemnation of Masonic organisations. In Spain, Fernando VII praised the clergy for its conduct during the constitutional period, and rewarded absolutist clerics who had been outspoken in their condemnation of the constitution. Archbishops who had inveighed against the constitution or participated in the civil war received honours: Veremundo Teixeiro of Valencia, for instance, was decorated with the Cross of Isabel la Católica. The regency had re-established all the monasteries closed down by the liberals, which also recovered their confiscated properties, while Jesuits were allowed to return. Bishops also set up independent 'inquisitorial' juntas to purge the kingdom, juntas that the king, concerned about their autonomous powers, only grudgingly accepted.[142] In the Kingdom of the Two Sicilies, meanwhile, it was rather the government that would charge the Catholic hierarchy with the purging from its ranks of liberal clerics. So-called *giunte di scrutinio* were set up under the supervision of the Church to establish which priests and monks had been members of secret societies. In Sicily the temporary reconciliation between the island's elites and the monarchy was sealed by the appointment of Cardinal Gravina, who had presided over the revolutionary provisional government in the initial stages of the revolution, as *luogotenente generale* of the island between March and July 1821, to re-establish order and supervise the giunte.[143]

However, this was only a temporary phenomenon. After the revolutions church–state relations in fact became increasingly difficult. First of all, both absolutist and constitutional governments continued to be committed to the erosion of church privileges. The determination of Pope Pius VII to centralise the governance of the Church and render bishops loyal to the pope rather than to monarchs failed to prevent the state from weakening church authority.[144] In Spain in 1823, bishops demanded the

libéral en Espagne, France et Italie dans la première moitié du XIXᵉ siècle: Colloque internationale 12/13/14 novembre 1987 (Aix-en-Provence: Université de Provence, 1989), pp. 323–42.

142. Callahan, *Church, Politics, and Society*, p. 140.

143. Labate, *Un decennio*, pp. 114ff.

144. Javier Francisco Ramón Solans, 'A Renewed Global Power: The Restoration of the Holy See and the Triumph of Ultramontanism, 1814–1848', and Andoni Artola 'Was a State–Church Alliance Really Possible? The Case of the Spanish Episcopate and the Crown (1814–1833)', both in *A History of the European Restorations: Culture, Society and*

reintroduction of the Holy Inquisition, but the king never went so far as actually to reinstate it. With the return of liberalism in 1836, the state waged an even more radical attack on church privileges.[145] In Portugal too, although Dom Miguel repealed the constitution, he did not reinstate the Holy Inquisition. He readmitted the Jesuits, but did not grant them any privileges or return any properties to them. With the defeat of Dom Miguel between 1833 and 1834, the new constitutional government decided to assume full control of all clerical appointments, from bishops to parish priests, dismissing all bishops chosen by Dom Miguel, closing down all monasteries with the exception of the nunneries, depriving even these of the right to accept new novices, and selling off their properties. The papal nuncio was expelled. This led to a schism within the Portuguese church. The pope refused to recognise the bishops appointed by the constitutional government, and some of the bishops appointed by Dom Miguel therefore continued to act in clandestinity. It was only in 1841 that this crisis was resolved, by a compromise between the Portuguese government and the papacy.[146]

Even in the context of ever-harsher conflict, however, a section of the clergy chose to support constitutional government. The events of the 1820s had irremediably modified the politics of the Catholic clergies, encouraging political activism independent of the official views of the pope. Even when there were dramatic confrontations between the Holy See and liberal or revolutionary governments, the clergy was by no means united in joining the counterrevolutionary front or in following papal instructions. In Naples and Sicily, in spite of the explicit papal condemnation of the Carboneria in 1821, priests continued to flock to the secret societies, whether the Carboneria or else new organisations established subsequently and in rivalry with it, and to take part in conspiratorial activities and uprisings. Their biographies often demonstrate a direct relationship between their support for revolution in 1820 and later events. Just to give one example: two of the main organisers of a failed 1828 uprising in the Cilento (an area south of the city of Salerno, not far from Naples) were clerics. Before plotting this uprising, the canon Antonio Maria De Luca

Religion, ed. Michael Broers and Ambrogio A. Caiani, 2 vols (London: Bloomsbury, 2019), 2, pp. 72–81, and 61–72.

145. Callahan, *Church, Politics, and Society*, pp. 158–66.

146. Manuel Braga da Cruz, 'As relações entre a Igreja e o Estado liberal: Do "cisma" à Concordata (1832–1848)', in *O liberalismo na Península Ibérica na primeira metade do século XIX*, ed. Miriam Halpern Pereira, Maria de Fátima Sá e Melo Ferreira and João B. Serra, 2 vols (Lisbon: Sá da Costa Editora, 1982), 1, pp. 223–35.

had been a protagonist of the 1799 Neapolitan revolution, and had been elected to the parliament in 1820.[147] Such itineraries are true also of many of the priests active in the uprisings that broke out in the provinces of the kingdom between 1847 and 1848.[148] Nor was this a uniquely Neapolitan phenomenon. During the schism of the Portuguese church between 1834 and 1841, when the Holy See refused to recognise the appointments made by the liberal governments, only a minority of clerics, in the north of the country, were actively hostile to the liberal regime.[149] Likewise in Spain, with the outbreak of the first Carlist civil war in 1834, only a minority of the regular and secular clergies actively supported the pretender and joined the insurrection.[150]

In some ways Greece continued to be different from Catholic countries. While the Catholic church was becoming a more centralised organisation, and the bishops' loyalty to the pope (over that to their monarchs) the norm, the recognition and consolidation of the Greek state confirmed the permanent divorce of its church from the patriarchate of Constantinople. In 1833 the regency that ruled on behalf of the new King Otto of Bavaria, then still a minor, formalised the separation of the Greek church from the patriarchate. Under this new settlement, the Church would respond directly to the king, its official head, and would be managed by a synod of bishops chosen by him directly. The king himself would also have the final approval of any episcopal appointment. At the same time, the new Greek administration set out to do what revolutionary governments in the rest of Europe had already started: namely, to suppress monastic communities and take over their properties. While during the revolution governments had seen monastic communities as key allies in their fight against the Ottomans, after 1832 the members of Otto's regency, and in particular Georg von Maurer, considered them not only an unnecessary burden upon society, but also a threat to the new regime. Given their loyalty to the patriarchate and sympathy for Russia, as well as their influence over the peasantry, they could be a source of sedition and undermine the new state. Between 1833 and 1834 the Bavarian administration therefore suppressed all monasteries with no more than six monks, confiscating their

147. Matteo Mazziotti, *La rivolta del Cilento nel 1828 narrata da documenti inediti* (Rome: Società Editrice Dante Alighieri, 1906).

148. Delpu, *Un autre Risorgimento*, pp. 264–71; Delpu 'La parole des prêtres, un outil de politisation révolutionnaire (Royaume des Deux-Siciles, 1799–1848)', in *Rhétorique et politisation, de la fin des Lumières au Printemps des Peuples*, ed. Sophie-Anne Leterrier and Olivier Tort (Arras: Artois Presses Université, 2021), pp. 197–210.

149. Ferreira, *Rebeldes*, pp. 75–81.

150. Callahan, *Church, Politics, and Society*, p. 150.

properties and forbidding donations to monastic communities, and closed down all but three nunneries. These events were not painless, and in fact they provoked a great deal of resistance, within society more widely as much as within the Church itself. Both the attack on monasticism and the establishment of an autocephalous church controlled by the state were deeply unpopular. The traditionalist wing of the Church, headed by Oikonomos, lamented the permanent separating off of a national church, which could ultimately only undermine Orthodoxy and facilitate the influence of Western missionaries. Priests and monks stirred up popular protests against the settlement for years to come. Yet in spite of these protests, the new church became the foremost defender of national ideology. In addition, neither the advocates of the national church nor its enemies questioned the identification between Orthodoxy and the new state. This is true also of those who resented Bavarian absolutism and hoped for a reintroduction of representative government.[151]

Perhaps the most enduring legacy of all of the 1820s revolutions was thus the notion that constitutional government required religiously homogeneous communities to survive. In spite of the fact that voices in favour of toleration became more common, especially within the left wing of the constitutional front, and among democrats and republicans in particular, all the constitutions that were introduced in Portugal, Spain, Naples and Greece between the 1830s and 1850s included a religious definition of the nation, confirming the direct link between religion and citizenship rights. In Portugal, all the constitutions introduced between 1826 and 1910 declared that cults other than the Catholic one could only be practised in private, by foreigners. In Spain, when after the 1836 revolution the progresistas managed to have approved a constitution that reflected their own values, they did not question the notion of the exclusively Catholic nature of the Spanish nation. This idea was retained and reinforced by the Spanish moderados, who considered religious toleration a destabilising source of conflict and disagreement in society, when they imposed their own brand of constitutionalism. In Naples the constitution introduced during the revolution of 1848 reaffirmed that no cult other than the Catholic one was permitted in the kingdom.[152] It was only in Piedmont

---

151. Frazee, *Orthodox Church*, pp. 104–15, 120–21, 125–27; Petropulos, *Politics and Statecraft*, pp. 180–92; Frary, *Russia*, pp. 118–120.

152. Jesús Millán y García-Varela and María Cruz Romeo Mateo, 'La nación católica en el liberalismo: Las perspectivas sobre la unidad religiosa en la España liberal, 1808–1868', *Historia y Política* 34 (2015): 183–209. For Portugal, see Miriam Halpern Pereira, 'Nación, ciudadanía y religión en Portugal (1820–1910)', *Ayer* 69 (2008): 277–302. For the Italian

that the promulgation of the Statuto Albertino in 1848 put an end to the discrimination suffered by religious minorities, the Protestant Waldensians and the Jews: for the first time, the members of these religious communities were granted full citizenship rights, by virtue of two separate decrees issued in February and March 1848. Thus, overall, the belief that the homogeneity of the nation expressed in religious terms was a boon to be protected represented another long-lasting legacy of the 1820 revolutions across southern Europe.

---

peninsula, Eugenio Federico Biagini, 'Citizenship and Religion in the Italian Constitutions, 1796–1849', *History of European Ideas* 37 (2011): 211–17.

Unfinished Business

THE AGE OF REVOLUTIONS IN SOUTHERN
EUROPE AFTER THE 1820S

THIS BOOK HAS sought to show the extent to which southern European societies became politicised to an unprecedented degree during the revolutions of the 1820s. New political practices and older forms of protest mobilised all ranks of society, including women. Although in Spain and Portugal in particular the constitution divided societies, it also attracted a substantial popular following. The role of the army, the clergy and of specific social groups such as artisans, sailors and peasants has been highlighted. Such mobilisation in favour of the constitution served sometimes to defend corporate rights or community and professional privileges that had been eroded, but also to advance the interests of social groups hostile to these. Although during these revolutions constitutional government was understood in different, even conflicting, ways, it gained novel support from public opinion not only in urban settings, but also in the countryside. Faced with conflicting expectations, revolutionaries did not seek to overturn the existing social order. In Naples, Spain, Sicily and Greece they sought simply to abolish or limit legal privileges and to promote equality before the law. This was carried out in a more radical fashion in Spain; more timidly in Portugal. Only a small minority of revolutionaries actively supported a substantial redistribution of land, for instance. At the same time, these revolutions marked the rise of a new political leadership, distinct from its predecessors, although such change was uneven. It was in Greece that the most radical revision of the social order took place, featuring as it did the replacement of an entire ruling class. In Naples, Spain and Portugal too, a new political elite emerged at the national level and, some evidence suggests, also at the local level. Conversely, in Sicily the revolution reaffirmed the supremacy of the corporate interests of the city of Palermo represented by the aristocracy and the artisans.

Whatever the conflicting expectations the revolutions had aroused, their end left a significant proportion of the populations of southern European countries unhappy with the political settlements that had eventually been reached, enforced as they were by foreign military and diplomatic intervention. The political mobilisation of the 1820s could only be temporarily suppressed. As a matter of fact, the regimes set up in the aftermath of the revolutions would prove no less unstable than the revolutionary ones had been. An analysis of the political vicissitudes and the turbulent history of the succeeding decades in Portugal, Spain, Naples and Greece serves to demonstrate, retrospectively, the enduring impact of the revolutions of the 1820s. The peculiar convergence of the various upheavals of the 1820s was not replicated in the years that followed. Nonetheless, Portugal, Spain, the Italian peninsula and Greece alike were shaken by many rebellions, revolutions and civil wars, lasting until the 1870s. Indeed, in intensity and frequency they far outnumber those erupting in the rest of Europe in the same period: a of period of intense instability that lasted for at least four decades. Its chronology overlapped, but did not coincide with, the dates conventionally associated with the age of revolutions in western Europe. With the exception of uprisings on the Italian peninsula, 1830 and 1848 were less important as revolutionary turning points than 1836, 1840, 1846 and 1854. A degree of stability across southern Europe was only achieved between the 1860s and 1870s, when arguably the revolutionary cycle initiated in the 1820s came to an end.

An important legacy of the 1820s was the fact that subsequent revolutions in the name of the constitution or against it continued to be led by military officers. Military intervention through the practice of the pronunciamiento remained the favourite (and most successful) tool to enforce a broad range of alternative political projects in all of these countries (with the exception of Naples) until at least the 1860s. Of equal importance, moreover, was that widespread mobilisation in favour of constitutional government, or the broadening of its popular base through a broader suffrage, often remained associated with demands to protect municipal autonomy and provincial self-rule against interference from the centre. Moreover, during these four decades after the 1820s revolutions, notions of a religiously homogeneous national community continued to be associated with demands for constitutional government, and defended by subsequent constitutional regimes. Finally, in each subsequent revolutionary upheaval, and every time a new constitution was introduced, the memory of the 1820s revolutions and their martyrs was mobilised to legitimise regime change and win popular backing. While the memory of the 1820s remained for a long time a divisive one, it was gradually integrated into the national canon of each country, and absorbed into the public discourse of the constitutional monarchies that were established across southern Europe by the 1860s and 1870s.

The 1830s represented at the same time a turning point for the movements in favour of constitutional government in southern Europe. Monarchical reluctance to grant constitutional government or to broaden its social basis led to a substantial realignment of the social and political forces in favour of change. What exacerbated the turbulence of the following decades was the emergence of novel forms of mass mobilisation, and new and conflicting political movements in favour of or against constitutionalism. On the left, a new programme that advocated democracy and republican government in the name of popular sovereignty and equal political rights took shape after the 1830s. It led to the development and consolidation of a new working-class sociability and of political parties that started openly to question monarchical power. Meanwhile a more conservative and anti-revolutionary brand of constitutionalism emerged, which conversely would challenge the legitimacy of popular mobilisation, popular sovereignty and revolution. Thus the divisions already existing among supporters of the constitution in the 1820s grew deeper in the following decades, crystallising as an increasingly binary opposition. The liberal family came to be split between a conservative strand and a more progressive one, and their respective supporters disagreed about how broad suffrage should be, about the powers to be vested in the monarch and in the parliament and about the desirability or otherwise of popular participation. In this new context, democracy and liberalism gradually became alternative political projects. This phenomenon was a function of an increasingly international language of politics, whose adoption in southern Europe was facilitated by the international character of the lives and culture of its political class. It was also a response to the subversive potential that various sectors within the urban and rural masses had manifested on the Iberian peninsula when siding with counterrevolution.[1]

1. On these concepts as tool of political mobilisation in southern Europe, see the relevant essays in Joanna Innes and Mark Philp, eds, *Re-imagining Democracy in the Mediterranean, 1780–1860* (Oxford: Oxford University Press, 2018), and in particular Philp and Eduardo Posada-Carbò, 'Liberalism and Democracy', pp. 179–204.

These new alternative projects were embraced both by the former revolutionaries of the 1820s and by a younger generation that had not directly experienced the uprisings of that momentous decade.

Regardless of political affiliations, the constitutions and the events of the 1820s represented the starting point for any subsequent reflection about how to find a new and enduring political settlement. It was while in exile, an experience shared by most revolutionary leaders from Naples, Piedmont, Sicily, Spain and Portugal, that the greater part of this retrospective analysis of the 1820s was conducted. Either through memoirs, through pamphlets or through articles that remained in manuscript form or were published abroad, the revolutionaries went back to that decade to reflect upon the causes of failure. This literary production turned the political battles that had divided the revolutionaries into a 'war of memory', one in which old enemies and rivals blamed each other and indulged in bitter recriminations regarding the failure of their political programmes. This literature combined a desire to celebrate, commemorate and discuss past events with a commitment to finding new political solutions. It was by learning from past mistakes that revolutionary programmes could be relaunched, sometimes with the same objectives and strategies that had been tested in that decade, and sometimes with new ones. This epilogue looks at the legacies of the 1820s through the lens of the personal experiences and individual trajectories of four revolutionaries who lived on to take part in the political upheavals of the following decades: the Greek Yannis Macriyannis (1797–1864); the Neapolitan Guglielmo Pepe (1783–1855); the Portuguese Bernardo de Sá Nogueira de Figueiredo, Viscount (from 1834) and Marquis (from 1864) of Sá da Bandeira (1795–1876); and the Spanish Antonio Alcalá Galiano (1798–1865). Pepe, Nogueira and Galiano all experienced exile abroad: Pepe lived most of his life abroad after 1821, Galiano was exiled intermittently in the 1820s, 1830s and 1840s and Nogueira lived abroad for a much shorter period during the 1820s. Another thing common to this group was the professional background of most of them. Macriyannis, Pepe and Nogueira had all been military officers during the 1820s, and continued their military careers beyond the that decade. Although their trajectories differed greatly, they all bear out the importance the military class continued to play in conceiving and implementing revolutionary change in their countries for the decades to come. Nogueira became a key protagonist in the unstable political life of his country from the 1830s until the end of his days, when the army finally stopped interfering in politics. Macriyannis, conversely, experienced persecution, temporary imprisonment and marginalisation for the greater

part of his life, but contributed at the same time to organising and supporting the two revolutions that reintroduced constitutional government
in Greece in 1843 and 1862. Pepe on the other hand failed to turn any of
his revolutionary plans into reality during his own lifetime, but did much
to advance the cause of Neapolitan and Italian patriotism through propaganda and advocacy abroad.

Antonio Alcalá Galiano is the only publicist and politician in this group
without a military pedigree. His biography, however, shines as much light
as any on the history of southern Europe up to the 1860s. His political
and intellectual trajectory demonstrates that in order to rescue constitutional government, many former revolutionaries were willing to abandon
revolution as a tool of political change, and were ready to exclude the majority of the population from participation in the decision-making process.
They did so firstly to find a compromise with the existing conservative
social forces and the monarchs, and secondly to ensure that their respective countries enjoyed social stability. Galiano, like many former radicals
of his generation and many conservatives of a subsequent one, became
convinced that moderate—or elitist—liberalism represented the best solution to the political and social turbulence produced by revolutions and
counterrevolutions. This brand of constitutional government, for which
Galiano worked intellectually and pragmatically as a politician, would be
tested by the 1860s not only in Spain, but also in Portugal, on the Italian
peninsula and in Greece.

Yannis Macriyannis and the betrayal
of the Greek revolution

A wave of memoirs of former fighters and a number of general histories
of the Greek revolution were published in its aftermath. Among them the
memoirs of General Yannis Macriyannis loom large. Macriyannis wrote
these between 1829 and 1840, and continued them between 1844 and
1850. Although these memoirs represented his own response to a number
of histories of the revolution, considered by him to be too partisan, and
although he had written them with a public audience in mind, at his death
they were still in manuscript form. Since their publication in 1903, the
quality of their style and language have earned them the reputation of a
classic text of modern Greek literature; indeed, a masterpiece. Composed
after the end of the revolution, they go back to the years of the war of independence to cover the political life of the new state until the 1850s, and
combine autobiographical notes and recollections of Macriyannis's own

military and political activities with historical reflections.[2] Born in 1797 to
a family of farmers and shepherds, he grew up in Livadia in Boeotia. As a
teenager he entered the service of a merchant who worked for Ali Pasha of
Yannina, but soon became independently wealthy thanks to his own commercial and speculative activities. On the eve of the revolution he became
a member of the Philiki Etaireia, and in 1821 he was temporarily arrested
by the Ottomans for conspiratorial activities.[3] Once released, he joined
the war in a number of different capacities to become in due course one
of its most prominent and renowned military leaders: he was responsible
for policing the city of Athens after its liberation in 1822. During the civil
wars he sided with the legislative assembly against Kolokotronis, and led
an expedition against the province of Arcadia in the Peloponnese that had
rebelled against the central government.[4] After Ibrahim's invasion of the
Peloponnese, Macriyannis was involved in the defence of the citadel of
Neokastro as a newly appointed general, and later of Nafplion.[5]

A profound sense of disappointment with the outcome of the revolution pervades the pages of his memoirs. For Macriyannis, the creation of
the new state had failed to meet the hopes of those who had fought for
its foundation: in particular the peasants and the *palikaria*—the rank-
and-file irregular groups of the war of independence, and their families.
Like other former revolutionary leaders such as Kolokotronis, Kolettis and
Mavrokordatos, Macriyannis became a protagonist in the political life of
his country after the revolution, remaining for most of it on the side of
the opposition. His biography coincided with Ioannis Kapodistrias's rule
as governor from 1828 until his murder in 1831, the government of the
Bavarian regency and the reign of King Otto, who ruled until 1843 as an
absolute monarch, and between that year and 1862 as a constitutional king.
The sequence of governments that ruled Greece in the decades following the
revolution left Macroyannis permanently frustrated and dissatisfied, as he
felt that all of them failed to meet the demands for social justice and popular participation that had been articulated by the revolution. This frustration turned him into a leading figure of the opposition to King Otto's
autocratic rule and a victim of Bavarian despotism, a protagonist of the
revolution of 1843 and a close observer of the 1862 revolution and the fall
of the Bavarian monarchy. Macriyannis's memoirs do not offer only the

2. I refer here to the French edition, Général Macriyannis, *Mémoires*, trans. with introduction and notes by Denis Kohler (Paris: Albin Michel, 1986).

3. Macriyannis, *Mémoires*, pp. 81–92.

4. Ibid., p. 170.

5. Ibid., pp. 185–86, 203–5.

author's own perspective on these first decades of the new Greek state. They provide insights into the expectations of large sectors of the population after the 1820s, and bear witness to the hostility towards the authoritarian nature of the new state's institutions of a part of its military and political leadership. They also demonstrate that the conflicts and disagreements opposing the military class, the westernised Greeks of the diaspora and the Phanariots during the revolution continued also in its aftermath.

One of the main reasons why Macriyannis felt the revolution had been betrayed was the failure of subsequent governments to reintegrate into society the veterans of the war of independence. Indeed, he became one of their foremost champions. This social problem haunted consecutive governments for at least twenty years after the revolution, and was an important cause of regional rebellions and crippling instability. At the end of the war of independence Kapodistrias had found himself having to deal with some twenty to thirty thousand former irregular fighters. The solution to this problem was closely related to those of the enforcement of law and order and the organisation of the armed forces of the new nation state. Particularly challenging was the reintegration into society of the irregular forces hailing from the provinces in Roumeli still under Ottoman rule. These constituted a cohort of refugees without permanent employment, all too prone to rioting, to joining armed bands, or to re-enlisting with the Ottoman authorities. Former war veterans along with new irregular groupings (often straying across the border with the Ottoman Empire) and bandits were the protagonists of a series of rebellions that marked the two decades following the end of the revolution: the civil war that broke out after Kapodistrias's murder in 1831, when Roumeliot troops invaded the Peloponnese; the captains' revolts of 1832; and the uprisings in Acarnania and Evrytania between 1835 and 1836. Irregular troops also contributed to the instability that led to the 1843 revolution and were the protagonists of insurgencies in 1847–48 in Acarnania. All of these events show just how difficult it turned out to be to demobilise the troops that had fought during the revolution. The roots of the problem were both financial and organisational: rebellions broke out when troops wanted to be paid regularly, or demanded land distribution, while all the time refusing to be integrated into the regular forces. Their professional complaints were often compounded by other grievances, from their inveterate hostility to taxation and conscription to their demands for constitutional reforms, and to their desire to retain local autonomy against interference from central government. Subsequent governments tried to find a solution to these problems, although only with limited success. In 1833 the

Bavarian regency proceeded to disband the remaining irregular armed groups. It set up a new gendarmerie and a larger regular army with a view to absorbing part of these disbanded formations. At the same time a crime of brigandage was officially introduced as a means of punishing irregular forces challenging the government. To resolve the question of the veterans, a commission was set up to assess their claims. As a consequence, eight hundred of their number were organised into a 'Royal Phalanx' and granted a small pension. Yet these measures did not put an end to the turbulence of the irregular forces, who continued to constitute a source of instability for a variety of reasons: many of them would not tolerate their integration into a regular army, while several of their leaders, even after having joined the army, retained their control and influence over their groups.[6] Macriyannis himself was involved in these efforts to reorganise the army. Having refused to join the gendarmerie in 1833, he was appointed a member of the committees entrusted with the task of organising the army in eastern Greece. However, he considered the efforts made to resolve the problem of the veterans to be inadequate. He denounced the fact that political interference and factionalism prevented an equitable distribution of pensions and rewards, and that former veterans with their families continued to live in destitution. He also attacked the government for persecuting former revolutionary fighters—among them Kolokotronis, who in 1834 was imprisoned, tried and condemned for treason, with a capital sentence— rather than rewarding them for their past services.[7]

Macriyannis's hostility towards the Bavarian regency and indeed, towards King Otto himself, was compounded by other factors that led broad sectors of public opinion increasingly to regard the regime as unpatriotic. First and foremost, the closure of monastic communities, along with the creation of a national church controlled by the state and independent from Constantinople, was construed as a direct attack upon religion. Secondly, the transformation of the Orthodox church into a national institution, whose governing body, the Synod of Bishops, was presided over by the monarch as its temporal head, and the closure or reduction of monasteries and nunneries turned out to be hugely unpopular. The regency saw both measures as part of a concerted effort to strengthen the state at the expense of any other competing authority, in line with its ideology inspired by 'enlightened absolutism', and was hoping that the sale of the monastic

6. On this theme, see Koliopoulos, *Brigands*; McGrew, *Land and Revolution*.

7. Macriyannis, *Mémoires*, pp. 304–7, 309, 316–17. In 1834 Kolokotronis was released.

properties would help to consolidate the state's parlous finances.[8] However, not only many members of the clergy, but also the general population resented these reforms. A number of peasant revolts on the Mani peninsula, in Messinia and Acarnania and on the islands of Spetses and Hydra erupted in protest at these measures. General Macryannis himself was highly critical of the closure of the monastic communities, a measure he considered to be an unjustified attack on those who had been at the forefront of the revolutionary efforts, many of whom had paid with their own lives for the liberation of Greece. He observed that, as a consequence of these closures, monks were now 'dying of hunger on the roads'.[9] The fact that the king himself was Catholic and refused to convert to Orthodoxy, and that he had allowed Protestant missionaries into the country, reinforced the belief that he was an enemy of the national faith.

What contributed more perhaps than any other factor to a sense of the revolution having been betrayed was the fact that the new Greek state was devoid of those constitutional guarantees and elements of popular governance that, in the eyes of Macriyannis, had represented, along with national emancipation, the main benefits of the anti-Ottoman uprising. As a matter of fact, Kapodistrias had ruled as a dictator, and the Bavarian monarchy similarly focused on establishing and reinforcing an administrative and centralised state without any form of representation whatsoever. These circumstances paved the way to the emergence of a pro-constitutional opposition, supported by a part of Greek society, which Macriyannis was quick to join. While at first welcoming the appointment of Kapodistrias as governor and then condemning his murder in 1831 (for twenty-six months until May 1830 he was head of the gendarmerie of Sparta and the Peloponnese), Macriyannis lamented the governor's decision to dissolve the legislative assembly.[10] For this reason, during the civil war that broke out after the death of Kapodistrias, he became a member of the constitutional front led by Kolettis, Koundouriotis and Zaimis against the incoming governor, Avgoustinos Kapodistrias, brother of Ioannis, and supported their temporary establishment of an alternative government. Once again hopeful that the establishment of the Bavarian monarchy could mark a new beginning for the country, he was soon to be disappointed. His demands for a constitution put him in direct collision

8. Charles A. Frazee, 'Church and State in Greece', in *Greece in Transition: Essays in the History of Modern Greece, 1821–1974*, ed. John T. A. Koumoulides (London: Zeno, 1977), pp. 128–52 at 133; Frary, *Russia*; Petropulos, *Politics and Statecraft*, pp. 180–92.

9. Macriyannis, *Mémoires*, pp. 314–15.

10. Ibid., pp. 255, 334.

with Joseph von Armansperg, one of the three members of the Bavarian regency, and arch-chancellor of the country during Otto's reign up until 1837. As a member of the Council of Athens, to which he had been elected in 1833, Macriyannis openly criticised the lack of a constitution. In 1837 he organised a public banquet with other former revolutionary fighters such as Koundouriotis and Kolokotronis to approve a petition in favour of a constitution, that was published in the press. As a consequence, Armansperg decided to put him under house arrest and to dissolve the city council.[11]

Given the impossibility of any public advocacy in favour of the constitution, and the king's own hostility to it, in the years that followed Macroyannis turned to clandestine opposition and took part in the concerted efforts to organise the revolution of September 1843. The revolutionary script followed by the Greek insurgents that year represented a variant of the southern European pronunciamientos of the 1820s. First, it had required the organisation of an extensive secret society network in the previous years (to the establishment of which Macriyannis made a substantial contribution); second, it was organised by army officers stationed in Athens and led by Dimitrios Kallergis, commander of the cavalry (Kallergis was another former revolutionary fighter, who in 1821 had left Crete to join the anti-Ottoman war). Third, it combined an army initiative with civilian mobilisation. Finally, like the events of 1820 and 1821 in Spain, Portugal, Piedmont and Naples, it was bloodless. Macriyannis himself had planned to take part in this military coup, but since the court had been informed about the conspiracy, the gendarmerie surrounded his house to prevent any military intervention. His arrest precipitated events: the other officers, fearing that the same would happen to them, decided to act at once. On 14 September, Kallergis led the national guard towards the royal palace and demanded the introduction of a constitution. Large crowds gathering in the square outside the palace supported his action.[12]

As a result, a national assembly summoned by the king (in which Macriyannis participated as an active member) approved an entirely new constitution. This document introduced a senate with life members appointed by the king, and a parliament elected by quasi-universal male suffrage (based on property ownership). At the same time it guaranteed substantial powers to the monarch, who held executive power and shared the right

11. Ibid., pp. 325–26.
12. Ibid., pp. 370–77. On these events, see also Petropulos, *Politics and Statecraft*, pp. 442–46.

to legislate with the two chambers.[13] This success notwithstanding, the constitutional practice subsequently established under Otto turned out to be far from popular. What soon came to be almost universally condemned was the so-called 'Otto system', a style of governance based on constant monarchical interference in the business of government, controlled by a royal clique, and in electoral processes, which almost invariably resulted in the selection of candidates backed by the monarch. Macriyannis blamed the prime minister, Ioannis Kolettis (1844–47), for keeping the parliament under his own control, and for calling for new elections whenever he wanted to further consolidate his power.[14] Royal interference in governmental affairs and elections, along with censorship of the press, were not the only causes for the discredit into which the regime fell, moreover. A prolonged economic crisis and the monarch's lack of commitment to the liberation of the Greek lands under Ottoman rule also contributed to his unpopularity.[15]

The early 1850s, like the late 1830s, represented years of personal defeat for Macriyannis. In 1852 the general was accused of plotting to murder the king and queen, and as a result he was arrested, tried, stripped of his military rank and condemned to death. In 1854 his sentence was first commuted to one of ten years' detention, and thanks to the intervention of Dimitrios Kallergis, he was subsequently released. At the same time Macriyannis became a symbol of the opposition to the regime, which demanded the liberation of the Greek territories under foreign rule as well as constitutional reform. In 1859, during a public tour of the island of Zante, in the British Ionian Islands, he was accorded a triumphal welcome by the local population. By 1860 the successful example of the Italian Risorgimento and the influence of the ideas and activities of Garibaldi and Mazzini in Greece added to the prevailing frustration with the existing regime, and provided an additional source of inspiration for those critical of it.[16]

13. On this constitution, see Petropulos, *Politics and Statecraft*, pp. 466–99, and on debates around it, Michalis Sotiropoulos, *Liberalism after the Revolution: The Intellectual Foundations of the Greek State, c. 1830–1880* (Cambridge: Cambridge University Press, 2023), pp. 132–65, 194–243.

14. Macriyannis, *Mémoires*, pp. 422–23.

15. Sakis Gekas, 'The Crisis of the Long 1850s and Regime Change in the Ionian Islands and the Kingdom of Greece', *The Historical Review/La Revue historique* 10 (2013): 57–84.

16. Gekas, 'Crisis'; Antonis Liakos, *L'unificazione italiana e la grande idea: Ideologia e azione dei movimenti nazionali in Italia e in Grecia, 1859–1871* (Florence: Aletheia, 1995), pp. 79–89, 146–48.

The opprobrium heaped upon the Bavarian monarchy was such that another revolution became all but inevitable. In 1862 a military revolt replaced the Bavarian dynasty with the Danish royal house of Holstein-Sonderberg. As in 1843, this uprising was the result of combined military and civilian intervention: it was sparked in February 1862 by the insurrection of the garrisons of Nafplion, Tripoli, Kythnos and Syros, supported by the local populations, and was followed by another in October that same year. Significantly, a new generation of radical students, merchants and officers were the protagonists of this revolution. Yet this generation looked to Macriyannis as a symbol of their own values and of the new order they were intent upon establishing. In one of the key public moments of the events of 1862, the old general was paraded through the streets of Athens by cheering crowds.[17] A new parliament elected in 1862 proceeded in 1864 to approve one of the most advanced charters in Europe: the new constitution abolished the senate and introduced a single parliament elected by universal male suffrage. While the 1844 constitution, like the 1814 French Charte, had been a document granted by the king, the 1864 constitution was more firmly grounded in the principle of national sovereignty. As a consequence it substantially reduced the powers the monarch had previously enjoyed.

The fact that some of the main protagonists of the 1821 uprising, Alexandros Mavrokordatos and Konstantinos Kanaris among them, sat in this new national assembly created a direct connection between that event and the debates in the course of which the new constitution was drafted.[18] But all of its plenipotentiaries, regardless of the generation to which they belonged, saw their work in relation to the Greek constitutional history inaugurated by the 1821 revolution. The memory of those events therefore haunted the proceedings of the new assembly. When discussing what to call it, some proposed the name 'Seventh National Assembly', counting the one established in 1821 at Epidavros as the first in the history of Greece. This idea was dropped, as no agreement could be reached as to which of the various national assemblies that had been summoned after 1827, but had never completed their work, should be included in the count. In the end the new body was simply named the 'Second National Assembly'. As one plenipotentiary explained when endeavouring to justify this choice, 'There are two eras: the first era is that of the fall of the Ottoman dynasty,

---

17. Macriyannis, *Mémoires*, pp. 512–13.

18. Mavrokordatos was in fact elected president of the committee charged with the drafting of the new constitution.

the second that of the fall of the Bavarian dynasty.'[19] What reinforced this sense of continuity between the 1820s and 1862 was also the claim that the new constitution, although not directly influenced by the constitutional texts of the Greek revolution, was in line with their founding principles. As the professor of law Nikolaos Saripolos argued during the proceedings of the national assembly, on the basis of the Greek revolutionary tradition elected deputies ought to be considered representatives of the nation, and not of their particular constituencies.[20] In April 1864 Macriyannis was elected deputy for Athens in the new parliament. In the same month, just a few days before passing away, he was reinstated in his military rank. The same students who had led the 1862 revolution attended his funeral en masse. By so doing, they were paying homage to the old combatant whose life had formed a bridge between the 1821 revolution and the new constitutional monarchy of King Georgios of the Hellenes. Macriyannis's death therefore seemed to confirm that the revolutionary cycle started in 1821 had finally come to an end that year.[21]

Bernardo de Sá Nogueira (Viscount and Marquis of Sá da Bandeira) and the search for political stability in Portugal

The reintroduction of absolutism to Portugal by Dom Miguel in 1828 led to a bloody civil war that came to an end only in 1834. In that year, Miguelismo as a political force was defeated for good. The Treaty of Évora Monte that Dom Miguel signed in May that year forced him to abdicate, stripped him of any royal status and drove him into exile for the rest of his life.[22] While hostility to liberalism persisted in Portuguese society, both among the popular classes and the elites, and absolutist riots flared up again in the decades that followed, as a political force it never again represented a serious threat to the constitutional monarchy. Although monarchical constitutionalism had won, however, what remained contentious, as in Spain, was the type of constitution that was to be adopted. The divisions

19. These debates can be found in Antonis Pantelis, Stefanos Koutsompinas and Triantafyllos Gerozisis, eds, Κείμενα συνταγματικής ιστορίας (Documents of constitutional history) (Athens: Ant. Sakkoulas, 1993), pp. 269–74, quotation at 273. See also Sotiropoulos, Liberalism, ch. 6.

20. Pantelis, Koutsompinas and Gerozisis, Κείμενα (Documents), p. 314. I am grateful to Michalis Sotiropoulos for pointing these documents out to me.

21. Denis Kohler, 'Introduction' in Macriyannis, Mémoires, pp. 11–78 at 49–50.

22. Lousada and Ferreira, D. Miguel, pp. 232–33.

within the liberal front led to a new cycle of political instability and a wave of civil wars and military coups that came to an end only in 1870. The Portuguese revolutions of the 1820s represented unfinished business precisely because the two constitutional options of that decade, the 1822 and the 1826 constitutions, split the constitutional front into two camps, one more radical and the other more conservative. With the end of the civil war and the defeat of Dom Miguel, these divisions within the liberal camp proved irreconcilable. The extent of royal powers vis-à-vis those of the parliament, the desirability of universal and direct or limited and indirect male suffrage, the existence of an upper chamber—in short, how far popular sovereignty should be constrained or limited—became the bones of contention that divided constitutionalists These questions opposed the 'Setembristas' (who in 1836 carried out a revolution against the reviled 1826 Carta) to the 'Cartistas'.

Another legacy of the 1820s was the enduring role of the army as a political broker, a role reinforced by the civil war and the defeat of Dom Miguel. Although in 1834 the size of the army was substantially reduced, the armed forces still physically occupied the country and were de facto controlling, even administering, many towns and villages. The liberal state needed them to survive against its enemies, as hostility towards constitutionalism and support for absolutism persisted at the local level among both popular classes and elites. This dependence of the liberal state on its officers enabled these to interfere systematically in its political life. As a consequence, even after 1834, no government was safe without the support of the army. Thus the troubled history of Portugal after the 1820s is first and foremost the history of competing constitutional movements that sometimes fought against each other, and sometimes attempted to reach a compromise and achieve a consensus around a single charter. It is also a history of civil wars, popular uprisings and military pronunciamientos carried out to settle these political disagreements, until 1870; and the army, national guard, popular mobilisation and the monarch all interacted to determine the success or failure of each revolutionary attempt. Every new government had to include an influential military leader, settle the army's grievances and purge it of its enemies in order to consolidate its own grip on the country. In this respect too, the 1820s inaugurated a long period of military intervention and military influence in politics.

As a leading officer of the Portuguese army and a prominent politician, Bernardo de Sá Nogueira was one of the key figures in all the conflicts that followed the end of Dom Miguel's reign. His personal career extended from the Peninsular War, to the failed pronunciamiento of the

Martinhada in November 1820, to his rise as prime minister in a pacified Portugal in 1836 and 1837, a position he temporarily held again in
1862, 1865, 1868–69 and 1870. His political and military trajectory offers a
counterpoint to that of another important *vintista* officer who continued
to be at the centre of Portuguese politics during the same tract of time:
General João Francisco de Saldanha Oliveira e Daun (Duke of Saldanha
from 1846).[23] While Nogueira was an advocate of the 1822 constitution
and a passionate champion of popular sovereignty, Saldanha became the
leading Cartista in the army, that is to say a supporter of the 1826 constitution. It was during the Biénio Cartista that Saldanha had been appointed
minister of war, and his dismissal from this post in 1827 had triggered
public protests. Nogueira tended to be more respectful of civilian power.
Saldanha was instead directly responsible for a number of both failed and
successful military coups between 1836 and 1870. The political history of
Portugal between the 1830s and the 1870s can be read through the opposition of and conflict between these two prominent officers.

Nogueira was a *fidalgo*, the aristocratic son of an *alcaide mor* (the
noblemen in charge of recruiting and organising troops at the local level) of
Cadaval. The war effort against the French (he fought in Spain as well
as in France) earned him promotions in the ranks of the army and nurtured
in him a commitment to political reform. His key role in the Martinhada,
the failed attempt to introduce the Spanish constitution in November 1820,
marked the end of any direct involvement in revolutionary politics during
the Triénio. Once released from prison thanks to a favourable vote of the
Cortes, Nogueira left Portugal to join the revolution in Naples. However,
the end of the revolution there prevented him from fulfilling his plans, and
as a consequence he opted for temporary exile in France, where he studied
natural sciences until 1824. Back in Portugal, he continued to serve the
army in various capacities, defending the second constitutional regime
against the Miguelistas in the civil war that raged between 1826 and 1827.
In 1828 he refused to serve in the army under Dom Miguel, left Portugal
for England and Brazil, along with the bulk of the liberal army, but joined
the liberal government on the island of Terceira in the Azores in 1829.
From there he took part in the campaign that led to the conquest of all
the islands and, more importantly he joined the expedition of 7,500 constitutional troops that landed in in 1832, as aide-de-camp to Dom Pedro

23. On Saldanha, see the entry 'Daun, João Carlos Gregório Domingos Vicente Francisco de Saldanha Oliveira e', in *Dicionário do vintismo e do primeiro cartismo (1821-23 e
1826-28)*, ed. Zília Osório de Castro, Isabel Cluny and Sara Marques Pereira, 2 vols (Lisbon:
Assembleia da República, 2002), 1, pp. 583-90.

himself, taking part in the war that led to the defeat of Dom Miguel two years later. Nogueira's diaries, which cover the entire period of the civil war from to 1826 to 1832, indeed represent an invaluable record of these events.[24]

It was thanks to his services to Dom Pedro that, with the end of the civil war, Nogueira rose to public prominence under the new queen, Dom Pedro's daughter Dona Maria II. In recognition for his role in the civil war, the queen gave him the title of Baron of Sá da Bandeira in 1833, and the following year that of Viscount (*visconde*). His political career started in 1835 with his temporary appointment, just for a few months, as minister of war. In the same year he was rewarded with a peerage, in recognition of his past services to the constitutional cause. However, Sá da Bandeira was not an enthusiastic supporter of the 1826 constitution reintroduced in 1834. In September 1836, in fact, an uprising led by the population of Lisbon and the national guard forced the queen to reintroduce the 1822 constitution. Sá da Bandeira became one of the two key figures of the new Setembrista regime, along with Manuel da Silva Passos ('Passos Manuel'). Between 1836 and 1839 he was minister of finance and of foreign affairs, and held the presidency of the council twice, roles that enabled him to guarantee the army's support for the constitution. The governments to which he belonged were determined to promote a markedly reformist agenda. They innovated in the sphere of the primary and secondary education as well as in military and technical training, put forward measures aimed at encouraging trade and, last but not least, they sought the abolition of slavery across the Portuguese Empire, a question about which Sá da Bandeira felt passionately.[25]

In spite of the victory of the revolution, the hostility of the queen and of sections of the army, who favoured the more moderate Carta to the 1822 constitution, threatened the survival of the regime from its outset. In November 1836 the queen had tried to reintroduce the Carta with the support of the British, General Saldanha and the Duke of Terceira; the following year the same military commanders led an unsuccessful pronunciamiento conducted by a provincial regiment with the same objective. In this context of instability, Sá da Bandeira decided to seek a reconciliation between all liberals and look for a new compromise. This was finally achieved in 1838. The 1838 constitution represented a synthesis of

24. Published as Bernardo de Sá Nogueira de Figueiredo, marquês de Sá da Bandeira, *Diário da guerra civil: 1826–1832*, ed. José Tengarrinha, 2 vols (Lisbon: Seara Nova, 1976).

25. Rui Branco, 'A vida política', in *História contemporânea de Portugal: 1808–2010*, vol. 2: *A construção nacional, 1834–1890*, ed. Pedro Tavares de Almeida (Lisbon: Fundación Mapfre/Editora Objectiva, 2013), pp. 31–74 at 36–37.

the competing priorities of the Cartistas and Setembristas. This constitution, which was in force until 1842, continued to abide by the principle of popular sovereignty by maintaining direct elections and broadening suffrage (which excluded only those with an income of less than 80,000 *réis* per year). At the same time it reintroduced a senate and, to appease the Cartistas and the queen, accorded the monarch the right of veto.[26]

However, this compromise did not last very long and for a number of reasons failed to stabilise the liberal state. The new constitutional regime and the ones that followed had to deal with a new popular opposition on the left, which had not existed in the 1820s. This new radical opposition was made up of the members of the national guard, the radical clubs of the capital and the *arsenalistas* (stevedores), who were even more critical of royal power, and occasionally veered towards outright support for republicanism. In March 1838 the national guard based in the arsenal of Lisbon mutinied, demanding guarantees that the revolution would not be undermined by the new government, and it was Sá da Bandeira who intervened at the head of three thousand troops to suppress the uprising in a violent clash that resulted in a hundred casualties.[27]

Aware that the queen would be on their side, the Cartistas did not hesitate to intervene again militarily and renege on the compromise reached in 1838. In 1842 António Bernardo da Costa Cabral, a former radical turned moderate, and minister of justice since 1839, led a military uprising in Porto that reintroduced the Carta, and held the premiership until 1846. Aware that the majority of the army was siding with Costa Cabral, Sá da Bandeira renounced his plans to lead a popular insurrection in Lisbon, fearing as he did that he would not have the support of a sufficient number of regiments, but became resolutely hostile to Costa Cabral.[28] The consolidation of the latter's power led to the marginalisation of the Setembristas, whom Cabral criticised for their alleged tendency to rely on street politics.[29] His victory therefore served to reignite the mutual distrust between the two main currents of Portuguese liberalism, and the determination of each to delegitimise the other, a process that invoked arguments and a language that dated back to the civil wars and military interventions of

26. Maria de Fátima Bonifácio, 'O Setembrismo corrigido e actualizado', *Penélope: Fazer e Desfazer História* 9 (1993): 309–21.

27. Simão José da Luz Soriano, *Vida do Marquez de Sá da Bandeira*, 2 vols (Lisbon: Sousa Neves, 1887–88), 2, pp. 141–44.

28. On these events, see Ramos, 'A revolução liberal', p. 504.

29. Maria de Fátima Bonifácio, *A segunda ascensão e queda de Costa Cabral, 1847–1851* (Lisbon: ICS, 2002).

the 1820s. Both parties in fact claimed to be the only lawful representatives of the nation, and accused each other of betraying the constitutional cause and the monarchy. In 1842 allegations in the governmental press that the Setembrista opposition supported the return of Dom Miguel and had held the queen prisoner led to a public response by Sá da Bandeira. In a number of articles he attacked Costa Cabral for acting against the wishes of the queen and against the constitution, for interfering in elections to control the parliament and for creating nothing less than a tyrannical government. For Sá da Bandeira, only a decision by the Cortes could have made the replacement of the 1822 constitution with the Carta a legal act. Costa Cabral claimed instead that the reintroduction of the Carta earlier that same year reflected only the spontaneous wishes of the entire nation and the army.[30]

Finally, continuing political instability was fuelled by popular resistance to the reforms introduced by all liberal governments in the 1830s and 1840s. As in Greece or in Spain, a combination of factors fostered rural revolts, banditry and guerrilla warfare: for example, reluctance to pay taxes, or hostility towards the administrative reorganisation that had abolished the majority of local councils and deprived them of any autonomy. At the local level, coalitions of different social groups, ranging from the peasants to clerics, provincial gentry and aristocrats, were capable of challenging state power and governmental controls. The armed forces took advantage of this almost chronic state of revolt in the provinces to justify their intervention, not only to re-establish law and order, but also to advance their own constitutional agenda in the name of popular grievances. In 1844 a military rebellion in Torres Novas led by Setembrista regiments was easily suppressed, and Costa Cabral seized the opportunity to purge the army of its Setembrista officers.[31] It was increasing popular turbulence that led to the resignation of Costa Cabral two years later, and soon afterwards to full-scale civil war. In 1846 an anti-government rebellion in the province of Minho, known as the Guerra da Patuleia, prompted by taxation and by a law prohibiting interment outside cemeteries, led to the establishment of local juntas that spread from the provinces of Minho and Trás-os-Montes to the rest of the kingdom, and reclaimed municipal autonomy. Its leaders and supporters rebelled in the name of the principles both of Setembrismo and of counterrevolutionary Miguelismo.[32] With

30. Soriano, *Vida do Marquez*, 2, pp. 190–211.

31. Ramos, 'A revolução liberal', p. 506.

32. Ferreira, *Rebeldes*; Maria de Fátima Bonifácio, *História da guerra civil da Patuleia* (Lisbon: Editorial Estampa, 1993).

Costa Cabral's resignation, a government presided over by the Marquis of Palmela but including Sá da Bandeira as minister of war and leader of the national guard was appointed to pacify the country. The Setembristas were promised that a constituent assembly would revise the Carta.[33] However, this pacification attempt failed and further civil war broke out. What triggered the war in October was the Duke of Saldanha's military expedition to Lisbon in defence of the Carta, an expedition backed by the queen. The Setembristas, who meanwhile had set up a provisional governmental junta in Porto, responded with their own military expeditions towards Lisbon, one from Porto and another led by Sá da Bandeira himself, that proceeded from the Algarve towards the north. This confrontation came to an end only thanks to the intervention of Spain and Britain and the military defeat of the Setembristas.[34]

The winner of the conflict, Saldanha, was now determined to find a compromise by creating a new and durable alliance between the Cartistas and the Setembristas that would isolate the radicals and stabilise the country. In 1851 Saldanha's successful military coup not only removed the much-hated Cabral, but also put an end to the cycle of political instability and military interventions that had begun in 1820. Sá da Bandeira publicly welcomed Saldanha's coup. Cabral's unpopularity had favoured Saldanha's pronunciamiento, but there were other reasons for the enduring nature of the settlement that followed. Saldanha promoted all officers irrespective of their political affiliations, laying the ground for the creation of an army that was no longer divided into factions and, crucially, would cease to intervene in government, delegating decisions entirely to the political class. In the same year Sá da Bandeira was appointed field marshal and also director of the military school.[35] Moreover, a new constitutional reform approved in 1852 revised the Carta by introducing direct suffrage and, in a bid to appease the Setembristas, lowered the voting threshold. These reforms inaugurated a new era of political peace, or *paz regeneradora*. They transformed the political landscape by creating a new liberal consensus supported by a moderate right-wing liberal party, the Partido Regenerador and, from 1853, a moderate left-wing party, the Partido Histórico. The two parties would recognise each other as legitimate candidates for government without the need for revolutionary interventions, and at the same time the political extremes would be marginalised.

33. Soriano, *Vida do Marquez*, 2, pp. 237–40.
34. Ibid., pp. 243–87.
35. Ibid., pp. 387–92. Bonifácio, *D. Maria II*, p. 226.

In this new context, the older political divisions dating back to the two constitutions of the 1820s lost their significance once and for all. The former Cartistas and Setembristas joined either the Partido Regenerador or the Partido Histórico. In the following decade, governments may have had a very short life, and the elections may have been called very frequently, but they took place in an atmosphere of mutual legitimation.[36]

These transformations changed the nature of military influence on politics, but did not put an end to it. Senior military officers continued to play an important role in government. Saldanha was a prominent leader of the Partido Regenerador, and in this capacity he was prime minister between 1851 and 1856. Between 1856 and 1859 it was the turn of the Partido Histórico to govern, under the leadership of the Duke of Loulé. Sá da Bandeira, although he had only joined the Partido Histórico in 1859, and otherwise remained on the margins of party politics on the left, in those years held the portfolios of the navy, war and public works.[37] In the new political landscape of the 1860s he continued to play an important role. He was briefly prime minister in 1862 and was made Marquis of Sá da Bandeira in 1864. He held the portfolio of war and that of the navy, along with the presidency of the council, in 1865. The opposition between the two parties came to an end in the mid-1860s when the moderate wings of the Partido Histórico and the Partido Regenerador merged. Sá da Bandeira refused to join the new party and created his own Partido Reformista, to their left. It was as leader of this new party that he was appointed prime minister again between 1868 and 1869. In these two decades he managed to accomplish one of his most cherished political ambitions, the abolition of slavery—a cause he had espoused, along with the reform of the empire in Africa, since the 1830s. As minister of the navy in 1858 he had set a date for the end of slavery, which was to be in twenty years' time. In 1869, however, as prime minister, he succeeded in abolishing it immediately and permanently, anticipating this date by nine years.[38]

Furthermore, to preserve its influence, the army replaced the use of force with direct participation in parliamentary politics. It was in the parliament that it defended its interests as a pressure group, and managed to do so very successfully. Between 1853 and 1856 no fewer than thirty-six

36. On *Regeneração*, see José Miguel Sardica, *A regeneração sob o signo do consenso: A política e os partidos entre 1851 e 1861* (Lisbon: ICS, 2001).

37. Sardica, *A regeneração*, pp. 105–40, 165–86, 211–18, 245–50.

38. João Pedro Marques, *Sá da Bandeira e o fim da escravidão: Vitória da moral, desforra do interesse* (Lisbon: ICS, 2008). On his colonial reform plans, see Paquette, *Imperial Portugal*, pp. 338–47, 364–71.

members of the army sat in the parliament as deputies; between 1858 and 1869 their numbers fluctuated between twenty and twenty-seven. Receiving requests from soldiers and officers, and interacting with the politicians of their groups, they managed to obtain a substantial pay rise for commissioned officers and the rank and file, and the abolition of purchase of remission from military service in 1865. In general, they systematically defended the existence of a well-trained and well-financed standing army. Sá da Bandeira supported all of these requests, either as minister of war or as prime minister. As he argued in 1866, the best way to defend the neutrality of Portugal was to ensure that it retained a well-equipped army and navy and a proper system of fortresses.[39] In this new political context the last attempt to resolve a political crisis through military means, which took place in 1870, was doomed to fail: that year, in fact, a military pronunciamiento organised by Saldanha closed the cycle of military interventions inaugurated in 1820. These events once again opposed Saldanha to Sá da Bandeira. In May 1870, at a time of increasing popular opposition and protest in the name of republican and democratic principles, Saldanha led several regiments to the Ajuda Palace at Lisbon, and forced the King Luís I to dismiss the government and appoint himself as prime minister. He then governed as a dictator by decree for three whole months, proposing a constitutional reform to neutralise popular radicalism, and advancing the project of 'Iberismo', the plan to merge Spain and Portugal under a single monarchy. Sá da Bandeira, however, gave his support to the king, who decided to dismiss Saldanha, sent him to London as ambassador and appointed his rival as prime minister. This was in fact Sá da Bandeira's last public commitment before his retirement from politics and his death in 1876. While his biography demonstrates the enduring influence of the military caste on Portuguese politics, it also sheds light on the way such influence changed in nature after the 1850s, when Portugal gradually moved towards a more stable and less contested constitutional settlement. Soon after his death, a committee was set up to raise funds for a statue in his honour, to which the royal family and the political elite of the country contributed. The statue was finally erected in 1886. In the consensual political climate of those years, during which political parties would alternate in government, the radicalism of his early life and his involvement in the civil wars were forgotten. What the statue celebrated was a number of

---

39. Isilda Braga da Costa Monteiro, 'The Military in the Chamber of Deputies, 1851–1870: Corporative Lines of Action in Defense of the Army', *E-Journal of Portuguese History* 8, no. 1 (2010): 1–22.

bipartisan virtues: his commitment to the defence of the nation during the war against the French and to liberal institutions, and the important part he had played in the abolition of slavery.[40]

Guglielmo Pepe: transnational fame and the endurance of Neapolitan patriotism

The international networks created during the simultaneous revolutionary waves of the 1820s did not peter out at the end of these revolutions, but remained active and were constantly deployed in the following years. In the Italian states constitutional government reappeared only briefly in 1830 in the Papal States and central duchies, and in Naples, Sicily only in 1848. The fact that monarchical absolutism was more resilient on the Italian peninsula than anywhere else in southern Europe turned exile into a semi-permanent condition for many revolutionaries, and encouraged conspiratorial activities abroad for a longer period than in the other states of the region. Guglielmo Pepe's biography bears witness to the transnational dimension of the southern European struggle for constitutional freedom beyond the 1820s. Exile provided opportunities not only for conspiracy, but also for public advocacy in favour of the cause of the regeneration of the Italian peninsula. As a consequence, Pepe's revolutionary politics were not confined to Neapolitan or Italian exiled revolutionaries, but engaged with liberal circles throughout Europe. Thus his status as an exile did not reduce his visibility and celebrity: on the contrary it contributed to his fame as one of the most popular international revolutionary figures of the first half of the nineteenth century.[41] As discussed in chapter ten above, the revolutions coincided with the establishment of a new transnational and pan-European public sphere, and with the celebration of a series of new heroes. While their end put a temporary stop to the development of political journalism in southern Europe, it continued to foster international cults of personality further north, where a much greater degree of freedom of the press was allowed. Pepe appears to have been directly involved in advancing his international fame by constructing a public image that would appeal to liberal audiences across the continent. His contacts in a variety of European countries enabled him to have his historical accounts translated from Italian into Spanish, French, English

40. On the erection of the statue, see Soriano, *Vida do Marquez*, 2, pp. 533, 546.

41. On this theme, I follow Gian Luca Fruci, '"Sol Garibaldi a te può dirsi uguale": Guglielmo Pepe, celebrità transnazionale e speaker internazionale del Risorgimento (1820–1855)', unpublished paper given at Cantieri di Storia IX SISSCO, Padua, 15 September 2017.

and German, and his memoirs published in France, Britain and Switzer-land.[42] In these writings he presented himself as the main protagonist and the symbol of the Neapolitan revolution, the incarnation of national aspirations for constitutional freedom; an international celebrity whose prestige and legitimacy owed a great deal to other transnational liberal icons such as General Lafayette and John Cam Hobhouse; and finally, as an exile on account of the love he bore both his Neapolitan and his Italian fatherlands. As he stated when completing these memoirs in 1846, 'in spite of this love, while she languishes in ignoble servitude, under Princes sub-ject to Austrian influence, and averse to liberal institutions, even should it be permitted me, I am resolved never to set my foot in Italy again'.[43]

Addressing foreign audiences provided an opportunity to challenge northern European scepticism about the Neapolitans' capacity to enjoy political freedom and to make European public opinion aware of the pre-dicament of southern Italy. But exile represented also a time to reflect on the causes of the failure of the revolution. Pepe did so first in a number of historical reconstructions of the key events of the Neapolitan revolu-tion, which were designed in large part to defend the role he had played in these events. One of these historical accounts addressed the king of the Two Sicilies directly, exhorting him to respect his oath of allegiance to

42. Guglielmo Pepe, *A Narrative of the Political and Military Events, Which Took Place at Naples, in 1820 and 1821; with Observations Explanatory of the National Conduct in General, and of His Own in Particular, during that Period; Addressed to His Majesty, the King of the Two Sicilies, by General William Pepe. With an Appendix of Official Documents, the Greater Part Hitherto Unpublished* (London: Treuttel and Würtz, Treuttel, Jun. and Richter, 1821); Pepe, *Relation des événements politiques et militaires qui ont eu lieu à Naples en 1820 et 1821 adressée à S. M. le Roi des Deux Siciles, par le général Guillaume Pépé, avec des remarques et des explications sur la conduite des Napolitains en général, et sur celle de l'auteur en particulier, pendant cette époque, suivie d'un recueil de documens officiels, la plupart inédits* (Paris: Crapelet, 1822); Pepe, *Memoria relativa á los sucesos políticos y militares de Nápoles en los años 1820 y 1821, con varias observaciones sobre la conducta de las naciones en general, y de la suya en particular; Dirigida a S.M. el rey de las dos Sicilias por el general D. Gullermo Pepe, y acompañada de documentos de oficio cuya mayor parte no se ha dado á luz hasta ahora* (Madrid: Imprenta de D. Miguel de Burgos, 1822); Pepe, *Relazione delle circostanze relative agli avvenimenti politici e militari in Napoli nel 1820 e 1821, diretta a s.m. il Re delle Due-Sicilie dal generale Guglielmo Pepe. Con le osservazioni sulla condotta della nazione* [. . .] *Accompagnata da documenti uffiziali* [. . .] *per la prima volta la luce* (Paris: Crapelet, 1822); Pepe, *Darstellung der politischen und militärischen Ereignisse in Neapel in den Jahren 1820 und 1821. Ein Sendschreiben an S.M. den König Beider-Sicilien, vom General Wilhelm Pepe. Mit einem Anhange offizieller, grösstentheils ungedruckter Aktenstücke*, trans. Friedrich Krug (Ilmenau: B. F. Voigt, 1822).

43. Pepe, *Memoirs*, 3, p. 367. An Italian edition was published in Paris as *Memorie del Generale Guglielmo Pepe intorno alla sua vita ed ai recenti casi d'Italia scritte da lui medesimo*, 2 vols (Paris, Baudry, 1847).

the constitution and to reintroduce it. The second, published in English alone, offered a more thorough examination of the causes of the failure of the revolution not only in Naples, but also in Spain, Portugal and Piedmont. While he admitted that, compared to northern Europe, Naples and southern Europe more generally had been corrupted by hundreds of years of despotism—he commented in particular on the negative influence of the papacy—Pepe told his international public that by 1820 the Neapolitans had become mature enough to enjoy constitutional government. The warm welcome they gave the constitution that year, as opposed to the hostility and violence displayed by the populace against the republic in 1799, bore witness to the maturity they had acquired in the meantime.[44] If, as he admitted, most had not joined the fight against the Austrians in 1821, this could not be attributed to their indifference to the constitution, but to the very fact that the prince in charge of the army himself seemed to be uninterested in defending his own country.[45] In fact for Pepe the problem of the revolution had not been a lack of popular support, but rather the mistake made by the Neapolitan parliament in placing its trust in the monarchy. First, it had agreed to let the monarch go to Laibach, where he betrayed the revolution and reneged on his oath. Second, out of excessive loyalty to the Cádiz Constitution, it left the command of the constitutional army to his son, a decision that led to its defeat in the face of the Austrian invasion.

During Pepe's exile the political disagreements and personal enmities already evident during the revolution were amplified, and came to be embodied in print. In what became a *guerre des plumes*, the exiled revolutionaries blamed each other for the failure of the constitutional experiment. Pepe's rival General Michele Carrascosa, for instance, castigated the Carboneria for having alienated the majority of the Neapolitan population from the revolution itself, an opinion that Pepe dismissed as groundless. Carrascosa also accused Pepe of representing the interests of a single faction and of displaying dictatorial tendencies, instead of defending the constitution.[46] Their disagreements led to a duel that took place in London in 1823, and put an end to their personal disagreements in

44. Pepe, 'Non-Establishment'.

45. Ibid., p. 278.

46. Ibid., p. 284. Compare to Michele Carrascosa, *Mémoires historiques, politiques et militaires sur la révolution du Royaume de Naples en 1820 et 1821 et sur les causes qui l'ont amenée accompagnés de pièces justificatives la plupart inédites par le général Carrascosa* (London: Treuttel, Würtz, Treuttel fils et Richter, 1823), p. 28.

the name of brotherhood and patriotism.[47] Other Neapolitan patriots explicitly blamed the Cádiz Constitution for having undermined the revolution. Pietro Colletta, for instance, not only agreed with Carrascosa that the Carboneria had damaged the revolution, transforming itself from a weapon against despotism into an 'instrument of servitude', but also went on to argue that the Cádiz Constitution was particularly unsuited to the populations of the kingdom, who were not ready to enjoy the excessive degree of liberty granted by it because of their intrinsic immaturity.[48] In his writings from exile Luigi Blanch, who in 1820 had gone on a mission to defend the Neapolitan revolution in various European capitals, agreed with Pepe that the southern peoples were fit for constitutional government. He was convinced that the transformation of society undertaken during the Napoleonic period had destroyed the foundations of absolutism, and that the monarchy had to find a new 'political constitution'. At the same time, however, he endorsed Colletta's opinion that the Spanish constitution was not suited to this purpose. For him the French Charte instead would have enjoyed legitimacy among all components of Neapolitan society, including its moderate elites and its old nobility. If the king had granted it, he might have prevented foreign intervention against the constitutional government.[49]

Exile also provided opportunities to relaunch the revolutionary movement, and offered a chance to build new bridges with foreign opinion makers, politicians and exiles from other countries in support of further conspiracies. Between 1830 and 1831 Pepe sought to take advantage of the new revolutionary context in France to revive his insurrectionary plans in the Mediterranean. In cooperation with Spanish exiles such as Antonio Alcalá Galiano and Francisco Javier de Istúriz, he had hoped to raise money to arm two thousand volunteers, and use the island of Corsica as a base from which to launch an expedition to Spain and to Calabria. The intention was to introduce a constitution in both countries. Having

---

47. 'Generals Pepe and Carrascosa', *The Annual Register, or a View of the History, Politics and Literature of the Year 1823*, no. 65 (London: Baldwin, Cradock and Joy, 1824), p. 25. On this event, see also Luca Manfredi, *L'uomo delle tre rivoluzioni: Vita e pensiero del generale Guglielmo Pepe* (Foggia: Bastogi, 2009), pp. 232–33.

48. Colletta wrote his history while in exile in Florence, where he died in 1831. It was published posthumously (1834). See Pietro Colletta, *Storia del reame di Napoli dal 1734 sino al 1825*, 4 vols (Lugano: Tipografia Elvetica, 1834), 4, pp. 221–22.

49. Luigi Blanch, 'La rivoluzione del 1820 e la reazione che ne seguì', in Blanch, *Scritti storici*, ed. Benedetto Croce, vol. 2: *Il regno di Napoli dalla restaurazione borbonica all'avvento di re Ferdinando II (1815–1830)* (Bari: Laterza, 1945), pp. 129–351 at 235–37.

sustained a correspondence with Lafayette for nine years or so, soon after the 1830 revolution Pepe finally met the old French general, then commander of the national guard in Paris. In spite of the backing the elderly general had given to his requests, Pepe nonetheless failed to obtain a loan from the French revolutionary government to support his project for southern Europe.[50] In the light of recent events in France, the Spanish constitution had begun to seem an obsolete document. Pepe's own constitutional thought changed during this same period, and was influenced in particular by his friend Lafayette's interpretation of the French constitution of 1830 as one that had in fact established a republican monarchy. In a book published in France in 1839, Pepe treated the creation of an Italian unitary state allied to France and Britain as an important stepping stone to the creation of a new geopolitical order in Europe. In his view what was now required to achieve this goal was a new 'democratic' representative monarchy, one stripped of any aristocratic privileges and sustained by a broad popular base, in accordance with the principles of the Orleanist constitutional monarchy.[51]

In spite of the failure of these plans in 1830 and 1831, what military strategy would best guarantee the success of an insurrection remained a central topic of debate for the exile community to which Pepe belonged. Once again, the ideas and military practices of the 1820s set the terms of the debate in the two succeeding decades. In 1830 a Piedmontese exile, Carlo Bianco di Saint Jorioz had revived the notion that a form of guerrilla warfare inspired by the Spanish anti-Napoleonic insurrection could be adopted in the territories of the Italian peninsula and deployed against its absolutist governments. His ideas were embraced also by the young Mazzini in the same years.[52] Meanwhile Pepe had become sceptical about the possibility of transferring this model to Italy, although he still held it to be vital to create a citizens' army in support of the revolution. In a number of essays on military strategy published in the same decade, he argued that the system of provincial militias he had set up during the 1820 revolution was the essential basis for a national insurrection. These militias, to be organised first in southern Italy, would then contribute to the exporting

50. Pepe, *Memoirs*, 3, pp. 288–307.

51. Guglielmo Pepe, 'L'Italie politique et ses rapports avec la France et l'Angleterre' [1839] (Venice: Imprimerie Naratovich, 1848), pp. 62–63.

52. See Carlo Angelo Bianco di Saint Jorioz, *Della guerra d'insurrezione per bande, applicata all'Italia* (n.p. [Italy], 1830); Giuseppe Mazzini, *Della guerra d'insurrezione conveniente all'Italia*, in Mazzini, *Scritti politici, editi ed inediti*, 31 vols (Imola: P. Galeati, 1907), 3, pp. 197–230.

of the revolution to the rest of the peninsula.[53] Pepe partly modified this opinion in 1840, when he admitted that guerrilla warfare might be of some use, but only as a subsidiary and secondary measure in support of regularly organised militias.

When revolution broke out again in the Kingdom of the Two Sicilies in 1848, it was neither the outcome of a military pronunciamiento supported by provincial militias, as had been the case in 1820, nor the product of an armed insurrection planned in exile. This time, it began with an insurrection in the capital of Sicily, Palermo, where revolutionaries once again introduced the 1812 Sicilian Constitution, thereby declaring the island independent. A few days later in Naples, a large and spontaneous popular mobilisation forced the king to introduce a constitution.[54] Unlike the events of the 1820s, those of 1848 belonged to a larger movement throughout the peninsula: popular protest and pressure from the elites led to the introduction of constitutions in all the Italian states. In the Papal States, in Piedmont and in Tuscany, but not in Naples, the reintroduction of constitutional government had been preceded by a wave of top-down reforms in 1847. These events also led to a series of attempts to organise a federation of Italian states. In these new circumstances, after eighteen years of absence, Pepe went to Naples, where the king offered him the honour of presiding over the first constitutional government. The majority of Neapolitan revolutionaries had demanded the reintroduction of the Spanish constitution—albeit with a number of modifications—but King Ferdinando II had conceded instead a 'Statuto' inspired by the French constitution of 1830. Faced with the king's resistance to the proposed modifications of the constitution, which would have entailed suspending the introduction of an upper chamber and broadening the suffrage, Pepe resigned from the post.[55] Instead, he accepted the task of leading the Neapolitan troops in the war declared by all the Italian states, under Piedmontese leadership, against Austria. Pepe attached great importance to this military expedition, being convinced that only by permanently expelling Austria from the peninsula could the defeat previously suffered by the constitutional government

53. See Guglielmo Pepe, *Memoria sui mezzi che menano alla italiana indipendenza* (Paris: Paulin, 1833); Pepe, *L'Italia militare* (Paris: Pihan de la Forest, 1836). On Pepe and this debate, see Angelo Matteo Caglioti, 'La nazione armata di Guglielmo Pepe', *Clio: Rivista Trimestale di Studi Storici* 47, no. 2 (2011): 185–211.

54. On these events see Enrico Francia, *1848: La rivoluzione del Risorgimento* (Bologna: Il Mulino, 2012); Mellone, *Napoli 1848*.

55. Manfredi, *L'uomo*, pp. 298–300.

in 1821 be avoided.[56] Once more he was to be disappointed: following the pope's decision to withdraw his support from the war, King Ferdinando II likewise decided to recall his troops. Pepe for his part refused to comply. With the very few soldiers who did not follow the king's order he then went on to Venice. There he fought with others in defence of Manin's republic, besieged by the Austrian army from June 1848 up until August 1849, when the revolutionary government surrendered.[57]

The end of the revolutions and the withdrawal of the constitution in Naples represented a turning point for the history of the Kingdom of the Two Sicilies and for Neapolitan liberalism. First of all, they put an end to any hopes of turning the Bourbon monarchy into a constitutional one. The brutal repression carried out by the king against the supporters of the constitution, who were either thrown into prison or exiled, led to the international isolation of his kingdom. Its dynasty was henceforth discredited in the eyes of international public opinion, which came to dismiss its rule as the most despotic in Europe. In the years to follow Turin, the capital of the only kingdom in the peninsula to retain a constitution after 1848, became the main centre of Italian nationalism, and attracted hundreds of exiles from the other Italian states. Pepe went first of all to Paris, where he lived until 1851, and then settled in the Kingdom of Sardinia. Moving between Nice, Genoa and Turin, he devoted his time once again to propaganda and conspiracy among exiled patriots of his and of a later generation. His memoirs of the latest round of revolutions, published in 1851, perpetuated his own idea that the freedom of Italy always started in the south, given the importance he attributed to the revolutionary mobilisation of Calabria in 1847.[58] They also contributed to the construction of an image of the Bourbons as oriental-style despots, a judgement widely endorsed by other contemporary accounts.

The events of these years led, secondly, to the marginalisation, if not the demise, of any insurrectional plans. They served to convince most patriots that the solution to the Neapolitan and Italian question lay in the hands of the Piedmontese monarchy and in the military and diplomatic initiatives of is moderate constitutional governments. An increasing number of exiled revolutionaries from Naples came to imagine a single unitary Italian state on the peninsula as the only way to guarantee constitutional

56. Guglielmo Pepe, *Delle rivoluzioni e delle guerre d'Italia nel 1847, 1848, 1849: Memorie del generale Guglielmo Pepe con aggiunta d'una prefazione e di note* (Turin: Luigi Arnaldi, 1850), pp. 131–32.

57. Manfredi, *L'uomo*, pp. 319–22, 329–65.

58. Pepe, *Delle rivoluzioni*; also Guglielmo Pepe, *Casi d'Italia negli anni 1847, 48 e 49: Continuazione delle memorie del generale Guglielmo Pepe* (Genoa: Ponthenier, 1851).

government in the south, at the expense of the survival of Kingdom of the Two Sicilies as an independent state. Yet Pepe's own views in the early 1850s show that Italian nationalism and Neapolitan constitutional patriotism did not necessarily become alternative options, nor did the former consign the latter to oblivion. Rather, these two patriotisms continued to be combined in different ways, in line with shifting circumstances. Although in the 1830s and 1840s Pepe had written about the desirability of a single Italian state covering the entire Italian peninsula, in the early 1850s he was still prepared to endorse plans to turn the Kingdom of the Two Sicilies into an independent constitutional monarchy under an alternative dynasty. In fact, he would seem to have been supportive of the ambitions of Lucien Murat, the son of Naples's former King Gioacchino (Joachim Murat), to replace the Bourbon dynasty: ambitions endorsed by a substantial group of exiled revolutionaries. In 1853 he organised a number of banquets in honour of Lucien in Nice, along with other Neapolitan patriots.[59] When Pepe died in 1855, the funeral orations delivered by his friends and fellow exiles celebrated him as a quintessential Italian patriot. They called to mind his defiant refusal in 1849 to follow his king's order, so as to continue the national war against the Austrians.[60] Three years later a statue of the general unveiled in a square in Turin portrayed him in the act of trampling on King Ferdinando's decree demanding the withdrawal of his army from the river Po. However, as his own request to be buried in Naples next to his brother Florestano suggests, he remained until the end a staunch supporter of Neapolitan constitutionalism as a stepping stone towards a broader Italian patriotism.

Antonio Alcalá Galiano and the transition to moderate liberalism

At the end of the revolutions some of their former protagonists came to believe that the failure of the revolutionary experiments of the 1820s had been due to their excessive radicalism. Representative government could only be reintroduced and would only last, they believed, if a new compromise between the forces of tradition and those supporting the revolution could be found. This compromise would protect some fundamental

59. On Pepe and Muratism, see Delpu, *Un autre Risorgimento*, pp. 401–4. On Muratism, see Fiorella Bartoccini, *Il murattismo: Speranze, timori e contrasti nella lotta per l'unità d'Italia* (Milan: Giuffrè, 1959).

60. On Pepe's funeral, see *Onori funebri renduti a Guglielmo Pepe* (Turin: Stamperia dell'Unione Tipografica Editrice, 1855).

liberties and maintain some form of parliamentary representation while at the same time excluding the majority of the population from political participation. It would also—crucially—grant the monarch substantial powers, in order to guarantee his or her support for the constitution, and to stabilise the political order against the threat of insurrection. In this attempt to establish constitutional regimes designed to reconcile liberty and order, avoid revolution and exclude the bulk of the population from political participation lay the essence of moderate liberalism. This was by no means a new idea, as some revolutionaries during the 1820s (in particular the Spanish moderados) had already advocated this solution. But in the decades to follow a larger number of supporters of representative government, including some who had not directly experienced the events of the 1820s, came to embrace it in Spain and in the rest of southern Europe. They resolutely rejected any revolutionary idea, and became even more critical of the notion of popular sovereignty than any of their number had been during the 1820s. They did so in the face of mounting political instability, further political radicalisation on the left and the right alike (in Spain and Portugal in particular), and out of fear of potential revolutionary threats (in Piedmont). Between the 1830s and the 1860s a number of constitutional settlements were inspired by the ideological tenets of moderate liberalism: in Portugal under the premiership of António da Costa Cabral (1841–46 and 1849–51), in Piedmont when a constitutional monarchy was established in 1848, in Greece in the period between 1843 and 1862 and in Spain during the so-called 'Década Moderada' between 1844 and 1854, and also intermittently in the 1850s and 1860s when moderates were in power.[61]

The political and intellectual biography of Antonio Alcalá Galiano shows that after the 1820s even a former exaltado writer could find it possible, in the name of stability and order, to abandon his commitment to participatory politics and embrace a new political settlement. After the Trienio itself, Galiano's career extended from the constitutional years under María Cristina's regency between 1834 and 1840, through the years of moderate governments between 1843 and 1854 and, after the 'Bienio Progresista' (1854–56), to those marked by the government of a new 'Unión Liberal'. It was interrupted by three periods of exile abroad.

61. Maria de Fátima Bonifácio, 'Costa Cabral no contexto do liberalismo doutrinário', *Análise Social* 28, no. 1 (1993): 1043–91. On Piedmontese moderates, see Roberto Romani, *Sensibilities of the Risorgimento: Reasons and Passions in Political Thought* (Leiden: Brill, 2018); Maurizio Isabella, 'Aristocratic Liberalism and Risorgimento: Cesare Balbo and Piedmontese Political Thought after 1848', *History of European Ideas* 39 (2013): 835–57. On the Greek case, see Sotiropoulos, *Liberalism*.

Galiano had been the author of Riego's manifesto of January 1820 and a leading figure among the exaltados; he was one of the most charismatic and celebrated orators of the Trienio, noteworthy for his public speeches in defence of the revolution and Riego's army at the Fontana de Oro and the Sociedad Landaburiana.[62] He had also been an active member of the Cortes. His most famous intervention as a deputy took place in the dramatic circumstances of the French invasion of 1823. Faced with the imminent arrival of the French army, the Cortes approved and adopted Galiano's suggestion that they declare the king temporarily incapacitated, so that against his will he could be transferred with them from Seville to Cádiz.[63]

At the end of the revolution Galiano left Spain with hundreds of other revolutionaries and went into exile in Britain. With the exception of a few months spent in the French capital, between 1823 and 1834 he lived in London, where he made a living as a journalist and professor of Spanish literature in the newly founded University College. In the British capital a lively debate about the reasons for the failure of the revolution, mirroring that taking place among the exiled Neapolitans, opposed the moderados to the exaltados.[64] In the London-based exile press, the exaltados claimed that moderation had paved the way to the counterrevolution, while the moderados for their part argued that the exaltados had undermined the constitution. Galiano intervened in this debate with a lengthy article published in 1824 in the leading Benthamite periodical *The Westminster Review*, in which he harshly criticised Britain for allowing France to put an end to the constitutional government. For Galiano, what had done most to undermine the constitutional regime had been the behaviour of the king, who had created a 'party of the chambers' exerting undue influence over governmental decisions. This behaviour had been made possible by flaws in the constitution itself, a document that gave the monarch excessive powers. Galiano also pointed to the resilience of social privileges and corporate interests, untouched by the revolution, that had further weakened the constitutional regime. Like most of his fellow exiles, however, he continued to defend the 1812 constitution as a valuable document. While arguing in favour of some revisions, he claimed that it had

---

62. For Galiano's biography, I follow here Raquel Sánchez García, *Alcalá Galiano y el liberalismo español* (Madrid: Centro de Estudios Políticos y Constitucionales, 2005). On his early political career, see pp. 105–14.

63. On the temporary deposition of the king, see Antonio Alcalá Galiano, *Recuerdos de un anciano* (Madrid: Luis Navarro, 1878), pp. 421–41.

64. Simal, *Emigrados*, pp. 197–210.

acquired a moral authority recognised by the majority of the population of Spain.[65] It was in its name that the exiles continued to be engaged in conspiratorial activities and revolutionary attempts that would replicate the model of the military pronunciamiento of 1820.[66]

After the death of Fernando VII in September 1833, constitutional government was finally reinstated in 1834 under the regency of María Cristina, and a bloody civil war broke out between her liberal supporters and those backing the absolutist pretender to the throne, Don Carlos. In these new circumstances the exiles who had fled Spain in 1823 and had been involved in a number of failed uprisings in the following years were granted an amnesty. Many of them, including Galiano, returned home, and to active political life. This novel context favoured political realignments and the creation of new moderate and progressive groupings with their own distinctive programmes and ideologies. In 1834 the regent granted a constitution—the 'Estatuto Real'—inspired by the French Charte of 1814, which introduced a bicameral system based on an upper chamber appointed by the regent and a lower chamber elected on the basis of a very limited franchise. The prime ministers who served under this constitution, from Francisco Martínez de la Rosa to Juan Álvarez Mendizábal, had all participated in the events of the Trienio. Although progressive liberals and moderates wished to revise the Estatuto, criticising it for its inadequate electoral laws or for its lack of an explicit list of rights, they had one and all ceased to consider the 1812 constitution to be a document suited to dealing with the problems of contemporary Spain. Galiano was elected to the Estamento de Procuradores, the lower chamber, and took part in the debates about a new electoral law relating to this level of the legislature. Having joined it as a progresista, by the beginning of 1836 he had been appointed minister of the navy in a short-lived moderado government led by another former exaltado turned moderado, Francisco Javier de Istúriz.[67] In 1836 a revolution precipitated by a number of insurrections across the provinces and culminating in the pronunciamiento of the Royal Guard at La Granja forced the regent to reintroduce the 1812 constitution with a view to discussion

65. Antonio Alcalá Galiano, 'Spain', *The Westminster Review* 1, no. 2 (1824): 289–336; Joaquín Varela Suanzes-Carpegna, 'El pensamiento constitucional español en el exilio: El abandono del modelo doceañista (1823–1833)', *Revista de Estudios Políticos* 88 (1995): 63–90.

66. Simal, *Emigrados*, pp. 311–26.

67. On this period of Galiano's life see, Sánchez García, *Alcalá Galiano*; pp. 189–236. On these events, see Isabel Burdiel, 'The Liberal Revolution, 1808–1843', in *Spanish History since 1808*, ed. José Álvarez Junco and Adrian Shubert (London: Bloomsbury, 2000), pp. 17–32, esp. 25–27.

regarding a new charter. As a compromise between progressive and moderate liberals, a new constitution was introduced in 1837. This document replaced the single parliament of the 1812 constitution with two chambers and a property-based suffrage in which only 5.5 per cent of the population had voting rights. Following the revolution of 1836 Galiano, like Istúriz, once again went into exile to England, but the following year he was back as a member of the newly elected Cortes.

The new constitution did not restore peace, however: Carlist forces managed to control Navarre, the Basque country and parts of Catalonia, where they enjoyed substantial popular support. A Carlist army even managed to approach Madrid. Only in 1840, with the Treaty of Vergara, did the civil war end and the Carlists cease represent a serious threat to the constitutional monarchy. That threat had served to reinforce another brand of provincial radicalism on the left, a constitutionalism that had its roots in municipal government and local militias, revived by the reintroduction of the municipal legislation of 1823, and equally capable of gaining the support of urban populations. Galiano's transition to moderate liberalism represented a response to the perceived threats represented by these alternative forms of popular mobilisation. In these new circumstances, Galiano became convinced that in order to survive, representative government would have to exclude the masses, and base itself on the capacities of the educated classes. It also required a powerful monarchical authority. While at the end of the Trienio Fernando's behaviour had convinced him that royal authority had to be limited, by the end of the 1830s Galiano had come to the conclusion that only a powerful executive and substantial monarchical prerogatives could defend constitutional government against the destabilising force of various popular radicalisms. From 1837 onwards he contributed to the shaping of a new, moderate political agenda through his active engagement with parliamentary politics and as an editor of a moderate periodical, *El Piloto*, along with Juan Donoso Cortés. After their parliamentary victory of 1839, Galiano condemned the progresistas in the pages of *El Piloto* for having encouraged popular disturbances and tumults, and advocated the repression of all forms of popular excess, on the grounds that they would otherwise lead to anarchy and tyranny. Democracy was denounced as the basis for despotism, an increasingly common idea amongst moderate liberals across Europe.[68] Central to the moderates' ambitions to control these countervailing radicalisms was a reform of the state that would reinforce state control over municipal

---

68. *El Piloto*, 23 March and 27 August 1839, quoted in Sánchez García, *Alcalá Galiano*, pp. 253–54.

authorities. While moderates disagreed about the desirability or otherwise of retaining the fueros—some supported them in order to obtain the support of Carlismo's social base while others, Galiano among them, favoured abolition—they all agreed on the desirability of limiting local autonomy. Galiano thus defended and supported the controversial reform presented to and voted for by the Congreso in 1840 that aimed at turning the alcaldes into government representatives and executors of ministerial decisions, and gave the government the right to dissolve the ayuntamientos.[69]

It was this reform that triggered a widespread reaction across the country against the moderate government and led to the exile of María Cristina and the establishment of General Baldomero Espartero's regency, which lasted three years. This period was marked by the emergence of a popular republicanism, whose supporters joined reading clubs, patriotic societies and secret organisations. While they advocated universal suffrage and popular sovereignty, these republicans were not nostalgic for the 1812 constitution, a document they criticised for the powers it granted to the king.[70] In 1841 the moderates had backed the military intervention of another general, Leopoldo O'Donnell, to remove Espartero, but this attempt had failed. Galiano, condemned for his participation in this failed pronunciamiento against Espartero to a sentence of ten years' imprisonment, went into exile for the third time in Paris and London. Only in the summer of 1843 did he return to Spain, when the military defeat of Espartero by General Ramón María Narváez inaugurated a full decade of moderate government.

The return of the moderates to power was marked by a constitutional reform that led to the ratification of the new document in 1845. This new charter, unlike the previous one, no longer made reference to national sovereignty, but instead placed sovereignty in the hands of the monarch and the Cortes, reinforcing the powers of the former. It also abolished the elective basis of the senate and transformed this chamber into one entirely appointed by the monarch. Municipal autonomy was curtailed and electoral reform further restricted suffrage to a mere 1 per cent of the population. Galiano fully supported the new regime. Although he would have preferred a senate that included also a hereditary aristocracy, he welcomed the transformation of the monarchy from one that, in his own words, had been sustained by democracy, to one sustained by mesocracy and aristocracy.[71]

---

69. See Galiano's speech on 2 June 1840, as published in *Diario de las sesiones de Cortes del Congreso de Diputados*, vol. 4 (Madrid: Imprenta Nacional 1840), pp. 19–20. On the context, see also Castro, *La revolución liberal*, p. 125.

70. Peyrou, *El republicanismo*, p. 121.

71. Sánchez García, *Alcalá Galiano*, p. 306.

While he did not himself hold any prominent ministerial office, he participated in the parliamentary life of the period as a member of the senate, to
which he was appointed by the queen in 1845. The only important institutional post he held during this Década Moderada was that of Spanish ambassador in Lisbon from 1851 to the end of the moderate government in 1854,
which was brought about by means of military intervention.

It was as an essayist and public intellectual that Galiano made his most
significant contribution during this period. From 1838 onwards he delivered cycles of public lectures on Spanish literature, history and politics at
the Ateneo de Madrid, one of the leading cultural institutions of the city
and a bastion of moderate political culture. In 1845 he become president of
the institution, and from 1846 he also held the chair of Spanish literature
there. In his *Lecciones de derecho político*, published in 1843 as a collection
of the lectures he had delivered at the Ateneo in the previous years, he
provided an authoritative theorical justification of moderatism, combining Burke's emphasis on the need to root institutions in history and society
with Bentham's utilitarianism.[72] He also reflected upon the history of his
own country, and in particular upon the events that followed the Napoleonic wars. He did so in a number of historical writings and pamphlets that
contributed to the creation of a moderates' historiography. In his monumental history of Spain, published between 1844 and 1846, he located the
events of 1820–23 in the context of the great European revolution that
had first affected Spain in 1808. In his view these events had dramatically
altered the customs of the country's population, undermining respect for
the upper classes and religion, and disseminating military insurrectionary practices. The attempts at restoration made by Fernando in 1814 and
1823 had been doomed to fail, as they could not stem or reverse these
dramatic but unavoidable changes.[73] For Galiano, following in the footsteps of Guizot's historical accounts of European civilisation, the history
of modern Spain was that of the birth and consolidation of representative
government. The mismatch between modern aspirations in society and
persisting traditional values accounted for the turbulence of Spanish history from the French invasion to the 1830s. That gap between society and

72. Antonio Alcalá Galiano, *Lecciones de derecho político constitucional* (Madrid: D. I.
Boix, 1843).

73. Antonio María Alcalá Galiano, *Historia de España desde los tiempos primitivos
hasta la mayoria de la Reina Doña Isabel II., redactada y anotada con arreglo à la que
escribio en Ingles el Doctor Dunham [. . .] Con una reseña de los historiadores Españoles
de mas nota por Don J. Donoso Cortés, y un discurso sobre la historia de nuestra nacion
por Don F. Martinez de la Rosa*, 7 vols (Madrid: Sociedad Literaria y Tipografica, 1844–46),
7, pp. 262–63.

representative institutions, he seemed to imply, had by the 1840s finally been filled, thanks to the existence of a constitutional regime better suited than any previous one to the needs of Spain.

The eruption of the 1848 revolutions in Europe and their impact on Spain would however undermine the social stability achieved under the moderate constitution. During that year the prime minister Narváez had reacted swiftly to suppress the urban insurrections in Madrid and Seville, and Carlist and republican disturbances in Catalonia.[74] Galiano was broadly sympathetic to the government's response. Although mindful of the risks posed by abuse of powers and the excessive use of force, he agreed with his friend Donoso Cortes that in such circumstances the establishment of a dictatorship was a legitimate option. Inspired once more by Guizot, he claimed in 1848 that, unlike the American revolution and the events of 1789 and 1830, which had been morally just, this latest wave of uprisings was wholly unjustified. Their dangerous outcome had been the collapse of monarchical power, the rise of the populace at the expense of the middle classes and the establishment of a democracy that would lead to the rule of tribunes and demagogues.[75] His fears regarding the threat posed by revolutionary instability were confirmed in 1854, when a military coup led to two years of government by the progresistas, marked by grassroots mobilisation of republican associations. It was precisely to contribute to the social stability of the country undermined by these new popular forces that in 1857 he wholeheartedly supported Narváez's reform of the senate. The reform introduced some hereditary peers to an upper chamber previously made up of life members only. Support for the inclusion of an aristocratic element in the constitution did not however prevent him seeing the rise of a commercial middle class in a favourable light. Galiano viewed this phenomenon as an additional source of stability for the constitutional monarchy. In the last years of his life he devoted much of his time, in fact, to advocating free trade, writing and giving public lectures on this topic, and contributing to the establishment of the Asociación para la Reforma de los Aranceles de Aduanas (Association for the reform of customs duties) in 1859. His direct engagement in politics lessened considerably as the years passed, but did not come to an end. He was sent briefly to the embassies of Turin and Lisbon as a diplomat between 1858 and 1859, and had to wait until 1864, at the very end of his life, to be appointed minister of public works in a government presided over by Narváez. In his final years,

74. Ignacio García de Paso García, 'El 1848 español: ¿Una excepción europea?', *Ayer* 106, no. 2 (2017): 185–206.

75. Antonio Alcalá Galiano, *Breves reflexiones sobre la indole de la crisis por que estan pasando los gobiernos y pueblos de Europa* (Madrid: Ramón Rodríguez de Rivera, 1848).

concern for the defence of authority led Galiano not just to accept, but to justify, the curtailment of individual rights. Indeed, it was in the name of the defence of authority that in 1864 he supported the government's decision to forbid a university professor from expressing opinions against the monarchy and the concordat with the Catholic church. The former advocate of freedom of the press during the Trienio now supported the dismissal of a professor who had criticised the queen, and of the rector of the university who had defended him.[76] During the night of 10 April 1865, travelling from home to his office by carriage, Galiano found himself in the midst of the public demonstrations organised by students in defence of their rector. Shaken by the experience, the following day he died while attending a meeting of the council of ministers. It was perhaps ironic that the ex-revolutionary Galiano should die in the wake of experiencing the sort of popular disorder that he had long come to consider to be the gravest threat to the stability of the constitutional order.[77]

This episode and the protest of the university professors led to a governmental crisis, and more generally precipitated the end of the compromise between moderates and progresistas that had existed since 1856. In fact, it paved the way to another period of military interventions, revolution and civil war. In 1868 a military uprising supported by both progressive and unionist officers dethroned Queen Isabel II, inaugurating the so-called 'revolutionary sexennium', a period of great political instability. The establishment in 1869 of a democratic monarchy under Amadeo, Duke of Aosta, with a new constitution, in turn produced a republican revolutionary opposition. After the abdication of King Amadeo in 1873 this republican opposition managed to gain power, if only for eleven months. Meanwhile a Carlist insurrection swept across many provinces, creating yet another source of social and political instability.[78]

Conclusion

The tempestuousness which marked the years after Galiano's death serves to remind us that the moderate attempt to stabilise the monarchy by drastically limiting popular participation did not go unchallenged. It shows that

76. Sánchez García, *Alcalá Galiano*, pp. 422–26. On this context, see Raymond Carr, *Spain 1808–1975*, 2nd edn (Oxford: Oxford University Press, 1982), pp. 296–97.

77. Alcalá Galiano, *Memorias*, 2, pp. 533–34.

78. On this period, see Carr, *Spain*, pp. 305–67; Demetrio Castro, 'The Left: From Liberalism to Democracy', in *Spanish History since 1808*, ed. José Álvarez Junco and Adrian Shubert (London: Bloomsbury, 2000), pp. 86–90.

to put an end to the cycle of revolutions, civil wars and counterrevolutions inaugurated during the 1820s proved extremely difficult; and this was the case throughout southern Europe. Greece was the only state where a degree of political stability under a constitutional regime based on universal suffrage had been established by 1864. The handing over of the Ionian Islands by Britain to Greece that same year, when the new King George was enthroned, further increased the popularity of the new constitutional regime. Over the next decade the state also managed to put an end to the chronic problem of banditry inherited from the Greek revolution.[79] But in the rest of southern Europe it was only after the 1860s that the social and political cleavages proliferating after the 1820s revolutions came to be resolved, and a substantial broadening of popular participation in the decision-making process was finally allowed. After that decade, the moderates' political project to confine voting rights to the social elites was eclipsed everywhere, with the exception of Italy. In Spain, the restoration of the Bourbon monarchy of 1875 produced yet another political compromise, this time based on the 1845 constitution that had divided sovereignty between the king and the parliament. While this constitution, approved in 1876, introduced universal suffrage, this latter feature was immediately withdrawn. It was finally reintroduced nine years later, however, in 1885.

The decade of the 1860s had been no less turbulent in Portugal. As mentioned above, republican uprisings broke out in 1868 in Porto, Lisbon and Braga, and continued in the capital until 1870, when a final military coup was attempted by the Duke of Saldanha. In 1876 two new parties—namely, the Partido Progressista created by a merger between the Reformista and the Histórico parties, and the Partido Republicano—were established on the left. However, their advocacy of electoral reform in the name of popular sovereignty did not lead to further instability and turmoil. To absorb their opposition and weaken their alliance, the prime minister Fontes Pereira de Melo approved in 1878 an electoral reform that reintroduced quasi-universal male suffrage. Granting all heads of families the right to vote, this electoral law finally reintroduced in Portugal the voting system first adopted in 1822.[80]

On the Italian peninsula, meanwhile, the conquest of the Kingdom of the Two Sicilies and its integration into the new Kingdom of Italy after

79. Gallant, *Edinburgh History*, pp. 151–53.

80. Pedro Tavares de Almeida, 'Electors, Voting and Representatives', in *Res publica: Citizenship and Political Representation in Portugal, 1820–1926*, ed. Fernando Catroga and Pedro Tavares de Almeida (Lisbon: Assembleia da República, 2011), pp. 60–89 at 62–63. On Portuguese republicanism, see Fernando Catroga, *O republicanismo em Portugal, da formação ao 5 de Outubro de 1910*, 2nd edn (Lisbon: Editorial Notícias, 2000).

Garibaldi's successful expedition in 1860 was not a painless event either. It gave rise to a civil war that lasted until the middle of that same decade. This bitter and bloody conflict showed the extent to which political loyalties in the Neapolitan provinces were sharply divided between those attached to the Bourbon absolute monarchy and those supportive of the new nation on grounds of the political freedoms it finally guaranteed. This was the first (and last) armed legitimist and counterrevolutionary movement to take place in southern Italy since the Napoleonic occupation.[81] Nor did the revolution of 1860 put an end to Sicily's yearning for autonomy from Naples: in 1860 the Palermitans supported Garibaldi's expedition in order that they might themselves be liberated from Neapolitan rule, but in 1866 they rose up again in the name of the independence of the island. Plebiscites based on male universal suffrage had sealed the legitimacy of a new Italian state by extending constitutional government to the former Kingdom of the Two Sicilies. However, the new electoral system of the Kingdom of Italy limited voting rights to a small percentage of its population. On the Italian peninsula moderate liberalism managed to impose its political agenda for a longer span of time than anywhere else, and the new political elites there resolutely refused to broaden political participation.[82]

Thus, seen retrospectively from the vantage point of the 1860s, the 1820s uprisings look like a transformational moment both in the history of constitutional government and in the Age of Revolutions in southern Europe. A similar combination of popular mobilisation and mass participation in electoral processes would not be easily replicated, as these features reappeared only much later on. Male universal suffrage had become a reality in Greece and Spain by the 1880s, but it would only be achieved again across all the southern peripheries of the continent at the beginning of the following century. As the biographies of the four revolutionaries from Greece, Portugal, Spain and Naples summarised above suggest, very few of those who had participated in the events of the 1820s would live to enjoy the same degree of political freedom again.

81. Carmine Pinto, *La guerra per il Mezzogiorno* (Bari: Laterza, 2019).

82. On the plebiscites and more generally on moderates, see Roberto Romani, 'Political Thought in Action: The Moderates in 1859', *Journal of Modern Italian Studies* 17, no. 5 (2012): 593–607; Romani, *Sensibilities*.

Note: dates for the Greek revolution listed in this chronology (and used in the text of this book) refer to the old Julian calendar, used at the time in the Ottoman Empire, and are given here in italic. The Julian calendar was twelve days behind the Gregorian calendar then employed in Europe, which is adopted for the rest of this chronology (including the Battle of Navarino).

1806

23 January	Ferdinando IV, king of Naples and Sicily, flees to Palermo under British protection. French troops of Marshal Masséna invade Naples in February.

1807

29 November	Departure of the fleet that takes the Portuguese royal family and court to Brazil.
30 November	Occupation of Lisbon by the French troops of General Junot.

1808

16 February	The French army invades Spain.
2 May	'Dos de Mayo' uprising against the French in Madrid. Beginning of the Peninsular War.
6 May	Fernando VII of Spain is forced to abdicate by Napoleon and is taken into custody in France at the Château de Valençay.

1809

4 March	Second French invasion of Portugal from the north, by Marshal Soult. Porto is occupied.

1810

June	Third French invasion of Portugal, through Beira, under command of Marshal Masséna.

1811

17 April	Definitive withdrawal of Masséna's troops from Portugal.

1812

19 March	The Spanish Cortes proclaim the Constitution of Cádiz.
May	The Treaty of Bucharest puts an end to war between Russia and Ottoman Empire started in 1806. Russia acquires Bessarabia.
19 July	The Sicilian parliament (three estates: *bracci*) starts drafting the Sicilian constitution. The charter receives the final royal assent on 25 May 1813.

1814

22 March   Fernando VII returns to Spain. On 4 May he abolishes the Constitution of Cádiz.

1815

17 June   The king returns to Naples as absolute sovereign with the new title of Ferdinando IV of the Two Sicilies.

1817

17 October   Execution of Gomes Freire de Andrade and those accused of the conspiracy against the regency of the Kindgom of Portugal.

1820

1 January   Pronunciamiento of Rafael Riego at Las Cabezas de San Juan, Spain.

2 July   Pronunciamiento of Michele Morelli and Giuseppe Salvati, based in Nola, Naples.

8 July   Luigi Minichini and General Guglielmo Pepe enter the city of Naples at the head of the constitutional army.

8–9 July   Royal Guards' failed attempt to prevent the meeting of the Cortes and to repeal the constitution in Madrid.

9 July   Opening of the Spanish Cortes. The king takes an oath to the constitution before the Chamber.

15 July   Popular insurrection breaks out in Palermo, capital of Sicily, in favour of the independence of the island from Naples.

4 August   Dissolution of Riego and Quiroga's constitutional army.

24 August   Pronunciamiento of Bernardo Correia de Castro e Sepúlveda and Colonel Sebastião Drago Valente de Brito Cabreira in Porto, Portugal.

31 August   Rafael Riego arrives in Madrid.

3 September   Public demonstrations and ceremonies for Riego in Madrid. Patriotic songs are sung in his honour in the theatre.

5 October   End of war between Palermo and Naples. A peace convention between the two parties is signed in the capital of Sicily.

23 October–
17 December   Congress of Troppau: a conference of the Quintuple. Alliance to discuss the suppression of the revolution in Naples.

1821

January   Congress of European powers starts at Laibach (Ljubljana). Prince Metternich decides on intervention to crush the revolution in Naples.

26 January   Meeting of the constituent Cortes in Lisbon.

26–29 January   Peloponnesian notables and members of the Philiki Etaireia meet at Vostitsa (Greece) to plan the revolution.

22 February–
6 March   General Alexandros Ypsilantis crosses the river Pruth into Moldavia and declares an insurrection against the Ottomans.

7 March	The Austrian army defeats General Pepe's Neapolitan constitutional army at Antrodoco, near Rieti.
10 March	Pronunciamento in Alessandria, Piedmont.
15–30 March	Beginning of the insurrection in the Peloponnese. Surrender of the Turkish garrisons to the insurgents in the towns of Kalavryta and Kalamata.
23–25 March	The Messinian senate issues an appeal to the European royal courts for help.
2 April	Defeat of the Piedmontese constitutional army at Novara.
10 April	The patriarch of Constantinople, Grigorios V, and prelates are executed there on Orthodox Easter Sunday.
8 May	The revolution is proclaimed by Lykourgos Logothetis on the island of Samos.
18 May	King Ferdinando returns to Naples as absolute monarch.
7 June	Defeat of Alexandros Ypsilantis's Sacred Band at Drăgășani, Wallachia.
4 July	Arrival of Dom João VI in Lisbon, from Brazil.
1 September	Dismissal of Rafael Riego as captain general of Aragon.
23 September	Theodoros Kolokotronis seizes Tripolitsa, capital of the Morea.
29 October	Cádiz insurrection. Protests in Seville are encouraged by the exaltados.
4 November	A regional assembly meets at Messolonghi and promulgates the Statute of the Senate of western continental Greece.
15 November	A regional assembly of eastern continental Greeks convenes at Salona (Amphissa) and approves the Statute of Areios Pagos.
20 December	The First National Assembly of revolutionary Greece meets at Piada (New Epidavros).

1822

1 January	The First National Assembly endorses the Provisional Constitution of Greece. On 15 January it issues the declaration of Greek independence.
30 March	Massacre of Chios carried out by Ottoman naval forces.
30 June	Closure of the Cortes in Madrid and uprising of the Royal Guard.
14 August	Spanish royalists establish a supreme regency (*regencia*) in La Seu d'Urgell, Catalonia.
25 October	The first siege of Messolonghi (western Greece) begins.

1823

18 January	Nafplion is made capital of revolutionary Greece.
30 March	The Second National Assembly convenes at Astros, Greece.
7 April	French troops cross the Bidasoa river into Spain.
23 April	The Spanish Cortes opens its sessions in Seville, and war is declared against France.

23 May	French troops in Madrid. The following day the Duke of Angoulême enters the city and appoints a regency.
27 May	The pronunciamiento of the Infante Dom Miguel in Vila Franca de Xira ends the first liberal Triénio in Portugal.
15 June	King Fernando VII is taken to Cádiz by the constitutional government of Spain.
26 June	The French army arrives at the gates of Cádiz.
1 October	Fernando VII's manifesto suspends the Spanish constitution and declares null and void all government acts since 7 March 1820.

1824

March	The first civil war breaks out in Greece.
30 April	Failed attempt at an ultra-royalist coup led by Dom Miguel, who is forced to leave Portugal and go into exile.
November	A second civil war breaks out in Greece, between Roumeliot and Peloponnesian notables and military chiefs.

1825

| 4 January | Death of Ferdinando, King of the Two Sicilies. His son Francesco ascends to the throne. |
| *15 April* | The second siege of the Greek city of Messolonghi begins. |

1826

10 March	Death of Dom João VI of Portugal.
4 April	A protocol is signed in St. Petersburg between Great Britain and Russia, in favour of an autonomous Greek state under nominal Ottoman suzerainty.
6 April	The Third National Assembly of Greece convenes at Epidavros.
10–11 April	Messolonghi is taken by Ottoman forces. The population leaves the city.
29 April	Dom Pedro IV grants the Constitutional Charter, or Carta, to Portugal. Rebellions by Miguelistas break out in the provinces.
2 May	Dom Pedro IV abdicates in favour of his daughter Dona Maria, on condition that she swear an oath to the constitution and marry her uncle, Dom Miguel.
1 August	Infanta Dona Isabel Maria becomes regent of Portugal on behalf of Dona Maria II.
5 October	Pronunciamiento of the Marquis of Chaves in Vila Real, Trás-os-Montes, followed by other pronunciamientos in Viseu, Vila Pouca de Aguiar and the Algarve, Portugal.
8 October	Elections to the Chamber of Deputies, Portugal.
23–25 October	Civil war breaks out in Portugal. Silveira invades Trás-os-Montes, and Teles Jordão occupies Beira and Magessi Alentejo.

29 October	Signing of a betrothal contract between Dona Maria II and Infante Dom Miguel of Portugal.
30 October	Opening of the constitutional Cortes, Portugal.
24 December	A five thousand-man division of the British army, commanded by General Sir William Henry Clinton, arrives in Lisbon, in support of the Portuguese constitutional regime. (It will return to Britain in April 1828.)

1827

March	Royalist revolt of the *agraviados* breaks out in Catalonia, Valencia, Aragon, the Basque country and Andalusia. It will be suppressed by September.
8–10 March	Absolutist forces arriving in Portugal from Spain are disarmed. End of the civil war in Portugal.
19 March	The Third National Assembly of Greece convenes at Troezena in the Peloponnese.
2 April	The Third National Assembly elects Ioannis Kapodistrias first head of state of free Greece.
1 May	The Third National Assembly endorses the political constitution of Greece.
6 July	Britain, France and Russia sign the Treaty of London for the pacification of Greece. The treaty commits the three powers to resolving 'the Greek question'.
24 July	*Archotadas*, constitutional riots in Lisbon in favour of General Saldanha.
20 October	The navies of Britain, France and Russia defeat the Turco-Egyptian fleet in a battle in the bay of Navarino.

1828

8 January	Ioannis Kapodistrias arrives in Greece as the new governor. He sets up his provisional state administration in Aegina.
22 February	Dom Miguel disembarks in Lisbon and swears an oath to the Portuguese constitution.
26 February	Infanta Isabel Maria, regent of Portugal, transfers her duties to her brother, Infante Dom Miguel.
13 March	Dom Miguel dissolves the Cortes of Portugal. The 'Hymn of the Constitution' is forbidden.
25 April	Absolutist riots in Lisbon. Acclamation of Dom Miguel by the senates of Lisbon, Coimbra and Aveiro.
3 May	Convocation of the traditional three estates of the kingdom in Lisbon. Dom Pedro, in Rio de Janeiro, abdicates and appoints Dom Miguel regent of Portugal on behalf of Dona Maria II.
16 May–2 July	Pronunciamiento of the garrison of Porto in favour of the Portuguese constitution, and establishment of a junta.

22 May	Restoration of the constitution of Portugal on the island of Terceira, in the Azores archipelago, and acclamation of Dom Pedro in Coimbra.
25 May	A pronunciamiento in the Algarve, Portugal, in defence of the Carta, is immediately suppressed.
June	Failed constitutional uprising in the province of Cilento, Naples.
7 July	Oath of Dom Miguel before the traditional three estates in Lisbon.

1829

14 February	Constitutional forces land on the island of Terceira; the Miguelist naval offensive is defeated in August.
8 March	Arrival of six hundred Portuguese emigrants in England.
7 May	Execution of participants in the May 1828 constitutional insurrection in Porto, Portugal.
June	Dom Pedro nominates a regency on the island of Terceira.
11 July	The Fourth National Assembly convenes at Argos, Greece.

1830

3 February	The three 'great powers' (Britain, France and Russia) sign the Protocol of London, establishing an independent Greek state under their guarantee.

1831

7 April	Dom Pedro is forced to abdicate the imperial crown of Brazil; he comes to Europe with his daughter.

GLOSSARY OF FOREIGN TERMS

The following is an alphabetical reference list of foreign terms recurrent in the text, which are italicised and defined at first occurrence and thereafter given in roman type.

alcalde. mayor (in Spain)

armatolikia. territories ruled on behalf of the Ottoman authorities by *armatoloi*

armatoloi. members of a Christian military class presiding over districts of Ottoman Roumeli

ayuntamiento. local or municipal council in Spain

baldios. communal lands owned by villages and local communities in Portugal

bande. irregular armed groups traditional to Sicily

barrios. neighbourhoods or districts of Spanish cities

câmara. local or municipal council in Portugal

capitão mor. a local notable in Portugal empowered under the *ordenanças* to draft soldiers

carbonari. members of the Carboneria secret society (established in southern Italy)

comarca. district into which each province was divided in Portugal

comuneros. members of the Comunería secret society (established in Spain)

concelho. subdivision of a *comarca* in Portugal

corregedor. royal official at the head of a Portuguese comarca

corregidor. civil servant appointed by the king as head of a municipal government in Spain

demogerontes. local administrators in Greece

deputazioni provinciali. equivalent in Italy to the Spanish *diputaciones provinciales*

diputaciones provinciales. provincial committees under the Spanish constitution of 1812

donatários. holders of seigneurial rights in Portuguese districts

exaltados. left-wing supporters of the constitution in Spain in 1820–23

fueros. privileges enjoyed by the Kingdom of Navarre and the provinces of the Basque country

giunta (local or national). committee set up at the beginning of the revolution in Piedmont and Naples

governadores (do reino). governors appointed to rule Portugal on behalf of the regent

intendente. representative of central government in Spain and Naples

intendenza. Neapolitan/Sicilian province governed by an *intendente*

jefe político. head of a *diputación provincial* under the Spanish constitution of 1812

juíz de fora. magistrate presiding over a *câmara* in Portugal

juíz do povo. leading official representing artisans corporation in Lisbon

junta (local or national). committee set up at the beginning of the revolution (in Spain)

kapakia. act of submission and mutual protection to end an armed conflict in Christian Ottoman lands

kapetanaioi or *kapoi.* armed men at the service of notables in the Peloponnese

kapudan pasha. grand admiral of the Ottoman navy

klepht. brigand or member of an armed band in the Ottoman lands

merindad. a lodge of the Comunería secret society

moderados. moderate-conservative supporters of the constitution in Spain in 1820–23

ordenanças. territorial organisation of the army in Portugal to draft soldiers

partida. guerrilla band in Spain

progresistas. left-wing supporters of the constitution in Spain after the 1830s

pronunciamiento. revolutionary proclamation by the army

realistas/realisti. supporters of the absolute monarchy in Portugal and Spain/Naples

regencia. royalist government set up in the name of the absolute monarch during the civil war in Spain in 1822

regidor. member of the municipal government in Spain

sociedades patrióticas. clubs or associations of constitutionalists in Portugal and Spain

tierras baldías y propias. communal lands owned by villages and municipal authorities in Spain (equivalent to the *terre demaniali* in Naples and Sicily)

Trienio. the three-year revolutionary period between 1820 and 1823 in Spain

Triénio. the three-year revolutionary period between 1820 and 1823 in Portugal

tertulia patriótica. a patriotic society (of supporters of the constitution) in Spain

turbe (carboniche). confraternities recruited from the popular classes in support of the Carboneria secret society

vendita. lodge of the Carboneria secret society

BIBLIOGRAPHY

Archives

ATHENS

BMA Benaki Museum, Archive
       of the War of Independence
BSA British School at Athens   Finlay Papers
GSA General State Archive   Administrative Committee
                                   Ministry of Religion
                                   Vlachoyannis Collection,
                                      Karaiskakis Archive

CATANIA

ASC Archivio di Stato di Catania   Miscellanea Risorgimentale
                                   Intendenza Borbonica
BCUC Biblioteca Civica Ursino   Raccolta di Fogli Sciolti

LISBON

AHM Arquivo Histórico Militar   Arquivo Particular de Sá da Bandeira
                                   Assuntos Militares Gerais
AHP Arquivo Histórico Parlamentar,
       Assembleia da República
ANTT Arquivo Nacional Torre do Tombo Intendência Geral de Polícia (IGP)
                                   Leis e Ordenações
                                   Ministério do Reino, Autos de Aclamação
                                   Ministério dos Negócios Eclesiásticos e
                                      da Justiça
                                   Ministério dos Negócios Estrangeiros
BNP Biblioteca Nacional de Portugal Manuscritos Reservados

LONDON

BL British Library   Church Papers, Add MS

MADRID

AAM Archivo Ayuntamiento de Madrid
AHN Archivo Histórico Nacional   Consejos Suprimidos
                                   Estado

[615]

CD   Congreso de los Diputados
APR   Archivo del Palacio Real   Papeles Reservados de Fernando VII

MILAN

MRM   Museo del Risorgimento,
        Civiche Raccolte Storiche

NAPLES

ASN   Archivio di Stato di Napoli   Borbone
                                  Ministero degli Affari Interni
                                  Polizia Generale
BNN   Biblioteca Nazionale di Napoli
SNSP   Società Napoletana di Storia Patria

PALERMO

ASP   Archivio di Stato di Palermo (Gancia)   Direzione Generale di Polizia
                                        Real Segreteria di Stato presso il
                                           Luogotenente Generale di Sicilia
           Archivio di Stato di Palermo (Catena)   Real Segreteria, Incartamenti
BCP   Biblioteca Comunale di Palermo   Manoscritti

RAGUSA

ASR   Archivio di Stato di Ragusa   Fondo Statella

TURIN

AST   Archivio di Stato di Torino   Materie Politiche per Rapporto
                                        all'Interno
                                    Segreteria di Stato Affari Interni,
                                    Alta Polizia

Periodicals

Astro da Lusitania
Correio do Porto
Diario de Barcelona
Diario de la Ciudad de Valencia
Diario de Madrid
Diario Mercantil de Cádiz
Εφημερίς Αιτωλική [*Efimeris Aitoliki*]
El Amigo de los Pobres

El Censor
El Conservador
El Eco de Padilla
El Látigo Liberal contra el Zurriago Indiscreto
El Liberal Guipuzcoano
El Piloto
El Restaurador
El Universal
El Zurriago
Ελληνικά Χρονικά [*Ellinika Chronika*]
Enciclopedia Ecclesiastica, e Morale: Opera Periodica, Compilata da G.V.T
Φίλος του Νόμου [*Filos tou Nomou*]
Gazeta de Lisboa
Gazeta de Madrid
Gazeta del Gobierno Imperial de Mexico
Gazzetta Piemontese
Genio Constitucional
Giornale Costituzionale del Regno delle Due Sicilie
Giornale del Regno delle Due Sicilie
Giornale la Fenice
Giornale Patriottico della Lucania Orientale
Giornale Patriottico di Sicilia
Il Censore
Il Corrispondente Costituzionale
L'Amico della Costituzione
L'Imparziale (Naples)
L'Imparziale Siciliano (Messina)
La Minerva Napolitana
La Sentinella Subalpina
La Voce del Popolo
La Voce del Secolo
Le Mercure du Dix-Neuvième Siècle
Le Spectateur Oriental: Feuille Littéraire, Critique et Commerciale
Miscelánea de Comercio, Política y Literatura
Mnemosine Constitucional
O Braz Corcunda e o Verdadeiro Constitucional
O Campeão Portuguez, ou O Amigo do Rei e do Povo
O Liberal
O Padre Amaro, ou Sovéla, Politica, Historica, e Literaria
O Patriota
O Punhal dos Corcundas
Σάλπιγξ Ελληνική [*Salpix Elliniki*]
Sociedad Patriótica Mallorquina
The Monthly Magazine; or, British Register
The Westminster Review

Primary Sources and Documentary Collections*

A.C.B.D., *Parlata dell'uomo sincero: Avviso alla più parte della nazione* (n.p., n.d. [1820])

Al parlamento nazionale, petizione del canonico Felice Racioppi di Apice in P.U. (Avellino, n.d.)

Alberti, Annibale, ed., *Atti del parlamento delle Due Sicilie, 1820-1821*, 6 vols (Bologna: Zanichelli, 1926-41)

Alcalá Galiano, Antonio María, *Apuntes para servir a la historia del origen y alzamiento del ejército destinado a Ultramar en 1 de Enero de 1820* (Madrid: Aguado y Compañía, 1821)

——, *Breves reflexiones sobre la índole de la crisis por que estan pasando los gobiernos y pueblos de Europa* (Madrid: Ramón Rodríguez de Rivera, 1848)

——, *Historia de España desde los tiempos primitivos hasta la mayoria de la Reina Doña Isabel II., redactada y anotada con arreglo à la que escribio en ingles el Doctor Dunham [. . .] Con una reseña de los historiadores Españoles de mas nota por Don J. Donoso Cortés, y un discurso sobre la historia de nuestra nacion por Don F. Martinez de la Rosa*, 7 vols (Madrid: Sociedad Literaria y Tipografica, 1844-46)

——, *Lecciones de derecho político constitucional* (Madrid: D. I. Boix, 1843)

——, *Memorias de Antonio Alcalá Galiano, publicadas por su hijo*, 2 vols (Madrid: E. Rubiños, 1886)

——, *Recuerdos de un anciano* (Madrid: Luis Navarro, 1878)

——, 'Spain', *The Westminster Review* 1, no. 2 (1824): 289-336

Allocuzione del sacerdote Don Luigi Ammendola, recitata nella parrochiale chiesa di S. Giuseppe di Otajano nel di' 16 luglio 1820 (Naples: Marotta, 1820)

Almeida Garrett, João Baptista da Silva Leitão de, *O dia vinte e quatro de Agosto* (Lisbon: Typ. Rollandiana, 1821)

——, *Viagens na minha terra*, with an introduction by João Gaspar Simões, vol. 1 of Almeida Garrett, *Obras completas de Almeida Garrett*, 10 vols (Lisbon: Círculo de Leitores, 1984 [1846])

Almeida y Sandoval, Cândido de, *O fanatismo e a intolerancia combatidos por hum filosofo Christão* (Lisbon: Imprensa Nacional, 1821)

Amari, Michele, *Studii su la storia di Sicilia dalla metà del XVIII secolo al 1820*, ed. Amelia Crisantino (Quaderni Mediterranea—ricerche storiche 15) (Palermo: Accademia nazionale di scienze, lettere e arti, 2010 [1842])

Andreotti, Davide, *Storia dei cosentini*, 3 vols (Naples: Salvatore Marchese, 1869-74)

Antoniou, David, ed., *Η εκπαίδευση κατά την Ελληνική Επανάσταση, 1821-27: Τεκμηριωτικά κείμενα* (Education during the Greek Revolution, 1821-27: Sources), 2 vols (Athens: Hellenic Parliament, 2002)

Aquarone, Alberto, Mario D'Addio and Guglielmo Negri, eds, *Le costituzioni italiane* (Milano: Edizioni di Comunità, 1958)

* Note that in the sections of the Bibliography that follow, Portuguese and Spanish surnames are by default listed alphabetically by the assumed patronymic: in the Portuguese case, this is the last surname given; in the Spanish case, it is the first. Thus, for example, António Monteiro Cardoso (Portuguese) is listed by 'Cardoso', and Francisco Carantoña Álvarez (Spanish) by 'Carantoña'.

Archives diplomatiques pour l'histoire du tems et des états: L'année 1821, 2 vols (Stuttgart and Tubingen: Librairie Cotta, 1822)

Αρχεία της Ελληνικής Παλιγγενεσίας (Archives of the Greek Regeneration), 25 vols (Athens: Library of the Hellenic Parliament, 1971–2012 [publication started initially in 1857]), also available at https://paligenesia.parliament.gr/ (accessed 15 August 2022)

Arcucci, Giovanni, *Rimostranza della Società dei Carbonari al sommo pontefice Pio VII* (Naples: Paci, 1820)

Astur, Eugenia, *Riego: Estudio histórico-político de la Revolución del año veinte* (Oviedo: Escuela Tipográfica de la Residencia Provincial de Niños, 1933)

Baillie, Marianne, *Lisbon in the Years 1821, 1822, and 1823*, 2 vols (London: John Murray, 1825)

Balsamo, Vincenzo, *Addizioni del traduttore: Sui deputati*, in Benjamin Constant, *Ragionamento di un elettore con se stesso* (Lecce: 1820)

——, *Sulla amministrazione civile* (Lecce: Vincenzo Marino, 1820)

Bartholdy, Jakob Salomon, *Memoirs of the Secret Societies of the South of Italy, Particularly the Carbonari* (London: John Murray, 1821)

Bayo, Estanislao de Kostka, *Historia de la vida y reinado de Fernando VII de España*, 3 vols (Madrid: Imprenta de Repullés, 1842)

Beolchi, Carlo, *Reminiscenze dell'esilio* (Turin: Tipografia Nazionale, 1852)

Bianco, Gerardo, *La rivoluzione siciliana del 1820 con documenti e carteggi inediti* (Florence: Bernardo Seeber Editore, 1905)

Bianco di Saint Jorioz, Carlo Angelo, *Della guerra d'insurrezione per bande, applicata all'Italia* (n.p. [Italy], 1830)

Blanch, Luigi, 'Luigi de' Medici come uomo di stato e amministratore', in Blanch, *Scritti storici*, ed. Benedetto Croce, vol. 2: *Il regno di Napoli dalla restaurazione borbonica all'avvento di re Ferdinando II (1815-1830)* (Bari: Laterza, 1945), pp. 1–126

——, 'La rivoluzione del 1820 e la reazione che ne seguì', in Blanch, *Scritti storici*, ed. Benedetto Croce, vol. 2: *Il regno di Napoli dalla restaurazione borbonica all'avvento di re Ferdinando II (1815-1830)* (Bari: Laterza, 1945), pp. 129–351

Blaquiere, Edward, *The Greek Revolution: Its Origins and Progress* (London: G. & W. B. Whittaker, 1824)

Botelho, Sebastião José Xavier, *Historia verdadeira dos acontecimentos da ilha da Madeira depois do memoravel dia 28 de Janeiro* (Lisbon: António Rodrigues Galhardo, 1821)

Buldain Jaca, Blanca Esther, *Las elecciones de 1820: La época y su publicistica* (Madrid: Ministerio del Interior, Secretaría General Técnica, 1993)

Cabreira, Drago Valente de Brito, *Relação histórica da revolução do Algarve contra os Francezes, que dolozamente invadirão Portugal no anno de 1807* (Lisbon: Typografia Lacerdina, 1809)

Cabrerizo, Mariano de, *Coleccion de canciones patrióticas que dedica al ciudadano Rafael del Riego y a los valientes que han seguido sus huellas* (Valencia: Venancio Olivares, 1822)

Campanile, Gennaro, *Allocuzione nel rendimento di grazie all'altissimo per l'ottenuta costituzione* (Naples, 15 July 1820)

Canzone nna accaseione da venuta de li cravonare a Nnapole (Naples, n.d.)

Capefigue, Jean Baptiste Honoré Raymond, *Récit des opérations de l'armée française en Espagne*, [. . .] (Paris: E. Guide, 1823)

Carrascosa, Michele, *Mémoires historiques, politiques et militaires sur la révolution du Royaume de Naples en 1820 et 1821 et sur les causes qui l'ont amenée accompagnés de pièces justificatives la plupart inédites par le général Carrascosa* (London: Treuttel, Würtz, Treuttel fils et Richter, 1823)

Catechismo patriottico estratto dalle opere di La Croix ed adattato al Regno delle Due Sicilie tradotto dal francese da Giovanni Taddej (Naples: Luca Marotta, 1820)

Catecismo patriotico para uso de todos cidadãos portugueses, de M. de la Croix, trans. Manuel Ferreira de Seabra, published in *O Patriota*, 22 and 29 October 1820

Catecismo político arreglado á la constitución de la monarquía española para illustracion del pueblo, instruccion de la juventud y uso de las escuelas de primeras letras (Barcelona: Piferrer, 1820 [1812])

Carta constitucional da monarchia portugueza (Lisbon: Impressão Regia, 1826)

Chagas, Cypriano José Rodrigues das, *As cortes ou os direitos do povo portuguez que dedica ao exercito* (Lisbon: Officina de António Rodrigues Galhardo, 1820)

Church, E. M., *Sir Richard Church in Italy and Greece* (Edinburgh and London: William Blackwood, 1895)

Church, Richard, 'Narrative by Sir R. Church of the War in Greece during his Tenure of the Command, 1827–29', in BL, Church Papers, Add MS 36563–65 (manuscript, 3 vols)

——, *Relazione dei fatti accaduti al tenente generale Riccardo Church in Palermo la notte del 15 luglio 1820* (Naples: Tipografia Francese, 1820)

Cienfuegos y Jovellanos, Francisco Xavier, 'Exhortacion del Señor Obispo de Cádiz al estallar la rebelión en la isla', 9 January 1820, in *Colección eclesiástica española*, 3, pp. 30–41

Clary, Michele Basilio, *Il liberalismo cristiano: Omelie sacro-politiche* (Messina: Giuseppe Pappalardo, 1821)

——[or Clari], *Orazione funebre in morte di Sua Maestà Ferdinando I* (Naples: Angelo Trani, 1825)

Clogg, Richard, *The Movement for Greek Independence, 1770–1821: A Collection of Documents* (London: Macmillan, 1976)

Código Penal Español (Madrid: Imprenta Nacional, 1822)

Colección eclesiástica española, 14 vols (Madrid: Imprenta de E. Aguado, 1823–24)

Colletta, Pietro, *Storia del reame di Napoli*, ed. Nino Cortese, 3 vols (Naples: Libreria Scientifica Editrice, 1953–57)

——, *Storia del reame di Napoli dal 1734 sino al 1825*, 4 vols (Lugano: Tipografia Elvetica, 1834)

Comstock, John Lee, *History of the Greek Revolution, Compiled from Official Documents of the Greek Government* (New York: W. W. Reed & Co., 1828)

Constitución política de la monarquía española, promulgada en Cádiz, á 19 de Marzo 1812 (Cádiz: Imprenta Real, 1812)

Constitution, loix, ordonnances des assemblées nationales des corps législatifs et du président de la Grèce (Athens: Imprimerie Royale, 1835)

Contoni, Apolinar, 'Cartilla de explicación de la constitución política de la monarquía española, para la instrucción de los niños de la parroquia de Santiago de la ciudad de Baza' [Seville, 1821], in *Catecismos políticos españoles arreglados a las constituciones del siglo XIX* (Madrid: Comunidad de Madrid, Consejería de Cultura, Secretaría General Técnica, 1989), pp. 203–11

Costa, José Daniel Rodrigues da, *Novidades de Lisboa dadas por Bento Aniceto, lavrador ao seu compadre: Cura da sua freguezia na provincia da Beira* (Lisbon: João Nunes Esteves, 1823)

Crotoniate, Michele Farina, *Della responsabilità de' deputati, ossia Breve osservazione sull'articolo 128 della costituzione delle Spagne* (Naples: Giovanni de Bonis, 1820)

D'Amato, Gabriele, *Panteon dei martiri della libertà italiana* (Turin: Gabriele D'Amato Editore, 1851)

Dakin, Douglas, *British Intelligence of Events in Greece, 1824-1827: A Documentary Collection* (Athens: Historical and Ethnological Society of Greece, 1959)

Daun, José Sebastião de Saldanha Oliveira e, *Diorama de Portugal nos 33 mezes constitucionaes, ou Golpe de vista sobre a revolução de 1820, a Constituição de 1822, a Restauração de 1823* [. . .] (Lisbon: Impressão Regia, 1823)

de Angelis, Francesco, *Storia del regno di Napoli sotto la dinastia borbonica*, 7 vols (Naples: G. Mosino, 1817–33)

De Attellis, Orazio, 'L'ottimestre costituzionale delle Due Sicilie' (manuscript, 1821), in BNN, MS VA 47/2

De Nicola, Carlo, *Diario napoletano 1798-1825*, ed. Renata De Lorenzo, 3 vols (Naples: Società napoletana di storia pPatria, repr. 1999 [1906])

De Vecchi, D., *La voce del cittadino* (Capua, 1821)

Debidour, Antonin, *Le Général Fabvier, sa vie militaire et politique* (Paris: Plon, 1904)

Del modo che tenne il principe di Paternò D. Giovanni Luigi Moncada per indurre il popolo di Palermo alla capitolazione col comandante delle armi del Re il ten. Col. D. Florestano Pepe segnata a 5 ottobre 1820 (n.p., n.d. [1821])

Delacroix, Jacques Vincent, *Catéchisme patriotique à l'usage de tous les citoyens françois, dédié aux états-généraux* (Paris: Guffier, 1789)

Dialogo tenuto verso la fine di giugno del corrente anno 1820 tra il patriota Lorenzo e l'arciprete D. Fabrizio (Naples, n.d.)

Diário das cortes geraes e extraordinárias da nação portugueza, 7 vols (Lisbon: Imprensa Nacional, 1821–22)

Diario de las actas y discusiones de las Córtes: Legislatura de 1820 y 1821, 13 vols (Madrid: Imprenta de las Cortes, 1820–21)

Diario de las sesiones de Cortes del Congreso de Diputados (Madrid: Imprenta Nacional, 1840)

Diccionario provisional de la constitucion política de la monarquía española (Madrid, 1820)

Dias, Augusto da Costa, ed., *Discursos sobre a liberdade de imprensa no primeiro parlamento português (1821)* (Lisbon: Editorial Estampa, 1978)

Dimakopoulos, Georgios, *Η Διοικητική οργάνωσις κατά την Ελληνικήν Επανάστασιν, 1821-1827* (Administrative organisation during the Greek revolution, 1821–1827) (Athens: Klisiouni Brothers, 1966)

Dimitriadis, Georgios, *Ιστορία της Σάμου συνταχθείσα και εκδοθείσα υπό Γεωργίου Δημητριάδου, Σαμίου ανότπτου [sic] των κατά την Επανάστασιν γεγονότων προς χρήσιν της φιλομαθούς νεολαίας προς ην ο συγγραφέας την παρούσαν ανατιθήσι* (History of Samos written and published by Georgios Dimitriadis, from Samos and a witness to the events of the revolution to be used by the educated youth to whom the writer dedicates this work) (Chalkis: Typ. Evripou, 1866)

Discorso di tre studenti sulle circostanze attuali (Naples, 1820)

Discurso de D. Manuel Maía de Acevedo, gefe político interino de Asturias, leido el dia 22 de Mayo en la Junta Electoral de Provincia (Oviedo: Oficina de Francisco Pérez Prieto, 1820)

Dufau, Pierre-Armand, *Collection des constitutions, chartes et lois fondamentales des peuples de l'Europe e des deux Amériques*, 7 vols (Paris: Picon et Didier, 1823–30)

El observador de las sociedades secretas (Madrid, n.d. [1822])

Emerson, James, Giuseppe Pecchio and William H. Humphreys, *A Picture of Greece in 1825*, 2 vols (London: Henry Colburn, 1826)

Examen critique des révolutions d'Espagne, de 1820 à 1823 et de 1836, 2 vols (Paris, 1837)

Exposição da lei natural, ou Catecismo do cidadão (Lisbon: Typografia Rollandiana, 1820)

Fauriel, Claude, *Chants populaires de la Grèce moderne*, 2 vols (Paris: Dondey-Dupré, 1824–25); English translation as *The Songs of Greece* (London: Longman, Hurst, Rees, Orme, Brown & Green, 1825)

Fernández Sarasola, Ignacio, ed., *Constituciones en la sombra: Proyectos constitucionales españoles (1809–1823)* (Oviedo: Universidad de Oviedo, 2014)

Ferrão, F. A. Fernandes da Silva, *Apologia dirigida à nação portuguesa para plena justificação do corpo dos Voluntarios Academicos do anno de 1826* (Coimbra: Imprensa de Trovão e Companhia, 1827)

Figueiredo, António Pereira de, *Os Sebastianistas combatidos, o egregio encoberto apparecido, o caso raro e maravilhoso acontecido* (Lisbon: J.F.M. de Campos, 1823)

Finlay, George, *History of the Greek Revolution*, 2 vols (London: W. Blackwood, 1861)

Fotakos (Chrysanthopoulos Fotios), *Βίος του Πάπα Φλέσα συγγραφείς μεν υπό Φωτάκου πρώτου υπασπιστού του Γέρω Κολοκοτρών εκδοθείς δε υπό Σ. Καλκάνδη* (Life of Papa Flessa written by Fotakos, first adjutant to Old Man Kolokotronis, published by S. Kalkandi) (Athens: Typois Nomimotitos, 1868)

Foteinos, Ilias, *Οι άθλοι της εν Βλαχία Ελληνικής Επαναστάσεως το 1821 έτος* (The feats of the Greek revolution of the year 1821 in Wallachia) (Leipzig, 1846)

Galanti, Luigi, *Catechismo costituzionale per uso del regno unito delle Sicilie* (Naples: Domenico Sangiacomo, 1820)

Gallardo, Bartolomé José, *Impugnacion joco-seria al folleto titulado Condiciones y semblanzas de los diputados a Cortes para la legislatura de 1820 y 1821* (Madrid: Libreria de Paz, 1821)

Galli, Florent, *Campagne du Général Mina en Catalogne* (Paris: Philippe, 1831)

Gamboa, Biagio, *Documenti storici*, attached to Gamboa, *Storia della rivoluzione*

——, *Storia della rivoluzione di Napoli entrante il luglio del 1820* (n.p.: Presso il Trani, n.d.)

García Zamora, Don Mariano, 'Breve discurso o sermon que en la misa de espíritusanto celebrada en la iglesia catedral de Cartagena sita en Murcia. [. . .] A los electores de partido' [1820], in *Sermones revolucionarios del Trienio Liberal (1820–1823)*, ed. Gérard Dufour (Alicante: Instituto de Cultura Juan Gil-Albert, Diputación de Alicante, 1991), pp. 85–97

'Generals Pepe and Carrascosa', *The Annual Register, or a View of the History, Politics and Literature of the Year 1823*, no. 65 (London: Baldwin, Cradock and Joy, 1824), p. 25

Germanos ('Palaion Patron Germanos', metropolitan of Patras [Georgios Ionnou Kozias]), *Απομνημονεύματα* (Memoirs) (Athens: Spyros Tsaggaris, 1900)

Gil Novales, Alberto, ed., *Rafael Riego: La Revolución de 1820, día a día* (Madrid: Tecnos, 1976)

Giordano, Antonio, *Idee generali sulla scelta de' deputati e pensieri di costituzione per un governo rappresentativo* (Naples: Tipografia di Porcelli, 1820)

Gordon, Thomas, *History of the Greek Revolution*, 2 vols (London: William Blackwood & T. Cadell, 1832)

Grasso, Salvatore, *La scola custetuzionale pe li piccirilli: Primma lezione cuntenuvazione de li penzieri de chillo che scrivette la primma chiacchiariata tra lu Sebeto e lu cuorpo de Napole* (Naples: Antonio Garruccio, 1820)

Gualterio, Filippo Antonio, *Gli ultimi rivolgimenti italiani: Memorie storiche con documenti inediti*, 4 vols (Florence: Le Monnier, 1852)

Herculano, Alexandre, *A voz do Profeta* [1837], now in *Opúsculos*, ed. Jorge Custódio and José Manuel Garcia, 5 vols (Lisbon: Presença, 1982–5), 1, pp. 43–77

Hortal, D. Tomas Martínez del, *Discurso pronunciado en Villanueva de la Serena el dia 8 de mayo de 1820 al congreso de electores parroquiales en la eleccion de electores de partido* (Madrid, 1820)

Hymno constitucional: Cantado no Real Theatro do Porto em Julho de 1826 (Porto: A. L. de Oliveira, 1826)

Idee sulla Sicilia (Naples: Reale Tipografia della Guerra, 1821)

Il Caldararo vinto dal Carbonaro (Naples, n.d.)

Illustração aos povos para fazerem com acerto as elleições dos deputados para a proxima legislatura, feita pela sociedade patriotica denominata Gabinete de Minerva (Lisbon, 6 August 1822)

Jourdain, Jean-Philippe-Paul, *Mémoires historiques et militaires sur les événements de la Grèce depuis 1822, jusqu'au combat de Navarin*, 2 vols (Paris: Brissot-Thivars, 1828)

Kasomoulis, Nikolaos, Ενθυμήματα στρατιωτικά της Επαναστάσεως των Ελλήνων, 1821–1833 (Military memoirs of the revolution of the Greeks, 1821–1833), ed. Yannis Vlachoyannis, 3 vols (Athens: Chorigia Pagkeiou Epitropis, 1939–42)

Katakouzinos, Georgios, Ὑπόμνημα του Πρίγκηπα Γεωργίου Κατακουζηνού' (Memorandum of Prince Georgios Katakouzinos), Kishinev, 28 October 1821, in Δύο πρίγκηπες στην Ελληνική Επανάσταση: Επιστολές αυτόπτη μάρτυρα και ένα υπόμνημα του Πρίγκηπα Γεωργίου Κατακουζηνού (Two princes in the Greek revolution: Letters of an eye witness and a memorandum by Prince Georgios Katakouzinos), ed. Vasilis Panayiotopoulos (Athens: Asini, 2015)

Kolokotrones [Kolokotronis], Theodoros, *Kolokotrones the Klepht and the Warrior: Sixty Years of Peril and Daring; An Autobiography*, trans. Elizabeth Mayhew Edmonds (London: T. F. Unwin, 1892)

Koumarianou, Aikaterini, ed., *Ο Τύπος στον Αγώνα, 1821–27* (The press in the 'Struggle', 1821–27), 3 vols (Athens: Ermis, 1971)

Kritovoulides, Kallinikos, *Narrative of the Cretan War of Independence, Vol. 1*, ed. A. Ioannides (London: n.pub., 1864)

L'ignoranza illuminata: Dialogo tra un carbonaro ed un contadino (Naples: Francesco del Vecchio, 1820)

La Ferrière, Édouard, *Les Constitutions d'Europe et d'Amérique* (Paris: Cotillon, 1869)

La rivoluzione piemontese dell'anno 1821: Nuovi documenti (in *Biblioteca di storia italiana recente 1800–1870*, vol. 11) (Turin: Bocca, 1923)

La voz de la patria: Observaciones que hace un español á los que hayan leido el papel titulado cosa sobre Comuneros (Málaga: Luis de Carreras, 1823)

Labate, Valentino, *Un decennio di Carboneria in Sicilia (1821-1831): Documenti* (Rome: Società Editrice Dante Alighieri, 1909)

Lamennais, Félicité de, *El dogma de los hombres libres: Palabras de un creyente* (Madrid: José Maria Repulles, 1836)

Lane Poole, Stanley, *Sir Richard Church* (London: Longmans, Green & Co., 1890)

Le trame de' preti di Bisceglie contra la libertà (Naples, 1820)

Leake, William Martin, *A Historical Outline of the Greek Revolution, with a Few Remarks on the Present State of Affairs in That Country* (London: John Murray, 1826)

Lehasca, Attanasio, *Cenno storico dei servigi prestati nel regno delle Due Sicilie dai greci epiroti albanesi e macedoni in epoche diverse* (Corfu, 1843)

Lettera dell'arcivescovo di Napoli al parlamento nazionale e risposta del parlamento (Naples, 1821)

Life and Correspondence of Major Cartwright, ed. F. D. Cartwright, 2 vols (London: Henry Colburn, 1826)

Lignos Antonios, ed., *Αρχείον της Κοινότητος Ύδρας, 1778-1832* (Archive of the community of Hydra, 1778-1832), 16 vols (Piraeus: Typois 'Sphairas', 1921-31)

Lobo, Joaquina Cândida de Sousa Calheiros, *Cathecismo religioso, moral e politico para instrucção do cidadão portuguez* (Coimbra: Imprensa da Universidade, 1822)

Lo que espera la España de sus representantes en el próximo congreso nacional (Madrid: Imprenta de Nuñez, 1820)

López Cepero, Manuel, *Catecismo religioso, moral y político* (Madrid: Imprenta de García, 1821)

Lucarelli, Raffaele, *Pretensioni de' siciliani confutate da un napolitano* (Naples, 1821)

'Luis de Borbon por la Divina Misericordia Presbítero Cardenal de la santa Iglesia Romana, del Título de Santa María de Scapa, Arzobispo de Toledo [. . .]', pastoral letter, 15 March 1820 (Madrid: Imprenta de la Compañía, 1820)

Macedo, José Agostinho de, *Sermão de acção de graças pelo restabelecimento da monarquia independente* (Lisbon: Impressão da Rua Formoza, 1823)

Macriyannis, Général [Yannis], *Mémoires*, trans. with introduction and notes by Denis Kohler (Paris: Albin Michel, 1986)

Maia, Joaquim José da Silva, *Memorias historicas, politicas e filosoficas da revolução do Porto em maio 1828* (Rio de Janeiro: Typographia de Laemmert, 1841)

Mamoukas, Andreas Z., ed., *Τα κατά την αναγέννησιν της Ελλάδος, ήτοι συλλογή των περί την αναγεννώμενην Ελλάδα συνταχθέντων πολιτευμάτων, νόμων και άλλων επισήμων πράξεων από του 1821 μέχρι τέλους του 1832* (On the regeneration of Greece: Collection of constitutions, laws and other formal acts of the regenerated Greece from 1821 to 1832), 11 vols (Athens: Vasiliko Typografeio, 1839-52)

Mangeruva [Mangiaruva], Andrea, *Avventure di un esule* (Palermo: Stamperia Console, 1849)

'Manifiesto del rey a la Nacion', 23 April 1823, in *Suplemento à la Gazeta Española del martes 29 de abril de 1823*, pp. 81-82

Manifiesto que da al público el teniente general Do Manuel Freyre para hacer conocer su conducta en le tiempo que tuvo el mando del egército reunido de Andalucía [. . .] (Seville: Imprenta Mayor, 1820)

Manifiesto y otros documentos de la Sociedad de Comuneros (Cádiz: Esteban Picardo, 1823)

Mavrocordato, Alexandre [Alexandros Mavrokordatos], *Coup d'œil sur la Turquie* (1820), in Anton von Prokesch-Osten, *Geschichte des Abfall der Griechen vom türkischen Reich im Jahre 1821* (Vienna: Gedold, 1867)

Mazzini, Giuseppe, *Della guerra d'insurrezione conveniente all'Italia*, in Mazzini, *Scritti politici, editi ed inediti*, 31 vols (Imola: P. Galeati, 1907), 3, pp. 197–230

Metaxas, Constantin, *Souvenirs de la Guerre de l'indépendance de la Grèce* (Paris: Ernest Leroux, 1887)

Millingen, Julius, *Memoirs of the Affairs of Greece, Containing an Account of the Military and Political Events which Occurred in 1823 and Following Years; With Various Anecdotes relating to Lord Byron* (London: John Rodwell, 1831)

Miñano y Bedoya, Sebastián, *Condiciones y semblanzas de los diputados a Cortes para la legislatura de 1820 y 1821* (Madrid: D. Juan Ramos y Compañía, 1821)

——, *Condiciones y semblanzas de los Sres. diputados a Cortes para los años de 1822 y 1823* (Madrid: Imprenta del Zurriago de don M. R. y Cerro, 1822)

——, *Histoire de la révolution d'Espagne de 1820 à 1823: Par un espagnol témoin oculaire*, trans. Ernest Poret, vicomte de Blosseville, Meissonier de Valcroissant and Andrés Muriel, 2 vols (Paris: J. G. Dentu, 1824)

Minichini, Luigi, *Luglio 1820: Cronaca di una rivoluzione*, ed. Mario Themelly (Rome: Bulzoni, 1979)

Miraflores, Manuel Pando Fernandez de Pinedo, marqués de, *Apuntes histórico-críticos para escribir la historia de la revolucion de España desde el año 1820 hasta 1823* (London: Richard Taylor, 1834)

——, *Documentos a los que se hace referencia en los apuntes histórico-críticos sobre la revolución de España*, vol. 1 (one vol. published) (London: Richard Taylor, 1834)

Miranda, Inocêncio António de, *O cidadão lusitano: Breve compendio, em que se demonstrão os fructos da constituição, e os deveres do cidadão constitucional, para com deos, para com o rei, para com a patria, e para com todos os seus concidadãos; Dialogo entre hum liberal, e hum servile—o Abbade Roberto e D. Julio* (Lisbon: Neves e filhos, 1822)

Mis apuntes sobre elecciones de diputados (Valencia, 1820)

Moltedo, Achille, *Dizionario geografico–storico–statistico de' comuni del regno delle Due Sicilie* (Naples: Gaetano Nobile, 1858)

Moscati, Ruggero, ed., *Guglielmo Pepe, 1797–1831*, vol. 1 (one vol. published) (Rome: Istituto per la storia del Risorgimento italiano, 1938)

Namorado, Maria and Alexandre Sousa Pinheiro, eds, *Legislação eleitoral portuguesa: Textos históricos (1820-1974)*, 2 vols (Lisbon: CNE, 1998)

Natale, Michele, *Inno carbonaro ed analogo* (Naples, n.d.)

Neves, José Acúrsio das, *História geral da invasão dos franceses em Portugal e da restauração deste reino* (Porto: Edições Afrontamento, 2008 [1810–11])

Nuova parlata de' catanesi contro i palermitani (Naples, 1820)

O parocho constitucional: Dialogo entre hum parocho de Riba-Tejo e hum cidadão liberal de Lisboa seu amigo (Lisbon: Imprensa Nacional), 1821

O reitor da freguezia da Sé de Coimbra, aos cidadãos seus parochianos, broasheet available online at http://purl.pt/1357 (accessed 14 August 2022)

Onori funebri renduti a Guglielmo Pepe (Turin: Stamperia dell'Unione Tipografica Editrice, 1855)

Palma, Alerino, *Κατήχησις πολιτική εις χρήσιν των Ελλήνων συνταχθείσα μεν ιταλιστί υπό του φιλέλληνος Κ. Α. Π. μεταφρασθείσα δε παρά Νικολάου Γ. Παγκαλάκη* (Political catechism for the use of the Greeks written in Italian by the philhellene K. A. P., translated by Nikolaos G. Pagkalakis) (Hydra, 1826)

Palmieri, Michele, *Le duc d'Orléans et les émigrés français en Sicile, ou Les italiens justifiés* (Paris: Delaunay et Dentu, 1831)

Palmieri, Niccolò, *Saggio storico e politico sulla costituzione del Regno di Sicilia infino al 1816 con un'appendice sulla rivoluzione del 1820*, with an introduction by Enzo Sciacca (Palermo: Edizioni della Regione Sicilia, 1972 [1847])

Pantelis, Antonis, Stefanos Koutsompinas and Triantafyllos Gerozisis, eds, *Κείμενα συνταγματικής ιστορίας* (Documents of constitutional history) (Athens: Ant. Sakkoulas, 1993)

Parish, Henry Headley, *The Diplomatic History of the Monarchy of Greece* (London: J. Hatchard & Son, 1838)

Paula, Francisco de, *Discurso que se pronunció en la insigne iglesia colegial de Xerez de la Frontera el domingo 7 de mayo de 1820, con motivo de las elecciones del partido de la misma ciudad* (Cádiz, 1820)

Pecchio, Giuseppe, *Anecdotes of the Spanish and Portuguese Revolutions* (London: G. & W. B. Whittaker, 1823)

——, *Relazione degli avvenimenti della Grecia nella primavera del 1825* (Lugano: Vannelli, 1826)

Pensieri politici di tre filantropi messinesi P. S. R., O. S. N., ed A. S. sul trattato conchiuso tra il comandante generale Florestano Pepe e lo ex-principe Paternò (Naples: Presso Giovanni de Bonis, 1820)

Pepe, Guglielmo, *A Narrative of the Political and Military Events, Which Took Place at Naples in 1820 and 1821; with Observations Explanatory of the National Conduct in General, and of His Own in Particular, during that Period; Addressed to His Majesty, the King of the Two Sicilies, by General William Pepe. With an Appendix of Official Documents, the Greater Part Hitherto Unpublished* (London: Treuttel and Würtz, Treuttel, Jun. and Richter, 1821)

——, *Casi d'Italia negli anni 1847, 48 e 49: Continuazione delle memorie del generale Guglielmo Pepe* (Genoa: Ponthenier, 1851)

——, *Darstellung der politischen und militärischen Ereignisse in Neapel in den Jahren 1820 und 1821. Ein Sendschreiben an S.M. den König Beider-Sicilien, vom General Wilhelm Pepe. Mit einem Anhange offizieller, grösstentheils ungedruckter Aktenstücke*, trans. Friedrich Krug (Ilmenau: B. F. Voigt, 1822)

——, *Delle rivoluzioni e delle guerre d'Italia nel 1847, 1848, 1849: Memorie del generale Guglielmo Pepe con aggiunta d'una prefazione e di note* (Turin: Luigi Arnaldi, 1850)

——, *L'Italia militare* (Paris: Pihan de la Forest, 1836)

——, *L'Italie politique et ses rapports avec la France et l'Angleterre* [1839] (Venice: Imprimerie Naratovich, 1848)

——, *Memoirs of General Pepe, Comprising the Principal Military and Political Events of Italy*, 3 vols (London: Schulze & Co., 1846)

——, *Memoria relativa á los sucesos políticos y militares de Nápoles en los años 1820 y 1821, con varias observaciones sobre la conducta de las naciones en general, y de la suya en particular; Dirigida a S.M. el rey de las dos Sicilias por el general D. Gullermo Pepe, y acompañada de documentos de oficio cuya mayor parte no se ha dado á luz hasta ahora* (Madrid: Imprenta de D. Miguel de Burgos, 1822)

——, *Memoria sui mezzi che menano alla italiana indipendenza* (Paris: Paulin, 1833)

——, *Memorie del Generale Guglielmo Pepe intorno alla sua vita ed ai recenti casi d'Italia scritte da lui medesimo*, 2 vols (Paris: Baudry, 1847)

——, *Relation des événements politiques et militaires qui ont eu lieu à Naples en 1820 et 1821 adressée à S. M. le Roi des Deux Siciles, par le général Guillaume Pépé, avec des remarques et des explications sur la conduite des Napolitains en général, et sur celle de l'auteur en particulier, pendant cette époque, suivie d'un recueil de documens officiels, la plupart inédits* (Paris: Crapelet, 1822)

——, *Relazione delle circostanze relative agli avvenimenti politici e militari in Napoli nel 1820 e 1821, diretta a s.m. il Re delle Due-Sicilie dal generale Guglielmo Pepe. Con le osservazioni sulla condotta della nazione* [...] *Accompagnata da documenti uffiziali* [...] *per la prima volta la luce* (Paris: Crapelet, 1822)

——, 'The Non-Establishment of Liberty in Spain, Naples, Portugal and Piedmont Explained', *The Pamphleteer* (London: A. J. Valpy, 1824), pp. 223–86

Pinelli, Ferdinando, *Storia militare del Piemonte*, 3 vols (Turin: Degiorgis, 1854–55)

Plagianakou Bekiari, Vasiliki and Aristotelis Stergellis, eds, *Αρχείο Ιωάννη Κωλέττη* (Archive of Ioannis Kolettis), 2 vols (Athens: Academy of Athens, 2002)

Plumari, Giuseppe, *Orazione funebre per il piissimo, clementissimo, invittissimo Ferdinando I* (Messina: Giuseppe Fiumara, 1825)

Polyzoidis, Anastasios, *Προσωρινό Πολίτευμα της Ελλάδος και σχέδιον οργανισμού των επαρχιών αυτής. Αμφότερα επιδιορθωμένα και επικυρωμένα υπό της Δευτέρας Εθνικής Νομοθετικής των Ελλήνων Συνελεύσεως εν Άστρει, οίς έπονται το πολιτικόν σύνταγμα της Βρεταννίας και το των Ηνωμένων Επικρατειών της Αμερικής, μετά της διατυπώσεως του συνεδρίου αυτών, εξ Αγγλικών και Γαλλικών συγγραμμάτων μεταφρασθέντα υπό Α. Πολυζωίδου* (Provisional polity of Greece and a plan of the organisation of its provinces. Both revised and ratified by the second National Assembly of the Greeks in Astros, accompanied by the political constitution of Britain and that of the United States of America, with the proceedings of their congresses, translated according to English and French treatises by Anastasios Polyzoidis) (Messolonghi: D. Mestheneos, 1824)

——*Κείμενα για τη δημοκρατία, 1824–1825* (Texts on democracy, 1824–1825), ed. Filimon Paionidis and Elpida Vogli (Athens: Ekdoseis Okto, 2011)

Pouqueville, François, *Histoire de la régénération de la Grèce*, 4 vols (Paris: Firmin Didot, 1825)

Protopsaltis, Emmanuel G., ed., *Ιστορικόν αρχείον Αλέξανδρου Μαυροκορδάτου* (Historical archive of Alexandros Mavrokordatos), 6 vols (Athens: Academy of Athens, 1963)

'Proyecto de decreto acerca de nueva demarcación de parroquías y dotación de párrocos', attached to the *Dictámen de la Comisión eclesiástica sobre el nuevo plan de iglesias metropolitanas y catedrales de la monarquía española, presentado á las Córtes el día 13 de mayo de 1821* (Madrid: Don Mateo Repullés, 1821)

Quiroga, Antonio, *Ejército nacional: Al ilustrísimo señor Obispo de Cádiz* (México: Oficina de D. Alejandro Valdés, 1820)

Raybaud, Maxime, *Mémoires sur la Grèce pour servir à l'histoire de la guerre d'indépendence* (Paris: Tournachon-Molin Libraire, 1834)

Refutação da constituição dos insurgentes (Lisbon: Simão Thaddeo Ferreira, 1823)

Relação de todos os individuos, que compozerão o Batalhão dos Voluntarios Academicos, organizado e armado no anno lectivo de 1826 para 1827 [. . .] *agora fielmente reimpressa, e accrescentada com algumas notas correctivas e illustrativas* (Coimbra: Real Imprensa da Universidade, 1828)

Relação dos festejos que tiverão lugar em Lisboa nos memoraveis dias 31 de julio, 1, 2 etc. de agosto de 1826 (Lisbon: J.F.M. de Campos, 1826)

Ricciardi, Giuseppe, *Martirologio italiano dal 1792 al 1847; libri dieci* (Florence: Le Monnier, 1860)

Riego Núñez, Eugenio Antonio del, *Obras póstumas poéticas de Don Eugenio Antonio del Riego Núñez* (London: Charles Wood, 1843)

Rimostranza dell'arcivescovo di Conza per la libertà della chiesa (Conza: Giuseppe De Bonis, 1821)

Rodriguez de Carassa, Eduardo José, *Oración fúnebre que en las solemnes exequias celebradas en el convento de religiosas de la encarnación (vulgo San Plácido). Por el alma de don Matías Vinuesa, capellán de honor de S.M., arcediano de Tarazona, y cura antes de Tamajon, asesinado en la cárcel en la tarde de 4 de mayo de 1821* (Madrid: Imprenta de Nuñez, 1823)

Romano, Andrea, ed., *Costituzione di Sicilia stabilita nel Generale Parlamento del 1812* (Soveria Mannelli: Rubbettino editore, 2000 [Palermo, 1813])

Romero Alpuente, Juan, *Historia de la revolución española y otros escritos*, ed. Alberto Gil Novales (Madrid: Centro de Estudios Constitucionales, 1989)

Sá da Bandeira, Bernardo de Sá Nogueira de Figueiredo, marquês de, *Diário da guerra civil: 1826–1832*, ed. José Tengarrinha, 2 vols (Lisbon: Seara Nova, 1976)

Saggio di costituzione di Benjamin Constant (Naples[?], 1820[?])

Salerno, Nicola, *Compendio della terapeutica costituzionale, ossia Ristretto ragionamento su la cura de' mali politici e legali nel nuovo governo costituzionale del regno di Napoli* (Naples: Giovanni de Bonis, 1820)

Sansone, Alfonso, *La rivoluzione del 1820 in Sicilia* (Palermo: Tipografia Fratelli Vena, 1888)

Santa Bárbara, António de, *Sermão em acção de graças pela desejada e muito feliz união da Junta Provisoria do Governo Supremo do Reino com o governo interino de Lisboa—verificada no 1.º de outubro de 1820, que na igreja dos monges benedictinos da cidade do Porto, e no dia 22 do mesmo mez, quando o corpo do commercio deu o maior testemunho da sua gratidão ao Deos dos exercitos por tão memorando beneficio*, included with *Relação da solemne acção de graças que o Corpo do Commercio da cidade do Porto ordenou se rendesse ao Altissimo dia 22 de Outubro, pela feliz união do Supremo Governo do Reino com o governo interino de Lisboa* (Coimbra: Real Imprensa da Universidade, 1821)

Santos, Clemente José dos, *Documentos para a história das Cortes gerais da nação portuguesa*, 8 vols (Lisbon: Imprensa Nacional, 1883–91)

Santos García Auñon, Ramón de los, *Teoría de una constitución política para España por un español* (Valencia, 1822); republished in Fernández Sarasola, *Constituciones en la sombra*, pp. 267–451

Sarao, Antonio, *Dialoghi sul governo democratico e costituzionale in rapporto al siculo* (Messina: Michalangelo Nobolo, 1821)

Silvestre, Francesco, *Per la morte di S.M. Ferdinando I* (Naples: Saverio Giordano, 1825)

Soriano, Simão José da Luz, *Vida do Marquez de Sá da Bandeira*, 2 vols (Lisbon: Sousa Neves, 1887–88)

Soutsos, Panagiotis, *Odes d'un jeune grec, suivies de six chants de guerre* (Paris: Emler Frères, 1828)

Soutzo, Alexandre, *Histoire de la révolution grecque* (Paris: Didot, 1829)

Stanhope, Leicester, *Greece during Lord Byron's Residence in That Country, in 1823 and 1824*, 2 vols (Paris: Galignani, 1825)

Stassano, Antonio, *Cronaca: Memorie storiche del Regno di Napoli dal 1798 al 1821*, ed. Roberto Marino and Mario Themelly (Naples: Istituto italiano per gli studi filosofici, 1996)

Testamento que fez à hora da morte a illustrissima e excellentissima senhora Dona Constituição à hora da sua morte (Lisbon: Impressão de A. L. da Oliveira, 1828)

The Provisional Constitution of Greece, Translated from the Second Edition of Corinth, Accompanied by the Original Greek; Preceded by a Letter to the Senate of the Grecian Confederation, and by a General View of the Origin and Progress of the Revolution, by a Grecian Eye-Witness; and Followed by Official Documents (London: John Murray, 1823)

Tisi, Pasquale, *Il quattro agosto a Posillipo* (Naples, 1820)

Tomadakis, Nikolaos V. and Anthoula A. Papadaki, eds, *Κρητικά ιστορικά έγγραφα, 1821–1830* (Historical Documents from Crete, 1821–1830), vol. 1 (one vol. published) (Athens: Ministry of Culture and the Sciences, 1974)

Toreno, Conde de, *Discursos parlamentarios*, ed. Joaquín Varela Suanzes-Carpegna (Oviedo: Junta General del Principado de Asturias, 2003)

Trikoupis, Spyridon, *Ιστορία της Ελληνικής Επαναστάσεως* (History of the Greek revolution), 2nd edn, 4 vols (London: Taylor and Francis, 1860–62)

Un siciliano alla nazione napoletana (Naples: Agnello Nobile, 1820)

Vacani, Camillo, *Storia delle campagne e degli assedj degl'Italiani in Ispagna dal 1808 al 1813*, 2 vols (Milan: Imperiale Regia Stamperia, 1823)

Vannucci, Atto, *I martiri della libertà italiana nel secolo decimo nono* (Florence: Società Editrice Fiorentina, 1848)

Vaudoncourt, Guillaume de, *Letters on the Internal Political State of Spain during the Years 1821, 22 and 23* (London: Lupton Relfe, 1824)

Ventura, Francesco, *De' diritti della Sicilia per la sua nazionale indipendenza* (Palermo: Reale Stamperia, 1821)

Vigo, Leonardo, *Problema di politica sulla indipendenza della Sicilia* (Palermo, 1821)

Voutier, Olivier, *Mémoires du Colonel Voutier sur la guerre actuelle des grecs* (Paris: Bossange Frères, 1823)

Walsh, Robert, *A Residence at Constantinople during a Period including the Commencement, Progress, and Termination of the Greek and Turkish Revolutions*, 2 vols (London: Westley and Davis, 1836)

Young, William, *Portugal in 1828, Comprising Sketches on the State of Private Society, and of Religion in that Kingdom under Dom Miguel* (London: Henry Colburn, 1828)

Ypsilanti, Alexandre [AlexandrosYpsilantis], *Correspondance inédite*, ed. Gregori Arš and Constantin Svolopoulos (Thessaloniki: Institute for Balkan Studies, 1999)

Ypsilanti, Nicolas, *Mémoires du prince Nicolas Ypsilanti: D'après le manuscrit no. 2144 de la Bibliothèque nationale de Grèce, publié par le Dr. D. Gr. Kambouroglous* (Athens: Librairie Française & Internationale G. Eleutheroudakis, n.d.)

Secondary Sources

Acampora, Angelo, *I moti del 1820-21 a Castellammare* (Castellammare di Stabia: Pianeta Giovani, 1985)

Adelman, Jeremy, 'An Age of Imperial Revolutions', *The American Historical Review* 113, no. 2 (2008): 319–40

———, *Sovereignty and Revolution in the Iberian Atlantic* (Princeton, NJ: Princeton University Press, 2006)

Aguilar, María Jesús, *La imagen del Trienio Liberal en Asturias* (Oviedo: Universidad de Oviedo, 1999)

Aksan, Virginia, *Ottoman Wars, 1700-1870: An Empire Besieged* (Harlow: Longman Pearson, 2007)

Alexandre, Valentim, *Os sentidos do Império: Questão nacional e questão colonial na crise do antigo regime português* (Porto: Edições Afrontamento, 1993)

Aliprantis, Christos, 'Lives in Exile: Foreign Political Refugees in Early Independent Greece (1830–53)', *Byzantine and Modern Greek Studies* 43, no. 2 (2019): 243–61

Alivizatos, Nikos, *Το Σύνταγμα και οι εχθροί του στη νεοελληνική ιστορία, 1800–2010* (The constitution and its enemies in modern Greek history, 1800–2010) (Athens: Polis, 2011)

Almeida, Pedro Tavares de, 'Electors, Voting and Representatives', in *Res publica: Citizenship and Political Representation in Portugal, 1820–1926*, ed. Fernando Catroga and Pedro Tavares de Almeida (Lisbon: Assembleia da República, 2011), pp. 60–89

———, ed., *Legislação eleitoral portuguesa, 1820–1926* (Lisbon: Imprensa Nacional-Casa da Moeda, 1998)

Almuiña Fernández, Celso, 'Clericalismo y anticlericalismo a través de la prensa española decimonónica', in Carlos Seco Serrano et al., *La cuestión social en la Iglesia española contemporánea* (Madrid: El Escorial, 1981), pp. 123–75

Angelomatis-Tsougarakis, Eleni, 'Women', in *The Greek Revolution: A Critical Dictionary*, ed. Paschalis M. Kitromilides and Constantinos Tsoukalas (Cambridge, MA: Harvard University Press, 2021), pp. 420–36

———, 'Women in the Greek War of Independence', in *Networks of Power in Modern Greece: Essays in Honour of John Campbell*, ed. Mark Mazower (London: Hurst Publishers, 2008), pp. 45–68

Annino, Antonio, 'Cádiz y la revolución territorial de los pueblos mexicanos 1812-1821', in *Historia de las elecciones en Iberoamérica, siglo XIX*, ed. Antonio Annino (Buenos Aires: Fondo de Cultura Económica, 1995), pp. 177–226

Anscombe, Frederick F., *State, Faith, and Nation in Ottoman and Post-Ottoman Lands* (Cambridge: Cambridge University Press, 2014)

———, 'The Balkan Revolutionary Age', *The Journal of Modern History* 84, no. 3 (2012): 572–606

Araújo, Ana Cristina, 'Revoltas e ideologias em conflito durante as invasões francesas', *Revista de História das Ideias* 7 (1985): 7–75

Argyriou, Astérios, *Les Exégès grecques de l'apocalypse à l'époque turque (1453-1821): Esquisse d'une historie des courants idéologiques au sein du people grec asservi* (Thessaloniki: Society for Macedonian Studies, 1982)

Armand-Hugon, Augusto, *Storia dei valdesi*, 2 vols (Turin: Claudiana, 1989)

Armitage, David, *Civil Wars: A History in Ideas* (New York: Alfred A. Knopf, 2017)

———, *The Declaration of Independence: A Global History* (Cambridge, MA: Harvard University Press, 2007)

Armitage, David and Sanjay Subrahmanyam, eds, *The Age of Revolutions in Global Context, c. 1760-1840* (Basingstoke: Palgrave Macmillan, 2010)

Arnabat Mata, Ramon, 'Cambios y continuidades en los ayuntamientos constitucionales del Trienio Liberal (1820–1823)', *Bulletin d'Histoire Contemporaine de l'Espagne* 54 (2020): 1–18

———, 'La contrarrevolución y la antirevolución', in *El Trienio Liberal (1820-1823)*, ed. Pedro Rújula and Ivana Frasquet (Granada: Comares Historia, 2020), pp. 285–307

———, 'La divulgación popular de la cultura liberal durante el Trienio (Cataluña, 1820–1823)', *Trienio* 41 (2003): 55–83

———, *La revolució de 1820 i el Trienni Liberal a Catalunya* (Vic: Eumo, 2001)

———, 'Los catalanes y la nación española durante el Trienio Liberal (1820–1823)', in *VII Simposio Internacional: Ciudadanía y nación en el mundo hispano contemporáneo*, ed. José Maria Portillo Valdés and Javier Ugarte (Vitoria, Instituto de Historia Social Valentín de Foronda, 2001), pp. 63–78

———, 'Propaganda antiliberal i lluita ideologica durant el Trienni Liberal a Catalunya (1820–1823)', *Recerques: Història, Economia i Cultura* 34 (1996): 7–28

———, 'Província, pàtria, nació i estat a l'inici de la revolució liberal (1820–1823)', in *Identitats nacionals i nacionalismes a l'estat espanyol a l'època contemporània*, ed. Sebastià Serra Busquets and Elisabeth Ripoll Gil (Palma de Mallorca, Institut d'Estudis Baleàrics, 2019), pp. 31–48

———, *Visca el rei i la religió! La primera guerra civil de la Catalunya contemporània* (Lleida: Pagès Editors, 2006)

Artola, Andoni 'Was a State–Church Alliance Really Possible? The Case of the Spanish Episcopate and the Crown (1814–1833)', in *A History of the European Restorations: Culture, Society and Religion*, ed. Michael Broers and Ambrogio A. Caiani, 2 vols (London: Bloomsbury, 2019), 2, pp. 61–72

Artola Gallego, Miguel, *La España de Fernando VII*, 2nd edn (Madrid: Espasa Calpe, 1999)

Assereto, Giovanni, 'Dall'antico regime all'unità', in *Storia d'Italia: Le regioni dall'Unità a oggi; La Liguria*, ed. Antonio Gibelli and Paride Rugafiori (Turin: Einaudi, 1994), pp. 161–98

Ausín Ciruelos, Alberto, 'Propaganda, periodismo y pueblo en armas: Las guerillas y sus líderes según la prensa de la guerra de Independencia (1808-1814)', *Aportes* 97 (2018): 7–43

Aymes, Jean-René, 'Du catéchisme religieux au catéchisme politique (fin du XVIII siècle–début du XIX)', in *École et Église en Espagne et en Amérique latine. Aspects idéologiques et institutionnels*, ed. Jean-René Aymes, Eve-Marie Fell and Jean-Louis Guerena (Tours: Presses Universitaires François-Rabelais, 1988), pp. 17–32

Azevedo, Julião Soares de, *Condições económicas da revolução portuguesa de 1820* (Lisbon: Básica Editora, 1976)

Baker, Keith Michael and Dan Edelstein, eds, *Scripting Revolution: A Historical Approach to the Comparative Study of Revolutions* (Stanford, CA: Stanford University Press, 2015)

Barberis, Walter, *Le armi del principe: La tradizione militare sabauda* (Turin: Einaudi, 1988)

Barkey, Karen, 'In the Lands of the Ottomans: Religion and Politics', in Stedman Jones and Katznelson, *Religion and the Political Imagination*, pp. 90–111

Baroja, Pío, *Siluetas románticas y otras historias de pillos y de extravagantes* (Madrid: Espasa Calpe, 1934)

Barone, Giuseppe, *L'oro di Busacca: Potere, ricchezza e povertà a Scicli (sec. XVI–XIX)* (Palermo: Sellerio, 1998)

Barrio Gozalo, Maximiliano, 'Los eclesiásticos afrancesados durante la Guerra de la Independencia', in *Las élites y la revolución de España (1808–1814): Estudios en homenaje al profesor Gérard Dufour*, ed. Armando Alberola and Isabel Larriba (Alicante: Publicaciones de la Universidad de Alicante, 2010), pp. 227–56

Barton, Gregory A., *Informal Empire and the Rise of One World Culture* (London: Palgrave Macmillan, 2014)

Bartoccini, Fiorella, *Il murattismo: Speranze, timori e contrasti nella lotta per l'unità d'Italia* (Milan: Giuffrè, 1959)

Bayly, Christopher, *Imperial Meridian: The British Empire and the World 1780–1830* (London: Routledge, 1989)

——, 'Rammohan Roy and the Advent of Constitutional Liberalism in India, 1800–30'. *Modern Intellectual History* 4, no. 1 (2007): 25–41

——, *Recovering Liberties: Indian Thought in the Age of Liberalism and Empire* (Cambridge: Cambridge University Press, 2011)

——, *The Birth of the Modern World 1780–1914: Global Connections and Comparisons* (Oxford: Blackwell, 2004)

Beales, Derek, *European Catholic Monasteries in the Age of Revolution, 1640–1815* (Cambridge: Cambridge University Press, 2003)

Beaton, Roderick, *Byron's War: Romantic Rebellion, Greek Revolution* (Cambridge: Cambridge University Press, 2013)

Beik, William, *Urban Protest in Seventeenth-Century France: The Culture of Retribution* (Cambridge: Cambridge University Press, 1997)

Benigno, Francesco, 'Rivolte in città', *Storica* 10 (1998): 164–70

Benton, Lauren and Lisa Ford, *Rage for Order: The British Empire and the Origins of International Law (1800–1850)* (Cambridge, MA: Harvard University Press, 2016)

Bernardes, Denis Antônio de Mendonça, *O patriotismo constitucional: Pernambuco 1820–1822* (São Paulo: Editora Universitária UFPE, 2001)

Bersano, Arturo, *Adelfi, federati e carbonari: Contributo all storia delle società segrete* (extracted from *Atti della reale accademia delle scienze di Torino*, vol. 45) (Turin: Vincenzo Bona, 1910)

Berti, Giuseppe, *I democratici e l'iniziativa meridionale nel Risorgimento* (Milan: Feltrinelli, 1962)

Bethencourt, Francisco, 'The Unstable Status of Sebastianism', in *Utopia in Portugal, Brazil, and Lusophone Africa*, ed. Francisco Bethencourt (Oxford: Peter Lang, 2015), pp. 43–69

Biagini, Eugenio Federico, 'Citizenship and Religion in the Italian Constitutions, 1796–1849', *History of European Ideas* 37 (2011): 211–17

Bitis, Alexander, *Russia and the Eastern Question: Army, Government, and Society, 1821–1833* (Oxford: Oxford University Press, 2006)

Blanco Valdés, Roberto L., *Rey, Cortes y fuerza armada en los orígines de la España liberal, 1808–1823* (Madrid: Siglo XXI de España, 1988)

Bloch, Marc, 'Reflexions d'un historien sur les fausses nouvelles de la guerre', *Revue de Synthèse Historique* 33 (1921): 13–35

Bonifácio, Maria de Fátima, *A segunda ascensão e queda de Costa Cabral, 1847–1851* (Lisbon: ICS, 2002)

———, 'Costa Cabral no contexto do liberalismo doutrinário', *Análise Social* 28, no. 1 (1993): 1043–91

———, *D. Maria II* (Lisbon: Círculo de Leitores, 2014)

———, *História da guerra civil da Patuleia* (Lisbon: Editorial Estampa, 1993)

———, 'O Setembrismo corrigido e actualizado', *Penélope: Fazer e Desfazer História* 9 (1993): 309–21

———, 'Os arsenalistas da Marinha na Revolução de Setembro, 1836', *Análise Social* 17, no. 65 (1981): 39–65

Bornate, Carlo, 'L'insurrezione di Genova nel marzo 1821', in *La rivoluzione piemontese dell'anno 1821*, pp. 331–468

———, 'La partecipazione degli studenti liguri ai moti del 1821 e la chiusura dell'università', in *Giovanni Ruffini e i suoi tempi: Studi e ricerche* (Genoa: Comitato regionale ligure della Società nazionale per la storia del Risorgimento, 1931), pp. 95–161

Boyd, Carolyn P., 'Un lugar de memoria olvidado: El Panteón de Hombres Ilustres en Madrid', *Historia y Política* 12 (2004): 15–39

Brady, Hugh, *Rome and the Neapolitan Revolution of 1820–21: A Study in Papal Neutrality* (New York: Columbia University Press, 1937)

Branco, Rui, 'A vida política', in *História contemporânea de Portugal: 1808–2010*, vol. 2: *A construção nacional, 1834–1890*, ed. Pedro Tavares de Almeida (Lisbon: Fundación Mapfre/Editora Objectiva, 2013), pp. 31–74

Braude, Benjamin and Bernard Lewis, eds, *Christians and Jews in the Ottoman Empire: The Functioning of a Plural Society* (New York: Holmes and Meier, 1982)

Brégianni, Catherine, 'L'influence maçonnique sur l'hellénisme durant la dernière période ottomane et les symboles de l'état grec', in *Diffusions et circulations des pratiques maçonniques, XVIII–XX siècle*, ed. Pierre-Yves Beaurepaire, Kenneth Loiselle, Jean-Marie Mercier and Thierry Zarcone (Paris: Classiques Garnier, 2012), pp. 285–99

Brennecke, Christiana, 'Internacionalismo liberal, romanticismo y sed de aventuras: La oposición inglesa y la causa de España en los años veinte del s. XIX', in *Segón Congrés Recerques: Enfrontaments civils; Postguerres i reconstruccions*, vol. 1 (Lleida: Associació Recerques, Pagès, 2002), pp. 459–74

Brewer, David, *The Greek War of Independence* (New York: Duckworth, 2001)

Brice, Catherine, ed., *Frères de sang, frères d'armes, frères ennemis: La fraternité en Italie (1824–1914)* (Rome: École française de Rome, 2017)

Broers, Michael, *The Politics of Religion in Napoleonic Italy: The War against God, 1801–1814* (London: Routledge, 2002)

Bron, Grégoire, 'Il Mediterraneo dei portoghesi all'inizio del secolo XIX: Diplomazia e internazionalismo liberale, 1808–1835', *Daedalus* 5 (2014): 214–42

Bruyère-Ostells, Walter, *La Grande Armée de la liberté* (Paris: Tallandier, 2009)

———, 'Réseaux maçonniques et para-maçonniques des officiers de la Grande Armée engagés dans les mouvements nationaux et libéraux', *Cahiers de la Méditerranée* 72 (2006): 153–69

Burdiel, Isabel, 'The Liberal Revolution, 1808–1843', in *Spanish History since 1808*, ed. José Álvarez Junco and Adrian Shubert (London: Bloomsbury, 2000), pp. 17–32

Bustos, Sophie, 'El 7 de julio de 1822: La contrarrevolución en marcha', *Revista Historia Autónoma* 4 (2014): 129–43

Buti, Vittorio, 'Albanesi al servizio del regno delle due Sicilie', *La Rassegna Italiana: Politica letteraria e artistica* 39 (1939): 151–57

Butrón Prida, Gonzalo, 'Fiesta y revolución: Las celebraciones políticas en el Cádiz liberal', in *La revolución liberal*, ed. Alberto Gil Novales (Madrid: Ediciones del Orto, 2001), pp. 159–77

———, 'From Hope to Defensiveness: The Foreign Policy of a Beleaguered Liberal Spain, 1820–1823', *The English Historical Review* 133, no. 562 (2018): 567–96

———, *Nuestra sagrada causa: El modelo gaditano en la revolución piamontesa de 1821* (Cádiz: Fundación Municipal de Cultura del Ayuntamiento de Cádiz, 2006)

———, 'Pueblo y élites en la crisis del absolutismo: Los Voluntarios Realistas', *Spagna Contemporanea* 25 (2004): 1–20

Butrón Prida, Gonzalo and Pedro Rújula, eds, *Los sitios en la Guerra de la Independencia: La lucha en las ciudades* (Madrid: Silex; Cádiz: Universidad de Cádiz, 2012)

Caetano, Marcelo, *Os antecedentes da reforma administrativa de 1832 (Mouzinho de Silveira)* (Lisbon: Universidade de Lisboa, 1967)

Caglioti, Angelo Matteo, 'La nazione armata di Guglielmo Pepe' *Clio: Rivista Trimestale di Studi Storici* 47, no. 2 (2011): 185–211

Caglioti, Luigia, *Vite parallele: Una minoranza protestante nell'Italia dell'Ottocento* (Bologna: Il Mulino, 2006)

Calaresu, Melissa, 'Images of Ancient Rome in Late Eighteenth-Century Neapolitan Historiography', *Journal of the History of Ideas* 58, no. 4 (1997): 641–61

Callahan, William J., *Church, Politics, and Society in Spain, 1750–1874* (Cambridge, MA: Harvard University Press, 1984)

Calles Hernández, Claudio, 'La lucha política durante el Trienio Liberal: El enfrentamiento electoral de diciembre de 1821 en Salamanca', *Salamanca: Revista de Estudios* 53 (2006): 71–134

Canal, Jordi, *El Carlismo*, 2nd edn (Barcelona: RBA, 2006)

Cancila, Orazio, *L'economia della Sicilia: Aspetti storici* (Milan: Il Saggiatore, 1992)

Candeloro, Giorgio, *Storia dell'Italia moderna*, vol. 2: *Dalla restaurazione alla rivoluzione nazionale*, 2nd edn (Milan: Feltrinelli, 1988)

Canella, Maria ed., *Armi e nazione: Dalla Repubblica Cisalpina al Regno d'Italia (1797–1914)* (Milan: FrancoAngeli, 2009)

Cantos Casaneve, Marieta, Fernando Durán López and Alberto Romero Ferrer, eds, *La guerra de pluma: Estudios sobre la prensa de Cádiz en el tiempo de las Cortes (1810–1814)*, 2 vols (Cádiz: Universidad de Cádiz, 2009)

Capela, José Viriato, Henrique Matos and Rogério Borralheiro, *O heróico patriotismo das províncias do norte: Os concelhos na Restauração de Portugal de 1808* (Monção: Casa Museu, Universidade do Minho, 2008)

Carantoña Álvarez, Francisco, 'Liberalismo y administración territorial: Los poderes local y provincial en el sistema constitucional de Cádiz', in *La revolución liberal*, ed. Alberto Gil Novales (Madrid: Ediciones del Orto, 2001), pp. 135–57

Cardoso, António Monteiro, *A revolução liberal em Trás-os-Montes (1820–1834): O povo e as elites* (Porto: Edições Afrontamento, 2007)

——, 'Notícias "aterradoras" e pasquins "incendiários": A circulação de rumores em Trás-os-Montes no tempo das lutas liberais', in *Contra-revolução, espírito público e opinião no sul da Europa: Séculos XVIII e XIX*, ed. Maria de Fátima Sá e Melo Ferreira (Lisbon: Centro de Estudos de História Contemporânea Portuguesa, 2009), pp. 109–16

Carey, Peter, *The Power of Prophecy: Prince Diponegoro and the End of the Old Order in Java, 1785–1855* (Leiden: Brill, 2008)

Carr, Raymond, *Spain 1808–1975*, 2nd edn (Oxford: Oxford University Press, 1982)

Casals Bergés, Quintí, *La representación parlamentaria en España durante el primer liberalismo (1810–1836)* (Lleida: Edicions de la Universitat de Lleida, 2014)

Cascão, Rui, 'A revolta de Maio de 1828 na Comarca de Coimbra: Contribuição para uma sociologia da revolução liberal', *Revista de História das Ideias* 7 (1985): 111–53

Cassino, Carmine, 'La comunità italiana in Portogallo tra rivoluzione e reazione (1820–1828)', *Memoria e Ricerca* 48 (2015): 121–41

——, '"Lisboa dos italianos": Presença italiana e práticas de nacionalidade nos primeiros trinta anos do século XIX', *Cadernos do Arquivo Municipal*, 2nd series, 3 (2015): 211–37

Castellano, Carolina, *Spazi pubblici, discorsi segreti: Istituzioni e settarismo nel Risorgimento italiano* (Trento: Tangram, 2013)

Castells, Irene, *La utopía insurrecional del liberalismo: Torrijos y las conspiraciones liberales de la década ominosa* (Barcelona, Editorial Crítica, 1989)

Castro, Concepción de, *La revolución liberal y los municipios españoles* (Madrid: Alianza Editorial, 1979)

Castro, Demetrio, 'The Left: From Liberalism to Democracy', in *Spanish History since 1808*, ed. José Álvarez Junco and Adrian Shubert (London: Bloomsbury, 2000), pp. 86–90

Catroga, Fernando, *O republicanismo em Portugal, da formação ao 5 de Outubro de 1910*, 2nd edn (Lisbon: Editorial Notícias, 2000)

Cazzaniga, Gian Mario, 'Origini ed evoluzioni dei rituali carbonari italiani', in *Storia d'Italia, Annali 21: La massoneria*, ed. Gian Mario Cazzaniga (Turin: Einaudi, 2006), pp. 559–78

Cebreiros Álvarez, Eduardo, 'Conflictos entre municipios gallegos durante el Trienio Liberal: La lucha por la capitalidad', *Revista de Dret Històric Català* 14 (2015): 149–81

Cecere, Domenico, 'Scritture del disastro e istanze di riforma nel regno di Napoli (1783): Alle origini delle politiche dell'emergenza', *Studi Storici* 58 (2017): 187–214

———, 'Suppliche, resistenze, protesta popolare: Le forme della lotta politica nella Calabria del settecento', *Quaderni Storici* NS 46, no. 138 (2011): 765–96

Cepeda Gómez, José, *El ejército español en la política (1787-1843): Conspiraciones y pronunciamientos en los comienzos de la España liberal* (Madrid: Fundación Universitaria Española, 1990)

Cestaro, Antonio, *Le diocesi di Conza e Campagna nell'età della Restaurazione* (Rome: Edizioni di Storia e Letteratura, 1971)

Christiansen, Eric, *The Origins of Military Power in Spain, 1800-1854* (Oxford: Oxford University Press, 1967)

Cingari, Gaetano, *Mezzogiorno e Risorgimento: La restaurazione a Napoli dal 1821 al 1830* (Rome: Laterza, 1976)

Ciuffoletti, Zeffiro, 'La massoneria napoleonica in Italia', in *La massoneria: La Storia, gli uomini, le idee*, ed. Zeffiro Ciuffoletti and Sergio Moravia (Milan: Bruno Mondadori, 2004), pp. 121–34

Clancy Smith, Julia, *Mediterraneans: North Africa and Europe in an Age of Migration, c. 1800-1900* (Berkeley, CA: University of California Press, 2011)

Clemente, Giuseppe, 'Nicola Intonti e i moti del 1820–21 in Capitanata', *La Capitanata* 22 (1984–85): 195–203

Clogg, Richard, 'Anti-Clericalism in Pre-Independence Greece, c. 1750–1821', in Clogg, *Anatolica: Studies in the Greek East in the 18th and 19th Centuries* (Aldershot: Routledge, 1996), ch. 8

———, 'The Correspondence of Adhamantios Korais with the British and Foreign Bible Society (1808)', in Clogg, *Anatolica: Studies in the Greek East in the 18th and 19th Centuries* (Aldershot: Routledge, 1996), ch. 16

———, 'The "Dhidhaskalia Patriki" (1798): An Orthodox Reaction to French Revolutionary Propaganda', in Clogg, *Anatolica: Studies in the Greek East in the 18th and 19th Centuries* (Aldershot: Routledge, 1996), ch. 5

Codesal Pérez, Matilde, *La ciudad de Zamora en el Trienio Liberal (1820-23)* (Zamora: Ayuntamiento de Zamora, 2008)

Colley, Linda, 'Empires of Writing: Britain. American and Constitutions, 1776–1848', *Law and History Review* 32, no. 2 (2014): 237–66

———, *The Gun, the Ship, and the Pen: Warfare, Constitutions, and the Making of the Modern World* (New York: W. W. Norton & Co., 2021)

Colombo, Adolfo, 'I moti di Alessandria nel 1821 secondo nuovi documenti', *Rivista di Storia, Arte, Archeologia per la Provincia di Alessandria* 31 (1922): 291–336

Comellas, José Luis, *Los primeros pronunciamientos en España* (Madrid: CSIC—Escuela de Historia Moderna, 1958)

Conejero López, Luisa, 'El clero de Málaga en el Trienio Liberal', *Baetica: Estudios de Arte, Geografía e Historia* 2, no. 2 (1979): 277–93

Conti, Fulvio, 'La massoneria e la costruzione della nazione italiana dal Risorgimento al fascismo', in *La massoneria: La storia, gli uomini, le idee*, ed. Zeffiro Ciuffoletti and Moravia (Milan: Bruno Mondadori, 2004), pp. 135–91

Cortese, Nino, 'Il governo napoletano e la rivoluzione siciliana del MDCCCXX–XX1', *Archivio Storico Messinese* NS 28–35, no. 1 (1934): 3–245

———, *L'esercito napoletano e le guerre napoleoniche: Spagna, Alto Adige, Russia, Germania* (Naples: Ricciardi, 1928)

——, *La prima rivoluzione separatista siciliana: 1820-1821* (Naples: Libreria Scientifica, 1951)

Costa, Fernando Dores, 'Army Size, Military Recruitment and Financing in Portugal during the Period of the Peninsular War—1808-1811' *E-Journal of Portuguese History* 6, no. 2 (2008): 31–57

——, 'Franceses e "jacobinos": Movimentações "populares" e medidas de polícia em 1808 e 1809; Uma "irrupção patriótica"?', *Ler História* 54 (2008): 95–132

——, 'O Conde de Palmela em Cádis (1810-1812)' *Ler História* 64 (2013): 87–109

——, 'The Peninsular War as a Diversion and the Role of the Portuguese in the British Strategy', *Portuguese Journal of Social Science* 22, no. 1 (2013): 3–24

Couderc, Anne, 'Nation et circonscription: Construire et nommer le territoire grec, 1832-1837', in *Nommer et classer dans les Balkans*, ed. Gilles de Rapper and Pierre Sintès (Athens: École française d'Athène, 2008), pp. 217–235

——, 'Religion et identité nationale en Grèce pendant la révolution d'indépendance (1821-1832): Le creuset ottoman et l'influence occidentale', in *La Perception de l'héritage ottoman dans les Balkans*, ed. Sylvie Gangloff (Paris: L'Harmattan, 2005), pp. 21–41

——, 'Structuration du territoire et formation des élites municipales en Grèce (1833–1843)', in *Construire des mondes: Élites et espaces en Méditerranée XVI–XX siècle*, ed. Paul Aubert, Gérard Chastagnaret and Olivier Raveux (Aix-en-Provence: Presses universitaires de Provence, 2005), pp. 163–184

Coverdale, John, *The Basque Phase of Spain's First Carlist War* (Princeton, NJ: Princeton University Press, 1984)

Crawley, Charles W., *The Question of Greek Independence: A Study of British Policy in the Near East, 1821-1833* (Cambridge: Cambridge University Press, 1930)

Crisantino, Amelia, *Introduzione agli 'Studii su la storia di Sicilia dalla metà del XVIII secolo al 1820' di Michele Amari* (Palermo: Mediterranea, 2010)

Cruz, Manuel Braga da, 'As relações entre a igreja e o estado liberal: Do "cisma" à Concordata (1832-1848)', in *O liberalismo na Península Ibérica na primeira metade do século XIX*, ed. Miriam Halpern Pereira, Maria de Fátima Sá e Melo Ferreira and João B. Serra, 2 vols (Lisbon: Sá da Costa Editora, 1982), 1, pp. 223–35

D'Alessandro, Domenico, 'Documenti inediti su Massoneria e Carboneria nel Regno delle Due Sicilie', in *Sentieri della libertà e della fratellanza ai tempi di Silvio Pellico*, ed. Aldo Mola (Foggia: Bastogi, 1994)

D'Alessandro, Vincenzo and Giuseppe Giarrizzo, *La Sicilia dal Vespro all'unità d'Italia* (Turin: UTET, 1989)

D'Elia, Costanza, 'Supplicanti e vandali: Testi scritti, testi non scritti, testi scritti dagli storici', *Quaderni Storici* NS 31, no. 92 (1996): 459–85

Dakin, Douglas, *British and American Philhellenes during the Greek War of Independence 1821-1833* (Thessaloniki: Institute for Balkan Studies, 1955)

——, *The Greek Struggle for Independence, 1821-1833* (Berkeley, CA: University of California Press, 1973)

Dalidakis, George and Peter Trudgill, *Sfakia: A History of the Region in its Cretan Context* (Heraklion: Mystis, 2015)

Daly, Gavin, *The British Soldier in the Peninsular War: Encounters with Spain and Portugal, 1808-1814* (Basingstoke: Palgrave Macmillan, 2013)

Darnton, Robert, 'An Early Information Society; News and the Media in Eighteenth-Century Paris', *The American Historical Review* 105, no. 1 (2000): 1–35

Daskalakis, Apostolos, '"Thourios Hymnos", le chant de la liberté de Rhigas Velestinlis', *Balkan Studies* 4 (1963): 315–346

Daum, Werner, *Oscillazioni dello spirito pubblico: Sfera pubblica, mercato librario e comunicazione nella rivoluzione del 1820-21 nel Regno delle Due Sicilie* (Naples: Società napoletana di storia patria, 2015)

'Daun, João Carlos Gregório Domingos Vicente Francisco de Saldanha Oliveira e', in *Dicionário do Vintismo e do primeiro Cartismo (1821-23 e 1826-28)*, ed. Zília Osório de Castro, Isabel Cluny and Sara Marques Pereira, 2 vols (Lisbon: Assembleia da República, 2002), 1, pp. 583–90

Davis, John A., '1799: The Santafede and the Crisis of the *ancien régime* in Southern Italy', in *Society and Politics in the Age of the Risorgimento*, ed. John A. Davis and Paul Ginsborg (Cambridge: Cambridge University Press, 1991), pp. 1–25

———, *Naples and Napoleon: Southern Italy and the European Revolutions (1780-1860)* (Oxford: Oxford University Press, 2006)

———, 'Rivolte popolari e controrivoluzioni nel Mezzogiorno continentale', in *Folle controrivoluzionarie: Le insorgenze populari nell'Italia giacobina e napoleonica*, ed. Anna Rao (Rome: Carocci, 1999), pp. 349–68

———, 'The Neapolitan Army during the *decennio francese*', *Rivista Italiana di Studi Napoleonici* 25, no. 1 (1988): 161–77

Davis, Robert C., *Christian Slaves, Muslim Masters: White Slavery in the Mediterranean, the Barbary Coast, and Italy, 1500-1800* (New York: Palgrave Macmillan, 2003)

de Dijn, Annelien, *French Political Thought from Montesquieu to Tocqueville: Liberty in a Levelled Society?* (Cambridge: Cambridge University Press, 2009)

De Francesco, Antonino, 'Church e il nastro giallo: L'immagine del 1820 in Sicilia nella storiografia del XIX secolo', *Rivista Italiana di Studi Napoleonici* 28 (1991): 23–90

———, *La guerra di Sicilia: Il distretto di Caltagirone nella rivoluzione del 1820-21* (Catania: Bonanno Editore, 1992)

———, 'Vulcano di patriottismo: Catania nella politica rivoluzionaria dell'ottocento', in *Catania: La grande Catania; La nobiltà virtuosa, la borghesia operosa*, ed. Enrico Iachello (Catania: Sanfilippo editore, 2010), pp. 323–31

De Lorenzo, Renata, 'La costruzione di un sistema patriottico: Protagonisti e memorialisti napoletani nella Guerra Spagnola', in *Gli Italiani in Spagna nella guerra napoleonica (1807-1813): I fatti, i testimoni, l'eredità*, ed. Vittorio Scotti Douglas (Alessandria: Edizioni dell'Orso, 2006), pp. 217–53

———, *Murat* (Rome: Salerno Editrice, 2011)

De Silva, Kingsley M., *A History of Sri Lanka* (London: C. Hurst & Co., 1981)

Della Peruta, Franco, *Esercito e società nell'Italia napoleonica: Dalla Cisalpina al regno d'Italia* (Milan: FrancoAngeli, 1996)

———, 'War and Society in Napoleonic Italy: The Armies of the Kingdom of Italy at Home and Abroad', in *Society and Politics in the Age of the Risorgimento: Essays in Honour of Denis Mack Smith*, ed. John A. Davis and Paul Ginsborg and (Cambridge: Cambridge University Press, 2002), pp. 26–47

Delpu, Pierre-Marie, 'Eroi e martiri: La circolazione delle figure celebri della rivoluzione napoletana nell'Europa liberale, 1820-1825', *Rivista Storica Italiana* 130, no. 2 (2018): 587–614

———, 'La Parole des prêtres, un outil de politisation révolutionnaire (Royaume des Deux-Siciles, 1799–1848)', in *Rhétorique et politisation, de la fin des Lumières au Printemps des Peuples*, ed. Sophie-Anne Leterrier and Olivier Tort (Arras: Artois Presses Université, 2021), pp. 197–210

———, 'Patriotisme libéral et nation catholique: Les Prêtres libéraux dans la révolution napolitaine de 1820–1821', *Studi Storici* 58 (2017): 545–71

———, *Un autre Risorgimento: La Formation du monde libéral dans le royaume des Deux-Siciles (1815–1856)* (Rome: Collection de l'École française de Rome, 2019)

Demange, Christian, *El Dos de Mayo: Mito y fiesta nacional (1808–1958)* (Madrid: Madrid: Centro de Estudios Políticos y Constitucionales, 2004)

Desan, Susan, Lynn Hunt and William Max Nelson, eds, *The French Revolution in Global Perspective* (Ithaca, NY: Cornell University Press, 2013)

Despotopoulos, Alexandros, 'Ἡ Ἑλληνική Ἐπανάσταση (1821–1830)' (The Greek revolution, 1821–1830), in *Ἱστορία του Ἑλληνικού Ἔθνους* (History of the Greek nation), ed. Christopoulos Giorgos and Bastias Ioannis, 17 vols (Athens: Ekdotiki Athinon, 1970–2000), 12: *Ἡ Ἑλληνική Ἐπανάσταση και η ίδρυση του ελληνικού κράτους* (The Greek revolution and the foundation of the Greek state)

Di Fiore, Laura, *Alla frontiera: Confini e documenti di identità nel Mezzogiorno continentale preunitario* (Soveria Mannelli: Rubbettino, 2013)

Dialla, Ada, 'Imperial Rhetoric and Revolutionary Practice: The Greek 1821', *Historein* 20, no. 1 (2021), DOI: https://doi.org/10.12681/historein.27480

Dias, Pedro Augusto, *Subsidios para a história politica do Porto* (Porto: Typographia Central, 1896)

Díez Morrás, Francisco Javier, *'La Antorcha de la libertad resplandece': La Sociedad Patriótica de Logroño y los inicios del liberalismo* (Logroño: Ayuntamiento de Logroño, 2016)

Dimitropoulos, Dimitris, 'Pirates during a Revolution: The Many Faces of Piracy and the Reaction of Local Communities', in *Corsairs and Pirates in the Eastern Mediterranean. Fifteenth–Nineteenth Centuries*, ed. Gelina Harlaftis, Dimitris Dimitropoulos and David J. Starkey (Athens: AdVenture SA, 2016), pp. 29–40

———, *Θεόδωρος Κολοκοτρώνης* (Theodoros Kolokotronis) (Athens: Ta Nea, Istoriki Vivliothiki, 2009)

———, 'Πειρατές στη στεριά; Πρόσφυγες, καταδρομείς και καθημερινότητα των παράκτιων οικισμών στα χρόνια του Αγώνα' (Pirates ashore? Refugees, irregulars and everyday life in coastal areas during the war of independence), in *Όψεις της Ελληνικής Επανάστασης του 1821: Πρακτικά Συνεδρίου, Αθήνα 12 και 13 Ιουνίου 2015* (Aspects of the Greek Revolution of 1821: Proceedings of a conference, Athens, 12 and 13 June 2015), ed. Dimitris Dimitropoulos, Christos Loukos and Panagiotis Michailaris (Athens: EMNE, 2018), pp. 87–105

Dito, Oreste, *Massoneria, Carboneria ed altre società segrete nella storia del Risorgimento italiano* (Turin: Casa editrice nazionale, Roux e Viarengo, 1905)

Dueñas García, Francisco, 'El sitio de Barcelona de 1823', in *El municipi de Barcelona i els combats pel govern de la ciutat*, ed. Joan Roca Albert (Barcelona: Proa, 1997)

Dufour, Gérard, 'Estudio preliminar y presentación', in *Sermones revolucionarios del Trienio Liberal (1820–1823)*, ed. Gérard Dufour (Alicante: Instituto de Cultura Juan Gil-Albert, Diputación de Alicante, 1991), pp. 7–57

———, 'La emigración a Francia del clero afrancesado', in Dufour, José A. Ferrer Benimeli, Leandro Higueruela del Pino and Emilio La Parra López, *El clero afrancesado: Actas de la Mesa Redonda, Aix-en-Provence, 25 de enero de 1985* (Aix-en-Provence: Université de Provence, 1986), pp. 163–206

Dym, Jordana, *From Sovereign Villages to National States: Cities, State, and Federation in Central America, 1759–1839* (Albuquerque, NM: University of New Mexico Press, 2006)

Efthymiou, Maroula, 'Cursing with a Message: The Case of Georgios Karaiskakis in 1823', *Historein* 2 (2000): 173–82

Elorza, Antonio, 'La ideología moderada en el Trienio Liberal', *Quadernos Hispanoamericanos* 288 (1974): 584–652

Esdaile, Charles J., 'El levantamiento español', in Esdaile and Javier Tusell, *Época contemporánea: 1808–2004*, vol. 6 of John Lynch, ed., *Historia de España*, 6 vols (Barcelona: Crítica, 2001), pp. 13–31

———, *Fighting Napoleon: Guerrillas, Bandits and Adventurers in Spain, 1808–1814* (New Haven, CT: Yale University Press, 2004)

———, 'Heroes or Villains Revisited: Fresh Thoughts on *la guerrilla*', in *The Peninsular War: Aspects of the Struggle for the Iberian Peninsula*, ed. Ian Fletcher (Staplehurst: Spellmount, 1998), pp. 93–114

———, 'Popular Mobilisation in Spain, 1808–1810: A Reassessment', in *Collaboration and Resistance in Napoleonic Europe: State Formation in an Age of Upheaval, c.1800–1815*, ed. Michael Rowe (New York: Palgrave Macmillan, 2003), pp. 90–106

———, *The Spanish Army in the Peninsular War* (Manchester: Manchester University Press, 1988)

Falcetta, Angela, *Ortodossi nel Mediterraneo cattolico: Frontiere, reti, comunità nel Regno di Napoli (1700–1821)* (Rome: Viella, 2016)

Faria, Ana Mouta, 'A condição do clero português durante a primeira experiência de implantação do liberalismo: As influências do processo revolucionário francês e seus limites', *Revista Portuguesa de História* 23 (1987): 301–31

———, 'A hierarquia episcopal e o vintismo', *Análise Social* 27, nos 116–117 (1992): 285–328

———, *Os liberais na estrada de Damasco: Clero, igreja e religião numa conjuntura revolucionária (1820–1823)* (Lisbon: Fundação Calouste Gulbenkian, 2006)

Feliu i Montfort, Gaspar, *La clerecia catalana durant el Trienni Liberal* (Barcelona: Institut d'Estudis Catalans, 1972)

Fernandes, Paulo Jorge da Silva, 'Elites locais e poder municipal: Do antigo regime ao liberalismo', *Análise Social* 41, no. 178 (2006): 55–73

Fernández Sarasola, Ignacio, *La Constitución de Cádiz: Orígen, contenido y proyección internacional* (Madrid: Centro de Estudios Políticos y Constitucionales, 2001)

———, 'Opinión pública y libertades de expresión en el constitucionalismo español (1726–1845)', *Historia Constitucional* 7 (2006): 160–86

Fernández Sebastián, Javier, *La génesis del fuerismo: Prensa e ideas políticas en la crisis del Antiguo Régimen (País Vasco, 1750–1840)* (Madrid: Siglo XXI de España, 1991)

———, 'Toleration and Freedom of Expression in the Hispanic World between Enlightenment and Liberalism', *Past and Present* 211 (2011): 159–97

Ferreira, Maria de Fátima Sá e Melo, 'A política na rua: Festa liberal e festa contrarevolucionária no Portugal do século XIX', in *A Rua: Espaço, tempo, sociabilidade*, ed. Graça Índias Cordeiro and Frédéric Vidal (Lisbon: Livros Horizonte, 2008), pp. 155–64

———, 'Nuestra Señora de Rocha de Carnaxide: Una devoción del miguelismo', in *Discursos y devociones religiosas en la Península Ibérica, 1780–1860: De la crisis del Antiguo Régimen a la consolidación del Liberalismo*, ed. Rafael Serrano García, Ángel de Prado Moura and Elisabel Larriba (Valladolid: Ediciones de la Universidad de Valladolid, 2014), pp. 151–61

———, *Rebeldes e insubmissos: Resistências populares ao liberalismo (1834–1844)* (Porto: Edições Afrontamento, 2000)

———, '"Vencidos pero no convencidos": Movilización, acción colectiva y identidad en el Miguelismo', *Historia Social* 49 (2004): 73–95

Ferrer Benimeli, José A., *Masonería española contemporánea, 1800–1868*, 2 vols (Madrid: Siglo XXI de España, 1980)

———, *Masonería, Iglesia e ilustración: Un conflicto ideológico-político-religioso*, 4 vols (Madrid: Fundación Universitaria Española, 1977)

Fiestas Loza, Alicia, 'La libertad de imprenta en las dos primeras etapas del liberalismo español', *Anuario de Historia del Derecho Español* 59 (1989): 351–491

Fiume, Giovanna, 'Bandits, Violence, and the Organization of Power in Sicily in the Early Nineteenth Century', in *Society and Politics in the Age of the Risorgimento: Essays in Honour of Denis Mack Smith*, ed. John A. Davis and Paul Ginsborg (Cambridge: Cambridge University Press, 1991), pp. 70–91

———, *Le bande armate in Sicilia, 1819–1849: Violenza e organizzazione del potere* (Palermo: Annali della Facoltà di lettere e filosofia di Palermo, 1984)

Fleming, Katherine, *Greece: A Jewish History* (Princeton, NJ: Princeton University Press, 2008)

———, *The Muslim Bonaparte: Diplomacy and Orientalism in Ali Pasha's Greece* (Princeton, NJ: Princeton University Press, 1999)

Fontana, Josep, *De en medio del tiempo: La segunda restauración española 1823–1834*, 2nd edn (Barcelona: Crítica, 2013)

———, *La quiebra de la monarquía absoluta, 1814–1820* (Barcelona: Crítica, 2002)

———, *La revolució de 1820 a Catalunya* (Barcelona: Rafael Dalmau, 1961)

Fowler, Will, ed., *Forceful Negotiations: The Origins of the Pronunciamiento in Nineteenth-Century Mexico* (Lincoln, NE: University of Nebraska Press, 2010)

Francia, Enrico, *1848: La rivoluzione del Risorgimento* (Bologna: Il Mulino, 2012)

Frangos, George Dimitrios, 'The Philiki Etairia: A Premature National Coalition', in *The Struggle for Greek Independence: Essays to Mark the 150th Anniversary of the Greek War of Independence*, ed. Richard Clogg (Hamden, CT: Archon Books, 1973), pp. 83–103

Frary, Lucien J., *Russia and the Making of Modern Greek Identity, 1821–1844* (Oxford: Oxford University Press, 2015)

———, 'Slaves of the Sultan: Russian Ransoming of Christian Captives during the Greek Revolution, 1821–1830', in *Russian–Ottoman Borderlands: The Eastern Question Reconsidered*, ed. Lucien J. Frary and Mara Kozelsky (Madison, WI: University of Wisconsin Press, 2014), pp. 101–30

Fraser, Ronald, *Napoleon's Cursed War: Popular Resistance in the Spanish Peninsular War* (London: Verso, 2008)

Frazee, Charles A., 'Church and State in Greece', in *Greece in Transition: Essays in the History of Modern Greece, 1821–1974*, ed. John T. A. Koumoulides (London: Zeno, 1977), pp. 128–52

———, *The Orthodox Church and Independent Greece, 1821–1852* (Cambridge: Cambridge University Press, 1969)

Fruci, Gian Luca, 'Democracy in Italy: From Egalitarian Republicanism to Plebiscitarian Monarchy', in Innes and Philp, *Re-imagining Democracy*, pp. 25–50

Fuentes, Juan Francisco, 'De la sociabilidad censitaria a la sociabilidad popular en la España liberal', in *Sociabilidad y liberalismo en la España del siglo XIX*, ed. Juan Francisco Fuentes and Lluís Roura, pp. 207–24

———, 'El liberalismo radical ante la unidad religiosa', in *Libéralisme chrétien et catholicisme libéral en Espagne, France et Italie dans la première moitié du XIXe siècle: Colloque internationale 12/13/14 novembre 1987* (Aix-en-Provence: Université de Provence, 1989), pp. 127–41

———, 'Estructura de la prensa española en el Trienio Liberal: Difusión y tendencias', *Trienio* 24 (1994): 165–96

———, 'La fiesta revolucionaria en el Trienio Liberal español (1820–1823)', *Historia Social* 78 (2014): 43–59

———, 'La formación de la clase política del iberalismo español: Análisis de los cargos públicos del Trienio Liberal', *Historia Constitucional* 3 (2002): 1–37

Fuentes, Juan Francisco and Pilar Garí, *Amazonas de la libertad: Mujeres liberales contra Fernando VII* (Madrid: Marcial Pons, 2014)

Fuentes, Juan Francisco and Javier Fernández Sebastián, *Historia del periodismo español: Prensa, política y opinión pública en la España contemporánea* (Madrid: Síntesis, 1997)

Fureix, Emmanuel, 'L'Iconoclasme: Une pratique politique (1814–1848)?', in *La Politique sans en avoir l'air: Aspects de la politique informelle. XIXe–XXIe siècles*, ed. Laurent Le Gall, François Ploux and Michel Offerlé (Rennes: Presses Universitaires de Rennes, 2012), pp. 117–32

———, *L'Œil blessé: Politiques de l'iconoclasme après la Révolution française* (Ceyzérieu: Éditions Champ Vallon, 2019)

Gabiani, Niccola, *Il vescovo d'Asti ed i moti del 1821* (Asti: Paglieri e Raspi, 1921)

Galasso, Giuseppe, *Storia del regno di Napoli*, 5 vols (Turin: UTET, 2006–7)

Gallant, Thomas W., *The Edinburgh History of the Greeks, 1768 to 1913: The Long Nineteenth Century* (Edinburgh: Edinburgh University Press, 2015)

Gambasin, Angelo, *Religiosa magnificenza e plebe in Sicilia nel XIX secolo* (Rome: Edizioni di Storia e Letteratura, 1979)

García de Paso García, Ignacio, 'El 1848 español: ¿Una excepción europea?', *Ayer* 106, no. 2 (2017): 185–206

García León, José M., *La milicia nacional en Cádiz durante el Trienio Liberal 1820–1823* (Cádiz: Caja de Ahorros de Cádiz, 1983)

Garriga, Carlos and Marta Lorente, *Cádiz 1812: La constitución jurisdiccional* (Madrid: Centro de Estudios Políticos y Constitucionales, 2007)

Gasparolo, Francesco, 'Il primo moto rivoluzionario del 21 in Alessandria', *Rivista di Storia, Arte, Archeologia per la Provincia di Alessandria* 30 (1921): 3–31

Gekas, Sakis, 'The Crisis of the Long 1850s and Regime Change in the Ionian Islands and the Kingdom of Greece', *The Historical Review/La Revue Historique* 10 (2013): 57–84

——, *Xenocracy: States, Class and Colonialism in the Ionian Islands, 1815–1864* (New York: Berghahn, 2016)

Ghervas, Stella, *Reinventer la tradition: Alexandre Stourdza et l'Europe de la Sainte Alliance* (Paris: Honoré Champion, 2008)

Giarrizzo, Giuseppe, 'La Sicilia dal Cinquecento all'unità d'Italia', in D'Alessandro and Giarrizzo, *La Sicilia*, pp. 692–730

Gil Novales, Alberto, *El Trienio Liberal* (Madrid: Siglo XXI España, 1980)

——, 'Rafael Riego', in *Diccionario biográfico del Trienio Liberal*, ed. Alberto Gil Novales (Madrid: Ediciones El Museo Universal, 1991), pp. 562–63

——, *Las sociedades patrióticas (1820–1823): Las libertades de expresión y de reunión en el origen de los partidos políticos*, 2 vols (Madrid: Tecnos, 1975)

Gin, Emilio, *L'aquila, il giglio e il compasso: Profili di lotta politica ed associazionismo settario nelle Due Sicilie (1806–1821)* (Mercato San Severino: Edizioni del Paguro, 2007)

Giordano, Bruno, 'La scuola militare di Modena in età napoleonica (1798–1820)', in *Istituzioni e cultura in età napoleonica*, ed. Elena Brambilla, Carlo Capra and Aurora Scotti (Milan: FrancoAngeli, 2008), pp. 295–315

Glover, Michael, *A Very Slippery Fellow: The Life of Sir Robert Wilson, 1777–1849* (Oxford: Oxford University Press, 1978)

Gómez Rivero, Ricardo, *Las elecciones municipales en el Trienio Liberal* (Madrid: Boletín Oficial del Estado, 2015)

González Casanovas, José Antonio, *Las diputaciones provinciales en España: Historia política de las diputaciones desde 1812 hasta 1985* (Madrid: Mancomunidad General de Diputaciones de Régimen Común, 1986)

Granata, Sebastiano Angelo, '"L'empia masnada": Bande armate e conflitti civili nella zona etnea', in *Una rivoluzione 'globale': Mobilitazione politica, conflitti civili e bande armate nel; Mezzogiorno del 1820*, ed. Sebastiano Angelo Granata (Milan: FrancoAngeli, 2021), pp. 157–89

Grenet, Mathieu, '"Grecs de nation", sujets ottomans: Expérience diasporique et entre-deux identitaires, 1770–1830, in *Les Musulmans dans l'histoire de l'Europe. Passages, et contacts en Méditerranée*, ed. Jocelyne Dakhlia and Wolfgang Kaiser, 2 vols (Paris: Albin Michel, 2013), 2, pp. 311–44

——, 'La Loge et l'étranger: Les Grecs dans la franc-maçonnerie marseillaise au début du XIXᵉ siècle', *Cahiers de la Méditerranée* 72 (2006): 225–43

Grieco, Giuseppe, 'British Imperialism and Southern Liberalism: Re-shaping the Mediterranean Space: 1817–1823', *Global Intellectual History* 3, no. 2 (2018): 202–30

Grimaldi, Antonella, 'L'insurrezione genovese del 1849', *Rassegna Storica del Risorgimento* 95 (2008): 323–78

Guaita, Aurelio, *División territorial y descentralización* (Madrid: Instituto de Estudios de Administración Local, 1975)

Guerci, Luciano, *Istruire nelle verità repubblicane: La letteratura politica per il popolo nell'Italia in rivoluzione, 1796–1799* (Bologna: Il Mulino, 1999)

Guillén Gómez, Antonio, *Una aproximación al Trienio Liberal en Almería: La milicia nacional voluntaria (1820–1823)* (Almería: Instituto de Estudios Almerienses, 2000)

Hagemann, Karen, *Revisiting Prussia's Wars against Napoleon: History, Culture and Memory* (Cambridge: Cambrdige University Press, 2015)

Hamnett, Brian (R.), 'Joaquín Lorenzo Villanueva, de católico ilustrado a católico liberal: El dilema de la transición', in *Visiones del liberalismo: Política, identidad y cultura en la España del siglo XIX*, ed. Alda Blanco and Guy Thompson (Valencia: Universitat de València, 2008), pp. 19–42

——, *La política española en una época revolucionaria, 1790–1820* (Mexico City: Fondo de Cultura Económica, 2011)

——, *The End of Iberian Rule on the American Continent, 1770–1830* (Cambridge: Cambridge University Press, 2017)

——, *The Enlightenment in Iberia and Ibero-America* (Cardiff: University of Wales Press, 2017)

Hatziiossif, Christos, 'Conjunctural Crisis and Structural Problems in the Greek Merchant Marine in the 19th Century: Reaction of the State and Private Interests', *Journal of the Greek Diaspora* 12 (1985): 5–20

Hatzopoulos, Konstantinos, 'Οι επαναστατικές προκηρύξεις του Αλ. Υψηλάντη: Προβλήματα σχετικά με την εκτύπωση τους' (The revolutionary declarations of Al. Ypsilantis: Problems with their publication), *Ελληνικά* [*Ellinika*] 33, no. 2 (1981): 320–73

Hatzopoulos, Marios, 'Oracular Prophecy and the Politics of Toppling Ottoman Rule in South-east Europe', *The Historical Review/La Revue Historique* 8 (2011): 95–116

Hespanha, António Manuel, *Guiando a mão invisível: Direitos, Estado e lei no liberalismo monárquico português* (Coimbra: Almedina, 2004)

——, 'O constitucionalismo monárquico português: Breve síntese', *Historia Constitucional* 13 (2012): 477–526

Hill, Peter, 'How Global was the Age of Revolutions? The Case of Mount Lebanon, 1821', *Journal of Global History* 16, no. 1 (2021): 65–84

——, 'Mount Lebanon and Greece: Mediterranean Crosscurrents, 1821–1841', *Historein* 20, no. 1 (2021), DOI: https://doi.org/10.12681/historein.24937

Hiotis, Panayotis, *Ιστορία του Ιονίου Κράτους από συστάσεως αυτού μέχρις ενώσεως (ετη 1815–1864)* (History of the Ionian State from its establishment to unification (the years 1815–1864)), 2 vols (Zakynthos: Typografeion Eptanisos, 1874)

Hippler, Thomas, *Citizens, Soldiers and National Armies: Military Service in France and Germany* (London: Routledge, 2008)

Hobsbawm, Eric, *The Age of Revolution: 1789–1848* (London: Weidenfeld & Nicolson, 1962)

Hocquellet, Richard, 'Elites locales y levantamiento patriótico: La composición de las juntas provinciales en 1808', *Historia y Política* 19 (2008): 129–50

Hopkin, David, *Voices of the People in Nineteenth-Century France* (Cambridge: Cambridge University Press, 2012)

Hunt, Lynn, *The Family Romance of the French Revolution* (Berkeley, CA: University of California Press, 1992)

Iachello, Enrico, 'Centralisation étatique et pouvoir local en Sicile au XIX siècle', *Annales* 49, no. 1 (1994): 241–66

Idoate, Florencio, 'La merindad de Tudela durante la guerra realista', *Príncipe de Viana* 27, nos 104–5 (1966): 277–300

Iglesias Rogers, Graciela, *British Liberators in the Age of Napoleon: Volunteering under the Spanish Flag in the Peninsular War* (London: Bloomsbury, 2013)

Innes, Joanna, 'L'"éducation nationale" dans les îles Britanniques, 1765–1815: Variations britanniques et irlandaises sur un thème européen', *Annales* 5 (2010): 1087–116

———, 'Popular Consent and the European Order', in Innes and Philp, *Re-imagining Democracy*, pp. 271–99

Innes, Joanna and Mark Philp, eds, *Re-imagining Democracy in the Mediterranean, 1780–1860* (Oxford: Oxford University Press, 2018)

Isabella, Maurizio, 'Aristocratic Liberalism and Risorgimento: Cesare Balbo and Piedmontese Political Thought after 1848', *History of European Ideas* 39 (2013): 835–85

———, *Risorgimento in Exile: Italian Émigrés and the Liberal International* (Oxford: Oxford University Press, 2009)

Isabella, Maurizio and Konstantina Zanou, eds, *Mediterranean Diasporas: Ideas and Politics in the Long Nineteenth Century* (London: Bloomsbury, 2015)

Jacob, Margaret C., *Living the Enlightenment: Freemasonry and Politics in Eighteenth-Century Europe* (New York: Oxford University Press, 1991)

Jensen, Oskar Cox, *Napoleon and British Song, 1797–1822* (London: Palgrave Macmillan, 2015)

Kaltchas, Nicholas, *Introduction to the Constitutional History of Modern Greece* (New York: Columbia University Press, 1940)

Kallivretakis, Leonidas, 'Athens in the 19th Century: From Regional Town of the Ottoman Empire to Capital of the Kingdom of Greece' (17 June 2017), available at https://brewminate.com/athens-in-the-19th-century-from-regional-town-of-the-ottoman-empire-to-capital-of-the-kingdom-of-greece/ (accessed 14 August 2022)

Karakatsouli, Anna, 'Μαχητές της ελευθερίας' και 1821: Η Ελληνική Επανάσταση στη διεθνική της διάσταση ('Freedom fighters' and 1821: The Greek war of independence in its transnational dimension) (Athens: Pedio, 2016)

Karamanolakis, Vangelis, 'The University of Athens and Greek Antiquity (1837–1937)', in *Re-imagining the Past: Antiquity and Modern Greek Culture*, ed. Dimitris Tziovas (Oxford: Oxford University Press, 2014), pp. 112–27

Katsiardi-Hering, Olga, 'Diaspora and Self-Representation: The Case Study of Greek People's Identity, Fifteenth–Nineteenth Centuries', in *Human Diversity in Context*, ed. Cinzia Ferrini (Trieste: EUT, 2020), pp. 239–65

———, 'Greek Merchant Colonies in Central and South-Eastern Europe in the Eighteenth and early Nineteenth Centuries', in *Merchant Colonies in the Early Modern Period*, ed. Victor Zakharov, Gelina Harlaftis and Olga Katsiardi-Hering (London: Pickering & Chatto, 2012), pp. 127–80

———, Η ελληνική παροικία της Τεργέστης (1751–1830) (The Greek community of Trieste (1751–1830)), 2 vols (Athens: University of Athens, 1986)

Kitromilides, Paschalis, 'Athos and the Enlightenment', in Kitromilides, *An Orthodox Commonwealth: Symbolic Legacies and Cultural Encounters in Southeastern Europe* (Aldershot: Routledge, 2007), pp. 257–72

———, *Enlightenment and Revolution: The Making of Modern Greece* (Cambridge, MA: Harvard University Press, 2013)

———, *Enlightenment, Nationalism, Orthodoxy: Studies in the Culture and Political Thought of South-Eastern Europe* (Aldershot: Routledge, 1994)

———, 'From Orthodox Commonwealth to National Communities: Greek–Russian Intellectual and Ecclesiastical Ties in the Ottoman Era', in Kitromilides, *An Orthodox Commonwealth: Symbolic Legacies and Cultural Encounters in Southeastern Europe* (Aldershot: Routledge, 2007), pp. 1–18

———, 'Itineraries in the World of the Enlightenment: Adamantios Korais from Smyrna via Montpellier to Paris', in *Adamantios Korais and the European Enlightenment*, ed. Paschalis Kitromilides (Oxford: Voltaire Foundation, 2010)

———, 'Orthodoxy and the West: Reformation to Enlightenment', in *The Cambridge History of Christianity*, vol.5: *Eastern Christianity*, ed. Michael Angold (Cambridge: Cambridge University Press), pp. 187–208

———, 'Η Φιλική Εταιρεία και η πολιτική γεωγραφία του Διαφωτισμού' (The Philiki Etaireia and the political geography of the Enlightenment), in *Οι πόλεις των Φιλικών: Οι αστικές διαδρομές ενός επαναστατικού φαινομένου; Πρακτικά ημερίδας, Αθήνα, 14 Ιανουαρίου 2015* (The cities of the Philikoi: The urban trajectories of a revolutionary phenomenon; Proceedings of a conference, Athens, 14 January 2015), ed. Olga Katsiardi-Hering (Athens: The Hellenic Parliament Foundation, 2018), pp. 25–35

Kohler, Denis, 'Introduction', in Macriyannis, *Mémoires*, pp. 11–78

Koliopoulos, John F., *Brigands with a Cause: Brigandage and Irredentism in Modern Greece, 1821–1912* (Oxford: Oxford University Press, 1987)

Kontogeorgis, Dimitris, 'Μεταξύ πανδούρων και βογιάρων: Οι Φιλικοί στο Βουκουρέστι και στο Ιάσιο' (Between pandouroi and boyars: The Philikoi in Bucharest and in Jassy), in *Οι πόλεις των Φιλικών: Οι αστικές διαδρομές ενός επαναστατικού φαινομένου, Πρακτικά ημερίδας, Αθήνα, 14 Ιανουαρίου 2015* (The cities of the Philikoi: The urban trajectories of a revolutionary phenomenon; Proceedings of a conference, Athens, 14 January 2015), ed. Olga Katsiardi-Hering (Athens: The Hellenic Parliament Foundation, 2018), pp. 57–76

Korinthios, Gianni, *I greci di Napoli del meridione d'Italia dal XV al XX secolo* (Cagliari: AMED, 2012)

———, *I liberali napoletani e la rivoluzione greca (1821–1830)* (Naples: IISF, 1990)

Kostantaras, Dean J., 'Christian Elites of the Peloponnese and the Ottoman State, 1715–1821', *European History Quarterly* 43, no. 4 (2013): 628–56

Kostis, Kostas, *History's Spoiled Children: The Formation of the Modern Greek State* (London: Hurst, 2018)

Kotsonis, Yannis, *Η Ελληνική Επανάσταση και οι αυτοκρατορίες: Η Γαλλία και οι Έλληνες, 1797–1830* (The Greek revolution and the empires: France and the Greeks, 1797–1830) (Athens: Alexandreia, 2020)

Koumarianou, Aikaterini, 'Εισαγωγή' (Introduction) to Koumarianou, *Ο Τύπος στον Αγώνα* (The press in the 'Struggle'), 1, pp. 12–30

Koumarianou, Catherine [Aikaterini Koumarianou], 'The Contribution of the Intelligentsia to the Greek Independence Movement, 1798–1821', in Clogg, *Movement for Greek Independence*, pp. 67–86

Kremmydas, Vasilis, 'Προεπαναστατικές πραγματικότητες: Η οικονομική κρίση και η πορεία προς το 21' (Pre-revolutionary realities: The economic crisis and the path to 1821), *Μνήμων* [*Mnimon*] 24, no. 2 (2002): 71–84

La Parra López, Emilio, 'El eco de Lamennais en el progresismo español: Larra y Joaquín María López', in *Libéralisme chrétien et catholicisme libéral en Espagne,*

France et Italie dans la première moitié du XIXe siècle: Colloque internationale 12/13/14 novembre 1987 (Aix-en-Provence: Université de Provence, 1989), pp. 323–42

——, *El primer liberalismo español y la Iglesia: Las Cortes de Cádiz* (Alicante: Instituto de Cultura Juan Gil-Albert, 1985)

——, 'El rey ante sus súbditos: Presencia de Fernando VII en el espacio público', *Historia Constitucional* 20 (2019): 3–23

——, *Fernando VII: Un rey deseado y detestado* (Barcelona: Tusquets Editores, 2018)

——, 'La canción del *Trágala*: Cultura y política popular en el inicio de la revolución liberal en España', *Les travaux du CERC en Ligne*, no. 6 (2009), in *La Réception des cultures de masse et des cultures populaires en Espagne (XVII–XX siècles)*, ed. S. Salaün and F. Etienvre, available at https://crec-paris3.fr/wp-content/uploads/2011/07/actes-03-La-Parra.pdf (accessed 14 August 2022)

——, 'La metamorfosis de la imagen del rey Fernando VII entre los primeros liberales', in *Cortes y revolución en el primer liberalismo español*, ed. Francisco Acosta Ramírez (Jaén: Publicaciones de la Universidad de Jaén, 2006), pp. 73–96

——, *Los Cien Mil Hijos de San Luis: El ocaso del primer impulso liberal en España* (Madrid: Síntesis, 2007)

——, 'Ni restaurada, ni abolida: Los últimos años de la Inquisición española (1823–1834)', *Ayer* 108 (2017): 153–75

Labate, Valentino, *Un decennio di Carboneria in Sicilia (1821–1831)* (Rome: Società Editrice Dante Alighieri, 1904)

Laiou, Sophia, 'Political Processes on the Island of Samos Prior to the Greek War of Independence and the Reaction of the Sublime Porte: The Karmanioloi-Kallikantzaroi Conflict', in *Political Initiatives 'From the Bottom Up' in the Ottoman Empire*, ed. Antonis Anastasopoulos (Rethymno: Crete University Press, 2012), pp. 91–105

Lappas, Kostas, 'Πατριαρχική σύνοδος περί "Καθαιρέσεως των φιλοσοφικών μαθημάτων" το Μάρτιο του 1821: Μια μαρτυρία του Κωνσταντίνου Οικονόμου' (Patriarchal synod on 'The deposition of the philosophical courses' in March 1821: A testimony by Konstantinos Oikonomou), *Μνήμων [Mnimon]* 11 (1987): 123–53

Laudani, Simona, *'Quegli strani accadimenti': La rivolta di Palermo del 1773* (Rome: Viella, 2005)

Lehner, Ulrich L. and Printy, Michael, eds, *A Companion to the Catholic Enlightenment in Europe* (Leiden: Brill, 2010)

Lepre, Aurelio, 'Classi, movimenti politici e lotta di classe nel Mezzogiorno dalla fine del Settecento al 1860', *Studi Storici* 16, no. 2 (1975): 340–77

——, *La rivoluzione napoletana del 1820–21* (Rome: Editori Riuniti, 1967)

Levati, Stefano 'Politica, affarismo ed esercito: La lotta per il potere nel Ministero della guerra durante la Seconda Repubblica Cisalpina e la Repubblica Italiana (giugno 1800–maggio 1805)', in *L'affaire Ceroni: Ordine militare e cospirazione politica nella Milano di Bonaparte*, ed. Stefano Levati (Milan: Guerini e Associati, 2005), pp. 65–96

Levy, Avigdor, 'The Officer Corps in Sultan Mahmud II's New Ottoman Army, 1826–39', *International Journal of Middle East Studies* 2, no. 1 (1971): 21–39

Liakos, Antonis, *L'unificazione italiana e la grande idea: Ideologia e azione dei movimenti nazionali in Italia e in Grecia, 1859–1871* (Florence: Aletheia, 1995)

Linz, Juan, José Ramón Montero and Antonia Ruiz, 'Elecciones y política', in *Estadísticas históricas de España: Siglo XIX–XX*, ed. Albert Carreras and Xavier Tafunell, 2nd edn, 3 vols (Bilbao: Fundación BBVA, 2005,), 1, pp. 1027–1154

Llanos Aramburu, Félix, *El Trienio Liberal en Guipúzcoa (1820–1823)* (San Sebastián: Facultad de Filosofía y Letras, Universidad de Deusto, 1998)

López García, José Miguel, *El motín contra Esquilache* (Madrid: Alianza Editorial, 2006)

Lorente Sariñena, Marta, *Las infracciones a la constitución de 1812* (Madrid: Centro de Estudios Constitucionales, 1988)

Loukos, Christos, *Αλέξανδρος Μαυροκορδάτος* (Alexandros Mavrokordatos) (Athens: Ta Nea Istoriki Vivliothiki, 2010)

Lousada, Maria Alexandre, 'A contra-revolução e os lugares da luta política: Lisboa em 1828' in *Contra-revolução, espírito público e opinião no sul da Europa: Séculos XVIII e XIX*, ed. Maria de Fátima Sá e Melo Ferreira (Lisbon: Centro de Estudos de História Contemporânea Portuguesa, 2009), pp. 83–108

——, 'Imprensa e política: Alguns dados sobre a imprensa periódica portuguesa durante as lutas liberais (1820–1834)', *Finisterra* 24, no. 47 (1989): 88–104

——, 'Public Space and Popular Sociability in Lisbon in the Early 19th Century', *Santa Barbara Portuguese Studies* 4 (1997): 220–32

——, 'Sobre a alimentação popular urbana no início do século XIX: Tabernas e casas de pasto lisboetas', in *Desenvolvimento económico e mudança social: Portugal nos últimos dois séculos; Homenagem a Miriam Halpern Pereira* ed. José Vicente Serrão, Magda A. Pinheiro and Maria de Fátima Sá e Melo Ferreira (Lisbon: ICS, 2009), pp. 227–48

Lousada, Maria Alexandre and Maria de Fátima Sá e Melo Ferreira, *D. Miguel* (Lisbon: Círculo de Leitores, 2009)

Lousada, Maria Alexandre and Nuno Gonçalo Monteiro, 'Revoltas absolutistas e movimentação camponesa no Norte, 1826–1827 (algumas notas)', in *O liberalismo na Península Ibérica na primeira metade do século XIX*, ed. Miriam Halpern Pereira, Maria de Fátima Sá e Melo Ferreira and João B. Serra, 2 vols (Lisbon: Sá da Costa Editora, 1982), 2, pp. 169–82

Luis, Jean-Philippe, *L'Utopie réactionnaire: Épuration et modernisation de l'état dans l'Espagne de la fin de l'ancien régime (1823/1834)* (Madrid: Casa de Velázquez, 2002)

Makrides, Vasilios N., 'The Enlightenment in the Greek Orthodox East: Appropriation, Dilemmas, Ambiguities', in *Enlightenment and religion in the Orthodox World*, ed. Paschalis Kitromilides (Oxford: Voltaire Foundation, 2016), pp. 17–44

Manessis, Aristovoulos, *Deux États nés en 1830: Ressemblances et dissemblances constitutionnelles entre la Belgique et la Grèce* (Brussels: Maison Ferdinand Larcier, 1959)

Manfredi, Luca, *L'uomo delle tre rivoluzioni: Vita e pensiero del generale Guglielmo Pepe* (Foggia: Bastogi, 2009)

Manique, António Pedro, *Mouzinho da Silveira: Liberalismo e administração pública* (Lisbon: Livros Horizonte, 1989)

Marichal, Juan, 'From Pistoia to Cádiz: A Generation's Itinerary, 1786–1812', in *The Ibero-American Enlightenment*, ed. Alfred Owen Aldridge (Urbana, IL: University of Illinois Press, 1971), pp. 97–110

Marques, António Henrique de Oliveira, *História da Maçonaria em Portugal*, 3 vols (Lisbon: Editorial Presença, 1990–97)

Marques, Fernando Pereira, *Exército e sociedade em Portugal no declínio do antigo regime e advento do liberalismo* (Lisbon: A Regra do Jogo, 1981)

———, *Exército, mudança e modernização na primeira metade do século XIX* (Lisbon: Cosmos, Instituto de Defesa Nacional, 1999)

Marques, João Francisco, 'O clero nortenho e as invasões francesas: Patriotismo e resistência regional', *Revista de História* 9 (1989): 165–246

Marques, João Pedro, *Sá da Bandeira e o fim da escravidão: Vitória da moral, desforra do interesse* (Lisbon: ICS, 2008)

Marsengo, Giorgio and Giuseppe Parlato, *Dizionario dei piemontesi compromessi nei moti del 1821*, 2 vols (Turin: Istituto per la storia del Risorgimento italiano, 1982)

Martín-Cleto, Julio Porres, 'Curiosidades Toledanas', *Toletum: Boletín de la Real Academia de Bellas Artes y Ciencias Históricas de Toledo* 42 (2000): 9–42

Mas Galvañ, Cayetano, 'La democracia templada según un "clérigo del lugar": Perfiles biográficos e ideológicos de D. Ramón de los Santos García', in Fernández Sarasola, *Constituciones en la sombra*, pp. 211–66

Mason, Laura, *Singing the French Revolution: Popular Culture and Politics 1787–1799* (Ithaca, NY: Cornell University Press, 1996)

Mastroberti, Francesco, *Pierre-Joseph Briot: Un giacobino tra amministrazione e politica (1771–1827)* (Naples: Jovene, 1998)

Matos, Sérgio Campos, 'Linguagem do patriotismo em Portugal: Da crise do Antigo Regime à I República', in *Linguagens e fronteiras do poder*, ed. Miriam Halpern Pereira, José Murilo de Carvalho, Maria João Vaz and Gladys Sabina Ribeiro (Lisbon: Centro de Estudos de História Contemporânea Portuguesa, 2012), pp. 35–52

Maturi, Walter, *Il concordato del 1818 tra Santa Sede e le Due Sicilie* (Florence: Le Monnier, 1929)

———, *Il Principe di Canosa* (Florence: Le Monnier, 1944)

Mazarakis-Ainian, Ioannis K., *Η ιστορία της ελληνικής σημαίας* (The history of the Greek flag) (Athens: National Historical Museum, 2007)

Mazower, Mark, *Salonica: City of Ghosts; Christians, Muslims, and Jews, 1430–1950* (London: Harper Collins, 2004)

———, *The Greek Revolution: 1821 and the Making of Modern Europe* (London: Penguin Books, 2021)

———, 'Villagers, Notables and Imperial Collapse: The Virgin Mary on Tinos' in *Networks of Power in Modern Greece: Essays in Honour of John Campbell*, ed. Mark Mazower (London: Hurst Publishers, 2008), pp. 69–87

Mazurel, Hervé, *Vertiges de la guerre: Byron, les philhellènes et le mirage grec* (Paris: Les Belles Lettres, 2013)

Mazziotti, Matteo, *La rivolta del Cilento nel 1828 narrata da documenti inediti* (Rome: Società Editrice Dante Alighieri, 1906)

McGrew, William W., *Land and Revolution in Modern Greece 1800–1881: The Transition in the Tenure and Exploitation of Land from Ottoman Rule to Independence* (Kent, OH: The Kent State University Press, 1985)

Meletopoulos, John, *The Greek Navy in 1821* (Athens: Commercial Credit Bank, 1971)

Mcllo, Evaldo Cabral de, *A outra Independência: O federalismo pernambucano de 1817 a 1824* (São Paulo: Editora 34, 2004)

Mellone, Viviana, *Napoli 1848: Il movimento radicale e la rivoluzione* (Milan: FrancoAngeli, 2017)

Meriggi, Marco, *Gli Stati italiani prima dell'unità: Una storia istituzionale* (Bologna: Il Mulino, 2011)

——, *La nazione populista: Il mezzogiorno e i Borboni dal 1848 all'Unità* (Bologna: Il Mulino, 2021)

Mesquita, José Carlos Vilhena, 'A instauração do liberalismo em Portugal numa visão global socioeconómica: A participação do Algarve', in *Estudos 1. Faculdade de Economia da Universidade do Algarve* (Faro: Faculdade de Economia da Universidade do Algarve, 2004), pp. 23–48

Michael, Michalis N., 'The Loss of an Ottoman Traditional Order and the Reactions to a Changing Ottoman World: A New Interpretation of the 1821 Events in Cyprus', *International Review of Turkish Studies* 3 (2013): 8–36

Michailaris, Panagiotis and Vassilis Panagiotopoulos, *Κληρικοί στον Αγώνα: Παλαιών Πατρών Γερμανός, Ιγνάτιος Ουγγροβλαχίας, Νεόφυτος Βάμβας* (Clerics in the 'Struggle': Palaion Patron Germanos, Ignatios Ouggrovlachias, Neophytus Vamvas) (Athens: Ta Nea/Istoriki Vivliothiki, 2010)

Michailidis, Iakovos D., 'The Formation of Greek Citizenship (19th Century)', in *Citizenship in Historical Perspective*, ed. Steven G. Ellis, Gudmundur Halfdanarson and Ann Katherine Isaacs (Pisa: Edizioni Plus, 2006), pp. 155–62

Millán y García-Varela, Jesús, 'Autoritat, opinió i mobilització a l'Oriola del Trienni: Una aproximació als significats del liberalisme', *Pasado y Memoria: Revista de Historia Contemporanea* 10 (2011): 219–41

Millán y García-Varela, Jesús and María Cruz Romeo Mateo, 'La nación católica en el liberalismo: Las perspectivas sobre la unidad religiosa en la España liberal, 1808–1868', *Historia y Política* 34 (2015): 183–209

Mina Apat, María Cruz, *Fueros y revolución liberal en Navarra* (Madrid: Alianza Editorial, 1981)

Moliner Prada, Antonio, *Revolución burguesa y movimiento juntero en España* (Lleida: Milenio, 1997)

Monteiro, Isilda Braga da Costa, 'The Military in the Chamber of Deputies, 1851–1870: Corporative Lines of Action in Defense of the Army', *E-Journal of Portuguese History* 8, no. 1 (2010): 1–22

Monteiro, Nuno Gonçalo, *Elites e poder entre o Antigo Regime e o Liberalismo*, 3rd edn (Lisbon: ICS, 2012)

——, 'Lavradores, frades e forais: Revolução liberal e regime senhorial na comarca de Alcobaça (1820–24)', in Monteiro, *Elites*, pp. 221–99

——, 'Societat rural i actituds polítiques a Portugal (1820–1834)', in *Carlisme i moviments absolutistes*, ed. Josep Maria Fradera, Jesús Millán and Ramón Garrabou (Girona: Editorial Eumo, 1990), pp. 127–50

Monti, Gennaro Maria, *Stato e Chiesa durante la rivoluzione napoletana del 1820–21* (Milan: Vita e Pensiero, 1939)

Montoya, Pío de, *La intervención del clero vasco en las contiendas civiles 1820–1823* (San Sebastián: Editorial Txertoa, 1971)

Montroni, Giovanni, 'Linguaggi di regalità: L'uso pubblico della retorica a Napoli nel primo ottocento', *Contemporanea* 1 (1998): 703–30

Morange, Claude, 'Opinión pública: Cara y cruz del concepto en el primer iberalismo español', in *Sociabilidad y liberalismo en la España del siglo XIX*, ed. Juan Francisco Fuentes and Lluís Roura (Lérida: Milenio, 2001) pp. 117–46

——, 'Teoría y práctica de la libertad de la prensa durante el Trienio Constitucional: El caso de "El Censor" (1820–1823)', in *La prensa en la revolución liberal: España, Portugal y America Latina*, ed. Alberto Gil Novales (Madrid: Universidad Complutense de Madrid, 1983), pp. 203–32

——, *Una conspiración fallida y una Constitución nonnata (1819)* (Madrid: Centro de Estudios Políticos y Constitucionales, 2006)

Morelli, Antonio, *Michele Morelli e la rivoluzione napoletana*, 2nd edn (Bologna: Cappelli, 1969)

Moscati, Ruggero, 'La questione greca e il governo napoletano', *Rassegna Storica del Risorgimento* 20, no. 1 (1933): 21–49

Musi, Aurelio, 'L'amministrazione locale del regno di Napoli: Dall' "università" d'antico regime alla "comune" del decennio murattiano', *Clio: Rivista Trimestale di Studi Storici* 27, no. 3 (1991): 501–13

Narciso, Enrico, 'Illuminismo e cultura sannita nel secolo XVIII', in *Illuminismo meridionale e comunità locali*, ed. Enrico Narciso (Naples: Guida, 1988), pp. 25–62

Newitt, Malyn, 'Lord Beresford and the Gomes Freire conspiracy', in Newitt and Robson, *Lord Beresford*, pp. 111–34

——, 'Lord Beresford and the governadores of Portugal', in Newitt and Robson, *Lord Beresford*, pp. 89–109

Newitt, Malyn and Martin Robson, *Lord Beresford and British Intervention in Portugal, 1807–1820* (Lisbon: ICS, 2004)

Nicolini, Fausto, *Aspetti della vita italo-spagnuola nel Cinque e Seicento* (Naples: Guida, 1934)

Nieto Sánchez, José A. and Álvaro París Martín, 'La participación popular en la crisis política de la monarquía: Del motín contra Godoy al 2 de mayo de 1808 en Madrid', *Investigaciones Históricas: Época Moderna y Contemporánea* 37 (2017): 109–48

——, 'Transformaciones laborales y tensión social en Madrid: 1750–1836', *Revista Encuentros Latinoamericanos* 6, no. 1 (2012): 210–74

Oddo, Francesco Luigi, *Le maestranze di Palermo: Aspetti e momenti di vita politico/sociale (sec. XII–XIX)* (Palermo: Accademia nazionale di scienze, lettere e arti, 1991)

Offord, Derek, 'The Response of the Russian Decembrists to Spanish Politics in the Age of Fernand VII', *Historia Constitucional* 13 (2012): 163–91

Ozouf, Mona, 'Fraternité', in *Dictionnaire critique de la révolution française*, ed. François Furet and Mona Ozouf (Paris: Flammarion, 1988), pp. 731–40

——, *La fête révolutionnaire, 1789–1799* (Paris: Gallimard, 1976)

Palacios Cerezales, Diego, '"Assinem assinem, que a alma não tem sexo!" Petição coletiva e cidadania feminina no Portugal constitucional (1820–1910)', *Análise Social* 205, no. 4 (2012): 740–65

——, 'Embodying Public Opinion: From Petitions to Mass Meetings in Nineteenth-century Portugal', *E-Journal of Portuguese History* 9, no. 1 (2011): 1–19, http://www

.brown.edu/Departments/Portuguese_Brazilian_Studies/ejph/html/Summer11
.html (accessed 14 August 2022)

———, 'Re-imagining Petitioning in Spain (1808–1823)', *Social Science History* 43, no. 3 (2019): 487–508

Papagiorgis, Kostis, *Τα καπάκια: Βαρνακιώτης, Καραϊσκάκης, Ανδρούτσος* (*Kapakia*: Varnakiotis, Karaiskakis, Androutsos) (Athens: Kastaniotis, 2003)

Pappas, Nicholas Charles, *Greeks in Russian Military Service in the Late Eighteenth and Early Nineteenth Centuries* (Thessaloniki: Institute for Balkan Studies, 1991)

Paquette, Gabriel, *Imperial Portugal in the Age of Atlantic Revolutions: The Luso-Brazilian World c. 1770–1850* (Cambridge: Cambridge University Press, 2013)

———, 'The Brazilian Origins of the 1826 Portuguese Constitution', *European History Quarterly* 41, no. 3 (2011): 444–71

París Martín, Álvaro, 'Artesanos y política en Madrid durante el resistible ascenso del liberalismo (1808–1833)', *Theomai* 31 (2015): 43–62

———, 'El fin del Trienio: Contrarrevolución popular y terror blanco en el Madrid de 1823', *Ayer*, forthcomimg (2022), DOI: https://doi.org/10.55509/ayer/902

———, 'Los Voluntarios Realistas de Madrid: Politización popular y violencia contrarrevolucionaria (1823–1833)', in Rújula and Ramón Solans, *El desafío*, pp. 89–123

———, 'Milicia nacional', in *El Trienio Liberal (1820–1823): Una mirada política*, ed. Pedro Rújula and Ivana Frasquet (Granada: Editorial Comares, 2020), pp. 213–38

———, 'Royalist Women in the Marketplace: Work, Gender and Popular Counter-revolution in Southern Europe (1814–1830)', in *Popular Agency and Politicisation in Nineteenth-Century Europe: Beyond the Vote*, ed. Oriol Luján and Diego Palacios Cerezales (London: Palgrave Macmillan, 2023), pp. 55–77

París Martín, Álvaro and Jordi Roca Vernet, 'Green Ribbons and Red Berets: Political Objects and Clothing in Spain (1808–1843)', in *Political Objects in the Age of Revolution: Material Culture, National Identities, Political Practices*, ed. Carlotta Sorba and Enrico Francia (Rome: Viella, 2021), pp. 61–96

Pata, Arnaldo da Silva Marques, *Revolução e cidadania: Organização, funcionamento e ideologia da Guarda Nacional (1820–39)* (Lisbon: Colibri, 2004)

Payne, Stanley G., *Politics and the Military in Modern Spain* (Stanford, CA: Stanford University Press, 1967)

Pécout, Gilles, 'International Volunteers and the Risorgimento', *Journal of Modern Italian Studies* 14, no. 4 (special issue) (2009): 395–522

———, 'Philhellenism in Italy: Political Friendship and the Italian Volunteers in the Mediterranean in the Nineteenth Century', *Journal of Modern Italian Studies* 9, no. 4 (2004): 405–27

Pedreira, Jorge and Fernando Dores Costa, *D. João VI: O Clemente* (Lisbon: Círculo de Leitores, 2006)

Pereira, Miriam Halpern, 'Artesãos, operários e o liberalismo: Dos privilégios corporativos para o direito ao trabalho', in Pereira, *Do Estado liberal ao Estado-providência: Um século em Portugal* (Bauru: EDUSC, 2012), pp. 105–80

———, 'Nación, ciudadanía y religión en Portugal (1820–1910)', *Ayer* 69 (2008): 277–302

———, *Negociantes, fabricantes e artesãos entre velhas e novas instituições: Estudo e documentos*, vol. 2 of Pereira, ed., *A crise do antigo regime e as Cortes constituintes*, 5 vols (Lisbon: João Sá da Costa, 1992)

—, *Sob o signo da Revolução de 1820: Economia e sociedade* (Lisbon: Assembleia da República, 2020)

Pereira, Miriam Halpern and Ana Cristina Araújo, eds, *Gomes Freire e as vésperas da Revolução de 1820* (Lisbon: Biblioteca Nacional de Portugal, 2018)

Pérez Garzón, Juan Sisinio, 'Absolutismo y clases sociales: Los Voluntarios Realistas de Madrid (1823–1833)', *Anales del Instituto de Estudios Madrileños* 15 (1978): 295–310

—, *Milicia nacional y revolución burguesa: El prototipo madrileño, 1808–1874* (Madrid: Consejo Superior de Investigaciones Científicas, 1978)

Pérez Núñez, Javier, 'Conmemorar la nación desde abajo: Las celebraciones patrióticas del Madrid progresista, 1836–1840', *Historia y Política* 35 (2016): 177–202

Perreau-Saussine, Emile, *Catholicism and Democracy: An Essay in the History of Political Thought* (Princeton, NJ: Princeton University Press, 2011)

Petropulos, John Anthony, *Politics and Statecraft in the Kingdom of Greece, 1833–1843* (Princeton, NJ: Princeton University Press, 1968)

Peyrou, Florencia, *El republicanismo popular en España, 1840–1843* (Cádiz: Universidad de Cádiz, 2002)

—, 'Los orígines del federalismo en España: Del liberalismo al republicanismo 1808–1868', *Espacio, tiempo y forma, Serie V, Historia Contemporánea* 22 (2010) (*República y monarquía en la fundación de las naciones contemporáneas: América Latina, España y Portugal*, ed. Àngeles Lario): 257–78

—, *Tribunos del pueblo: Demócratas y republicanos durante el reinado de Isabel II* (Madrid: Centro de Estudios Políticos y Constitucionales, 2008)

Philliou, Christine M., *Biography of an Empire: Governing Ottomans in an Age of Revolution* (Berkeley, CA: University of California Press, 2010)

Philp, Mark, *Radical Conduct: Politics, Sociability and Equality in London, 1789–1815* (Cambridge: Cambridge University Press, 2020)

Philp, Mark and Eduardo Posada-Carbó, 'Liberalism and Democracy', in Innes and Philp, *Re-imagining Democracy*, pp. 179–204

Pieri, Piero, *Storia militare del Risorgimento* (Turin: Einaudi, 1962)

Pinheiro, Magda, *O liberalismo nos espaços públicos: A memória das revoluções liberais através dos monumentos que a celebram* (Oeiras: Celta, 2000)

Pinto, Carmine, *La guerra per il Mezzogiorno* (Bari: Laterza, 2019)

——'Silvati, Giuseppe', in *Dizionario biografico degli italiani* (Rome: Istituto della Enciclopedia Italiana, 2018), vol. 92, pp. 622–25

Pissis, Nikolas, 'Investments in the Greek Merchant Marine (1783–1821)', in *Merchants in the Ottoman Empire*, ed. Suraiya Faroqhi and Gilles Veinstein (Leuven: Peeters, 2008), pp. 151–64

Ploux, François, *De bouche à oreille: Naissance et propagation des rumeurs dans la France du XIXe siècle* (Paris: Aubier, 2003)

Portillo Valdés, José M., *Crisis atlántica: Autonomía e independencia en la crisis de la monarquía hispana* (Madrid: Marcial Pons, 2006)

—, *Revolución de nación: Orígenes de la cultura constitucional en España, 1780–1812* (Madrid: Centro de Estudios Políticos y Constitucionales, 2000)

Prousis, Theophilus C., *British Consular Reports from the Ottoman Levant in an Age of Upheaval, 1815–1830* (Istanbul: ISIS, 2008)

——, *Russian Society and the Greek Revolution* (DeKalb, IL: Northern Illinois University Press, 1994)

Rabow-Edling, Susanna, 'The Decembrist Movement and the Spanish Constitution of 1812', *Historia Constitucional* 13 (2012): 143–61

Radich, Maria Carlos, 'Formas de organização politica: Sociedades patrióticas e clubes politicos, 1820–1836', in *O liberalismo na Península Ibérica na primeira metade do século XIX*, ed. Miriam Halpern Pereira, Maria de Fátima Sá e Melo Ferreira and João B. Serra, 2 vols (Lisbon: Sá da Costa Editora, 1982), 1, pp. 117–41

Ramón Solans, Francisco Javier, 'A Renewed Global Power: The Restoration of the Holy See and the Triumph of Ultramontanism, 1814–1848', in *A History of the European Restorations: Culture, Society and Religion*, ed. Michael Broers and Ambrogio A. Caiani, 2 vols (London: Bloomsbury, 2019), 2, pp. 72–81

Ramos, Rui, 'A revolução liberal (1834–1851)', in *História de Portugal*, ed. Rui Ramos, Bernardo Vasconcelos e Sousa and Nuno Gonçalo Monteiro (Lisbon: A Esfera dos Livros, 2017), pp. 491–519

——, 'A Tale of One City? Local Civic Traditions under Liberal and Republican Rule in Portugal', *Citizenship Studies* 11 (2007): 173–86

Rao, Anna Maria, 'La massoneria nel Regno di Napoli', in *Storia d'Italia, Annali 21: La massoneria*, ed. Gian Mario Cazzaniga (Turin: Einaudi, 2006), pp. 513–42

Reis, António do Carmo, *Invasões francesas: As revoltas do Porto contra Junot* (Lisbon: Editorial Notícias, 1991)

Renda, Francesco, *Risorgimento e classi popolari in Sicilia, 1820–1821* (Milan: Feltrinelli, 1968)

Revuelta Gonzalez, Manuel, *Política religiosa de los liberales en el siglo XIX: Trienio Liberal* (Madrid: CSIC—Escuela de Historia Moderna, 1973)

Riall, Lucy, *Eroi maschili, virilità e forme della guerra*, in *Il Risorgimento*, ed. Alberto Banti, and Paul Ginsborg (Turin: Einaudi, 2007)

——, *Under the Volcano: Empire and Revolution in a Sicilian Town* (Oxford: Oxford University Press, 2013)

Río Aldaz, Ramón del, 'Camperols foralistes i contraris a la revolució burgesa? Un mite que s'esfondra a Navarra'. *Recerques: Història, Economia, Cultura* 22 (1989): 25–44

——, *Orígenes de la guerra carlista en Navarra (1820–1824)* (Pamplona: Gobierno de Navarra, Institución Príncipe de Viana, 1987)

Rizopoulos, Andreas, 'Activités maçonniques avec arrière-plan politique—et réciproquement—en Grèce au XIXᵉ siècle', *Cahiers de la Méditerranée* 72 (2006): 203–24

Rizopoulos, Christos and Andreas Rizopoulos, *Φιλέλληνες και Έλληνες τέκτονες το 1821* (Philhellenes and Greek freemasons in 1821), 2nd edn (Athens: Tetraktys, 2008)

Robert, Vincent, *Le Temps des banquets: Politique et symbolique d'une génération (1818–1848)* (Paris: Publications de la Sorbonne, 2010)

Rocco, Ciro, 'La crisi dei prezzi nel regno di Napoli nel 1820–21', in *Il Mezzogiorno preunitario: Economia, società, istituzioni*, ed. Angelo Massafra (Bari: Edizioni Dedalo, 1988), pp. 169–79

Rodríguez López-Brea, Carlos María, *Don Luis de Borbón: El cardenal de los liberales, 1777–1823* (Toledo: Junta de Comunidades de Castilla-La Mancha, 2002)

——, 'La Constitución de Cádiz y el proceso revolucionario en las Dos Sicilias (1820–1821)', *Historia Contemporánea* 47 (2013): 561–94

——, 'La Iglesia española y la Guerra de la Independencia: Desmontando algunos tópicos', *Historia Contemporánea* 35 (2007): 743–63

——, 'La Santa Sede y los movimientos revolucionarios europeos de 1820: Los casos napolitano y español', *Ayer* 45 (2002): 251–74

Roessel, David, *In Byron's Shadow: Modern Greece in the English and American Imagination* (Oxford: Oxford University Press, 2001)

Romani, Roberto, 'Political Thought in Action: The Moderates in 1859', *Journal of Modern Italian Studies* 17, no. 5 (2012): 593–607

——, *Sensibilities of the Risorgimento: Reasons and Passions in Political Thought* (Leiden: Brill, 2018)

Romeo, Rosario, 'Momenti e problemi della Restaurazione nel Regno delle Due Sicilie (1815–1820)', *Rivista Storica Italiana* 57 (1955): 366–417

Romeo Mateo, María Cruz, *Entre el orden y la revolución: La formación de la burguesía liberal en la crisis de la monarquía absoluta (1814–1833)* (Alicante: Instituto de Cultura Juan Gil Albert, 1993)

——, 'Memoria y política en el liberalismo progresista', *Historia y Política* 17 (2007): 69–88

Rosa, Mario, ed., *Cattolicesimo e lumi nel Settecento italiano* (Rome: Herder, 1981)

Rosanvallon, Pierre, *La Démocratie inachevée: Histoire de la souveraineté du peuple en France* (Paris: Gallimard, 2000)

——, *La rivoluzione dell'uguaglianza: Storia del suffagio universale in Francia* (Milan: Anabasi, 1994)

Rosen, Frederick, *Bentham, Byron and Greece: Constitutionalism, Nationalism, and Early Liberal Political Thought* (Oxford: Oxford University Press, 1992)

Rosenblatt, Helena, *Liberal Values: Benjamin Constant and the Politics of Religion* (Cambridge: Cambridge University Press, 2008)

——, 'The Christian Enlightenment', in *The Cambridge History of Christianity*, vol. 7: *Enlightenment, Reawakening and Revolution, 1660–1815*, ed. Stewart J. Brown and Timothy Tacket (Cambridge: Cambridge University Press, 2006), pp. 283–301

Rospocher, Massimo, *Oltre la sfera pubblica: Lo spazio della politica nell'Europa moderna* (Bologna: Il Mulino, 2013)

Rosselli, John, *Lord William Bentinck and the British Occupation of Sicily, 1811–1814* (Cambridge: Cambridge University Press, 1956)

Rudorff, Raymond, *War to the Death: The Sieges of Saragossa, 1808–1809* (London: Purnell Book Services Ltd, 1974)

Ruiz Jiménez, Marta, *El liberalismo exaltado: La confederación de comuneros españoles durante el Trienio Liberal* (Madrid: Editorial Fundamentos, 2007)

——, 'La confederación de comuneros españoles en el Trienio Liberal (1821–23)', *Trienio* 35 (2000): 155–86

Rújula, Pedro, *Constitución o muerte: El Trienio Liberal y los levantamientos realistas en Aragón (1820–1823)* (Zaragoza: Edizions de l'Astral, 2000)

——, *Contrarrevolución, realismo y Carlismo en Aragón y el Maestrazgo,1820–1840* (Zaragoza: Prensas de la Universidad de Zaragoza, 1998)

——, 'Una monarchia populista? Potere assoluto e ricorso al popolo nella restaurazione spagnola di Fernando VII', *Memoria e Ricerca: Rivista di Storia Contemporanea* 27, no. 62 (2019): 421–35

Rújula, Pedro and Manuel Chust, *El Trienio Liberal en la monarquía hispánica: Revolución e independencia (1820–1823)* (Madrid: Catarata, 2020)

Rújula, Pedro and Javier Ramón Solans, eds, *El desafío de la revolución: Reaccionarios, antiliberales y contrarrevolucionarios (siglos XVIII y XIX)* (Granada: Editorial Comares, 2017)

Runciman, Steven, *The Great Church in Captivity: A Study of the Patriarchate of Constantinople from the Eve of the Turkish Conquest to the Greek War of Independence*, 2nd edn (Cambridge: Cambridge University Press, 1985 [1968])

Sá, Victor de, *A crise do liberalismo e as primeiras manifestações das ideias socialistas em Portugal (1820–1852)* (Lisbon: Seara Nova, 1969)

Sakellariou, Michael B., Ἕνας συνταγματικός δημοκράτης ηγέτης κατά την Επανάσταση του 21: ο Γ. Λυκούργος Λογοθέτης της Σάμου (1722–1850) (A constitutional democrat leader during the revolution of 1821: G. Lykourgos Logothetis of Samos (1772–1850)) (Irakleion: Crete University Press, 2014)

Sánchez García, Raquel, *Alcalá Galiano y el liberalismo español* (Madrid: Centro de Estudios Políticos y Constitucionales, 2005)

Sánchez Hita, Beatriz, 'Libertad de prensa y lucha de partidos en el Trienio Constitucional: Los procesos contra el *Diario Gaditano* de José Joaquín de Clararrosa', *El Argonauta Español* 2 (2005), DOI: https://doi.org/10.4000/argonauta.1194

Sánchez Mantero, Rafael, 'Gibraltar, refugio de liberales exiliados', *Revista de Historia Contemporánea* 1 (1982): 81–107

——, *Los Cien Mil Hijos de San Luis y las relaciones franco–españolas* (Seville: Editorial Universidad de Sevilla, 1981)

Sánchez Martín, Víctor, 'Creación, construcción y dudas sobre la imagen del héroe revolucionario y del monarca constitucional en 1820', in *Culturas políticas monárquicas en la España liberal: Discursos, representaciones y prácticas (1808–1902)* ed. Encarna García Monerris, Mónica Moreno Seco and Juan Ignacio Benedicto (Valencia: Universitat de València, 2013), pp. 59–88

——, ' "Que nada importa que yo sufra", o La servidumbre de Riego: Mito y lucha política entre moderados y exaltados durante el Trienio Constitucional', *Ayer*, forthcoming (2022), DOI: https://doi.org/10.55509/ayer/900

Sánchez Romero, Gregorio, *Revolución y reacción en el nordeste de la región de Murcia* (Murcia: Real Academia Alfonso X El Sabio, 2001)

Santos, Cândido dos, *Jansenismo e antijansenismo nos finais do Antigo Regime* (Porto: CITCEM, 2011)

Santos, Fernando Piteira, *Geografia e economia da revolução de 1820* (Lisbon: Edições Europa-América, 1962)

Sardica, José Miguel, *A Europa napoleónica e Portugal: Messianismo revolucionário, política, guerra e opinião pública* (Lisbon: Tribuna da História, 2011)

——, *A regeneração sob o signo do consenso: A política e os partidos entre 1851 e 1861* (Lisbon: ICS, 2001)

Sauch Cruz, Núria, *Guerrillers i bàndols civils entre l'Ebre i el maestrat: La formació d'un país carlista (1808–1844)* (Barcelona: Publicacions de l'Abadia de Montserrat, 2004)

Scalisi, Lina and Arianna Rotondo, 'La città del buongoverno', in *Catania: La grande Catania; La nobiltà virtuosa, la borghesia operosa*, ed. Enrico Iachello (Catania: Sanfilippo editore, 2010), pp. 13–30

Scaramella, Pierroberto, *Il cittadino ecclesiastico: Il clero nella repubblica napoletana del 1799* (Naples: Vivarium, 2000)

Schettini, Glauco, 'Un rito rivoluzionario: I banchetti per i poveri in Emilia Romagna, 1797–1798', *Contemporanea* 18 (2015): 197–220

Schroeder, Paul W., *The Transformation of European Politics 1763–1848* (Oxford: Oxford University Press, 1994)

Schwartz, Stuart B., *All Can Be Saved: Religious Tolerance and Salvation in the Iberian Atlantic World* (New Haven, CT: Yale University Press, 2008)

Sciambra, M., 'Prime vicende della comunità greco-albanese di Palermo e suoi rapporti con l'oriente bizantino', *Bollettino della Badia Greca di Grottaferrata* 16, no. 5 (1962): 102–4

Scirocco, Alfonso, 'Il problema dell'autonomia locale nel Mezzogiorno durante la rivoluzione del 1820–21', in *Studi in memoria di Nino Cortese* (Rome: Istituto per la storia del Risorgimento italiano, 1976), pp. 485–528

Segre, Arturo, 'L'episodio di S. Salvario', in *La rivoluzione piemontese dell'anno 1821*, pp. 251–319

Serrão, Joaquim Veríssimo, *A Instauração do Liberalismo (1807–1832)* (*História de Portugal*, vol. 7) (Lisbon: Editorial Verbo, 1984)

Serrão, Joel, 'D. Miguel' in *Dicionário de História de Portugal*, ed. Joel Serrão, 4 vols (Lisbon: Iniciativas Editoriais, 1971), 3, pp. 55–58

Sifneos, Evrydiki, 'Preparing the Greek Revolution in Odessa in the 1820s: Tastes, Markets and Political Liberalism', *The Historical Review/La Revue Historique* 11 (2014): 139–70

Signorelli, Alfio, *Catania borghese nell'età del Risorgimento* (Milan: FrancoAngeli, 2015)

———, 'Partecipazione e generazioni in Sicilia dalla costituzione del 1812 all'unità', in *Rileggere l'Ottocento: Risorgimento e nazione*, ed. Maria Luisa Betri (Turin: Carocci, 2011), pp. 203–23

Silbert, Albert, *Le Portugal méditerranéen à la fin de l'ancien régime: XVIIIᵉ siècle-début du XIXᵉ siècle; Contribution à l'histoire agraire comparée*, 2 vols (Lisbon: SEVPEN, 1966)

———, *Le Problème agraire portugais au temps des premières cortes libérales (1821–1823)* (Paris: Fondation Calouste Gulbenkian, 1985)

Silva, Armando Barreiros Malheiro da, *Miguelismo: Ideologia e mito* (Coimbra: Edições Minerva, 1993)

———, 'O clero regular e a "usurpação": Subsídios para uma história sócio-política do Miguelismo', *Revista de História das Ideias* 9 (1987): 529–630

Simal, Juan Luis, 'Conspiración, revolución, y contrarrevolución en España, 1814–1824', *Rivista Storica Italiana* 130, no. 2 (2018): 526–56

———, *Emigrados: España y el exilio internacional, 1814–1834* (Madrid: Centro de Estudios Políticos y Constitucionales, 2013)

Sivasundaram, Sujit, *Waves across the South: A New History of Revolution and Empire* (London: William Collins, 2020)

Skopetea, Ellie, *Το 'Πρότυπο Βασίλειο' και η 'Μεγάλη Ιδέα': Όψεις του εθνικού προβλήματος στην Ελλάδα, 1830–1880* (The 'Model Kingdom' and the 'Great Idea': Aspects of the national problem in Greece, 1830–1880) (Athens: Polytypo, 1988)

Sluga, Glenda, *The Invention of International Order: Remaking Europe after Napoleon* (Princeton, NJ: Princeton University Press, 2021)

Sofianos, Dimitrios, Ἐγκύκλιοι (Αὐγουστος 1821–Ιανουάριος 1822) του Οικουμενικού Πατριάρχη Ευγενίου ʹΒ περί δουλική υποταγής των Ελλήνων στον οθωμανό κατακτητήʹ (Encyclicals [August 1821–January 1822] of the ecumenical patriarch Evgenios II recommending to the Greeks submission to Ottoman rule), *Δελτίο του Κέντρου Ερεύνης της Ιστορίας του Νεότερου Ελληνισμού* [*Deltio tou Kentrou Erevnis tis Istorias tou Neoterou Ellinismou*] 2 (2000): 19–43

Soler, Emilio, Francisco Sevillano and Emilio La Parra López, eds, *Diarios de viaje de Fernando VII (1823 y 1827–1828)* (Alicante: Universidad de Alicante, 2013)

Sòriga, Renato, *Le società segrete, l'emigrazione politica e i primi moti per l'indipendenza* (Modena: Società tipografica modenese, 1942)

Sotiropoulos, Michalis, *Liberalism after the Revolution: The Intellectual Foundations of the Greek State, c. 1830–1880* (Cambridge: Cambridge University Press, 2023)

———, '"United we stand, divided we fall": Sovereignty and Government during the Greek Revolution (1821–28)', *Historein* 20, no. 1 (2021), DOI: https://doi.org/10.12681/historein.24928

Sotiropoulos, Michalis and Antonis Hadjikyriacou, '*Patris, Ethnos,* and *Demos*: Representation and Political Participation in the Greek World', in Innes and Philp, *Reimagining Democracy*, pp. 99–126

———, '"Βαδίζοντας προς τη μάχη ανάποδα": Οι πολιτικές αντιλήψεις του 1821 και η Εποχή των Επαναστάσεωνʹ ('Walking backwards into battle': Political concepts of 1821 and the Age of Revolutions), *Μνήμων* [*Mnimon*] 32 (2021): 77–109

Spadoni, Domenico, *Una trama e un tentativo rivoluzionario dello stato romano nel 1820–21* (Rome: Albrighi e Segati, 1910)

Spagnoletti, Angelantonio, 'Centri e periferie nello stato napoletano nel primo Ottocento', in *Il Mezzogiorno preunitario: Economia, società, istituzioni*, ed. Angelo Massafra (Bari: Edizioni Dedalo, 1988), pp. 379–92

———, *Storia del Regno delle Due Sicilie* (Bologna: Il Mulino, 2008)

Späth, Jens, 'Promotori del liberalismo: I parlamenti del regno di Spagna e del Regno delle Due Sicilie, 1820–1823', *Rivista Storica Italiana* 130, no. 2 (2018): 615–38

———, *Revolution in Europa 1820–23: Verfassung und Verfassungskultur in den Königreichen Spanien, beider Sizilien und Sardinien-Piemont* (Cologne: SH Verlag, 2012)

———, 'Turning Constitutional History Upside Down: The 1820s Revolutions in the Mediterranean', in *Re-mapping Centre and Periphery: Asymmetrical Encounters in European and Global Contexts*, ed. Tessa Hauswedell, Axel Körner and Ulrich Tiedau (London: UCL Press, 2019), pp. 111–34

Sperber, Jonathan, *Revolutionary Europe, 1780–1850* (Harlow: Longman, 2000)

St. Clair, William, *That Greece Might Still Be Free: The Philhellenes in the War of Independence* (Cambridge: Open Book Publishers, 2008)

Stathis, Panagiotis, 'From Klephts and Armatoloi to Revolutionaries', in *Ottoman Rule and the Balkans 1760–1850: Conflict, Transformation, Adaptation; Proceedings of an International Conference held in Rethymno, Greece, 13–14 December 2003*, ed. Antonis Anastasopoulos and Elias Kolovos (Rethymno: University of Crete, Department of History and Archaeology, 2007), pp. 167–79

Stedman Jones, Gareth and Ira Katznelson, eds, *Religion and the Political Imagination* (Cambridge: Cambridge University Press, 2010)

Stewart, Charles, 'Dreaming of Buried Icons in the Kingdom of Greece', in *Networks of Power in Modern Greece: Essays in Honour of John Campbell*, ed. Mark Mazower (London: Hurst Publishers, 2008), pp. 89–108

Stites, Richard, 'Decembrists with a Spanish Accent', *Kritika: Explorations in Russian and Eurasian History* 12, no. 1 (2011): 5–23

——, *The Four Horsemen: Riding to Liberty in Port-Napoleonic Europe* (Oxford: Oxford University Press, 2014)

Suanzes-Carpegna, Joaquín Varela, 'El constitucionalismo español y portugués durante la primera mitad del siglo XIX (un estudio comparado)', *Estudos Íbero-Americanos* 33, no. 1 (2007): 38–85

——, 'El pensamiento constitucional español en el exilio: El abandono del modelo doceañista (1823–1833)', *Revista de Estudios Políticos* 88 (1995): 63–90

——, *La monarquía doceañista (1810–1837)* (Madrid: Marcial Pons, 2013)

——, 'Nació, representació i articulació territorial de l'Estat a les Corts de Cadis', *Afers* 68 (2011): 47–70

Subrahmanyam, Sanjay, *Explorations in Connected History: From the Tagus to the Ganges* (New Delhi: Oxford University Press, 2005)

Tengarrinha, José, *Da liberdade mitificada à liberdade subvertida: Uma exploração no interior da repressão à imprensa periódica de 1820 a 1828* (Lisbon: Edições Colibri, 1993)

——, 'La batalla de las ideas: Conservadores y reformistas en Portugal (1808–1810)', in *Guerra de ideas. Política y cultura en la España de la Guerra de la independencia*, ed. Pedro Rújula and Jordi Canal (Madrid: Marcial Pons Historia, 2011), pp. 57–72

——, *Movimentos populares agrários em Portugal (1751–1825)*, 2 vols (Lisbon: Publicações Europa-América, 1994)

——, *Nova história da imprensa portuguesa das origens a 1865* (Lisbon: Círculo de Leitores, 2013)

Ternavasio, Marcela, *Gobernar la revolución: Poderes en disputa en el Río de la Plata, 1810–1816* (Buenos Aires: Siglo XXI, 2007)

Teruel Gregorio de Tejada, Manuel, *Obispos liberales: La utopía de un proyecto, 1820–1823* (Lleida: Milenio, 1996)

Themelly, Mario, 'Introduzione', in Minichini, *Luglio 1820*, pp. i–lxxi

Themudo Barata, Manuel, 'A subversão organiza-se a nível nacional', in *Nova História militar de Portugal*, ed. Manuel Themudo Barata and Nuno Severiano Teixeira, 5 vols (Lisbon: Círculo de Leitores, 2003–4), 3, pp. 164–74

Thibaud, Clément, *Républiques en armes: Les armées de Bolívar dans les guerres d'indépendance du Venezuela et de la Colombie* (Rennes: Presses Universitaires de Rennes, 2006)

Todorov, Nikolai, 'Quelques renseignements sur les insurgés grecs dans les Principautés danubiennes en 1821', in Μελετήματα στη μνήμη Βασιλείου Λαούρδα/*Essays in Memory of Basil Laourdas* (Thessaloniki, 1975), pp. 471–77

——, *The Balkan City, 1400–1900* (Seattle: University of Washington Press, 1983)

Torras, Jaime, *Liberalismo y rebeldía campesina, 1820–1823* (Barcelona: Ariel, 1976)

Torre, Joseba de la, 'Nekazal klaseak, antzinako erregimenaren krisia eta iraultza burgesa nafarroan'/'Clases campesinas, crisis del Antiguo Régimen y revolución burguesa en Navarra', in *Zumalakarregi Museoa: Azterketa historikoak/Museo*

Zumalakarregi: Estudios históricos, 2 vols (San Sebastián: Diputación Foral de Gipuzkoa, 1992), 2, pp. 189–208

Trajkov, Veselin 'La coopération bulgaro-grecque dans les luttes de libération nationale', in *Πνευματικές και πολιτιστικές σχέσεις Ελλήνων και Βουλγάρων από τα μέσα του ΙΕ΄αιώνα έως τα μέσα του ΙΘ΄αιώνα* (Spiritual and cultural relationships between Greeks and Bulgarians from the middle of the 15th to the 19th century) (Thessaloniki: Institute for Balkan Studies, 1980), pp. 47–53

Tzakis, Dionysis, *Γεώργιος Καραϊσκάκης* (Georgios Karaiskakis) (Athens: Ta Nea, Istoriki Vivliothiki, 2009)

Ulloa, Pietro Calà, 'Sulle rivoluzioni del reame di Napoli: Ricordi' (manuscript, Naples, 1872), vol. 2, in BNN, MS XI F 42–43

Ursinus, Michael, *Grievance Administration (şikayet) in an Ottoman Province: The Kaymakam of Roumelia's 'Record Book of Complaints' of 1781–1783* (London: RoutledgeCurzon, 2005)

Vakalopoulos, Apostolos, *Φήμες και διαδόσεις κατά την Ελληνική Επανάσταση του 1821: Συμβολή στην ψυχολογία των ελληνικών επαναστατικών όχλων* (Rumours and news during the Greek Revolution of 1821: A contribution to the psychology of the revolutionary masses) (Thessaloniki: Triantafyllou, 1947)

———, *Τα ελληνικά στρατεύματα του 1821: Οργάνωση, ηγεσία, τακτική, ήθη, ψυχολογία* (The Greek troops of 1821: Leadership, organisation, tactics, customs, psychology) (Thessaloniki: Politeia, 1948)

Valente, Vasco Pulido, *Ir prò maneta: A revolta contra os franceses (1808)* (Lisbon: Aletheia Editores, 2007)

———, 'O povo em armas: A revolta nacional de 1808–1809', *Análise Social* 15, no. 57 (1979): 7–48

———, 'Os levantamentos "Miguelistas" contra a Carta Constitucional (1826–27)', *Análise Social* 30, no. 133 (1995): 631–51

———, *Os militares e a política (1820–1856)* (Lisbon: Imprensa Nacional, 2005)

Valín Fernández, Alberto J. V, 'Masonería y movimento liberal en la sublevación coruñesa del 1820, en apoyo del pronunciamiento de Rafael Riego', in *Ejército, pueblo y constitución: Homenaje al General Rafael Riego*, ed. Alberto Gil Novales (Madrid: Anejos de la Revista Trienio [Ilustración y Liberalismo], 1987), pp. 157–79

Van Kley, Dale K., 'From the Catholic Enlightenment to the Risorgimento: The Exchange between Nicola Spedalieri and Pietro Tamburini, 1791–1797', *Past and Present* 222 (2014): 109–62

———, *The Religious Origins of the French Revolution: From Calvin to the Civil Constitution, 1570–1791* (Basingstoke: Palgrave, 2000)

Van Steen, Gonda, 'Anniversaries', in *The Greek Revolution: A Critical Dictionary*, ed. Paschalis M. Kitromilides and Constantinos Tsoukalas (Cambridge, MA: Harvard University Press, 2021), pp. 694–707

Vargues, Isabel Nobre, *A aprendizagem da cidadania em Portugal (1820–1823)* (Coimbra: Livraria Minerva Editora, 1997)

Vasconcelos, Paulo Alexandre, 'A memória do liberalismo no espaço público do Porto (Santo Ildefonso, Bonfim e Campanhã)', in *Omni Tempore: Atas dos encontros da Primavera 2017* (Porto: Universidade do Porto, Faculdade de Letras, 2018), pp. 447–72

Vasdravellis, John, *The Greek Struggle for Independence: The Macedonians in the Revolution of 1821* (Thessaloniki: Institute of Balkan Studies, 1968)

Venturi, Franco, 'Le rivoluzioni liberali', in *Le rivoluzioni borghesi*, ed. Ruggiero Romano, 5 vols (Milan: Fratelli Fabbri, 1973), 4, pp. 193–208

Verdelho, Telmo dos Santos, *As palavras e as ideias na Revolução Liberal de 1820* (Coimbra: Instituto Nacional de Investigação Científica, 1981)

Verdo, Geneviève, 'L'Organisation des souverainetés provinciales dans l'Amérique indépendante: Le cas de la république de Córdoba, 1776–1827', *Annales* 69, no. 2 (2014): 349–81

Veremis, Thanos, *The Military in Greek Politics: From Independence to Democracy* (London: Hurst & Co., 1997)

Vernet, Jordi Roca, 'Fiestas cívicas en la revolución liberal: Entusiasmo y popularidad del régimen', *Historia Social* 86 (2016): 71–90

———, 'From the *Cortes* to the Cities, Exercising and Representing Popular Sovereignty: Barcelona during the *Trienio Liberal* (1820–23)', in *1812 Echoes: The Cadiz Constitution in Hispanic History, Culture and Politics*, ed. Stephen G. H. Roberts and Adam Sharman (Newcastle upon Tyne: Cambridge Scholars, 2013), pp. 130–49

———, *La Barcelona revolucionària i liberal: Exaltats, milicians i conspiradors* (Barcelona: Pagès Editors, 2011)

———, 'Las fiestas cívicas del Trienio Progresista (1840–1843): Progresistas enfrentados y desafío a la Regencia', *Historia Contemporánea* 56 (2018): 7–45

———, 'Las imágenes de la cultura política liberal durante el Trienio (1820–1823): El caso de Barcelona', *Cuadernos de Ilustración y Romanticismo* 10 (2002): 185–220

Verrengia, Paola, 'Le istituzioni a Napoli e la rivoluzione del 1820–21', in *Il Mezzogiorno preunitario. Economia, societá, istituzioni*, ed. Angelo Massafra (Bari: Edizioni Dedalo, 1988), pp. 549–64

Vick, Brian, *The Congress of Vienna: Power and Politics after Napoleon* (Cambridge, MA: Harvard University Press, 2016)

Vieira, Benedicta Maria Duque, *O problema político português no tempo das primeiras Cortes liberais: Estudos e documentos*, vol. 1 of Miriam Halpern Pereira, ed., *A crise do Antigo Regime e as Cortes constituintes*, 5 vols (Lisbon: João Sá da Costa, 1992)

Vinci, Stefano, 'Dal Parlamento al decurionato: L'amministrazione dei comuni del regno di Napoli nel decennio francese', *Archivio Storico del Sannio* 13 (2008): 189–218

Vovelle, Michel, *Les métamorphoses de la fête en Provence de 1750 à 1820* (Paris: Aubier/ Flammarion, 1976)

Wilson, James, 'Reappropriation, Resistance, and British Autocracy in Sri Lanka, 1820–1850', *The Historical Journal* 60, no. 1 (2017): 47–69

Woodhouse, Cristopher Montague, *The Battle of Navarino* (London: Hoddler & Stoughton, 1965)

Woolf, Larry, *Enlightenment and the Orthodox World: Western Perspectives on the Orthodox Church in Eastern Europe* (Athens: Centre for Neohellenic Research, 2000)

Woolf, Stuart, *Napoleon's Integration of Europe* (London: Routledge, 1993)

Yakovaki, Nassia, 'Ο Λόγιος Ερμής ως τόπος διαμόρφωσης του ελληνικού κοινού' (The *Logios Ermis* as a *topos* for the shaping of the Greek public), in *Λόγος και χρόνος* στη νεοελληνική γραμματεία (18ος—19ος αιώνας): Πρακτικά συνεδρίου προς τιμήν του Αλέξη Πολίτη, Ρέθυμνο, 12–14 Απριλίου 2013 (Discourse and time in modern Greek letters (18th–19th centuries): Proceedings of a conference in honour of Alexis Politis, Rethymno, 12–14 April 2013), ed. Stefanos Kaklamanis, Alexis Kalokairinos and Dimitris Polychronakis (Irakleion: Crete University Press, 2015), pp. 207–38

——, 'Οδυσσός, Κωνσταντινούπολη, Ισμαήλι: Τρεις οργανωτικοί σταθμοί ενός αχαρτογράφητου δρομολογίου' (Odessa, Constantinople, Izmail: Three organisational centres of an uncharted trajectory), in Οι πόλεις των Φιλικών: Οι αστικές διαδρομές ενός επαναστατικού φαινομένου, Πρακτικά ημερίδας, Αθήνα, 14 Ιανουαρίου 2015 (The cities of the Philikoi: The urban trajectories of a revolutionary phenomenon; Proceedings of a conference, Athens, 14 January 2015), ed. Olga Katsiardi-Hering (Athens: The Hellenic Parliament Foundation, 2018), pp. 173–200

Yaycioglu, Ali, *Partners of the Empire: The Crisis of the Ottoman Order in the Age of Revolutions* (Stanford, CA: Stanford University Press, 2016)

Zaghi, Carlo, *L'Italia di Napoleone* (Turin: UTET, 1989)

Zanou, Konstantina, 'Imperial Nationalism and Orthodox Enlightenment: A Diasporic Story between the Ionian Islands, Russia and Greece, ca. 1800–1830', in Isabella and Zanou, *Mediterranean Diasporas*, pp. 111–34

——, 'Profughi Ciprioti a Venezia e Trieste dopo il 1821 (nuovi elementi provenienti dalle carte Mustoxidi a Corfú)', in *Giornate per Cipro* (Padua: Garangola, 2007), pp. 39–62

——, *Transnational Patriotism in the Mediterranean, 1800–1850: Stammering the Nation* (Oxford: Oxford University Press, 2018)

Zavala, Iris M., *Masones, comuneros y carbonarios* (Madrid: Siglo XXI de España, 1971)

Zito, Gaetano, 'Benedettini a Catania tra conflitti e riforma: La visita abbaziale del 1822 a S. Nicola l'Arena', in *Monastica et Humanistica. Scritti in onore di Gregorio Penco O.S.B.*, ed. Francesco G. B. Trolese (Cesena: Badia di Santa Maria del Monte, 2003), pp. 519–60

Unpublished Papers

Fruci, Gian Luca, '"Sol Garibaldi a te può dirsi uguale": Guglielmo Pepe, celebrità transnazionale e speaker internazionale del Risorgimento (1820–1855)', unpublished paper given at Cantieri di Storia IX SISSCO, Padua, 15 September 2017

Petmezas, Socrates D., 'The Land Issue in the Greek War of Independence: A Reappraisal', working paper, presented at conference '1821: What Made It Greek and Revolutionary?', organised by Yannis Kotsonis and Ada Dialla, Athens, July 2018

Unpublished Master's and Doctoral Dissertations

Arruda, Paulo Henrique de Magalhães, 'Hipólito José da Costa, the Freemason', PhD dissertation, King's College London, 2016

Bron, Grégoire, 'Révolution et nation entre le Portugal et l'Italie: Les Relations politiques luso-italiennes des Lumières à l'Internationale libérale de 1830', doctoral dissertation, Paris EPHE and Lisbon ISCTE, 2013

Cassino, Carmine, 'Portugal e a Itália: Emigração, nação e memória (1800–1832)', doctoral dissertation, Universidade de Lisboa, 2015

Di Mauro, Luca, 'Le Secret et Polichinelle, ou Culture et pratiques de la clandestinité politique à Naples au début du XIX siècle (1799–1821)', doctoral dissertation, Sorbonne Université, Paris, 2015

Frangos, George Dimitrios, 'The Philike Etaireia 1814–1821: A Social and Historical Analysis', PhD dissertation, Columbia University, 1971

Grieco, Giuseppe, 'The British Empire and the Two Sicilies: Constitutions and International Law in the Revolutionary Mediterranean, ca. 1800–60', PhD dissertation, Queen Mary University of London, 2022

Ilikak, Sukru Huseyin, 'A Radical Rethinking of Empire: Ottoman State and Society during the Greek War of Independence (1821–1826)', PhD dissertation, Harvard University, 2011

Lousada, Maria Alexandre, 'O Miguelismo (1828–1834): O discurso político e o apoio da nobreza titulada', Master's thesis, Faculdade de Letras, Universidade de Lisboa, Lisbon, 1987

Manikas, Konstantinos I., 'The Relations between Orthodoxy and Roman Catholicism in Greece during the Revolution (1821–1827): Contribution to the History of the Church in Greece', doctoral dissertation, University of Athens, 2001

Marino, Dario, 'La "nostra politica rigenerazione": Petizioni e rivoluzione nel Regno delle Due Sicilie (1820–21)', doctoral dissertation, University of Salerno, 2022

Mesquita, José Carlos Vilhena, 'O Algarve no processo histórico do liberalismo português (A economia e a sociedade 1820–1842)', 2 vols, doctoral dissertation, Universidade do Algarve, Faro, 1997

Mondejar, Michel, 'Alliances et conflits au sein des sociétés secrètes libérales: La Confédération des chevaliers comuneros, ou les limites de l'illusion démocratique durant le triennat constitutionnel 1820–1823', doctoral thesis, Université de Provence, 2007

San Narciso Martín, David, 'La monarquía ante la nación: Representaciones ceremoniales del poder en España (1814–1868)', doctoral dissertation, Universidad Complutense de Madrid, 2020

Sánchez Martín, Víctor, 'Rafael del Riego: Símbolo de la revolución liberal', doctoral dissertation, University of Alicante, 2016

Varo Montilla, Francisco, 'La causa del Palmar: Conspiración y levantamiento de 1819', doctoral dissertation, UNED, Madrid, 2009, available at http://e-spacio.uned.es /fez/view/tesisuned:GeoHis-Fvaro (accessed 14 August 2022)

INDEX

Note: page numbers in *italics* refer to illustrations.